MESSIANISM
in the
TALMUDIC ERA

MESSIANISM
in the
TALMUDIC ERA

Selected with an Introduction

by

LEO LANDMAN

KTAV PUBLISHING HOUSE, INC.
NEW YORK
1979

Library of Congress Cataloging in Publication Data

Main entry under title:

Messianism in the Talmudic era.

    Includes bibliographical references.
    1. Messiah — Addresses, essays, lectures.
2. Messianic era (Judaism) — Addresses, essays, lectures.
3. Judaism — History — Talmudic period, 10–425 — Addresses,
essays, lectures. I. Landman, Leo.
BM615.M44   296.3'3   79–17379
ISBN 0–87068–445–0

To my beloved Parents
Shirley and Bernard Landman
who first taught me to
listen for the footsteps of the Messiah

Table of Contents

Acknowledgments

The editor is deeply grateful to the following for their generosity in granting permission to reprint the articles in this volume:

"The Five Methods" by A. H. Silver, *A History of Messianic Speculation in Israel* (Boston: Beacon Press, 1959) and reprinted by permission of Dr. Daniel Jeremy Silver.

"The Origin of the Messianic Hope in Israel" by H. P. Smith, *American Journal of Theology,* vol. 14, 1910.

"The Sources of Israel's Messianic Hope" by Hugo Gressman, *American Journal of Theology,* vol. 17, 1913.

At the End of the Days" by Hans Kosmala, *Annual of the Swedish Theological Institute* and reprinted by permission of E. J. Brill and Prof. Hans Kosmala.

Excerpts from *Galut veGeulah beSifruth Yisrael* by M. Waxman (Ogen Press, 1952) and reprinted by permission of M. Waxman.

"The Doctrine of the Two Messiahs in Sectarian Literature in the Time of the Second Commonwealth" by J. Liver, *Harvard Theological Review,* vol. 52, 1969, and reprinted by permission of *Harvard Theological Review,* copyright by the president and fellows of Harvard College.

"The Messiah of Ephraim and the Premature Exodus of the Tribe of Ephraim" by J. Heinemann, *Harvard Theological Review,* vol. 68, 1975, and reprinted by permission of *Harvard Theological Review,* copyright by the president and fellows of Harvard College and by permission of Prof. J. Heinemann.

"The Origin of the Idea of the Messiah" by Solomon Zeitlin, *In Time of Harvest* (New York, 1963) and reprinted by permission of Dr. Daniel Jeremy Silver.

"The Assumption of Moses and the Revolt of Bar Kokba." by Solomon Zeitlin, *Jewish Quarterly Review,* vol. 38, 1947.

"The Essenes and Messianic Expectations" by Solomon Zeitlin, *Jewish Quarterly Review,* vol. 45, 1954.

"The Origin of Jewish Eschatology" by N. Schmidt, *Journal of Biblical Literature,* vol. 41, 1922, and reprinted by permission of the Society for Biblical Literature.

"Recent Study of the Term 'Son of Man'" by N. Schmidt, *Journal of Biblical Literature,* vol. 45, 1926, and reprinted by permission of the Society of Biblical Literature.

"Messianismus und Mysterienreligion" by I. Heinemann, *Monatsschrift für Geschichte und Wissenschaft des Judentums,* vol. 69, 1925.

"Jewish Expectations about the Messiah According to the Fourth Gospel" by Marnius De Jonge, *New Testament Studies,* vol. 19, 1972, and reprinted by permission of Cambridge University Press.

" Jewish Messianic Belief in Justin Martyr's *Dialogue with Trypho,*" by A. J. B. Higgins, *Novum Testamentum,* vol. 9, 1967, and reprinted by permission of E. J. Brill, Leiden.

"Mashehu al R. Judah Aḥave d'R. Sella Ḥasida" by M. Ber, *Sinai,* vol. 48, 1961, and reprinted by permission of *Sinai.*

"Conception of the Ideal Kingdom Without a Messiah" by J. Drummond, *The Jewish Messiah* (London, 1897) and published by Green and Co.

Excerpts from *The Messianic Idea in Israel* (New York, 1955) by J. Klausner and reprinted by permission of Macmillan Publishing Co., Inc., copyright 1955.

Excerpts from *The Messianic Idea in Judaism* (New York, 1971) by Gershom Scholem and reprinted by permission of Schocken Books, Inc., copyright 1971.

"Power" by Jacob Neusner, *There We Sat Down* (New York, 1972) and reprinted by permission of Prof. Jacob Neusner.

Excerpts from *The Setting of the Sermon on the Mount* by W. D. Davies and reprinted by permission of Cambridge University Press, copyright 1964.

Introduction

Maimonides, in his usual clear and precise style, summed up the Jewish belief in a Messiah and in the expectancy of his momentary arrival. In the twelfth of his thirteen principles, Maimonides stated: *Ani ma'amin be'emunah she'lemah be'biath ha'moshiah. Ve'af al pi she'yith'ma'meah, im kol zeh ahake lo be'kol yom she'yabo* ("I believe with perfect faith in the coming of the Messiah, and though he tarry, yet I await daily his coming").

That the belief in the Messiah became a deep-rooted principle in Jewish life, allowing Jews to withstand and overcome the terribly tragic moments in their history, was best evidenced in the reports from the concentration camps at Treblinka, Maidanek, Birkenau, and the infamous Auschwitz, where millions of Jews went to the gas chambers and crematoria while chanting the words of Maimonides' twelfth principle—*Ani ma'amin,* "I believe with perfect faith in the coming of the Messiah . . ."

I. The Origin of the Jewish Messianic Belief

Since the belief in the coming of the Messiah is so deeply ingrained in the Jewish people, it becomes indeed strange to note how obscure the origin of the Messianic belief is. Many theories have suggested that the origin is not even to be found in Jewish sources. Some have said that the *Aharith ha-Yamim,* "the End of the Days," of Isaiah and Daniel was influenced by the ideas of Zarathustra. The world will be redeemed when Angra-Mainus, the god of evil, is defeated. Ahura-Mazda, the god of good, with the help of Saoshiant, the Messiah, will judge mankind. Then, the kingdom of Ahura-Mazda will bring joy and bliss to all mankind. The Persians also have a Day of Judgment, reward and punishment after death, and a Messianic era. However, in the philosophies of Zarathustra there are three Saoshiants, three Messiahs, all of the seed of Zarathustra, none of which compares to the one Messiah, or even to the two Messiahs (Messiah ben Joseph and Messiah ben David) of Judaism.

xi

Gressman, though with scant evidence, claims that the Messianic idea, based on the idea of a godly wonderchild who will redeem, comes from Egyptian or Babylonian sources. Heinemann and Klausner opposed this view. They concluded that neither in Egyptian nor in Babylonian literature do we find any sources for a Messiah. All references are to specific kings. All such foreign sources are meaningless because Isaiah speaks of an earthly, human being and not a supernatural phenomenon. For more detailed reading, we urge the reader to study the works of Oesterley, Hölscher, Dürr, and Smith found in the bibliography.

The term *mashiah* in the Bible is never used to connote the eschatological figure of a Messiah. It is found thirty-nine times. Once it refers to Cyrus (Isaiah 45:1) and some thirty times to the kings of Israel and Judea. The term also refers to the High Priest, as in Leviticus 4:3, 6:22; Daniel 9:25–6. None of these Biblical passages, whether they refer to the kings or to the High Priests, have any Messianic connotation. The term means "anointed" or "consecrated." It is for this reason that the king was never just called *mashiah*, but *mashiah hashem*, "consecrated to God." During the Second Commonwealth, neither priests nor kings were anointed.

In many ways, the belief in a Messiah in Judaism prior to the Middle Ages was different than belief in the Unity of God, Immortality, etc. True, they all were theological in nature, but the Messianic idea was more political than spiritual. It was linked to God because Jewish ideology linked everything to God. History itself was the expression of God's Will in the world. However, basically, it was political.

All religions set up some sort of relationship between man and God. Judaism saw this relationship as a pact (*brith*). It was an agreement imposing clauses and stipulations on each party to the pact. The basic agreement between Jewry and God was that Israel was to obey the Will of God, Who in turn promised to protect, provide for, and glorify Israel. According to this theory, if you conform to the Will of God, all will be well. Any evil that befalls man is a punishment placed upon the individual by the other party, the wronged party to the contract. This is clearly articulated throughout the Books of Moses (e.g., the fiery exhortations known as the *Tokhahah*) and the prophets (e.g., the Book of Judges). If Israel elects to be good, all sorts of good things will follow; if not, then the reverse will be true. When Israel left Egypt and accepted the Torah at Sinai, wonderful rewards were to be theirs. When Israel strayed, the destruction of the Temple, the epitome of punishment, naturally followed.

At the destruction of the First Temple and in the ensuing Persian era, two things occurred. The theory which saw Jewish sin and rebellion as an abrogation of the pact (covenant), and the destruction of the Temple as the punishment thereof, put Jewry into a dilemma. If the covenant was broken, then there could be no *raison d'etre* for Israel's continuation. Secondly, this theory gave no comfort to martyrdom. If Israel is no more, then all hope is removed.

Jews were in a bad state at that time, and a new theory developed. It is hard to say from where it came. Some feel that it was triggered by Jewish contact with Persia, but refurbished by Jews, just as Maimonides Judaized Aristotelian ideas. The idea developed that if Jewry is punished, even defeated, the people is not "sent" into exile, but God is defeated "with you." He goes into exile "with you." It provided the alternative that both He and Israel could stage a comeback. The covenant, however, was not broken. Hope was kept intact. The martyr was defeated in the battle *for* God, not slain *by* God.

Accordingly, when Israel rebelled against God and was forced into exile, God, as partner to the covenant, also went into exile. There ensued the constant debate as to who was at fault. ומפני חטאנו גלינו מארצינו ("And because of our sins were we driven from our land") placed the blame squarely upon Israel itself. On the other hand, זכור את הברית ("Remember the covenant") put the fault to God, Who deserted the people.

Although, at the time of the destruction of the Second Temple, Jews were aware of the earlier destruction and the fact that it did not mark the end of Jewish life, R. Yoḥanan b. Zakkai, as leader of the Jewish community in Judea and founder of Yavneh, had to combat the strong feeling still held by some that the destruction meant that Jewry was rejected by God. According to some scholars, e.g., Klausner, R. Yoḥanan b. Zakkai, before his death, supposedly said: "Clear the house [of utensils] because of impurity and prepare a throne for Hezekiah, King of Judah, who comes." This indicated that R. Yoḥanan b. Zakkai believed the coming of the Messiah to be imminent. This also was the understanding of Ferdinand Weber in his *System der altsynagogalen palästinischen Theologie*, (Leipzig, 1880), p. 341. Burkitt, in his *Jewish and Christian Apocalypses*, on the basis of Gen. R. 44, 22, concluded that R. Yoḥanan b. Zakkai renounced all apocalyptic ideas. On the other hand, based on the same source, Burkitt stated that R. 'Akiba believed the Kingdom of God to be at hand. His conclusions may be ignored since the cited source is not clear as to which sage held the views mentioned. Even A. Marmorstein's statement that R. Yoḥanan b. Zakkai expected the Messiah to come at any moment since he based many of his ordinances on such an expect-ancy, (for example, in *R.H.* 30a he said—"speedily the Temple will be rebuilt,") cannot be taken seriously. It is true that during this time, up until the Bar Kokhba revolt, Jews believed the Temple would be speedily rebuilt. However, there was nothing Messianic about this belief. It was based on political and religious hope and nothing more. Urbach sees R. Yoḥanan b. Zakkai as opposing the Messianic belief. There were those who urged the attempt to rebuild the Temple and proclaim that the Mes-siah would come soon. It was against these that R. Yoḥanan b. Zakkai said (*ARN* II, 3): אם יאמרו לך הילדים נלך ונבנה בית המקדש אל תשמע להם ואם יאמרו לך הזקנים בוא ונסתר בית המקדש שמע להם מפני שבנין ילדים סתירה וסתירת זקנים בנין. ("If youth say to you, 'Come, let us build the Temple,' do not listen to them. If the aged say to you, 'Come, let us destroy the Temple,' listen to them. For the building of youth is destruction, while the destruction of the aged is construction"). Furthermore, R. Yoḥanan b. Zakkai also stated: אם היתה נטיעה בתוך ידך ויאמרו לך הרי לך המשיח בא ונטע את הנטיעה ואחרי כן צא והקבילו ("If a plant is in your hand and it is told to you that the Messiah is here, come and plant and then go forth to receive him"). Urbach sees the first statement as being against the immediate rebuilding of the Tem-ple and the second as being against the urgency of the arrival of the Mes-siah.

That Hezekiah was assigned the role of Messiah was believed by some, perhaps because of the miraculous destruction of Sennacherib's army. In any case, R. Yoḥanan b. Zakkai saw Hezekiah in this role, despite the contention of both Goldin and Schechter that the words quoted after R. Yoḥanan b. Zakkai's death (see *Ber.* 28b; PT *Soṭa IX,* 17; PT *A. Z. III,* 1) were not his own. Certainly, the amora R. Hillel saw Hezekiah in the Messianic role. (See *Sanh.* 98b; also, the exposition of Bar Ḳappara, *ibid.* 94a; G. F. Moore, *Judaism* II, [Cambridge, 1966] p. 347.) L. Ginzberg (*Legends* VI, 365, n. 67) offers a different explanation. Hezekiah was a scholar on a throne. R. Yoḥanan b. Zakkai may have thought of Hezekiah coming to meet him at the entrance to a better life. A similar incident is described in the Talmud (*B.K.* 111b), where Raba hoped R. Oshaya would come to meet him because he, Raba, had ex-plained one of R. Oshaya's *halakhot.* Ginzberg also suggests that the Hezekiah in question was Hezekiah the Galilean. Geiger (*Jüdische Zeitschrift* VIII, 35) agreed. This Hezekiah was the one killed by Herod.

Hezekiah was also looked upon as a Messianic figure in the argument between the Jews and Trypho as pictured by Justin Martyr in his *Dialogues with Trypho.* The verse in Psalms 110 was attributed to Jesus by

Trypho, while the Jews said it referred to Hezekiah. The commentaries of the Middle Ages were also divided as to whom the verse refers. Thus, Rashi, following the sages, referred it to Abraham or Melchiẓedek, while Ibn Ezra claimed it spoke of David.

Another view of the Hezekiah vision is offered by Y. Iben-Shmuel (*Midrashei Geulah* [Tel Aviv, 1954], pp. 47–49), who sees R. Yoḥanan b. Zakkai forecasting an impending invasion from Parthia, while he attempted to alert the people to the redemption to come via Parthia. This theory is not borne out either by history or by the relationship of Rome and Parthia during this period, and certainly not by R. Yoḥanan b. Zakkai's attitudes, expressed elsewhere, to Parthia and Rome. The reader is also urged to read the views expressed by Louis Finkelstein (*Akiba,* pp. 70–71) and J. Neusner (*A Life of R. Yohanan b. Zakkai* [1962], pp. 228 ff.).

Finkelstein feels that R. Yoḥanan b. Zakkai was not satisfied with the academy he built. He apparently did not realize that Yavneh not only saved but enhanced Jewish culture. At the end of his life, he agonized whether or not he could have done more for his people while confronting Vespasian. Should he not have attempted to save the Temple and the country? He recalled Hezekiah in whose time the country was saved from Assyria. Why could he not have done as much and saved the country from Rome? Suddenly, he realized that all was well. His work had been approved. King Hezekiah, whom he had wanted to emulate, was there to welcome him. "Set the throne for Hezekiah . . . " J. Neusner agreed with Finkelstein. He saw Yavneh as the sapling one had to plant even when the Messiah is about to arrive.

Despite the fact that in the later periods both Christians and Jews variously interpreted and inferred Messianic overtones from certain Biblical passages, the former attributing these to Jesus, the latter to the future Messiah, there are many who feel that while the concept of redemption is Biblical, the figure of an eschatological Messiah is not found in the Bible. We have devoted a section to this theme. Space prevented us from dealing with the statement of R. Hillel: *Ain mashiah le'Yisrael* . . . (*Sanh.* 99a). By his statement, the sage aroused the concern of the medieval scholars. By that time, the belief in the Messiah had been well established, and a statement that there is no Messiah certainly had to be explained. How was it possible for someone of that early period to deny a basic tenet of Jewish thinking?

Rashi, in order to somehow justify the inclusion of an individual in the Talmud who appeared to contradict accepted theology, and who was titled *rabbi,* claimed that R. Hillel did not deny redemption but felt that God Himself would perform that act and would not delegate the task to a Messiah. R. David Bonvier, a student of Naḥmanides, in his commentary to the tractate *Sanhedrin,* adds to what Rashi had said, that R. Hillel could not have thought that no redemption at all would come and Israel would disappear among the nations of the world. This could not be since the promise for the "ingathering of the exiles" was assured. God would appear immediately after the "ingathering," revive the dead, etc. A Messiah was not necessary to conquer the nations. Ibn Ḥabbib, in his Introduction to *Ayn Yaaḳob,* claims that Rashi only meant to defend R. Hillel against the charge of heresy.

R. Shem Ṭob Shprot (*Pardes Rimonim,* p. 35) claimed that R. Hillel's statement was meant to hold true only if Israel remained unfit for redemption. Although the Messiah would also arrive even if Israel was not fit for redemption, this would depend upon the "merit of the fathers" (*zekhut aboth*). This, R. Hillel felt, ran out and was completely depleted at the end of the First Temple. Whatever merits owing to King David remained, ended with Hezekiah. The result, then, would be that since Israel was unfit for redemption and no longer had any "merit of the fathers," there would be no Messiah for Israel. In his *Torat ha'Olah,* the author continues to say that God would nevertheless bring redemption for His own sake, in order not to desecrate His Divine Name.

Joseph Albo (*Ikkarim* I, p. 11) poses the dilemma in precise terms. If R. Hillel was justified that the Messianic expectations had all been fulfilled during the reign of King Hezekiah, then why was R. Joseph so vehemently opposed to him and why chastise him so severely? Albo concludes that R. Hillel, even though he did not believe in a Messiah, was not considered a heretic. Apparently, the concept of a Messiah was not an essential in Jewish theology, and therefore anyone who denies the principle from an honest and sincere, albeit erroneous, viewpoint is not to be considered a heretic, although he would be deemed a sinner. Ibn Zimra (IV, 186) felt that R. Hillel had erred in his thinking and therefore was to be considered as one constrained (*anuss*) and not responsible for his actions or thoughts. Our bibliography contains many works that deal with this problem.

Neusner, on the other hand, concludes that R. Yoḥanan b. Zakkai brought forth a new approach. He felt that Rome was too powerful to encourage any resistance to her dominion, which would be futile. As leader of the Jewish community, he had to combat the strong feelings held by some, that the destruction meant they had been rejected by God. To the contrary, he taught that punishment follows sin but that redemption follows repentance. Observance of God's Will prevents the conquest of Israel; disobedience, equals subjection. Accordingly, R. Yoḥanan b. Zakkai's passive approach was not advocated for the sake of security but rather because he thought that this was a more effective means of engaging in a redemption program.

According to Neusner, the same approach was taken by Rab and Samuel in the Sasanian era of third-century Babylonia. Jews at that time were again keenly sensitive to the problem of how to hasten the advent of the Messianic era. Samuel in Babylonia, like R. Yoḥanan b. Zakkai before him, emphasized that a precarious political position required extraordinary efforts on the part of Jews to reestablish, expand, and intensify their religious standards. In doing so, he felt, Jewry would hasten the eventual redemption. Thus, Samuel exclaimed: אמתי שישראל משליכין דברי תורה לארץ, המלכות העכו"ם הזאת גוזרת ומצלחת ("While Israel casts the words of Torah to the ground, these idolatrous kingdoms will decree and succeed").

Rab also declared that when Israel improves its moral life, it will improve its historical conditions as well. All of these declarations had the effect of transferring the people's minds from political to moral issues. Neusner cites numerous passages which demonstrate this passive approach. Thus, he cited PT *R.H.* III, 8, 59a; *Lam. R. Proem* II; *Sukah* 29b and other sources. However, the critical passage to the entire structure presented by Neusner hails from *Sanhedrin* 97b concerning their debate as to what will bring about the redemption. אמר רב כלו כל הקיצין ואין הדבר תלוי אלא בתשובה ומעשים טובים. ושמואל אמר דיו לאבל שיעמוד באבלו —"Rab said: All the predestined dates [for redemption] have passed and the matter depends only on repentence and good deeds. But Samuel maintained: It is sufficient for a mourner to keep his mourning."

It is clear, that Samuel meant that living in the exile itself merited redemption, even should Israel not repent. The Talmud equated this dispute to the tannaitic views expressed by R. Eliezer and R. Joshua which we will cite below. In any case, Neusner feels that both Rab and Samuel here advise the people to attempt to endure. Even Rab, who might have agreed that perhaps once the arrival of the Messiah depended upon a date alone, now felt that all dates had been passed and therefore, what was now required was repentance and endurance. Both preached a passive approach. It is difficult to differ with the cogent, ingenious arguments of Neusner. His analysis is superb and broad in scope. However, if one looks at R. Rabbinovicz, *Varae Lectiones* p. 280, note 300, a variant reading has R. Joshua b. Levi as the author of this statement instead of Samuel. It would appear that this reading is the correct one. The story of R. Joshua b. Levi meeting Elijah at the entrance to the cave of R. Simeon b. Yohai and his subsequent meeting with the Messiah in Rome (or in the South of Judea) is related right after Rab's statement. R. Joshua b. Levi disagreed with Rab and argued that a Jew's exile existence, like a mourner's even without penitence and good deeds, will redeem him. According to the text, the narrator was R. Alexandrai, the frequent transmitter of R. Joshua b. Levi's thoughts. He, too, like R. Joshua b. Levi, felt that Israel would be redeemed even without repentance. His statement is cited in *Tanh. Va'era* 6 and *Ex. R.* 5, 18. If our assumptions are correct, then the position of Samuel as pictured by Neusner must be questioned. Furthermore, Neusner claims that while Samuel warned of catastrophies which would accompany the Messiah and that the Messianic age would contain no miraculous changes but that the poor would still be poor, etc., Rab, on the other hand, forecast that conditions would change drastically and for the better. Unfortunately, the passages cited, *Ketubot* 112b and especially *Berakhot* 17a, refer to *Olam Haba'ah.* Neusner also claims that Samuel discouraged public fasts other than the ninth of Ab since such fasts aroused the people's hopes for better days and they might act on such hopes. Neusner, here, confused two statements made by Samuel. The one he cited, *Pesaḥim* 54b אין תענית ציבור בבבל, aside from the historical difficulties it presents, as has been noted by A. Marmorstein, "Amidah of Fast Days," *JQR* (January, 1925), pp. 409ff., certainly would not substantiate Neusner's view. First, if any fast would arouse the hopes of the people, it would be the ninth day of Ab. Many have seen this as the reason behind R. Judah the Prince's attempt to nullify this fast (or at least, when it was transferred from the Sabbath to Sunday). One should also see the views expressed by the classical commentaries such as the Tosafot, *Ta'anit* 11b, *s.v. ayn;* Nissim Gerondi, *ad loc.;* and Meiri, *ad loc.* In any case, Samuel here was against granting the technical תענית ציבור, a "public fast" to additional fast days, and was not against fasts by the populace. In another statement, *Ta'anit* 11a אמר שמואל כל היושב בתענית נקרא חוטא, Samuel expressed his opposition to asceticism rather than to any overzealous Messianic hopes that might drive the people to foolish and risky activism. A similar view was expressed by the tannaitic R. Eleazar Ha-Kappor. [See also the editor's "The Guilt-Offering of the Defiled Nazrite," *JQR* (April, 1970), vol. LX, pp. 345–52.]

Despite these exceptions, we do agree with Neusner's basic conclusion, at least as far as Samuel is concerned. He was the champion of establishing good working relationships with the reigning power and of playing down everything that might arouse activistic approaches. His ruling that *keriah* (renting one's garment when in mourning) was not required for Jews who fought alongside the Romans and who were slain in battle (*M.K.* 26a) demonstrates this. Obedience to the reigning power was part of his *modus vivendi*. (See *B.B.* 3b and his major principle of *Dina D'Malkhuta Dina*. This principle surely emphasizes a recognition of the just nature of the governmental edicts, taxes and courts).

However, we disagree with Neusner's assessment of Rab's viewpoint. Rab opposed Samuel's friendship with Shapur. He accused Shapur of extortion (*B.M.* 70b and the commentators *ad. loc.* Even though *Ex. R.* 31, 10 would indicate that this statement was uttered in praise of Shapur, however, W. Bacher, *Die Agada der Babylonischen Amoräer*, 23 correctly sees this as sarcastically phrased). Rab, basically, was anti-Persian. He saw the Messiah as being of the Davidic line, like the Nasi, and therefore tied the Messianic expectations to Judea rather than to Babylonia. Thus, he also said: "Persia will eventually fall into the hands of Rome." (*Sanhedrin*, 98b, *Yoma*, 10a). Equally, he said that it would be better to be under Rome than Persia (*Shabbat*, 11a). Neusner's matter-of-fact acceptance of the text of *Horiyot*, 11b as a Palestinian affirmation of the Babylonian claim to be descendants of David is also questionable. The entire text is reversed in the Palestinian *Midrash Ve-Hizhir* (for details see my *Jewish Law in the Diaspora: Confrontation and Accommodation*).

The students of R. Yoḥanan b. Zakkai, R. Eliezer b. Hyrcanus and R. Joshua, equally disputed this issue concerning redemption. ר׳ אליעזר אומר אם ישראל עושין תשובה נגאלין ואם לאו אין נגאלין. א״ל ר״י אם אין עושין תשובה אין נגאלין? אלא הקב״ה מעמיד להן מלך שגזירותיו קשות כהמן וישראל עושין תשובה ומחזירין למוטב (R. Eliezer said: "If Israel repents they will be redeemed; if not, they will not be redeemed." R. Joshua said to him: "If they do not repent, they will not be redeemed? The Holy One, blessed be He, will place over them a king whose decrees will be as harsh as Haman's and the Israelites will repent and return to doing good" [*Sanh.* 97b–98a]).

It is quite clear that the view of R. Eliezer is that the redemption is directly dependent upon repentance. With it, the redemption will come; without it, Israel will not be redeemed. The problem is the view of R. Joshua. From his question, 'And if Israel does not repent, will they not be redeemed?,' it would seem that his view is that whether or not Israel repents, the redemption will come. R. Joshua could not conceive of God allowing Israel to languish in an eternal exile. The problem arises with the last part of the statement concerning the installation of a king whose decrees will be like Haman's. If these words are part of R. Joshua's statement, does he then agree with R. Eliezer that repentance is an essential prerequisite and should Israel not initiate repentance on its own, God will send a wicked king whose decrees will provoke Israel to turn to God whether they want to or not? In other words, the only distinction between R. Eliezer and R. Joshua is whether or not Israel must repent of their own accord. Should they fail to do so, R. Eliezer claims that God will not intervene, while R. Joshua claims that God will forcefully induce Israel to repent. Consequently, both agree that redemption without repentance is an impossibility. The Palestinian Talmud rejects this entirely. Its text reads as follows: . . . אם אין ישראל עושין תשובה אין נגאלין לעולם, ''If Israel does not repent, it will never be redeemed.'' To which R. Joshua retorted: וכי אם יעמדו ישראל ולא יעשו תשובה אינן נגאלין לעולם, ''If Israel stands pat and does not repent, will they never be redeemed?'' Now, instead of the next word reading ''*elah*-but'', which would merely continue the words of R. Joshua, the Palestinian Talmud's text states א"ל, that is, R. Eliezer responded that a king will arise whose decrees will be as Haman's, etc. One can easily see the cause for the scribal confusion between the word אלא and the abbreviation of א"ל. In any case, according to the Palestinian Talmud, the dispute is far more sharp. R. Eliezer requires repentance as a prerequisite to redemption while R. Joshua does not. It was R. Eliezer who added that if Israel does not repent by its own volition, God will intervene and cause Israel's repentence by means of an evil king. However, to R. Joshua, redemption is completely in God's hands. He will decide when it is to come about and Israel's deeds have no bearing on the matter.

The Talmud then cites a series of biblical verses, ostensibly cited by the two disputants, to substantiate their points of view. The last of these verses was cited by R. Joshua. The Talmud then ends the discussion with איסתלק ר' אליעזר—R. Eliezer went away or שתק ר"א—R. Eliezer kept silent. Most commentaries see this ending as a sign that R. Eliezer conceded the argument in favor of R. Joshua. His silence was considered tantamount to admission that R. Joshua was correct. The problem with this interpretation is that subsequently, all the amoraim and the later sages accepted R. Eliezer's point of view, namely, that the Messianic age will only be ushered in by Israel's repentance.

We therefore suggest that the phrase at the end of the Talmudic discussion did not signify capitulation, but rather that R. Eliezer walked

away from the discussion convinced that there was no point in continuing
the dispute. Another verse, or yet another verse would not alter the
stance taken by each of the disputants. R. Eliezer did not concede his
position; rather, he recognized the futility in continuing the attempt to
win over the other side.

The same sages also disputed the time of the redemption. R. Eliezer
maintained redemption will arrive in the month of Tishrei, while R.
Joshua said it will be in Nisan. These were not two unrelated disputes but
were really part of the same outlooks. R. Eliezer did not intend his statement to be taken literally. To him, redemption without repentance was
inconceivable. Since no one can foretell when Israel will repent, no specific time can be forecast when the redemption will come. R. Eliezer felt
that redemption was totally an internal affair, not at all dependent upon
God's Will but upon Israel's moral behavior. He, therefore, pointed to
the month of Tishrei, indicating a period of penitence. In fact, R. Eliezer
added בר״ה בטלה עבודה מאבותינו במצרים—"it was on Rosh Hashanah that
slavery was ended in Egypt and our ancestors ceased their toil", as if to
say, even if the Exodus took place in Nisan, slavery ended in Tishrei.

In essence, then, R. Eliezer felt that redemption is clearly dependent
upon repentance. It is not an eschatological phenomenon which has its
own existence. It has no fixed time. Redemption will come when Jews
repent. R. Joshua opposed this view. It is inconceivable to him that Israel
will not be redeemed even if she does not repent. He felt that redemption
is an independent phenomenon and will arrive no matter what Israel does
or does not do. He paralleled the first redemption with the ultimate one.
Just as the first redemption from Egypt came about even though the
Israelites were steeped in iniquity and did not repent their ways, yet God
redeemed them, so it will come about at the end when Israel will be redeemed even without repentance no matter how deeply entrenched in spiritual mire they might be. To R. Joshua, the redemption was totally re-
legated to God, Who will decide the time of the Messiah's arrival. Again,
just as with the Egyptian Exodus a specific date was designated, so also
will the Messiah arrive at a specific date, known only to God. *Tanḥuma*
(Beḥuḳotai, ed. Buber, 3) adds to R. Joshua's statement: בין עושין תשובה
ובין שאין עושין כיון שהגיע הקץ מיד נגאלין ("Whether they repent or not, as soon
as the End comes, they will be redeemed"). According to Urbach, the
redemption in question refers to the Messianic age. R. Eliezer has no
עת הקץ—no "End." As a result, there is no point to attempt to calculate
when this "End" will come. Contrariwise, R. Joshua makes room for

the מחשבי קצין—the calculators of the "End." His view also allows for the *Heblei mashiah*, the birth pangs of the Messiah, which are to precede the advent of the Messiah.

The redemption of which these sages spoke referred to the natural restoration of peace, political autonomy, and freedom, the restoration of the Temple, etc., none of which is eschatological in nature. Even the harsh king was not meant to be a miraculous occurrence, but a gradual process compared to the gradual rise of Haman. This king, like Haman, will take advantage of circumstances that will place him in power. He will bide his time and find the right moment to issue his evil decrees. These will eventually become so fierce that they will make Israel look heavenward for redemption. This is repentance. However, neither sage spoke of an eschatological, Messianic redemption.

When one examines rabbinic sources, both tannaitic and amoraic, it becomes evident that the sages rejected R. Joshua's view. They concluded that God can redeem Israel even prior to the "End." They also did not fully agree with R. Eliezer's view. They believed that God's grace could overcome all. Finding themselves in the post–Bar Kokhba era, they compared themselves to the period of the Exodus. Just as Israel then was not fit for redemption, yet the redemption came, so it was possible in their own day. For additional information, we recommend that the reader look at the view expressed in the *Mekhilta* (*Bo* V, 5, ed. Hurwitz, p. 14) and A. Marmorstein, "The Idea of Redemption in the Aggada of the Tannaim and Amoraim" (in Hebrew, *Memorial Volume Studies in Jewish Theology* [London, 1950], p. 17–76).

Jacob Neusner, (*op. cit.* p. 54), presents an intriguing interpretation of the intense struggle for power between the Babylonian Exilarchs and the rabbis. He claims that the basis of the power of the Exilarchs was the "Messiah Myth," while the power of the rabbis rested on the "Torah Myth." Thus, as one example, Neusner interprets R. Naḥman's statement (*Sanh.* 98b): אי מן חייא הוא כגון אנא שנא׳ והיה אדירו ממנו ומושלו מקרבו יצא ("If the Messiah is of the living, then he is one as I, for it is said, 'And their nobles shall be of themselves, and their governors shall proceed from their midst' [Jer. 30:21]"). In other words, R. Naḥman felt that if the Exilarchate is considered self-rule, its existence fulfills Jeremiah's promise that the Messianic era is to be when Jews govern themselves. In this manner he interpreted the phrase "nobles shall be of themselves, governors shall proceed from their midst." To him, the Exilarch was the scion of David and governed. His edicts are legitimate and must be obeyed. Obedience, therefore, fulfills the Messianic role. The Exilarch's power was not seen in terms of Persian power but as totally legitimate from the standpoint of Jewish tradition.

On the other hand, Neusner claims, the rabbis saw observance of the Torah as the prerequisite to the advent of the Messianic age. This Torah, first revealed to Moses, then handed over to the prophets and eventually received by the sages, was best understood by the latter, who expressed the full Will of God. Since the rule of the rabbis was based on Torah, it was not mere governing that was of greatest import but the qualities of justice, righteousness, etc.

The pivotal point of their dispute was that the sages claimed the redemption can only come by means of a moral reformation, which was basically the core of their rule. The Exilarchs saw themselves as the "stand-ins" for the Messiah. As long as they ruled, "the scepter had not departed." They were the link between David of the past and David of the future.

In the generation before the destruction of the Second Temple, there were some vague indications of Messianic movements. Greenstone concluded that the time was acute for the advent of a Messiah. However, he feels that this was due to the cruelty of the Roman procurators. They forced some Jews to join the Ebionites or the Nazarenes, whose central philosophy revolved around a Messiah; some were slaughtered by the Romans when they joined demagogues with Messianic claims, men such as Theudas and Simon of Cyprus; while others, who attempted to resist Titus, had not time left for Messianic ideas. It seems to this writer, however, that these Messianic indications were not due to increased Roman persecutions but to the popular belief that the chronology of that day was ripe for Messianism. For detailed information, the reader might consult the work by A. Z. Eshkoli cited in the bibliography.

II. Natural and Supernatural Messianism

The idea of a Messiah in Judaism centered around a human figure. He may have been assigned exceptional qualities of wisdom and understanding; he was to bring peace and a just life to Israel and to mankind, but he was never more than a being of flesh and blood. Israel will be redeemed from all oppression; the yoke of the exile will be removed; the exiles will be gathered-in; the kingship of Israel will be restored and the world will recognize the sovereignty of God. None of these will be brought about by means other than natural ones. The third-century amora, Samuel, best described it when he said (*Ber.* 34b): אין בין עולם הזה לימות המשיח אלא שיעבוד מלכויות בלבד ("There is no difference between this world and the Days of the Messiah except the bondage of foreign powers"). Even those who spoke of a supernatural Messianic era, which would be preceded by supernatural events and a radical transformation of the world, still spoke of it as being this-worldly.

Some sages, who accepted the supernatural nature of the Messianic era, claimed (*Pes. R.* 2,3): עתידה ירושלים להיות כא״י, וא״י ככל העולם כולו ("In the future, Jerusalem will be expanded to the size of Eretz Yisrael and Eretz Yisrael as the entire world"). Another statement said that the expansion of Jerusalem will equal the amount a horse travels in one half a day (*Pes.* 50a). Nevertheless, all Jews will come to pray in Jerusalem because the clouds will carry them and bring them to their destination. All kinds of fantastic tales were spun. Jerusalem will be filled with precious stones and anyone may take of them to his heart's desire. In monetary disputes between two Jews, both will come to Jerusalem to adjudicate their dispute before the Messiah. However, as soon as they cross the border into Jerusalem, their dispute will be settled. The defendant will pay the demand with the jewels of Jerusalem (*Pes. d'R. Kahane* 127a).

Despite these and other miraculous tales, it was believed that life during the Messianic age would still be normal. The Messiah will build the Temple; the priests will sacrifice therein; the Levites will chant the Psalms and the Torah will be the same. All of these are amoraic statements. In fact, in tannaitic literature, the Messiah has no miraculous powers. He is no wonder-worker. These miraculous descriptions of the Messianic age are, therefore, the vivid imagination of what Jews thought the Messianic age would be like. Similar traditions were found in the Pseudepigraphal literature, which was not the literature of the mainstream of Judaism. Despite the fact that some statements, such as the passage related in the name of R. Gamaliel (*Shab.* 30b and *Ket.* 111b), appear to be tannaitic, they can easily be shown to be of amoraic origin. Many of these passages of the amoraim were prefaced by the phrase אל תתמה ("Do not be astounded . . . "). Phrases such as these obviously show that the author himself recognized the exaggeration in which he was about to engage.

III. Jewish and Christian Doctrines of the Messiah

The idea of the Messiah in Christianity stemmed almost completely from the apocalyptic, supernatural expression of the Messianic hope. It is totally based on the personality of the Messiah. Because of the political failure of Jesus and the fear of Roman power, political redemption was looked upon as a Jewish problem, while spiritual redemption was considered a world problem.

Whereas Klausner, despite some basic differences, still described the redemption ideas of Judaism and Christianity as essentially the same, G. Scholem, on the other hand, saw them as totally different, and therefore their ideas of the Messiah are totally different. In Judaism, redemption was a public, outer event, which was to take place on the stage of human history. In Christianity, redemption concerns the private world of every individual, the spiritual world within the soul of a person. In Judaism, Messianism was to take place in the distant future and at the end of history, while in Christianity it is the basis of the historical process.

Judaism and Christianity also differed in one other major point. To Christianity, the following words of Jeremiah were uniquely significant: לא כברית אשר כרתי את אבותם ביום החזיקי בידם להוציאם מארץ מצרים אשר המה הפרו את בריתי ואנכי בעלתי בם נאום ד'. כי זאת הברית אשר אכרת את בית ישראל אחרי הימים ההם נאם ד' נתתי את תורתי בקרבם ועל לבם אכתבנה והייתי להם לא-להים והמה יהיו לי לעם ("Not according to the covenant that I made with their fathers in the day that I took them by the hand to bring them out of the land of Egypt; which my covenant they broke, although I was a lord over them, saith the Lord. But this shall be the covenant that I will make with the House of Israel; After those days, saith the Lord, I will put my law in the inward parts, and write it in their hearts; and will be their God, and they will be my people" [Jer. 31:31–32]).

Christians saw this as a declaration that law-and-book religion would be abrogated and at the End all such restricting things would vanish. Instead, recognition of God that stems from within a person will take its place and will not be based on the letter of the law. Christianity saw a "new covenant," where inward fulfillment of the old code would be possible. It was no longer necessary to have an external law, but all will depend on the inner, human personality. The stress and emphasis was placed upon such phrases as "in the heart" and the "inner parts."

A utopian Messianism always implied that the End would culminate in the perfection of Jewish law. Only in the Messianic age can all of *halakhah* be fulfilled. The phrase *hilkhata le'meshiḥa* meant that Jewish law could only be realized in its totality in a world ruled by the Messiah. It is true that Torah was not considered subject to change. It was a *Torah temimah* and eternal. Nevertheless, there were those who concluded that the Messiah would enhance the understanding of the present Torah and allow everyone to come to a closer comprehension of the Divine. On the other hand, since the Messiah would usher in a period where the good ultimately triumphs and where no evil exists, there were those who wondered: Why bother with the *mitzvoth?* After all, their purpose is essentially to allow for the discrimination between good and evil. Christianity, therefore, concluded that the Messianic age ushers jn a time of anarchy, freedom from religious law. All of Paulinian theology was based on the idea that the law is to be abrogated with the advent of the Messiah. The crux of the difference between Jewish and Christian religion hinges on this one basic principle.

The question to which Paul addressed himself was not just the problem of πνεῦμα, the spirit of the law, versus γραμμα, the letter of the law. The Messianic fulfillment led Paul to conclude that the time had come for the annulment of the Torah. With the advent of a Messiah, he felt, men had no longer a need for a Torah to be liberated from sin. All that would be achieved by the Messiah.

R. Bultmann (in his *Theologie des Neuen Testaments* [Tübingen, 1953], p. 55) describes the early Christian community as having an ambivalent attitude to Torah. They might even have been afraid to accept Paul's ideas about shedding Torah law. Urbach, in his book *The Sages,* claims that Jews were not yet concerned with Christian theology but were ready to point out their inconsistencies. Urbach feels that this was the purpose of the sarcastic tale told concerning Imma Shalom and her brother R. Gamaliel.

> Imma Shalom, R. Eliezer's wife, was the sister of R. Gamaliel. In her neighborhood, there was a certain philosopher who had a good reputation that he did not accept bribes. They sought to expose him so she brought him a golden lamp and said to him, "I desire that a share be given me in my father's estate." He said to them, "Divide it." He [R. Gamaliel] said to him, "It is decreed for us, 'Where there is a son, a daughter does not inherit.'" He replied, "From the day that you were exiled from your land, the Law of Moses has been taken away, and the law of the Evangelion has been given, and in it is written, 'A son and a daughter inherit equally.'" The next day, he [R. Gamaliel] brought him a Libyan ass. He [the judge] said to them, "Look at the end of the book and in it is written, 'I came not to destroy the Law of Moses nor to add to the Law of Moses,' and in it is written, 'A daughter does not inherit where there is a son.'" She said to him, "Let your light shine as a lamp!" R. Gamaliel said to her, "The ass has come and knocked over the lamp!" [*Shab.* 116a–b]

We disagree with Urbach's assessment of the incident. First of all, during the period of R. Gamaliel there was great concern with Christian inroads. The *Birkhat Haminim* (the blessing against the apostates), the changes in terminology as well as ritual, and many other indications all show this great concern. The story of Imma Shalom and R. Gamaliel also helps point out their anti-Paulinian ideas. These, of course, became stronger by the end of the tannaitic era, when Christian ideology also became more clear and set along the teachings of Paul. Thus, concerning Psalm 136, which contains twenty-six verses, each of which gives thanks to the Almighty and uses the word *hodu* ("Give thanks"), R. Joshua b. Levi said: "To what do these twenty-six *hodus* ['give thanks'] correspond? To the twenty-six generations which the Holy One, blessed be He, created in His world; though he did not give them the Torah, He sustained them by His grace." This statement refers to the twenty-six generations from Adam to Moses, who could not sustain themselves by their deeds since no Torah had yet been given, yet who nevertheless were sustained by God's grace. It obviously shows that grace was required as long as Torah had not yet been given. It opposes the Paulinian idea that Torah was supplanted by grace.

The term בר אנש, usually and erroneously translated "son of man," has great significance to Christian theology and has had many interpretations. We offer one interpretation by N. Schmidt, who does not see this as a Messianic term, in the third section of this book. Others, such as Bacon, Dalman, Klausner, P. Parker, and Edwin A. Abbott, agree with him. In opposition, Eduard Meyer and R. H. Charles argue that the phrase cannot just mean "man," since in the New Testament the "son of man" was given authority to forgive sin and is lord over the Sabbath.

Prof. M. S. Enslin, in his *The Prophet from Nazareth* (New York, 1961), partially recognized that in these cases the only proper translation is "man" and not "son of man." Prof. Zeitlin pointed out (*JQR,* October 1961, p. 188 and elsewhere) that the translation of this phrase as "son of man" is based on a mistranslation. The Aramaic has the meaning of "man," while the Greek translators of the Gospels thought that בר אנש meant "son of man."

IV. The Two Messiahs

The Bar Kokhba revolt gave great impetus to the Messianic idea. Despite his central role as leader of Palestinian Jewry, we know almost nothing about the life of Bar Kokhba. Who was he? What was his name? How did he conduct himself up to and during the rebellion? All we really know about him is that he was killed in battle when Betar fell. We are not even sure of his name. In the Talmud, he is referred to as Bar Kokhba and Bar Kosiba. Some of the Jewish Chroniclers, as, for example Ibn Daud in his *Sefer Hakabbalah,* call him Bar Kosiba, while others, such as Gedaliah Ibn Yahya in his *Shalsheleth Hakabbalah,* call him Bar Kokhba. Justin Martyr, who lived during this period, calls him $\beta\alpha\rho\chi\omega\chi\acute{\epsilon}\beta\alpha\varsigma$. Yet many modern scholars have insisted that his name was Bar Kosiba and that Kosiba was either his father or the town of his birth. For a full discussion of these sources, we urge the reader to study the work by S. Yeivin entitled *Milhemeth Bar Kokhba.* Yeivin concluded that Bar Kosiba was so named because of the community from which he hailed, since he could find no such Hebrew name as Kosiba. Indeed, the Jews of that era avoided all names that had some evil or sinister connotation (*Sanh.* 82b). Similarly, Bar Kokhba must also stem from his community since there is no Hebrew name Kokhba. Yeivin, then, speculates upon two communities—one of which, *Ka'u'kab,* about 12.5 kilometers northeast of Zezun, is mentioned by the Church Fathers. The second, in the Galilee, is an Arab town by the same name about 4 kilometers northwest of Kufr Manda. This last-named community is in the vicinity of Nazareth, where many families claimed to be descended from the House of David. According to Christian tradition, the Romans, during the time of Hadrian and Domitian, searched for descendants of the Davidic family in the vicinity of Nazareth. It follows, says Yeivin, that Bar Kokhba considered himself to be a descendant of the House of David. Without this the sages, especially R. Akiba, would never have supported him or considered him to be the Messiah.

Contrariwise, S. Zeitlin, in an article entitled "Bar Kokba and Bar Kozeba" (*JQR,* vol. XLIII [July 1952], pp. 77–82), points out that when the sages of that period wanted to describe the place from which someone hailed, they used the word *ish* followed by the name of city. For example, there were תדוס איש רומי, יוסי בן יועזר איש צרידה, יעקב איש כפר סכניא and others. However, the word *bar* is never used for this purpose in tannaitic writings, the New Testament, or Josephus. Secondly, had his name been Kozeba, those opposed would surely have played up the connotation of liar and claimed failure for the rebellion right from the outset. Thus, Zeitlin concluded that his surname was Bar Kokhba and his proper name was Simon, as evident from the coins that bore his name. Why was he called Bar Kokhba? R. Akiba considered him to be the Messiah and interpreted the words in Numbers 24:17—דרך כוכב מיעקב ("There shall step forth a star out of Jacob")—as referring to the leader of the revolt.

Klausner emphasizes that the fact that Bar Kokhba was accepted even though he was not of Davidic origin merely highlights how strong the Messianic hopes were at that time. It proves to him also that this era emphasized the political aspect of the Messianic hope only.

There is no question that Klausner erred regarding Bar Kokhba's non-Davidic origin. The exchange between R. Akiba and Yoḥanan b. Torta, where the latter argued: "Akiba! Grass will grow on your cheeks but the Son of David will not have come," proves the error. Had Bar Kokhba not been a scion of the House of David, Yoḥanan b. Torta could easily have demolished R. Akiba's support of Bar Kokhba. The fact is that no one would have accepted Bar Kokhba without Davidic background. However, Bar Kokhba's statement as he went to battle, ריבונה דעלמא לא תסעוד ולא תכסוף ("Master of the World, we do not need Your assistance, but do not help our enemy"—PT Taan. 4, 68d; compare with Lam. R. II, 2, where it was said by two brothers and not Bar Kokhba), indicates that this was not a spiritual but rather a political, national revolt. It was probably for this reason that many of the sages opposed R. Akiba and the revolt.

The traumatic experience of Bar Kokhba's failure and the persecutions that followed brought sharp reactions to the Messianic hopes. With the Bar Kokhba rebellion ending in disaster, the concept of two Messiahs, the Messiah b. Joseph and the Messiah b. David, seems to have been created. Their origin and purpose have been the subject of great debate. We have devoted one section to the analysis of this phenomenon in Jewish life. Scholars have been faced with the reality that two Messiahs are mentioned in Jewish eschatology. However, the sources are scant and little information is available to us. The first question to be answered is: When did the idea of a second Messiah develop? If, as many scholars feel, the idea originated after the Bar Kokhba revolt, then the following additional questions must be resolved:

1. What was the purpose of a second Messiah?
2. Why did this idea develop just at this time?
3. Why was the second Messiah of the tribe of Joseph?
4. Why was he to die in battle?
5. Is there a connection between the dying Messiah b. Joseph and the suffering servant of Christianity?

We have presented two articles that deal with the subject from different standpoints. Other works on this theme, such as the writings of Aptowitzer, Ginzberg, Dix, Wieder, Kuhn, Von Wunde, Moore, and Hurwitz, are presented in the bibliography. Some of them trace this idea to different time periods. Some speak of a Messiah of Judah (Israel) and of Aaron, Melchizedek, Elijah, etc. Still others felt there were many Messiahs in early history. Klausner here expands his theory to include both Messiahs. To him, the Messiah b. Joseph served as the political Messiah, while the Messiah b. David served as a spiritual Messiah. However, Klausner fails to answer the many questions we listed above.

V. Messianic Phenomena: Speculation and Calculations

One problem which was never quite resolved in Jewish thinking concerned the arrival of the Messiah. Was the Messianic idea dependent upon human action, and therefore could the Messiah be induced to arrive at any time, or did the Messianic dream not include human responsibility and determination to do something about its realization, but was left to the complete discretion of God? Messianic activism, lured by utopian ends, always urged man's participation in his own destiny. Many rabbinic sages, however, warned against "forcing the End," threats that were resented by the revolutionary minds.

Those who left the Messianic arrival completely to God encouraged calculations as to the Messiah's arrival date. Much opposition arose. Some were opposed because they feared popular disillusionment when calculated dates came and went without the Messiah's arrival, thus the statement of R. Jonathan: תפח עצמן של מחשבי קיצין ("May the bones of the calculators of the End rot"). The opposition of others was prompted by the fear of possible misuse of such calculations by those who falsely claimed Messiahship. Finally, Christian polemicists often used such calculations to prove the Messiahship of Jesus. We have presented a number of articles which concern themselves with such calculations and their methods.

The last section of the book is a collection of various ideas that were associated with Messianism. Certainly not enough is included, but at least the reader will be able to sample some of the themes discussed. Judaism speaks of *heblei mashiah*, the birth pangs of the Messiah. Christianity speaks of a "suffering servant." However, these are not to be interchanged. The Jewish idea of *heblei mashiah* refers to the suffering that is to be visited upon the world prior to the advent of the Messiah. Nor is the War of Gog and Magog, whether at the beginning or the end of the Messianic age, to be misconstrued as part of a "suffering messiah" theory. In Judaism, it was thought of as the last struggle between the forces of good and evil. All of these events are to be this-worldly. We have also included brief articles concerning the regeneration of the world.

It has been pointed out that eschatology and myth are related to each other. Myth gives a picture of the unknown past. It graphically describes the origin of things. More than that, it projects a particular story into its universal or ideal sense. Eschatology does the same, except that, instead of the past, it deals with the future. Since it is impossible for people to assess the past or the future except through their imaginations, we tend to see the past or the future in terms of an ideal past and an ideal future.

It becomes quite evident, then, how a kind of Messianic parallelism between the ideal past and the ideal future arose. Prompted by a host of national disasters, loss of land, loss of independence, loss of Temple, etc., combined with a firm determination to continue existence as a people, the Messianic idea became prominent in Jewish life. Probably far more responsible was the firm belief that God is a God of Justice, and inherent in His very existence is the restoration of Israel which He had promised. In order to vindicate his own Name—ומביא גואל לבני בניהם למען שמו—and fulfill His own Word, God will send a redeemer.

The sages recognized this parallelism. They spoke of the Exodus as the *geulah rishonah,* the "first redemption," and Moses as the *goel rishon,* the "first redeemer." They spoke of the Messianic age as the *geulah aharona,* the "ultimate redemption," and the Messiah as the *goel aharon,* the "ultimate redeemer" (*Gen. R.* 85; *Exod. R.* I; *Tanh., Shemot* 8; *Tazriah* 8; *Sanh.* 19b). Just as Moses was raised in the House of Pharaoh in Egypt, so the Messiah will be in Rome. Both had to appear and then hide. Just as Moses crossed from Midian to Egypt riding on an ass, so will the Messiah arrive riding on an ass. Just as Moses gave water in the desert, so the Messiah will make rivers flow in the desert (*Koh. R.* I, 9).

Since the golden age of ancient Jewry took place during the Davidic days, and the Messianic idea became the Jewish hope to regain the "good old days," it is no wonder that David, or the scion of David, was to be the Messiah. Furthermore, being essentially a political idea, it was tied to the real, historical line of David, King of Israel. How did David reach this status? First of all, as we have stated, the Davidic age was considered, politically or otherwise, the best of all ages. Secondly, the unique position

of Judah in terms of leadership was enunciated as early as the Blessings of
Jacob at the end of Genesis. Space does not allow us to discuss the important phrase עד כי יבא שילה ("until he will come to Shilo" – Gen. 49:10) and
the key word "Shilo," which still has not clearly been defined, thereby
leaving the entire passage, at best, ambiguous. Furthermore, Nathan the
prophet forecast (II Sam. 7:16):ונאמן ביתך וממלכתך עד עולם לפניך כסאך יהיה נכון
עד עולם ("And thy house and thy kingdom shall be established forever
before thee; thy throne shall be established forever").

It was accepted that authority was here granted to the Davidic House
to be the kings over Israel, as well as the Divine promise for their eternal
existence. In some instances, this was interpreted to refer to specific kings
who historically fulfilled the prophecy. In time, since reality had not really sated Jewish expectancy, the prophecy was reinterpreted, adjusted, and
cast forward in time to an eschatological fulfillment.

These, except for the last, are all amoraic statements. In the earlier
period, as in the amoraic period, it appears that the Messianic idea, important as it may have been, had not assumed the status of a creed. Individuals, and perhaps even groups of sages, had deep feelings concerning the Messianic idea, but the fact remains that R. Judah the Prince did
not include the Messianic idea in the Mishnah. The two references that
are made are not clear. Once it is found in the tractate *Sotah* 49b, which is
not a Mishnah but a baraita, and a second time in the tractate *Berakhoth*
12b, where it refers to *Olam Habaah,* the Future World, and not to the
Messianic age, as can be determined by a comparison between this text
and the text of the Palestinian Talmud. In any case, the fact that R. Judah
omitted from Mishnah *Sanhedrin* a statement concerning the Messianic
belief equal to the statements made concerning the belief in *Torah min
Shomayim* (the Divine, heavenly origin of Torah) and Resurrection, leads
one to wonder what the status of the Messianic idea really was at the
beginning of the third century of the common era.

The literature on the subject of Messianism in the Talmudic era is
vast. The problem an editor of a volume such as this one faces is not what
to include but what to leave out. The constraints on this work, such as the
size of the volume and the limitation as to the number of articles permitted in a language other than English, are crucial. In addition, problems of
copyright limited the selections severely. Important areas, such as the
place and functions of Elijah, the differences between *Olam Habaah* (the
World to Come) and *Yemoth Hamashiah* (the Messianic days), the Messiah in prayer, and many more had to be omitted. We have attempted to
include some of the omitted material in our bibliography.

One word about the blurred definitions of the terms *Olam Habaah* and *Yemoth Hamashiah*. In rabbinic sources they are often interchanged, while at other times they stand for different concepts. Modern scholars have differed. While Klausner considers them to be different, Schürer sees them as one and the same. There is no doubt that Klausner is correct. Both terms refer to a time to come, and therefore the confusion arose. One possible sign that might distinguish the terms is this: if the statement contains either material or political hopes, it refers to the Messianic age; however, if there are also references to resurrection, life after death, Garden of Eden, Gehenna, etc., it refers to *Olam Habaah*. Hruby, whose article we have included, sees *Olam Habaah* as not being connected to Israel's national expectations. It is a personal expectation, dependent upon the Justice of God, individual merit, the concept of Reward and Punishment, and the eternity of the soul. It is true that individual merit does not allow itself to be separated from the ultimate fate of the entire nation. God's justice encompasses both nation and individual. However, an individual's fate depends upon his own moral status and not upon a redeemer. The conclusion, then, is that entrance to *Olam Habaah* is the reward for the righteous, who do so via resurrection. The sinners are punished by having no part in resurrection. There are numerous discussions by the sages concerning who will or will not have a share in *Olam Habaah,* but never once is there such a discussion concerning the Messianic era.

The first clear mention of resurrection in the Bible is in the Book of Daniel (12:1): ובעת ההיא ימלט עמך כל הנמצא כתוב בספר. ורבים מישני אדמת עפר יקיצו לחיי עולם ואלה לחרפות לדראון עולם והמשכילים יזהירו כזהר הרקיע ומצדיקי הרבים ככוכבים לעולם ועד. (" . . . and at that time, your people shall be delivered, everyone that shall be found written in the book. And many of them that sleep in the dust of the earth shall awake, some to everlasting life and some to shame and everlasting contempt. And they that are wise shall shine as the brightness of the skies; and they that turn many to righteousness as the stars for ever and ever").

Accordingly, both righteous and wicked share in resurrection. Later on, Josephus attributed the belief in resurrection to the Pharisees. Thus, he stated: "They also believe that souls have an immortal vigor in them, and that under the earth there will be rewards and punishments according as they have lived virtuously or viciously in this life; and the latter are to be detained in everlasting prison, but the former shall have power to revive and live again" (*Ant.* 18. 1, 3).

Scholars differ as to the exact meaning of Josephus. Did the Pharisees believe in physical resurrection of the body or in immortality of the soul? Urbach, Dodd, and others believe that the passage refers to *Tehiyat haMetim,* the return of the soul to the body which is revived. Immortality of the soul, Josephus attributed to the Essenes, who believed that the soul escapes from the body at death. Thus, to Urbach, *Tehiyat haMetim* takes place *before* reward and punishment in *Olam Habaah.* S. Zeitlin, on the other hand, believed that the Pharisees postulated immortality of the soul but did not subscribe to a physical resurrection. Even the term *Tehiyat haMetim* does not refer to physical resurrection.

In later days, according to some, there appears to have been a connection between Elijah and resurrection (*Sotah* 49b; *PT Shab.* I, 5; *PT Shek.* II, end). In some instances, resurrection is assigned to God Himself (*Midr. Tehillim* 93). Other questions, such as whether or not resurrection applies to non-Jews as well, and whether it occurs in Eretz Yisrael first, are also discussed.

The phrase *Aharith haYamim* ("at the end of days") has had a variety of interpretations. Gressman and Volz said that all prophets, including the pre-exilic ones, were eschatologists. Others, among them Hölscher and Mowinckel, maintain that none of the prophets were eschatologists. Both of these schools hold that the phrase in question refers to a time when this world comes to an end. We have presented the views of Kosmala, who feels that *Aharith haYamim* is the time furthest away, the extreme, the time which comes last. The term *aher,* he claims, means that something else "follows." Thus, in Deuteronomy 11:12, the recurring agricultural years are described as *reshith* and *aharith,* where each end has a new beginning that follows. Furthermore, the word *haYamim* is never used in the sense of absolute time. The word *haYom* means "today." Therefore, *haYamim* means "the days of the present time." As a result, *Aharith haYamim* indicates a period that has not yet occurred but will come at the extreme end of this age.

A word about my beloved teacher, who also became my friend, Dr. Solomon Zeitlin, of blessed memory. When I began this project he encouraged me, as he always did in my academic career, as well as in my personal life. He always gave freely of his time and was ever ready to discuss whatever problems or issues confronted me. The void he has left has not been filled, nor could it have been, by anyone else. I sorely miss him.

I wish to commend KTAV PUBLISHING HOUSE for rendering outstanding service to the field of Jewish scholarship. The company, by reprinting Jewish scholarly works, has made inaccessible material available, has gathered scattered material into concise and handy volumes, and generally has aided scholarship by its productions.

I wish to thank the entire library staff at Yeshiva University for their constant help.

I cannot end this Introduction without expressing my firm hope that the present State of Israel be indeed the *athalta de-Geulah,* the beginning of the first rays of redemption for the people of Israel and for all mankind.

June, 1978

Leo Landman
Yeshiva University

I

The Origin of the
Jewish Messianic Belief

THE SOURCES OF ISRAEL'S MESSIANIC HOPE

HUGO GRESSMANN

University of Berlin, Berlin, Germany

1. *Authenticity.*—The prophet's word is the poet's word. The first evidence of this is the repetition of thought in the *parallelismus membrorum*, the second is the distinct rhythm, however we may minutely define its character. Hence for the interpretation of the prophets we must not apply the laws of prose, as in the interpretation of the Old Testament stories, but the laws of poesy, which are different from those of prose. However, as there are different kinds of prose, so it is necessary to determine exactly the idea of *prophetic poesy*. This has not yet been done with the exactitude which is necessary to meet the problem of the history of Israel's literature.[1]

Here may be noted only one point of view, in which the prophetic books are in sharp contrast with the narrative books. The prose of the Old Testament is not of ornate but of plain style; it is lacking in epithets, ornamented speech, figures, and comparisons; in short, it wants the "inner forms" of poesy. The beauty of Hebraic prose consists only in the arrangement of the independent tale— and not in that of the collections or books of tales—and in concise logical and artistic construction, the parts of which are necessary to the context as a whole and the limits of which are sharply fixed. There is not a detail too many, nor one too few; they touch one

---

[1] For the history of literature and for the method of scientific definition terms of art are necessary, which should be used with exact signification. I have looked for such terms in Skinner's *Genesis*, but do not find them. We ought to distinguish, for purposes of explanation, quite exactly between myths, tales, or stories, legends (in Hebraic, *midrash*), fairy tales, fables, sentences, or proverbs (originally of wise men), etc.; furthermore between tales, historical tales (by word of mouth), and historiography (written historical tales), etc. There is only one history of Israelitish literature of this sort, that by Hermann Gunkel (in *Die Kultur der Gegenwart*, edited by Paul Hinneberg. Berlin, 1906, pp. 51 ff.). A good beginning is made by Richard G. Moulton, *The Literary Study of the Bible*, revised ed., London (1899). The history of Israelitish literature is in the main a history of style.

another like the wheels of a watch. Therefore, for the commentator, who should be a reproducing artist, it is comparatively easy to discover incoherence in the artistic whole, to perceive fissures and clefts, to show gaps and to supply that which is lacking, to remove inorganic additions, and to set apart secondary work. Such criticism is quite inapplicable to the books of the prophets. Although they are artists and their creations are not without an inner logic and a constraint of outer form, yet *the abrupt, hasty, and unquiet style is characteristic of prophetic poesy* in contrast with the clear, mature, and quiet manner of the prose writers. This difference is to be interpreted by the fact that the prophets are always of a troubled temper and are seized in their innermost soul. They are ever pronouncing their deliverances in excitation and passion, torn by the tempest of furious wrath or overpowered by the ardor of enthusiastic love. Their words are vibrant with the blessed paroxysms of communion with God and the secret mysteries of ecstasy. He who would understand them may not approach with sober and cool intellect, but he himself must feel something of this emotion; above all, he must have in mind that the psychic laws for excited men are different from those for normal ones. The *visionary* element brings the prophets near to the dreamers; their lyric is dream-lyric, their poesy is dream-poesy. Hence it is not only false, but even absurd, to transfer the principles of higher criticism, well approved in the interpretation of the Hexateuch, to prophetic poesy, which is governed by its own laws.

In spite of their intense experiences, the prophets in the expression of their thoughts adhere to the traditional forms, just as do the modern poets, who likewise, notwithstanding their boundless individualism, seldom break through the bars of the usual poetic types. The determination of the various forms of prophetic speech is again a task in the literary study of the Bible, which has scarcely been undertaken as yet. First of all, it is to be considered that the prophetic writings are not books of great, universal conception like the Homeric Epos, but every book is a collection, or an anthology of many prophetic poems by the same or by different authors. Unhappily, these poems are preserved in continuous text without any marks to separate one song from another. It is, therefore, *the first duty of exegesis, to fix the beginning and the end of each prophetic poem;* for without this preliminary work interpretation is impossible.   Imagine Goethe's lyrics printed like Isaiah's songs! Only a barbarian would do such a thing. But he would be no less a barbarian who would venture to treat Goethe's poems thus disfigured as if they had an inner unity, or who would undertake to comment upon an arbitrary combination of several songs having no connection with one another.   Is not that inter-preter then also a barbarian who applies such a method to Isaiah?

By good hap, the task that arises here for the history of litera-ture is not so difficult as it seems at first sight.   In determining the prophetic poems, we not only avail ourselves of identity of situa-tion and of aesthetic judgments; but we obtain another approach from the typical introductions and conclusions which frame all the songs and indicate their type.   "Thus Jahve has spoken" is said usually in the beginning; "for the mouth of Jahve has spoken it" is added frequently at the end.   A collection and investigation of such phrases and similar formulae and their importance for fixing the limits of prophetic poems is a pressing necessity in order to advance our understanding of the prophets and to forward the progress of literary study. He who has an eye for such things soon observes that the songs are generally very short.   In modern literary usage we should not call them "poems," but simply "sentences" or "words."   The prophets were no "rhetoricians" nor "preachers," but *poets of little sentences* orally pronounced.

For our purpose there are to be considered among the many species of prophetic poesy only two, and they meet us in all the prophetic books: the "threats" and the "promises."   These are in direct contrast with each other both in content and in temper. The threats predict ill fortune, the promises, on the contrary, good fortune for Israel.   In the threats, therefore, lives the wrath of the prophet against the sins of Israel; hence the threats are mostly combined with "denunciatory words," to give plausibility to the coming calamity.   The promises, however, are filled with the love of the prophet for his people; hence they are often joined with an "exhortation" to bring the hearers back to the right way and to lead them to happiness.   Each of the two species has run its

5

own course of development, which a study of the material would readily reveal. This too is a new problem of literary study well rewarding labor.

The promises are as different from the threats as love-songs from funeral songs. Certainly the two species are sometimes combined in the same poem, but usually they are independent of each other. Unless peculiar reasons force us, *we have no right to establish a connection between the threat and the promise;* for a poem, rounded in itself, should not be joined with another poem, likewise finished in itself. This simple consideration disposes of nearly all the arguments against the authenticity of the promises, or the messianic hopes almost identical with them. It is said that the prophe could not threaten and promise at one and the same time. But in fact, he does not. The conjunction of the two is purely arbitrary. But there is no reason why the prophet should not threaten at one time and promise at another time, as the poet may now mourn the death of his friend, and again may sing as a lover.

It may be objected that these comparisons are lame. The prophet predicting to his people sometimes ill fortune, sometimes good fortune could not be filled now with burning wrath and then with glowing love for Israel. Why not? Also in this case he is like the poet; both are *animated by changing moods.* Is this surprising in such impassioned men as the prophets? They were no dogmatists obliged to avoid contradictions; they did not endeavor, for the most part, to declare their opinions systematically, so much so that it is impossible for us to apprehend all the details. Commonly the threats are spoken as absolutely as the promises; now the whole people shall be ruined without anyone being saved; again the prosperity of the new time shall be such that no one shall be lost. These prophecies exclude each other, but besides them we find a series of connecting sentences showing us how the prophets fitted them each to the other. That a great calamity would break upon Israel, they were always assured; they were doubtful only of one point, whether Jerusalem would escape the coming destruction or not. But after the ill fortune the good fortune would follow; yet not inevitably, but only if the remnant should repent. This thought Isaiah has embodied in the name of his son

6

(Isa. 7:3). If Israel does good, Jahve will be gracious "to the remnant of Joseph" (Amos 5:15); if Jerusalem is purified in the melting furnace, then it shall return as it was at the beginning (Isa. 1:25, 26).

Though threat and promise may be found separately, yet calamity and prosperity form a chronological unity which, however, is not always clearly stated, because it is to be completed as a matter of course: first calamity, then prosperity. By this consecution the logical contradiction of threat and promise is annulled. At any rate, it was dependent upon the prophets' inner experiences and moods, whether they were putting themselves in the time of ill fortune, painting horrid pictures of terror, or whether they were plunging into the time of happiness that was to follow later on. Now a cursory glance teaches us that with the greater prophets the threats are much more frequent than the promises. Hence it follows that the canonical prophets were *predominantly announcers of calamity.* Jeremiah (28:8) intimates that they were exclusively so. But he has said this in his conflict with "the prophet of grace," Hananiah, and in polemics one likes to be pointed and one is inclined to sharpen the contrast. According to the vision of his vocation Jeremiah was called to be a prophet (1:10), not only "to destroy, to ruin, and to demolish," but also "to build and to plant." It is characteristic that the negation is placed first. The greater prophets were, it is true, announcers of grace and good fortune, but they were so only in the second place. There was a time or there were situations, when they denied the grace of God totally, or when they clothed their idea of the great misery that was to come in such harsh words that the grace of God seemed to be excluded. Nor are we allowed to forget their controversy with their prophet-brethren who announced the contrary. Even this exaggeration knowing neither indulgence nor restraint reveals its very prophetic character, for it results from the passion of these men who did not think the golden mean to be the best way. In calmer moments they accepted the legitimacy of the expectation of good fortune that existed in Israel (Amos 5:14, "as you have said"); but they thought the realization of this prophecy to be possible only by the conversion of Israel. It is no hazard, on the contrary, it is worthy of notice that we never meet these announcements in the form of "threats," due to the wrath of the prophets, but nearly always in the "exhortations" that result from a milder disposition of soul.

Even these *limited prophecies* are so characteristic that their authenticity is not to be doubted. But if we think the coexistence of complete denial and limited acknowledgment of God's grace to be authentic tradition, we have no scruples in crediting the greater prophets with being the authors of *the promises* or messianic hopes, *which have no limit at all.* If the prophets were only announcers of calamity, had they only come to ruin and to demolish, then was their god an enigmatical God, and his doing was as senseless as the work of a peasant who is always ploughing and never seeding (Isa. 28:22–29). God, who governs not only the history of Israel but that of the whole world, would never have *inflamed* the prophets if his plan had been *the eternal No.* They would never have understood him, if he had spoken *his eternal Yes* only for the heathen. Though the sinful Israelites might be as indifferent to him as the Negroes (Amos 9:7), yet there was an Israel of faith and hope which the prophets could not give up. They did not know how it was to come; they felt no obligation to paint the future with scientific exactitude, but they were sure of one thing: though God should bring to ruin his whole people, yet would he find means sufficient to awaken from even the stones seed of Abraham. If we deprive the prophets of this idea, we make them demigods whose feet do not touch the earth.

Surely the expectation of God's grace must be understood as a matter of faith and a certitude of soul; but it is impossible to declare its origin by this fact, for the messianic hope has its root in the soil of popular imagination which is older than all prophecy. For this we not only have internal arguments, but Amos says plainly: "Then Jahve the God Zebaoth will be with you *as you have said*" (5:14); and still more distinctly: "Woe to those *wishing near* the day of Jahve" (5:18). Consequently, there were already people at the time of Amos who knew of the day of Jahve and longed for it as a day of light and happiness. These words are not sufficient to reconstruct the *popular expectation of grace;* one is obliged to add all the other traits of the prophecies which may certainly or probably be traced back to popular ideas. That is all the more reason why one should not form one's opinion in advance without having a comprehensive survey of the traditional facts.

If we look back from this preliminary knowledge, we understand now much more easily why the prophets, at least sometimes, gave promises. They were men of flesh and blood, and therefore sons of their time; they were earth-born and could not deny their origin in spite of the isolated grandeur of their thoughts which led them up to a giddy height. The messianic prophecies which are with difficulty adapted to the sphere of the prophet's ideas are certainly taken in part from the popular tradition. But if in reality they were spoken by the greater prophets in whose books they are to be read, we expect as a matter of course that they will show traces of prophetic spirit and that their religion and ethics will be much more elevated. Meditating upon the promises, two irrepressible questions that are always to be kept in sight present themselves to us: What ideas has the prophet taken from others? How much has he transformed them and adapted them to the actual situation?

2. *Contents.*—I confine myself to the pre-exilic promises in which the Messiah himself is spoken of, treating the others only as may be necessary. The most instructive is Mic. 5:1–5, a passage which, from the mention of Asshur, surely dates from the Assyrian time, and which therefore may have been written by Micah about the time of Hezekiah. From the smallest district,[1] so it is written there in a spirited antithesis, the Messiah, the greatest king, shall come. Beth Ephrath is the native place of David. Consequently the prophet does not expect a descendant of David, but the return of David himself. The ruler of the last days is at the same time the ruler of the first days, a new antithesis which can be applied to David only *cum grano salis* and which is transferred to him from

---

[1] I read with others in vs. 1, ואתה בית אפרת הצעיר באלפי יהודה; vs. 4, remove והיה זה שלום, a gloss to the preceding וישבו, and read באדמתנו וְהֵקִים הקים על), "to establish over," like Jer. 23:4; the subject is Jahve or his Messiah). The ending כו", being on the margin, has come into the text at a wrong place; it belongs to vs. 5, where is to be read הצילנו and furthermore בפתיחות. In vs. 3, remove יהוה, and in vs. 5, ארץ, *metri causa*.

9

another one. "Therefore," because the Messiah is to be born, "he [Jahve] gives them up" (the Israelites of the north). And so it must be, for, as everybody knows, the time of good fortune is immediately preceded by a time of ill fortune. The author alludes to ideas well known, otherwise he could not continue with the conclusive "therefore." One ought to imagine the birth of the Messiah to be the beginning of happiness. But only, when the distress has risen to the utmost, "she who travaileth will bring forth." The prophets speaks ἐν μυστηρίῳ; for who the queen-mother of the Messiah is, he does not know. The new birth of David is a great secret, blessed be the woman that bears him! Micah's dependence upon Isaiah is excluded by the fact that the greater prophets committed no plagiarism; and, what is more, Mic. 5:4 ff. contains ideas which we do not find in Isaiah. The first consequence of the messianic time is the reconstruction of Israel into a united nation: "Then the rest of its [Israel's] brethren will return to the sons of Israel." The Israelites of the north are already in the exile; hence this promise is pronounced after 722 B.C. Secondly, the Messiah, the pious king, will govern his people in the name and by the power of Jahve, and so his kingdom will be a kingdom of peace and will extend over the whole world. All nations are subject to the Messiah, even the Assyrians. If they are coming to subject Judah, as they did Northern Israel, then it will be the worse for them; for in that case, the Messiah has come to save Judah from this great distress. The author therefore expected the return of David soon after the conquest of Samaria, before Asshur had advanced the second time to menace Judah. Here, too, we find older ideas that cannot be fully explained by the situation of the contemporary history, for it is said: When Asshur dares enter the sacred, inviolable Judah, then "seven princes and eight human governors" will be established to rule over "the country of Nimrod" with sword and iron, and never more will they dare cross the plans of Jahve and disturb the peace of the world.

In the promise of Micah the combination of the Messiah with David who shall bring back prosperity to the united Israel, is dependent upon the contemporary history. Behind this idea of David's return, however, we recognize the older mythological thought of *the returning primeval king.* To him is also attributed the kingdom of peace and the world-dominion which cannot have had its origin in the remembrance of David's time. The Assyrians being the worst enemies of the Israelites, their subjection is easily explained by the state of the contemporary history. But behind this we find another idea which is a great deal older and which may be explained by mythological parallels which become clear only in later times: the Messiah can establish his kingdom only when *the satanic powers* are subjugated. While usually one shepherd is sufficient to tend a flock, the satanic Asshur must have seven or eight princes to rule it with iron scepters. So the time of prosperity is preceded by a terrible time of distress.

This promise of Micah touches closely the promise of Isaiah 7:10–17, which was not written down by the prophet himself but by one of his disciples.[1] According to the context, Isaiah had announced to Ahaz the deliverance from the calamity prepared by the Ephraimites and Arameans. As vss. 10 ff. belong to the same time (about 732 B.C.), we expect a promise. Now Isaiah wants to give a sign that he may show himself a prophet sent by God. Ahaz, however, resists him, because he will not tempt God. The prophet is highly irritated, for this resistance is an offense to Jahve. Therefore he himself will tell of a miracle that Jahve is going to perform. This introduction must be followed by a terrible threat against Ahaz. The man who wrote this down thought the following oracle to be a promise for Judah, but a threat against Ahaz. His conception must be ours, however the situation may have been invented. Any exegesis that does not do justice to this double-character of the passage is unsuccessful.[2] A young wife is pregnant, she will bear a son and will call him Immanuel;

---

[1] Compare vs. 13, ויאמר, the third (not the first!) person singular, and vs. 3, אל־ישעיהו. He who corrects to the first person falsifies the tradition. From this is to be explained the peculiar vs. 10, ויוסף יהוה; the "redactor" identifies Isaiah with Jahve and heightens the consciousness of the prophet a little. Isaiah is here degraded to a worker of miracles, and a magician.

[2] Vs. 14, העלמה = "a young wife"; the article is an idiom of the Hebraic. Vs. 15 from לדעתו till בטב is a gloss (cf. vs. 16). From vs. 17 remove ועל־עמך; for "over thee and thy family" belong together. The verse becomes meaningless through the words "over thy people." Remove את מלך אשור with others.

11

he will eat honey and milk. Before the boy has grown up, Ephraim and Aram will be devasted. But God will bring upon Ahaz and his family days such as have not been since the division of the kingdom. Nothing but the birth of Immanuel can be the miracle; no other sign is spoken of in the oracle. Indeed, he is a mysterious boy, for his birth warrants the destruction of the enemies. Immanuel can be no other than the Messiah, with whom the days of happiness *must* come for Judah. Here we recognize distinctly that the messianic hope is particularly Judaistic; the happiness of Judah can begin only after the destruction of Northern Israel. As with Micah, so here the coming of the Messiah is preceded by a time of calamity. There the Assyrians menaced Judah, but here the Syrians and Ephraimites. In both cases the scheme is the same: first calamity, then fortune; only its content is changed to the contemporary historical situation. It was the enormity of the distress that awakened in the prophets the belief that they would live in the "last days," and which made them sure that the Messiah was already conceived. If human help seemed to be impossible, the marvelous child, the Messiah, was to be born. Hence it is clear what an immense danger the Syro-Ephraimitish war must have been for Judah; in those times the hearts of the king and of the people trembled, "as the trees of the wood tremble in the storm." Isaiah agreed with this idea, but his feelings were opposite to those of the others, for he expected the intervention of Jahve and the speedy appearance of the Messiah. *For this reason* he demanded of the king "quietness" and "faith" (7:4, 9). Like Micah, Isaiah, too, speaks in a mysterious manner of the young wife who shall bear. Nobody knows who she is, not even the prophet; only one thing is known, that in the immediate future the Messiah shall be born of a woman. Contrary to Micah, we here have nothing of David's return; it even seems to be excluded, for finally the prophet turns against the governing dynasty: it shall see worse days than at the time of the kingdom's division, when in Northern Israel a foreign dynasty mounted the throne.[1] With these words,

[1] The words "since Ephraim left Judah" are well understood, if they are transferred to the dynasty and not to the people of Judah. For the people had suffered worse things in the time before David than after the division of the kingdom. Here is clearly meant: "Such evil days as never before."

12

the fall of the Davidic dynasty is announced: when the Messiah mounts the throne, then "the scepter will be taken from Judah," as is already said in other words in Gen. 49:10. When Herod hears that the Messiah is born, he orders the child to be killed because now the end of his dynasty has come.

So the promise of Isaiah is interpreted from the historical situation. Yet there remain still some mysterious traits which apparently are not necessary and which therefore must belong to an older popular tradition. Why does Isaiah speak of the *queen-mother of the Messiah?* This strikes us the more forcibly as Micah, independently of Isaiah, uses the same term; remarkable, too, is the fact that neither mentions the father, as if the child had no father. At any rate, we must think of a mysterious birth, without identifying it with the Persian motive of the "virginal conception." Moreover, why are "milk and honey," the food of the Messiah spoken of? We should like to pass over this detail, for it is of no importance for the context. But according to the independent oracle (7:21, 22), "milk and honey" are the food of the saved people and a sign of the prosperity of the new time.[1] Hence, when Immanuel eats milk and honey, the messianic time has come. These two traits (the mother and the food) disprove the usual interpretation of Immanuel being a creation of Isaiah to make evident the shortness of the time.

Also Isa. 9:1–6 is a promise,[2] which becomes extremely clear by noting the final clause: "May the zeal of Jahve do this." In his faith, the prophet thinks it to be already present. He has certainly hoped that it would come soon; for he never would have sung songs of the end of the days if he had thought this end to be far off. At first, in three pictures he describes the great joy as being near: As the dead will rejoice when they see the "great light" of the sun in the Hades, as the reapers shout when they are gathering in a rich harvest, as the warriors exult when they are

---

[1] 7:18–19 (cf. the introduction, והיה ביום ההוא); 7:20 (ביום ההוא); 7:21–22 (והיה ביום ההוא), and 7:23–25 (והיה ביום ההוא) are independent oracles, partly "threats," partly "promises."

[2] Vs. 2, read הגילה; vs. 3, מוטת; vs. 4, מגאלה; vs. 6, למרבה המישור, according to the parallel שלום.

distributing a great booty, so will the people rejoice, when Jahve appears to break the yoke of the tyrant. That is the first deed Jahve does; the insupportable burden of the foreign yoke has an end. Here, too, the new time is the salvation from a time of misery; just because of this, the joy will be endless. Secondly, the prophet adds the destruction of the war-boots and the war-mantles, a poetic paraphrase of the fact that war will have an end forever. It begins the kingdom of peace, the quietness of which shall never more be disturbed. The third is the most grandiose: Then a child shall be born who will mount the throne of David, in order to rule with justice through all eternity. Also here the Messiah's birth is spoken of in dark, mysterious words. He is said to sit on the throne of David, to renew the splendor of the old Davidic kingdom, but it is not said that he is a descendant of David's house. At any rate, he is not thought to be the prince royal, the son of the reigning king, whose birth could not be celebrated ἐν μυστηρίῳ. The Messiah, being the king of eternity, has no successors.

Ideas depending upon the situation of the time are not at all to be recognized in this oracle, and therefore it cannot be dated exactly. But we have no urgent argument against the authorship of Isaiah, in whose book it is found. Nevertheless it may be said that the contents of this prophecy are much older than Isaiah. The prophet might very well have expected a king who should break the yoke of Judah's enemies, but for what reason should he hope that there would never again be war? This supposes a complete conversion and a change of man and civilization which is not to be explained psychologically by the situation of the contemporary or of the future time. Neither here nor anywhere else does Isaiah present any economic or humanistic reason which might have produced this belief in him. We might record the prophetic piety which thinks absolute confidence in God to be incompatible with confidence in armies and horses, but even from this the idea of universal peace cannot have its origin; for then the foreign nations menacing Israel would have been supposed to be equal to the prophets in their faith. Here it is not at all religion that is spoken of. On the contrary, the peace of the world is as evident as the destruction of the enemies. Besides this, we have to explain why Isaiah endowed his Messiah with demigod-like attributes: "Marvelous of counsel, God of battle, father of eternity, prince of peace." No other than Isaiah has insisted upon the unequaled grandeur of Jahve; only God is majestic, and in his presence all men, even the kings, are "flesh and not spirit." How could the same prophet transfer the attribute of God, the *El Gibbor*, to the king that was to come?

The third messianic prophecy of Isa. 11:1–9 throws light on the origin of the ideas and leads back to Micah.[1] At first Isaiah *celebrates* the king himself who will sprout forth from "the tree-stump of Jesse." As David has come from the root of Jesse, so the Messiah will be no other than a David *redivivus*. This was also our interpretation of Mic. 5:1 ff. Furthermore, Ezek. 34:23 f.; 37:24 f. says the same thing bluntly (cf. Hos. 3:5). The threat against Ahaz may be easily connected with it; for the image of the tree-stump announces that the reigning dynasty will be dethroned. But there may have been two different ideas; sometimes the Messiah is David himself, sometimes, however, a "sprout" for David. It is worthy of note that the prophet never speaks of David's "son" or "descendant," but always of David himself or of a "sprout," grafted to Jesse's or David's tree like a *foreign* sprig. Why should Isaiah not have pronounced different views of such vague things, of which nobody knows anything? The chief matter is the glorification of Jahve and his Messiah *in Jerusalem*. The new king that will then come will surpass the rulers of the present; he will possess the spirit of Jahve seven fold, superhuman knowledge and titanic power. Secondly, Isaiah celebrates *the return of paradise*. He does not do this bluntly, for this would be prosaic. The antique, primitive style demanded concrete images which expressed well the abstract ideas. When the wild animals become domestic, they change their nature and become like those of the Golden Age, in the land of the gods. And when men are no longer sinners, they too obtain a new nature and become like the innocent children of paradise. Hence we may retrospectively conclude that the end of war and the beginning of universal peace are psychologically to be interpreted from mytho-

---

[1] Vs. 1, read יפרח; remove vs. 3a; vs. 4, read עריץ; vs. 6, רעים (instead of ומריא); vs. 7, תתרעינה; vs. 8, מערת, parallel to חור.

logical and popular ideas and not from prophetic ones. Besides this, we may conclude that even the Messiah here painted is in reality not David but the king of the primeval times. So the end is the return of the beginning.

The same conclusion is suggested to us by Mic. 5:1 ff. It is made still clearer for us, if we add Isa. 1:21–26.[1] At first the prophet here threatens Jerusalem with retribution, because justice has been prostituted. But he adds then a promise in the event of Jerusalem's conversion. If it is purified in the melting-furnace, "then I will make thy judges as they were in the beginning and thy advisers as in the commencement." This can be no allusion either to Solomon or to David; for the time of Solomon was, it is true, known by its justice, but it was not "in the beginning." We might think the time of David to be the time of commencement, but we nowhere hear of any particular deed of justice of David nor of his counselors. Perhaps we might think of the time of Moses, which often appeared to the prophets an ideal time, but it is only the time of the "young love" between Jahve and Israel, and therefore important only in a religious sense, never in an ethical or forensic relation. So we have no alternative but to take the words in their proper sense: "the beginning" is the beginning of the world. As in other places the king of the primitive time, so here the state of the primeval time is glorified for its justice. The end returns to the beginning. So we see that all the ideas of the messianic end-time which do not depend upon the historical situation, have their origin in the ideas of the Golden Age or the paradise. In reality, they are of mythological origin, though we meet them in a historical form and sometimes inserted with specific prophetic ideas. Most of the hopes were already current among the people; by the prophets they were merely changed, adapted to the circumstances of the historical situation, and deepened ethically and religiously. The analysis of the messianic hopes confirms and completes at the same time the account of Amos that the expectation of a happy time was alive in the hearts of his contemporaries.

---

[1] Vss. 21–24, a threat (vss. 21–23, introduction or scolding-word; vs. 24, *corpus* or oracle); vss. 25–26, promise. The two belong together, as the first and the last line show. For vs. 25 read: מֵעָלַיִךְ and בָּכָר .

3. *Origin.*—The first question is, whether the source of the messianic hope lies on Israelitish ground or not. This question is answered by a comparison of the messianic prophecies with the ideas of paradise. For we suspect that the two are identical, or at any rate correspond with each other in the main, because the colors portraying the end-time are taken from the beginning time. We may give up the full congruence, since only a part of the Israelitish paradise-tales is extant. Besides Gen. chaps. 1–3, there may have been many other tales, of which we know nothing; moreover, Gen. chaps. 1–3 existed in many forms, before these chapters got their present canonical form. But even if we have regard to these possibilities, there must be some agreement between the beginning time and the end-time. We do in fact find it so in some particulars. The messianic hopes of a *universal peace* in the world of men and animals surpass, it is true, what is told in the Israelitish tales of the Golden Age. But some traits of the present tradition teach us that there once were tales of paradise in accordance with the expectations of the end-time; the dry precepts concerning food (Gen. 1:29; 2:16) are the last survival of a poetic tale about the peace of the Golden Age, unspoiled by any shedding of blood. The tale of Cain and Abel (Gen. 4:1 ff.), though having another origin, tells us, in its present position (immediately after the expulsion from Eden!), who the first murderer was. Then grew up the institutions of civilized life, among them the gild of metal-workers, who created the sword and with the sword the practice of blood-revenge (Gen. 4:22 ff.). Thus mankind fell into the deepest depths of sin, and withdrew from the blessed peace of paradise; but at the end of the days mankind will return to the conditions of the beginning.

The ideal food of the messianic time is *milk and honey* (Isa. 7:15, 21 f.; Amos 9:13; Joel 4:18). The men of paradise ate fruits of trees (Gen. 1:29; in 2:16 corn is added). This idea is scarcely originated by the Israelites or by the Palestinians, but in a land of tropical climate, the inhabitants of which are living upon banana trees or date-palms. The food-ideal of the Israelitish peasants was bread in the morning and flesh in the evening (I Kings 17:6), because corn was produced and cattle breeding was pursued.

17

Milk and honey are, however, still today the main food of the Beduins and were longed for by the Israelites as long as they tented like nomads on the outskirts of cultivated land. Hence for its fertility they called Palestine the land where milk and honey flow instead of water, like the land of the gods. This messianic hope is to be understood from Israelitish views, although being the opposite of the pictures of paradise known to us. Besides this we meet other expectations more exactly in agreement with the economic circumstances of Palestine. In the end-time there will be an abundance of wine (Gen. 49:11; Amos 9:13 f.), of corn (Amos 9:13; Isa. 4:2), of figs and olive-trees (Hos. 2:23 f.; Mic. 4:4). All the more peculiar is the mention of milk and honey.

But we find other ideas which cannot at all be of Israelitish origin. The return of paradise is combined with *the return of the paradise-king*. Genesis knows nothing of a primeval king, and in this case it is not permissible to complete the tradition, for the older Israelites may certainly be said not to have known a paradise-king, because the basis of such an idea was missing. Israel could be told of a paradise-king only since the time of Saul or David; i.e., since a kingdom existed in Israel. If the tradition be ever so much transformed, Moses and Joshua are not made kings, to say nothing of the first man. It corresponds with the family life of their own tribal society, that the Israelites conceive paradise as including only the family of Adam. Therefore the idea of the primeval king must have its source among a people whose kingdom is rooted in the oldest times, even out of mind, who cannot at all imagine a life without a king and for whom it is necessary to think of the first man as the first king. So our eyes turn from Israel to the extremely old kingdoms of the nearer Orient, to Egypt and Babylonia.[1]

To this may be added a second argument, *the deification of the Messiah*. Some traces are found, it is true, that even in Israel the reigning rulers were extolled like gods or sons of gods, although not as often as in Egypt (Pss. 2, 45, 110, which are not messianic). But such courtly ideas are not to be supposed in the case of the prophets

---

[1] It may be briefly noted that similar ideas are likewise found in Greek literature; cf. Hesiod: ἔργα καὶ ἡμέραι 111. But are they of Greek origin?

who dared to tell the kings their faults in such a manner that they sometimes offend the royalist sensibilities of modern men. The more peculiar, then, is the fact that they have adorned the messianic king without scruple with such godlike attributes as "God of battle" or "father of eternity," with epithets usually reserved for Jahve alone. We shall understand this best by presuming that the prophets are depending upon an older tradition. This tradition is created by men who were accustomed to elevate their kings into the god's sphere and who made no great difference between a king and a god. As Israel borrowed the institution of kingship from the peoples of the nearer Orient, so it may have accepted too the expectation of the messianic god-king, perhaps through the channel of the Canaanites. In this respect the prophets were not afraid to draw upon Israel's popular hopes, because the godlike attributes were applied not to the king of the present, but of the end-time, to Him who was to bring the beginning of God's kingdom. The less the contemporary ruler accomplished the prophetic ideal, the more in contrast the prophets liked to exalt the Messiah.

The idea of the Messiah, since it is not of Israelitish origin, we think to have been first borrowed from the Canaanites, for at any rate the Canaanites performed the part of mediators, if we suppose a foreign source. The very close connection between the Messiah and David's dynasty teaches us that Israel's messianic hopes got their first stamp in Jerusalem or in Judah, because the Northern Israelites were not immediately interested in a Judaic dynasty. So in the first place, our eyes turn to the Canaanitish past of Jerusalem. Unhappily, the tales of this town never having been gathered, we know of its past less than of many other little villages in Northern Israel or in the Negeb. Only by the way, do we hear of *Melchizedek*, and this very same man causes us to raise the question whether he is thought to be the primeval king. This is likely, for he is made the contemporary of Abraham and not of Joshua or of David (Gen. 14:18 ff.). As Abraham is the ancestor of the Israelites, so Melchizedek may have been the ancestor of Jerusalem's kings or the founder of Jerusalem's dynasty. According to the court-style, the first king must have reigned in the first time, and there is documentary evidence in Ps. 110:4, where a pre-exilic king of

Jerusalem is celebrated in an unusual manner, probably on the day of his accession to the throne. An oracle announces him to be "a priest of eternity like Melchizedek." The contemporary ruler is being glorified here as the messianic king of the end-time, Melchizedek being regarded as the demigod-like king of the first time. It does not matter if this priest-king is made by Gen. chap. 14 the contemporary of Abraham. Perhaps we may suppose that likewise all the other demigod-like attributes of Ps. 110 are transferred from Melchizedek to the reigning ruler. Then Melchizedek would be born "upon the holy mountains" (of the sky) like the Babylonian gods or kings.[1] In this case it would be allowable to combine the ideas of the Canaanite, or more exactly of the Jerusalemite court-style with those of Babylonia.

Up to this time unmistakable traces of a paradise-king in Babylonia are missing; with great probability, however, we may refer to the *myth of Adapa* which was found in the Egyptian archives of Tell-el Amarna. That this myth was known in Palestine, the paradise-tale shows us; for the main motive (the loss of immortality) is borrowed from the Adapa myth, though considerably darkened. For this reason Adapa must be the primeval king, if he be never so called. Characteristically, the Israelites have made the "king" a simple "man." According to the introduction of the myth, the wise Adapa was not only a priest (baker, cup-bearer, and cook), but also king of Eridu, "to make known the lots [?] of the land," "created the ruler [?] of mankind"; his commandments were transgressed by no one; his was a blessed time. But he wants immortality—only this thing. When he has lost it forever, Anu cannot give him the royal dignity, as it is usually interpreted. On the contrary, Anu seems to prophesy his return at the end of the days: "Then Anu disposed for him [?] the fate, to cast forth rays of his government even unto the future of the days." Since Sennacherib calls himself the second "Adapa," from this point of

---

[1] I read Ps. 110:3:

ביום הָלֶדֶת לך ‖ בהררי קדש ‖ מרחם שַׁחַר ‖ כַּטָל וִלְדְתִּיךָ ‖

"On thy birthday I begot thee on the holy mountains like dew from the womb of Aurora" (another *Helal ben Schachar*). Perhaps Isa. 1:26 and Jer. 23:6 allude to the time and the name of Melchizedek. Possibly we find Jerusalemite primeval tales in Ps. 46, 76; Isa. 28:14–22; it must suffice to indicate this.

20

view as well Adapa must be the primeval king returning at the end-time. Besides this we know nothing of Babylonian prophecies either of an unhappy time or of a happy time, aside from a late notice from Berossus in Seneca.

On the contrary, we now possess *Egyptian prophecies* of many times from 2000 B.C. to 300 A.D.[1] Most interesting is the fact that threats and promises are connected here as in the Old Testament. Up to this time no critic has dared to deny the genuineness of the "messianic hopes" of the Egyptians. Should not that which is correct for the Egyptian prophets be suitable also to those of Israel? Therefore threat and promise belong together antithetically; the time of happiness cannot be better painted than against the background of the time of distress. This antithesis has become a typical style, not only for the Egyptians but also for the Israelites. The scheme is fixed, but its content ever changes according to the historical situation. The characteristic difference in the oracles of the two peoples is that the Egyptians only repeat the usual phrases, while the Israelites transform the type individually here as everywhere. Therefore the messianic prophecies in Israel had a long and important **history, while in** Egypt they remained unaltered through the centuries. Because of this long continuance of prophecy, Egypt is thought to be the land of its origin, since the oldest text, surely prophetic, was there delivered about 2000 B.C. This is by no means the earliest possible date, for the prophetic scheme must be still older, inasmuch as ill fortune and good fortune are there strung together without any interposition. From this self-revelation we may recognize the typical character of this prophecy. Moreover, it is remarkable that we meet cosmical elements in the picture of the calamity: "At that time the sun will shine [only] one hour; one cannot see, when it will be midday." So the distress is not exclusively of a political sort; the picture seems to depend upon the expectation of a world-catastrophe, similar to the Israelitish prophecies. Amos 8:9 may be compared with the oracle just cited. It is curious that Amos

---

[1] The texts are gathered conveniently by Ranke in *Altorientalische Texte und Bilder*, edited by Gressmann, Part I, pp. 204 ff. From this book are taken, too, the above-cited translations of the Babylonian texts by Ungnad.

8:8 furnishes a comparison with the Nile, an image of Egyptian origin. Further we may recall to mind Amos 9:11: the hut of David broken down shall be repaired, that is: Northern Israel and Judah shall be connected again. Compare with this the Egyptian prophecy: "He shall gain the crown of Upper Egypt and win for himself the crown of Lower Egypt." Similarly as the mother of Immanuel is spoken of, so here "the wife from Nubia" is mentioned, who will bear the messianic king, and so on. But all these details cannot in themselves prove a dependence of Israelitish prophecy upon Egyptian; for it is possible that in all these cases there is an analogous development.

A connection between the messianic hope of Israel and that of Egypt would be necessary, if there was in Egypt too a king of the first time, whose return was expected. In fact, we find allusions to a tale that once the god Re ruled on earth over man and gods. Deserving of regard is the hypothesis of Gardiner,[1] that the wise Ipuwêr, who (the first time) like an Egyptian Nathan censures the king for the evil and ill fortune of his reign, then paints the ideal of a good king. The first time he says: "It is confusion that thou bringest throughout the land together with the noise of tumult. . . . . Thou hast spoken falsehood. . . . . Would that thou mightest taste some of the miseries, then wouldst thou say . . . ." Afterward he says: ". . . . lack of people . . . . Re . . . . He bringeth [?] coolness to that which is hot. It is said: he is the herdsman of mankind. No evil is in his heart. When his herds are few, he passes the day to gather them together, their hearts being on fire [?]. Would that he had perceived their nature [?] in the first generation [of men]; then he would have suppressed evil, he would have stretched forth his arms against it, he would have destroyed their seed [??] and their inheritance." It is likely these words are to be regarded "as a description of Re, whom ancient legends regarded as the first king of Egypt, and whose reign was looked back upon as a sort of Golden Age" (Gardiner). Unfortunately there is no proof that the Egyptians expected a return of Re and the lost paradise, or that the messianic king was painted by the prophets with the colors of the god-king Re. But

[1] Alan H. Gardiner, *The Admonitions of an Egyptian Sage.* Leipzig, 1909.

according to all we know hitherto, such a hope does not seem to be excluded, especially since the reigning kings were respected as natural sons of Re.

Hence we cannot yet pass a sure judgment concerning the origin of the messianic hope. The probability is more in favor of Egypt than Babylonia, although there may have been similar expectations throughout the nearer Orient;[1] and, moreover, in Palestine the influences of Egypt and Babylonia may have crossed. Now, looking over the whole material, we may search out *the psychological roots*. The last outlet for the messianic hope we have found is the conception of the returning paradise and of the returning paradise-king. This is not to be separated from the idea of the world's destruction and the return of chaos; certainly it may be said that the end of the world is the *prius* and has caused the return of the Golden Age. Whence these thoughts grew up is a problem in itself, not to be solved by the way. At any rate, in the later times these ideas are in existence; they are handed down from generation to generation, and are more or less active. The only development is that the mythological ideas are historicized always anew; that is, they are applied to the situations of any time, but only under the constraint of important historical events, and by these they are modified. This we may illustrate best through the development of an analogous idea. About the time of Jesus the conception is current that the coming of the Christ is to be preceded by the satanic Antichrist. When a man like Nero arises persecuting Christianity with great cruelty, he is regarded by the Christians as the Antichrist. Thus the conception of the returning Nero is to be explained. When Napoleon crushed Germany with iron fist, the idea of the Antichrist revived again, but now Napoleon was the Antichrist. This shows the imposing grandeur of Napoleon, however destructive he may have been. According to this, the Babylonians, the Assyrians, and still earlier the Ephraimites and Syrians were thought to be the satanic powers, with whom chaos returns. The battles of God with Tiâmat, Leviathan, and other dragons are to be repeated in the end-time;

---

[1] In the inscription of the Hittite king *KLM* newly published I cannot discover any messianic element. There is only the style of antithesis *largely spread*.

23

and every time when the world trembled with fear of foreign conquerors or re-echoed the endless calls to arms, poets or prophets alluded to the battles of the last days. In the same manner the idea of the returning paradise-king changed from time to time. When David gained the love of Israel, and as the remembrance of his person and his kingdom continued, the returning paradise-king became the returning David. And when Frederick Barbarossa got the love of the Germans, they expected the returning *Kaiser Rotbart* from the *Kyffhäuser*. So this idea is the last shout of the "messianic" hope.

The grandeur of Israel's prophets is not imperiled by the supposition or the proof of dependence upon older ideas. Nathan's boldness in the presence of David is admirable, even if Ipuwêr, the Egyptian sage, should have thrown a similar "Thou liest" into the face of his king. And Isaiah's prophecies of the Messiah do not lose any of their ethico-religious depth, even if the Egyptians and the Canaanites already knew a messianic hope. Israel's prophets have embodied their finest and sublimest thoughts in the Messiah's person; and like bright threads of gold the prophetic ideas are woven into the purple robe of the popular faith. All that we call "fleshly" messianic hope is of popular origin; of this sort are the ideas of the coming kingdom, when the whole world will do homage to Israel, when the treasures of the nations shall be gathered to Jerusalem, and when foreign kings shall build the golden gates of the city. The greater prophets, however, emphasized justice regnant over the king, the officers, and the whole people; the kingdom of peace, when all disquietude is over, and every war is ended; the fear of God beaming forth from Jerusalem and giving light to all the nations; and the blessedness of God's children living in sinless innocence and performing their duties for his name's sake.

The Source and Beginnings
of the Messianic Idea

by JOSEPH KLAUSNER

TO THE three good gifts which the people Israel have left as an inheritance to the entire world: monotheism, refined morality, and the prophets of truth and righteousness—a fourth gift must be added: *belief in the Messiah.*

No other nation in the world knew a belief like this. To be sure, various Christian theologians, and likewise a number of other independent scholars, have attempted to rob Israel of its prior right to the belief in the Messiah, and to confer it upon the Assyrians, the Egyptians, or the Persians.[1] But even those who defend the cause of

[1] See on this, first of all, in the important book of H. Gressmann, *Der Ursprung der israelitisch-jüdischen Eschatologie*, Göttingen, 1905, pp. 36, 160, 190, 206, 215, 245, 247, Note 2; A. Jeremias, *Handbuch der altorientalischen Geisteskultur*, Leipzig, 1913, pp. 205–225; E. Sellin, *Die israelitisch-jüdische Heilandserwartung*, Berlin, 1909, pp. 38–46. Wilhelm Bousset (*Die jüdische Apokalyptik*, 1903; Bousset-Gressmann, *Die Religion des Judentums im Neutestamentlichen Zeitalter*, 3rd ed., 1926, p. 226) attempted to prove that the Jewish Messiah of the period of the Second Temple resembles the Persian "Saoshyant"; and P. Volz (*Die vorexilische Jahveprophetie und der Messias*, Göttingen, 1897) supposes that the prophets had no ideal of a King-Messiah until Ezekiel. Against Gressmann in particular see Nathanael Schmidt, "The Origin of Jewish Eschatology" (*Journal of Biblical Literature*, XLI [1922], 102–114). Against Gressmann, Jeremias, Sellin, *et al.*, see E. Koenig, *Die messianischen Weissagungen des Alten Testaments*, Stuttgart, 1923, pp. 20–25; and against Volz even Gressmann himself has come out (in his book mentioned above, pp. 238–250). Rudolf Kittel, who inclines toward early Babylonian-Egyptian influence, limits it strictly, seeing it only as a *possibility*, since the *essential* marks of the Hebrew Messianic expectation are lacking in both the Babylonian and the Egyptian literature (see R. Kittel, *Geschichte des Volkes Israel*, 5th ed., Gotha, 1922, II, 256–257, note 3). See also G. Kittel, *Die Probleme des palaestinischen Spätjudentums und das Urchristentum*, Stuttgart, 1926, pp. 75–85.

13

Babylonian influence are forced to confess that in the Sumero-Babylonian literature there is no "clear expectation of the restoration of the good conditions of Paradise, by which history might be consummated." [2] And those who insist that the first ancient stimulus came to the Hebrew Messianic idea from the Egyptians, the Persians, or the Babylonians also see the exceedingly great advantage of the Jewish Messianic ideals. [3] The most original people in the world—the Greek people—did not have any real Messianic expectation; and the *Fourth Eclogue* of Vergil is so late that there can be no doubt of the influence of the ancient Jewish Sibyl upon this Roman poet, or even of the influence—direct or indirect—of the prophets of Israel in Greek translation. Moreover, the threefold Persian Saoshyant is also completely remote from the Jewish Messiah, for Zoroaster lived at a time so late (*c.* 660–583 B.C.E.*) that it is hard to believe that the three "Messiahs" (Saoshyants), all of whom had to be sons of Zoroaster, were the ones who brought into being the Hebrew Messianic expectation, which we see already fully developed in the time of Isaiah and even before. [4]

How is it possible to explain this wonderful phenomenon: the marvelous development of the Messianic idea in the midst of a unique people, Israel, to such a degree that there is nothing like it in any other nation?

The answer to this question is to be sought in the ancient history of the Israelite people.

The Messianic expectation is the *Golden Age in the future.* But all the ancient peoples except Israel could tell only of a *Golden Age in the past.* Many philosophers and students of religions have been amazed at the marvelous fact that all ancient peoples praised and exalted the Age of Gold which is already past, but only the people Israel related wonders about the Golden Age *which is still to come.* The happy state of the first man in the Garden of Eden was so short

---

* Before the Christian Era.

[2] See W. Eichrodt, *Die Hoffnung des ewigen Friedens in alten Israel*, Gütersloh, 1920, p. 155 (also p. 142).

[3] See A. Jeremias, *op. cit.*, p. 225; Sellin, *op. cit.*, pp. 42–43, 44–45.

[4] See J. Scheftelowitz, *Die altpersische Religion und das Judentum*, Giessen, 1920, pp. 197, 202–203.

that it is difficult to call it an "Age." The cause of this difference between Israel and the other peoples is made understandable to us when we consider the ancient historical traditions of the people Israel.

The ancient, primitive history of every people is regularly pictured in its imagination as a period of happiness and tranquillity, as is pictured the period of childhood in the mind of every person whose childhood was not most unfortunate. Not so the ancient history of the people Israel. Dark was the childhood of this people destined for tribulation. The Patriarchs were forced to move from country to country time after time because of severe famine in their homeland. While they were wandering in foreign lands, they suffered from the insolence and tyranny of the kings of those lands (Pharaoh, Abimelech, Shechem son of Hamor). A short time after the death of the Patriarchs began the Egyptian bondage, with all its terrible oppressions. No nation on earth knew such sufferings in its early youth. Israelite history in its earliest time became a history of afflictions. The people Israel did not have a *glorious past*, hence it was forced to direct its gaze toward a *glorious future*. It longed for one to ransom and deliver it from its afflictions and troubles. It yearned for a *redeemer and savior*. And such a savior appeared in the form of *Moses*.

The name Moses [Heb. *Mosheh*] itself, according to popular etymology, indicates one who brings out or ransoms.[5] The Talmud calls him "savior of Israel."[6] It is not our concern here to investigate whether there is a historical kernel in the stories about the Patriarchs, nor whether the oppression in Egypt is entirely or only partly historical and whether the exodus from Egypt under the leadership of Moses is historical fact or only legend. Sufficient here is the fact that at a very early time, relatively speaking, the traditions about the Egyptian captivity and the Exodus were very well established in the nation. In the mind of the nation, therefore, its whole childhood was considered, at a relatively early time, as having been filled with af-

---

[5] Therefore he is not called Mashui ["drawn," passive voice], as the phrase "Because I drew him out of the water" (Exod. 2:10) would require; this was already noted by the ancient interpreters. Actually, of course, Mosheh is thought to be an Egyptian word, which is a part of the names of a number of Egyptian kings (Thutmose, Ahmose, *et al.*).

[6] Sotah 12b (see also 11b and 13a); Sanhedrin 101b.

flictions, oppression, and servitude. It was inevitable that the stories
of oppression, as we find them in the first sections of the Book of
Exodus, should make a strong impression on the entire people Israel.
It was also inevitable that the people should feel compelled to accord
the very greatest glory and honor to the exalted and grandiose personality of *the first deliverer*. This was the man Moses, this the great
deliverer, who not only ransomed Israel from all its *material* troubles
and from *political* servitude, but also redeemed it from its ignorance
and its spiritual bondage. He was not only a guide and leader of the
Israelite people; he was also a lawgiver and prophet. The exalted picture of Moses necessarily, therefore, impressed itself upon the spirit
of the nation and became a symbol of the redeemer in general. Political
salvation and spiritual redemption of necessity were combined in the
consciousness of the nation to become one great work of redemption. Thus was born the redemptive dualism which necessarily put
its stamp upon the redeemer of the future, *the expected Messiah*.

Various scholars assert that the Messianic idea could have been born
only after kings ruled in Israel, since the prophets portrayed the
Messiah as a mighty king and an exalted ruler.[7] But they forget, first,
that the prophets do not call the redeemer by the name "Messiah,"[8]
and hence in the time of the prophets the "anointing" of the kings
was not a clear sign of the redeemer; and secondly, that the spiritual-
ethical characteristics of the Messiah, which in the last analysis are
fundamental in the prophetic portrayal of the Messiah—precisely
these characteristics are hard to find not only in the kings of Israel
but also in the kings of Judah. Yet precisely these characteristics were
found in Moses.

Moreover, in Moses were embodied not only the spiritual characteristics of the Messiah but also his political characteristics. Moses
was not only a lawgiver; he was also a leader of the nation, over the
fate of which the Most High had made him ruler. He fought the
people's wars against Amalek, against Sihon and Og, and against the
kings of Midian. Though he himself did not command the army in

---

[7] See F. Giesebrecht, *Beiträge zur Jesajakritik*, 1890, p. 26. Cf. also *Dor Dor ve-
Doreshav* by I. H. Weiss, I, 28–34.
[8] See above, Chap. I, p. 8.

the war against Amalek and Midian, nevertheless Joshua, the son of Nun, and Phinehas, the son of Eleazar, fought according to his directions and under his supervision. In the Talmud and Midrash he is called "king" a number of times.[9] The designation "warrior" fits him no less than that of "sage." [10] He would impose the death sentence upon those meriting judicial death; he was the head of the nation in times of peace and its commander-in-chief in times of war. To be sure, these were not the main characteristics of Moses. And so it is with the characteristics of the Messiah: the ethico-spiritual character-istics are the principal ones, but the political characteristics are not lacking.

The authors of the Talmud and Midrash, with their fine national feeling, perceived the relation and connexion between the Messianic expectation and the exodus from Egypt, between the Messiah and Moses. They name Moses "the first redeemer" [11] in contrast to the Messiah, who is "the last redeemer." [12] They compare Moses to the Messiah in various phraseology: [13] for example, just as Moses brought redemption to his people, so also will Messiah bring redemption; [14] just as Moses was brought up in the house of Pharaoh among the enemies of his people, so also will Messiah dwell in the city of Rome, among the destroyers of his land; [15] just as Moses, after revealing him-self to his brethren in Egypt and announcing to them that deliverance was near, was forced to go into hiding for a time, so also will Messiah be forced to hide himself after the first revelations; [16] just as Moses crossed from Midian to Egypt riding on an ass (Exod. 4:20), so also will Messiah come riding on an ass; just as Moses caused manna to

---

[9] See, e.g., Zeḥahim 102b; Seder Olam Rabbah, Chap. 4.

[10] See Nedarim 38a and Shabbath 92a.

[11] Ruth Rabbah 2:14 on the text "And Boaz said unto her."

[12] Genesis Rabbah, Chap. 85.

[13] "Rab said: The world was created only on David's account. Samuel said: On *Moses'* account; R. Johanan said: For the sake of *the Messiah*" (Sanhedrin 98b).

[14] Genesis Rabbah, Chap. 85; Exodus Rabbah, Chap. 1; Tanhuma, Shemoth, 8.

[15] Exodus Rabbah, Chap. 1; Tanhuma, Shemoth, 8, and Tazri'a, 8. Cf. also San-hedrin 19b.

[16] Numbers Rabbah, Chap. 11; Song of Songs Rabbah, on the text "My beloved is like a gazelle" (2:9); Pesikta Rabbathi, Chap. 36 (ed. M. Friedmann, pp. 161–162).

rain from the sky, so will Messiah bring forth different kinds of food in a miraculous way; and just as Moses gave to the children of Israel wells and springs of water in the wilderness, so also will Messiah make streams of water flow in the desert.[17] Not only this, but the acceptance of suffering because of the iniquities of others, which late Jewish legend attributes to the Messiah, is in the Talmud and is also attributed to our master Moses.[18] (This may be called "suffering for atonement;" Christian scholars call it "vicarious suffering," and in Christianity this idea has become an important article of faith.)

The phrases cited from the Talmud and Midrash, which mostly belong to the Amoraim and were spoken at a very late time, cannot, of course, be used as historical proof that the belief in the Messiah actually sprang from the marvelous traditions about Moses the first redeemer. I have cited them here only to show that these traditions about "the savior of Israel," who brought out his people from the first captivity, comprise the authentic *embryo* from which the Messianic idea of necessity developed. Even at a relatively late time, in the period of the Amoraim, the connexion between the first redeemer and the last redeemer was still felt and recognized by the sages of Israel. The oppression and afflictions in which the first traditions of the history of Israel began inevitably brought forth within Israel the strong yearning for redemption.[19] And the first traditions about the first redeemer necessarily left their stamp upon this yearning, that is to say, upon the ideals of redemption. Thus were brought forth within Israel both the impersonal Messianic expectation and the personal Messiah. For the ideal of redemption is the Messianic expectation, and the *personal* ideal of redemption is the belief in the Messiah.

This lofty ideal, of which Moses inevitably became a symbol,

17 Koheleth Rabbah 1:9, on the text "That which hath been"; Midrash Shemuel, Chap. 14 (ed. Buber, p. 90). The prophet Elijah, the herald of the coming of the Messiah, is also compared with Moses in a number of ways, because Elijah is also the chosen of the LORD and also in a certain sense a redeemer. See the citation of passages in the Italian work of Castelli, *Il Messia*, pp. 197–198; cf. also pp. 213–214.

18 See Berakoth 32a, and at length in Sotah, end of Chap. 1 (14a).

19 This does not exclude the possibility that the element of *retribution* in the Messianic idea has in it some of "the odor of the soil of Palestine," as Gressmann showed in two excellent books. See H. Gressmann, *Eschatologie*, p. 192; *Palaestinas Erdgeruch in der israelitischen Religion*, Berlin, 1909.

owing to the development of events in Israelite history, gained strength and struck deep root in the nation. Never did a young and conquering people endure afflictions and troubles in the land which it had subdued by sword and bow, as endured the people Israel after the death of Joshua. The former inhabitants of the land, who were thought to have been conquered, continued to subdue and oppress different tribes of Israel one after the other. "And the children of Israel cried to the LORD"—we find this expression in the Book of Judges time after time. The period of heroes is the earliest historical period of every people; but not even one other people can tell in its early legends about such numerous afflictions and oppressions as can the people Israel. Now when the cry of the oppressed people would ascend to heaven, "The LORD would raise up a *savior* for the children of Israel"—thus relates the Book of Judges. Redeemer after redeemer helped them. These were the "judges" who did not judge at all, just as the "judges" (*suffetae*) of the Carthaginians, offspring of the Tyrians, did not judge. The "judges" were political saviors: noble fighters, bold heroes, and temporary rulers, mostly in times of war only, but sometimes (as we find in Gideon) also in times of peace. These "saviors" had the political characteristics of Moses and in their prowess in war they even surpassed him; but the spiritual-ethical characteristics of Moses were lacking. Each one of the judges was a temporary "Messiah" of his tribe or of a number of tribes in the political sense but not in the spiritual sense. Each was a kind of little but successful Bar-Cochba. Samuel, the last judge, had all the spiritual characteristics of Moses. It is well known how excessively the men of the Talmud praise him; [20] but the political characteristics were lacking. The first Israelite king, Saul, son of Kish, lacked the spiritual characteristics of a Messiah. To be sure, he is called in the Scriptures "the LORD's anointed"; but I have already said that these words must be understood in their plain meaning: he was the LORD's chosen one and was anointed as king. [21]

The true prototype of the Messiah was the second Israelite king, David, son of Jesse. His great political talents, by means of which he

[20] See, e.g., Nedarim 38a.
[21] See, above, beginning of Chap. I, p. 7.

succeeded in unifying all the tribes of Israel and making them one great and powerful nation according to the conceptions of his time, his marvelous heroism and courage, as revealed in his extensive wars against all the neighbors of Israel, and his glorious victories in which he defeated all those peoples to whom Israel had been subject until his time—all these things were necessary to make him in the eyes of the people the greatest political savior of all those who defended Israel at any time.

But his spiritual characteristics also fitted him to become in the eyes of the people the ideal type of the King-Messiah. In spite of the fact that cruelty is imputed to him with respect to the Moabites and Ammonites, whom he measured with the line and made to pass under saws and axes of iron, or with respect to the sons of Rizpah, daughter of Aiah, whom he commanded to be hanged, and the like; and in spite of the affair of Bath-sheba, which the Scriptures did not cover up, David was in the last analysis—if we judge him according to his time and according to the characteristics of Oriental monarchs—an ideal king. Following the severe words of Ernest Renan about David,[22] it has been in latter years almost a fashion to belittle the importance of David and to diminish his historical stature. How do these scholars support their case? Only from the discreditable deeds which are related about him in the Bible. But, if they give credence to the narratives of the Bible, if they admit that it does not spare even those in whom it delights, telling the "bitter truth" about them, why do they not give credence also to those numerous passages in the Bible in which the figure of David appears before us full of light and splendor? In the Bible we see David doing deeds of cruelty, but we likewise see him confessing his sins and repenting of them, loving even his rebellious son Absalom more than his own life; requiting Saul, who hated him, with mercy when Saul's life was in his hands and lamenting over his death after he was slain; permitting the prophet Nathan to say everything that was on his mind; and wholeheartedly concerning himself about the national religion.

To be sure, popular legend exaggerated too much in praising him and his good qualities, and was not satisfied until it made him the

22 See *Histoire du peuple d'Israel*, I, 411–451.

author of various hymns in the Book of Psalms. Yet this fact alone, that popular imagination expanded and exalted this national hero not only as a king possessing outstanding political talents but also as the possessor of superior religio-ethical qualities—this fact alone proves that undoubtedly David was a man of the very highest attainments. *Ex nihilo nihil fit.* Outstanding political abilities together with these religio-ethical qualities made David the *authentic* prototype of the redeemer and the founder of that ruling family one of whose descendants the Messiah must be. Not only did the name "son of David" become a standing title of the King-Messiah, but also the name "David" itself. The prophet Hosea says, concerning the Messianic age, "Afterward shall the children of Israel return, and seek the LORD their God, and David their king" (Hos. 3:5). And in the Talmud there is an opinion that the expected Messiah will be David himself or will be called by the name "David." [23]

Meanwhile, prophecy was developing in Israel, and in the kingdoms of Ephraim and Judah arose prophets who broadened and deepened the conceptions of the tribes of Israel. In this process the Messianic expectation received an almost entirely new form.

In fact, *the Messianic expectation is the positive element in the message of the prophets.* As reprovers and preachers, the prophets were by necessity great masters of negation. King Ahab charges one of the prophets of the LORD that "he doth not prophesy good concerning me, but evil" (I Kings 22:8). The whole struggle of the true prophets against the false prophets revolved around this point only, that the false prophets envisioned what the people wanted them to envision: prosperity and happiness and peace in the present. And they praised the deeds of kings, princes, and people at the time when the true prophets were dissatisfied with the present, and were denouncing in very harsh words both the deeds of the people and the deeds of those standing at their head. Before the eyes of these true prophets was hovering a high ideal, from which the forces of the

---

[23] Yer. Berakoth, Chap. 2, Hal. 1, *in the Baraitha,* which, to be sure, appears to be not very early; cf. the words of R. Judah in the name of Rab and of R. Papa in Sanhedrin 95*b*, and the symbolic saying, "David King of Israel is alive and vigorous," which was transmitted by Rabbi (Rosh Ha-Shanah 25*a*). Below, in Part III, Chap. VII, I have enlarged on this.

time were completely remote, not even attempting or seeking to approach it. The *existing situation* was bad in the eyes of these prophets;
only what *should be*—and according to their conviction it also *could
be*—was good. The bad, therefore, was in the *present*, and the good
in the *future;* the bad was in *actuality*, and the good in the *ideal*.

The hoped-for good, the ideal, which will be the actuality in the
future—this is the Messianic expectation in its full depth. Thus the
strong contrast between the actual and the ideal deepened and
broadened the early Messianic expectation and made it a universal
and eternal conception.[24] The more the prophets were dissatisfied
with the present, the more they were embittered against conditions
existing in their day and were impelled to warn the people, to prophesy an evil day, with troubles and distress, the more would their hearts,
crushed and sick at the ruin of their people, seek comfort in visions
and imaginings of "the end of [these] days." There, in the world of
the future, their imaginations would soar to the skies, and the ideal
which was living in their noble hearts would become for them complete actuality. So with this future actuality they would comfort the
unhappy people, who had to endure so much from foes and adversaries without and from proclaimers of easy times, deceivers, and
false teachers within. The great love and compassion which filled their
kindly hearts—though so often they had to harden themselves against
their beloved people, to call them all sorts of dishonorable names,
and to prophesy all the evils in the world against them—would flood
over into the Messianic conceptions and fill them with light and
splendor, national power, and spiritual exaltation.

But not only this. The prophets also introduced into the Messianic
expectation the humanitarian-universal and spiritual-ethical elements, which at the beginning had made little impression on it. Up
to the time of the prophets, the savior was mostly a strong deliverer
of his people from political oppression. But the prophets, who sought

---

[24] Gunkel, Gressmann, and Sellin (in their books cited above, p. 13, Note 1)
have shown almost certainly that the basic Messianic ideas were long antecedent
to the prophets, and it is actually possible that the beginning of these ideas is
mythological and comes from Egypt and Babylonia; but what they are now—
the hope of the nation and the consolation of humanity—they were made by
the prophets. On this no doubt can be cast.

always righteousness and justice and whose wide range of vision took in the whole world, broadened and deepened this idea also. Up to the time of the prophets, the nation had been most conscious of *political wrong*, which had manifested itself in the evils of oppression and captivity. The prophets, who carried the banner of truth and righteousness in their time, were the first in Israel who began to feel that there is in the world a greater evil than this: *personal evil*, that is to say, the wrong which man does to his fellow man. This perception brought them to the conviction that evil is not accidental, and also that it does not pass away when the end of oppression and subjection to another people arrives; and redemption from this personal evil was the chief of all their aspirations. It is no wonder, then, that for the most part the prophets thought of the redemption from personal evil as a *personal redemption*. Thus the man who will bring this redemption, the Messiah, had to be the embodiment of the highest righteousness, which tolerates no evil. Therefore, the Messiah became more and more not only a pre-eminent political ruler, but also a man of pre-eminent moral qualities.

Now, since evil is not political alone and is not accidental and transitory, since it is human, it is thus stamped upon the spirits of all men; therefore it is spiritual and universally human. (Natural catastrophe is not taken into account, since this sort of evil comes from God as a punishment for the evil deeds of men.) Therefore, salvation and redemption from this evil must also be spiritual and universal. In such wise the Messianic idea, without destroying its political attributes, became more and more spiritual, and without destroying its nationalist characteristics became more and more universal. The dreams of the people Israel became at the hands of the prophets the dreams of all humanity. Redemption encompasses not alone the people Israel and its land, but likewise all peoples and all lands. This is the goal of universal righteousness, of which the prophets were the supreme exponents.

The sages of Greece also recognized the evil in the world, and from Socrates to the last of the Stoics, the philosophers longed for redemption from this evil. But since the evil they saw was more the *natural* evil, from which there is no flight or escape and for which no human being is really to be blamed, therefore they sought deliverance in other ways. The Stoics and Cynics taught that salvation from the evil in this world is to be sought and found in *salvation from the world itself*, that is, in flight from the storms and passions of this world. Christianity, which was compounded of Judaism and Greek philosophy, has a redeemer of the world, but along with this there are also ascetics who are saved from the evil in the world by flight from the world to desert places and monasteries. Judaism, seeking redemption from the personal evil in this world, found it in *improvement of the world* by a personal Messiah alone. The personality of the Messiah became more and more elevated in the time of the prophets and the time of the Tannaim, finally reaching tremendous power and eminence. The Messiah had the attributes of a king, inherited from Moses, the judges, and David; to these were added also the attributes of a *prophet*.

Thus the Messiah, as I have said, became a truly pre-eminent man, to the extent that the *Jewish* imagination could picture him: he was supreme in strength and heroism; he was also supreme in moral qualities. A great personality, which is incomparably higher and stronger than ordinary people, a personality to which all very willingly make themselves subject and which can overcome all things, but for these very reasons feeling a very strong sense of obligation—this is the pre-eminent man of Judaism. Of a pre-eminent man like this it is possible to say, "Thou hast made him a little lower than God." For from a pre-eminent man like this to God is but a step. But this step Judaism did *not* take. It formed within the limits of a humanity, which is continually raising itself up, the ideal of flesh and blood, "the idea of the ultimate limit of man" (in the language of Kant), this great personality, only by means of which and by the help of which can redemption and salvation come to humanity—the King-Messiah.

There is yet another great universal conception included in the Messianic expectation.

We have already seen that the Israelite nation, which had a history of afflictions from the beginning of its growth, dreamed about a Golden Age, which was not behind it but before it. This Golden

Age was called "the end of the days" ["latter days," "final days," "final time," and so on]. As long as these "coming days" had not arrived, the development of the nation was still *incomplete;* particularly so after its land, political power, sanctuary, and language had been destroyed. Judaism is, therefore, *imperfect* or, more correctly, lacking completion. And thus it will continue to be until it returns to its own land, until its sanctuary is rebuilt, and until its exiles are gathered in from the four corners of the earth—and until "the earth shall be full of the knowledge of the LORD as the waters cover the sea," and "the wolf shall dwell with the lamb" [Isa. 11:6, 9]. Development and completion, therefore, were laid in the foundation of Judaism by means of the Messianic idea. And since the completion of the Jewish nation is connected with the completion of all humanity which must "be full of the knowledge of the LORD" and cease from wars and oppression, therefore included in the Messianic expectation is that concept of a general going-forward, which neither the Greeks nor any other peoples knew; in other words, the idea of progress in the broadest and most exalted sense.[25]

Truly the Messianic idea is the most glistening jewel in the glorious crown of Judaism!

[25] There are objectors who would argue that this conclusion is the product of the idea of progress in which the liberal nineteenth century believed so completely but which is now difficult to maintain, in view of all that has happened in world history; actually, however, the Messianic idea is an idea of sudden, catastrophic change. These objectors should be reminded of the matter of the *repentance* which precedes the *redemption;* in the repentance required in the Messianic age a basic element is the demand for *moral reform*—and this is the very foundation of the idea of progress.

THE ORIGIN OF JEWISH ESCHATOLOGY

NATHANIEL SCHMIDT

CORNELL UNIVERSITY

ESCHATOLOGY is the doctrine concerning the last things (τὰ ἔσχατα, *novissima*, האחרית). It deals with man's condition after death, the destiny of nations, and the end of the world. The Oxford dictionary defines it as "the department of theological science concerned with 'the four last things': death, judgment, heaven and hell". This is obviously too narrow a definition. In so far as eschatology has to do with religious ideas it is, indeed, a part of theology. But even without religious stimulus man's mind projects itself into the future as well as into the past. His scientific study of nature and his philosophy are as likely as his religion to occupy themselves with things to come. In the field of religious eschatology there are more things than the four mentioned. Even in Jewish and Christian eschatological thought, a place should be given to such conceptions as the Messiah, the kingdom of heaven on earth, the intermediate state, the resurrection, the destruction of the world, the new heaven and the new earth. The sharp distinction between eschatology and messianism drawn by Hermann Cohen[1] cannot be maintained; and the last things on earth can surely not be left out. Other ideas are found in the eschatology of other religions. Hugo Gressmann[2] confines eschatology to the complex of ideas connected with the end of the world and the renovation of the world, excluding in principle all that concerns "death

---

[1] *Die Religion der Vernunft*, 1921. Cp. my observations on this important posthumous work in The Philosophical Review, Jan. 1922, pp. 68 ff.

[2] *Der Ursprung der israelitisch-jüdischen Eschatologie*, 1905.

and resurrection, in short the final destiny of the individual"
Such limitations do not seem justified either by etymology or.
usage.

But attention had been too exclusively given to the fate
of the individual. Even on the lower stages of religious development speculation upon things to come is not wholly limited
to man's condition after death. The shifting fortunes of war
and the varying success in obtaining · supplies give rise to
anxious or hopeful thoughts of what may befall the tribe.
Devastating floods, fires, cyclones, earthquakes, or volcanic
eruptions, and terror-inspiring eclipses of the heavenly bodies
suggest the possibility of a destruction of the world. But the
higher forms of eschatological thought presuppose a more
complex social organization and a closer observation of natural
phenomena. Hope of deliverance from foreign oppression is
keenest where it springs from a proud and outraged national
consciousness, kept alive by the memory of past greatness;
and dreams of empire are born of the example set by mighty
conquerors and rulers holding peoples in subjection. It is
especially myths of astrological origin that furnish material
for strongly developed eschatologies. Only prolonged observation of the movements of the planets and the sun's course
through the signs of the zodiac can render possible the thought
of a recurrence at the end of the present period of the events
connected with the world's origin, and the renovation of the
world after its destruction. Eschatology clearly develops with
the growth of man's intellectual and moral perceptions, his
larger social experience, and his expanding knowledge of nature.
While there is a general similarity, the outward forms vary
with the character of the environment and the peculiar genius
of each people. Ideas, like commodities and fashions, pass
from land to land, but if the native soil can produce them
a foreign origin must not too hastily be assumed.

These general considerations should be borne in mind in
approaching the subject of Jewish eschatology. No one questions that our extant literature reveals a marked difference
between earlier and later ideas in respect of man's condition
after death, Israel's destiny, and the future of the world. The

great prophets of the Assyrian and Chaldaean periods stand
forth in striking contrast with their predecessors and their
successors in the Persian and the Graeco-Roman periods.
Their tremendous emphasis upon the ethical demands of Yahwe
and their opposition to chauvinism and entangling foreign
alliances have set them apart and given them an epoch-making
significance. It is not strange, therefore, that modern interpreters have been inclined to look upon them chiefly as moral
teachers and to overlook the fact that they also were sooth-
sayers and politicians. Their eyes were always turned toward
the future, endeavoring to discern what Yahwe was about to
do in the earth, and watching with anxiety the fulfilment of
their prognostications of coming events. They took part in
the raging political party strife of their day, if not with violent
acts, as some who had gone before them, at least with fierce
denunciations and strong intimidations. But they were powerful
personalities, straightforward, fearless, and consistent. This has
led many investigators of the books ascribed to them to regard
as interpolations and additions sections that appeared to be
out of harmony with their distinctive style, their characteristic
cast of thought, and the historic situation that confronted them,
and especially to athetize passages containing eschatological
ideas foreign to the general tone and tenor of their oracles
and known to have flourished in much later times. These
passages have to do, not with the future of the individual, for
on this point even the supposed interpolators, with one single
exception (Isa. 26 19), still maintained the older view, but with
the future of Israel and of the world.

Against this critical treatment a reaction has recently set
in, led by Gunkel, Eichhorn, Gressmann, Bousset, and to some
extent Bertholet, Kittel and others. Having discovered in the
Hebrew Bible numerous unmistakable allusions to myths
apparently of Babylonian origin, in addition to those already
recognized as such, Hermann Gunkel[3] began to question the
current explanation of certain peculiar expressions as merely
figures of speech and to reject the *zeitgeschichtliche Methode,*

---

[3] *Schöpfung und Chaos,* 1895.

as Auberlen[4] had called it, that sees in many of them cryptic references to historic personalities. Suggestions in this direction were also made in academic lectures by that brilliant teacher, Albert Eichhorn. The same tendency was followed by Wilhelm Bousset,[5] though somewhat more guardedly and with stronger emphasis on possible Persian influence. Besides extending this manner of approach to many of the major problems of Old Testament exegesis, Hugo Gressmann[6] finally formulated a new theory and presented it in a work characterized by great learning, much ingenuity, and often rare insight. Briefly outlined, the theory is this. Long before the time of Amos many myths of foreign origin had found their way into Israel and Judah and attached themselves to the thought of Yahwe and his dealings with his people, the other nations, and the world. Most important among these was the conception of a coming destruction of the world by fire, preceded by an accumulation of plagues, and followed by a renewal of the world and the return of the terrestrial paradise, with its innocence and blessedness, ruled over by a semi-divine being, the first man. This idea probably originated in Persia, came through Elam (possibly as early as 2000 B. C.) to Babylonia, and then traveled with the Amorites to Palestine, where it had already been saturated with the Jewish spirit in the eighth century B. C. The great prophets applied the myth of the cosmic catastrophe locally, but because of their moral earnestness suppressed the supplementary myth of the cosmic restoration, except that in some passages they made concessions to the popular eschatology. The allusions in these passages cannot be understood unless one bears in mind the original myth. In the Graeco-Roman period this ancient mythical material was again utilized by the apocalyptic seers, and fresh accessions from abroad made it possible for them to rear a more elaborate structure.

A few typical illustrations must suffice to show the method of interpretation and the somewhat startling results. In Amos 5 18 the prophet declares: "Ah! ye who wish for the day of Yahwe!

---

[4] *Der Prophet Daniel und die Offenbarung Johannis*, 1854.
[5] *Die Religion des Judentums*, 1903, 1906 2; *Die jüdische Apokalyptik*, 1903.
[6] *l. c.*

Wherefore would ye have the day of Yahwe? It will be darkness, and not light". Zephaniah says (1 18): "their silver and their gold cannot save them on the day of Yahwe's wrath, when all the land will be consumed by the fire of his anger; for he shall make a terrible end of all that dwell in the land". The conclusion is drawn that "the day of Yahwe" was a technical term popularly understood to mean both the end of the world through fire and its restoration, bringing in the golden age, but that the people generally expected to escape from the conflagration and share in the good time to come, while the prophets were unwilling to hold out any such hope. The thought of this day of Yahwe is supposed to be of foreign origin. So also the idea of a "Remnant", which did not originate with Isaiah. The enemy from the north in Jeremiah and Zephaniah is not a definite people expected to come upon Judah from that direction, neither the Scythian nor the Chaldaean, but a mysterious being connected with the mountain of the gods in the north. "So gut der Nordberg gleich dem Götterberge ist, so gut ist der Nördliche ein göttliches Wesen" (p. 190): and so is also the king of the north in Dan. 11 40 ff., whom Porphyrius and others have identified with Antiochus IV Epiphanes. It is thought that an Israelitish origin for this divine being is excluded, "since it has for its foundation polytheism".

The child called Immanuel in Is. 7 grows up in a land where the people live on milk and honey. These are imported products. Palestine was not a land literally flowing with milk and honey. They are "Götterspeise" and belong to the land of the gods. Immanuel is a mythical figure. The divine mother was probably originally Ishtar, not Damkina or Hathor. The hero expected by Isaiah (9 1-6) is a human king and a god, a kind of "Halbgott". The mythical epithets point to Egypt where they are common in the royal protocols (p. 282). The court style used in reference to the reigning prince as well as the eschatological king could not have been invented in a small kingdom, but must have come from a world-power. In some of the Servant of Yahwe Songs, found in the appendix to the book of Isaiah, we have remains of a cult-song, referring originally to the death and resurrection of a god, probably

42

Hadad-Rimmon or Tammuz-Adonis. In some passages these reminiscences from a pagan cult are applied to the people of Israel. Like the mother of the Messiah, the Messiah himself is of foreign origin. The figure of a divine king could only be based on the apotheosis of kings, not found in Israel, but among its neighbours. "One like a man" (כבר אנש) in Dan. 7 13 is not Michael, the guardian angel of the people to whom the kingdom is to be given, as I endeavoured to show in a paper read before this Society,[7] but the highest angel, a semi-divine being, known as "the man", an abbreviation of "the first man", the king of paradise, originally a foreign god, possibly the Persian Gayōmarṭ (Bousset), but more likely some divinity surviving as an aeon in Gnostic speculation. This non-Jewish figure traveled to Palestine for the first time long before the days of Amos and Hosea, and a second time shortly before the Christian era.

Criticism in detail is not possible within the limits of this paper. A few suggestions, however, may be offered. There is no room for doubt that myths of Sumerian, Akkadian, Arrapa-chitian, Amoritish, Aramaean, Canaanitish, Hittite, Egyptian, Cretan, and Assyrian origin found their way into Palestine and may have become known in Israel and Judah. This must certainly be the case with the stories concerning the creation of the world and primeval times. Nor can it be questioned that the rich development of eschatology in the Hasmonaean and Roman periods was influenced by Persian and Greek speculation. But the assumption of a foreign origin whenever a peculiar looking conception presents itself may easily become an obsession. Real evidence of advanced eschatological thought outside of Israel in the early times contemplated by the theory does not yet exist, or is at least extremely rare. Gunkel[8] rightly observes: "Aus der Beobachtung der Präcession der Sonne erklärt sich ... die Gleichung von Urzeit und Endzeit, die in der Eschatologie eine solche Rolle spielt". It is quite uncertain, however, how early observers in Babylonia were able

[7] JBL, XIX, 1900, pp. 22 ff.
[8] *Genesis*,[2] p. 234.

to compute, even roughly, the precession of the equinoxes and consequently the cosmic year. Eduard Meyer[9] ascribes the division of the equator and the ecliptic into 360 degrees, and of the latter into the twelve signs of the zodiac, to the Chaldaeans in the first millennium B. C. and the more important progress in astronomy as well as astrology among them to the time of the Chaldaean Kingdom and the Achaemenian and Seleucid dynasties. According to Seneca,[10] Berosus maintained that "the world will burn when all the planets that now move in different courses come together in the Crab, so that they all stand in a straight line in the same sign, and the future flood will take place when the same conjunction occurs in Capricorn". How much older this conception is than the third century B. C. we cannot tell. If the idea of the cosmic catastrophe and the restoration of the world came from Persia, we have absolutely no datable documents to show when it first appeared there. Nor is there any evidence of its presence in Elamitic inscriptions or any indication of what could be identified as Persian influence in Elam in the remote period suggested.

The prophetic texts thus far discovered in Egypt do not show any idea of the destruction of the world through fire or reconstruction after such a catastrophe. They are important, however, because they clearly reveal the tendency of putting on the lips of ancient seers prophecies of historic events known to the real authors and of interpolating earlier texts, and also because the descriptions of present misery and future prosperity, in spite of the "Lust am Fabulieren" so characteristic of the Egyptians, keep within such modest bounds. A priest in the time of Snefru is credited with having predicted the coming of Ameni, probably Amenemhat I, and his successful reign, in a Petrograd papyrus and a wooden tablet at Cairo from the eighteenth dynasty. A demotic papyrus from the year 7 A. D. tells of the prophecies of calamity and Assyrian conquests uttered by a lamb in the 6th year of Bocchoris (c. 730 B. C.). The fragment of a Greek papyrus from the third century

---

[9] *Geschichte des Altertums*, I[3], 1913, pp. 591 ff.
[10] *Quaestiones naturales*, III, 29.

A. D. apparently contains a translation of a defense made before a king Amenophis by a potter accused of godlessness, who turns prophet, predicts disasters for Egypt, and then suddenly dies. Unless the whole production is very late, there is an interpolation threatening "the city on the sea"—as the reference to Agathos Daemon shows, clearly Alexandria— with so complete a destruction that fishermen will dry their nets where it once stood. It goes on to foretell the coming of a king from the east, set up by Isis, in whose reign there will be such blessedness that those who survive into that period will wish the dead to rise in order to share their joy. The time is obviously approaching when the movable year will coincide with the fixed year, the end of a Sothis-period in 139 A. D. One is tempted to think of a Jewish hand retouching an older text in the reign of Hadrian, or that of a native Egyptian having some familiarity with Jewish ideas and phraseology. "The Admonitions of Ipuwer", in a Leiden papyrus, though supposed by Lange, Breasted, and Eduard Meyer to contain "messianic" elements, do not seem to refer to the future at all, as Gardiner and Gressmann[11] have recognized. It is indeed astonishing that so few analogies to Jewish eschatological ideas have yet been found. It may be confidently expected that more will be discovered in course of time, giving a firmer foundation for theories of foreign influence, even where they seem today quite plausible.

There is no logical necessity for supposing that the notion of a destruction of the world through fire and a new creation, admittedly based on very advanced astronomical knowledge, must have preceded the simpler thought of local catastrophes. The more clearly it is perceived that Yahwe was regarded as manifesting himself in the earthquake, the cyclone, the volcanic eruption, the shirokko, the fire from heaven, and the pestilence, the more natural it is to assume that such plagues were expected as punishments for sin, whether alone or in groups, long before they were looked upon as signs of an impending cosmic conflagration. Similarly, the blessings of

11 *Altorientalische Texte und Bilder*, 1909, p. 210.

Yahwe, abundant harvests, plenty of flocks and herds, security
against wild beasts, victories in war, rich booty, health, long-
evity and numerous progeny, would be expected as gracious
rewards long before they were thought of in connection with
a restoration of the world after a cosmic conflagration and
a return of the terrestrial paradise. The day of Yahwe looked
for by the contemporaries of Amos may very well have been
a day of victory and consequent prosperity, and the day of
wrath, that fearful day, with which an Amos and a Zephaniah
threatened the people, need be no more than a day of terrible
defeat at the hands of foreign foes. If Yahwe afflicts them,
not only with war, but with all its hellish train, and hurls at
them the plagues that are his ancient agencies, this does not
necessarily imply that he destroys the whole universe. There
is no hint before Isaiah, either in Judah or among the other
nations, of a mythical Remnant. His expectation that only
few Judaeans would survive the devastating judgment to turn
to Yahwe, as those who perished failed to do, does not necessarily suggest an already extant eschatological conception,
nor a return from exile, nor the salvation of the elect.

It is perfectly natural that Jeremiah should have interpreted
his vision of the seething caldron as indicating the coming of
an enemy from the north, that he should have been ignorant
of the name of the Scythians approaching from that direction,
of their alliance with Assyria, and of their purpose to attack
Egypt rather than the Assyrian vassal-state, Judah, and that
he should have been convinced that Yahwe was watching over
the oracle he had given to fulfil it, and therefore applied it
later to the Chaldaeans. Nowhere, except in the thought of
Jeremiah and Zephaniah, is there an indication of any such
northern enemy. The court-style, which has been so illuminat-
ingly described by Gressmann, may indeed have been in part
borrowed. But the modesty of small courts can scarcely be
urged against Jewish originality. Isaiah may certainly have
expected that a young woman looking forward to motherhood
would call a son Immanuel, with the easy confidence which the
overthrow of Damascus and Samaria would inspire, and that
an Assyrian invasion would soon work such havoc in Judah

that a limited amount of milk and honey would suffice for
the few survivors in a land reduced to a desert. Of a mother-
goddess there is not the slightest suggestion; and though
Palestine may not literally be flowing with milk and honey,
this diet would not have to be imported from the land of the
gods. A shoot springing up from the root of Jesse obviously
presupposes the fall of the Davidic dynasty and the birth of
a scion of the old royal family on which the legitimatist hope
centered. Whether a "Götterkind" or not, it is not necessary
to think that the dominion would rest on his shoulders before
he had grown up. That the singer of the Servant of Yahwe,
even in some passages, drew upon a cult-song, celebrating the
death and resurrection of a foreign deity, seems an unnecessary hypothesis, however ingenious it may be. Semites love to
represent nations as individuals; and the death and quickening
to new life of a nation is a figure of speech that does not
necessarily imply complete extinction and an absolutely new
creation. If the resurrection had not been barred out from
the eschatological scheme, one would not have been startled
to find the bones in Ezekiel's valley interpreted as the *disjecta
membra* of a god, possibly Osiris.

Seeing that the everlasting kingdom is to be given to the
people of the saints of the Most High, or the exalted saints
(קדישי עליונין), the angelic nation, (and Gressmann himself admits
that the one like a man in Dan. 7 13, as everywhere else in
the book, is an angel), there appears to be no good reason
why we should not regard Michael, the guardian angel of his
people, as the highest of the angels. That he fights with the
guardian angels and former gods of the world-powers does
not militate against but rather strengthens this conclusion.
He may indeed have been a god originally, as Gressmann
thinks, and I suggested long ago. He was in course of time
merged with the Messiah. No evidence has been brought
forward to prove Gressmann's assertion that the Messiah was
once a foreign god (p. 282). The hope of an Anointed One,
either a righteous and victorious king who shall be a genuine
descendant of David, as in the Psalms of Solomon, or a high-
priestly ruler "of Aaron and Israel", as in the Zadokite

documents, is altogether explicable as a native growth. Neither
in Daniel, nor in the Parables of Enoch, nor in Baruch, nor
in IV Ezra can the original בר נשא "the man" have been a
title of either the angel or the Messiah. No arguments urged
from any side—and they have all been carefully considered—
have changed my conviction as to the essential soundness of the
position laid down for the first time in a paper presented to
this Society twenty-seven years ago[12] both as to the employment
of the term בר נשא in the original Aramaic texts of these
apocalypses and as to its use by Jesus. Especially Grotius,
Lagarde, Arnold Meyer and Eerdmans had paved the way.
The same conclusions were reached independently, though
published later, by Lietzmann; and they subsequently met with
the approval of Wellhausen. In various publications[13] I have
continued the discussion, dealing with such objections as have
been made. It has more recently been suggested that Jesus
may have used the term בן אדם; this seems to be precluded
by the definite article before the genitive in the Greek which
evidently seeks to render very literally the Aramaic phrase,
just as the Aramaic version by their ברה דנברא, ברה דאנשא,
and ברה דבר נשא seek to render word for word the Greek.
Dalman[14] recognizes that בר נשא was used by Jesus, and that
it was not a messianic title. He thinks that אנש rather than
בר אנש, was used in Galilean Aramaic in the first century
A. D. It is not impossible that one was used more frequently
than the other, though in the absence of texts from that century
it cannot be proved. His strange conjecture that, when it
actually was employed at that time, as by Jesus, it was not
understood, and not intended to be understood, in the sense
it always has wherever it occurs in any of the Aramaic dialects
certainly lacks all plausibility. In regard to the later apocalypses there is still too much confidence in the integrity and
accuracy of late versions, themselves sometimes made from
translations. This is not to be wondered at, when even in
the interpretation of the prophetic books the simple duty is

---

[12] Published in JBL, XV, 1896, pp. 36 ff.
[13] *Encyclopaedia Biblica*, 1903; *The Prophet of Nazareth*, 1905, etc.
[14] *Die Worte Jesu*, 1898.

neglected of comparing long-suspected passages with those that are all but universally recognized as genuine. It is too late to question that much mythical material of foreign origin was taken into the thought of Israel and adopted by its own religious genius, and there is no disposition to undervalue the real services rendered by scholars like Gunkel and Gressmann in detecting such alien elements. But some considerations are often overlooked. Before the prophets, and in spite of them, polytheism flourished in Israel; and there were native myths as well as foreign. Myths are what men say about the gods. What are the stories told about Yahwe himself but myths? Concerning the so-called "schools of the prophets" we know next to nothing. If the stories of Elijah and Elisha come from these "sons of the prophets", they reveal little that can be traced to a foreign origin, but have many mythical as well as legendary features. On the other hand, there is a tendency to underestimate the creative power and originality of the great prophets and of those who struggled with the problems of thought under the mighty ethical impulse they had given. In respect of man's condition after death the adoption of the Persian doctrine of a resurrection seems to have been prepared, not only by the belief that Yahwe had taken certain heroes directly up to heaven and brought others back from Sheol by empowering his prophets to raise them from the dead, but also by peculiar moral considerations. While Job himself resolutely brushes aside "the hope of man", he touches with infinite pathos upon the longing of the creator for the work of his hands that might lead him to call this creature back from Sheol into life. In the struggle for monotheism the simple explanation, in the appendix to Isaiah, that the other gods were simply stocks and stones did not satisfy. They were thought of as living beings reduced from their divine rank to be angels, among whom Yahwe must reign and rebellion be quelled. Thus justice was extended to the invisible world, and the way was paved for heaven and hell. In annotations to the prophecies against foreign nations, the idea of a return from exile was applied to some of them, and places of honor were given even to enemy nations by the side of Israel. When

8

the notion of a cosmic conflagration and a following restoration, an אחרית corresponding to the ראשית, appears in tangible form, the dominant note is the hope of a new heaven and a new earth, wherein dwelleth righteousness. This ethical motivation is of the greatest importance.

Toward an Understanding
of the Messianic Idea
in Judaism

GERSHOM SCHOLEM

I

ANY DISCUSSION OF the problems relating to Messianism is a delicate matter, for it is here that the essential conflict between Judaism and Christianity has developed and continues to exist. Although our discussion will not be concerned with this conflict, but rather with internally Jewish perspectives on Messianism, it will be of value to recall the central issue of this conflict. A totally different concept of redemption determines the attitude to Messianism in Judaism and in Christianity; what appears to the one as a proud indication of its understanding and a positive achievement of its message is most unequivocally belittled and disputed by the other. Judaism, in all of its forms and manifestations, has always maintained a concept of redemption as an event which takes place publicly, on the stage of history and within the community. It is an occurrence which takes place in the visible world and which cannot be conceived apart from such a visible appearance. In contrast, Christianity conceives of redemption as an event in the spiritual and unseen realm, an event which is reflected in the soul, in the private world of each individual, and which effects an inner transformation which need not correspond to anything outside. Even the *civitas dei* of Augustine, which within the confines of Christian dogmatics and in the interest of the Church has made the most far-reaching attempt both to retain and to reinterpret the Jewish categories of redemption, is a community of the mysteriously redeemed within an unredeemed world. What for the one stood unconditionally at the end of history as its most distant aim was for the other the true center of the historical process, even if that process was henceforth peculiarly decked out as *Heilsgeschichte*. The Church was

I

51

convinced that by perceiving redemption in this way it had overcome an external conception that was bound to the material world, and it had counterpoised a new conception that possessed higher dignity. But it was just this conviction that always seemed to Judaism to be anything but progress. The reinterpretation of the prophetic promises of the Bible to refer to a realm of inwardness, which seemed as remote as possible from any contents of these prophecies, always seemed to the religious thinkers of Judaism to be an illegitimate anticipation of something which could at best be seen as the interior side of an event basically taking place in the external world, but could never be cut off from the event itself. What appeared to the Christians as a deeper apprehension of the external realm appeared to the Jew as its liquidation and as a flight which sought to escape verification of the Messianic claim within its most empirical categories by means of a non-existent pure inwardness.

The history of the Messianic idea in Judaism has run its course within the framework of this idea's never-relinquished demand for fulfillment of its original vision. The considerations I would like to set forth in what follows concern the special tensions in the Messianic idea and their understanding in rabbinic Judaism. These tensions manifest themselves within a fixed tradition which we shall try to understand. But even where it is not stated explicitly, we shall often enough find as well a polemical side-glance, or an allusion, albeit concealed, to the claims of Christian Messianism. A number of the things which I would here like to sum up briefly are obvious and hardly constitute an object of learned controversy; of others, however, this can hardly be said, and much as the history of Messianism has been discussed, there is room for a sharper analysis of what it is that makes up the specific vitality of this phenomenon in the history of the Jewish religion. I shall not try to compete with historical and mythological analyses of the origins of Messianic belief in biblical texts or in the history of religion in general; such studies have been undertaken by outstanding scholars like Joseph Klausner, Willi Staerk, Hugo Gressmann, Sigmund Mowinckel, and many others.[1] The object of these remarks is not the initial development of the Messianic idea but the varying perspectives by which it became an effective force after its crystallization in historical Judaism. In this connection it must be emphasized that in the history of Judaism its influence has been exercised almost exclusively under the conditions of the exile as a primary reality of Jewish life and Jewish history. This reality lends its special coloring to each of the various conceptions with which we shall be dealing here.

Within rabbinic Judaism as a social and religious phenomenon three kinds of forces are active precisely at those points where it is the most alive: conservative, restorative, and utopian. The conservative forces are directed toward the preservation of that which exists and which, in the historical environment of Judaism, was always in danger. They are the most easily visible and immediately obvious forces that operate in this type of Judaism. They have established themselves most effectively in the world of *Halakhah,* in the construction and continuing preservation and development of religious law. This law determined the nature of the Jew's life in exile, the only frame in which a life in the light of Sinaitic revelation seemed possible, and it is not surprising that it drew to itself, above all, the conservative forces. The restorative forces are directed to the return and recreation of a past condition which comes to be felt as ideal. More precisely, they are directed to a condition pictured by the historical fantasy and the memory of the nation as circumstances of an ideal past. Here hope is turned backwards to the re-establishment of an original state of things and to a "life with the ancestors." But there are, in addition, forces which press forward and renew; they are nourished by a vision of the future and receive utopian inspiration. They aim at a state of things which has never yet existed. The problem of Messianism in historical Judaism appears within the field of influence of these forces. To be sure, the conservative tendencies, great and even crucial as their role and their significance were for the existence of the religious community of Judaism, have no part in the development of Messianism within this community. This is not true, however, of the two other tendencies which I characterize as restorative and utopian. Both tendencies are deeply intertwined and yet at the same time of a contradictory nature; the Messianic idea crystallizes only out of the two of them together. Neither is entirely absent in the historical and ideological manifestations of Messianism. Only the proportion between them is subject to the widest fluctuations. Among various groupings within Jewry entirely different points of application for such forces and tendencies are emphasized. There has never been in Judaism a measured harmony between the restorative and the utopian factor. Sometimes the one tendency appears with maximal emphasis while the other is reduced to a minimum, but we never find a "pure case" of exclusive influence or crystallization of one of these tendencies. The reason for this is clear: even the restorative force has a utopian factor, and in utopianism restorative factors are at work. The restorative tendency, per se, even when it understands itself as such—as for example in the case of Maimonides whose statements regarding the Messianic idea I shall shortly discuss in greater detail—is nourished to no small degree by a utopian impulse which now appears as projection upon the past instead of projection on the future. The reason for this, too, is clear. There is a common ground of Messianic hope. The utopianism which presents the Jew of that epoch with the vision of an ideal as he would like to see it realized, itself falls naturally into two categories. It can take on the radical form of the vision of a new content which is to be realized in a future that will in fact be nothing other than the restoration of what is ancient, bringing back that which had been lost; the ideal content of the past at the same time delivers the basis for the vision of the future. However, knowingly or unknowingly, certain elements creep into such a restoratively oriented utopianism which are not in the least restorative and which derive from the vision of a completely new state of the Messianic world. The completely new order has elements of the completely old, but even this old order does not consist of the actual past; rather, it is a past transformed and transfigured in a dream brightened by the rays of utopianism.[2] Thus the dialectically linked tension between the utopian and restorative factors provides us also with deep tensions in the forms of Messianism crystallized in rabbinic Judaism, to say nothing of the interiorization of these impulses in Jewish mysticism. I shall now elaborate several principal structures of these forms and in so doing try to clarify the tensions they express.

II

When the Messianic idea appears as a living force in the world of Judaism—especially in that of medieval Judaism, which seems so totally interwoven with the realm of the *Halakhah*—it always occurs in the closest connection with apocalypticism. In these instances the Messianic idea constitutes both a content of religious faith as such and also living, acute anticipation. Apocalypticism appears as the form necessarily created by acute Messianism.

It is self-evident and needs no justification that the Messianic idea came into being not only as the revelation of an abstract proposition regarding the hope of mankind for redemption, but rather in very specific historical circumstances. The predictions and messages of the biblical prophets come to an equal degree from revelation and from the suffering and desperation of those whom they addressed; they are spoken from the context of situations and again and again have proven effective in situations where the End, perceived in the immediate future, was thought about to break in abruptly at any moment. To be sure, the predictions of the prophets do not yet give us any kind of well-defined conception of Messianism. Rather we have a variety of different motifs in which the much emphasized utopian impulse—the vision of a better humanity at the End of Days—is interpenetrated with restorative impulses like the reinstitution of an ideally conceived Davidic kingdom. This Messianic message of the prophets addresses man as a whole and sets forth images of natural and historical events through which God speaks and in which the End of Days is announced or realized. These visions never involve the individual as such, nor do these declarations claim any special "secret" knowledge gained from an inner realm not accessible to every man. By contrast, the words of the apocalyptists represent a shift in this view of the content of prophecy. These anonymous authors of writings like the biblical book of Daniel, the two books of Enoch, Fourth Ezra, the Baruch apocalypses, or the Testaments of the Twelve Patriarchs—to name only a few documents of this at one time seemingly over-flourishing literature—encase the words of the ancient prophets in a frame which they mold and furnish in their own way.

Here God no longer shows the seer individual instances of historical occurrence or only a vision of history's end; rather he sees all of history from beginning to end with particular emphasis on the arrival of that new aeon which manifests itself and prevails in the Messianic events. The Pharisee Josephus had already seen Adam, the first man, as a prophet whose vision encompassed not only the flood in Noah's day but also the flood of fire at the end of time and thus included all of history.[3] The talmudic Aggadah saw things very much the same: God shows Adam—but also Abraham or Moses—the entire past and future, the current and the final aeon.[4] Likewise, the priest of the End of Days (the priestly Messiah) who appears in the Habakkuk commentary of the Dead Sea sectarians, will be able to interpret the visions of the ancient prophets regarding the total course of the history of Israel as all of their features now become fully visible. In this interpretation of the visions of the ancient prophets or even in the work of the apocalyptists themselves, motifs of current history, which refer to contemporary conditions and needs, are closely intertwined with those of an apocalyptic, eschatological nature, in which not only the experiences of the present exercise an influence, but often enough ancient mythical images are filled with utopian content. As students of apocalypticism have always noted correctly, in this process the new eschatology moves decisively beyond the ancient prophecies. Hosea, Amos, or Isaiah know only a single world, in which even the great events at the End of Days run their course. Their eschatology is of a national kind: it speaks of the re-establishment of the House of David, now in ruins, and of the future glory of an Israel returned to God; also of everlasting peace and the turning of all nations toward the one God of Israel and away from heathen cults and images. In contrast, apocalypticism produced the doctrine of the two aeons which follow one another and stand in antithetical relationship: this world and the world to come, the reign of darkness and the reign of light. The national antithesis between Israel and the heathens is broadened into a cosmic antithesis in which the realms of the holy and of sin, of purity and impurity, of life and death, of light and darkness, God and the anti-divine powers, stand opposed. A wider cosmic background is superadded to the national content of eschatology and it is here that the final struggle between Israel and the heathens takes place. There arise the conceptions of the Resurrection of the Dead, of reward and punishment in the Last Judgment, and of Paradise and Hell, in which notions of individual retribution at the End of Days occur in conjunction with promises and threats addressed to the nation. All these are conceptions which are now closely tied to the ancient prophecies. The words of the prophets, which in their original context appear so clear and direct, henceforth become riddles, allegories, and mysteries which are interpreted—one might say, deciphered—by an apocalyptic homiletic or an original apocalyptic vision. And thus we have the framework in which the Messianic idea now begins its historical influence.

But there is an additional factor. As the meaning of the Greek word indicates, apocalypses are revelations or disclosures of God's hidden knowledge of the End. That is to say, what reached the prophets as knowledge which could hardly be proclaimed with sufficient loudness and publicity, in the apocalypses becomes secret. It is one of those enigmas of Jewish religious history that have not been satisfactorily solved by any of the many attempts at explanation just what the real reason is for this metamorphosis which makes knowledge of the Messianic End, where it oversteps the prophetic framework of the biblical texts, into an esoteric form of knowing. Why does the apocalyptist conceal himself instead of shouting his vision into the face of the enemy power as did the prophets? Why does he load the responsibility for those visions, fraught with danger, on the heroes of biblical antiquity and why does he convey them only to the select or initiated? Is it politics? Is it a changed understanding of the nature of this knowing? There is something disturbing in this transcendence of the prophetic which at the same time carries along with it a narrowing of its realm of influence. It cannot be coincidental that for nearly a millennium this character of apocalyptic knowing has also been preserved by the heirs of the ancient apocalyptists within rabbinic Judaism. For them it takes its place at the side of the gnostic knowledge of the *merkabah,* the throne-world of God and its mysteries which, explosive as this knowledge in itself was, could be reported only in a whisper. Not without reason the writings of the *merkabah* mystics in Judaism always contain apocalyptic chapters.[5] The stronger the loss of historical reality in Judaism during the turmoil surrounding the destruction of the Second Temple and of the ancient world, the more intensive became consciousness of the cryptic character and mystery of the Messianic message, which indeed always referred precisely to the re-establishment of that lost reality although it also went beyond it.

In an almost natural way Messianic apocalypticism orders the old promises and traditions, along with the newly adhering motifs, interpretations, and reinterpretations, under the two aspects which the Messianic idea henceforth takes on and keeps in Jewish consciousness. These two aspects, which in fact are based on the words of the prophets themselves and are more or less visible there, concern the catastrophic and destructive nature of the redemption on the one hand and the utopianism of the content of realized Messianism on the other. Jewish Messianism is in its origins and by its nature—this cannot be sufficiently emphasized— a theory of catastrophe. This theory stresses the revolutionary, cataclysmic element in the transition from every historical present to the Messianic future. This transition itself becomes a problem in that, beginning with the words of the prophets Amos and Isaiah, the really non-transitional character of it is pointed up and emphasized. Isaiah's Day of the Lord (chapters 2 and 4) is a day of catastrophe and is described in visions which stress this catastrophic nature in the extreme. But we learn nothing about how that Day of the Lord, on which previous history ends and on which the world is shaken to its foundations, is related to the "End of Days" (promised at the beginning of chapter 2 of Isaiah) on which the House of the Lord shall be established at the top of the mountains and the peoples flow unto it.

The elements of the catastrophic and the visions of doom are present in peculiar fashion in the Messianic vision. On the one hand, they are applied to the transition or destruction in which the Messianic redemption is born—hence the ascription of the Jewish concept of "birth pangs of the Messiah" to this period. But, on the other hand, it is also applied to the terrors of the Last Judgment which in many of these descriptions concludes the Messianic period instead of accompanying its beginnings. And thus for the apocalyptist's glance the Messianic utopia may often become twofold. The new aeon and the days of the Messiah are no longer one (as they still are in some writings of this literature); rather they refer to two periods of which the one, the rule of the Messiah, really still belongs to this world; the other, however, already belongs entirely to the new aeon which begins with the Last Judgment. But this doubling of the stages of redemption is mostly the result of learned exegesis which seeks to put every saying of the Bible harmoniously into place. In an original vision catastrophe and utopia do not twice follow after each other, but it is precisely by their uniqueness that they bring to bear with full force the two sides of the Messianic event.

However, before I devote a few remarks to these two sides of the Messianic idea as they characterize Messianic apocalypticism, I must preface a word intended to correct a widespread misconception. I am referring to the distortion of historical circumstances, equally popular among both Jewish and Christian scholars, which lies in denying the continuation of the apocalyptic tradition in rabbinic Judaism. This distortion of intellectual history is quite understandable in terms of the anti-Jewish interests of Christian scholars as well as the anti-Christian interests of Jewish ones. It was in keeping with the tendencies of the former group to regard Judaism only as the antechamber of Christianity and to see it as moribund once it had brought forth Christianity. Their view led to the conception of a genuine continuation of Messianism via the apocalyptists in the new world of Christianity. But the other group, too, paid tribute to their own prejudices. They were the great Jewish scholars of the nineteenth and early twentieth centuries, who to a great extent determined the popular image of Judaism. In view of their concept of a purified and rational Judaism, they could only applaud the attempt to eliminate or liquidate apocalypticism from the realm of Judaism. Without regrets, they left the claim of apocalyptic continuity to a Christianity which, to their minds, gained nothing on that account. Historical truth was the price paid for the prejudices of both camps. Attempts to eliminate apocalypticism completely from the realm of rabbinic Judaism have not been lacking since the Middle Ages and in what follows we shall even deal with the most consequential of these attempts, that of Maimonides. Such attempts represent one tendency among other, entirely different ones which have also been active in the history of Judaism. By themselves these attempts can claim no value as a truthful representation of the historical reality of Judaism. For this denial of apocalypticism set out to suppress exceedingly vital elements in the realm of Judaism, elements filled with historical dynamism even if they combined destructive with constructive forces. The idea that all apocalyptic currents of the pre-Christian age flowed into Christianity and there found their real place is a fiction which cannot be maintained against more careful historical examination. Just after the origin of the known apocalypses, especially those of the first pre- and post-Christian centuries, an undiminished mighty stream of apocalypticism rushes forth within the Jewish rabbinic tradition; in part it flows into the channel of the talmudic and aggadic literature, in part it finds its expression in its own literature, preserved in Hebrew and Aramaic. There can be no talk of a discontinuity between these later apocalypses and those ancient ones whose Hebrew originals have until now remained lost and which have only been preserved in translations and in the adaptations of the Christian churches. While one may question to which Jewish circles these independent writings that preserve their pseudepigraphic literary form really belong—nothing in them contradicts the spiritual world of the rabbis even if it is not possible to bring them into close relationship with it—there remains no doubt about the entry of apocalyptic tradition into the House of Study and the range of ideas of the traditional scholars. Here the cover of anonymity is again thrown off, the secretive whisper turns into an open exchange of ideas, into formal instruction, and even into pointed epigrams whose authors, with their often well-known names, take responsibility for their words. The significance of these two sources of rabbinic apocalypticism for an understanding of Messianism in the world of the *Halakhah* cannot be estimated too highly.

I spoke of the catastrophic nature of redemption as a decisive characteristic of every such apocalypticism, which is then complemented by the utopian view of the content of realized redemption. Apocalyptic thinking always contains the elements of dread and consolation intertwined. The dread and peril of the End form an element of shock and of the shocking which induces extravagance. The terrors of the real historical experiences of the Jewish people are joined with images drawn from the heritage of myth or mythical fantasy. This is expressed with particular forcefulness in the concept of the birth pangs of the Messiah which in this case means the Messianic age. The paradoxical nature of this conception exists in the fact that the redemption which is born here is in no causal sense a result of previous history. It is precisely the lack of transition between history and the redemption which is always stressed by the prophets and apocalyptists. The Bible and the apocalyptic writers know of no progress in history leading to the redemption. The redemption is not the product of immanent developments such as we find it in modern Western reinterpretations of Messianism since the Enlightenment where, secularized as the belief in progress, Messianism still displayed unbroken and immense vigor. It is rather transcendence breaking in upon history, an intrusion in which history itself perishes, transformed in its ruin because it is struck by a beam of light shining into it from an outside source. The constructions of history in which the apocalyptists (as opposed to the prophets of the Bible) revel have nothing to do with modern conceptions of development or progress, and if there is anything which, in the view of these seers, history deserves, it can only be to perish. The apocalyptists have always cherished a pessimistic view of the world. Their optimism, their hope, is not directed to what history will bring forth, but to that which will arise in its ruin, free at last and undisguised.

To be sure, the "light of the Messiah" which is to shine wondrously into the world, is not always seen as breaking in with complete suddenness; it may become visible by gradations and stages, but these gradations and stages have nothing to do with the history that has gone before. "It is told of Rabbi Hiyya and Rabbi Simeon that they walked in the valley of Arbela early in the morning and saw the dawn breaking on the horizon. Thereupon Rabbi Hiyya said: 'So too is Israel's redemption; at first it will be only very slightly visible, then it will shine forth more

60

brightly, and only afterwards will it break forth in all of its glory.' "[6] Such a belief was very common among apocalyptic calculators in all ages whenever they sought schemata according to which the different stages of the redemption would occur within the frame of the Last Days. But the apocalyptic calculation which relied upon numbers and constellations expresses only one side of this point of view and many teachers repudiated it again and again, not without reason, though with little success. In opposition to it stands the no less powerful sentiment that the Messianic age cannot be calculated. This was most pointedly expressed in the words of a talmudic teacher of the third century: "Three things come unawares: the Messiah, a found article, and a scorpion."[7] And with sharper stress on the always possible End, the immediacy to God of each day, we find: "If Israel would repent even for a single day, they would be instantly redeemed and the Son of David would instantly come, for it says (Ps. 95:7) : *Today if you will listen to His voice.*"[8]

Such words add to the concept of the spontaneity of the redemption the idea, expressed in numerous moral dicta of the talmudic literature, that there are deeds which, as it were, help to bring about the redemption, somewhat like a midwife at a birth. Whoever does one thing or-another (whoever, for example, cites what he has heard, stating the name of his source), "he brings redemption into the world." But here it is not a matter of real causality, only of an already established frame for pointed, sententious formulations which are directed less at the Messianic redemption than at the moral value of the suggested conduct. Indeed, statements of this kind stand totally outside the realm of apocalyptic thought. They present a moralism which must have been welcomed by later reinterpretations of Messianism in the sense of a rational and sensible utopianism. But in fact there can be no preparation for the Messiah. He comes suddenly, unannounced, and precisely when he is least expected or when hope has long been abandoned.

This deep feeling of the impossibility of calculating the Messianic age has produced in the Messianic Aggadah the idea of the occultation of the Messiah, who is always already present somewhere and whom a profound legend, not without cause, allows to have been born on the day of the destruction of the Temple. Beginning at the moment of the deepest catastrophe there exists the chance for redemption. "Israel speaks to God: When will You redeem us? He answers: When you have sunk to the lowest level, at that time will I redeem you."[9] Corresponding to this continually present possibility is the concept of the Messiah who continually waits in hiding. It has taken many forms, though admittedly none more grand than that which, with extravagant anticipation, has transplanted the Messiah to the gates of Rome, where he dwells among the lepers and beggars of the Eternal City.[10] This truly staggering "rabbinic fable" stems from the second century, long before the Rome which has just destroyed the Temple and driven Israel into exile itself becomes the seat of the Vicar of Christ and of a Church seeking dominion by its claim to Messianic fulfillment. This symbolic antithesis between the true Messiah sitting at the gates of Rome and the head of Christendom, who reigns there, accompanies Jewish Messianic thought through the centuries. And more than once we learn that Messianic aspirants have made a pilgrimage to Rome in order to sit by the bridge in front of the Castel Sant' Angelo and thus enact this symbolic ritual.

III

This catastrophic character of the redemption, which is essential to the apocalyptic conception, is pictured in all of these texts and traditions in glaring images. It finds manifold expression: in world wars and revolutions, in epidemics, famine, and economic catastrophe; but to an equal degree in apostasy and the desecration of God's name, in forgetting of the Torah and the upsetting of all moral order to the point of dissolving the laws of nature.[11] Such apocalyptic paradoxes regarding the final catastrophe were accepted even into as sober a text as the Mishnah, the first canonical codification of the *Halakhah*.

In the footsteps of the Messiah [i.e., in the period of his arrival] presumption will increase and respect disappear. The empire will turn to heresy and there will be no moral reproof. The house of assembly will become a brothel, Galilee will be laid waste, and the people of the frontiers will wander from city to city and none will pity them. The wisdom of the scribes will become odious and those who shun sin will be despised; truth will nowhere be found. Boys will shame old men and old men will show deference to boys. "The son reviles the father, the daughter rises up against the mother . . . a man's enemies are the men of his own house" (Micah 7:6). The face of the generation is like the face of a dog [i.e., brazenness will reign]. On whom shall we then rely? On our Father in heaven.[12]

The pages of the Talmud tractate Sanhedrin which deal with the Messianic age are full of most extravagant formulations of this kind. They drive toward the point that the Messiah will come only in an age which is either totally pure or totally guilty and corrupt. Little wonder that in one such context the Talmud cites the bald statement of three famous teachers of the third and fourth centuries: "May he come, but I do not want to see him."[13]

Though the redemption, then, cannot be realized without dread and ruin, its positive aspect is provided with all the accents of utopianism. This utopianism seizes upon all the restorative hopes turned toward the past and describes an arc from the re-establishment of Israel and of the Davidic kingdom as a kingdom of God on earth to the re-establishment of the condition of Paradise as it is foreseen by many old Midrashim, but above all by the thought of Jewish mystics, for whom the analogy of First Days and Last Days possess living reality. But it does more than that. For already in the Messianic utopianism of Isaiah we find the Last Days conceived immeasurably more richly than any beginning. The condition of the world, wherein the earth will be full of the knowledge of the Lord as the waters cover the sea (Isa. 11:9), does not repeat anything that has ever been, but presents something new. The world of *tikkun*, the re-establishment of the harmonious condition of the world, which in the Lurianic Kabbalah is the Messianic world, still contains a strictly utopian impulse. That harmony which it reconstitutes does not at all correspond to any condition of things that has ever existed even in Paradise, but at most to a plan contained in the divine idea of Creation. This plan, however, even with the first stages of its realization, came up against that disturbance and hindrance of the cosmic process known as the "breaking of the vessels" which initiates the Lurianic myth. In reality, therefore, the Last Days realize a higher, richer, and more fulfilled condition than the First Days, and even the Kabbalists remain bound to a utopian conception. The contents of this utopia differ in the various circles. The model of a renewed humanity and of a renewed kingdom of David or of a descendant of David, which represents the prophetic legacy of Messianic utopianism, is often enough combined by the apocalyptists and mystics with a renewed condition of nature and even of the cosmos as a whole. The escapist and extravagant character of such utopianism, which undertakes to determine the content of redemption without having experienced it yet in fact, does of course subject it to the wild indulgence of fantasy. But it always retains that fascinating vitality to which no historical reality can do justice and which in times of darkness and persecution counterpoises the fulfilled image of wholeness to the piecemeal, wretched reality which was available to the Jew. Thus the images of the New Jerusalem that float before the eyes of the apocalyptists always contain more than was ever present in the old one, and the renewal of the world is simply more than its restoration.

In this connection, the talmudic teachers were already faced with the question whether one may "press for the End," that is to say, force its coming by one's own activity. Here we find a deep cleavage of opinion with regard to Messianism. The dream was not always accompanied by the determination to do something for its realization. On the contrary: it is one of the most important characteristics of Messianism that to the minds of a great many there was an abyss here. And this is not surprising since precisely in the biblical texts which served as the basis for the crystallization of the Messianic idea it is nowhere made dependent upon human activity. Neither Amos' Day of the Lord nor Isaiah's visions of the End of Days are deemed the results of such action. Likewise, the ancient apocalyptists, who undertook to disclose the secrets of the End, know nothing of this. In truth, everything is here attributed to God and it is just this that lends a special character to the contradiction between what is and what shall be. The warnings against human action which dares to bring about the redemption have always been most offensive to the revolutionary and to the one who "presses for the End," as the Jewish term would have it. But they do not lack legitimacy, and they are by no means only signs of weakness and possible cowardice (although they may sometimes be that as well).

In Song of Songs 2:7 we find the verse: "I adjure you, daughters of Jerusalem, by the gazelles and by the hinds of the field, do not awaken or stir up love until it is ready." Rabbi Helbo comments: "Four vows are contained here. The Israelites are adjured not to revolt against the kingdoms of the world [the secular powers], not to press for the End, not to reveal their mystery to the nations of the world, and not to come up from exile like a wall [in great masses]. But, if so, why does King Messiah come? To gather in the exiled of Israel."

Thus we read in the old Midrash to the Song of Songs.[14] But likewise the author of Fourth Ezra is exhorted by the angel: "You will certainly not want to hasten more than the Creator" (4:34).

This is the attitude of the spokesmen of that Messianism in Judaism which still placed all hope on unbroken faith in God. It corresponds to and originates from the afore-mentioned conception of the essential lack of relation between human history and the redemption. But we can understand why such an attitude was again and again in danger of being overrun by the apocalyptic certainty that the End had begun and all that was still required was the call to ingathering. Ever and again the revolutionary opinion that this attitude deserves to be overrun breaks through in the Messianic actions of individuals or entire movements. This is the Messianic activism in which utopianism becomes the lever by which to establish the Messianic kingdom. One may, perhaps, formulate the question which produced this division of minds more pointedly. It would then be: Can man master his own future? And the answer of the apocalyptist would be: no. But the enticement to action, the call to fulfillment, is inherent in this projection of the best in man upon his future, which is just what Jewish Messianism in its utopian elements so emphatically set forth.

And it is not surprising that beyond the repudiations and reservations of the theologians, historical recollection and. mythical legend together kept alive the memory of the Messianic ventures of Bar Kokhba or of Sabbatai Zevi, who created epochs in the history of Judaism. The legend of Rabbi Joseph de la Reyna, which long enjoyed great popularity,[15] pictures in extreme fashion an individual's enticement to Messianic action, an enticement which must fail because no one is capable of such action. It describes the undertaking of a great teacher in Israel, for whom the redemption is concentrated on shattering only one last barrier. But it must be done by magic, and it must fail for just this reason. This legend of the great magician and Kabbalist who captured Sammael, the devil, and thus could have brought about the redemption if he had not himself fallen under the devil's sway in the process, is a grand allegory on all "pressing for the End." Such Joseph de la Reynas have never been lacking in Jewish life, whether they remained hidden in some corner of the exile or, by exposing their identity and exaggerating their own magic, made the jump into world history.

This Messianic activism, incidentally, lies on that peculiar double line of mutual influence between Judaism and Christianity which goes hand in hand with inner tendencies of development in both religions. The political and chiliastic Messianism of important religious movements within Christianity often appears as a reflection of what is really Jewish Messianism. It is well known how vigorously such tendencies were decried as Judaizing heresies by their orthodox opponents in Catholicism and Protestantism alike. From a purely phenomenological point of view there is doubtless some truth to these reproaches, even if in historical reality these tendencies also arise spontaneously from attempts to take Messianism seriously and from a feeling of dissatisfaction with a Kingdom of God which is to lie within us and not about us. The more Christian Messianism—to use the words of a significant Protestant theologian, who with this formulation no doubt believed he had expressed something most positive [16]—presented itself as "this wondrous certainty of pure inwardness," the more strongly dissatisfaction with this view had to find itself referred back to the Jewish vision. And thus, again and again, such chiliastic and revolutionary Messianism as emerges, for example, among the Taborites, the Anabaptists, or the radical wing of the Puritans, draws its inspiration mainly from the Old Testament and not from Christian sources. To be sure, it is the Christian conviction regarding the redemption which has already come that lends this activism a special seriousness and its special vehemence—and thus its significance in world history. In the Jewish realm, from which it originates, this activism remains singular and strangely powerless precisely because it is aware of the radical difference between the unredeemed world of history and that of the Messianic redemption, as I have explained it above. Parallel to this line, along which Judaism has again and again furnished Christianity with political chiliastic Messianism, runs the other one, along which Christianity, for its part, has bequeathed to Judaism or aroused within it the tendency to discover a mystical aspect of the interiorization of the Messianic idea. To be sure, this aspect comes to the same degree from the inner movement and development of mysticism in Judaism itself, for which the Messianically promised reality must in addition appear as a symbol of an inner condition of the world and of man. It will always remain difficult to decide how much may be said of historical influence with regard to these two channels and how much must be ascribed to immanent movement within each one's own world of ideas.

The interiorization of the redemption remains a problem even where, unlike in Christianity, it did not serve to establish a thesis alleging that in the redemption something like a pure inwardness bursts forth. I have already stressed that it is indicative of the special position of Judaism in the history of religion that it thought nothing of such a chemically pure inwardness of redemption. I do not say: thought little, but thought nothing at all. An inwardness, which does not present itself in the most external realm and is not bound up with it in every way, was regarded here as of no value. According to the dialectics of Jewish mysticism, the drive to the essence was at the same time the drive outward. The re-establishment of all things in their proper place, which constitutes the redemption, produces a totality that knows nothing of such a division between inwardness and outwardness. The utopian element in Messianism refers to this totality and to it alone. Historically, this totality could be viewed with a double glance, cast upon the inner and outer aspect of the world, as in the Lurianic Kabbalah, so long as it was certain that one would not fall victim to the other. But it remains peculiar that this question concerning the inner aspect of the redemption should emerge so late in Judaism—though it finally does emerge with great vehemence. In the Middle Ages it played no role. Perhaps this is connected with the repudiation of the Christian claim which just at that time returned to the notion of the inwardness of redemption and insisted upon it, a notion which was so evidently refuted on the stage of history and therefore, as far as the churches were concerned, had no business being there.

IV

In the above, I have emphasized the two aspects of the Messianic idea which appear in rabbinic Judaism and provide it with ongoing apocalyptic inspiration: the catastrophic and the utopian. Yet the figure of the Messiah, in whom the fulfillment of redemption is concentrated, remains peculiarly vague; and this, I think, has good reason. Features of such varying historical and psychological origins are gathered into this medium of fulfillment and coexist within it that they do not furnish a clear picture of the man. One is almost tempted to say that his character is overdetermined and therefore has again become uncertain. Unlike Christian or Shiite Messianism, no memories of a real person are at work here which, though they might arouse the imagination and attract old images of expectation, nonetheless are always bound to something deeply personal. Jesus or the Hidden Imam, who once existed as persons, possess the unmistakable and unforgettable qualities of a person. This is just what the Jewish image of the Messiah, by its nature, cannot have since it can picture everything personal only in completely abstract fashion, having as yet no living experience on which to base it.

There is, however, a historical development in this character of the Messiah on which the two aspects stressed here shed a great deal of light. I am referring to the doubling of the figure of the Messiah, its split into a Messiah of the House of David and one of the House of Joseph. This conception of the "Messiah ben Joseph" was again discussed only a few years ago in a very interesting monograph by Siegmund Hurwitz which tries to explain its origins in psychological terms.[17] But I think it can best be understood in terms of those two aspects with which we have been concerned here. The Messiah ben Joseph is the dying Messiah who perishes in the Messianic catastrophe. The features of the catastrophic are gathered together in him. He fights and loses— but he does not suffer. The prophecy of Isaiah regarding the suffering servant of God is never applied to him. He is a redeemer who redeems nothing, in whom only the final battle with the powers of the world is crystallized. His destruction coincides with the destruction of history. By contrast, when the figure is split, all of the utopian interest is concentrated on the Messiah ben David. He is the one in whom what is new finally comes to the fore, who once and for all defeats the antichrist, and thus presents the purely positive side of this complex phenomenon. The more these two sides are made independent and emphasized, the more this doubling of the Messiah figure remains alive for the circles of apocalyptic Messianists even in later Judaism. The more this dualism becomes weakened, the less is the doubling mentioned, and the special figure of the Messiah ben Joseph becomes superfluous and meaningless.

Such mitigations of the dualism occur even in the talmudic literature itself. Much as apocalyptic imagination fascinated many rabbinic teachers, and varied as its continuing influence was in medieval Judaism, more sober conceptions remained alive as well. There were many who felt repulsed by apocalypticism. Their attitude is most sharply expressed by the strictly anti-apocalyptical definition of the Babylonian teacher Samuel of the first half of the third century, which is often referred to in the Talmud: "The only difference between this aeon and the Days of the Messiah is the subjection [of Israel] to the nations." [18] This obviously polemical utterance provides the cue for a tendency with which we shall still have to deal in terms of its effect and its crystallization in the powerful formulations of Maimonides.

Such counter-tendencies have not, however, been able to hamper the continuing effectiveness of radical apocalyptic, utopian currents in Jewish Messianism. On the contrary, one might say that this apocalypticism was deeply rooted in popular forms of Judaism that were widespread during the Middle Ages. The esoteric element increasingly spills out into the popular domain. Apocalyptic productivity stretches from the third century down to the period of the Crusades. Important products of the Kabbalistic literature still clearly manifest the continuing influence of this apocalyptic element, as indeed many of its parts represent a productive continuation of the old Aggadah, though on a new level. We must of course take into account that a number of such products of popular apocalypticism fell victim to rabbinical censorship. This censorship, though not constituted in any institutional form, was no doubt effective. Much that was written in the Middle Ages did not at all suit the fancy of the responsible leadership, and sometimes we learn of ideas and writings, which did not gain entry into the "higher literature," only via fortuitously preserved letters or some hidden quotation. This popular apocalypticism presents itself to us as propaganda literature. In a time of gloom and oppression it seeks to bring consolation and hope, and thereby it necessarily generates extravagances. There is an anarchic element in the very nature of Messianic utopianism: the dissolution of old ties which lose their meaning in the new context of Messianic freedom. The total novelty for which utopianism hopes enters thus into a momentous tension with the world of bonds and laws which is the world of *Halakhah*.

The relationship between the Jewish *Halakhah* and Messianism is indeed filled with such tension. On the one hand, Messianic utopianism presents itself as the completion and perfection of *Halakhah*. It is to perfect what cannot yet find expression in the *Halakhah* as the law of an unredeemed world. Thus, for example, only in Messianic times will all those parts of the law which are not realizable under the conditions of the exile become capable of fufillment. And thus there seems to be no antagonism created at all between what can be provisionally fulfilled in the law and what can only be fulfilled Messianically. The one calls for the other, and the concept of a Messianic *Halakhah* in the Talmud's terms, i.e., one which can be taught and fufilled only in the Days of the Messiah, is by no means merely an empty phrase; it represents a very real content. The law as such can be fulfilled in its total plenitude only in a redeemed world. But there is doubtless another side to the matter as well. For apocalypticism and its inherent mythology tore open a window on a world which the *Halakhah* rather preferred to leave shrouded in the mists of uncertainty. The vision of Messianic renewal and freedom was by its nature inclined to produce the question of what it would do to the status of Torah and of the *Halakhah* which was dependent on it. This question, which the men of *Halakhah* could consider only with misgivings, is necessarily raised by rabbinic apocalypticism. For even if the Torah was regarded as not subject to change, the problem of its practical application in the Messianic age had to emerge within such conceptions as well. And here indeed it was easier to assume that the divine "Yoke of the Torah" would become heavier rather than lighter. For at that time a great deal would become capable of fulfillment for the first time which under the conditions of the exile, in which the *Halakhah* had largely developed, was not at all realizable. At the same time, the conception of a "Torah of the Messiah," as it appears in the talmudic literature, drew in its wake yet another conception: that of a more complete development of the reasons for the commandments, which only the Messiah will be able to explain.[19] Both understanding of the Torah and its fulfillment will thus be infinitely richer than they are now. But along with this, there were bound to be motifs which carried this new understanding to the level of a deeper, even purely mystical comprehension of the world of the law. The greater the assumption of changes in nature or of revolutions in man's moral character—which latter were determined by the extinction of the destructive power of the evil inclination in the Messianic age—the greater did the modification also have to become which under such circumstances affected the operation of the law. A positive commandment or a prohibition could scarcely still be the same when it no longer had for its object the separation of good and evil to which man was called, but rather arose from the Messianic spontaneity of human freedom purely flowing forth. Since by its nature this freedom realizes only the good, it has no real need for all those "fences" and restrictions with which the *Halakhah* was surrounded in order to secure it from the temptations of evil. At this point there arises the possibility of a turning from the restorative conception of the final re-establishment of the reign of law to a utopian view in which restrictive traits will no longer be determinative and decisive, but be replaced by certain as yet totally unpredictable traits which will reveal entirely new aspects of free fulfillment. Thus an anarchic element enters Messianic utopianism. The Pauline "freedom of the children of God" is a form in which such a turning meant leaving Judaism behind. But this was by no means the only form of these conceptions, which appear in Messianism again and again with dialectical necessity. Finally, the anarchic element is also joined by the antinomian potentialities which are latent in Messianic utopianism. (See "Redemption Through Sin.")

The opposition between restorative and purely utopian, radical elements in the conception of the Messianic Torah brings an element of uncertainty into the *Halakhah*'s attitude to Messianism. The battle lines are by no means clearly drawn. Unfortunately, a penetrating and serious study of this relationship of the medieval *Halakhah* to Messianism is one of the most important yet unfulfilled desiderata of the scientific study of Judaism. As far as I can see, no one has taken an interest in doing it. If I may trust my own very incompetent judgment—really only an impression— I would say that many of the great men of *Halakhah* are completely entwined in the realm of popular apocalypticism when they come to speak of the redemption. For a number of them, apocalypticism is not a foreign element and is not felt to be in contradiction to the realm of the *Halakhah*. From the point of view of the *Halakhah*, to be sure, Judaism appears as a well-ordered house, and it is a profound truth that a well-ordered house is a dangerous thing. Something of Messianic apocalypticism penetrates into this house; perhaps I can best describe it as a kind of anarchic breeze. A window is open through which the winds blow in, and it is not quite certain just what they bring in with them. As vital as this anarchic airing may have been for the house of the law, it is certainly easy to understand the reticence and misgivings with which other significant representatives of *Halakhah* regarded everything that makes up Messianic utopianism. Many, as I have said, were deeply involved with apocalypticism; but among many others one can notice an equally deep uneasiness with regard to the perspectives it reveals. As long as Messianism appeared only as an abstract hope, as an element totally deferred to the future which had no living significance for the life of the Jew in the present, the opposition between the essentially conservative rabbinic and the never completely defined Messianic authority, which was to be established from entirely new dimensions of the utopian, could remain without real tension; indeed, there could be attempts to create a certain harmony between such authorities. But whenever there was an actual eruption of such hope, that is to say, in every historical hour in which the Messianic idea entered the mind as a power with direct influence, the tension which exists between these two forms of religious authority immediately became noticeable. These things could be united in pure thought, or at least they could be preserved next to one another, but they could not be united in their execution. Observing the appearance of such tension in the Messianic movements of the twelfth century with their concomitant antinomianism, among the followers of David Alroy in Kurdistan or among those of the Messiah who appeared at that time in Yemen, no doubt influenced Maimonides' attitude when with such great energy he set about to restrict the scope of Messianic utopianism to an absolute minimum.

The emergence of such radical contents in the Messianic idea can be most clearly seen in a medieval work in which *Halakhah* and *Kabbalah* are very closely intertwined. I am thinking of the book *Ra'ya Mehemna*, which belongs to the most recent layer of the literature that is gathered together in the *Zohar* and which came into being in the last years of the thirteenth or the first years of the fourteenth century. The author, who is a Kabbalist deeply rooted in the *Halakhah*, here deals with the mystical reasons for the commandments and prohibitions of the Torah. But his book is also written out of an acute Messianic expectation which possesses all of the urgency of the imminently impending End. He is not, however, motivated in the least by an interest in the catastrophic aspect of the redemption, of which he has not discovered any new, independent features, but rather in the utopian content which in anticipation he seeks to formulate. Here an anarchic vision of liberation from the restrictions which the Torah has laid upon the Jew in an unredeemed world, and above all in the exile, plays a central role. The author expresses his vision by means of old biblical symbols which now become types for the different status of things in the unredeemed world and in the Messianic age.

These symbols are the Tree of Life and the Tree of Knowledge, or the Tree of Knowledge of Good and Evil, which because its fruit brings about death is also called the Tree of Death. These trees, respectively, control the state of the world, be it the state of Creation as such or of the Torah, which as the divine law governs and determines it. Standing in the center of Paradise and representing higher orders of things, the trees control a great deal more than just existence in the Garden of Eden. Since the Fall of Adam, the world is no longer ruled by the Tree of Life as it had been in the beginning, but by the Tree of Knowledge. The Tree of Life represents the pure, unbroken power of the holy, the diffusion of the divine life through all worlds and the communication of all living things with their divine source. There is no admixture of evil in it, no "shells" which dam up and choke life, no death, and no restriction. But since the Fall of Adam, since the time when the forbidden fruit of the Tree of Knowledge was eaten, the world is ruled by the mystery of this second tree in which both good and evil have their place. Hence, under the rule of this Tree, the world contains differentiated spheres: the holy and the profane, the pure and the impure, the permitted and the forbidden, the living and the dead, the divine and the demonic. Although the Torah, the revelation of God's providence, is in essence one and immutable, it manifests itself in every state of the world in a manner befitting this state. Our comprehension of revelation is presently tied to the Tree of Knowledge and presents itself as the positive law of the Torah and as the realm of the *Halakhah*. Its meaning appears to us now in what is commanded and what is prohibited and in everything which follows from this basic distinction. The power of evil, of destruction and death, has become real in the free will of· man. The purpose of the law, which as it were constitutes the Torah as it can be read in the light—or shadow!—of the Tree of Knowledge, is to confine this power if not to overcome it entirely. But in the Messianic redemption the full glory of the utopian again breaks forth, although characteristically and in keeping with the idea of the Tree of Life it is conceived as a restoration of the state of things in Paradise. In a world in which the power of evil has been broken, all those differentiations also disappear which had been derived from it. In a world in which only the pure life still reigns, obstructions to the stream of life, which solidify it in externals and in "shells," no longer have any validity or significance. In the present state of the world the Torah must appear on many levels of meaning; even the mystical meaning, by which the insightful individual is permitted a glance at least into its hidden life and into his own connection with this life, is necessarily bound to the phenomena of even the most external realm. Therefore, in exile, *Halakhah* and Kabbalah always remain mutually related. But when the world will again be subject to the law of the Tree of Life, the face of *Halakhah* itself will change. Where everything is holy there will no longer be need of restrictions and prohibitions, and whatever appear as such today will either vanish or reveal a totally new, as yet undiscovered, aspect of pure positiveness. In this conception, the redemption now appears as the manifestation of something deeply spiritual, as a spiritual revolution which discloses the mystical content and significance of the Torah as its real and true literal meaning. Mystical utopia takes the place of the national and political utopia without actually abrogating it, but as a kernel which has now begun to sprout. The author revels in the contrast between the "Torah of the Exile" and the "Torah of Redemption": the latter alone will disclose the undistorted and living meaning of the entire Torah in its infinite fullness. But he does not elucidate any transition between these two kinds of manifestation or between the conditions in the two states of the world which are expressed in these two aspects of the one "complete Torah of God." The utopian vision in rabbinic Judaism was driven no further than this, and scarcely could have been.

THE ORIGIN OF THE MESSIANIC HOPE IN ISRAEL

PROFESSOR HENRY PRESERVED SMITH, D.D.
Meadville Theological School, Meadville, Pa.

Frequent seditious attempts of the Jews in the first century of our era are evidence of an intense hatred for their rulers such as may be expected when a conquered people is harshly treated. But they are evidence of something more than this common and natural hatred. Josephus says that in the crowning struggle his countrymen were moved by an oracle which predicted that about that time one from their land should become ruler of the world. The very day that Jerusalem fell into the hands of the besiegers a prophet proclaimed that the people should go up to the temple there to receive signs of their deliverance. Reports had spread as far as Rome itself that the fates would give the rule of the world to men from the East. Josephus,[1] writing after the disastrous issue, could perhaps persuade himself that the oracle was, as he calls it, ambiguous. He can hardly have believed that it referred to Vespasian though he is bold enough to assert this. A Jew familiar with the Scriptures could not seriously think that the prophets looked for a gentile Messiah. The historian was willing to flatter the ruling house, and also to count on the ignorance of his readers. The material in our hands enables us to say that the messianic hope which inspired the revolt in the year 70, and the even more remarkable one sixty years later, was anything but ambiguous, and to say also that it did not refer to a Roman monarch.

---

[1] The material from Josephus, Tacitus, and Suetonius has often been cited and discussed, recently by Lagrange, *Le messianisme chez les Juifs* (Paris, 1909), 1–27.

337

Its strength and vitality are attested by the later history of the Jews. Although the rabbis learned not to try to set up the kingdom by force their expectation of a deliverer has never abated. This expectation passed over to the church, not only as something fulfilled in Christ, but as something yet to have its consummation in his second advent. It helped to convince Jews and Christians that Mohammed was the crown and seal of the line of prophets. It persists in Islam in the dream of a Mahdi, and the enthusiasm with which almost every century welcomes a pretender to that title shows the tenacity of the idea.

The vitality of the messianic hope has made messianic prophecy an important subject of study among Jews and among Christians. The Talmud affirms that the prophets spoke only of the days of the Messiah,[2] and Christian scholars have assumed this to be self-evident and have built their systems of interpretation upon it. The early disciples of Jesus naturally found the main importance of the Old Testament in its adumbrations of their Savior. The allegorical method of interpretation enabled them to find these adumbrations in many places where a more sober exegesis cannot follow. How firmly rooted the tradition became may be seen in any Roman Catholic treatise of the present day[3] or in the more conservative Protestant discussions. The most elaborate presentation of the material from this point of view is still that of Schöttgen,[4] who confutes the Jews by showing how their rabbis have in all points affirmed the Protestant orthodoxy of the eighteenth century. More recent scholars have freely drawn upon Schöttgen, and the traditional theory was vigorously reasserted by Hengstenberg, whose elaborate *Christology of the Old Testament* avows that "the beginnings of messianic prophecy go back to the earliest times; that in every period the prediction breaks out

[2] Sanhedrin, 99a. In connection with this, mention is made of a certain Rabbi Hillel who held that Israel had its Messiah in the days of Hezekiah—an attempt to find a historical interpretation for Isaiah's Immanuel. But the theory is mentioned only to be rejected.

[3] For example, Hetzenauer, *Theologia Biblica*, I, 574–611 (1908), or Lémann, *Histoire complète de l'idée messianique chez le peuple d'Israel* (1909).

[4] Christiani Schoettgenii *Horae Hebraicae et Talmudicae in Theologiam Judaeorum de Messia impensae*, Tomus II, 1742. The substance of this second volume of Schöttgen's great work was published by himself in German in 1748.

afresh; that the prophetic writings present it not sporadically and occasionally only, but that it forms the soul and center of all their declarations."[5]

The older rationalism had already entered a protest against the exegetical methods of the scholastic theologians. Herder pointed out the unnaturalness of making isolated verses predictive of the Messiah, without regard to the context in which they are found.[6] One of the earliest treatises to bear the title "Biblical Theology" says: "We make a mistake when we prove too much, make everything predictive of the Messiah, and claim to understand all that the prophets have said, when in fact we do not possess the discourses of the prophets in their original order."[7] What the author means he makes clear when he further says that it is an unprofitable employment to force unwilling prophecies to describe Jesus' vestment, his place of birth, or his triumphal entrance into Jerusalem. Much better is it to show that the hand of Providence is convincingly manifest in the whole Old Testament economy preparing for the advent of Jesus. Radical thinkers, however, were not willing to concede even this much, and at least one of them went so far as to deny that there was a well-defined messianic idea in Judaism at the advent of Jesus. So extreme a statement was easily shown to be false.[8]

The mediating theologians of the last century saw that many of the traditional positions must be given up, but they seem not to have been able to take a really historical view of the problem. Too often they expelled the old allegory only to admit it again under the name of a type.[9] Our own time is better able to appreciate the problem because our critical results are more assured, because we distinguish more sharply between religion and dogma, and because our knowledge of the ancient East is more complete. It falls to us to distinguish clearly the various elements which tradition heaped up, labeling the whole as messianic. Without hesitation we lay aside as irrelevant

[5] *Christologie des alten Testamentes*[2], III, 2, p. 1.

[6] See the eighteenth of his *Briefe das Studium der Theologie betreffend*.

[7] Ammon, *Biblische Theologie*[2], II (1801), 22, 25.

[8] The statement of Bruno Bauer is known to me only by Zeller's refutation in his *Theologische Jahrbücher* for 1843.

[9] The best representative of this school is perhaps Riehm whose essay on "Messianic Prophecy" was first published in the *Studien und Kritiken* in 1865 and 1869.

77

a considerable number of texts which have been classed as messianic, such as the *Protevangelium,* and the Blessing of Noah.

Further, in order to get a clear view of the messianic hope in Israel we must leave out of view all that Christian theology has affirmed about a suffering Messiah. Whether the doctrine of vicarious atonement was held by Old Testament writers is an inquiry of the greatest importance. But it must not be confused with the inquiry into the messianic hope. There is no evidence that the Jews ever conceived of a suffering Messiah until after Bar Kochba had failed in his attempt to set up the kingdom. Even then the conception was so foreign to tradition that two Messiahs were postulated —the Messiah ben Joseph is to fall in the war against Gog, and thus prepare the way for Messiah ben David. But this Messiah ben Joseph is not the atoning Savior of Christian belief, although it is possible that Christian insistence on the messianic interpretation of Isa., chap. 53, may have turned attention to the need of such a prophetic personality.[10] In any case he does not belong in a discussion of the messianic hope in Israel. It need hardly be added that the phrase "birth pangs of the Messiah" found in Jewish authors has nothing to do with the sufferings of the Messiah, but refers only to the woes which precede his advent.

The expectation of the Jews at the beginning of our era is most definitely set forth in the passage which follows, and which must have been known to Josephus for he was a member of the Pharisaic school:

"Behold, O Lord, and raise up to them their king, the son of David, in the time which thou, O God, knowest; that he may reign over Israel thy servant; and gird him with strength that he may break in pieces the unjust rulers; may purge Jerusalem from the heathen which trample her down to destroy her; in wisdom and righteousness may he thrust out sinners from the inheritance, crush the proud spirit of the sinners as potter's vessels; and with a rod of iron shall he break all their substance. He shall destroy the ungodly nations with the word of his mouth so that at his rebuke the nations shall flee before him, and he shall convict the sinners in the thought of their own hearts. And he shall gather together a holy

---

[10] The most recent discussion of rabbinical theories is given by Klausner, *Die messianischen Vorstellungen des Jüdischen Volkes im Zeitalter der Tannaiten* (1904). The work of Lagrange already cited covers a wider range. The Kabbalistic theories of atonement on which Schöttgen laid so much stress, as confirming Christian doctrine, are now known to be of mediaeval origin, and they show dependence on Christian speculation.

people whom he shall lead in righteousness, and shall judge the tribes of the people that has been sanctified by the Lord his God. And he shall not suffer iniquity to dwell in the midst of them; and none that knoweth wickedness shall abide with them. For he shall take knowledge of them that they are all sons of their God, and shall apportion them in the land according to their tribes; and the stranger and the sojourner shall dwell with them no more. He shall judge the nations and the peoples with the wisdom of his righteousness; and he shall hold the nations under his yoke to serve him. And he shall glorify the Lord in a place to be seen of the whole earth; and he shall purge Jerusalem and make it sacred even as it was at the beginning; so that the nations shall come from the ends of the earth to see her glory, bringing as gifts her sons which had fainted, and they shall see the glory with which God has glorified her. And he as righteous king, taught by God, shall be over them, and there shall be no unrighteousness among them in his days, because they are all holy and the Messiah of the Lord is their king."[11]

As we read these words and the rest of the psalm of which they are a part, we realize the vitality of the hope which sustained the Jews under so many trials, and which was ready to respond to the proclamation of the Baptist. Certainly there is here more than the interpretation of some ambiguous oracle. But when we try to follow this hope backward to discover its genesis and growth we find that in its definite form, as the expectation of a king of David's line, it was by no means a constant factor in Israel's religion. To this extent the treatment of messianic prophecy by the theologians has been misleading. In the canonical books of the Old Testament the name Messiah is nowhere applied to the expected deliverer unless in one or two of the Psalms. The hope of the people was fixed rather on the kingdom of God than on the Son of David. And under this broad term—the kingdom of God—were included various and heterogeneous details. One writer will be content with the return of the scattered sons of Israel to Palestine; another sets his heart on the purification of the land from gentile defilements; a third pictures the temple rebuilt with more than its pristine splendor. The catalogue would include the divine protection of Jerusalem from invasion, a supernatural chastisement of invading armies, the subjugation of the nations under Israel, the constant performance of the Levitical ritual without flaw, the physical reconstruction of the land so that the temple mount shall dominate the whole region, the fruitfulness of the land heightened to the marvelous, and the visible presence of

[11] Psalms of Solomon 17:23–36.

God himself in his sanctuary. The restoration of the line of David is, in comparison with some of these, rather an inconspicuous feature of the program. Very rarely is a single member of the dynasty singled out and clothed with something of superhuman brightness. To be really fruitful our study of the subject must not attempt to combine all the features into a single messianic picture, but must try to discover which one was prominent in any particular period of Israel's history.

The great prophets of the eighth century found the hope of a better future already cherished by the people at large. The remarkable thing is that they set themselves against it as a delusion. Its existence is easily accounted for. Tradition delighted to tell of the warlike deeds of Yahweh, Israel's leader in the conquest of the land. The storm which caused the rout of Sisera was Yahweh's charge at the head of the hosts of heaven. Joshua's great victory at Beth Horon was due to the direct intervention of the God to whom he prayed. When Jonathan made his single-handed attack on the Philistines an earthquake spread terror in the enemies' camp. Yahweh had the extraordinary forces of nature at his command and there will come a time when he will use them effectively for the vindication of his people in some decisive action. Such was the popular expectation of the day of Yahweh.[12]

The opposition of the great prophets to this expectation was not motived by any doubt of the power of Yahweh. In faith they were at one with their contemporaries. Where they differed was in the conception of God's ethical requirements, resulting in a vivid sense of sin. In the people's hope they found the great obstacle to their preaching—to encourage the hope of prosperity would have been to cut the nerve of their own message. They held that Yahweh's resources of storm and earthquake would be drawn upon not for the deliverance but for the punishment of Israel. Amos makes the day of Yahweh the reverse of what the people were looking for—a day of darkness rather than light. Isaiah makes the day a day of visitation on all that is proud and lifted up: "And the loftiness of man shall be bowed down, and the haughtiness of man shall be humbled and Yahweh alone shall be exalted in that day."[13] There is no evidence

---

[12] See the study entitled "The Day of Yahweh," by J. M. P. Smith, *American Journal of Theology*, V, 505–33.

[13] Isa. 2:12–22, cf. Amos 5:18–20.

that in the prophet's thought the exaltation of Yahweh required the preservation of Israel. Quite the contrary; the exaltation of Yahweh will be complete in that his justice is visited first on the nation most near to him: "Yahweh of Hosts is exalted by justice, and God the Holy One is seen to be holy by righteousness." And what this means is made clear: "I will tell you what I will do to my vineyard; I will take away the hedge thereof and it shall be eaten up; I will break down the wall thereof and it shall be trodden down; and I will lay it waste, it shall not be pruned nor hoed; but there shall come up briars and thorns; I will even command the clouds that they rain no rain upon it."[14] It is difficult to see what would be left of a vineyard after such treatment. Many parallels might be cited to show, what this passage shows plainly enough, that these prophets refused to entertain the thought of future deliverance.

Those prophets who voiced the popular optimism were branded as false prophets. Jeremiah gives us explicit testimony as to the message of a true prophet: "The prophets which were before me and before thee of old prophesied against many countries and against great kingdoms of war and of evil and of pestilence; the prophet who prophesies of prosperity, when the word of that prophet comes to pass then shall it be known that Yahweh has sent him."[15] Micah was in full accord with this declaration and the words in which he announced the destruction of Jerusalem and the desolation of the temple hill were long remembered. In the mind of all these preachers, fidelity to the ethical character of Yahweh involved as a logical necessity determined opposition to the optimism of the people at large.

There was then no messianic hope among these earlier prophets, and the doubts expressed by many critics as to the date of so-called messianic passages now imbedded in their books are well founded. We should be wrong in requiring of these men a cast-iron consistency; they were men like ourselves and keenly alive to the signs of the times. Jeremiah reveals to us the struggle between the yearnings of the patriot and the dictates of conscience. Hope may sometimes have kindled in them when the people showed a better mind. The very faith which prompted to a dark view of Israel's future suggested that even-

---

[14] Isa. 5:5 f.; cf. vs. 16. [15] Jer. 28:8 f.

handed justice would at some time call the Assyrian to account, and
thus give Israel some relief. The perception that a few in Israel
remained faithful among the many faithless led Isaiah to reflect on
the remnant that would escape the impending catastrophe. He had
also a band of disciples to whom he committed his instruction[16] in
the confidence that the future had something in store for them. He
called his son Shearjashub to intimate his faith that a remnant would
repent.

But a moment's reflection shows how far short this falls of what
we call the messianic hope. That a mere remnant will repent only
throws into prominence the mass which refuses to repent, and which
must perish; that a small circle of right-minded men will care for
the prophetic word and preserve it to future generations does not
imply that either the nation or the kingship will survive. The most
explicit declaration which we can with some confidence ascribe to
Isaiah is this: "I will turn my hand upon thee and thoroughly purge
away thy dross, and take away thy baser metal; and I will restore
thy judges as at the first and thy counsellors as in the beginning;
afterwards thou shalt be called City of righteousness, Faithful Town."
Some maintain that such an expression implies the continuance of
the kingship, but this is far from obvious. The traditions of Israel
knew of a time when there was no king. The tone in which Hosea
alludes to kings and princes shows that he had no tenderness for the
monarchy. Nahum, Zephaniah, and Jeremiah have no care for any
political institution. Deuteronomy allows the people to choose a king
but evidently does it as a concession to human weakness. These
facts speak plainly enough; the earlier prophets had no clear and
consistent hope of a messianic kingdom even in the broad sense of the
term. If the people cherished the idea that Yahweh had bound
himself by a covenant to preserve and strengthen Israel the prophets
were quick to show that a covenant broken by one party ceases to be
binding on the other.

The predictions of disaster were abundantly fulfilled in the fall
of Jerusalem, and with that event prophets of the old school lost their
vocation. It is to the eternal credit of Ezekiel that he understood
the emergency and rose to it. Having begun his career as a prophet

[16] Isa. 8:16–18.

of calamity he changed his tone to meet new conditions when the catastrophe actually fell. We are at first sight tempted to think that the hope of a restoration was simply the old confidence in the day of Yahweh. But it is a question whether that hope was strong enough to survive the events of 586. As long as Jerusalem stood the exiles cherished the old hope, as we know from Jeremiah's denunciations. But with the fall of the city the hope disappeared. The people said: "Yahweh has forsaken the land." They believed themselves to be suffering the penalty for the long series of sins committed by their ancestors: "The fathers have eaten sour grapes and the children's teeth are set on edge." They saw nothing to hope for: "Our transgressions and our sins weigh us down; how then can we live? . . . . Our bones are dried up and our hope is lost; we are clean cut off." To meet such a state of mind the prophet needed more than the discredited hope of a day of Yahweh. To promise that disheartened band of exiles a new Gideon would have been grotesque even to their apprehension.

We have every reason to suppose therefore that Ezekiel's program of restoration was the product of his own vital religious faith confronting the facts of the exile. He believed with the others that Yahweh had forsaken his land, but he could not believe that he would permanently remain away from it. Living among the heathen the prophet was compelled to realize, as his predecessors had not realized, that Yahweh's name suffered from the scoffs of his enemies. They said: "These are the people of Yahweh yet they had to go out of his land." The honor of Israel's God suffered under these aspersions and must be vindicated: "Not for your sake do I act, O house of Israel, but for my sacred name which you have profaned among the nations whither you have gone. And I will sanctify my great name which has been profaned."[17] The nations which supposed Yahweh too weak to protect his own must be convinced by some signal example of his power. And this means much more than the old "day of Yahweh." A victory over the gentiles would not guarantee the sanctity of the Name which Ezekiel has at heart; that must be secured by a radical overturning in the physical world and an equally radical renewal in the hearts of men.

[17] Ezek. 36:20–23 and elsewhere.

The reason why Ezekiel could not conceive Yahweh to be permanently a voluntary exile from Palestine must be sought in the priestly habit of his mind. To the ritualist a sanctuary has a *character indelebilis*. Yahweh having once chosen his dwelling at Jerusalem that place became forever sacred. To think of it as permanently given over to pollution would be a constant pain to the devout soul. Moreover, to Ezekiel there was special fitness in Yahweh's choice of Palestine. It was in his geography the central point of the whole earth, from which Yahweh could best supervise his universe: "This is Jerusalem; I have set her in the midst of the nations and the countries are round about her."[18] Even the temporary absence of Yahweh could not deprive his land of its sacredness. The sacredness had been polluted by Israel and Judah; hence the judgment that had been meted out to them. But to suppose that the choice of God can be nullified by the action of man is impossible.

It is probable that Ezekiel was influenced by the primitive conception of the covenant between Yahweh and his people. According to the earliest narrative Yahweh agreed to go into the land with the people, on condition that they make the land a fit place of residence for him. But this was precisely what they had not done; they had eaten with the blood, had worshiped other gods, had brought uncircumcised foreigners into the temple, had buried the corpses of their kings under the walls of his house. If these things are avoided in the future there is no reason why Yahweh may not again dwell in the land. And to guard against these things is the object of Ezekiel's regulations. What he seeks is not a kingdom of God but a sanctuary properly served by a priesthood and guarded against the intrusion of anything profane. Israel's vocation is to be the temple-keeper of Yahweh. A prince is set over them and he is to continue the line of David, but he is only incidental to the priestly function of the nation—he is sort of temple steward to provide decent material for the sacrifice. Some police duties are also assigned to him, but he is really an insignificant figure in the new commonwealth.[19]

[18] 5:5. The navel of the earth is still pointed out in the Church of the Holy Sepulchre.

[19] It cannot be said that Ezekiel had any enthusiasm for the line of David, and it has even been suggested that the allusions to David (34:23 f. and 37:25) are later interpolations. But this is a precarious supposition.

Almost if not quite all the details of Ezekiel's program are intelligible from the premises with which he starts out. The vindication of Yahweh's name requires some exemplary judgment on the heathen. This necessity is met by the vision of Gog. The purification of the land requires the expulsion of the Edomites. The preservation of the temple's sanctity must be guarded by its change of location and by the settling of the priests and Levites about it. We cannot now discuss these matters; the thing of importance is that the firm faith of the prophet inspired his fellow-exiles and they began to cherish his hope. In the fragments of their literature which had survived the catastrophe they found it recorded that their God was gracious and forgiving. Ezekiel himself had assured them that he had no pleasure in the death of the wicked. The first activity of the exiles, we may suppose, was to scrutinize the records of the past to find food for hope. The promises made to the patriarchs were read as though they did not refer only to the first conquest of Canaan. The oracle ascribed to Balaam mentioned a star out of Jacob and a scepter out of Israel which should smite all the corners of Moab. It might well be that this word of God was yet to be fulfilled. Isaiah had predicted punishment for the proud heart of the king of Assyria. The equal pride of Babylon must in like manner call down the divine vengeance.

With these thoughts in mind we can see the exiles scanning the political horizon for some sign of the expected deliverance. At the appearance of Cyrus before Babylon a poet among them uttered the joyful cry which now appears among the discourses of Isaiah.[20] The author sees the day of Yahweh approaching. Israel's God has summoned the Medes to perform his purpose upon Babylon. The doomed city is to meet the fate of Sodom and Gomorrha. Instead of being populous with men it will be the haunt of the desert demons and of savage beasts. The restoration of Israel will follow: "They shall take them captive whose captives they were, and shall rule over their oppressors." The leading thought is not that of Ezekiel but is purely political, and the taunt song in which the restored Zion exults over the humiliation of her enemy savors much more of human passion than of religious enthusiasm. The old hope of a day of Yahweh

[20] Isa., chaps. 13 and 14:1–22.

seems to have asserted itself. The long denunciation of Babylon which is now appended to the book of Jeremiah, breathes the same spirit.[21]

Religiously this national and particularistic hope is of small value. As a welcome contrast we turn to the elevated and spiritual poems which now form the second half of the book of Isaiah. This writer takes Ezekiel's thought of Yahweh's return to dwell among his people but frees it from its ritual limitations. Israel's God will reveal himself as the true God by himself leading his people back home. They will go forth in joy; the mountains will break forth before them into singing; the nations will see the glory thus revealed; Jerusalem will be rebuilt in splendor, her foundations of precious stones; the sanctity of the city will be inviolable, for no uncircumcised or unclean person will enter there. This might be construed as a more poetical presentation of Ezekiel's vision. But we read further that Israel will be a priestly nation for all the world, a light for the gentiles, and a bringer of salvation to all the earth. The picture becomes transcendental when it shows us a new heavens and a new earth; that the city will need no light from sun or moon; that Yahweh will be her everlasting light and her God her splendor.

Along with Deutero-Isaiah we may consider the kindred passages which speak of the return of paradise, and of all nations coming to the house of Yahweh to be taught of his ways.[22] In one we read of Yahweh's vengeance upon Edom and the accompanying wrath upon all nature. The theophany is accompanied as in the old days by convulsions in heaven and earth. There follows a transformation of the desert so that the ransomed of Yahweh may return and come to Zion with everlasting joy upon their heads.

The sketch shows, if it shows anything, that the originators of the messianic hope pay scarcely any attention to a messianic king. Ezekiel accepts a prince as a necessary evil; Deutero-Isaiah ignores him altogether.[23] But the hope of a restoration once having been formulated the thoughts of the exiles naturally turned to the monarch. If in the ideals of early Hebrew writers the tribal organization was thought to be the best, contact with the great oriental states showed

[21] Chaps. 50 and 51.

[22] Isa., chaps. 34, 35; Isa. 2:2-4 (Mic. 4:1-4).

[23] The only reference to David in Deutero-Isaiah is a purely historical one—55:3.

how impracticable was any other political system than the kingship. In an autocracy the welfare of the people depends in large measure on the character and ability of the monarch. In the fine phrase of Hammurabi, the king is commissioned by the gods "to let justice prevail in the land, to destroy the wicked and the evil, to prevent the strong from oppressing the weak." Some at least of the kings of Judah had interpreted their vocation in this way. David was the national hero, and his dynasty was the object of loyal devotion. The long captivity of Jehoiachin conferred upon him the glory of martyrdom, and the tragic fate of Zedekiah gave him a special place in the hearts of his countrymen. It cannot surprise us then that the hope of a return brought with it the idea of the restoration of the dynasty. The imprudent action of Haggai and Zechariah in hailing Zerubbabel as the expected one shows that the expectation was already formulated.

How the expectation had become current is evident from several passages now imbedded in the prophetical books. We have already noticed that the exiles turned to the remains of their literature for consolation, if haply they might find some word of hope among the messages of the prophets. The more obscure of the early oracles would perhaps receive the most attention. The venerable poem put into the mouth of the dying Jacob assured the scepter to Judah and gave him right to the obedience of the nations.[24] The Jew in exile could hardly rest in the thought that this inspired prediction had exhausted its meaning in the brief triumph of David over Edom and Moab. It now received a messianic interpretation.

Among the prophecies of Isaiah was one about the child Immanuel which gave opportunity for study. The original purpose of the prophet was no more than to assure Ahaz of speedy relief from his foes. The historical exigency was a matter of no moment to the later reader, but the mysterious child continued to occupy his thoughts. The meaning of the name was in itself a comfort to the believer.

Knowing ancient literary methods as we do we are not surprised to find this Immanuel prophecy overlaid by accretions of late date which more or less distinctly show that it had received a messianic

---

[24] Gen. 49:10. It is not necessary to enter into a discussion of the obscure reference to Shiloh. The more than forty dissertations known to Schöttgen on this passage have been followed by numerous later studies without discovering a satisfactory interpretation.

interpretation. The most distinct is now the climax of the section.[25] In the belief that the day of redemption has already dawned the writer hails the child who is born with the lofty name—Wonder-counsellor, Hero-God, Father-of-eternity, Prince-of-peace. He adds that there shall be no end of his welfare on the throne of David. Here for the first time we have a full-fledged messianic prediction; a member of the house of David is about to re-establish the royal power and to rule with justice and righteousness. As Yahweh's representative he may claim the loftiest titles, which moreover are quite in accord with oriental court usage. What was expected of him is made clear by the prediction of a shoot from the stock of Jesse: "With righteousness shall he judge the poor, and decide with equity for the meek of the land."[26] Many scholars accept this passage as a genuine word of Isaiah the son of Amoz. But it is immediately followed by an evidently post-exilic passage, its description of the expected paradise is evidently of the tenor of Deutero-Isaiah, and the phrase "stock of Jesse" seems impossible in the mouth of the older Isaiah. All these indications date it in the later rather than the earlier period.

We may bring into connection with these two passages some other insertions in the prophetical books. Hosea's assurance that the children of Israel will repent and seek David their king[27] must be one such insertion. At the end of the book of Amos we read a promise that the ruined tent of David shall be again erected, and that the exiles shall be brought back to their land.[28] The book of Jeremiah repeats the prediction of a righteous branch for David[29] in two places whose late date must be obvious to every reader. That the hope of the author fixed itself on the dynasty must be evident from the direct assertion that David shall never want a man to sit upon the throne of the house of Israel. Another writer declares that a king shall rule in righteousness and princes shall rule in justice, making it evident that he looked for a just administration rather than a supernaturally endowed individual who should hold the throne for an indefinite period.

Our review shows us that in the exilic and post-exilic period there was a definite expectation of the restored Jewish commonwealth of

[25] Isa. 9:1–6 (vss. 2–7 in the English).

[26] Isa. 11:1–10.   [27] Hos. 3:5.   [28] Amos 9:11–15.   [29] Jer. 23:5–8; 33:14–18.

which the dynasty of David should have the rule. This expectation received new life and a different form in the Maccabean persecution. Testimony is given by the Book of Daniel. Here we find an anxious inquiry for the date at which the kingdom of God will come. The seventy weeks are derived from the seventy years of Jeremiah which had long passed without having brought the promised redemption. The broader outlook of the author on the world's history and his deep conviction of the degeneracy of his times cause him to seek something more than the traditional restoration of Israel to its own land. In his view the purpose of God must include the destruction of the gentile empires and the universality of the rule of Israel: "The kingdom and the greatness of the kingdom shall be given to the people of the saints of the Most High."[30] The stone which is cut out of the mountain grows until it fills the whole earth. After the great beast is destroyed one like a man is brought near the Ancient of Days: "And there was given him dominion and glory and a kingdom, that all the peoples, nations, and languages should serve him." It should be clear that this figure *like a man* is a personification of Israel. Such a personification is in strict accord with the rest of the vision, and in his own explanation of the vision the writer makes his meaning clear.

The largeness of his scheme, but not the prominence of a personal Messiah, is the advance made by this writer. His idea of a dramatic judgment of the nations is part of his larger scheme, and this impressed other thinkers of about the same period. In a passage now incorporated in the Book of Isaiah we learn that the judgment reaches the unfaithful or disobedient angels. Another pictures the Name of Yahweh coming from afar burning with anger, to wreak his vengeance on the heathen, for whom a fire is prepared. A supplement to the same book naïvely sets forth the gratification of the saints when they look upon the bodies of transgressors burned in the unquenchable fire and gnawed by the undying worm.[31] This implies that the judgment is held at Jerusalem, which in fact is asserted by Deutero-Zechariah, and apparently by Joel.[32] The only reference to a messianic king in all this apocalyptic literature is Zechariah's announcement of a king coming in lowly guise as Prince of Peace.[33]

[30] Dan. 7:27; cf. 2:44; 12:1-3.
[31] Isa. 66:24; cf. 24:21 and 30:27-33.
[32] Zech. 14:12-15; Joel 3:12-16.
[33] Zech. 9:9 f.

When we turn to the Book of Psalms we find a vivid hope of the kingdom of God, but little about a Messiah. The kingdom is conceived as already present, in so far as Yahweh is rightful king and judge of all the earth. His throne is in the heavens, and his kingdom rules over all; from that throne he looks down upon the children of men; he gives food to the hungry, frees the prisoners, opens the eyes of the blind, executes justice for the oppressed, and turns the way of the wicked upside down. The hard facts of life seem indeed to contradict the theory, but the believer comforts himself with the thought that in a little while the judge will ascend the throne and gather the nations around him, there to decide their fate and vindicate his people. The impassioned prayer that Yahweh will intervene actively with shield and spear, will bow the heavens and come down, will renew his mighty deeds of old, show the inward struggle of those who were holding onto their faith amidst the taunts of an unbelieving world.[34] In very few cases is the Messiah mentioned, and in some at least of these it is evident that the term is applied to the nation rather than to an individual. This is not strange when we think of the meaning of the word—the Anointed. Who could so truly lay claim to the title as the faithful people whom Yahweh had chosen for himself, and had appointed to do his work in the world? It is Israel therefore who sits upon the sacred hill of Zion, and boasts of the divine decree. The parallelism in such a verse as this—"Yahweh is strength to his people, and a fortress of salvation to his anointed"— is sufficient to show the author's thought.

Still the ideal king, whom we have already met as a member of the Davidic house, is occasionally mentioned. The well-known seventy-second psalm is a prayer for his success as warrior and ruler, culminating in the wish that his name may endure forever. In other psalms Yahweh is reminded that his covenant with David promised him an enduring throne and is then asked where is the fulfilment.[35] The restoration of the dynasty is the utmost which the writers expect or desire. The most distinctly individualistic of all the so-called messianic psalms gives the monarch priestly as well as kingly power, but it is doubtful whether the author had the Messiah in mind at all.

[34] The passages are so familiar that it is needless to give references.
[35] Pss. 89 and 132.

The Old Testament Apocrypha show the messianic expectation in the form which we find in the Book of Psalms. Yahweh is king; he will reign in Jerusalem; the righteous will dwell there and the nations will bring gifts. Tobit expects the streets to be paved with sapphire; Baruch looks for a day of judgment; Ben Sira hopes for a return of the exiles, the rule of the house of David, and an everlasting covenant. The Books of Maccabees allude to the throne of David, and the raising-up of a prophet to guide Israel. According to Wisdom the righteous are to judge the heathen, and the God of Israel will be king.[36] In the circle in which these books originated the messianic hope cannot have been very ardently cherished.

Among the Pseudepigrapha however we find some passages of special interest. Among them we should put first the one from the Psalms of Solomon already quoted. In the disorders from which Palestine suffered after the death of Pompey, when the weakness of the Hasmoneans became evident, the thoughts of the pious turned with ardent longing to the promise of a Davidic king. This psalm describes the Maccabean princes as usurpers who laid waste the throne of David and who were punished for their presumption. Then follows the prayer for the expected son of David, who will restore the purity of Jerusalem and so enable the holy nation to accomplish its mission as God's own people and the guardian of his worship. This is the logical culmination of the messianic hope in the proper sense of that term. It looks for a king possessed of the divine grace, powerful enough to secure the independence of his nation, and wise enough to rule with justice. He is not more than David himself had been, according to tradition, and if the author reflected at all upon the length of life allotted to him he doubtless thought of him as reaching a good old age and then being gathered to his fathers, leaving a son to succeed him and carry on his reign of peace and righteousness. In other words this character has nothing transcendental about it.

Very different is the picture presented by some apocalyptic writings of this period.[37] Chief of these is the collection which passes under

---

[36] Tobit 13:10 and vss. 16–18; Baruch 2:34 f. and 4:36; Ecclus. 47:11; I Macc. 2:57; 4:46; 14:41; II Macc. 2:17 f.; Wisdom 3:8.

[37] It is unnecessary to cite those passages of the Sibylline books which allude to the messianic time. They really add nothing to our knowledge.

the name of Enoch. That this book is made up from several sources is generally recognized and is evident from the various views of the Messiah which it presents. At the culmination of the animal vision, which is dated with some confidence in the latter part of the second century B.C., the Messiah appears as a white bull.[38] Whether an individual is intended or whether the dynasty is presented in this form, is open to doubt. The figure is not important to the author's scheme, for it takes no part in the judgment, or in the conquest of the heathen. A great advance on this view is marked however by a section which we may call the messianic book of Enoch and which is dated about the middle of the first pre-Christian century.[39] In his vision Enoch sees the Elect One of righteousness and faith. "And I saw his dwelling place under the wings of the Lord of Spirits and all the elect before him are resplendent as lights of fire." This passage alone would not prove that the Messiah is pre-existent, for Enoch is seeing what is to come to pass at the end of days. But in the second similitude we learn that the name of the Son of Man was named before the Lord of Spirits *before the stars of heaven were made*, and that he has been chosen and hidden before him before the creation of the world and forever more. This is more than an ideal pre-existence. The Son of Man has now become a heavenly being, and it is he who will judge the world: "He will raise the mighty from their thrones and will grind to powder the teeth of the sinners."[40]

That the Messiah is the Son of God is intimated in a single passage of Enoch, and is more fully developed in IV Ezra, where we read: "For my Son the Messiah will be revealed and all those who are with him, and will rejoice those who remain four hundred years. Afterwards my Son the Messiah will die, and all who have human breath."[41] After this comes the universal resurrection.

In a later chapter of this book we read that the Messiah who rebukes the Roman Empire has been kept by the Most High for the end of days, and that then he will bring the nations before his judgment seat and after rebuking will destroy them; but he will redeem

---

[38] Enoch 90:37 f. [39] Chaps. 37–71.

[40] Chaps. 46 and 48; cf. 51:3 and 61:8. The identification of Enoch himself with the Son of Man in 71:14 is a vagary not yet satisfactorily explained.

[41] IV Ezra 7:28 f.; cf. Enoch 105:2.

the remnant of the Jews[42] and give them joy until the end, the Day of Judgment. In still another passage it is said that the man who ascends from the sea is the one whom the Most High has kept for a long time by whom he will redeem the creation, and he is again called My Son.[43]

We have now traced the messianic hope in Israel from its beginning down to its completion in the first century of our era. The question inevitably suggests itself whether this hope is something which we may claim as distinctively Jewish, or whether it is only a part of the oriental view of the universe, originating in Babylon and borrowed by the Hebrews. To answer this question correctly it is necessary to do more than to point out some details in which Babylonian and Hebrew thought resemble each other. Our endeavor ought first to approach the subject from the point of view of Hebrew religion and see whether the messianic hope is intelligible as part of the system which Jewish thinkers were providentially called to work out for the world. Putting the question in this way, we need not hesitate to say that the messianic hope is a necessary part of the Jewish religion.

It is not of course possible to deny that Israel shared the views of its neighbors on many points where we moderns have very different ideas. What is sometimes called the oriental view of the universe was only the view common to all mankind until the time when modern science compelled men to a new cosmology. All mankind until recently held that the earth was the center of the whole universe; that the gods were principally concerned with what goes on here; that there was a certain correspondence between the movements of the stars and the fate of nations and individuals. The idea of predictive prophecy was not confined to the Hebrews. The whole ancient world was full of presages and oracles; the foretelling of events had a larger place in the history of Greek cities than in that of Israel. In Egypt there were recorded forecasts of national success or disaster—one such was given by the mouth of an inspired lamb. In Assyria and Babylonia divination was reduced to a science.[44]

[42] IV Ezra 12:32–34. The words of the Syriac, "Who shall arise out of the seed of David," are not in the Latin.

[43] 13:26; cf. vs. 37.

[44] Gressmann, *Altorientalische Texte und Bilder*, I, 205–9; *Keilinschriftliche Bibliothek*, VI, 69.

The Sibylline books are evidence that at the beginning of our era intelligent people were ready to give credence to such oracles all over the Roman world. Josephus claims prophetic gifts for himself, something which strikes us as ludicrous, but there is no reason to suppose that he does not take himself quite seriously.

This general scheme of things was held by the Hebrews in common with their neighbors. It was not a question of one borrowing from the other. And the same is true of the belief that God is most clearly revealed in the extraordinary events of nature. Hebrew religious faith saw in Yahweh the Savior of his people, who came to their help in the storm and the earthquake. So the Babylonian found in Marduk the conqueror of forces hostile to man, and related the myth in which he triumphed over Tiamat. Allusions to Yahweh as smiter of the dragon, of Rahab, and of the crooked serpent,[45] show that similar stories circulated among the Hebrews. But why should we say with a recent author that the "prophetic eschatology uses symbols which are mythological in their nature and not Israelitic"? Why should the religious faith of Israel not be vital enough to picture its God as a warrior victorious over a dragon? A real religious faith must have an active God as its object.

We underrate the vitality of faith when we insist that all its expressions must be literary reminiscences. In the particular case of the messianic hope we may be sure that the men who were looking for salvation from the miseries of the Exile were very little concerned about literary reminiscences. This is eminently true of the two men to whom we owe the messianic hope—Ezekiel and Deutero-Isaiah. Ezekiel we see to be a man saturated with traditional ideas, the last man, one would say, to borrow Babylonian mythological conceptions. Recent scholars are inclined to see in his vision of Gog remains of a myth. But Ezekiel in his youth had known of the Scythian invasion which came to the very border of Judah. In vision he sees over again that terrible enemy threatening to overflow the land, this time to be checked by an act of Yahweh which would vindicate his power and secure the peace of his people for all time. No other source for this and the other visions need be sought than the prophet's firm faith in the power of Yahweh and in his fidelity to his chosen people. And

[45] Isa. 27:1; 51:9; Amos 9:2.

the same is true of Deutero-Isaiah. The theory of an extra-Israelite origin for the hopes of these two great prophets finds no justification in the facts.

The passages inserted in the earlier part of Isaiah's book need some attention. It has recently been urged, for example, that the Immanuel prophecy has the appearance of something "designed to meet an expectation already in the air."[46] By this is meant that the people of Jerusalem were already looking for a deliverer, a hero to be born of a virgin, and that Isaiah encouraged them to believe that he was about to appear. But if this were so, how obscurely the prophet expressed himself! Could not the great orator have said in a few words that this was his meaning? Even if he had said that the expected wonderful child was about to be born, would that have given Ahaz assurance that the impending siege of Jerusalem would come to nought? When we make the prophet a framer of enigmas we deprive him of his merits as a clear expounder of the will of God.

With somewhat more of probability an eschatological tradition of extra-Israelite origin is by some discovered in the ninth chapter of Isaiah.[47] The program of the author is the one already familiar to us: First comes a great overturning, and the people that has walked in darkness sees a great light; the yoke of the oppressor is broken; the garment rolled in blood and the arms of the invader are given to the flames. Then comes the birth of the deliverer, the child of wonderful name, and the kingdom of peace is ushered in. No reason can be assigned for making this a foreign importation except the exalted name given the child. To understand this name we need only remind ourselves that even the common man in Israel did not hesitate to call his child "Brother-of-Yahweh" or "Son-of-Yahweh," and that in the royal family we meet such names as "Strength-of-Yahweh" and "Righteousness-of-Yahweh." Moreover, the king was in all Hebrew tradition the Anointed of Yahweh, his representative, partaking of his sanctity. If now at some great crisis a seer had the confidence that the ideal king was as hand there was nothing extravagant in his use of the words of the text. Extra-Israelite tradition is not needed to account for his language.

[46] Burney, *Journal of Theological Studies* (1909), 582.

[47] Gressmann, *Ursprung der israelitisch-jüdischen Eschatologie*, 279; Oesterley, *Evolution of the Messianic Idea in Israel*, 222.

Descriptions of the good time coming which we now read in the eleventh and the thirty-fifth chapters of Isaiah are sometimes supposed to be borrowed from gentile descriptions of the Golden Age. To understand these chapters we must notice that each forms the climax of a group of prophecies. The editors of the prophetic books evidently planned to conclude each section with an encouraging prediction. Thus Amos, Hosea, Zechariah, and the several sections of Isaiah end each with a messianic prophecy. We have seen reason to believe that these editors wrought subsequently to the great Deutero-Isaiah; in fact they all used Deutero-Isaianic ideas, adding however a more distinct expectation of the messianic king. Now, the features of the two chapters we are considering which seem to be borrowed from pictures of the golden age, are precisely those of Deutero-Isaiah. But these we have decided to be the fruit of a strong religious faith expressed with the glow of a poetic temperament.

Up to this point, therefore, we have reason to believe that the messianic hope is an original production of the Israelite prophets. With the Book of Daniel, to which we now come, the case is somewhat different. At the time of its writing the Jews had long been in contact with Persian and Greek thought, and that they had been influenced by the ideas of the people among whom they lived is shown by evidence in our possession. We are prepared to find traces of such influence even in so thoroughly a Jewish book as Daniel. The author bases his scheme of history on the Number Four—the great image is made up of the four metals: gold, silver, bronze, and iron. We are reminded at once of the sequence of the four ages of the world in Greek writers. The Persian eschatology also knows four ages of the world each of three thousand years. The coincidence is too striking to be accidental. Yet we may say that the author of Daniel uses the scheme in a way to show his originality, for he does not make the whole duration of the world consist of four periods, but only the time from the reign of Nebuchadrezzar to the Maccabean Age.

The Number Four appears again in the vision of the beasts, and the beasts themselves look so like mythological survivals that we suspect gentile influence. Yet it would be easy to make too much of this superficial resemblance. The comparison of a hostile invader to a savage beast is so natural that it had been used long before Daniel.

The earlier prophets had likened the enemy to a lion issuing from his lair, or to the wolves of the desert. One detail in Daniel, however, does not accord with the figure—these beasts come out of the sea, which is not the home of lions or leopards. This we may admit to be a survival from Babylonian mythology, which makes Tiamat, the personified ocean, the mother of all sorts of monsters. The fourth beast of Daniel also looks like a mythological monster, "a beast terrible and powerful, which had great iron teeth; it broke in pieces and stamped the residue with its feet." We are justified in saying that there is here also a possible survival from early myths. But we must remember that the gentile influence was not direct; the myths had passed into folklore and had long ceased to be recognized as what they had been in their origin. In fact it would have horrified the apocalyptic writers to think that they were in any way influenced by heathen ideas.

The Persian religion had a well-developed theory of the last things, including a judgment at the end of the present age, a resurrection of the dead, the coming of a Savior, the creation of a new heaven and a new earth, and the setting-up of the kingdom of the good divinity. This scheme is known to us only through post-Christian documents, and its earlier stages are still under investigation. It is impossible to say therefore what influence it exercised on Jewish thought. In almost every respect the ideas of Daniel are less developed. Daniel knows of no personal Messiah; he expects only a partial resurrection; he ignores entirely the picturesque bridge over which according to the Mazdeans the souls are to go after death. We must conclude that direct Mazdean influence on Daniel is slight.[48]

The phrase "Son of Man" used by Daniel is supposed by some to be a mythological survival. The language of Daniel is "one like a son of man" which, as is well known, means simply "one like a man." As was shown above, this figure is a personification like the animals which appear in the same vision. The author chooses a man to represent the restored nation of Israel in order to show that this kingdom is as superior to the empires of the world as a man is above the beasts. The only thing that needs to be explained is the

[48] This is the opinion of Charles, *Critical History of the Doctrine of a Future Life,* 136. This author recognizes also that the doctrine of a resurrection found in Isa., chap. 26, cannot be derived from a Persian source.

coming on the clouds of heaven. Because of this feature some scholars identify the Son of Man with an angel, perhaps Michael, the guardian angel of Israel,[49] while others think of a pre-existent judge and ruler of the world, originally a god, now an emanation of the godhead.[50] Neither hypothesis is convincing. The author thought of the Israel which was to receive the kingdom as dwelling at a distance from Jerusalem; that the exiles should fly as a dove to their home was a thought familiar to all readers of Deutero-Isaiah; to bring the man out of the sea whence the beasts had ascended would seem to make him no better than the heathen powers. An angelic figure would have come *with* the Ancient of Days, and not have waited until the judgment was past. Giving due weight to all these considerations we see that this Son of Man is explicable as an organic part of the vision and is not a loan from gentile sources.

Finally, the pre-existent Messiah of Enoch and Ezra is explicable as an exegetical development from the Son of Man of Daniel and the Son of Yahweh of the second psalm. That the apocalyptic writers busied themselves with the earlier literature needs no demonstration. The figure of the Son of Man when once interpreted of an individual was sure to attract devout speculation. The ideal pre-existence of many things became about this time a postulate of the scribes. The ideal existence of the mysterious deliverer and ruler easily objectified itself as a real existence under the wings of the divinity. In this case therefore as in the others we are not compelled to assume gentile influences to account for the exalted messianic expectation.

Our conclusion is that the messianic hope in its various forms is a product of Hebrew and Jewish religious faith. This faith rested upon the mercy and fidelity of Israel's God and on his election of a people in whom his glory should be manifested. In the struggle which this faith went through to maintain itself under heathen oppression the hope gradually developed until it reached the transcendental form which it assumes in the latest documents. Here and there, in minor details, it may have been influenced by mythological survivals, but these survivals had already passed into folklore and do not in any case affect the substance of the hope.

[49] Schmidt, *JBL*, XIX, 22-27.

[50] Clemen, *Religionsgeschichtliche Erklärung des Neuen Testamentes*, 117, 122.

The Origin of the Idea of the Messiah

SOLOMON ZEITLIN

*

THERE IS A saying in the Talmud "either the sword or the book." [1] This could be interpreted that one who seeks to combat injustice and is a fighter for ideas and ideals cannot produce great scholarly works. On the other hand a true scholar cannot engage in public affairs, for his place is in an ivory tower. Dr. Abba Hillel Silver has shown that this saying refers only to the average person, not to a person of superior intellect and gifted with original ideas. Such a person combines valor in fighting for his ideas and ideals and those faculties required to produce scholarly works of permanent value.

Doctor Abba Hillel Silver, who is approaching his seventieth birthday, has devoted his life to the service of the Jews. He was the main champion in defending the Jewish rights in *Eretz Israel* (Palestine) before the United Nations. History will record the great indebtedness which the State of Israel owes to him.

While Dr. Silver was engaged in the struggle for the rights of the Jews he, at the same time, produced scholarly works in which he displayed sound learning and showed keen historical insight. He has a masterful style and exhibits great courage in expounding his views.

The first of Dr. Silver's scholarly works was *A History of Messianic Speculation in Israel,* in which he traces the messianic speculations among the Jews from the end of the first century to that of the seventeenth century. This book shows a vast knowledge of the sources and literature of this period as well as the author's acute mind in dealing with this complicated subject. Some of his other books are *Religion in a Changing World, Where Judaism Differed,* and the latest, *Moses and the Original Torah,* in which Moses is presented as a living reality, a challenge which very few scholars have been able to accomplish. All of Dr. Silver's works are of lasting value.

In the volume dedicated in honor of Doctor Abba Hillel Silver's seventieth birthday, it is fitting to have an article on the origin of the

1 Abodah Zarah 17.

idea of a messiah, since the first fruit of Dr. Silver's thought was on
the messianic expectation.

I

The messianic expectation among the Jews was both a blessing and
a curse. The hope for a messiah gave them strength and courage during the centuries of the Middle Ages, dark ages, in their privations
and degradations. They underwent great sufferings but they hoped
that this would not be prolonged. They believed that the Promised
Messiah would come soon, redeem them from their misery, and bring
them back to their homeland, the Land of Israel, where the kingdom
of Israel would be reestablished under the scepter of a scion of the
family of David. Their motto was "to hope and to suffer." The expectation of a Messiah, indeed, made their survival possible. It kept alive the
hope that at a not too distant time the Messiah would come. They
besought God in their prayers to hasten the coming of the promised
Messiah.

On the other hand, the longing and expectation of the Messiah
brought misfortune and suffering to the Jews. Many opportunists and
adventurers, observing the persecution and degradation of the Jews
and being aware of their hopes for a Messiah, took advantage of the
situation by proclaiming themselves either messiahs or prophets of
messiahs. These messianic movements were catastrophic to the Jews.
One of the latest was Sabbatai Zevi's messianic movement in the
seventeenth century. Almost all the Jews of that period succumbed to
it, rich and poor. Even the intelligent classes—bankers, doctors, and
rabbis, believed Sabbatai Zevi to be the true messiah. The propaganda for this movement was led by one Nathan, who proclaimed
himself to be a prophet. He was a demagogue, adventurer, and forger.
He showed great ability, we may say genius, in the organization of
the movement. Sabbatai Zevi's messianic movement was calamitous
to the Jews as were all the others. In fact, the Jews have not yet fully
recovered from the aftereffects of the collapse of the Sabbataian
movement.

True, there were men who honestly believed themselves to be
messiahs. They arrived at this belief because of their ascetic way of
living and through their engrossment in the studies of mysticism and
Kabbala. They fasted and prayed and thus their minds became deranged—they saw visions that God destined them to be messiahs to
redeem His people and lead them to the Promised Land. This type of
false messiah also brought great suffering to the Jews. The messianic
expectation, as stated previously, was both a blessing and a curse. It

was a tower of strength for survival during the dark ages and it also brought great suffering.

II

The word *Mashiah*, messiah, *christos* in Greek, has the connotation of being anointed. We learn from the Bible that Aaron, the first priest; the Tabernacle and the vessels in it were anointed with oil.[2] The anointment signified that they were divine and belonged to Yahweh. The Prophet Samuel anointed Saul, the first king, and in doing so said, "Is it not that Yahweh hath anointed thee to be a *nagid* over His inheritance." [3] Saul thus became divine and thus became *Mashiah* of Yahweh.[4] Later when the Prophet Samuel anointed David to become king, the same nomenclature, *Mashiah* of Yahweh, was given to him.[5] God promised David that the kingship would be an inheritance of his family and would last forever.[6]

The term *Mashiah* was not only applied to the Jewish kings and high priest but also to foreign kings. Cyrus, the king of Persia, was called the *Mashiah* of Yahweh.[7] The word *Mashiah* was used in the Bible as an adjective, not as a noun. The term "messiah" as a noun appears only in the late apocalyptic literature and in the New Testament. On the other hand, during the Second Commonwealth neither the kings nor the priests were anointed with oil. Therefore an explanation is necessary as to how the term *Mashiah*, "messiah," appears later in the Hebrew literature as a person and aroused the idea in the minds of the people that God would send a *Mashiah*.

The early Church Fathers, to prove that Jesus was the true messiah, *Christos*, maintained that there were references to Jesus as the messiah in the Pentateuch and in the other books of the Bible. To combat the views of the Church Fathers the rabbis interpreted the same verses as containing prophecies of the Jewish *Mashiah*. To cite a few examples: The verse in Genesis 49:10 reads, "The scepter shall not depart from Judah, Nor the ruler's staff from between his feet, As long as men come to Shiloh; And unto him shall the opinions of the people be." Origen interpreted this passage as referring to the "Christ of God," Jesus.[8] The Targum, according to Jonathan, interprets it as referring to the Jewish *Mashiah*. The verse in Isaiah 11:1 reads, "And there shall come forth a shoot of the stock of Jesse and

---

2 Exodus 40:9–15.
3 I. Samuel 10:1.
4 *Ibid.*, 26:11.
5 *Ibid.*, 16:13; II Samuel 19:22.
6 *Ibid.*, 7:8–16.

7 Cf. Isaiah 45:1. "Thus said Yahweh to his *mashiah* to Cyrus."
8 *Against Celsus*, B. 1, 53. "For He came for whom these things were reserved, the Christ of God."

a twig shall grow forth out of his roots." Justin Martyr interpreted this verse as a prophecy for the coming of Jesus.[9] The rabbis interpreted it as referring to the coming of the Jewish *Mashiah*. In Chapter 53 of Isaiah the suffering of the servant of Yahweh is described. The Church Fathers interpreted it as referring to the Passion of Jesus. Barnabas, one of the Apostolic Fathers, interpreted this chapter as referring partly to Israel and partly to Jesus.[10] Origen, in his treatise Against Celsus, said that the Jews believed that the prophecies in this chapter referred to the whole people of Israel regarded as one individual. He denied this contention and held that the prophecies and suffering related in this chapter referred to the sufferings and the death of Jesus Christ.[11] The Targum, according to Jonathan, interpreted this chapter as referring to *Mashiah,* the Jewish Messiah.

The Church Fathers as well as the rabbis injected their ideas of the messiah into the Biblical passages. However, as we have previously stated, there is no indication anywhere in the Bible of the coming of a personal messiah, natural or supernatural. The word *Mashiah* appears in the Bible several times. It has the connotation of anointed and refers to the high priest [12] or to the king, of the family of David. In the Book of Psalms the word *Mashiah* is found several times. It appears in Chapter 84:10, "Look upon the face of Thine *Mashiah*." This seems to refer to the anointed high priest. In Chapter 89:39, "But Thou hast cast off and rejected, Thou hast been wroth with Thine *Mashiah*." This seems to refer to the family of David. Similarly in verse 52 the word *Mashiah* refers to the family of David. Again in Chapter 105:15, "Touch not My *Mashiah* and do My prophets no harm." This refers to the anointed priest. The psalmist beseeches the people not to harm the priest and the prophet. It seems that this verse is dislocated and should come at the end of the chapter. In the book of Lamentations 4:20, we read, "The breath of our nostrils, the anointed of the *Mashiah* of Yahweh, was taken in their pits; of whom we said: 'Under his shadow we shall live among the nations.'" The words "*Mashiah* of Yahweh" refer to King Josiah. In the book of Daniel the word *mashiah* occurs twice. In one place the author designates *mashiah* as *nagid*, ruler.[13] This undoubtedly is a reference to the high priest who, during the Second Commonwealth, was the spiritual as well as the secular ruler of the people.[14] In the other place the

9 Cf. *The First Apology*, 32. "A flower has sprung from the root of Jesse this Christ."

10 *The Epistle of Barnabas*, 5. "For the scripture concerning him relates partly to Israel, partly to us, and it speaks thus: 'He was wounded for our iniquities. . . .'"

11 B. 1.55. ". . . My Jewish opponent replied that these predictions bore reference to the whole people. . . . And who is this person save Jesus

author wrote, "And after three score and two weeks shall the *mashiaḥ* be cut off." [15] Here the author refers to the elimination of the priesthood of the Zadokite family. The book of Daniel, as we have it today, was composed after Judah Makkabee purified the Temple.[16] These passages were cited to show that in the Bible the word *mashiaḥ* has the connotation of anointed and refers to the high priests or to the kings of the family of David. Modern theologians, Christian and Jewish, have injected the idea of the expectation of a personal, supernatural messiah into the Biblical passages. All histories of the Second Commonwealth are vitiated with the idea of messianic expectations.

True, the prophets do speak of a millennium—a period of happiness and prosperity when there will be no more wars between nations, and people will live in peace with one another. But this is not an expectation of a personal messiah. We must differentiate between a millennium and a messiah. The Prophet Isaiah, who according to tradition was of the family of David,[17] voiced a longing for a period when a descendant of Jesse, that is, of the family of David, imbued with the spirit of Yahweh, would rule. That day would be the time of the millennium, when "The wolf shall dwell with the lamb, and the leopard shall lie down with the kid; and the calf and the young lion and the fatling together; and a little child shall lead them" (11:6–10). There are messianic expectations in this passage. Isaiah hoped that a time would come when the Jews would prosper and live in peace as before at the time of King Solomon, a descendant of Jesse. Isaiah was a great patriot and nationalist. As a parallel we may cite the hope of a devotee of the Bourbon dynasty that the grandeur of France will be restored as in the time of Louis XIV.

That the Jews during the first part of the Second Commonwealth did not have the expectation of a personal messiah is evident from the literature produced during that period. The word *mashiaḥ* does not occur in the book of Ben Sirah nor does it occur in the other apocryphal literature—Tobit, Judith, The Wisdom of Solomon, I Maccabees. In the latter it is stated that when the high priesthood was given to Simon the Hasmonean, a clause was inserted, "Until a true prophet will arrive in Israel." [18] From this we may deduce that Jews believed prophecy would be restored but there is no indication that they expected a messiah. Even in II Maccabees, wherein physical resurrection [19] and the hope that all Jews would be gathered in Judaea

---

Christ, by whose stripes they who
  believe on Him are healed."
12 Cf. Leviticus 4:3.
13 9:25.
14 Cf. also I Chronicles 9:11.

15 9:26.
16 Cf. I *Maccabees*, ed. Dropsie, p. 32.
17 Talmud Megillah 10.
18 Chap. 14:41.
19 See Chap. 7.

are given prominence, the word *mashiah* does not occur—the author believed this would be accomplished through the intervention of God.

The term "messiah" occurs only in the apocalyptic literature; once in the Testament of the Twelve Patriarchs,[20] twice in the Book of Enoch,[21] and twice in the last two chapters of the Psalms of Solomon.[22] The first two books mentioned as well as the last two chapters of the Psalms of Solomon (17th–18th) were written after the time of Herod. We may even assume that "Lord Messiah" in Chapter 17 is a later Christian interpolation.[23] The word "messiah" also occurs in IV Ezra[24] and the Apocalypsis of Baruch.[25] the messiah is portrayed in this literature as being a scion of David who will rule over Israel and free the Jews from their foreign yoke. The Jews believed that the messiah would be a supernatural being and yet a son of David. In the Book of Enoch the son of David is named "the anointed of God," [26] "the Elect One," [27] "the Son of Man," [28] "the Son of God." [29]

This, then, is our paradox. The idea of a supernatural messiah is mentioned only in the apocalyptic books which were considered "outside books," profane—there had been an edict against reading them [30] —nevertheless the idea of a messiah possessing supernatural power became deeply rooted among the Jews, almost an article of faith. What were the forces which gave rise to the idea of a supernatural messiah? We have pointed out that the term *mashiah* had the connotation of high priest, or King David and his son Solomon, who had been anointed with oil. What were the causes which brought about this persistent idea of a supernatural messiah? Ideas which have a profound influence and are lasting are not created in a vacuum or by the whim of a person, however important he may be.

To comprehend the origin of the idea of a supernatural messiah we must briefly review the political and spiritual conditions which prevailed at the time of the Restoration. At the head of the exiles who returned from Babylonia were two men, who represented influential political factions with diametrical ideological views. One was Joshua, the grandson of Seraiah, the high priest who had been killed by the Babylonians, representing the high priesthood. The other leader was Zerubbabel, the grandson of King Jehoiachin, representing the Davidic royal family. A clash developed between these two factions

---

20 *The Testament of Reuben*, 6:8.
21 48:10; 52:4.
22 17:6; 18:8.
23 Cf. H. E. Ryle and M. R. James, *Psalms of the Pharisees commonly called the Psalms of Solomon*, ad loc.

24 Cf. 5:29; 12:32.
25 29:3; 39:7; 40:1; 70:9. Cf. also S. Zeitlin, "The Apocrypha," *Jewish Quarterly Review*, 1947, pp. 239–248.
26 48:10.
27 49:2; 51:1.

as to how the Judaean community should be organized. The adherents of Joshua maintained that the community should be ruled by the high priest, the vicar of God. In other words that it be established as a theocracy. The followers of Zerubbabel held that the new community should be ruled by a scion of the family of David. The ideology of Joshua triumphed. Zerubbabel disappeared from the political and religious arena. The Judaean community was established as a theocracy.[31]

Although the Judaean community took the form of a theocracy, the idea that a scion of the family of David should rule over Israel was not obliterated from the minds of the people. Many Judaeans still hoped that ultimately the Judaean State would be ruled by a descendant of the family of David. This hope was cherished especially among the lower classes. It was so deeply held among the Judaeans that the author of I Maccabees, in giving the Testament of Mattathias the Hasmonean, said that David "inherited the throne of an everlasting kingdom." [32] Similarly Ben Sirah, writing in his book about Phineas, the grandson of Aaron to whom God gave the high priesthood forever, said that God made a covenant with David, the son of Jesse, to whom he gave an everlasting kingdom.[33]

The followers of Joshua were of the high priestly family of the Zadokites, the Sadducees. They were strict adherents to the written law. Although they recognized the unwritten law then in vogue, they did not hold it binding. To them only the laws of the Torah were binding. Since they strictly followed the Torah they held that Yahweh is an ethnic God, the God of the descendants of Abraham, Isaac, and Jacob, with whom He made a covenant and whose children He brought out of Egypt. Hence they still called the Temple built after the Restoration the House of Yahweh, using the same nomenclature applied to the Temple built by King Solomon. The followers of Zerubbabel maintained that the unwritten laws are on a par with the written laws, the Torah. They held that anyone who transgressed the unwritten laws would be liable to punishment as if he had transgressed the written laws.[34]

The group that held that the oral law is on a par with the Pentateuchal laws; that the new community should be established under the leadership of a scion of the Davidic family and not under the

28 62:14; 69:26.
29 69:4; 105:2.
30 M. Sanhedrin 11:1.
31 Cf. S. Zeitlin, *The Rise and Fall of the Judaean State*, 1962, pp. 6–12.
32 I Maccabees 2:57.
33 47:11.
34 Cf. S. Zeitlin, "The Pharisees," *Jewish Quarterly Review*, October, 1961, pp. 97–129; idem., op. cit.

leadership of a high priest; and that Yahweh is the God of all peoples and not an ethnic god was considered heretical by the Zadokites, the high priestly family. This group was called *Perushim*, Pharisees, separatists, by the Zadokites who maintained that they separated themselves from the Judaeans, the people of Yahweh. Down to the successful revolt under the leadership of the Hasmoneans the Pharisees had no influence over the affairs of the Judaean community but they had the confidence of the rank and file of the people.[35]

The Pharisees endeavored to solve the vexing problems of individuals—why did the righteous suffer and the wicked prosper? They taught the people that there was a future world where there would be reward and punishment—the reward for good deeds in this world and punishment for the wicked. They also impressed upon the minds of the people that the soul is immortal. The physical body dies but the soul lives forever. These theological views gave meaning and essence to the lives of the people, for they now felt that their good deeds in life were not in vain and were certain that they would be rewarded for them. That life in this world is passing while the future world is eternal became an article of faith. During the entire period of the Second Commonwealth the Pharisees stressed the views that one day leadership over the Jews would be vested in a scion of the family of David, and that there would be reward for the righteous and punishment for the wicked in the future world.

When the Hasmoneans succeeded in throwing off the yoke of the Syrians and eliminated the high priesthood of the Zadokite family, the influence of the Pharisees ascended. Daniel's words that the *mashiah* will be cut off, that is,[36] eliminated, refers to the abolishment of the high priesthood of the Zadokite family.

When the Judaean Commonwealth was established in 141 B.C.E. the Great Synagogue confirmed the high priesthood of Simon, the Hasmonean, and proclaimed him the ruler of the State. In this declaration there was a clause "until a true prophet will arise in Israel." The kingship was not given to him. With this act theocracy was abolished. But the view that Judaea should be a theocratic state was not entirely obliterated from the minds of all the people. Some of them longed for its re-creation. When the Roman general, Pompey, was in Syria, a deputation of Judaeans came to him asking that the kingship of Judaea be abolished and that the affairs of the community be placed in the hands of the high priest as in the olden days when the high priest was ecclesiastic as well as civil ruler over the people.[37]

35 *Ibid.*
36 9:26.

37 *Antiquities* 14. 3.2 (41).
38 *Ibid.*, 17. 11:2. (313–314).

In other words, they wanted Judaea to be a theocratic state. Similarly, after the death of Herod a deputation of Judaeans went to Augustus Caesar with the same petition.[38]

When Jannaeus Alexander assumed the kingship over Judaea the Pharisees bitterly opposed him. This brought about a civil war which ended tragically for the state. The Pharisees recognized that their struggle first with Jannaeus Alexander and later their participation in the civil war between John Hyrcanus and Aristobolus was catastrophic, so they abandoned political activity, devoting themselves to religion. They became quietists and legalists. However, there were groups among the Pharisees who continued to fight for the freedom of Judaea. Josephus tells that when Judaea was made a province of Rome in the year 6 c.e., Quirinus was sent by Rome to take a census of Judaea with a view to levying taxes upon the people. This aroused great opposition among the Judaeans. A man named Judas of Galilee organized a new group whose doctrines Josephus called the Fourth Philosophy.[39] This group was so named because Josephus deals with the Essenes, Sadducees, and Pharisees as philosophies, and names this group as the Fourth Philosophy. Josephus wrote about this group, "These men agree in all other things with the Pharasaic notions; but they have an inviolable attachment to liberty and say that God is to be their only ruler and Lord." He further said that Judas "incited his countrymen to revolt, upbraiding them as cowards for consenting to pay tribute to the Romans and tolerating mortal masters after having God for their Lord." [40] The followers of Judas from time to time resorted to seditious acts against the Romans. They also acted vigorously against their countrymen who submitted to the Romans. They considered as traitors such Judaeans who betrayed the freedom of their people. They held that terror must oppose terror.

Not being able to engage in open battle against the Romans and their followers, the Judaeans, the members of the Fourth Philosophy, resorted to the use of the *sica* (a short dagger) to assassinate those who favored peace with the enemy. From their use of the *sica* they received the name Sicarii [41] (not to be confused with the Zealots). Josephus referred to the Sicarii as robbers, brigands. He maintained that they were responsible for the destruction of the Judaean state and the burning of the Temple.

Of course the verdict of Josephus is a gross distortion of realities, for he himself said that hunger for freedom and liberty had motivated their actions. A speech which Josephus put in the mouth of Eleazar, son of Jairus, the last leader of the Fourth Philosophy before the fall

39 *Ibid.*, 18. 1.1(1–5); (23–25); *Jew-ish War* 2: 8.1 (107–108).

40 *Antiquities* 18. 1.6 (23–24).

41 *Ibid.*, 20. 8.10 (185–186).

of Masada, could not have come from the mouth of an ordinary robber: "Long since, my brave men, we determined neither to serve the Romans nor any other save God, for He alone is man's true and righteous Lord." He concluded his speech with the following, "For it is death which gives liberty to the soul and permits it to depart to its own pure abode, there to be free from all calamity; but so long as it is imprisoned in a mortal body tainted with all its miseries, it is in sober truth dead, for association with what is mortal ill befits that which is divine." [42] An ordinary brigand could not have uttered such noble sentiments, as Josephus would have us believe.

Josephus mentioned another group which he called wicked as were the members of the Fourth Philosophy. He gave no name to this group. In writing about these two groups he said that although their hands were purer than those of the Sicarii their intentions were more impious. "Deceivers and imposters under pretense of divine inspiration, fostering revolutionary changes," he said of them. "They persuaded the people to act like madmen, and led them out into the desert under the belief that God would there give them tokens of deliverance." [43]

This group was the Apocalyptists. Its members believed in the revelation of God and, therefore, the appelation of Apocalyptists is appropriate. The Apocalyptists as well as the members of the Fourth Philosophy, the Sicarii, were offshoots of the Pharisees. These two groups had the same objectives: to free the Judaeans from the yoke of the Romans as well as from the Herodean dynasty. They both maintained that God is the only ruler over man, but they differed in their methods of advocating this view. The members of the Fourth Philosophy held that terror must oppose terror. To free the Judaeans and destroy their adversaries, force and violence, even murder, were justified. The Apocalyptists were opposed to acts of terror and the use of violence. They preached love, their watchword was, "If one seeketh to do evil unto you, do well unto him and pray for him." [44] The Apocalyptists were God-fearing people who believed that God had not forsaken the Judaeans but only chastised them. They believed that He would reestablish Israel under His anointed *Mashiah*, that a scion of the family of David would rule in Zion and destroy the persecutors of His people as well as all the sinners. They considered *Mashiah* the anointed of Yahweh, not an ordinary human being, but

---

42 *Jewish War* 7. 8.6–7 (321–380).
43 *Ibid.*, 2. 13. 4 (259).
44 See *The Testament of the Twelve Patriarchs; The Testament of*

Joseph 18.2.
45 Cf. *Enoch* 51:2. "For in those days, the elect one shall arise and shall choose the righteous and the holy

one possessed of supernatural powers.[45] The Apocalyptists, aware of the might of Rome, knew that the Judaeans could not free themselves from the Romans by force. They believed that God would perform miracles to free His people. They introduced the idea of a supernatural *mashiah*, who would reveal himself in due time, vanquish the Romans, free Israel, and sit on the throne of his father David. Then the millennium would come, looked forward to by the prophets of old.

The Apocalyptists were a mystic religious group. Mysticism is belief in truths which are beyond comprehension and understanding. People whose minds are deranged by physical or mental suffering are led to join such groups, and in doing so they become fanatics. On the other hand, opportunists and adventurers join such groups out of selfish motives. Josephus refers to one, Theodas, who "persuaded a great part of the people to take their effects with them and follow him to the river Jordan, for he told them he was a prophet, and that he would by his command divide the river, and afford them an easy passage over it. Many were deluded by his words." [46] He also wrote about a man from Egypt who claimed to be a prophet. He "advised the people to come along with him to the Mount of Olives where he will perform miracles."[47] The Apocalyptists, however, in general were sincere, pious people. They believed that their revelations were given by angels and through supernatural powers, that the kingdom of God was approaching, and that the *Mashiah* of Yahweh would reveal himself in all his glory.

The normative Pharisees opposed both the Sicarii and the Apocalyptists. They may not have shared the view of Josephus that the Apocalyptists were imposters, charlatans, but they maintained that the Apocalyptists were deceiving themselves; that their views were in opposition to the true views of the Pharisees; and hence that the Judaeans would be led astray. The Pharisees believed that God would some day free His people from the Roman yoke, that the kingship would again be in the hands of *Mashiah* of Yahweh, a scion of David, but that the king would not possess supernatural power and would not perform miracles. In this view they greatly differed from the Apocalyptists.

The terms "*Mashiah* of Yahweh" and "son of David" are synonymous and interchangeable. The term *mashiah* in the Bible refers to David and his descendants. The author of Lamentations, deploring

from among them . . . and the elect one shall in those days sit on My Throne." See *Psalms of Solomon* 17:23, "Raise up unto them their king, the son of David."
46 See *Antiquities* 20. 5. 1 (97–99).
47 *Jewish War* 2. 13. 5 (261–262); Cf. also *Acts* 21:38.

the untimely death of King Josiah, calls him the *Mashiah* of Yah-weh.[48] The Talmud says that Rabbi Akiba called Bar Kokba "King *Mashiah.*" One of Rabbi Akiba's colleagues said to him, "Grass will grow through thy jaws, and the time of the son of David has not come."[49] The term "son of David" and "king *mashiah*" are synony-mous.

The gospels according to both Matthew [50] and Luke [51] trace the genealogy of Jesus to David, while Mark, who does not give the gene-alogy, states that Jesus is the son of David.[52] John, who stresses the view that Jesus was the son of God, nevertheless wrote, "But some said, Shall Christ come out of Galilee? Hath not the scripture said, that Christ cometh out of the seed of David and out of the town of Bethlehem where David was?" [53] According to the gospels Jesus was greeted with the words, "Blessed be the kingdom of our father David," "Hosanna to the son of David." [54] On the cross on which Jesus was crucified the words "Jesus of Nazareth, king of the Judaeans" were inscribed in Hebrew, Greek, and Latin.[55] *Mashiah,* messiah, Christ were synonymous in their minds with "son of David" and "king of the Judaeans."

After the burning of the Temple, and particularly after the tragic collapse of the Bar Kokba revolt, the belief in a supernatural messiah who would rebuild the Temple and restore the Jewish state gained sway over the minds of the people. This was their only hope. Physical revolts ended in catastrophe and they looked for their salvation, re-demption, to a supernatural *mashiah.* Not all the sages,[56] however, shared this view and it never became an article of faith. Rabbi Judah the Prince, in codifying the Mishnah, does not refer to the belief in a *mashiah.* Reference is once made to the days of *mashiah.*[57] In the Mishnah it is stated that those who do not believe in Revelation and resurrection will not have a share in the world to come.[58] Denial of the coming of *mashiah* is not included in this category. Many Tan-naim and Amoraim, however, believed in the coming of the *Mashiah*

---

48 4:20.
49 *Yerushalmi. Taanit 4; Midrash R. Lamentations* 2.
50 1:1–16:
51 3:24–31.
52 12:35.
53 7:41–42.
54 *Mark* 11:10; *Matt.* 21:9.
55 *Iesus Nazarenus, Rex Iudaeorum.*
56 Cf. also Maimonides *Mishne Torah, Hilkot Melachim.* Maimonides held that Messiah would be a mortal, a king, a descendant of the house of David, a man wiser than Solo-mon, and a prophet next in great-ness to Moses.
57 *Mishnah Berachot* 1.6. The phrase, "the footsteps of the *mashiah*" oc-curs in the *Mishnah Sotah* 9. 15. This part, however, is a later addi-tion; the name of Rabbi Phineas ben Jair is mentioned in this Mishnah which indicates that it was interpolated after the time of Rabbi Judah.
58 *Mishnah Sanhedrin* 10. 1.

and even indulged in predictions as to the time when he will reveal himself.

Belief in a supernatural *mashiah,* a scion of the family of David, was first brought forth by the Apocalyptic Pharisaic group. It did not greatly influence the Judaeans during the Second Commonwealth, but after the destruction of the Second Temple, and particularly after the revolt of Bar Kokba, it gained stimulus and shaped the life of the Jewish people throughout the centuries. The idea of a supernatural *mashiah* became the cornerstone of Jewish survival, as is admirably portrayed by Doctor Abba Hillel Silver in his book *A History of Messianic Speculation in Israel.*

II

Natural and Supernatural Messianism

Conception of the Ideal Kingdom Without a Messiah

by JAMES DRUMMOND

It is now time to inquire into the character of the Messianic kingdom itself. At our very entrance upon this subject a preliminary question meets us which demands our careful consideration. While our authorities concur in the recognition of a future ideal kingdom, it is, to say the least, extremely doubtful whether they all recognise a Messiah as standing at its head. It will be best to consider first the cases in which this uncertainty exists, and then, whichever way our decision may turn, we may appeal to our authorities in the chronological order whenever they throw light on the particular subject of which we may be treating.

The Book of Daniel is the first which asks for an impartial investigation ; but how to secure impartiality in the present instance it is not so easy to determine. It is not fair to charge a critic with partiality because he believes, as he thinks upon sufficient grounds, that the book contains a prediction of several historical events which took place centuries after its composition, and that we are bound to accept all interpretations which are found in the New Testament. But it is evident that such a judgment may very seriously affect the meaning which we attach to the text, and so far as we are swayed by it, we may be led quite unconsciously to repudiate a sense which we should otherwise derive from the words before us. It therefore seems more truly impartial to take the book simply as we find it, and endeavour to learn by a literary procedure what it was that the author meant to communicate to his readers. If the result prove to be inconsistent with the above assumptions, then it is, so far as it goes, an evidence against their truth; while if it prove to be favourable to them, it will be a stronger support than an interpretation which has been avowedly made in subjection to their restraints. Hengstenberg, however, wishes to throw the blame of partiality upon those who question the traditional interpretation. He says,—'So far as the rationalistic commentators were concerned, besides their general inclination to limit the number of Messianic prophecies as far as possible, there were special reasons why they should reject a Messianic explanation in the present case, if they could find any possible excuse for doing so. They assign its composition to as late a date as the period of the Maccabees. But according to the current theory, which I have shown to be erroneous in my work ' für Beibehaltung der Apocryphen,' there is not a single trace of the expectation of a personal Messiah to be found in the apocryphal books. This belief is said to have been altogether extinct in the days of the writers of the Apocrypha. If therefore there is any Messianic prophecy in the Book of Daniel, according to this theory it must be altogether erroneous to assign it to a Maccabean origin.' [1] Now Hitzig undoubtedly uses the assumed date of the book as conclusive against the Messianic interpretation, [2] and so far as this consideration affected his judgment in inter-

---

[1] *Christology of the Old Testament: translated by James Martin:* Clark, Edinburgh, 1858, vol. iii. p. 87. My references will be to this edition and volume.

[2] S. 116.

preting the text, he was, though on the opposite side, under the influence of precisely the same kind of partiality as more orthodox critics. This, however, is no reason for refusing to adopt the purely literary method, and to interrogate the book without reference to external conditions. We shall not be exposed to the bias which Hengstenberg points out, if we consider Hitzig's argument unsound ; and for my own part I cannot see why, even if the Messianic belief had died out as completely as he supposes, the writer of Daniel might not have endeavoured to revive it in the minds of his countrymen.

The first passage for which a Messianic meaning is claimed is at the end of Daniel's vision of the four beasts, and runs thus : ' I saw in the night visions, and, behold, [one] like a son of man [not ' *the* son of man,' as in the Authorised Version] came with the clouds of heaven, and came to the Ancient of days, and they brought him near before him. And there was given him dominion, and glory, and a kingdom, that all people, nations, and languages, should serve him : his dominion is an everlasting dominion, which shall not pass away, and his kingdom that which shall not be destroyed.' [1]   Now when we refer to the context to enable us to interpret this passage, we may guide our judgment both by the parallelism of the vision itself and by the explanation of it which is given in the succeeding portion of the chapter. In the vision four beasts are seen, which represent the brutal might of four successive heathen kingdoms; and as these beasts are altogether symbolical, we naturally expect the higher power which is to take their place to be also symbolically represented. What more suitable to succeed the savage beasts than the human form, drawing its life from heaven, and receiving its dominion from the Ancient

[1] vii. 13, 14.

of days? The vision itself, therefore, suggests that the 'son of man' stands for the ideal Israel, for whom the empire of the world was destined in the counsels of God. But no, says Hengstenberg,[1] 'on the contrary the analogy favours the Messianic interpretation. The four beasts do not represent kingdoms without heads, but "four kings."'[2] 'Hence, according to the analogy, we are not to look in this instance for a kingdom (ver. 27) without a king, a sovereign people.'[3] This remark of Hengstenberg's really strengthens the case against himself. How is it that Daniel is content to speak of the four heathen monarchies as 'four kings,' although the individual kings were of no importance, while in the case of the people over whom he is supposed to place a superhuman head, the pre-existent Messiah, he changes his mode of description, and says not a word about a king? This surely suggests to us the notion, not altogether foreign to Old Testament thought, of a pure theocracy, in which the Ancient of days would himself come and dwell as sole king upon his holy mountain; and we have in this suggestion a sufficient answer to Oehler's not very astute remark that in any case 'the kingdom is not to be thought of without its king.'[4]

In these observations we have partly anticipated our notice of the interpretation of the dream. In this the beasts are expressly referred to, but unfortunately the 'son of man' is not again mentioned. There are, however, three different verses in which the concluding part of the vision is explained,[5] and in all of these the dominion

---

[1] Hengstenberg's treatment is so copious and elaborate that in the following discussion I have taken him as the representative of the traditional interpretations, and have guided my arguments by reference to his. Some other views will, however, be noticed as we proceed.

[2] vii. 17.   [3] P. 89.

[4] Herzog, *Messias*, S. 416.   [5] Verses 18, 22, 27.

is assigned to ' the saints of the Most High,' without the
faintest allusion to a Messiah ; and accordingly, if we are
to allow the author to be his own interpreter, we must
believe that the ' son of man ' and ' the saints of the Most
High ' are identical.   The only answer which Hilgenfeld
makes to this argument is, ' but surely the Messiah is
precisely the head of this people,'[1] a remark which
merely takes for granted the thing to be proved.   Hengstenberg says, ' The error committed in the statement of
this argument is, that the passage under review is severed
from the entire course of prophecy, and no attention is
paid to the relation in which Daniel himself declares that
he stood to the prophets who preceded him ; compare ix.
6 . . . and 10.   It was a fundamental idea of prophecy
that the future salvation was to be bestowed upon the
people of the saints of the Most High, through the medium
of the Messiah ; that it did not belong to the people as a
body, but to the people as united under Christ their head.
. . .   If Daniel could assume that this was already known,
he had no reason to fear that he would be misunderstood,
when he afterwards attributed to the people of the saints
of the Most High, what he had previously written of the
Messiah.   No true Israelite would have misunderstood
him, even if he had not expressly mentioned the Messiah
before, and thus guarded against any misapprehension.'[2]
In this reply Hengstenberg scarcely meets the point of
the adverse argument.   The question is not whether
Daniel could have attributed to the saints of the Most
High what he had previously written of the Messiah, but
whether he had previously written anything of the
Messiah ; and the argument is that the total failure to
notice the Messiah throughout a long interpretation of
the dream, although there is a reiterated recurrence to

[1] *Jüd. Apol.* S. 46.   [2] Pp. 88–9.

its supposed Messianic portion, is an evidence in favour of the non-Messianic explanation. Hengstenberg has given no reason for this failure, which is the more extraordinary if we say, with Hilgenfeld,[1] that ' it was the principal aim of the author to bring this [the Messianic kingdom] livingly before the soul of his compatriots.

Our surprise is not diminished when we look more closely at the vision and its interpretation. If the ' son of man ' be the Messiah, he is here presented in a way which, so far as we know, is wholly new. The imagery of the ancient prophets, towards whom Daniel is said to have so carefully maintained his relations, is discarded, and instead of one sprung from the stem of Jesse, heir to the throne of David, we have a mysterious being, coming in cloudy grandeur to rule over the whole world, while the people of Israel are passed by without the most cursory notice. Now if anything required explanation, surely this did, especially as Hengstenberg was not at hand to point out that the second coming of the Messiah was intended, a fact which is studiously concealed in the vision itself. The presumption which is thus created that this mysterious allusion could not be left without elucidation is strengthened when we find that the fourth beast, with his ten horns and his little horn, receives such ample notice. How is it that the impiety of the little horn, the type of Antichrist, is portrayed with such individual features, while on the opposite side the great mediator vanishes utterly from view, and the Ancient of days and the chosen people completely fill the scene? This silence in regard to the Messiah Hengstenberg does not so much as pretend to explain.

It may be said, however, that Daniel's connection

[1] *Jüd. Apok.* S. 46.

with the prophets renders it improbable that he can have been without the Messianic belief. In this consideration there is some weight. But we have already seen that the prophets are by no means unanimous in what Hengstenberg is pleased to lay down as ' a fundamental idea of prophecy ; ' and as the writer has certainly not followed the old prophetic type, there is no difficulty in believing that he may have reverted to the still older idea of a pure theocracy, in which, though human leaders might be necessary, none should be distinguished with special Messianic dignity. Whether he did so or not must be judged simply from his own statements. The passage to which appeal is made with the greatest confidence yields to those who do not thrust into it a meaning derived from other sources a picture of world-wide dominion exercised by the saints under the immediate government of the Almighty himself; and this interpretation is confirmed by the two parallel passages in which the kingdom is referred to. In ii. 44 we are told that ' in the days of these kings shall the God of heaven set up a kingdom which shall never be destroyed : and the kingdom shall not be left to other people, but it shall break in pieces and consume all these kingdoms, and it shall stand for ever.' There is nothing in this inconsistent with the Messianic conception ; but had the Messiah been a prominent figure in the writer's thoughts, he would probably have been alluded to on so suitable an occasion. It is of more consequence, however, that in the other passage we find a mediator actually named, and that this is not the Messiah, but the archangel Michael. Having stated that the king of the north [Antiochus Epiphanes] should come to his end, and none should help him, the writer proceeds, ' And at that time shall Michael stand up, the great prince which standeth for the children

121

of thy people;'[1] and it is evident from the whole scope
of the passage, and particularly from the reference to the
resurrection, that here also 'the time of the end' is described.   It is surely incredible that if the writer believed
in a supernatural Messiah, he could be content to accord
to him only an obscure description, occupying a couple
of verses, and then at the close of his book not only omit
to say a word about him, but introduce Michael by name
as the heavenly mediator to whom the Israelites were to
look for deliverance.

Hengstenberg, however, produces arguments on the
opposite side, which appear even to Hilgenfeld pretty
much to the point,[2] and it is possible that these may
more than counterbalance the evidence already adduced.   In the first place he appeals to the 'history
of Biblical interpretation.'   'It was supported by the
whole of the early Christian Church with very few
exceptions.'[3]   As the early Christian Church had no
better means of interpreting the passage than we have
ourselves, and as it was the most natural thing possible
for them to give it a Messianic interpretation, I do not
see that there is any force in this argument.   But he
adds, 'the Jews were certainly interested in opposing it,
as Christ had so expressly declared himself to be the Son
of Man.   Yet with the exception of Abenezra, they are
unanimous in supporting this exposition.'[4]   When the
Messianic idea was fully developed, and when sound
principles of interpretation were systematically disregarded,
it is not surprising that the Jews adopted this into the
number of Messianic passages.   They may have done
so before the time of Christ, though in support of this
supposition we cannot appeal to the Book of Enoch, the

[1] xii. 1.   [2] 'Ziemlich treffend:' *Jüd. Apok.* S. 46, Anm. 2.
[3] Pp. 86–7.   [4] P. 87.

passages in that work relating to the Son of man being probably of later date. But even in this case the question is whether the national point of view may not have been altered after the power of the Romans began to make itself felt, and whether the Book of Daniel may not have been forced by a new interpretation into conformity with the changed circumstances of the people. As this is part of the question at issue, it is irrelevant to appeal to Jewish exegesis which does not go back beyond the Roman period. In regard to the bias of the Jews Hengstenberg is clearly wrong. The Messiah coming in the clouds presented so marked a contrast to the crucified Jesus that the passage in Daniel was used in refutation of the Christian claim ; and the recourse to a second coming, however satisfactory to Christians, could appear to a Jew little better than a makeshift. In the dialogue with Tryphon [1] Justin Martyr quotes this passage at length to illustrate the glory of Christ ; and what is the Jew's reply ? [2] 'These and similar scriptures compel us to expect in glory and greatness him who as a son of man receives the eternal kingdom from the Ancient of days ; but this so-called Christ of yours has been dishonoured and inglorious, so that he even fell under the extreme curse that is contained in the law of God, for he was crucified.' I think, therefore, that we need not abandon our own judgment in deference to that of the Talmudists.

In support of the presumption which he thinks is created by the 'history of Biblical interpretation' Hengstenberg adduces four 'positive arguments.'

'1. The ideal personality of the nation would have been more particularly pointed out at the very outset ; otherwise everyone would understand the passage as referring to the actual person of the Messiah. The elevation of the

[1] Ch. 31.   [2] Ch. 32.

people had hitherto been inseparably connected with the royal house of David; and earlier prophets had invariably pointed to the Son of David as the author of its future glory. If, therefore, Daniel ascribed this future exaltation first to the Son of man, and then to the nation, he could only intend that the former of these should be understood as referring to the Messiah.'[1] This argument conveniently assumes the very point which is under discussion, namely that the Messianic belief was existing in full vigour at the time when the book was written. And we may venture to say on the other hand, that it was only under the suggestion of a pre-existing belief that a Messianic interpretation could possibly have arisen. But in addition to this *petitio principii* the argument is strangely inconsequential:—the people always expected the Messiah to appear in the person of one of the royal house of David; therefore they could not possibly suppose that one like a son of man coming with the clouds of heaven could be other than the Messiah. Where is the identity or resemblance between these two ideas? Even in the Talmud, where the Messianic sense is admitted, the contrast between this and an earlier view is felt to require explanation:—'Rabbi Yehoshua' ben Levi threw two verses against one another: " Behold he will come in the clouds of heaven as the Son of man," and " He is poor, sitting on an ass."—If they [the Israelites] are deserving, [he will come] on the clouds of heaven; if they are not deserving, poor, sitting on an ass.'[2] I think, therefore, that the Messianic interpretation is not the first which would occur to an Israelite who had always expected the Messiah to rise out of the stem of Jesse; and Hengstenberg's argument consequently falls to the ground.

' 2. His coming in the clouds of heaven is decisive. The anti-Messianic expositors have not only to explain,

[1] P. 89. [2] *Synhed.* 98a.

how Israel could be in heaven, . . . but how it could become possessed of omnipotent judicial power. For it is this that is indicated by his coming with the clouds.'[1] We have here two arguments in the form of one. The first, that Israel could not be in heaven, seems to me, I must be excused for saying, 'decisive' of nothing but the inconceivably prosaic character of the man who can resort to it ; as though the glowing dreams of a prophet and poet were to be as dry and literal as the dreary lucubrations of a modern theologian. Will, then, Hengstenberg explain how the Lord could 'cast down from heaven unto the earth the beauty of Israel,'[2] if Israel had never been in heaven, and how Babylon could have 'fallen from heaven,'[3] and how Capernaum can have been 'exalted unto heaven'?[4] He must also explain how kings could be beasts, and come up from the sea. But leaving this trifling, let us look at the writer's own thought. First he sees the four winds of heaven striving upon the great sea, and four great beasts coming up from the sea, and exercising successive dominion till the Ancient of days appears, and passes judgment upon them ; and then, in contrast to these beasts, born from the wilderness of ocean amid tumult and tempest, and wielding their brute power in a selfish and impious tyranny, another form, bearing the mild and devout lineaments of a man, comes with the pomp and glory of heaven to receive from the Ancient of days an eternal kingdom. The heaven is the proper contrast to the sea, as the human form is to the bestial, and the beauty and significance of the vision would be seriously marred if this feature were removed.

As to the second portion of the argument, it is a pure assumption to say that coming with the clouds denotes

[1] Pp. 89–90. See also Pusey, p. 85 *sq.*   [2] Lam. ii. 1.
[3] Isai. xiv. 12.   [4] Matt. xi. 23.

'omnipotent judicial power.' A few pages farther back, indeed, Hengstenberg says that 'in the symbolical language of the Bible the clouds represent judgment,'[1] and again, 'the Messiah appears upon the clouds of heaven; he is, therefore, an almighty judge, even *before* the dominion is given to him.'[2] It is a strange principle of exegesis which ascribes an unalterable meaning to the figurative language of poetry, and it may seem hardly worth while to refer to one or two other ideas represented by clouds. As one might expect in a hot climate, the word is used to symbolise refreshment and coolness; 'The Lord will create upon every dwelling place of mount Zion . . . a cloud and smoke by day,'[3] *i.e.* to serve as a welcome shade. Again, as something transient, though dark and threatening, the cloud becomes a symbol of forgiven sin: 'I have blotted out, as a thick cloud, thy transgressions, and, as a cloud, thy sins.'[4] And in reference to God himself it denotes that He is for a time inaccessible to the petitions of men: 'Thou hast covered thyself with a cloud, that our prayer should not pass through.'[5] That from the magnificence of cloudy scenery it should be used to symbolise the divine majesty, and from the terrors of the thunder-storm be mingled with the concomitants of divine judgment, is only what we should expect; but to say that therefore anyone who seems in a night-vision to come with the clouds must be an omnipotent judge is merely idle assertion. That the language in Daniel is intended to indicate the heavenly exaltation of the 'one like a son of man,' and the solemn inauguration of a divine kingdom upon earth, is evident without going beyond the limits of the passage itself; but we must observe that the Son of man is not represented as coming

[1] P. 83. [2] P. 84. [3] Isai. iv. 5.
[4] Isai. xliv. 22. [5] Lam. iii. 41.

down to earth, as we should expect a judge to do, but as coming to the Ancient of days ; and therefore, if we may venture to follow the leading of the words themselves instead of a traditional theology, the idea presented is not that of an almighty being coming in his own right to rule the world, but rather that of one who has been raised up from the earth, and is borne along with the clouds to the throne of the Eternal, in order to receive by divine grant a kingdom which others had claimed by their own lawless force. As Hengstenberg is fond of Jewish interpretation, we may appeal in support of this view to Fourth Ezra, in which the being like a man comes up ' out of the heart of the sea,' and afterwards flies 'with the clouds of heaven ; ' and his goal is ' the top of mount Zion,' which, we may remember, was believed to be the dwelling-place of God.[1] This view is further confirmed by the fact that the judgment is supposed to have already taken place,[2] and if the writer meant to imply that this judgment was conducted by the Son of man, he has certainly expressed himself with the most studied ob- scurity. The conception which we have thus reached, though not inconsistent with the Jewish belief in the Messiah, is perfectly suitable to the ideal Israel. Heng- stenberg's ' decisive ' argument, therefore, can satisfy only those who are already convinced.

Before leaving this argument, however, it may be worth while to hazard a further remark. If the plea could be sustained that coming with the clouds represents judicial power, then we have only to turn to verse 22 to find that ' judgment was given to the saints of the Most High.' Though this may perhaps mean that justice was

---

[1] xiii. 3 (in all the versions but the Latin, in which there is evidently a lacuna), 5, 25, 35.
[2] Verse 10.

done to the saints, something may be said on behalf of the idea that the power of judgment was committed to them. The word here used is רֹעֵא; and as the same word is twice used in this very chapter to denote the supreme judgment,[1] we might expect the same sense to be preserved throughout.[2] In this case the saints would be expressly invested by the writer himself with that judicial power the supposed possession of which by the ' son of man ' is regarded as such a conclusive proof that he cannot be identical with them. That the idea was not foreign to Jewish thought, that judgment, in a subordinate sense, might be committed to the Israelites, we learn from the Book of Enoch : ' Afterwards there will be another week, the eighth, that of righteousness, and there shall be given to it a sword, in order that judgment and righteousness may be exercised on those who act violently, and the sinners shall be given over into the hands of the righteous.'[3] The final judgment is not to take place till the tenth week ; but at an earlier time the sword of judgment is entrusted to the righteous. Thus, even if we admit Hengstenberg's statement that the ' clouds represent judgment,' his conclusion is invalid.

' 3. Israel could not appropriately be compared to a son of man. Such a comparison presupposes that there was a difference as well as a resemblance.'[4] If we are in this way to press the particle of comparison, כ, the argument is directly opposed to the purpose for which it is used. Christ was a *real* son of man, as Hengstenberg of course admits ; and therefore, whatever he may have

---

[1] Verses 10 and 26.

[2] So Mr. Fuller understands it, explaining it by the rule, ' quod facit per alterum, facit per se.' *Speaker's Com.* vi. p. 330.

[3] xci. 12. See also xcv. 3, ' that you [the righteous] may exercise judgment on them [the sinners] as you will.'

[4] P. 90.

been besides, we cannot say that he *resembled* a son of man. A man is a great deal more than a biped ; yet it would be absurd to say that he resembled a biped. The description, accordingly, though not inconsistent with the idea of a wholly supernatural Messiah, who was not a true son of man, completely excludes Hengstenberg's Messiah. On the other hand, it precisely suits a per- sonified people, who are not a son of man, but only *as it were* a son of man. In the passage already quoted from Fourth Ezra, in the Æthiopic, Arabic, and Armenian versions, it is the wind which rises up from the sea like a man, though after this has occurred the mysterious being is spoken of as a man. This suggests the thought that perhaps the writer of Daniel may have meant by his comparison that it was not a real man of flesh and blood that appeared in the clouds, but rather a grand cloudy form that shaped itself out of the ascending vapours, till it seemed the glorified heavenly reflection of ideal humanity. On the other hand, if he meant the Messiah, I have seen no satisfactory reason for his using the particle of comparison at all. It would have been more natural to have said simply, ' I saw the Son of man.'

' 4. In the other passages of this book, in which anyone is described as being like the children of men, it is not an ideal person, but a real person, who is spoken of. The same remark applies to Ezek. i. 26.' [1] The analogy of four passages, even if they were like the pre- sent one, could hardly establish a rule. But in all four instances the expression is quite different. And here again the argument turns against Hengstenberg ; for the comparison is invariably used in reference to those who were in no sense men—to God in Ezekiel, and to angels in Daniel.[2]

[1] P. 90.   [2] viii. 15 ; x. 16, 18.

Such are the arguments by which the Messianic interpretation is defended, and which appear satisfactory even to such a critic as Hilgenfeld. To my own mind they appear simply worthless; and therefore the considerations which led us to assign a different meaning to the passage remain unimpaired.

The next passage in which the Messiah is by some critics supposed to appear is viii. 15 *sq.* At the end of the vision of the ram and the goat Daniel 'heard one saint speaking, and another saint said unto that certain saint which spake, How long shall be the vision concerning the daily sacrifice?' When Daniel had heard the answer, there stood before him 'as the appearance of a man [גָּבֶר]. And I heard a man's voice between the banks of Ulai, which called, and said, Gabriel, make this man to understand the vision.' Oehler[1] and Hilgenfeld[2] think that this person with the man's voice can be no other than the Son of man of vii. 13. With the interpretation, however, which we have given to the latter passage, all plea for this opinion falls away. There is nothing in the narrative itself to suggest anything but the presence of two angelic beings, one of whom assumed the visible appearance of a man, and is evidently Gabriel, while the other is known to be at hand only by the voice which is heard above the middle of the river. To assume that the owner of this voice is the Messiah is indeed to build one's theories in the air.

This passage is, however, connected with a later vision, which Daniel saw 'by the side of the great river, which is Hiddekel.'[3] Here appeared 'a certain man clothed in linen, whose loins were girded with fine gold of Uphaz.' Now the linen dress denotes the priestly

---

[1] Herzog, *Messias*, S. 417.   [2] *Jüd. Apok.* S. 47.
[3] x. 4 *sq.*

R

office, and the gold indicates the rank of a prince ; and
thus, according to Hilgenfeld,[1] is indicated a character
precisely suited to the Messianic conception in the
Maccabean time, when the high-priest had so long pre-
sided over the nation. These tokens, however, are not
inconsistent with the dignity of an archangel. Michael
also is ' one of the chief princes,'[2] and if we have no
other reference in Daniel to the priestly functions of the
angels, it would not be unsuitable to ascribe them to
those who stood nearest to the throne of God.[3] With
these articles of dress all resemblance to the Messiah
ceases. This being, whoever he is, belongs wholly to
the celestial realm. He is there engaged in conflict with
the angel-prince of the kingdom of Persia. With the help
of Michael he was able to leave the contest for a time, in
order to make revelations to Daniel ; but when this duty
is accomplished, he must return to the fight. His revelation is long and minute, and extends to the time of the
resurrection ; yet nowhere does he give the faintest hint
of any personal participation in the earthly fortunes of
Israel. The people are Daniel's people,[4] and Michael is
their heavenly prince.[5] How anything could be more
unlike the Messiah it is difficult to conceive ; and indeed
the total absence of Messianic promise throughout this
elaborate description of ' what shall befall thy people in
the latter days '[6] seems to me to be conclusive evidence
that, if the writer believed in a Messiah at all, he regarded
him as so subordinate to the general glory of Israel that
it was not worth while to introduce him on the scene ;
and it is most probable that the Messianic idea had lost all

---

[1] *Jüd. Apok.*, S. 49.   [2] Verse 13.
[3] Hitzig appropriately refers to Rev. viii. 2, 3.
[4] x. 14 ; xii. 1.   [5] x. 21. xii. 1.   [6] x. 14.

hold on the mind of the people, and had not yet re-shaped itself from the pictures in the ancient prophecies.

We come now to a passage the interpretation of which is beset with difficulties, ix. 24–27.[1] To this Hengstenberg devotes all his strength in a laboured exposition and argument, which occupy, in the translation, more than 170 pages. As it is not necessary for us to imitate this minuteness in order to arrive at rational grounds for deciding between the Messianic and non-Messianic interpretations, I propose to start by presenting Hengstenberg's translation, and accepting it with the exception of a few points which seriously affect the decision of the controversy.

The following, then, is his rendering, a few of his explanations which are needed to make the sense clear being given in brackets:—'Seventy weeks are cut off [definitely and precisely determined] upon thy people and upon thy holy city, to shut in [forgive, cover up] transgression, and to seal up sins [remove them from the sight of God], and to cover iniquity, and to bring eternal righteousness; and to seal up vision and prophet [not, as most suppose, to fulfil or confirm them, but to put them aside as no longer necessary], and to anoint a Holy of Holies. And thou shalt know and understand: from the going forth of the word to restore and to build Jerusalem unto an anointed one, a prince, are seven weeks and sixty-two weeks: the street is restored and built, and firmly determined;[2] but in narrow times. And after the sixty-two weeks an anointed one will be cut off; and there is not to him [Christ, owing to his rejection, has no

---

[1] Various opinions on this passage may be seen collected in the *Speaker's Commentary,* 'Excursus on the Seventy Weeks,' vi. pp. 360-365. They are given with candour and good taste; but the Excursus can hardly be said to contribute anything to the criticism of the subject.

[2] Dr. Pusey prefers ' street and wall shall be restored and builded,' p. 173.

rule over the covenant-people];[1] and the city and the
sanctuary the people of a prince, the coming one, will
destroy; and it will end in the flood,[2] and to the end
there is war, decree of ruins. And one week will confirm
the covenant to the many [or, he will confirm the covenant to the many one week], and the middle of the week
will [or, in the middle of the week will he] cause sacrifice
and burnt-offering to cease, and the destroyer comes over
the summit of abominations, and indeed until that which
is completed and determined shall pour down upon the
desolate places.'[3]

According to the view of the Messianic interpreters
we have here a literal prophecy of the coming of Christ,
of his death, and of the destruction of Jerusalem by the
Romans. By the anointing of a holy of holies Hengstenberg understands the communication of the Spirit to
Christ. He frankly admits that 'in the whole Bible
קֹדֶשׁ קָדָשִׁים is never applied to a person, but only to
things;'[4] but he thinks that 'Christ is here represented
as a most holy thing,' and that this interpretation is
justified by 1 Chron. xxiii. 13, where he believes that the
expression is used of Aaron and his sons,[5] and by Luke i.
35, where Christ is described as τὸ γεννώμενον ἅγιον.[6]

---

[1] Or, as Dr. Pusey explains it, 'the city and the sanctuary shall be his no
more:' pp. 176 and 184–5.

[2] The words 'the end thereof shall be with a flood' (as the A. V. has it)
Mr. Fuller refers to the destruction, not of the city, but of the prince, and
he thinks they should be rendered 'the prince that shall come and shall find
his end in the (not " a ") flood,' the flood being used for the 'army,' or as
typical of divine punishment. P. 358.

[3] Mr. Fuller thinks that the last word in 27, whether it be taken as 'a
desolate one' or as 'desolator,' refers to the Nagid (the prince). He who
had been a desolator becomes desolate. P 360.

[4] P. 123.

[5] Translating, 'Aaron was set apart to sanctify him as a most holy one,
he and his sons for ever.' P. 119.

[6] 'The Greek Versions . . . distinctly understand the words in dispute
in a personal sense.' Speaker's Com., where the words are cited, vi. p. 361.

He refers ' an anointed one' in each instance to Christ, and ' a prince, the coming one,' to Titus. He adopts as the beginning of the seventy weeks the year in which Nehemiah offered his prayer for the restoration of Jerusalem, on the ground that the actual restoration of the city was not commenced before that time.[1] It was in answer to this prayer that the divine decree went forth to rebuild the city. Now this event took place in the 20th year of Artaxerxes, that is, as Hengstenberg endeavours to prove, in the year 455 B.C.[2] The last clause in verse 25, he believes, must describe the events of the seven weeks just mentioned, and he infers that ' the restoration of the city is said to occupy the whole seven weeks, and to be completed when they close.' The year 455 B.C. corresponds with 299 from the foundation of Rome. Add to this sixty-nine weeks, or 483 years, and we reach 782 A.U.C., the year in which Christ began his ministry. Arguments are adduced to show that Christ's ministry really lasted three years and a half,[3] at the close of which he put an end, by his death, to the Jewish sacrifices, in conformity with verse 27.

The principal points in the non-Messianic interpretation may be briefly stated. The seventy weeks are adopted by the writer as an interpretation of the seventy years of Jeremiah, and terminate in the time of Antiochus Epiphanes. If we take as the earliest point of departure for our calculation the year 606 B.C., when Judæa fell under the Chaldean power, we reach the year 116 B.C., which is half a century too late. We thus encounter a

---

[1] P. 202 sq.

[2] Dr. Pusey assigns to this event the year 444 B.C. (pp. 169–170, with note 6). He dates, in preference, from the commission of Ezra in the seventh year of Artaxerxes, 457 B.C. (pp. 169 and 172), so that in his initial point of reckoning he differs only by two years from Hengstenberg.

[3] P. 240 sq.

serious chronological difficulty, which must be brought
under discussion farther on. 'An anointed one, a prince,'
is Cyrus who is to appear at the end of seven weeks, this
period being separated by the punctuation from the sixty-
two weeks. The second 'anointed,' who is to be 'cut
off,' is either Seleucus IV., who died in 175 B.C., or the
high-priest Onias III., who was killed most probably in
171 B.C. The last week terminates in 164 B.C.; and in the
midst of this period of seven years Antiochus Epiphanes
captured Jerusalem and put a stop to the sacrifices.

Before proceeding to the evidence which must guide
our judgment in deciding between these two views, we
must make a remark about the method of inquiry.
Hengstenberg tries to create a prejudice against the non-
Messianic interpreters by using these words :—' There is
a hint at the genesis of these views in the words of
Hitzig : " after the death of Jesus the Son of man (vii.
13), it was inevitable that those who regarded him as the
Messiah, should interpret the words 'the anointed one
shall be cut off' as pointing to him." It was necessary
at any price to set aside the exposition which owed its
origin to faith ; for the simple reason that they had got
rid of faith itself.' [1] This insolent speech (as I must term
it) does not tend to awaken our confidence in the candour
of the critic who makes it. Men are not to be charged with
want of faith because they see no reason to believe that
the minute prediction of the chronology of future events
is an element in real prophecy. Whatever difficulties
stand in the way of such a supposition are opposed to the
Messianic interpretation ; and if these difficulties be considerable, they certainly impose upon honest men the
duty of freshly examining the passage, to see whether the
old interpretation be the only one that is tenable. At the

[1] P. 250.

same time we must be careful not to allow this reflection
to bias our exegetical judgment. We must endeavour
to determine simply from the book itself and its correspondence with historical facts what it was that the
writer meant, and for the time being maintain an attitude
of indifference towards the theory of special prediction.
On the other hand we must be equally careful not to be
biassed by the traditional interpretation; for Hitzig's very
just remark shows that, on the supposition of its being
wrong, we can fully account for its existence. With
these remarks we may proceed to an investigation of the
evidence.

We must notice, in the first place, certain phrases to
which appeal is made, but which seem to me to afford no
evidence either way. The first is, 'to anoint a holy of
holies.' We have already seen the way in which Hengstenberg applies this to Christ. On the other hand it
is referred to the temple or to the altar, and to the
restoration of the national worship, after the victories of
Judas Maccabæus. The expression here used is applied
to the altar in Exodus xxix. 37; and in Leviticus viii. 11
it is said that this was consecrated by anointing with oil.
To this Hengstenberg replies that the term is much more
extensive than the temple or the altar, and therefore could
not be used alone to denote either of these. 'It would be
only by a mere guess, and without any foundation whatever, that the expression could be understood as referring
to the temple itself,' or to the altar.[1] '*Every interpretation which is based upon a mere conjecture must for that
very reason be rejected.*'[1] Now it may be quite true that
the term would not at once suggest either of these
meanings to a reader remote from the scenes to which
it relates; but, I imagine, some such meaning would

[1] P. 120.

immediately occur to those who had either just witnessed or were eagerly expecting the reconsecration of the temple amid popular rejoicing and thanksgiving.[1] The expression, however, need not be limited, but may refer to the dedication of all that the Jews considered most holy in connection with the temple-worship. In any case Hengstenberg's interpretation must fall before his own canon. Was any reader not previously biassed likely to think of the Messiah when his eye lighted on the anointing of a most holy *thing*? Nowhere else is the Messiah so called, and it is only by a process of forcing that the words can be made to suit him. Hengstenberg further objects that 'the outward dedication of the outward temple and altar is not in harmony with the other communications of divine grace, promised in the context. They are all of a spiritual nature,' &c.[2] To this it is a sufficient answer to say that the expression and embodiment of spiritual blessings in an outward temple is not inconsistent with Jewish thought, and we know from the history of the Maccabees how strong was the attachment of the religious party to the sanctuary and its worship. Hengstenberg's other objections, founded on the chronology, and on the supposed prediction of the total destruction of the temple, as they have a bearing on the whole passage, will be considered in another connection.

The expressions, 'an anointed, a prince' in verse 25, and 'an anointed' in verse 26, do not necessarily refer to the Messiah. The former might certainly be applied to Cyrus, who was called the Lord's anointed by the later Isaiah;[3] and if it be doubtful whether the latter could denote a heathen king who had conferred no benefits upon Israel, it would be a suitable designation of a high-

---

[1] See the description in 1 Mac. iv. 52 *sq.*
[2] P. 121.
[3] xlv. 1.

priest. Hengstenberg's arguments to prove that these terms must signify the Messiah have so little force that we need not pause to notice them. On the other hand, it may very fairly be contended that the absence of the article furnishes no light argument against the Messianic interpretation, and that especially its absence in the second instance, together with the want of any term answering to ' prince,' shows that the two anointed ones are not the same. This difficulty, however, might perhaps be got over, if the preponderant evidence pointed to a different conclusion.

Hengstenberg lays great stress on the general Messianic character of the opening verse. But this is not disputed. The writer undoubtedly looks forward to an ideal kingdom as earnestly as any of the prophets. The only question in this respect is whether he places a Messiah at the head of that kingdom.

We must now turn to the more general considerations which may be alleged in favour of each view.

We may notice first those which render it probable that the fulfilment of the prophecy is to be sought in connection with Antiochus Epiphanes. The ample description in chapters xi. and xii. seems to me almost decisive of the question. There, as we have seen, there is not only no mention of the Messiah, but the great consummation of the world's history is connected with Antiochus, and the last solemn prophecy in the whole book relates to the suspension of the daily sacrifice in his time. How could the ultimate limit of the author's view be more clearly indicated? Again, how are we to believe that the author could dwell at such great length and with such reiteration on the brief episode of Antiochus, and yet confine himself to the most meagre and obscure allusions to the Messiah? There is something utterly gro-

tesque in the supposition that a man should be miraculously
commissioned hundreds of years before to predict such
ample details about an ephemeral tyrant, and to tell
about the world's great Redeemer that he should come
in a certain year, and that he should be cut off, that he
should confirm the covenant for one week, and cause
sacrifice to cease, and not another word about a life so
rich in everlasting results. Surely so wonderful a gift
can never have been so eccentric in its action.

Once more, there are certain obvious correspondences
between this passage and the prophecies which confessedly
relate to Antiochus, and these make it probable that we
are to seek the solution in the same events. In verse 27
we are told that sacrifice should cease in the middle of
the seventieth week. Three years and a half, therefore,
are left before the bringing in of everlasting righteousness.
Now this is the period elsewhere assigned to the suspension of the sacrifices under Antiochus.[1] This is certainly
a singular coincidence, if different events are really
referred to. Certain characteristic expressions also are
here used. וְעַל כְּנַף שִׁקּוּצִים מְשֹׁמֵם ('over the summit of
abominations [comes] a desolator,' or, if we are guided
by the corresponding phrases, and admit a slight change
of reading, ' over the summit of abominations of the desolator') reminds us of הַפֶּשַׁע שֹׁמֵם ('the transgression of
the desolator') in viii. 13, הַשִּׁקּוּץ מְשֹׁמֵם ('the abomination
of the desolator') in xi. 31, and שִׁקּוּץ שֹׁמֵם ('the abomination of the desolator') in xii. 11. These resemblances
might no doubt point to a parallelism between the Syrian
and the Roman invasions; but taken by themselves they
would certainly lead us to suppose that the writer was
referring to the same event throughout.

---

[1] vii 25; viii. 14; xii. 7, 11. In the statements in these passages there
are minor differences; but as they do not affect the general conclusion, we
need not pause to discuss them.

The above reasons, viewed in combination, appear to me to possess great force; but we must now see how far they are counterbalanced by objections to the view which they seem so firmly to support. Hengstenberg advances no fewer than eleven arguments against the Maccabean interpretation, of which, while some are of slight importance, one or two possess considerable weight. These we must now survey in their order.

1. He says, 'We cannot see how the supposed Pseudo-Daniel could possibly regard the prophecies of Jeremiah as unfulfilled, and so be induced to make them the subject of a parody These prophecies contain no Messianic elements whatever.'[1]   It is quite possible, however, that the writer may have believed that the prophecy had been literally fulfilled, and yet have supposed that it contained a deeper sense in which it had not yet found its accomplishment.[2] Jeremiah certainly connects the return from the Captivity with the most glowing anticipations of the Messianic time in chapters xxx. and xxxi.; and it would not have been at all inconsistent with ancient modes of interpretation to conclude that, while the seventy years literally ended with the return from Babylon, they must be mystically extended to embrace the happier period.   It seems evident also that there must have been some connection in the writer's mind between the seventy years of verse 2 and the seventy weeks of 24, and that the recurrence of the seventy is not a mere coincidence.   Indeed there is no apparent reason for his mentioning the prophecy of Jeremiah at all except as a ground on which to erect his own These remarks may serve at the same time as a reply to the next argument.

[1] P. 251.

[2] This supposition sufficiently meets Dr. Pusey's appeal to Ezra i. 1 as evidence that the Jews regarded the prophecy as fulfilled.   Pp. 192–3.

2. 'A mystic interpretation like this, "for seventy years write quickly 490," is so evidently a mere caprice, that no author could have adopted it, unless he intended to make fun of Jeremiah.' According to this criticism a good many Jewish interpreters must have wished to make fun of their Scriptures. But perhaps Hengstenberg is only making fun of himself.

3. The initial point of the seventy weeks ought to be the same as that of Jeremiah's seventy years, and this is conceded by many anti-Messianic expositors; but then the difficulty arises that no divine command to rebuild Jerusalem was given at that time. If appeal is made, as it is by Hilgenfeld,[1] to Jeremiah xxv., where the prophecy is assigned to the fourth year of Jehoiakim, 606 B.C., the rejoinder is made that the prophet in that passage says nothing about the rebuilding of the city. To escape this difficulty Hitzig appeals to Jeremiah xxx. and xxxi., where the rebuilding of the city is expressly mentioned;[2] but he thus lays himself open to the objection that he adopts a different initial point for the seventy weeks, namely 588 B.C. I believe the solution of the difficulty is to be found in identifying the 'commandment,' or rather 'word,' of verse 25 with the 'word of the Lord' in verse 2; for limiting the desolations of Jerusalem to a period of seventy years is tantamount to a promise to restore it when that period has elapsed. When Dr. Pusey ridicules the idea of thus calling the 'prophecy of that temporary desolation *a word* or promise *to restore and rebuild it,*'[3] he forgets that this is the very view presented by Ezra i. 1–2, where the decree of Cyrus to build the house of the Lord is represented as the fulfilment of 'the word of the Lord by the mouth of Jeremiah.' That the prediction about the seventy years is the one

[1] *Jüd. Apol.* S. 29.   [2] xxx. 18; xxxi. 4, 38.   [3] P. 195.

here referred to is evident from the parallel passage in 2 Chronicles xxxvi. 21–23, where it is expressly mentioned. It is clear, therefore, that the words of Jeremiah were understood not so much as a prophecy that Jerusalem should lie waste as in the sense of a promise that it should be restored after a certain time.

4. 'The fact that, in ver. 24, there is an evident antithesis to ver. 2, where it is said that seventy years are to be accomplished upon the ruins of Jerusalem, militates against the assumption, that the destruction is taken as the point of commencement. How can the years, which are to be accomplished *upon the ruins*, be included in those which are to be accomplished *upon the city*?' The antithesis between the two verses is not evident except to those who agree with Hengstenberg; to those who take the other view it is the parallelism that is evident. That the 'desolations' and 'the city' are not antithetic is sufficiently proved by verse 18, 'open thine eyes, and behold our desolations, and the city which is called by thy name.'

5. 'דְּבָר, without the article, cannot properly be referred to the definite announcement made by Jeremiah.' In a passage where the article is so often omitted, when, if Hengstenberg be correct, we should expect it, this difficulty can have but little weight. The indefiniteness is peculiarly appropriate here, if, as I have suggested, the 'word' in question was rather implied than distinctly announced by Jeremiah. Dr. Pusey strangely says, '*a decree to restore and build Jerusalem* is, according to these theories, not to be any decree or commandment of God, but a prophetic promise.'[1] But surely a prophetic promise is at least as divine as the decree of an eastern despot; and what God has promised, he may very well

[1] P. 194.

be said to have decreed. When Dr. Pusey says there is
'no more ground to select a prophecy of Jeremiah . . .
than one of Micah or Isaiah,'[1] he seems quite to forget
that the chapter opens with a reference to the דְּבַר־יְהוָֹה
that came to Jeremiah.

6. The two periods ought to terminate with the same
event; but 'of the blessings, which are spoken of in
ver. 24, . . . not one is mentioned by Jeremiah.' On
the contrary, the most essential blessings are fully mentioned by Jeremiah, not indeed in immediate verbal connection with the seventy years, but in connection with
the return from the Captivity : 'I will forgive their iniquity,
and I will remember their sin no more.'[2]

7. We come now to the most serious objection. If
we count the seventy weeks from the earliest admissible
date, 606 B.C., they carry us about half a century too far.
Hitzig endeavours to escape this difficulty by regarding
the seven weeks as included within the sixty-two, and
reckoning them from 588 to 539 B.C. It is not a serious
objection to this that Cyrus did not restore the Jews till
the year 536 ; for the author may not have thought it
necessary to introduce fractions into his longer periods,
although he does so in the last week, where the division
was of more importance. The inclusion of the seven
weeks is recommended by the fact that the sixty-two
weeks, reckoned from 606 B.C., exactly suit the chronology.
But this suitability is qualified by the following consideration. According to Hitzig's punctuation the city is
to be rebuilt during the sixty-two weeks; and therefore
we should expect them to begin with the return from the
Captivity. And again, it is a very arbitrary and artificial
way of dealing with the seventy weeks to treat them as
not continuous. No one could possibly imagine such an

[1] P. 195.   [2] xxxi. 34. See the whole chapter.

interpretation from a simple study of the passage itself; and it is difficult to suppose that the writer can have intended that of which he gives not the slightest hint. The same objection applies to the variation of Hilgenfeld, who reckons the seven weeks and the sixty-two weeks from the same initial point, 606 B.C., ending the seven weeks with the victory of Cyrus over Astyages the Median in 558 B.C.[1]

Ewald escapes from these difficulties, but in a manner which seems no less arbitrary. He supposes that the author, having arrived at the idea of seventy weeks, acts on the belief that the week was the divine measure of time, and that every week must have its sabbath of divine peace and favour. From the midst of the seventy weeks, therefore, must be withdrawn seventy years representing the sabbaths, leaving the remainder as the time of affliction. Having thus curtailed the period given by the writer himself, Ewald starts with the year 588 B.C. Seven weeks, or forty-nine years (for here the sabbaths are not omitted), bring us to 539. The sixty-two weeks, or 434 years, extend to 105 B C. Subtract seventy years, and we are carried back to 175. The remaining week ends with 168 B.C; and the half-week, which Ewald regards as a lucky hit on the part of the author, represents a short transition period before the Messianic time comes in. Of this curious shortening of the time there is not a hint in the text; but this is no difficulty to Ewald: if there is not, there ought to be; it is evident that the passage must originally have had some closing words, and these no doubt made everything clear.[2] All this is to imagine rather than to interpret.

Delitzsch, following Hofmann and Wieseler, thinks the seven weeks are to be placed at the end, not at the

---

[1] *Jüd. Apok.* S. 30.   [2] *Proph. d. A. B.* iii. S. 423 *sq.*

beginning of the seventy, and that they consequently come after the time of Epiphanes, and indicate the interval between him and Christ.   But this not only seems quite opposed to the plain meaning of the text, but introduces the insuperable difficulty that the seven weeks must equal at least 160 years.[1]

Can we, then, suppose that the author made a serious chronological mistake?   This supposition is not easily admitted, for, as Ewald points out,[2] the succession of the high-priests, and the observance of the festivals, and of the sabbatical years, must have caused the preservation of a correct chronology.   It seems evident, however, that the author did not choose the period of seventy weeks purely on chronological grounds; and it is quite possible that amid the excitement of national disaster he had neither the wish nor the opportunity to estimate with precision the lapse of time.   Dr. Pusey appears to treat the supposition of error as something impious.   In eking out his own theory it no doubt would be so.   But if the work be of Maccabean origin, and if its inspiration concern itself with great principles, and not with the dry details of history, we may reasonably expect a certain amount of error and difficulty, such as we find in other apocalyptic books.   To conclude that the Book of Enoch was written by Enoch because, on the supposition of its late date, it presents difficulties in the solution of which critics are by no means agreed, would be obviously absurd; yet Tertullian, had he known what variety of opinion critics would express, might, like Dr. Pusey, have indulged in some cheap merriment at their expense.   On the other hand, a single error, however minute, is incom-

[1] Herzog, *Daniel*, S. 283 *sq*.   Other attempted explanations may be seen in Dr. Pusey's work, p. 195 *sq*.
[2] *Proph. d. A. B.* iii. p. 423.

patible with the theory of miraculous prediction; and this must not be forgotten in estimating the force of objections urged from the opposite sides.

We, have then, in the chronology the one serious objection to the Maccabean interpretation. The question whether this objection is to be considered fatal, or to be treated merely as a difficulty the solution of which is uncertain, depends upon another question yet to be examined, whether any better interpretation is open to our choice.

We may notice in this connection an objection insisted upon by Hengstenberg in regard to the sixty-two weeks.[1] He correctly maintains that the only legitimate translation, if these weeks be connected with the building of the city, is, 'during sixty-two weeks;' and he asks 'how could the restoration of the streets, which was accomplished, according to the testimony of history, in a much shorter time, . . . be described as occupying the whole period of 434 years?' In reply to this we may observe, in the first place, that Hengstenberg himself makes the rebuilding occupy exactly forty-nine years,[2] for which there is no historical warrant whatever. Jerusalem must have been made a habitable city in a much shorter time. The building of a town, however, is a continuous process, which we cannot say has been finished at any particular moment. The restoration of Jerusalem might very well be spoken of as continuing, though 'in troublous times,' throughout the whole period from the Captivity to the reign of Antiochus Epiphanes, who again overwhelmed it in ruin.

8. 'If the prophecy relates to the Maccabean era, how is it that it contains no allusion whatever to an event

[1] P. 138 *sq.*

[2] Dr. Pusey, with his different initial point, manages to extract the same time. Pp. 174-5.

S

which is mentioned in all the other prophecies of Daniel
connected with this period, the restoration of the state
and temple?' It would be well if Hengstenberg had
pointed out the passages on which he relied for this
statement. In the prophecy in xi. and xii. I cannot find
any express assertion that the temple will be restored.
The vision of the ram and the goat also, in viii., ends
with the abolition of the daily sacrifice, though Daniel
then hears one saint telling another that after a certain
time the sanctuary should be cleansed. On the other
hand, in the present passage verse 24 surely implies that
all the calamities of the people and the holy city will be
over at the end of seventy weeks, and it was not necessary to repeat this at the conclusion of the prophecy.

9. Hengstenberg points out some difficulties in the
way of applying the words, ' an anointed one shall be cut
off,' to either Alexander or Seleucus Philopator ; but he
says nothing about their application to Onias.

10. He appeals to the unanimous testimony of Jewish
tradition. But the Jews must, at a very early period,
have been forced to adopt a non-Maccabean interpretation ; for they saw that the everlasting righteousness had
not come ; and they were not prepared to admit that the
writer was mistaken. This remark might apply even to
the time when the first Book of Maccabees was written,
though the alleged references of that book to the
other prophecies of Daniel, while this is not alluded to,
might be sufficiently explained by the greater clearness
and fulness with which they dwell on the disasters of the
time.[1]

---

[1] Mr. Fuller, however, understands 1 Mac. i. 54, as referring to this
passage, and says, ' the LXX. by its [sic] curious reading of v. 26—μετὰ ἑπτὰ
καὶ ἑβδομήκοντα καὶ ἑξήκοντα δύο, i.e. "after 139 years" (139 Seleucid æra or
B.C. 174)—refer [sic] the passage to the same period :' Excursus on the

11. The ' non-Messianic interpretation will continue false, so long as the word of Christ is true,—that is, to all eternity.' This statement is made on the ground that Matthew xxiv. 15 and Mark xiii. 14 contain an allusion to this prophecy, and ' it is quoted by the Lord as an actual prophecy which had still to be fulfilled, so far as the destruction of the city and temple was concerned.' I must not shrink from noticing this objection, though I cannot but regret that that great and holy name is dragged into a mere critical discussion. If this appeal to authority is to prohibit the exercise of our own judgments, why has Hengstenberg wearied himself and his readers with such a dreary quantity of superfluous matter? The fact is that, when it suits him, ' he does not trouble himself about the authority of the Lord ' any more than Hitzig, whom he treats with such contempt. On philological grounds he renders מְשֹׁמֵם ' destroyer,' although Christ renders it τῆς ἐρημώσεως, ' desolation,' and he does not think it incumbent on him to maintain that שִׁקּוּצִים is in the singular number because in the New Testament it is translated τὸ βδέλυγμα. To the argument, however, there are even for Christians three answers. First, it is possible to acknowledge and revere the spiritual authority of Christ without supposing that it was any part of his office to pronounce ex-cathedra judgments upon questions of

Seventy Weeks, *Speaker's Com.* vi. p. 360. According to this the *oldest* Jewish interpretation supported the modern view. The reading referred to, however, is not what is generally found in editions of the LXX. Those of Wechelius (Frankfort, 1597), of Grabe (1707-1720), of Reineccius (Leipzig, 1730), of Holmes (fourth vol. Oxford, 1827), and of Tischendorf (Leipzig, 1850) all read μετὰ τὰς ἑβδομάδας τὰς ἑξηκονταδύο, and none of them mentions the other reading. That the text of the ordinary printed LXX. agrees here with the Codex Vaticanus is confirmed by the recent fac-simile edition of that MS. by Vercellone and Cozza (Rome, 1868-72). I have found the ' curious reading ' only in a work entitled *Daniel secundum Septuaginta ex tetraplis Origenis nunc primum editus e singulari Chisiano codice annorum supra* IↃCCC. Romæ, CIↃ IↃ CCLXXII.

s 2

interpretation and criticism. Secondly, Christ does not really express any opinion about the original meaning of the prophecy. He *applies* it no doubt to the destruction which was still future ; but it is quite conceivable that he may have regarded the passage as descriptive of the time of Epiphanes, and yet have gathered from it the wider conviction that the ' abomination of desolation ' in the holy place was the sure sign of national ruin. And lastly, the passage in which the reference to Daniel occurs is one of those in which we can least be certain that his words have been correctly reported.

The general conclusion, then, at which we arrive is that the Maccabean interpretation is supported by arguments of great strength, but is opposed by a serious chronological difficulty. We must now turn to the other interpretation, and see what can be urged for and against it.

Let us look first at the more general considerations which arise from the position of the passage in the book. These are all opposed to the Messianic exposition. In addition to those already noticed we may observe the following. The chronology which is given would be utterly valueless to Daniel ; for the seventy weeks would be reckoned from an undetermined point in the future. This hardly corresponds with the profession of Gabriel, that he came to give Daniel ' skill and understanding.' Again, the prayer to which this revelation is an answer is opposed to Hengstenberg's idea that the writer fully accepted the literal and complete fulfilment of Jeremiah's prophecy. Had he done so, and been the real Daniel, he would have believed that the ' desolations of Jerusalem ' had nearly reached their allotted term. But of this there is not a sign in the prayer :—' Let thine anger and thy fury be turned away from thy city Jerusalem, thy holy

mountain ; ' ' O my God, incline thine ear and hear ;
open thine eyes, and behold our desolations, and the
city which is called by thy name. . . O Lord, forgive ;
O Lord, hearken and do ; defer not, for thine own sake,
O my God.' These are not the words of one who is
calmly trusting in the speedy fulfilment of a divine promise ;
but they exactly suit the state of mind of one who felt that
the prophecy in its plain sense did not harmonise with
the facts, and who longed to extract from it some gleam
of present hope. And yet again, the revelation made by
Gabriel is obviously intended as an answer to the prayer
for the speedy restoration of Jerusalem ; but on the
Messianic interpretation it leaves undetermined the one
thing that Daniel wanted to know, and deals instead with
things that he had not referred to. It consoles him by
telling him that the city will be irretrievably ruined, and
the sacrifices abolished for ever ; and the bald allusions
to the Messiah are not calculated to impart either comfort
or hope. Thus the evidence in favour of the Messianic
view must be found wholly within the passage itself,
and in the precision with which its various parts accom-
modate themselves to historical facts.

There are only two points in which the Messianic interpretation seems at first sight to possess a decided
advantage, and one of these vanishes on a closer examination. The first is the accuracy with which the
sixty-nine weeks fit themselves into the real chronology,
if at least Hengstenberg be right in his elaborate calculations, and if we are content to ignore the decree of Cyrus.
These particulars we need not criticise, but leave him in the
full enjoyment of his one telling argument. The second
point is that, according to this prophecy, the city and
temple are to be ' irremediably destroyed,' whereas in the
time of Epiphanes they were ' merely subjected to a severe

visitation.'[1] Now there is no statement whatever that
the destruction of the city is final, and Hengstenberg's
conclusion is merely an inference from the usage of
certain words. On the other hand, verse 24, especially
when taken in connection with the preceding prayer,
seems to imply in no doubtful way that the people and
the city were, on the expiration of seventy weeks, to
enter into the enjoyment of everlasting righteousness ;
and if we have been right in our explanation of ' a holy
of holies,' the reconsecration of the temple is expressly
referred to. We cannot escape from this plain inference
by appealing to poetic phrases, especially as Hengstenberg
himself does not deny the applicability of these phrases
to the Babylonian destruction, which was certainly not
' irremediable.' But it may be worth our while to turn
to 1st Maccabees to see whether the proceedings of
Antiochus were of such an innocuous character that the
language of Daniel could not be properly applied to them.
We are there told that ' when they [the people of Jerusa-
lem] had given him credence, he fell suddenly upon the
city, and smote it very sore, and destroyed much people
of Israel. And when he had taken the spoils of the city,
he set it on fire, and pulled down the houses and walls
thereof on every side. But the women and children
took they captive, and possessed the cattle.'[2] The
' sanctuary was laid waste like a wilderness.'[3] This
disaster was regarded as a judgment. The dying
Mattathias said to his sons, ' Now hath pride and rebuke
gotten strength, and the time of destruction, and the
wrath of indignation,' and he therefore exhorts them to
be ' zealous for the law ; '[4] and Judas turned ' away
wrath from Israel ' by ' destroying the ungodly.'[5]

---

[1] P. 263. [2] i. 30–32. [3] ἠρημώθη ὡς ἔρημος, i. 39. See also ii. 12.
[4] ii. 40. [5] iii. 8.

Meanwhile 'Jerusalem lay void as a wilderness,[1] . . . the sanctuary also was trodden down.'[2] The people looked upon this as a terrible affliction. On their return to the ruined city, ' when they saw the sanctuary desolate,[3] and the altar profaned, and the gates burnt up, and shrubs growing in the courts as in a forest or on one of the mountains, yea, and the priests' chambers pulled down ; they rent their clothes, and made great lamentation, and cast ashes upon their heads.'[4] As the altar had been defiled, they thought it best to pull it down, and build a new one,[5] and ' new holy vessels ' had to be made.[6] The rebuilding of the fortifications is also expressly mentioned.[7] It is clear, therefore, that the Syrian treatment of Jerusalem was not a mere temporary occupation, which could not be justly compared with the Babylonian and Roman destructions. It aimed at the utter ruin of the Jewish polity ;[8] the fortifications of the city were levelled with the ground, the houses were burned or pulled down ; and if the shell of the sanctuary was left standing amid its desolations, it was only that it might be 'trodden down' with unholy feet, and 'profaned' with the heathen 'abomination of desolation.'[9] There is nothing, then, in the language of Daniel which is too strong to describe

[1] Ἔρημος.   [2] iii. 45. See also 51.
[3] Ἠρημωμένον.   [4] iv. 38, 39.
[5] iv. 44-7.   [6] iv. 49.
[7] iv. 60 ; vi. 7.   [8] i. 41-53.

[9] i. 54; see also vi. 7. Yet all this becomes with Dr. Pusey,—' shall fire some houses in the city, yet leaving it, as a whole, unhurt and inhabited as before [for which he refers to i. 38 and 55], and displacing not one stone or ornament of the temple, nay nor touching it ; for the idol-altar was built on the brazen altar outside' (p. 228). On this I forbear to remark, beyond stating that the account of i. 38 is that ' the inhabitants of Jerusalem fled on account of them, and it became a habitation of foreigners.' But before this we are informed that the enemy, after their destruction of the houses, ' built the city of David with a great wall,' and placed there a sinful nation, apparently to act as a garrison : i. 33, 34. That is, part of the city was spared for military purposes.

this invasion, which in its purposes was the most formidable that the Jews ever experienced, and in its actual results was fraught with calamities, which ' poured down' upon the desolate sanctuary, and had come upon the city with the sudden violence of a ' flood.' [1] Hengstenberg's argument therefore falls to the ground.

We must now ask how far the Messianic interpretation really answers to the statements in the text. The following considerations seem to me completely fatal to it. In order to estimate them at their full value we must remember that, by the hypothesis, this is a miraculous prophecy, and therefore, if its claims are to be sustained, it must be perfectly accurate in every part. You cannot defend your prophet by pleading errors which might be venial in an historian.

1. The Messianic kingdom did not begin, as stated in verse 24, nor was Christ anointed at the end of seventy weeks, but at the end of sixty-nine. It is no answer to say, with Hengstenberg,[2] that the prophecy was not fulfilled till ' the people of the covenant' personally appropriated the proffered reconciliation, and that Christ's anointing must be extended to the opening period of the Christian Church. This sort of answer would be equally good if the seventy had been seven hundred or seven thousand. What was there exactly seven years after Christ's baptism that we should say he had not been really anointed till then? Is it an orthodox dogma that Christ was anointed three years and a half after the ascension?

2. There is nothing in the text to account for the division of the sixty-nine weeks into seven and sixty-two. It is very easy to assume that the seven weeks are meant

---

[1] I am content to leave Hengstenberg the benefit of the doubt as to the reference of ' the flood.'

[2] P. 127.

for the building of the city ; but there is not a word to
that effect, and there is no historical reason for assigning
to it exactly that time.

3. Christ was not cut off till some time had elapsed
after the expiration of the sixty-two weeks, but it is certainly implied in the text that 'an anointed' was to be
cut off at the close of that period.   Thus verse 26 makes
his death contemporaneous with his appearance, and 27
makes it three years and a half later.   Dr. Pusey, oblivious
of the difficulty which he thus creates, says, 'Once, in the
future, at the end of the seventy weeks, there should be
an atoning for all iniquity.' [1]   Yet according to his own
interpretation, the atoning took place, not at the end of
seventy weeks, but in the middle of the seventieth.

4. The destruction of Jerusalem by the Romans did
not take place at the end of the sixty-two weeks, or
indeed till a considerable time after the close of the
seventy.   To say that 'when Christ was put to death
Jerusalem ceased to be the holy city,' [2] is no answer ; for
that is not what the prophecy is supposed to affirm, but
that the army of Titus will come and destroy the city ;
and this event was not coincident with Christ's death, and
still less with his baptism.   This interpretation, therefore,
makes Daniel a false prophet.

5. Christ did not cause the sacrifices to cease at the
time of his death.   Here it may be said with some
plausibility, that the sacrificial rites ceased 'so far as
everything essential was concerned.' [3]   But the prophecy
has all the appearance of relating to the objective fact ;
and we cannot suppose that a prophet who knew the
exact time of Christ's death would indicate it only by
connecting it, to the great confusion of his readers, with
an event which took place long afterwards.   The sacrifices

[1] P. 179.   [2] Hengst. p. 166.   [3] Ibid.

were stopped by the soldiers of Titus; and if we are to judge from the rest of the book, this kind of hostile stoppage is the only one which Daniel could have anticipated.

6. Hengstenberg can assign no meaning whatever to the second half of the last week. He tries to account in a sort of way for sixty-nine and a half weeks; but the prophecy speaks of seventy, and as no intelligible reason can be given for fixing on the middle of the fourth year after Christ's death as the moment when everlasting righteousness should be brought in, the interpretation breaks down hopelessly in a most essential point. Hengstenberg's lame suggestion is that 'the terminal point of the confirmation of the covenant is, more or less, a vanishing one, and therefore does not admit of being chronologically determined, with any minute precision.'[1] But unfortunately the prophet does determine it with minute precision, and fixes on a point of time distinguished by no historical event. Dr. Pusey thinks 'the remaining 3½ years probably mark the time during which the Gospel was preached to the Jews, before the preaching to the Samaritans showed that the special privileges of the Jews were at an end, and that the Gospel embraced the world. We have not,' he adds, 'the chronological data to fix it.'[2] Those who think that the grand climax of Daniel's prophecies was 'the preaching to the Samaritans' are probably beyond the reach of argument.

7. It is, as we have already observed, clearly implied in verse 24 that the people of Daniel and the holy city, and, for anything that appears, they alone are to enjoy the blessings which are promised after the lapse of seventy weeks.

[1] P. 240.   [2] P. 170.

These objections, which singly are very weighty, appear to me, when taken in combination, to be perfectly conclusive. The Maccabean interpretation, therefore, is left without a rival; and accordingly we are justified in accepting it, even though we cannot satisfactorily dispose of the chronological difficulty.

Our general conclusion, then, is that the Book of Daniel, though it portrays an ideal kingdom, fails to place its sovereignty in the hands of a Messiah.

In the Book of Wisdom there is one passage to which a Messianic interpretation has been given. It is that in which the treatment of the righteous man by the wicked is described.[1] Bad and unbelieving men are represented as expressing their hatred of one who is just, because he reproves their evil ways; and this just person has been supposed to be the Messiah. The closing verses[2] are the most significant :—' He pronounceth the end of the just to be blessed, and maketh his boast that God is his Father. Let us see if his words be true : and let us prove what shall happen in the end of him. For if the just man be the son of God, he will help him, and deliver him from the hand of his enemies. Let us examine him with despitefulness and torture, that we may know his meekness and prove his patience. Let us condemn him with a shameful death.' It is not surprising that these words were applied to Christ; but it is quite evident that in the original connection the righteous man is simply the representative of a class, and that no particular individual is alluded to. The absence of the Messiah from this book might seem to be less significant than in the case of Daniel, because the future glory of the righteous appears in a much less definite shape. Nevertheless that glory is so

[1] ii. 10–20.   [2] 16–20.

distinctly alluded to that a writer who held the Messianic hope could hardly have failed to utter it. He insists on the immortality of the righteous, and predicts that 'they shall judge the nations, and have dominion over the people, and their Lord shall reign for ever,'[1] and that they shall 'receive a glorious kingdom, and a beautiful crown from the Lord's hand.'[2] Nothing would have been more natural than to blend with these anticipations some allusion to the coming of the Messiah and the establishment of his rule; and we must therefore suppose either that the author did not entertain the Messianic hope, or that it occupied such a subordinate place in his mind that he did not think it worth mentioning.

In the first Book of Maccabees we similarly fail to discover the Messiah. Appeal has been made to ii. 57, where Mattathias, in reminding his sons of ancient examples of virtue, says, 'David in his mercy inherited the throne of a kingdom for ever;' but the most that we could infer from this is that Mattathias expected the royal line of David to be restored, and to rule without further interruption, and he might not unsuitably have referred to the Messiah as the great restorer, had he believed in him. Two other passages also are cited, in which reference is made to the future coming of a prophet. In the first[3] it is said that the people put away the stones of the old altar, which they had pulled down on account of its defilement, 'until a prophet should come to give answer concerning them.' In the second[4] we are told that 'the Jews and the priests were well pleased that Simon should be governor and high-priest for ever until a faithful prophet should arise.' In both instances the word 'prophet' is without the article, and the passages express nothing

---

[1] iii. 8.   [2] v. 16.
[3] iv. 46.   [4] xiv. 41.

more than the hope that the gift of prophecy, which had passed away, might be at some time restored.

Equally silent about the Messiah is the second Book of Maccabees, though the author expresses his earnest hope that the scattered Israelites will soon be brought together, through the divine pity, into the sacred place.[1] We shall see farther on that the Messianic idea was not altogether unknown to the Maccabean period; but it is certainly remarkable that it should appear only in a couple of dreamy or poetic books, the Book of Enoch and the Sibylline Oracles, while it is conspicuously absent not only from historical and didactic works, but from the great prophetical utterance of the age. We must conclude that it was just beginning to shape itself dimly in enthusiastic minds, and had not yet been accepted as a popular faith. The speedy triumph of the Maccabees satisfied for a time the aspirations of the people; and a longer period of suffering and disappointment was needed to develope the hope of a Messiah into a passion among the masses of the nation, and into a doctrine in the schools of the learned.

The Assumption of Moses is another book where we look in vain for the belief in a Messiah; for Hilgenfeld's notion that he is to be found in Taxo[2] is too whimsical to require serious notice.[3] We cannot, of course, tell what the author may have said in the portion of the work which has not survived; but in x. 26–28 he declares that God's kingdom will appear, and that God will come and take vengeance on the Gentiles, and exalt Israel to the stars, so that he could not have had a more suitable place for introducing the Messiah. We may with much probability conclude that he was not one of those who accepted the Messianic belief.

---

[1] ii. 18.　　　　[2] ix. 24, 25.　　　　[3] *Mess. Jud.* p. 467.

The Book of Jubilees is equally destitute of all traces of the Messiah. It is remarkable that the writer omits the blessings which Jacob pronounced upon his sons, though these would have opened to him a fine field for eschatological excursions. He just touches the tempting theme, but makes no disclosure of future events:— 'Israel blessed his sons before he died, and told them everything that should happen to them in the land of Egypt, and that should come upon them in the last days; he told them everything, and blessed them.'[1] It is extremely disappointing that we have not his exposition of the prophecy about Judah, and one cannot but suppose that there was some purpose in the omission. I can hardly help suspecting that he passed over this portion of Genesis on account of its accepted Messianic meaning, which he did not approve, and yet was not willing openly to contradict, and on account of its curse on Levi; for he invents blessings of his own for Levi and Judah, and, to avoid the obvious inconsistency with Genesis, puts them into the mouth of Isaac. In these, Levi takes the first place. His descendants are to be 'lords and princes and presidents to the holy seed of the children of Jacob.' They are to 'speak the word of the Lord,' and to tell his ways to Jacob, and are to stand nearest to the Lord. Judah also is to take a high position, but one political rather than religious. He is to tread down all who hate him. He is to be a lord over the sons of Jacob, he and one of his sons. His name, and the name of his sons, is to overspread the earth, and he is to be the terror of the Gentiles. Through him help and deliverance are to come to Israel, and, when he sits on the throne of honour, his righteousness shall be great.[2] This is certainly like a deliberate omission of the Messianic doctrine.

[1] Ch. xlv.   [2] Ch. xxxi.

There are also several other passages relating to the future of Israel in which the author, had he accepted this doctrine, might have been expected to introduce it.[1]

Turning to a different class of literature, we must notice two passages of Philo's, in which some have supposed that there is a reference to the Messiah. The first is in the *De Exsecrationibus*, § 9. Philo is speaking of the sudden reformation of the Israelites scattered among their enemies in all parts of the world, and their consequent return to their own land; and he says that they will be 'led by an appearance[2] more divine than the naturally human, invisible indeed to others, and manifest to those only who are being saved.' Dähne assumes that this superhuman leader is the Messiah; and from the analogy between the appearance here described, and the pillar of cloud and fire which led the Israelites through the wilderness, and which Philo allegorized into the Logos, he thinks it not improbable that the Logos is referred to in the present passage, and that thus the identification of the Logos with the Messiah was made by Philo.[3] Gfrörer is much more confident that the Logos is intended, but does not admit that he was identified by Philo with the Messiah.[4] It seems to me that the true effect of this passage is to induce a doubt whether Philo believed in a Messiah at all. If he entertained such a belief, this is certainly an occasion on which we should expect to find it clearly expressed. But this vision,

---

[1] Ch. i. S. 232; ch. xix. S. 16; ch. xxi. S. 19; chs. xxii., xxiii., and ch. xxxii. S. 42. Among the apocalyptic works the fourth book of the *Sib. Oracles* also is without a Messiah, notwithstanding its eschatological passages, which will be noticed farther on. This is the more remarkable as it belongs to the same period as Fourth Ezra and the Apoc. of Baruch.

[2] Ὄψεως.

[3] *Geschichtliche Darstellung der jüdisch-alexandrinischen Religions-Philosophie*, 1834, i. S. 437–8.

[4] *Philo u. d. al. Theos.* i. S. 528–530.

apparently of human form, but supernatural in its lineaments, and invisible to all but the sons of Israel, fulfilling
moreover the sole function of guide to the Holy Land,
does not correspond with any accepted type of the
Messiah.

The other passage to which appeal is made seems at
first sight to offer a more certain testimony. It occurs
in the course of a long eschatological description in the
De Praemiis et Poenis, § 16. Referring to the final overthrow of those who disturb the world's peace, Philo says,
'For a man shall go forth, says the oracle, leading an
army and waging war, and shall conquer great and populous nations,[1] God having sent upon his saints a fitting
help. Now this is undaunted courage of soul and the
mightiest strength of body, of which either is terrible to
enemies, but, if both be united, they are absolutely irresistible.' In this conquering warrior Gfrörer[2] and
Schürer[3] find the Messiah. But it should be observed
that the individual warrior is mentioned only in the quotation from Numbers; and if, with Oehler,[4] we regard
what follows as an explanation of the oracle, he is immediately allegorized into a mere symbol of courage and
strength. Throughout the whole passage there is not, in
Philo's own words, a single allusion to the Messiah ; and
I must therefore regard it as the most probable conclusion that, while Philo shared in the ideal hopes of his
race, he did not expect these hopes to be concentrated
and fulfilled in any supreme personality.

Even among the later teachers the belief in the
Messiah encountered some opposition. It is related that
when R. Akiba acknowledged the Messiahship of Bar-

---

[1] This is taken loosely from the LXX. ; Num. xxiv. 7.
[2] *Philo u. d. al. Theos.* i. S. 530.
[3] *Lehrb. d. n. Zeity.* S. 575.   [4] Herzog, *Messias*, S. 425.

Cochba, Rabbi Yochanan ben Toretha said to him, 'Grass will grow on thy cheeks, and the Son of David will not have come.'[1] At a still later period R. Hillel (that is, Hillel II. who lived in the time of Constantine [2]) said, 'There will be no Messiah for Israel, because they have enjoyed him already in the days of Hezekiah.' Rab Yoseph, however, refuted this :—'May God pardon R. Hillel. When was Hezekiah? In the first house [during the time of the first Temple]; but Zechariah prophesied in the second house,' allusion being made to the prophecy that Israel's king should come sitting on an ass.[3]

The above evidence, when fairly construed, seems sufficient to prove that the belief in a Messiah was far from being universally entertained among the Jews, especially before the time of Christ. Nor can we say that it was rejected only by some particular party; for we have failed to discover it in apocalyptic, haggadistic, didactic, historical, and philosophical works, and have found it disputed even in the schools of the Rabbis. But now we must turn our attention to those books in which it receives a more or less complete recognition.

[1] Jer. Ta'anith iv. 8 (5 in the modern editions).

[2] The accuracy of this statement is open to question, but need not be here discussed.

[3] *Synhed.* 99*a*.

Messianismus und Mysterienreligion.

Von I. H e i n e m a n n in Breslau.

> Es wandert eine schöne Sage
> Wie Veilchenduft auf Erden um;
> Wie sehnend eine Liebesklage,
> Geht sie bei Tag und Nacht herum.
> Das ist das Lied vom Völkerfrieden
> Und von der Menschheit letztem Glück;
> Von goldner Zeit, die einst hienieden —
> Der Traum als Wahrheit kehrt zurück;
> Wo ewig alle Völker beten
> Zu einem König, Gott und Hirt;
> Von jenem Tag, wo den Propheten
> Ihr göttlich Recht gesprochen wird.

Mit diesen Worten Gottfried Kellers schließt Eduard Norden[1] sein Buch „Die Geburt des Kindes", das zur Deutung der Zukunftshoffnungen eines römischen Dichters die Eschatologie ägyptischer und griechischer Mysterien, jüdischer Prophetien und urchristlicher Lehren heranzuziehen sucht. Aber wenn das Dichterwort dafür spricht, daß allenthalben, wo Menschen wohnen, eben aus der gemeinsamen Wurzel des Menschentums die verwandte Hoffnung aufsprießt, so glaubt Norden in Anknüpfung an ältere, weit zurückhaltendere Annahmen, daß zwischen diesen Eschatologien unmittelbare u r s ä c h l i c h e Beziehungen bestehen, daß insbesondere ein ägyptisches Mysterium von einem göttlichen Erlöserkinde ihnen zugrunde liegt und auf den jüdischen wie den hellenistisch-römischen Kulturkreis gewirkt hat. So wird die geschichtliche Beziehung zwischen Vergil und Jesaja, an die das Mittelalter glaubte, in ungeahnter Weise wieder erneuert, wenn auch in völlig neuer Form: die Uebereinstimmung beider, die zur Erhebung Vergils unter die Propheten führte, beruht nicht darauf, daß beide Christus geweissagt hätten, also nicht auf dem gleichen Blicke in die Zukunft, sondern auf der Wirkung der gleichen Vergangenheit, des gleichen Zaubers uralter Mysterienweisheit.

Es gehört zu den unvermeidlichen Schwächen kulturvergleichender Untersuchungen, wie der vorliegenden, daß sie den Forscher nötigen, über sein Fachgebiet hinauszugehen und sich auf Forschungsgebiete zu wagen, deren Quellen ihm nicht zugänglich sind. Norden ist einer unserer führenden klassischen Philologen; und doch bildet die Altertumswissenschaft nur e i n e n Pfeiler seines Gebäudes, die Hebraistik den anderen — und die Orientalistik den Bogen, der beide überspannt und verbindet. Den gleichen Bogen hat inzwischen,

---

[1] Nur mit Verfassernamen werden im folgenden angeführt: Eduard N o r d e n , Die Geburt des Kindes. Studien der Bibliothek Warburg III, Leipzig und Berlin, Teubner, 1924, 171 S. — Wilhelm W e b e r , Der Prophet und sein Gott, Beihefte zum Alten Orient Heft 3, Leipzig, Hinrichs, 1925, 158 S. — R. K i t t e l , Die hellenistische Mysterienreligion und das Alte Testament, Beiträge zur Wiss. vom A. T. Neue Folge, Heft 7, Berlin, Stuttgart, Leipzig, W. Kohlhammer, 1924, 100 S. — L. D ü r r , Ursprung und Ausbau der israelitisch-jüdischen Heilandserwartung, Berlin, Schwetschke, 1925, 161 S.

vom hebraistischen Ufer her, Rudolf Kittel zu spannen gesucht. Wir versuchen im folgenden, über ihre Forschungen kritisch zu berichten — unter gleichzeitiger Berücksichtigung der altphilologischen und der hebraistischen Grundlegung. Wir beschränken uns demgemäß — zugleich dem Interessengebiet dieser Zeitschrift entsprechend — auf die Grundfrage: f i n d e n s i c h i m — biblischen und nachbiblischen — J u d e n t u m Spuren derselben E r l ö -s u n g s l e h r e, die auch auf das k l a s s i s c h e A l t e r t u m gewirkt hat?

Hören wir zunächst Kittel und Norden, die — im Beweisgang und in Einzelergebnissen von einander abweichend — beide zu einer b e j a h e n d e n Antwort gelangen.

Vergil weissagt in der vierten Ekloge das unmittelbare Bevorstehen einer Zeit des Friedens und Segens in Menschen- und Tierreich im Anschluß an die bevorstehende Geburt eines Knaben. Unter diesem Knaben verstand das Mittelalter Jesus, und in der Tat darf man nach Norden nicht auf einen Prinzen oder einen Sohn des angeredeten Konsuls Pollio raten: der Knabe, der als „Sohn des Juppiter" angeredet und nach der letzten Zeile des Gedichtes „zur Tischgemeinschaft mit Göttern, zur Lagergemeinschaft mit einer Göttin" berufen ist, muß ein überirdisches Wesen sein[1]. Woher hat nun der Dichter diese — ebenso unrömische wie ungriechische — Vorstellung des Götterkindes als Friedensbringer? Norden antwortet: aus der ä g y p t i s c h e n Eschatologie. Von hier aus hat sich die Verehrung des kindlichen Gottes Har = Horus verbreitet; die befremdlichen Wendungen, daß das Götterkind „die Taten seines göttlichen Vaters lesen" (Norden 134 ff.) und „Leben empfangen" werde (Norden 121), entsprechen genau ägyptischer Redeweise. Nun weist aber Norden mit großem Scharfsinn darauf hin, daß Vergil z w e i Z e i t p u n k t e unterscheidet, zwischen welche der Amtsantritt des Konsuls Pollio fällt: einen bereits e i n g e t r e t e n e n, an welchem Apollon = Helios die Herrschaft übernommen hat (*tuus iam regnat Apollo*), einen zukünftigen, jedoch unmittelbar b e v o r -s t e h e n d e n, an welchem das Götterkind, zugleich aber eine „neue Weltordnung geboren werden wird". Auch diese Teilung wird aus Aegypten verständlich. Nach dem Bericht des Kirchenvaters Epiphanios (Norden 24 ff.) feierte man in Alexandrien das Geburtsfest des Sonnengottes am 24/5. Dezember durch einen mystischen Akt, bei dem die Gemeinde in die Worte ausbrach: „Die Jungfrau hat geboren: zunimmt das Licht". Ein zweites Fest wurde, gleichfalls in Alexandrien, in der Nacht vom 5/6. Januar begangen; diesmal lautete nach Epiphanios der Ruf: „zu dieser Stunde gebar heute die Jungfrau den A i o n", d. h. die (neue) Zeit. Beide Feste, schließt Norden weiter, müssen aus vorchristlicher Zeit stammen. Das erste Fest hieß Kikellia: und ein Fest dieses Namens — ohne Angaben über seinen Ritus — finden wir bereits im Jahre 239/8 v. Ch. (Norden 25). Aber — so schließt Norden weiter

---

[1] Auch wenn man Nordens Erklärung nicht in vollem Umfang anerkennt (vgl. Deubner, Gnomon I 166 ff.), sind natürlich mythische Züge in Vergils Bilde unbestreitbar; und nur darauf kommt es für das folgende an.

— auch die Verlegung des C h a n u k k a f e s t e s auf den 25.
Kislew, der etwa dem 25. Dezember entspricht, erklärt sich am
einleuchtendsten durch die Annahme, daß ein Sonnwendfest übernommen und umgestaltet worden ist. Und den Mythos von der
jungfräulichen Mutter, meint Norden, kennt bereits Philon. Ja,
wir können vielleicht in erheblich frühere Zeiten zurückgehen. Jene
beiden, zeitlich nahen und im Ritual verwandten Feste scheinen
aus einer einzigen Feier erwachsen zu sein. Nun hat man berechnet,
daß bei der Neugründung des ägyptischen mittleren Reiches i. J.
1996 die Wintersonnenwende etwa auf den 6. Januar jul. Kal. fiel
(Norden 38); im 4. vorchristlichen Jahrhundert fiel es auf den 24/5.
Dezember. Aus der doppelten Feier der Sonnenwende am richtigen
und am kirchlich überlieferten Tage wäre also die Doppelfeier erwachsen.

Diese uralte ägyptische Lehre von der Geburt des Sonnengottes
und einer neuen Zeit um die Wintersonnenwende hat also nach
Norden dreimal auf das Judentum gewirkt: auf J e s a j a s Bot-
schaft vom Knaben Immanuel als Bringer eines „neuen Aion", auf
die M a k k a b ä e r bei der Festsetzung des Chanukkafestes und
auf P h i l o n s allegorische Schrifterklärung.

Diese Forschungen führt Rudolf K i t t e l als Alttestamentler
weiter. Er läßt die Philonstellen beiseite; in der Chanukkafrage
äußert er sich kurz zustimmend; vor allem faßt er die Jesajastelle
ins Auge. Zunächst sei die griechische U e b e r s e t z u n g Jes 7₁₁,
nach welcher „die Jungfrau" den Immanuel gebären wird, von dem
Mysterienglauben an jungfräuliche Mütter beeinflußt. Aber der
Ruf des Hierophanten in Eleusis: „einen heiligen Knaben hat die
Herrin geboren, die Starke einen Starken" (wie ihn Kittel zitiert),
spricht dafür, daß schon J e s a j a , der „ein junges Weib" zur Mutter
eines Heldensohnes macht, unter dem Einfluß der Mystik steht.
Ja, schon vorprophetische Vorstellungen erhalten aus den Mysterienreligionen ihre Erklärung: Abrahams אל עולם Gen 21₃₃ bedeutet
„Gott Ewigkeit" und ist mit jenem Gott Aion identisch, dem wir
bereits begegneten. Aber auch die Hoffnung auf Verleihung von
„Licht" und „Leben" durch Gott und auf ein jenseitiges Weiter-
leben in Gemeinschaft mit ihm, die wir in manchen Psalmen vor-
auszusetzen haben (Kittel 92 f.), könnte von der Mysteriensprache
und -lehre beeinflußt sein — so wesentlich und bedeutungsvoll
natürlich die Unterschiede zwischen „diesem vermutungsweise an-
genommenen jüdischen" und dem hellenischen Mysterienglauben
offenbar sind (Kittel 95 f.).

Eine so tiefgehende Beeinflussung des antiken Judentums durch
die Mysterienreligionen, wie Norden und Kittel sie annehmen, wird
der jüdische Leser, der den Blick auf die Gesamterscheinung des
Judentums gerichtet hält, keinesfalls von vornherein für unwahrscheinlich halten. So hätten sich beide Forscher wohl auf den Zu-
satz der LXX zu Deut 23₁₈ (₁₇), der die Teilnahme an Mysterien
verbietet, zum Beweise dafür berufen können, daß schon im Altertum die Mysterienreligionen eine gewisse Anziehungskraft auf jüdische
Kreise übten. Und für das Mittelalter ist eine Wechselwirkung
zwischen Mystik und Judentum erwiesen. Daß in der Kabbala und

22*

in ihren Vorläufern, also insbesondere im Buch Jezira, sehr viel hellenistische Mystik steckt, bedarf für den, der mit gnostischen und neupythagoreischen Vorstellungen vertraut ist, wenn auch noch immer der Darlegung im einzelnen, so doch nicht mehr des grundsätzlichen Beweises. Aber weit über die Kreise der eigentlichen Mystiker hinaus hat der Glaube an zauberkräftige Namen[1], hat Buchstaben-[2] und Zahlenmystik und vor allem der Glaube an geheime astrologische Zusammenhänge trotz des Einspruchs großer Rationalisten auf die Philosophie, die Bibelerklärung, ja, die volkstümliche Redeweise[3] des Judentums gewirkt. Unter dem Einfluß der hermetischen Schriften steht, wie zwei der besten Kenner der Philosophie des jüdischen Mittelalters erwiesen haben[4], eine psychologische Schrift, die den gefeierten Namen des Bachja ibn Pakuda trug; gleiches gilt, wie ich demnächst an anderer Stelle zeigen zu können hoffe[5], von einem Abschnitt der echten Hauptschrift dieses Denkers. Und auch wenn neuere Vermutungen über den Einfluß ägyptischer und iranischer Erlösungsmysterien auf Philon von Alexandrien nicht ausreichend begründet scheinen, so wird man doch fragen müssen, ob das starke Ueberwiegen des Jenseitsgedankens im nachbiblischen Judentum, verglichen mit dem biblischen, ob also etwa die Auffassung dieser Welt als Vorhalle zu jener (Abot IV 16), nicht mit einer Jenseitsstimmung in Zusammenhang steht, die von den Mysterienreligionen her auf Philosophie und Frömmigkeit des ausgehenden Altertums Einfluß gewann. — Aber wie die Mystik der Umwelt auf das Judentum, so hat umgekehrt die Kabbala stark auf nichtjüdische Kreise gewirkt; es hat also eben die Wechselwirkung im Mittelalter stattgefunden, die namentlich Kittel für das Altertum vermutet.

Allein gerade der Vergleich zwischen diesen und den für das Altertum behaupteten Beziehungen führt bei näherem Zusehen zu starken Bedenken. Für das Mittelalter sind die V o r s t e l l u n g e n a l s s o l c h e sicher bezeugt, z. T. sogar, wie bei den Wirkungen der Kabbala auf die Renaissance, die Brücken zwischen der jüdischen und der nichtjüdischen Welt. Dagegen findet sich für diejenigen mystischen Vorstellungen, deren Abhängigkeit vom Heidentum Norden und Kittel behaupten, n i c h t e i n e i n z i g e s v ö l l i g s i c h e r e s Z e u g n i s. Aionkultus, Sonnenwendfest, Götterkind — von diesen Begriffen ist im Judentum an keiner unzweideutigen Stelle die Rede, insbesondere nicht in Verbindung mit der messianischen Hoffnung, von der doch wahrlich oft genug gesprochen wird. Philon z. B., der doch auch als Kronzeuge für Nordens An-

---

[1] Vgl. B. Jacob, Im Namen Gottes, vor allem auch über den Einfluß der ägyptischen Namensspekulation.

[2] Dornseiff, Das Alphabet[2] 1925 (dazu MGWJ 1923, 279).

[3] Der astrologische Ursprung von מזל טוב wird freilich kaum deutlicher empfunden als bei Laune, jovial oder Humor.

[4] D. Kaufmann, Studien über Gabirol (1899) 54, 1; Goldziher, Abh. d. Gött. Ges. d. W. 1907, 9*.

[5] In einer Arbeit über die Frage nach dem Sinn des Lebens in der hellenistischen und jüdischen Philosophie, die voraussichtlich als Beilage zum nächsten Jahresbericht des Jüdisch-theologischen Seminars in Breslau erscheinen wird.

sicht aufgerufen wird, entwickelt seine Lehre von der Heilszeit ohne jede Anspielung auf dergleichen[1]. Allgemeiner wird man sagen dürfen, daß im Judentum — mag man an die Bildersprache der Bibel oder an die Verirrungen astralen Glaubens denken — die Sonne kaum eine größere Bedeutung gewonnen hat als andere Himmelskörper und keinesfalls in der Weise dominiert, wie in Aegypten seit Chuenaten; auch was Philon über sie sagt, entstammt griechischer Lehre, die, mag sie orientalisch beeinflußt sein, in streng wissenschaftlicher Beobachtung ihre Rechtfertigung suchte[2]. Angenommen also, Norden und Kittel hätten in vollem Umfange Recht, so stünde es mit diesen Keimen, die in das Judentum eingedrungen wären, ganz anders als etwa mit der Astrologie: sie hätten sich nicht entwickelt, sondern derart „verkapselt", wie es die Aerzte wohl nennen, daß der Körper irgend welche Spuren ihrer Wirkung nicht gemerkt hat.

Aber freilich: unmöglich wäre das nicht. Wir haben daher in die Prüfung der einzelnen Aufstellungen einzutreten.

1. Der Gott Aion. Daß der israelitische Monotheismus „keinen Untergott neben Jhv" anerkennen kann, gibt Kittel S. 79 zu. Aber nach seiner Ansicht sind El Betel, El schaddai, Chaj roî, El eljon und El ʻolam lokale Gottheiten der alten Kanaaniter, die „mit Jhv verschmolzen wurden, der ihre Eigenschaften annahm" (S. 76). Danach wäre der El ʻolam — wenn Kittel recht hätte — nicht als israelitische, sondern als vorisraelitische Gottheit anzusehen, von der jedoch der Gott Israels die Eigenschaft der Ueberlegenheit über zeitliche Schranken „angenommen hätte".

Nun ist leider in keiner Weise zu zeigen, daß el ʻolam mehr zu bedeuten braucht als „der Gott der Urzeit", der, wie Kittel die herkömmliche Ansicht ganz richtig ausdrückt, „aus grauer Vorzeit in die Gegenwart hinein — und aus ihr in die ferne Zukunft hinüberreicht". Das wäre der Begriff eines ewigen Gottes, wie er schon für die „Unsterblichen" bei Homer vorausgesetzt werden darf, aber noch lange kein „Gott der Zeit". Gegen die Wiedergabe mit „Gott Ewigkeit" bei Kittel (S. 77 unten und 78) wären sogar schwerste grammatische Bedenken geltend zu machen, wenn sie etwa als Uebersetzung gemeint wäre[3]. Und wenn Damaskios als phönizischen Gott die „nichtalternde Zeit" nennt, so gehört Mut dazu, aus einer Notiz des 6. nachchristlichen Jahrhunderts auf vorprophetische Vorstellungen — eines Nachbarvolkes zu schließen. Wenn endlich Philon von Byblos den El der Phönizier mit „Kronos, dem Sohn des Uranos und seiner Schwester Ge" gleichsetzt, so beweist dieser Synkretismus nicht einmal, daß er diesen Kronos für einen Gott Chronos, einen Gott der Zeit, gehalten hat, wohl aber wird, gerade

---

[1] Vgl. B r é h i e r s Darstellung, Les idées de Philon 2 ff.

[2] Vgl. Heinemann, Poseidonios' metaph. Schriften I 128, 2, wo auf weiteres verwiesen ist; dazu Dieterich, Abraxas 54 und über Poseidonios' Lehre von der Sonne Reinhardt, Poseidonios 132, 205.|

[3] Nach den Analogien für Bezeichnung von Göttern und Königen müßte es האל עולם oder noch besser עולם האל heißen. Flußbezeichnungen wie נהר פרת stehen auf anderem Blatt.

durch Kittels Verwertung dieser Nachricht, anschaulich, wieso sich die Annahme eines phönizischen Zeitgottes bilden konnte.

Aber selbst angenommen, die Kanaanäer hätten einen Gott Ewigkeit gehabt — kann Kittel im Ernst meinen, die Huldigung des 90. Psalms an den Gott, der von Ewigkeit zu Ewigkeit waltet, sei nur durch „Uebernahme" dieser Gottesvorstellung zu erklären? Der Gott Israels ist erhaben über die Zeit, wie über den Raum; und so wenig wie seine Allgegenwart, so wenig brauchte man seine Ewigkeit aus dem Heidentum zu lernen. Gerade der 90. Psalm zeigt, wie aus dem schmerzlichen Bewußtsein der zeitlichen Beschränkung alles menschlichen Daseins der ehrfurchtsvolle Aufblick zu dem aller Schranke entzogenen Gott erwächst.

2. Das Sonnwendfest Chanukka. Bekanntlich erklären die Makkabäerbücher[1], denen Josephus und Megillat Taanit zustimmen, die Einsetzung des Chanukkafestes auf den 25. Kislew rein geschichtlich: an diesem Tage sei der Altar von Antiochos verunreinigt, an ihm wieder geweiht worden. Wellhausen[2] hatte jedoch die Ueberlieferung angefochten, weil sie „schwankend" sei — in dem Brief II Makk 1_{18} werde die Altarweihe durch Nehemia auf dies Datum verlegt — und den Festritus nicht ausreichend erkläre; da nun II Makk 6_8 von einem Dionysosfest die Rede ist, zu dessen Feier die Juden gezwungen wurden, so meint er, an diesem Tage habe ein heidnisches Fest stattgefunden, das man später judaisiert und „entgiftet" habe. Norden S. 26 stimmt ihm im allgemeinen zu, weist aber den in der Tat merkwürdigen Versuch zurück, diesen Dionysos mit dem Zeus Olympios zu identifizieren, dem der Altar geweiht wurde: das ursprüngliche Fest sei einer Sonnengottheit gewidmet gewesen und „kann sehr wohl wesensverwandt mit dem alexandrinischen" Sonnwendfeste gewesen sein. Kittel S. 20 glaubt zwar, daß das Entweihungsdatum verläßlich sei und auf guter Ueberlieferung beruhe; aber der Grund für die Vornahme der Entweihung am Sonnwendtage könne nur sein, daß Antiochos ein altes Sonnwendfest habe begehen wollen; überdies spreche der Name Chanukka für Zusammenhang mit Chanoch, der 365 Jahre alt geworden (Gen 5_{23}), also wohl als Sonnenheros zu betrachten sei.

In der Tat liegt zum Zweifel an dem Entweihungsdatum — mindestens daran, daß an diesem Tage irgend ein besonders verletzender Akt im Tempel vorging — nicht der geringste Anlaß vor. So sehr man bekanntlich geneigt war, auf bestehende Trauertage, wie den 17. Tammus oder den 9. Ab, traurige Ereignisse der Geschichte zu verlegen[3] — offensichtlich aus dem Glauben an den Charakter bestimmter Tage heraus[4], aus dem sich auch die Erzählungen von Fertigstellung des Stiftszeltes[5] und der Tempelweihe des Nehemia am

---

[1] I 4_{52} ff.; II 10_5; weiteres bei Schürer GdjV. I 209.
[2] Nachr. d. Gött. Ges. d. W. 1905, 131.
[3] „Je fünf traurige Dinge haben sich am 17. Tammus und am 9. Ab ereignet": Mischna Taanit IV 1.
[4] Ueber die weite Verbreitung dieses Glaubens im Altertum vgl. Hirzel, Philologus Sppl. XI 462.
[5] Pesiqta rabb. VI, 24a, b Friedmann; angeführt bei Aptowitzer, Kain und Abel 141.

25. Kislew erklären —, so überflüssig und beispiellos wäre im Judentum die Verlegung eines t r a u r i g e n Ereignisses auf einen
F r e u d e n t a g. Zur „Entgiftung" hätte die Verlegung der Weihe
auf den 25. Kislew ja genügt. Will man weiter behaupten, daß
Antiochos diesen Tag aus besonderem Anlaß gewählt habe, daß er
also einen heidnischen Feiertag beging, der im Jahre 168 auf den
25. Kislew des jüdischen Mondjahres fiel, so ist dagegen nichts ein-
zuwenden. Nur beweist ein Schritt des Antiochos Epiphanes, zumal
einer, den er zum Tort aller überlieferungstreuen Juden tat, nichts
für den jüdischen Volksglauben. Und die Festhaltung des Tages
durch die Makkabäer ist ganz gewiß nicht aus Rücksicht auf die
Götter des Antiochos erfolgt.

Aber es besteht natürlich auch die Möglichkeit, daß es im alten
Israel ein W i n t e r f e s t gab und daß es die Makkabäer mit ihrem
Einweihungsfest verbanden, „wie die Einweihung des salomonischen
Tempels an das Laubhüttenfest angeschlossen wurde"[1]. So hat
einer der besten Kenner der Midraschliteratur — ohne Wellhausens
Aufsatz heranzuziehen und ohne seinerseits bei Norden und Kittel
Beachtung zu finden — aus manchen Aggadastellen schließen zu
dürfen geglaubt, daß Chanukka ein sehr altes Wintersaatfest gewesen
sei[2]. Uns kann hier nur die Frage beschäftigen, ob dies Volksfest,
falls es ein solches gab, einen s o l a r e n Charakter trug. In der
Tat mag es — nicht nur christlichen Gelehrten — naheliegen, nach-
dem Useners Zurückführung des Weihnachtsfestes auf die Sonnenwende sich anscheinend durchgesetzt hat, den 25. Kislew ebenso
zu deuten wie den 25. Dezember. Aber der z w e i t e n Dezember-
hälfte entspricht gar nicht der K i s l e w, sondern weit eher der
T e b e t; während der letzten 19 Jahre fiel der 25. Kislew fünfzehn-
mal vor die Sonnenwende, viermal auf sie oder nach ihr[3]; kein Wunder,
daß in mischnischen Quellen die winterliche Wende die W e n d e
d e s T e b e t heißt[4]. Und was den Ritus anlangt, so spricht die
Anzündung von Lichtern, die zwar erst aus dem ersten nachchristlichen Jahrhundert bezeugt ist, aber sehr wohl älter sein kann[5],
nicht eindeutig f ü r eine Sonnwendfeier — sie ist auch für den
Ritus des Wasserschöpfens am Hüttenfeste überliefert, der offenbar
eine Fruchtbarkeitsfeier darstellt[6] —, dagegen ist die achttägige
Dauer und auch die Verwendung von Pflanzengewinden, die mindestens für die erste Abhaltung gut bezeugt ist[7], bei einem solaren

---

[1] Aptowitzer, Kain und Abel, Wien und Leipzig 1922, 36.

[2] Aptowitzer 33 ff., dessen Vermutung mir freilich an dem Festritus
keine Stütze zu finden scheint.

[3] Die Daten sind: 1, 18, 8, 26, 16, 5, 24, 13, 2, 20, 19/XII, 29/XI, 17,
6, 26, 15, 3, 22, 12/XII.

[4] Belege in den Wörterbüchern.

[5] Anders Krauß REJ XXX (1905) 32 ff.; Leszynsky, MGWJ 1911, 404,
deren Ansicht mir nicht zwingend erwiesen scheint; immerhin ist es nicht
richtig, wenn Norden und Kittel so verfahren, als ob der frühe Ursprung des
Lichtzündens überliefert sei.

[6] Grunwald im Jahrbuch für jüdische Volkskunde 1924.

[7] Nach II Makk 10₆ hat man die e r s t e Tempelweihe „nach Art des
Laubhüttenfestes" mit Festgewinden, wie sie für den ersten Tag dieses Festes
vorgeschrieben sind, aber tatsächlich 7 Tage lang verwendet wurden, begangen.
Wenn nun 1₉ und ₁₈ das Weihefest als das „Hüttenfest des Kislew" bezeichnet

Fest unverständlich. So bleibt denn nur die Ableitung von Chanoch, dessen Gleichsetzung mit Helios offenbar auf schwachen Füßen steht (die Heranziehung des phrygischen Gottes Anakos, der auch Nanakos hieß und von dem man gleichfalls nicht weiß, ob er ein Sonnengott war[1], zeigt, daß sich Kittel der Schwäche seiner Position bewußt ist) und die schon deswegen ausscheidet, weil Ableitungen mit *âh* von Personennamen zur Bezeichnung der Herkunft nicht möglich sind: wer könnte das Purimfest als Esthera oder Mordechaja bezeichnen!

3. Der Glaube an die Jungfrauengeburt bei den hellenistischen Juden. Auf getrennten Wegen gelangen Norden und Kittel zu der Annahme, daß die hellenistischen Juden an ein Mysterium von der Jungfrauengeburt des Messias geglaubt haben.

Norden beruft sich auf Leisegangs Forschungen, die den Lesern dieser Zeitschrift bereits aus einer anderen Abhandlung[2] bekannt geworden sind. Leider aber gibt er den Inhalt der betr. Philonstellen höchst ungenau wieder. „Gott steigt", so schreibt er S. 78, „in den Schoß sterblicher Frauen hinab, um mit ihnen zu zeugen. Die Vorstellung ihrer Jungfräulichkeit ist ihm derart bestimmt gegeben, daß er die Sagen der Patriarchenzeit durch Allegorisieren in einem selbst für ihn fast unerhörten Maße vergewaltigen muß". In Wahrheit ist für Philon jede „Zeugung" Symbol geistiger Befruchtung, wie jede Nahrungsaufnahme Symbol geistigen Zuwachses, jede äußere Entfernung Symbol innerer Entfremdung. So deutet er den Verkehr Abrahams mit Hagar genau wie seine stoischen Vorgänger den der Freier mit den Mägden der Penelope. Und Wendungen wie diese, daß Gott „den Mutterschoß öffnet" oder „Sara heimsucht", geben ihm Veranlassung, seine Lieblingslehre in die Bibel hineinzudeuten: daß nicht der Mensch der Vater der guten Gedanken ist, die in ihm aufsteigen, sondern Gott. In diesem Sinne hat Gott mit Lea, Zippora, Hanna gezeugt, ohne daß von deren Jungfräulichkeit die Rede wäre. Dagegen heißt es von Sara, daß für sie „die Weise der Frauen aufhörte" (Gen 18₁₁). Diesen Vers deutet Philon entweder so, daß Sara zu einem übermenschlichen Wesen oder (nach 4 Stellen) zu einem Mann oder (nach 3 Stellen) zu einer Jungfrau geworden sei; an einer weiteren Stelle läßt er die Frage, was aus ihr geworden sei, offen[3]. Der exegetische Spielraum, den der Bibelvers bot, ist also voll ausgenutzt; an eine Tradition, daß Gott nur

wird, so hat man daraus wohl mit Recht geschlossen (Krauß S. 28 ff., der weitere Literatur anführt), daß dieser Ritus noch eine Zeitlang festgehalten wurde. Aber als „Ersatz des Hüttenfestes" hätte man (trotz II Makk 10₆) das Fest schon deshalb nicht ansehen dürfen, weil die Verwendung des Hauptsymbols dieses Festes, der Hütte, natürlich nicht möglich war. Ich halte auch die Bezeichnung „Hüttenfest des Kislew" durchaus nicht für eine offizielle, und glaube, daß sie von den Verfassern des Briefes gewählt war, um das Fest den hellenistischen Juden durch Anlehnung an ein auch ihnen heiliges Fest zu empfehlen.

[1] Kittel 20₁.

[2] Heinemann MGWJ. 1922, 274 ff., wo auch B e l e g e und nähere Ausführungen z u m f o l g e n d e n zu finden sind.

[3] Die Stellen sind a. a. O. aufgezählt.

mit Jungfrauen zeuge, ist Philon nicht einmal bei Sara gebunden, geschweige sonst[1].

Kittel S. 14 findet, wenn der Uebersetzer von Jes 7₁₄ statt des Textwortes עלמה = *Jungweib*: παρθένος = *Jungfrau* gebe, so müsse „in der Zeit und der Umgebung des Uebersetzers die Vorstellung herrschend" gewesen sein, „die Mutter des Erlösers sei eine Jungfrau". Das erkläre sich daraus, daß Ischtar, „d i e Göttin schlechtweg, mehr und mehr als jungfräuliche Göttin gedacht wurde" (S. 72). Leider läßt Kittel unausgesprochen, ob er dem Uebersetzer den Glauben an eine ü b e r n a t ü r l i c h e Z e u g u n g zuschreiben will, den Norden bei Philon voraussetzt. Wäre dies Kittels Meinung, so müßte man entgegenhalten, daß die Lehre von einem zeugenden Gott im wörtlichen Sinne dem hellenistischen Judentum nicht minder fremd war als dem palästinischen, also keinesfalls als „f e s t - s t e h e n d" (Kittel S. 14) angesehen werden kann; vom Messias insbesondere wissen wir, daß er aus Davids Hause stammen sollte (gerade auf Grund der Jesaja-Stellen), d. h., wie die Stammbäume der Evangelien deutlich, zeigen, daß sein Vater als Davidide galt. Hält man aber fest, daß für den Uebersetzer Immanuels Vater unzweifelhaft ein Mensch war (wie auch Kittel anzunehmen scheint)[1], so ist es völlig unnötig, zur Erklärung der Uebersetzung die Muttergöttin Ischtar zu bemühen, für deren besondere Schätzung im Judentum — und für deren Verbindung mit dem Messiasglauben — Kittel nicht den leisesten Anhaltspunkt bringt, wiewohl es sich doch um eine „feststehende" Vorstellung handeln soll! Die Uebersetzung παρθένος ist gar nicht so unmöglich, wie Kittel annimmt (wenn ich sie auch persönlich nicht für richtig halte); ein durchaus unbefangener Gelehrter wie Greßmann[2] schreibt: „Ob die Mutter als Frau oder ‚Jungfrau‘ gedacht ist, läßt sich nicht entscheiden, da עלמה beides heißen kann"; das Wort, das außer an unserer Jesajastelle n i e von einer E h e f r a u gebraucht wird, scheint nur solche junge Frauen zu bezeichnen, die noch nicht geboren haben[3]; es ist also noch enger als unser *Mädchen* oder gar lat. *puella*, das doch nicht selten für παρθένος steht. In der Thora wird es einmal sicher, ein anderes Mal höchstwahrscheinlich[4] von einer Jungfrau gebraucht; an allen anderen Bibelstellen ist die gleiche Uebersetzung möglich, außer Hoheslied 6₈, wo von Mädchen, die Salomos Freuden teilen, die Rede ist. Wenn also der Uebersetzer glaubte, daß Jesaja das Weib in seiner höchsten Frische meine, so ist das mindestens nicht unverständlicher, wie wenn manche Bibelerklärer, Juden und Nichtjuden, geglaubt haben, רֵעַ auch ohne exegetischen Zwang als den Volksgenossen auffassen zu müssen.

---

[1] Gegen Nordens Versuch, aus dem Vorkommen von ἐπισκιάζειν im Lukasevangelium und bei Philon auf ein von beiden benutztes Mysterium zu schließen, vgl. Allgeier, Hist. Jahrbuch 1925, 1 ff.

[2] Ursprung der Eschatologie 284.

[3] Vgl. Haupt bei Gesenius-Buhl, der auf بنين verweist.

[4] Gen 24₄₃, Ex 2₈. Spr 30₁₉ בעלמה :דרך־גבר ist eine Auffassung im Sinne von Jes 62₅ mindestens möglich.

4. Der Ursprung des Messiasglaubens. Wenn also auch im hellenistischen Judentum Spuren des heidnischen Messiasmysteriums nicht nachweisbar sind — steht etwa bereits der Glaube J e s a j a s unter der Wirkung derselben ägyptischen Mysterien, die auch auf das Abendland gewirkt haben?

Auch in dieser Frage gelangen Kittel und Norden auf getrennten Wegen zu dem gleichen bejahenden Ergebnis.

Wenn Kittel glaubt, die Erwartung eines Wunderknaben, mit dessen Geburt eine neue Zeit anbricht, sei älter als Jesaja, so ist diese Möglichkeit keineswegs auszuschließen. Das argumentum ex silentio ist bei den jammervollen Resten althebräischen Schrifttums unbedingt zu verwerfen, mag es die kritische Theologie zum „Beweis" der Jugend irgend einer Einrichtung verwenden oder der schlichte Bibelleser zur Grundlage unwissenschaftlicher Vorstellungen machen. — Sehr bedenklich ist es aber, wenn Kittel S. 10 zum Beweis für das Alter der Vorstellung die drei Weissagungen von der Geburt eines Sohnes Jes 7$_{14}$, Gen 16$_{11}$ und Ri 13$_3$ (an Hagar und die Mutter Simsons) nebeneinanderstellt, um zu beweisen, daß die Worte „du bist schwanger und wirst einen Sohn gebären" '(auf welche sich die Uebereinstimmung beschränkt) zum „Stil der Beschreibung des Heilbringers und Bringers einer neuen Zeit" gehörten (S. 65). Hier wird man wirklich an das zornige Wort eines geistreichen Philologen[1] von den „unmoralischen Parallelennetzen" erinnert. „Bringer einer neuen Zeit" ist Simson nicht und Ismael trotz aller dialektischen Künste erst recht nicht[2]. Angenommen, die Aehnlichkeit des Wortlauts bedürfte der Erklärung, so genügt die Annahme, daß die Genesisstelle auf Jesaja und Richterbuch gewirkt hat.

Neben diese drei Stellen, die beweisen sollen, daß es in Israel und womöglich bei den streitbaren Beduinen (S. 11) im 8. Jahrhundert einen feststehenden Ausdruck der Heils- und Erlöserwartung gab, stellt Kittel aber einen Ausruf der griechischen Mysterien. Er schreibt S. 24: „Hippolytos berichtet, der Hierophant in Eleusis breche aus in den Festruf: E i n e n h e i l i g e n K n a b e n h a t d i e H e r r i n g e b o r e n , d i e S t a r k e e i n e n S t a r k e n . Und weiter: D a s i s t n ä m l i c h d i e J u n g f r a u , d i e s c h w a n g e r w a r , empfing und e i n e n S o h n g e b a r ." Jeder Leser muß den Eindruck haben, daß die — von Kittel selbst! — gesperrten Worte nach dem Bericht eines zuverlässigen Gewährsmannes wirklich von dem H i e r o p h a n t e n g e s p r o c h e n worden sind. Und er wird den Schluß für unausweichlich halten, daß auch in Eleusis anfangs eine „Starke" (= Jesajas עלמה), dann eine Jungfrau als Mutter eines göttlichen Erlöserkindes bezeichnet wurde (Kittel 65 ff.), daß also Jesaja — unbewußt natürlich (S. 68) — die Horus-Osirisgestalt verwertet, die auch auf Eleusis wirkt, während an der Umbiegung zur Jungfrau wieder die Muttergöttin

---

[1] Karl Reinhardt, Poseidonios 379.
[2] S. 11 zitiert Kittel Gen 16$_{12}$ „dessen Hand gegen jedermann ist" (von Ismael) — ohne die Fortsetzung „und die Hand aller ist wider ihn". In der Tat: zu der Meinung, daß in Ismael etwas von einem Erlöser „durchklingt", paßt sie wie die Faust aufs Auge.

Ischtar die Schuld trägt (S. 72). Die Bedenken, die Kittel selbst
bei der Entwicklung dieser Hypothese gekommen sind, werden dem
Leser nicht ausschlaggebend scheinen, bis er — den angeblichen
„Bericht des Hippolytos" über die Mysterien von Eleusis einmal
nachschlägt. Da ergibt sich folgendes: Hippolytos redet im V. Buch
seiner „Widerlegung der Ketzer", insbesondere in dem uns angehenden
8. Kapitel über „die bewundernswürdigen G n o s t i k e r , die
Erfinder einer neuen Sprachwissenschaft" (§ 1), die erst Homer mit
der Bibel (der von ihnen ausgelegten natürlich!) identifizieren
(§ 1—8), dann thrakische (§ 9—22), phrygische (§ 23—38) und schließ-
lich eleusische[1] Mysterien (§ 39—45). Durchweg gehen diese
(naassenischen) Gnostiker von Nachrichten oder Zitaten aus, die
sie deuten und mit Bibelstellen zusammenbringen; die Absicht,
gewissenhaft über jene Kulte zu berichten, liegt ihnen selbstverständlich fern. Nun kann in diesem Wirrsal natürlich manches
Korn echter Ueberlieferung enthalten sein, das wir nutzen dürfen.
Aber Voraussetzung für unsere Verwertung ist doch die Scheidung
des B e r i c h t s von den Z u s ä t z e n u n d D e u t u n g e n der
„neuen Sprachwissenschaft". Tut man das, so ergibt sich, daß
w e i t e r n i c h t s überliefert ist als der Ausruf des Hierophanten:
„Einen heiligen Knaben hat die Herrin geboren, Brimo den Brimos"
(§ 40). A l l e s a n d e r e ist gnostischer Z u s a t z; insbesondere
ist der Schlußsatz § 45: „dies ist die Jungfrau, die einen Sohn
gebiert, keinen psychischen, keinen körperlichen, sondern den seligen
Aion der Aione" (die letzten Worte fehlen bei Kittel!) natürlich
kein Priesterruf, sondern einer der gnostischen Versuche, die „Herrin"
§ 40 mit der „pneumatischen, himmlischen, höheren Geburt" (§ 41),
unter Heranziehung von Bibelstellen, die auf Mysterien bezogen
werden, gleichzusetzen. So darf sich denn Kittel (66, 1) nicht wundern,
wenn die Philologen seither auch die Glosse zum Priesterruf „eine
Starke einen Starken" nicht als authentisch angesehen, vielmehr
über das Wesen der Brimo nicht die „neue", sondern ihre eigene
Sprachwissenschaft befragt und aus der sonstigen Erwähnung der
Göttin und der Bedeutung der Wurzel von βριμοῦσϑαι ermittelt
haben, daß das Wort nicht die *Starke*, sondern die *Schnaubende,*
Grimmige bedeutet und wahrscheinlich eine Unterweltsgottheit bezeichnet. Die Uebereinstimmung zwischen dem Priesterruf und
der Jesajastelle beschränkt sich demnach darauf, daß hier wie dort
das Zeitwort *gebären* (in verschiedenen Tempora) mit einem männ-
lichen Objekt verbunden wird.

Während also die seither betrachteten scheinbaren Ueberein-
stimmungen zwischen jüdischen und heidnischen Anschauungen auf
sehr zweifelhaften oder erweislich falschen Deutungen der Urkunden
beruhen, ist der Versuch erheblich ernster zu nehmen, unzweifelhaft
vorhandene Aehnlichkeiten zum Ausgangspunkt quellenkritischer
Vermutungen zu machen. Solche Aehnlichkeiten bestehen zwischen
Vergil und Jesaja. Beide bringen das neue Zeitalter mit der Geburt
eines Wunderkindes in Verbindung; beide versprechen sich von ihm
Frieden — nicht nur für die Menschheit, sondern auch für die Tiere.

---

[1] Ueber ihre Wertschätzung durch die Naassener vgl. V 7,34, 20 .

Nun ist zwar bei Vergil nicht von einem friedlichen Z u s a m m e n - l e b e n der zahmen und der wilden Tiere die Rede, sondern „die Herden werden den Löwen nicht fürchten; vergehen wird die Schlange und das trügerische Giftkraut; assyrische Unschuldsstauden[1] werden überall erwachsen": es wird also der U n t e r g a n g alles Schädlichen geweissagt. Aber gerade diese Abweichung im einzelnen beweist nach Norden (51 ff.), daß nicht Jesaja oder die ihm folgende jüdische Sibylle (III 748 ff.) auf Vergil gewirkt hat; vielmehr ist, da Zufall ausgeschlossen scheint, die Nachwirkung derselben ägyptischen Mysterien anzunehmen, denen auch Jesaja — bei aller Selbständigkeit in der Formung — doch seine Bildersprache zu verdanken scheint.

Die Forschungen, auf die sich Norden bezieht, haben von Hugo Greßmanns Buch „Der Ursprung der israelitisch-jüdischen Eschatologie" (1905) ihren Ausgang genommen. Während namentlich Wellhausen das Vorhandensein vorexilischer Messiashoffnungen bestritt und die messianischen Stellen der älteren Prophetenbücher samt und sonders für unecht erklärte, erwies Greßmann, daß der Glaube an einen „Tag Gottes" nicht nur vorexilisch, sondern insofern „vorprophetisch" ist, als bereits Amos diesen Begriff als seinen Hörern bekannt voraussetzt. Der „p r o p h e t i s c h e n" Stufe der Heilshoffnung liegt also eine „v o l k s t ü m l i c h e" voraus, für welche der Tag Gottes (nach Amos 5_{18} ff.) lediglich ein „Tag des Lichtes" für Israel war. Erst die Propheten haben ihn zu einem Tage gerechten und furchtbaren Gerichtes gemacht und dadurch die volkstümliche Idee unerhört vertieft, auf der gegebenen Klaviatur ihre eigene Melodie gespielt (Greßmann 152 ff.). Aber auch die volkstümliche Stufe ist nicht die älteste. Sie beruht nach Greßmann auf der Erwartung großen „Heils" und „Unheils", die wir in manchen ägyptischen und babylonischen Texten finden. Mittelbar haben diese n i c h t j ü d i s c h e n Vorstellungen auch auf die prophetische Stufe gewirkt; der „Hofstil" und der „eschatologische Stil" der Sprachen der Weltreiche erklärt manche etwas überschwenglich klingende Wendung der Bibel (Greßmann 250 ff., 260 ff., 305 ff.) und manche Dunkelheit der Immanuelweissagung Jes 7_{14} ff. (S. 272 ff.).

Dreierlei scheint Greßmann erwiesen zu haben: das hohe Alter der messianischen Hoffnung, die Existenz einer vorprophetischen volkstümlichen Stufe, die Einwirkung mancher sprachlicher Wendungen aus den Sprachen, aus denen das Hebräische ja auch Fremdwörter entlehnt hat. Wenn Marduk einen Fürsten sucht, „ihn zu fassen bei seiner Hand; Kurasch berief er mit Namen", so hat Greßmann S. 251 Recht, auf Jes 45_1 ff. zu verweisen, wo es von demselben Kyros heißt, Gott habe ihn bei der Hand gefaßt und mit Namen gerufen. Und wenn — um ein von ihm nicht angeführtes Beispiel zu nennen — nach Jes 11_{15} Gott den Fluß Aegyptens in sieben Bäche zerschlagen wird und betreten lassen wird mit Sandalen, so wird es schwerlich Zufall sein, wenn es in einem Papyrus heißt: Der Fluß Aegyptens ist leer; man kann zu Fuß durchgehen" (Dürr 8).

---

[1] Amomum ist eine Balsamstaude (Weber 87, 3); doch wird die Etymologie natürlich empfunden.

Auch wenn etwa das ägyptische Wort für Leben einen besonders vollen Klang hat und alle Seligkeit einschließt, so mag es ganz wohl auf den Gebrauch von חיים an manchen Stellen gewirkt haben (vgl. Norden 119 ff., Kittel 86 ff.). Aber diese Feststellungen und Kombinationen berühren nicht den Kern unserer Frage. Verwertung von Wendungen beweist nicht die Uebernahme von Vorstellungen, am wenigsten bei Denkern von außergewöhnlicher Selbständigkeit. Es bleibt nach wie vor die Frage offen: stammt die Idee eines göttlichen E r l ö s e r k i n d e s und des T i e r f r i e d e n s aus ägyptischer oder babylonischer Quelle?

Schon dem Leser des Greßmannschen Buches muß auffallen, daß er weder hieroglyphische noch keilschriftliche Texte für die genannten Züge zu bringen vermag. Noch deutlicher wird der Tatbestand durch die Schrift von D ü r r , der des Aegyptischen, des Assyrischen und des Hebräischen mächtig ist. Die Zusammenstellung und Prüfung der Texte (1—37) führt ihn zu dem Ergebnis, daß es in Aegypten überhaupt keine Weissagungen einer glücklichen Endzeit gegeben hat; höchstens hat man einem König in der Weise gehuldigt, daß man seine Ruhmestaten in der Form eines vaticinium ex eventu gefeiert hat. Aehnlich steht es in Babylonien, nur daß dort die Könige gern „als von der Gottheit ausersehen und vorausbestimmt" bezeichnet werden. Aber „von einem großen und wunderbaren gottmenschlichen Herrscher der Endzeit" finden wir nach Dürr keine Spur; „alles, was man bis jetzt von einer orientalischen Erlösererwartung redet, ist lediglich Konstruktion"[1]. Insbesondere f e h l t natürlich jede Andeutung eines wunderbaren K n a b e n , an dessen Geburt der neue Aion geknüpft sei. Und gleiches gilt vom T i e r f r i e d e n . Die Glücksschilderungen halten sich durchaus in den Grenzen des in diesem Aion Möglichen (wie etwa diejenigen der Thora): „Die Aehre ward fünf Sechstel Ellen lang, die Ernte gelang, die Feldfrucht gedieh; es triefte die Fülle, Ueberfluß wurde aufgehäuft" (Dürr 17). „Inmitten von Stadt und Haus nahm kein Mensch die Habe seines Nächsten mit Gewalt weg; weder war da ein Räuber, der Blut vergoß, noch wurde eine Gewalttat verübt" (S. 18). In diesem Stil sind sämtliche Schilderungen, die seither bekannt geworden sind, gehalten. Die von uns gesuchten Züge — Wunderkind und Tierfrieden — sind also nicht nur seither nicht aufgewiesen: sie würden in diese durchaus realistisch gehaltenen Schilderungen gar nicht hineinpassen.

Man hat freilich geglaubt, daß die volkstümliche Vorstellung vom Tage Gottes aus sich unerklärlich sei und das Bestehen einer mythischen Vorstufe voraussetze. Auch dies — bei unserer geringen Kenntnis altjüdischen Volksglaubens nicht gerade zwingende — Argument weist Dürr 38 ff. zurück. Aus dem Vertrauen auf Jhv als den Herrscher und Retter seines Volkes mußte sich ergeben, daß der Gottestag ein Tag des Heils und des Unheils war: des Heils für Israel, des Unheils für seine Feinde. Erst die Propheten haben — auch nach Dürr — diese rein nationale Hoffnung im ethischen Sinne umgestaltet und gerade Israel als Folge seiner Sünden das

---

[1] Dürr S. 27, Anm. 33 nach Sellin.

Unheil verkündet. Eine solche Ableitung ist jedenfalls m ö g l i c h; keinesfalls kann also die jüdische Volksvorstellung als mittelbares Zeugnis für das Vorhandensein eines heidnisch-orientalischen Erlösungsmythos angesehen werden.

Und auch die Jesajastelle über Immanuel setzt keineswegs einen heidnischen Mythos von einem göttlichen Erlöserkind voraus. Gewiß heben die Attribute אל גבור, אבי עד den Erlöser über Menschenmaße hinaus[1] — wenn auch darüber erfreulicherweise Uebereinstimmung zu herrschen scheint, daß sie Jesaja[2] nicht in rein mythischem Sinn verstanden haben kann. Aber die Vermutung, daß seine Redeweise durch nichtjüdischen Huldigungsstil bestimmt sei, liegt sicherlich nahe, zumal wenn man bedenkt, daß das mittelhebräische Ajektiv אֱלֹהִי *göttlich* unter arabischem Einfluß (gebildet und) von unzweifelhaften Anhängern des strengsten Monotheismus auf Menschen jeden Bekenntnisses angewandt worden ist[3]. In der Tat sind in Aegypten „Prädikate wie: der große Gott, Herr über die Unendlichkeit, Fürst der Ewigkeit" ganz geläufig (Greßmann 282) — aber nicht von halbmythischen Wesen, sondern vom i r d i s c h e n H e r r s c h e r. Ihre Anwendung auf Menschen in der Bibel ist allerdings äußerst selten (Greßmann 256 ff.), aber doch nicht auf messianische Texte beschränkt[4]. Nicht der leiseste Anhaltspunkt spricht also dafür, daß die ägyptische Darstellung glücklicher Zeiten den Boden des Realen verlassen und neben den Herrscher ein überirdisches Wunderkind gestellt habe[5]. Unter Nordens Belegen für ägyptischen Kinderkult[6] steht kein einziger mit eschatologischen Schilderungen in Verbindung.

An diesen Feststellungen kann natürlich auch die Heranziehung eines lateinischen Textes des letzten vorchristlichen Jahrhunderts nichts ändern, zumal mittelbarer Einfluß biblischer Vorstellungen auf Vergil trotz Nordens sehr temperamentvoller Ablehnung durchaus möglich ist: die XV viri sacris faciundis, deren Einfluß auf unsere

---

[1] Die Schwierigkeit geht am besten aus der Tatsache hervor, daß der Targum und die mittelalterlichen jüdischen Erklärer sich dagegen sträuben, diese Attribute auf das Kind zu beziehen. Dagegen scheint man (z. B. Kittel S. 12) auf „Milch und Honig" zu viel Gewicht zu legen. Darin hat Greßmann 212, 1 sicher Recht, daß der Ausdruck nicht überall „Götternahrung" bezeichnet.

[2] Neuere Zweifel an der Echtheit der Stelle beschäftigen uns hier nicht· Denn „prophetisch" im edelsten Sinne ist diese Weissagung in jedem Fall. Ueberdies hat doch der Name „Gottmituns" nur einen Sinn, wenn sein Träger zu „uns" gehört, also durchaus Mensch ist.

[3] Die Anwendung des Adjektivs, das in seinen beiden Bedeutungen الوهي genau entspricht, scheint nach Ben Jehudas Thesaurus s. v. auf den arabischen Kulturkreis beschränkt zu sein und sich vorwiegend in Uebersetzungen zu finden.

[4] Für die Beziehung von Psalm 45,7 כסאך אלהים עולם ועד auf den König hätte sich Greßmann nicht erst auf Gunkel, sondern bereits auf — Raschi berufen können.

[5] Im Gegensatz gegen Kittel treffe ich mich mit Weber 99, 4 zusammen; doch vgl. das im Text folgende.

[6] S. 73 ff. über Har.

Ekloge Weber mehrfach betont[1], waren „Kenner der Kultur des Ostens"; daß zu den orientalischen Religionen, die gelehrte Zeitgenossen des Dichters kannten, das Judentum gehörte, hat gerade Norden[2] eingehend erwiesen; und zu den biblischen Bildern, nicht nur das vom T i e r f r i e d e n , sondern auch der Heilszeit gehört auch das V e r s c h w i n d e n des Unkrauts und seine Ersetzung durch Edelgewächs[3]. Weshalb weiterhin die heidnische Sibylle nicht von ihrer römerfeindlichen jüdischen Kollegin gelernt haben soll, ist gleichfalls nicht einzusehen. Trotzdem ist die Annahme irgendwelchen orientalischen Einflusses zur Erklärung der Uebereinstimmung mit Jesaja m. E. ganz überflüssig. In Nordens Untersuchung[4] stehen ganz bescheiden unter dem Text zwei Dichterstellen: eine aus Aristophanes: „nicht eher wird Frieden werden, als bis der Wolf das Lamm freit", eine aus Theokrit: „es kommt ein Tag, da der scharfgezähnte Wolf dem schlafenden Hirschkalb nichts zu leide tut." Weder Norden noch sonst jemand, der antike Utopien kennt — die Geschichte vom Schlaraffenland steht bekanntlich bereits bei einem attischen Komiker — möchte hier an Entlehnung eines ägyptischen Mysteriums denken. Vielmehr ist das Bestreben, die Natur gleichsam dem Ergehen des Menschen anzupassen, allgemein menschlich und im besonderen aus Griechenland — dafür gibt Norden 58 einige Parallelen — und aus Palästina bezeugt[5]; aus ihm ließe es sich befriedigend erklären, wenn Jesaja und — in anderer Weise! — Aristophanes dem Menschenfrieden den Tierfrieden zum Hintergrunde gibt und Vergil nicht nur den Menschen, sondern auch die Tiere von Sorge befreit.

Eher verspricht das umfassende Material, das W e b e r vorlegt, die Aufdeckung größerer kulturgeschichtlicher Zusammenhänge. Während sich Norden im wesentlichen auf Aegypten und die eigentliche Göttersage beschränkt, zieht Weber die altgriechische Vorstellung vom Weisen als „unsterblichem Gott" (85 f.) und vor allem persische und indische Legenden über die wunderbare Zeugung und Geburt des Weisen (84$_1$ und 89) heran. Von hier aus fällt auf Vergil unzweifelhaft starkes Licht — noch stärkeres, als im Rahmen unserer Besprechung gezeigt werden kann. So gewinnt die von Norden S. 65 nicht ausgewertete Tatsache Bedeutung, daß das

---

[1] Weber S. 90 ff. Leider f e h l t ein I n d e x , so daß sich die anderen Stellen schwer nachschlagen lassen!

[2] Festgabe von Fachgenossen Harnack dargebracht 292 ff. Die Einwände, die ich (an anderer Stelle) gegen seine Strabonanalyse machen werde, ändern nichts am Hauptergebnis, soweit es für uns in Betracht kommt. Uebrigens hatte Norden selbst früher (N. Jbb. 1913, 657$_4$) Einwirkung der Jesajastelle mit großer Bestimmtheit angenommen.

[3] Jes 55$_{13}$: Statt des Dorngeheges wird die Zypresse aufsteigen, statt des Unkrauts die Myrte.

[4] S. 52, 1: Aristophanes Frieden 1075 f.; Theokrit Herakliskos 86 f.

[5] Einiges über „die A n t e i l n a h m e d e r p h y s i s c h e n W e l t a n d e n S c h i c k s a l e n d e s M e n s c h e n " hat V. Aptowitzer MGWJ 1920, 227 ff. zusammengestellt. Der gleiche Gelehrte bereitet eine u m - f a s s e n d e A r b e i t über dies Thema vor und hat mir gestattet, das von ihm gesammelte h e l l e n i s t i s c h e Material zu vervollständigen. Ich möchte daher an dieser Stelle Nordens Parallelen nicht ergänzen.

Lächeln des Kindes bei der Geburt (V. 60 der Ekloge)[1] sich auch bei Zoroaster findet (Weber 107), und es ist vielleicht kein Zufall, daß bei der Geburt Buddhas junge Löwen unschädlich werden und überhaupt die Natur Anteil nimmt (S. 115 f.). Auch daß man den Weisen gern als übermenschliches Wesen ansah und in ihm die Unschuld des Urmenschen wieder aufleben ließ, wäre leicht noch eingehender zu zeigen als Weber es tut. Aber für die Frage nach den etwaigen Vorläufern der p r o p h e t i s c h e n Erlöserhoffnung ergibt sich kaum ein Anhaltspunkt. Weber (S. 99₄) legt Gewicht darauf, daß auch bei Jesaja, wie in der Buddhalegende (S. 89), ein Seher vor dem König steht und daß der Vater des Immanuel bei Jesaja nicht genannt ist; wenn „auf seiner Schulter die Herrschaft liegt", so bedeutet das die „Auszeichnung seines Körpers durch herrliche Merkmale" (S. 137 unter 3), die als Zeichen der Zeugung durch die Sonne in der buddhistischen Legende gilt; nicht der Mythos von einem „Gotteskinde", also einem kindlichen Gottwesen wie Har, sondern der von einem „Herrschergott" und seiner göttlichen Zeugung schwebt (nach Weber) dem Propheten vor, ist jedoch von ihm „seinen Anschauungen", die „keine weitergehende Mythologisierung vertrugen", angepaßt worden. Man sieht: die einzige bezeichnende Uebereinstimmung zwischen der Jesajastelle und den Erzählungen von der Geburt der Wundermänner bestünde in der Auffassung des „Zeichens der Herrschaft" — wenn sie erwiesen oder auch nur möglich wäre. Sie traut Jesaja zu, daß er den Mythos von der fleischlichen Zeugung des Erlösers durch eine Gottheit als bekannt und berechtigt anerkannt hätte — während gleichzeitig das Fehlen der u n z w e i f e l h a f t mythischen Züge aus der Gegnerschaft desselben Jesaja gegen die Mythologisierung hergeleitet wird. Ehe man zu solchen Widersprüchen greift, wird man sich bei der üblichen Erklärung beruhigen, daß das Symbol — etwa der Mantel — der Herrschaft auf der Schulter des Erlösers liegt. — Immerhin können für den Bibelforscher, den nicht nur Jesajas Vorstellungswelt, sondern auch diejenige seiner Hörer interessiert, Nachweisungen wie diejenigen, die Weber zusammenstellt, bei kritischer Sichtung und Weiterführung von Wert werden. Es wäre denkbar, daß die Vorstellung eines wunderbaren Weisen bereits im 8. Jahrhundert im Orient vorhanden war und auch von solchen israelitischen Kreisen, die ihre mythische Ausdrucksform verwarfen, soweit geteilt wurde, daß sich Jesaja auf sie beziehen konnte; falls also etwa die Attribute des Immanuel nicht an höfischen Huldigungsstil anknüpfen sollten, sondern an das Lob weiser Männer, so wären sie im Hinblick auf den späteren Sprachgebrauch von אלהי vom Weisen und auf die Ehrfurcht, die gegenüber dem Lehrer gefordert wurde[2], gut erklärlich.

---

[1] Falls nämlich dort *qui non risere parenti* (statt *cui n. r. parentes*) zu lesen ist; doch vgl. gegen Norden D e u b n e r , Gnomon I 166.
[2] Pirqe abot IV 12: „Es sei dir die Ehrfurcht vor deinem Lehrer wie die Ehrfurcht vor Gott". Auch bekannte palästinische und hellenistisch-jüdische Aussprüche über Elternehrung, die der Ehrung Gottes gleichsteht, gehören wohl hierher, da man in den Eltern vorwiegend die Erzieher sah; vgl. Heinemann, Schriften der jüd.-hell. Literatur II 170, 2.

5. Jüdische Mysterienstimmung.

Mystische Frömmigkeit unterscheidet sich von derjenigen der positiven Religionen durch ihre Grundauffassung des Verhältnisses von Gott und Mensch. Finden sich im biblischen Judentum Anklänge an die mystische Religionsauffassung?

Kittel bejaht die Frage — ohne sich über die in jedem Falle verbleibenden Unterschiede zu täuschen. Schade nur, daß alles, was er über diese U n t e r s c h i e d e lehrt — insbesondere zwischen dem Quietismus der Mystik und dem ethischen Aktivismus der prophetischen Frömmigkeit — auf einer Fülle unbestreitbarer T a t - s a c h e n beruht, während für die angeblich m y s t i s c h e n Züge selbst nur s c h w a c h e und u n s i c h e r e S t ü t z e n aufzuzeigen sind.

Was Kittel S. 84 f. über das Einswerden mit Gott sagt, ist durchaus zu billigen. „Männer Gottes" kennt auch das Judentum: aber der Unterschied zwischen ihnen und den Helden des Mysterienglaubens ist (zumal doch die Wunder stets Gott, nie den Propheten zugeschrieben werden) derart, daß es sich nur um „äußerliche Berührung" (Kittel 85) mit dem Mysterienglauben handelt. Lehrreich ist auch, was über das „Schauen Gottes" gesagt wird, insbesondere der Nachweis, daß es ein solches Schauen in dem geistigen Sinn, in dem es natürlich auch Kittel in der Bibel versteht, schon in Aegypten und Babylonien gegeben hat[1]; aber ein solches Schauen, das sich aus der Betrachtung des Götterbildes durch Vergeistigung entwickelt haben mag, ist für die Mysterienreligionen nicht kennzeichnend. Aehnlich steht es mit der biblischen Jenseitshoffnung. Es verdient immerhin Beachtung, wenn ein Gelehrter der kritischen Schule den Schluß des 17. Psalms („beim Erwachen darf ich mich sattsehen Deines Anblickes") — mit Raschi — auf das Erwachen vom Todesschlaf bezieht. Stichhaltiger scheint die Deutung der berühmten Worte Ps 73$_{25}$: „Wen habe ich i m H i m m e l — und neben dir liegt mir nichts an der Erde" auf j e n s e i t i g e und diesseitige Seligkeit. Solche Verbundenheit mit Gott hat der Dichter nach Vers 17 durch den Eintritt in die מקדשי אל erlangt, also wohl, wie Jer 51$_{51}$, die heiligen Hallen, das Heiligtum Gottes. Aber auch wenn man das Wort mit Kittel — ohne jede Parallele — als „heilige Lehren" deuten dürfte, so wäre man durch die Uebersetzung der LXX μυστήρια θεοῦ noch lange nicht berechtigt, an Mysterien im technischen Sinn zu denken; am wenigsten wäre es Kittel, der den Uebersetzungsfehler der LXX Jes 7$_{14}$, wie wir wissen, auf Beeinflussung des U e b e r s e t z e r s durch die Mysterienreligionen zurückführt; ganz abgesehen davon, daß die hellenistischen Juden das Wort μυστήρια nicht selten in ganz abgegriffenem Sinne brauchen, wie an der von Kittel herangezogenen Stelle Weish. Sal. 2$_{22}$ sicher den Gottlosen nicht Unkenntnis der Mysterien vorgeworfen wird.

Kann also von einer Einwirkung der Mysterienreligionen auf die jüdische Frömmigkeit keine Rede sein, so könnte sich höchstens fragen, ob die Wirkung, die das J u d e n t u m allgemein auf die

---

[1] Kittel 89, 2 gibt Literatur-Nachweise.

Frömmigkeit des H e l l e n i s m u s geübt hat, sich auch auf die
M y s t e r i e n r e l i g i o n e n erstreckt und zu ihrer V e r g e i s t i -
g u n g geführt hat. Das wäre denkbar, zumal im Hinblick auf die
Häufigkeit des Namens Iao in Zauberpapyri; beweisbar ist es nicht.
Die Ethisierung des Mysterienglaubens beginnt mit Platon; wir
haben Anlaß zu vermuten, daß auch Poseidonios an ihr einen ge-
wissen Anteil nahm; nichts nötigt uns, jüdischen Einfluß auf die
höheren Formen der mystischen Spekulation anzunehmen.

Die Prüfung der Vermutungen Nordens und Kittels führt also
zu negativem Ergebnis. Ihre Annahme, daß es im J u d e n t u m
Lehren gegeben habe, die denen der heidnischen Mysterienreligionen
verwandt waren, beruht zum größten Teil auf Mißverständnis (so
bezüglich des Gottes Aion, des angeblichen Sonnwendfestes und
der jungfräulichen Geburt); soweit sich verwandte Zukunftshoffnungen finden — nicht nur in der Bibel und im Hellenentum,
sondern auch im ferneren Orient — haben sie sich wesentlich
unabhängig von einander entwickelt. Gottfried Keller, der
Dichter, wird dem Tatbestand besser gerecht als die Philologen.
Es bleibt nur die Möglichkeit und Wahrscheinlichkeit bestehen,
daß die Bildersprache der Propheten, zumal in den messianischen
Reden, durch einen Stil bestimmt ist, der auf Könige und
vielleicht auf weise Religionsstifter anderer Völker Anwendung
gefunden hatte, und daß der Glaube an die jenseitige Verbundenheit mit Gott bereits für manche Psalmen vorausgesetzt
werden darf. Nicht einmal soviel ist zuzugeben, daß es sich um
eine Reihe ganz blasser Symptome handle, die auf einen einheit-
lichen Tatbestand weisen und sich dadurch gegenseitig verstärken.
Denn an intimen Zusammenhang der besprochenen h e i d n i s c h e n
Vorstellungen untereinander wird man höchstens dann glauben
können, wenn man Nordens Ansicht teilt, daß Vergil bezw. seine
sibyllische Quelle nur aus e i n e m — dem ägyptischen — Mysterien-
kreis geschöpft habe. Aber das ist durch Bolls Bedenken gegen den
Zusammenhang zwischen Ekloge und ägyptischem Sonnenglauben[1],
namentlich aber durch Webers Hinweis auf die persischen und
indischen Parallelen sowie auf die Bedeutung der XVviri für die
Ekloge äußerst unwahrscheinlich geworden; es ist also anzunehmen,
daß Vergil Elemente verbunden hat, die ursprünglich nicht mehr
mit einander zu tun hatten, wie die Sage von Dido mit
der Kyklopengeschichte oder der philosophischen Lehre vom
Jenseits, die er in der Aeneis zu verschmelzen weiß. Wie dem
aber sei — die Spuren mystischen Glaubens, die man im J u d e n -
t u m hat finden wollen, verweisen keineswegs auf einander: der
Gott Ewigkeit, das Sonnwendfest Chanukka, der Jungfernsohn
Isaak haben weder mit einander noch mit der Messiasidee das leiseste
zu tun. Auch vom schwächsten Indizienbeweis ist also keine Spur
zu finden.

Dies negative Ergebnis hat aber natürlich seine positive Seite.
Es gilt ja nicht nur, die T a t s a c h e der Einwirkung fremder Mystik

---

[1] DLZ. 1924, 773.

auf das Judentum festzustellen, sondern auch ihre G r e n z e n zu ermitteln und zu der Eigenart des Judentums in Beziehung zu setzen. In diesem Falle hat offenbar das polytheistische Element in den Vorstellungen, von denen die Rede war, derart abstoßend gewirkt, daß es nicht einmal zu einer Umformung in jüdischem Sinne gekommen ist. Den verallgemeinernden Schluß, daß das Judentum aus der Kultur der Umwelt nur gewählt habe, was ihm gemäß war, und verworfen, was ihm nicht entsprach, lassen leider die Tatsachen nicht zu; die Strenge jüdischer Selbstkritik denkt bekanntlich anders[1]; aber freilich lag der Monotheismus dem Juden, auch dem hellenisierten, derart im Blute, daß Anschauungen, die diesem widerstrebten, keine Anziehungskraft auf ihn üben konnten.

JEWISH MESSIANIC BELIEF IN JUSTIN MARTYR'S *DIALOGUE WITH TRYPHO*

BY

A. J. B. HIGGINS

Leeds

This question has often been discussed, usually with the chief emphasis on the value of the Dialogue as a source for Jewish belief in a suffering Messiah in the second century, and as a pointer to the possible existence of this belief in and before the time of Jesus. While necessarily taking account of this, the main purpose of the present study is to focus attention more on another aspect of Jewish conceptions according to Justin, namely, the Son of man and the two advents of the Messiah.

Although a discussion of this kind between a Christian and a Jew might seem rather improbable after the Bar Cochba revolt (A.D. 132-135), which resulted in a final estrangement between Jews and Christians owing to the refusal of the latter to participate in it, it is by no means ruled out as impossible. Trypho may or may not be Rabbi Tarphon [1]), a contemporary of Justin. If he is, then it was later Jewish tradition which made him a martyr in the war [2]). But acceptance of the identification would not necessarily involve accepting all the statements attributed to Trypho as reliable expressions of contemporary Jewish beliefs. And even if Justin had a discussion [3]) with this man, there would be no reason to regard the Dialogue as an accurate report of it. HARNACK, in his important study, held it as of secondary importance whether Justin owed his

---

[1]) The identification has been assumed by many scholars, e.g., E. SCHÜRER, *The Jewish People in the Time of Jesus Christ*, II. i (1901), 377; II.ii (1901), 186, n. 94; B. ALTANER, *Patrology* (1960), 122 f. It has been questioned by E. R. GOODENOUGH, *The Theology of Justin Martyr* (1923), 90-92; A. L. WILLIAMS, *Justin Martyr, The Dialogue with Trypho* (1930), xxv; E. SJÖBERG, *Der verborgene Menschensohn in den Evangelien* (1955), 81, n.1; N. HYLDAHL, "Tryphon und Tarphon", *Studia Theologica* 10 (1957), 77-88; J. JEREMIAS, *The Servant of God*[2] (1965), 74, n. 314.

[2]) Cf. SCHÜRER, *op. cit.*, II. i, 377.

[3]) At Ephesus, according to Eusebius, *H. E.* iv. 18.6, towards the end of the war (Dialogue 1.3).

knowledge to a particular Jew like Tarphon or to tradition, but accepted the Jewish ideas and objections as authentic [1]). He listed numerous agreements with Jewish scriptural exegesis [2]), though a not inconsiderable number of divergences are also mentioned. There is no doubt that Justin knew very well what messianic beliefs were current among Jews in his day, and he sometimes states them correctly. But whenever the opportunity presents itself, his zeal as a Christian apologist gets the upper hand, and he attributes to his Jewish interlocutor ideas which he could not possibly have entertained [3]).

In 49.1 Trypho declares: καὶ γὰρ πάντες ἡμεῖς τὸν Χριστὸν ἄνθρωπον ἐξ ἀνθρώπων προσδοκῶμεν γενήσεσθαι. This was in fact the prevalent Jewish expectation, and here the Dialogue is perfectly reliable. In opposition to Christian claims for Jesus, the tendency in post-Christian Judaism was to tone down messianic dogma and to emphasize the human nature of the Messiah [4]). But even more important is the necessarily associated denial by Trypho of the pre-existence and the divinity of the Messiah. He asserts:

"For you utter many blasphemies, in that you seek to persuade us that this crucified man was with Moses and Aaron, and spoke to them in the pillar of the cloud; then that he became man, was crucified..." (38.1); "For when you say that this Messiah existed as God before the ages, then that he submitted to be born and become man, yet that he is not man of men (Greek ἀνθρώπου), this appears to me to be not merely paradoxical, but also foolish" (48.1).

It is further in accordance with Jewish belief that Trypho declares:

---

[1]) A. von HARNACK, *Judentum und Judenchristentum in Justins Dialog mit Trypho*, *TU* xxxix, 1 (1913), 53 f.; cf. 90: "Es ist ein sehr bedeutendes Material, welches wir für die Kenntnis des Judentums (und Judenchristentums) und seines Verhältnisses zum Christentum um das J. 160 aus dem Dialog gewonnen haben".

[2]) *Op. cit.*, 61 ff., after GOLDFAHN.

[3]) Cf. SJÖBERG, *op. cit.*, 82; S. MOWINCKEL, *He That Cometh* (1956), 328, n.1. L. GOPPELT, *Christentum und Judentum im ersten und zweiten Jahrhundert* (1954), 289, writes: "Justin kennt das zeitgenössische Judentum auf Grund seiner palästinensischen Herkunft und tatsächlich durchgefochtener Streitgespräche so gut wie kein Vertreter der Heidenkirche bis Origenes". But this favourable estimate takes no account of Justin's apologetic methods. On Justin's knowledge of Palestinian Judaism see also W. A. SHOTWELL, *The Biblical Exegesis of Justin Martin* (1965), 71 ff.

[4]) Cf. SCHÜRER, *op. cit.*, II. ii. 162; HARNACK, *op. cit.*, 91.

"But Messiah — if he has indeed been born, and exists anywhere—
is unknown, and does not even know himself, and has no power until Elijah
comes to anoint him, and make him manifest to all" (8.4) [1].

The idea of the hidden or unknown Messiah is found in Rabbinic
literature in various forms [2]. It is important, however, that it is
not only that Trypho, while really believing that the Messiah has
not yet come (ἐκ δὲ τοῦ μηδὲ Ἠλίαν ἐληλυθέναι οὐδὲ τοῦτον ἀποφαίνομαι
εἶναι (49.1)), allows the possibility that he may be already on earth,
but concealed (8.4). Justin himself says that he is aware of this
attitude of the Jews.

"And I am likewise aware that they [the Jewish teachers] maintain
he has not yet come; or if they say that he has come, they assert that it is
not known who he is; but when he shall become manifest and glorious, then
it shall be known who he is" (110.1).

Here again, therefore, the Dialogue is reliable evidence for
contemporary Jewish belief [3].

It might then be asked whether the work, if it correctly represents
the conceptions of the human and the hidden Messiah, can be expected to be good evidence of other aspects of Jewish messianic
belief. But here Justin is simply reporting Jewish beliefs as facts,
and is not writing as an apologist for Christianity. It is quite a
different story when we turn to other aspects of messianic thought
as Justin has made Trypho express them.

---

[1] These and other passages are based on the translation in *Ante-Nicene
Christian Library* ii (1870). I have used the text edition by E. J. GOODSPEED,
Die ältesten Apologeten: Texte mit kurzen Einleitungen (1914). On this form
of the role of Elijah (cf. 49.1: Καὶ γὰρ πάντες ἡμεῖς τὸν Χριστὸν ἄνθρωπον ἐξ
ἀνθρώπων προσδοκῶμεν γενήσεσθαι, καὶ τὸν Ἠλίαν χρῖσαι αὐτὸν ἐλθόντα), cf. SB
iv. 797f.: certain Rabbinic passages suggest that it is "nicht unwahrscheinlich, dass die Erwartung, Elias werde einst den Messias salben, hier u. da
jüdischerseits ausgesprochen worden ist". The idea would follow naturally
from that of Elijah as the eschatological high priest, on which see J. JEREMIAS,
art. "Ἠλ(ε)ίας", *TWNT* ii. 934 f.; *SB* iv. 462f., 789-792. It was at any rate
a widespread belief that Elijah would precede the Messiah, cf. MOWINCKEL,
op. cit., 299.
[2] Cf. SJÖBERG, *op. cit.*, 73, 80 f.; MOWINCKEL, *op. cit.*, 305 f., with references; JEREMIAS, *The Servant of God*², 60, n. 252.
[3] That the thought of the hidden Messiah was already current in the
first century is proved by John vii 27, on which see C. K. BARRETT, *The
Gospel according to St John* (1955), 266: "John (who uses the objection of
this verse in order to lead up to the pronouncement of the next) probably
used the well-known Jewish belief but adapted it to his own thought of a
supernatural, heavenly redeemer".

In 31.1 Justin declares that Christ will come on the clouds as the Son of man according to Daniel's prophecy, which he then quotes (Dan. vii 9-28). Trypho then says:

"Sir, these and similar scriptures compel us to await someone glorious and great, him who as Son of man receives from the Ancient of Days the everlasting kingdom [1]). But this so-called Messiah of yours was so dishonoured and inglorious as to have incurred the final curse in the law of God, for he was crucified" (32.1).

Does Trypho mean that he personally is convinced by Justin's argument that the passage from Daniel is messianic, or that the Jews so understand it in any case? Or are the words merely put into Trypho's mouth for the sake of the argument?

We have seen that Trypho denies the pre-existence and the divinity of the Messiah, and correctly expresses the Jewish belief in a Messiah who will be "a man from men". This is consistent and, moreover, compatible with the thought that the Messiah would suffer, which Trypho also expresses (see below). It is true that there are Rabbinic passages [2]) which make use of Dan. vii, but they do little more than admit that the figure in Dan. vii 13 points to the Messiah like other prophecies (Ps. xxi 6; Jer. xxx 21; Amos ix 11; Zech. ix 9), with no emphasis on the Son of man as a superhuman Messiah from heaven, on verse 13 in particular, or on Son of man as a messianic title. But Trypho's declaration is hardly comparable with these, following immediately as it does on Justin's quotation from Dan. vii; it implies that Dan. vii 13 is fully understood, as in Christian interpretation, to refer to the Son of man-Messiah from heaven. The inconsistency of this admission of Trypho's with the notion of a purely human Messiah on the one hand, and with the denial of the Messiah's pre-existence and divinity on the other, is evident. It is impossible to reconcile this denial with the acceptance of a messianic view of Dan. vii, for such a view cannot but imply a supernatural figure, as in 1 Enoch 37-71 and 2 Esdras 13. We may say, then, that Trypho's words in 32.1 cannot be taken to mean that the Jews understood the passage

[1]) H. J. SCHOEPS, Theologie und Geschichte des Judenchristentums (1949), 78, n. 4, implies that this is valueless as evidence for Jewish views, since it is in a Christian book.
[2]) SB i. 66 f., 486, 956-959; cf. G. DALMAN, The Words of Jesus (1902), 245-247.

to refer to the Messiah [1]), nor that Trypho himself was convinced by Justin's arguments, because subsequently (in 38 and 48, as we have seen) he denies that the Jews thought of the Messiah as a celestial and pre-existent being. We are bound to the second alternative, that Justin has put these words into Trypho's mouth for the sake of the argument.

That this is the case is fully borne out by a consideration of the conceptions, both attributed to the Jew in the Dialogue, of the Messiah's two advents and of his sufferings—conceptions, it should be emphasized, closely related to one another.

If the conclusion reached about the idea of the Son of man is correct, confidence is also shaken in those passages where Trypho the Jew refers to the sufferings of the Messiah, a conception just as characteristic of Christian belief as that of the Son of man, although, of course, the idea of a suffering Messiah might, *prima facie*, be a true picture of Jewish belief and an aspect of the expectation of a *human* Messiah. The passage to which appeal is chiefly made reads as follows:

"Then Trypho remarked, 'Be assured that all our nation waits for the Messiah; and we admit that all the scriptures which you have quoted refer to him. Moreover, I also admit that the name of Jesus, by which the son of Nave (Nun) was called, has inclined me very strongly to adopt this view. But whether the Messiah should be so shamefully crucified, this we are in doubt about. For whosoever is crucified is said in the law to be accursed, so that I am exceedingly incredulous on this point. It is quite clear, indeed, that the scriptures announce that the Messiah had to suffer; but we wish to learn if you can prove to us whether it was by the suffering cursed in the law'.

"I replied to him, 'If the Messiah was not to suffer, and the prophets had not foretold that he would be led to death on account of the sins of the people, and be dishonoured and scourged, and reckoned among the transgressors, and be led as a sheep to the slaughter, whose generation, the prophet says, no man can declare, then you would have good cause to wonder. But if these are to be characteristic of him and mark him out to all, how is it possible for us to do anything else than believe in him most confidently? And will not as many as have understood the writings of the prophets, whenever they hear merely that he was crucified, say that this is he and no other?' " (89).

" 'Bring us on, then', said Trypho, 'by the scriptures, that we may also be persuaded by you; for we know that he should suffer and be led as a sheep. But prove to us whether he must be crucified and die so disgracefully and so dishonourably by the death cursed in the law. For we cannot bring ourselves even to think of this' " (90.1).

---

[1]) Cf. T. W. MANSON, "I do not think that we can infer anything from this passage concerning the Jewish interpretation of Dan. vii current in Justin's day", "The Son of Man in Daniel, Enoch and the Gospels" (1949), *Studies in the Gospels and Epistles*, ed. M. BLACK (1962), 128.

But it would be misleading to take this passage in isolation. JEREMIAS [1]) maintains that Justin's "report seems to be trustworthy that the final parting of ways occurred not over the preliminary question of whether the Messiah was παθητός, but the Christian doctrine that he had not only suffered, but died on the cross, a death upon which God had laid his curse". But JEREMIAS does not appear to be certain. We must, he says, "be on our guard against the statements of an apologist", but they must not "be dismissed too lightly". Again, "Justin's statements must not be pressed". In fact, the most reasonable assumption is that Justin simply attributes to Trypho the stock and authentic Jewish objection to a crucified Messiah (cf. 1 Cor. i 23).

Admittedly Trypho elsewhere concedes that the Messiah must suffer.

"Let these things be as you say, namely, that it was foretold Messiah would suffer, and is called a stone, and after his first advent (παρουσία), in which it had been announced he would suffer, would come in glory and be judge finally of all, and eternal king and priest. Now show if this man is he of whom these prophecies were made" (36.1).

"You have sufficiently proved by means of the scriptures previously quoted by you, that it is declared in the scriptures that the Messiah must suffer, and come again with glory, and receive the eternal kingdom over all the nations, every kingdom being made subject to him. Now show us that this man is he" (39.7).

The substance of both these utterances is in the main identical, with one notable difference. In the former Trypho concedes Justin's point of view for the sake of argument, in the latter he goes further and confesses himself *convinced* by Justin's use of scripture. All he still demands is proof that the Christian Messiah is the Messiah in question.

---

[1]) *The Servant of God* [2], 74; cf. SCHÜRER, *op. cit.*, II. ii. 185; HARNACK, *op. cit.*, 74, n. 3; W. D. DAVIES, *Paul and Rabbinic Judaism* (1948), 280 f. Opinions on the trustworthiness of Trypho's utterance as an index to Jewish belief in a suffering Messiah continue to differ widely. HENRY SCOTT HOLLAND wrote: "Trypho easily allows the *suffering* of the Christ, though it is hard to say whether he held this before Justin's proofs or not" (art. "St. Justinus Martyr", *A Dictionary of Christian Biography* (ed. W. SMITH and H. WACE) iii (1882), 584b). But SJÖBERG, *op. cit.*, 254 ("Als Zeuge für den Glauben an den leidenden Messias im Judentum sollte Justin ausscheiden") agrees with older writers like V. H. STANTON (*The Jewish and the Christian Messiah* (1886), 123) in regarding the Dialogue as a very weak witness to Jewish belief in a suffering Messiah. C. GUIGNEBERT, *The Jewish World in the Time of Jesus* (1939), 148, n.1, is also quite right in taking Trypho's words as in reality those of the apologist himself.

In both these passages we have, in addition to the thought of the sufferings of the Messiah, that of his two advents. The combination of this latter Christian idea [1]) with that of the suffering Messiah in itself casts serious doubts on the reliability of Trypho's admission in 90.1 that the Messiah must suffer. Is the idea of the Messiah's two advents, one in humility and suffering, the other with glory and power, conceivable in Judaism?

The nearest approach [2]) is to be found in sayings attributed to two third-century Rabbis. According to Rabbi Johanan the Messiah is for a time driven from his rule by the heathen, and so may be said to suffer, but he resumes it again. Rabbi Levi said the last redeemer, like the first (Moses) will be revealed and then be hidden for a time before his final appearance [3]). These resemblances, however, besides being considerably later than the Dialogue, are not true parallels at all, because the Messiah already at his (first) coming enters upon his rule, to resume it later after a period of concealment. There is no question of the Messiah, as in Christianity, only entering upon his rule after a previous advent attended by humility and suffering, much less of a departure into heaven before a second victorious advent. It is true that Trypho's utterances, in so far as they make no actual reference to the Messiah's exaltation into heaven before his assumption of kingship, might conceivably be viewed as in this respect fully in accord with Jewish ideas. Moreover, Justin's report in 68 that the Jewish teachers (implying discussions with Jews other than Trypho) agree that the scriptures he adduces prove that the Messiah "was to suffer and to be worshipped" and that "he will come to suffer and to reign", omits not only this feature but possibly also that of two advents. Nevertheless, in view of other passages no reliance whatever can in fact be placed on these omissions, as if they implied agreement with Jewish belief.

In the first place, we have already seen that Justin attributes to Trypho the expectation of the Son of man from heaven depicted

---

[1]) See Justin's own statements of it in chapters 14, 32, 40, 49, 52, 110, and cf. *Apol.* I, 52.3: δύο γὰρ αὐτοῦ παρουσίας προεκήρυξαν οἱ προφῆται· μίαν μέν, τὴν ἤδη γενομένην, ὡς ἀτίμου καὶ παθητοῦ ἀνθρώπου, τὴν δὲ δευτέραν, ὅταν μετὰ δόξης ἐξ οὐρανῶν μετὰ τῆς ἀγγελικῆς αὐτοῦ στρατιᾶς παραγενήσεσθαι κεκήρυκται.

[2]) The doctrine of the two Messiahs is irrelevant unless, as has been held, Messiah ben Joseph and Messiah ben David are identical; cf. H. ODEBERG, 3 *Enoch* (1928), Part II, 145.

[3]) *SB* ii. 284 f.; cf. SJÖBERG, *op. cit.*, 87-9.

in the vision in Dan. vii. Secondly, 68 includes statements very similar to those in 36 and 39, one of which explicitly mentions and the other clearly implies the idea of two advents. But it is in 68.9 that Justin goes so far as to say of the Jewish teachers:

"And since they are compelled, they agree that whatever scriptures we mention to them, which expressly prove that the Messiah was to suffer and to be worshipped and (to be called) God, and which I have already recited to you, do refer to Messiah, but they venture to assert that this man is not the Messiah. But they admit that he will come to suffer [1]) and to reign and to be worshipped as God".

How could Jews possibly have believed that the Messiah after his sufferings would be worshipped as God? This is patently Christian. That the thought of two advents ascribed to Trypho is simply the Christian doctrine is finally proved when Justin himself declares:

"O unreasoning men, understanding not what has been proved by all these passages, that two advents (παρουσίαι) of his have been announced, one, in which he is set forth as suffering and inglorious and dishonoured and crucified, the second, in which he shall come from heaven with glory" (110.2) [2]).

The fact is that Justin has overplayed his role of Christian apologist. Trypho is even represented as impressed by the possibility that the Messiah's name should be Jesus (89.1, quoted earlier). The Dialogue is reliable only when Trypho expresses the otherwise known Jewish beliefs in a Messiah who would be entirely human, and who would be hidden for a period before his manifestation to the world. This reliability ceases when it comes to the notion not only of a suffering Messiah, but of a Son of man-Messiah and of a Messiah who would appear twice, first in humiliation and then in power and glory. The messianic ideas expressed by Trypho bristle with inconsistencies which no amount of ingenuity can resolve into a harmonious picture. This is due to the ill-matched combination of genuinely Jewish beliefs and of Christian doctrines which Justin has put into Trypho's mouth for apologetic purposes.

---

[1]) "The earliest evidence for the belief that Messiah suffers appears to be Pesiqta Rabbathi on Zech. ix 9. As it now stands this seems to be from about the ninth century A.D.", SHOTWELL, op. cit., 76.

[2]) ἀλόγιστοι, μὴ συνιέντες, ὅπερ διὰ πάντων τῶν λόγων ἀποδέδεικται, ὅτι δύο παρουσίαι αὐτοῦ κατηγγελμέναι εἰσί· μία μέν, ἐν ᾗ παθητὸς καὶ ἄδοξος καὶ ἄτιμος καὶ σταυρούμενος κεκήρυκται, ἡ δὲ δευτέρα, ἐν ᾗ μετὰ δόξης ἀπὸ τῶν οὐρανῶν παρέσται. Compare with this the closely similar passage in *Apol.* I, 52.3 quoted above on page 304, note 1.

Allusions to the Messianic Idea
in the Pentateuch and Former Prophets
by JOSEPH KLAUSNER

JEWISH SCRIPTURAL interpretation and Christian theology join together in one aspiration—to find the Messianic idea in many Biblical passages where in truth there is not even a hint of it. In the very first chapters of the Book of Genesis, ancient Jewish and Christian scholars found such Messianic prophecies. In the curse upon the serpent (Gen. 3:14-15), especially in the words, "They shall bruise thy head and thou shalt bruise their heel," both the Targum attributed to Jonathan ben Uzziel and the Targum Yerushalmi saw an indication that the people Israel would conquer Sammael "in the days of the King-Messiah." Correspondingly, the church father Irenaeus found that these words indicated the Christian redeemer: it is the seed of the woman which is the enemy of the serpent, the serpent being Satan and the impulse to evil ("And I will put enmity between thee and the woman, and between thy seed and her seed"); and if the serpent, that is, Satan, shall bruise man first ("head"), then finally ("heel") man shall bruise him. Also in the blessing by Noah, "Blessed be the LORD, the God of Shem. . . . God shall enlarge Japheth and he shall dwell in the tents of Shem" (Gen. 9:26-27), the theologians have sought to find a hint of the Messiah, who will come forth from Shem and through whom the sons of Japheth also will acknowledge the God of Shem.[1] The Christian theologians actually find a hint like this in

[1] See in the book of Castelli, *Il Messia*, pp. 37-38, and especially Note 1 on p. 37.

26

the promises: "A prophet will the LORD thy God raise up unto thee, from the midst of thee, of thy brethren, like unto me"; and "I will raise them up a prophet from among their brethren, like unto thee, and I will put My words in his mouth" (Deut. 18:15 and 18);[2] also in the "Redeemer" in Job (19:25): "I know that my Redeemer liveth, and at the last He will rise upon the dust."

All these examples, and very many more like them, are theological interpretations, which it is fitting merely to mention before we pass on to the matter of genuinely Messianic Biblical passages. When we reach the Talmudic period, which coincides in time with the rise of Christianity, we shall be forced to concern ourselves again with interpretations like these, since they greatly influenced the people of that period. They had historical value, therefore, only in a very late time. Biblical verses of this kind, which were mistakenly considered to be Messianic, had a significant Messianic influence upon people of later generations; but at the time when they were written they had no Messianic purpose.

However, there are verses which, although considered Messianic only through error and by interpretation, nevertheless have a definite value in the history of the development of the Messianic idea from the beginning. They, likewise, did not exhibit a clear Messianic intent; yet they were the embryonic material from which the Messianic idea was afterward formed, under the influence of historical events. Such are, first of all, the verses containing the blessing of the LORD upon Abraham, Isaac, and Jacob:

And I will make of thee a great nation, and I will bless thee and make thy name great, and be thou a blessing . . . and in thee shall all the families of the earth be blessed (Gen. 12:2-3).

And I will multiply thy seed as the stars of heaven . . . and by thy seed shall all nations of the earth bless themselves (Gen. 26:4).

And thy seed shall be as the dust of the earth. . . . And in thee and in thy seed shall all the families of the earth be blessed (Gen. 28:14).

[2] See John 5:46; 6:14; 7:40; Acts 3:22; 7:37. Cf. also Matt. 11:3; 17:5; Luke 7:19, 9:35. For details see Hühn, *Die messian. Weissag.* I, pp. 141-143.

If we find in most of the Messianic expectations of the prophetic period, on the one hand, the prophetic promise that the people Israel will spread and increase and attain earthly happiness, and on the other hand, that Israel will be a light to the nations and from its land will go forth instruction to all peoples—then the *embryonic* material of these Messianic expectations is already to be found in the verses just cited. All the nations of the earth and all the families of mankind will be blessed by Israel—this is the kind of prophetic promise which has a nationalistic and universalistic quality at one and the same time; in other words, that quality which belongs to the Messianic idea in its entirety.

Thus it is also with the verses "Then ye shall be Mine own treasure from among all peoples," and "Ye shall be unto Me a kingdom of priests and a holy nation" (Exodus 19:5-6). This is not the Messianic expectation as it was pictured later, but from expressions like these the national and universal Messianic expectation grew. It is impossible to determine with certainty when these verses were written. But in all probability they preceded the writings of those prophets whose books are preserved to us, since according even to the most extreme Biblical critics the verses quoted belong to the Yahwist (J) and Elohist (E) sources, which preceded by a considerable time Amos and Hosea.[3] Therefore it is possible to see in these verses and verses like them the basis upon which little by little all Jewish Messianism was built. So from this point of view these verses have great importance in the history of the Messianic idea.

Of similar importance also are the well known verses (II Sam. 7:8-16 and I Chron. 17:7-14) in which Nathan the prophet assures David, "Thy throne shall be established forever" and "Thy house and thy kingdom shall be made sure forever." During his discourse the prophet says: "And I will appoint a place for My people Israel, and I will plant them, that they may dwell in their own place . . . neither shall the children of wickedness afflict them any more, as at the first" (II Sam. 7:10). If the Messianic idea in the prophetic period and in all later periods is almost never portrayed without mentioning "the kingdom of the house of David," and the name "son of David"

[3] See O. Eissfeldt, *Hexateuch-Synopse*, Leipzig, 1922, pp. 19*, 48*, 52-53*.

(or even "David") became almost the essential personal name of the Messiah [4]—then we can see that the belief in the victory of the house of David and in its everlasting sovereignty is already to be found in these verses.[5]

Traces of the belief that the Messiah will come forth from the house of David and that his kingdom will be an everlasting kingdom are also sought by Jewish and Christian theologians in the Blessing of Jacob, as bestowed upon Judah (Gen. 49:10):

> The sceptre shall not depart from Judah,
> Nor the ruler's staff from between his feet,
> Until Shiloh come;
> And unto him shall the obedience of the peoples be.

A whole literature has been written about this verse, and there is even a good-sized book on the different interpretations of the word "Shiloh." [6] Undoubtedly the part of the verse in which this word appears is very difficult to explain. The majority of modern Biblical exegetes read, according to the Targums Onkelos and Yerushalmi, the Syriac Peshitto, the translations of Aquila and Symmachus, and the interpretations of Rashi and Abravanel, not "Shiloh" but "*shello*" (the one to whom), and consider superfluous the words "and unto him" which follow Shiloh; they are only an interpretative addition to the expression "until shall come the one to whom shall be the obedience (that is, submission) of the peoples" ("peoples" meaning, as many times in the Bible, the tribes of Israel). This interpretation is particularly supported by the Septuagint, which translated "until Shiloh come" by ἕως ἂν ἔλθῃ τὰ ἀποκείμενα αὐτῷ.[7] But this interpretation, in spite of the fact that there is a certain scientific foundation for it, is not acceptable.

It is likewise difficult to consider the text in error and to read with Gressmann [8] *mōshelōh* (his ruler) instead of "Shiloh." Nearer the

---

[4] See above, pp. 20–21.

[5] See on this, E. Koenig, *Die messian. Weissag. d. A.T.*, 1923, pp. 132–142.

[6] A. Poznansky, *Schiloh: Ein Beitrag zur Geschichte der Messiaslehre*, Leipzig, 1904.

[7] "Until shall come the things stored up for him." See the book of Stade, *Geschichte des Volkes Israel*, I, 158ff.

[8] H. Gressmann, *Eschatologie*, pp. 263, 287.

truth is another interpretation, according to which the meaning intended in the word "Shiloh" is *Solomon, the son of David.* "Shiloh" is from the root SHLH, which is related both in meaning and in origin to the root SHLM, from which the name "Solomon" (*Shelomoh* in Hebrew) is formed.[9] And since all recent scholars conclude that the Blessing of Jacob was not composed before the period of the monarchy, it may be conjectured that it was composed in the time of Solomon. After the brilliant victories of David, which subdued many peoples, "the kingdom was established in the hand of Solomon," according to the witness of Scripture (I Kings 2:46). He did not have to fight any more; the submission of neighboring peoples was assured (compare "the rod that smote thee," Isa. 14:29). If we remember the promise of Nathan the prophet, mentioned above, the words in this verse will be understood in their plain meaning: "The sceptre shall not depart from Judah, nor the ruler's staff from between his feet, until Shiloh (Solomon) comes, and unto him shall be the obedience (submission) of the peoples." To be sure, Judah, like any of the larger tribes, always had rulers and lawgivers for itself; but the tribe of Judah had "the obedience of the peoples" only in the time of Solomon. There are no Messianic allusions, therefore, in this verse;[10] yet it is one of those Biblical passages upon which were based the Messianic expectations of later times. It, like the words of Nathan the prophet, strengthened the faith that the kingdom of the house of David would endure forever, rising up time after time to return to its pristine glory.[11]

From the same period and of the same nature are the well known verses in the section on Balaam:

> I see him, but not now;
> I behold him, but not nigh;
> There shall step forth [12] a star out of Jacob,
> And a sceptre shall rise out of Israel,
> And shall smite through the corners of Moab,

[9] The Christian theologian Hengstenberg has already translated "Shiloh" by the name Friedrich, i.e., man of *peace and security.*

[10] In spite of the opinion of Gressmann (*op. cit.*, p. 288), who thinks the old traditional view—that we have here a Messianic promise—correct.

[11] See also Castelli, *op. cit.*, pp. 38–41.

[12] Wellhausen reads *zārah*, "shine forth."

And break down all the sons of Seth.
And Edom shall be a possession,
Seir also, even his enemies,[13] shall be a possession;
While Israel doeth valiantly.
And out of Jacob shall one have dominion
And shall destroy the remnant from the city.
(Numbers 24:17–19).

All this was interpreted in a Messianic sense by the early Christians.[14] But more especially did the Sages of the Talmud see Messianic indications in them. It is well known that Rabbi Akiba said of Simon ben-Coziba, "A star has gone forth out of Jacob"; from this circumstance, apparently, this Messiah acquired the name Bar-Cochba, "son of a star." [15] But actually, these words refer to David.[16] This is what is called in Latin *vaticinium ex eventu* (prophecy out of the event). David was the first to conquer Edom; he also struck Moab a decisive blow.

In the same passage, a little before the verses just discussed (Num. 24:7), there is mention of Agag ("his king shall be higher than Agag"),[17] who was conquered and all but destroyed by Saul, as is well known. Some verses farther on (Num. 24:20–24), Amalek and its downfall are mentioned ("Amalek was the first of the nations, but his end shall come to destruction"); there is also mention of the victory of Asshur (Assyria) over the Kenites ("Nevertheless the Kenite shall be wasted, until Asshur shall carry thee away captive"); likewise of ships from the island of Cyprus ("Kittim," in Assyrian "Gutium") which shall harass Asshur ("But ships shall come from the coast of Kittim, and shall afflict Asshur"). All this shows that it is

[13] In the opinion of many Biblical scholars, the words "his enemies" belong to the end of the verse thus: "from the city of his enemies."
[14] See Matt. 2:2; Luke 1:78; Acts 22:16.
[15] Yer. Taanith, Chap. 4, Hal. 8; Lamentations Rabbah on the text "The LORD hath swallowed up" (2:2). See J. Klausner, *When a Nation Fights for Its Freedom* [in Hebrew], 5th ed., Tel-Aviv, 5707 [1947], pp. 167–169, in contrast to S. Yeivin, *The War of Bar-Cochba* [in Hebrew], Jerusalem, 5706, pp. 54–56.
[16] See Rashi and Ibn-Ezra on this passage; the Christian scholar Grotius also agrees with this view. In the opinion of Sellin (*Heilandserwartung*, 1909, pp. 10–12), this is a Messianic prophecy even earlier than the time of David, since a king is not mentioned in it, and it is very difficult in its idioms.
[17] In the Septuagint "Gog" is written in place of this. But "Gog" came to Ezekiel from an ancient legend (Sellin, *op. cit.*, p. 10).

impossible to date the Balaam passages before the period of David and Solomon.[18] And everything which we find in all these passages was realized in David, as has already been observed by medieval Jewish interpreters. There is no doubt, therefore, that it is impossible to consider these passages as Messianic in themselves. But also there is no doubt, in my opinion, that the exaggerated hopes about the glorious future of the people Israel, its greatness, its power, and its broad area of authority in days to come, as expressed in these verses, are the embryonic material out of which was afterward formed the Messianic idea in all its majesty and splendor.

Also considered as Messianic are those passages in the Books of Leviticus and Deuteronomy which contain the conditional blessing and curse (Lev. 26:3–45; Deut. 28:1–68, also Deut. 30:3–10) and which, according to the opinion of Biblical critics, are later than the first of the writing prophets. The Tannaitic Midrash, *Siphra*, on the section *Behukkothai* ("In My Statutes," beginning at Lev. 26:3), interprets all the words of the blessing as referring to the Messianic age.[19] In a certain sense this is correct. The great good, which God will pour out upon His people in the Messianic age, will come only as a result of the keeping of the statutes. Such was the opinion of the prophets and such is also the opinion of many of the Sages of the Talmud.[20] But still more Messianic is the assurance that comes after the terrific rebuke: "And yet for all that, when they are in the land of their enemies, I will not reject them, neither will I abhor them, to destroy them utterly, and to break my covenant with them; for I am the LORD their God," and so on (Lev. 26:44). This is the great promise, that the people Israel will endure forever, and after all the misery which it will undergo for its iniquities, it will rouse itself and be restored to its pristine glory. This matter is thoroughly explained in the Book of Deuteronomy:

[18] Against the opinions of David Kahana in his treatise *Introduction to the Balaam Passage* [in Hebrew] (Lvov, 5643 [1883]), of Sellin (see the preceding note), and of Hommel in his book *Die altisraelitische Ueberlieferung in inschriftlicher Beleuchtung*, München, 1897.
[19] See below, Part II, Chap. X.
[20] See below, Part III, Chap. IV.

Then the LORD thy God will turn thy captivity, and have compassion upon thee, and will return and gather thee from all the peoples, whither the LORD thy God hath scattered thee. If any of thine that are dispersed be in the uttermost parts of heaven, from thence will the LORD thy God gather thee, and from thence will He fetch thee. And the LORD thy God will bring thee into the land which thy fathers possessed, and thou shalt possess it; and He will do thee good, and multiply thee above thy fathers (Deut. 30:3–5).

The idea of "the return to Zion"—that hope of redemption and faith in the return of the natives to their own country, which is the cornerstone of the Jewish Messianic ideal—is found here almost in its entirety. This is not at all surprising. The Book of Deuteronomy is not earlier than the books of those prophets whose prophecies were collected together and preserved to us. Verses such as "The LORD will bring thee, and *thy king* whom thou shalt set over thee, unto a nation that thou hast not known, thou nor thy fathers" (Deut. 28:36) do not allow the possibility of dating the Book of Deuteronomy *in its entirety* before the fall of Samaria (individual elements could be more ancient). In the Book of Leviticus—of which the "rebuke section" is later even than Deuteronomy, in the opinion of Biblical critics (upon which doubt may still be cast), who attribute it to the Priestly Code —the idea of "the return to Zion" is not expressed with complete clarity. Nevertheless, a Messianic expectation is also to be seen in the assurance, "When they are in the land of their enemies, I will not reject them, neither will I abhor them, to destroy them utterly, and to break my covenant with them." Not yet here—nor in the Book of Deuteronomy—is the hope that a period of universal bliss and general ethical perfection will come upon mankind. Also still lacking is any hint of a personal Messiah. But already here *is* a strong hope that the Jewish nation will not sink down in sin and be lost among the Gentile nations.

With a strong hand and an outstretched arm, the LORD will rule over His nation, according to the words of Ezekiel. He will *force* it, by severe troubles and afflictions, to offer complete repentance. Then He will renew His covenant with it, which is to say that He will restore it to its own land and to its pristine glory, and it will again be "a

197

kingdom of priests and a holy nation." This is not only the nucleus from which grew many other Messianic expectations; it is the cornerstone of the hope for revival.[21] Moreover, the well known conception of "the birth pangs of the Messiah," to precede the future redemption, is already embodied in these passages, which are not so early, yet in any case contain an early prophetic deposit.

The fact that we did not find the Messianic idea expressed in all its fullness at a time earlier than the period of the monarchy cannot be considered a contradiction of the opinion expressed above,[22] that the Messianic idea is the result of the history of afflictions which began for Israel in its early youth, and that the personal Messiah is the product of the early traditions about Moses, the first redeemer. The Messianic idea is a complex of hopes for the future; it can, therefore, be embodied only in the words of prophecy. And there are almost no words of prophecy left to us from before the period of the monarchy, in spite of the fact that undoubtedly there were prophets in Israel before this period. In the Pentateuch and in the Former Prophets it is not possible even to seek for hopes for the future based on the Messianic idea, because these books are not collections of prophetic visions, but compilations of popular traditions, histories, and legends. To be sure, in places in the Pentateuch and Former Prophets where prophetic oracles do occur, we have found indications of Messianic expectations.[23]

This and one other thing.

The Messianic idea, whatever its origin, was not created in a day as we have it now. It grew, it developed little by little, while various periods of time passed by. Undoubtedly, in the early period there was yearning for a Messiah—a simple longing to be redeemed from victorious and oppressive enemies; I have already indicated above that every one of the judges was a temporary Messiah for his tribe or for

---

[21] See Castelli, op. cit., pp. 41–43. On the passages wrongly thought to be Messianic, see in general in this book, pp. 34–76; also Hühn, op. cit., I, 134–156. On the Psalms which are wrongly considered to be Messianic, and on "the servant of the LORD" in Isa. 52–53, I shall speak in the following chapters.

[22] See above, Chap. II, pp. 19–22.

[23] Such an indication may *possibly* be found also in the last verse of the prayer of Hannah (I Sam. 2:10).

a group of tribes.[24] In the time of David and Solomon this longing was increased and extended. But the Messianic idea did not reach its highest development before the time of Amos and Hosea. This is in the nature of things. The prophets had to reach an exceedingly great height in order that the Messianic ideal might become broad and lofty, spiritual and universal. I have already said that the personal Messiah has in him both kingly and prophetic attributes. Thus the more the prophetic standard was elevated, the more the whole Messianic idea was exalted and ennobled.

I did wish to emphasize one thing at the end of this chapter: if we see that Amos and Hosea—and a little later Isaiah and Micah—already had a very highly developed Messianic ideal, then we *must* suppose that this ideal was not born at one moment, but developed during the course of several generations before the time of Jeroboam II (son of Joash) and Uzziah son of Amaziah. And in at least half of the Messianic verses cited in the present chapter can be seen, in my opinion, those elements from which grew all those lofty Messianic expectations that are the glory and pride of Hebrew prophecy in its golden age.[25]

[24] See above, p. 19.
[25] These ideas, which were completely new when I published them for the first time (in *Ha-Shiloah*, Vol. 12, of the year 1903), have become acceptable views in recent years, owing to the researches of Gunkel, Gressmann, Sellin, Eichrodt, Kittel, *et al.*, who of course, to our sorrow, did not read modern Hebrew.

Daniel

(C. 167–164 B.C.E.) [1]

by JOSEPH KLAUSNER

AFTER "THE day of small things," lasting from the time of Ezra and Nehemiah almost to the middle of the Seleucid period, "the day of big things" came back. For "the small things"—as they appeared to the eye—prepared for and made possible the larger things. At the end of the Persian period (424–333) Judah gradually bestirred herself out of her depressed condition; during the rule of Alexander the Great and his successors (333–301) and the rule of the Ptolemies in Judah (301–198), Judah began to flourish; and during the rule of the first Seleucids (198–175) she achieved prosperity and wealth (the Tobiads).

This material success brought in its wake a vigorous cultural development: at that time were composed many of the Psalms, the Song of Songs, Koheleth, Esther, Ben-Sira. Jewish "Wisdom," having become at that time a kind of world-view mediating between theology, philosophy, and the practical understanding of life, was deepened and rounded out by the Greek thought which had penetrated into Palestine. The life of the individual became richer and fuller, a spirit of ease was felt in the land, and the space within the

---

[1] Actually, it would be proper to give here the Messianic expectations in the Book of Ben-Sira, which in any case cannot be later than the years 200–180, and so is prior to the Book of Daniel; but I do not wish to mix the Apocryphal and Pseudepigraphical books with those that were received within the canon of Holy Scripture.

walls with which Ezra and Nehemiah had surrounded their people became too restricted for the Jewish aristocracy.

Hellenism, which brought with it the beautified and broadened life, also brought much licentiousness: the acceptance of a foreign culture is always accompanied by a certain superficiality and frivolousness, inasmuch as it is hard to penetrate to the *heart* of the foreign culture, which is the fruit of the historical development, the racial characteristics, and the peculiar life-circumstances of the foreign people; but it is very easy to adopt the *external* symbols of the foreign culture.

So it has been always and everywhere, and so it was also in Judah in Ptolemaic and Seleucid times. In the time of Seleucus IV Philopator (187–175), the overseer of the Temple, Simon [or Simeon], "Prince of the Sanctuary," incited Heliodorus against the Temple treasury and against Onias III; and in the time of Antiochus IV Epiphanes (175–164), Yeshua-Jason bought the high-priesthood for money and established a gymnasium in Jerusalem (174–171); then Menelaus paid a higher price for the high-priesthood and received it from the king (171–170).

Antiochus came to Jerusalem during his first campaign against Egypt (170) and plundered the Temple. In the year 168 he sent to Jerusalem Apollonius, who conducted massacres in the cities of Judah, forced people to violate the religious laws (after greater Hellenization they violated them willingly), stopped the continual burnt-offerings, and on the 15th of ̇Kislev (168) set up "the detestable thing that causeth appalment" [Dan. 11:31, 12:11] beside the altar, upon which on the 25th of Kislev was offered as a sacrifice—a swine. The whole land, which had been fairly quiet for three hundred years, was filled with the moans of the tortured. The betrayers increased, but along with them the "pious" (Hasidim) and the holy, who actually died the death of martyrs; also "they that turn the many to righteousness" [Dan. 12:3], that is, those who aroused others to stand by their convictions and to die for the sanctity of Judaism, which at that time was already a complete and lofty world-view. Mattithiah [Mattathias] son of Yohanan Hashmonai [John Hasmoneus] arose as one that would "turn the many to righteousness" with sword in hand (167–166). He was followed by his son Judah the Maccabee [Judas Maccabeus], who even during the first two years of his political activity (166–164) was able to accomplish such great things as to amaze with his prowess Jews and Syrians alike. It was apparent that with a little more effort he would succeed in gaining control of the city and the sanctuary and in restoring Judaism to its former dignity.

And in the natal hour of great things like this, as in every hour of great men and extraordinary events, there appeared a great new book —great in its value for the time and for future generations. This book is the one we now have bearing the name "the Book of Daniel."

Ezekiel (14:14, 20) speaks of three righteous men, "Noah, Daniel, and Job"; and in another place (28:3) he says to the prince of Tyre, "Behold, thou art wiser than Daniel!" From these passages it appears clear that this Daniel was famous in the nation in Ezekiel's time as a righteous man and a great sage; could this be the Daniel of whom it is related in the Book of Daniel (1:1–6) that he was brought to Babylon *as a youth* "in the third year of the reign of Jehoiakim"? Ezekiel went into exile with the exile of *Jehoiachin* and began to prophesy in the fifth year of this exile, being then, apparently, thirty years of age (Ezek. 1:1–2); and if he had previously prophesied in Jerusalem he was then all the more not a youth. Thus he was not in any case younger than Daniel. So how could he speak of Daniel as being a righteous and wise man famous in his own time, and mention him immediately after Noah? Now most scholars have concluded that the reference is to "Danel," the righteous judge in the Ugaritic texts.

Moreover, the author of the Book of Daniel could not have been a prophet of the time of the Babylonian exile and the return to Zion —for various reasons. *First,* the historical data in Daniel in everything having to do with the time of the Babylonian exile and the Persian empire are full of startling errors: the conquest of Jehoiakim by Nebuchadrezzar is not mentioned in Kings at all, and from II Chronicles (36:3, 10) it appears that Nebuchadrezzar came up against him not in the third year of his reign but at the end of it; Belshazzar is here the son of Nebuchadrezzar, ruling after him (5:2, 11), while in fact the king after Nebuchadrezzar was Evil-Merodach his son, and

Belshazzar was the first-born son of Nabunaid; Darius is called "the
Mede" (6:1, Eng. 5:31, and 11:1) and "Darius the son of Ahasuerus
of the seed of the Medes" (9:1), while actually he was a Persian and
not the son of Ahasuerus at all; only four kings arise in Persia after
Darius the Mede or including him (11:2), while in fact seven kings
ruled after him.

In contrast to this we find in Daniel 8 and 11 almost exact details
of the events that took place from the time of Alexander the Great
to Antiochus Epiphanes. We find here "the king of Greece," who
conquers the kings of Persia and Media, and at his death "his kingdom
. . . shall be divided toward the four winds of heaven" (the four
kingdoms that were founded after the death of Alexander the Great,
particularly after the battle of Ipsus in the year 301); the wars of
"the kings of the south" (the Ptolemies) with "the kings of the north"
(the Seleucids) in the time of Ptolemy II Philadelphus (285–247)
and Antiochus II Theos (261–247) and following; the doings of
Antiochus IV Epiphanes in all his relations with Egypt and Judah,
the stoppage of the continual burnt-offering, the setting-up of "the
detestable thing that causeth appalment," those who "do wickedly
against the covenant," and the "wise among the people" who "cause
the many to understand"; and even the "little help" with which these
"wise" ones have been helped by Mattathias and Judas (11:7–42).
Only the end of Antiochus is not known clearly by the author of the
Book of Daniel,[2] and he also does not yet know exactly the time of
the dedication of the Temple by Judas Maccabeus.[3] All these things
demonstrate that we have before us not a prophet of the time of the

[2] According to 11:45, Antiochus should have died approaching Palestine, but
he actually died at the end of the year 164 in a distant Persian city. See on this
Budde, *Geschichte der althebr. Litt.*, pp. 328–330; Steuernagel, *Einleitung*, pp. 560–
661; Bernfeld, *Introduction*, II, 201–222; J. Klausner, *History of the Second
Temple*, III, 36, Note 1. Bernfeld goes so far as to agree with Lagarde that Daniel
7 was written at the time of the siege of Jerusalem by the Emperor Vespasian (*op.
cit.*, II, 215–220). See in detail H. H. Rowley, *Darius the Mede and the Four
World Empires in the Book of Daniel*, Cardiff, 1935.
[3] See Schürer, *Geschichte*, III⁴, 264–265. And not according to the opinion of
Hühn, *Die messian. Weissag.*, I, 77, Note 7, that in Daniel 8:14 the Dedication is
already indicated, since actually the words "then shall the sanctuary be victorious" [or "cleansed"] are only *a hope for the future*, like the rest of the verses
containing computations, and not an account of an established fact (see on this
Marti, *Daniel*, 1901, p. 60).

Babylonian exile, but an apocalyptist of the time of Antiochus Epiphanes, who composed his book near the year 164 B.C.E. (approximately 167–166 B.C.E.).

Second, it is said in the Book of Daniel that the time has come "to seal [finish] vision and prophet" (9:24)—something that could not have been said in the days of Ezekiel and Deutero-Isaiah. In the Book of Daniel the angels are called by personal names: "the man Gabriel" (9:21) and "Michael, the great prince who standeth for the children of thy people" (12:1; 10:21). Also in it are "the prince of the kingdom of Persia" and "the prince of Greece" (10:13, 20). In it (12:2) comes for the first time *the belief in the resurrection of the dead* in a clear and decisive form. And finally, in it Daniel is praised because he did not defile himself with the king's food and wine, but was nourished only by vegetables and water (1:8–16); and because "his windows were open in his upper chamber toward Jerusalem, and he kneeled upon his knees three times a day and prayed and gave thanks before his God" (6:11).

Third, in its Hebrew language occur late words such as *miqtsath* (part, 1:2), *hayyeb* (endanger, 1:10); *hathakh* in the sense of "determine" or "decree" (9:24), *rasham* (inscribe, 10:21), *hattamid* in the sense of "the continual burnt-offering" (8:11), and so on. Its Aramaic language is later than that of Ezra. And finally, there are in it *Greek words*, such as *kaitheros* [lyre], *sumponeyah* [bagpipe or dulcimer] and *pesanterin* [psaltery] (3:5).[4]

Fourth, the Book of Daniel stands in the collection of the Prophets after Ezekiel only in the Septuagint, while in the *Hebrew*, the original Holy Scriptures, it stands not among the Prophets but among the Writings—which clearly proves that it was written at a late date, when the collection of the Prophets was already finished and closed. Only the Gospels[5] call the author of the book "Daniel the prophet," while in ancient Jewish literature he is not considered as a prophet, or at least he is not called by that name. Finally, Ben-Sira, who speaks much of Noah (44:17–18) and mentions Job (49:9) along with

---

[4] See the brief introduction to the commentary on the Book of Daniel by Meir Lambert (*The Bible with Scientific Commentary*, ed. A. Kahana), Kiev, 1906.
[5] Matt. 24:15; Mark 13:14.

Ezekiel,[6] does not notice Daniel (who comes in Ezekiel along with Noah and Job, as mentioned above) with even one word.

If we·take these facts into consideration, we must confess that the Daniel mentioned in Ezekiel, or the Daniel mentioned in Ezra (8:2) as one of those returning from exile and in Nehemiah (10:7) as one of those making the covenant and setting their seal upon it, could not have been the author of the book before us. The actual author of this book lived in the time of the persecution by Antiochus Epiphanes, as was already recognized by Porphyry (233–305 c.e.) almost seventeen centuries ago;[7] and in order to strengthen the people in their faith, he felt the urge to tell them, in a series of scrolls, about Daniel, who also suffered persecution for his religion, and in whose time also certain kings (Nebuchadrezzar, Belshazzar, and Darius) forbade the observance of the ceremonial laws, showed impudence toward God, and plundered the vessels of the Temple, just as Antiochus had done in their own time. This author perceived from the beginning the troubles that would come upon Israel, but he also foresaw by the Holy Spirit that the troubles would not be prolonged and that salvation was soon to come.[8] Thus Daniel became the progenitor of two new types of literature that flourished like mushrooms from Hasmonean times until the rebellion of Bar-Cochba: (1) the "outside books" in general, which are called the "Pseudepigrapha" because they are attributed to ancient worthies (the Book of Enoch, the Book of Baruch, IV Ezra, and so on); and (2) the special kind of these books called by the name "revelation" or "apocalypse" because they contain prophecy of the future in the form of "revelations," "visions," and "appearances" filled with enigmatic figures of

---

[6] See what has been written on this by David Kahana in his article, "The Hebrew Ben-Sira and Its Texts" [in Hebrew] (*Ha-Shiloah*, XVIII, 366).

[7] This fact has been transmitted to us by one of the Church Fathers, Jerome (*Prologus in Danielem*); also in his commentary on Daniel 7:7 (Ed. Migne, Col. 530).

[8] There is, to be sure, an opinion that Daniel 1–6 was written at the time of the Babylonian exile and afterward by the earlier Daniel, while only Daniel 7–12 was composed in the time of Antiochus. But it is difficult to agree with this, since there is already found in Daniel 2 "the Vision of the Four Kingdoms," of which the fourth is undoubtedly the kingdom of Greece (Schürer, *op. cit.*, III[4], 265), and this vision is completely parallel with Daniel 7 (Budde, *op. cit.*, pp. 332–333). See also Rowley, *op. cit.*, pp. 2–5, 176–178.

speech, which are actually a review of what is past, but purport to be *a look into the future*, a glimpse of things to come.[9]

From what we have said, it follows as a matter of course that almost all of Daniel is Messianic in spirit; but Chapters 2, 6–9, and 12 are Messianic in essence.

In Chapter 2 there comes as the interpretation of the dream of Nebuchadrezzar by Daniel "the vision of the four kingdoms." The first kingdom is that of Nebuchadrezzar (kingdom of Babylonia), the second is the kingdom of Media (the author of the Book of Daniel thought that Darius *the Mede* preceded Cyrus *the Persian*), the third is the kingdom of Persia, and the fourth is the kingdom of Greece, which will be "a divided kingdom" (2:41): the kingdom of Greece will be divided into the kingdom of the Ptolemies and the kingdom of the Seleucids.

And in the days of those kings shall the God of heaven set up a kingdom, which shall never be destroyed; nor shall the kingdom be left to another people; it shall break in pieces and consume all these kingdoms, but it shall stand for ever (2:44).

This kingdom is *the world-wide Messianic kingdom*. It is described in more brilliant colors in the dream of Daniel in Chapter 7, which is known as "the vision of the four beasts."

Four beasts come up from the sea. The first beast is a lion—the kingdom of Babylonia, the strongest of the kingdoms; the second is a bear—the kingdom of Media; the third is a leopard—the kingdom of Persia; and the fourth beast, "diverse from all the beasts that were before it," "dreadful and terrible and strong exceedingly, having great iron teeth, devouring and breaking in pieces and stamping the remains with its feet," and equipped with "ten horns" (7:7), is the kingdom of Greece. Its ten horns are the ten kings (as known to the author of the Book of Daniel) that ruled from Alexander the Great to Antiochus Epiphanes. In the opinion of most interpreters they are: Alexander the Great, Seleucus I (Nicator), Antiochus I (Soter), Antiochus II (Theos), Seleucus II (Callinicus), Seleucus III (Cer-

---

[9] See for details on this J. Klausner, "Outside Books" [in Hebrew] (*Otsar ha-Yahadut, Hoveret le-Dogma*, Warsaw, 1906, pp. 97ff.).

aunus), Antiochus III (the Great), Heliodorus, Seleucus IV (Philopator), and Demetrius I (Soter).[10]

From the midst of these ten horns comes forth "another horn, a
little one" (7:8), or, as it is said farther on in Hebrew, "a little horn"
(8:9), in which are "eyes like the eyes of a man, and a mouth speaking
great things" (7:8). However, the LORD, the "ancient of days,"
sits upon His throne for judgment *and books are opened*, the horn
speaks "great words," but "because of the voice" of these words (that
is, as a punishment for them) the beast is slain, its body is destroyed,
and it is given to be completely burned with fire; as for the rest of the
beasts, only their dominion is taken away, while their lives are "prolonged for a season and a time" (7:9–12). Then the scene continues
thus:

> I saw in visions of the night,
> And behold there came *with the clouds of heaven*
> *One like unto a son of man*,
> And he came even to the Ancient of days,
> And he was brought near before Him.
> And there was given him dominion,
> And glory, and a kingdom,
> That all the peoples, nations, and languages
> Should serve him;
> His dominion is an everlasting dominion,
>   which shall not pass away, ,
> And his kingdom that which shall not be destroyed (7:13–14).

Daniel asks one of those standing before the LORD to tell him the
interpretation of the matter, and this one explains to him that the
four beasts are four kings (in the sense of kingdoms), and that after
them "*the saints of the Most High* shall receive the kingdom, and
possess the kingdom for ever, even for ever and ever" (7:18).

It is clear that the "son of man" [meaning "human being"] coming
"with the clouds of heaven," whose kingdom is an everlasting kingdom, is the same as these "saints of the Most High," for Verse 18 is
only an explanation of Verse 14. Since the rest of the peoples possessing kingdoms (the Babylonians, the Medes, the Persians, and the

[10] See the aforesaid commentary of R. Meir Lambert on Daniel 7:7 (p. 14);
Marti, *op. cit.*, pp. 49–51; Rowley, *op. cit.*, pp. 98–124.

Greeks) were portrayed as devouring *beasts* coming up from the sea, the righteous but oppressed people Israel was portrayed as a *human being* coming from heaven with the clouds. This conclusion will not be denied by anyone who takes the plain meaning of Scripture.[11]

But in a comparatively short time after the composition of the Book of Daniel it was thought among the Jews that this "son of man" was the Messiah. This is not surprising: a "human being" that could approach the throne of God and that could be given "dominion, and glory, and a kingdom" and whom all the peoples would serve and whose dominion would be an everlasting dominion could not possibly be other than the King-Messiah.[12] So thinks the author of the Ethiopic book of Enoch (Chapters 37–71, which are among the earlier ones), and of this Jesus *hints* in his use of "the son of man" in the Gospels;[13] according to the Gospel writers, he said that in the Messianic age "they will see the son of man coming on the clouds of heaven with power and great glory."[14] Actually, there is no *individual Messiah* in Daniel: the entire people Israel is the Messiah that will exercise everlasting dominion throughout the whole world. This is to be seen again in the details about the little horn with the "mouth speaking great things," which is nothing else, according to the explanation in Daniel itself, than a cruel and impudent king. Of him it is said:

And he shall speak words against the Most High, and shall wear out the saints of the Most High; and he shall think *to change the seasons and the law;* and they shall be given into his hand until *a time and times and half a time.* But the judgment shall sit, and his dominion shall be taken away, to

[11] This is opposed by Gressmann, *Eschatologie,* pp. 334–365, who of course was right about the mythological elements in the "son of man with the clouds of heaven," but was not right in his conclusion that the meaning of "son of man" here was *the Messiah from the very beginning.* This is also the answer to the argument of W.·Bousset, *Die Religion des Judentums im späthellenistischen Zeitalter,* 3rd ed., ed. Gressmann, Tübingen, 1926, pp. 265–268; 352–355.

[12] This is the natural cause of the ancient and widespread error which Gressmann (*op. cit.,* pp. 337–339) and Bousset (*loc. cit.*) cannot understand.

[13] I have emphasized the word "hints" because complete clarity could not have been present, since in Ezekiel the term "son of man" is on no account used in this sense (see J. Klausner, *Jesus of Nazareth,* 5th [Hebrew] ed., Jerusalem, 1945, pp. 266–268 [Eng. ed., pp. 256–257], and the additions at the end of the book, pp. 500–501 [not in Eng. ed.]).

[14] See Matt. 24:30; Mark 13:26; Luke 21:27, etc.

be consumed and to be destroyed unto the end. And the kingdom and the dominion, and the greatness of the kingdoms under the whole heaven, shall be given to *the people of the saints of the Most High;* their kingdom is an everlasting kingdom, and all dominions shall serve and obey them (7:25–27).

It is clear that the one spoken of here is Antiochus Epiphanes, the only Greek king who thought "to change the seasons and the law"; and that in the "son of man" coming "with the clouds of heaven" Daniel sees "the people of the saints of the Most High," that is to say, the entire people Israel, which at first will be delivered over to Antiochus "until a time and times and half a time" (see below), but afterward will be given world-wide Messianic dominion.

The same ideas are set forth in the Hebrew language in Chapter 8, where are mentioned "the king of Greece" (8:21)—Alexander the Great—and "a king of fierce countenance and understanding stratagems" (8:23)—Antiochus the man of "culture," who destroyed "them that are mighty and the people of *the saints*," who relied upon "his cunning" and destroyed many "in time of security" (8:24–25), and by whom "the continual burnt-offering was taken away, and the place of [the] sanctuary was cast down" (8:11). There is also in this chapter something like an explanation of "a time and times and half a time": the continual burnt-offering will be taken away and Baal-Shamayim ("the detestable thing"—or "transgression"—"that causeth appalment") [15] will be set up upon [or beside] the altar "unto two thousand and three hundred evenings and mornings; then shall the sanctuary be victorious" (8:13–14). This means 1,150 days, amounting to a little less than three and a half (lunar) years, the equivalent of "a time and times and half a time," or "a time, times, and a half," as it is in the Hebrew part of Daniel (12:7). But at the end of Daniel we find:

And from the time that the continual burnt-offering shall be taken away, and the detestable thing that causeth appalment [16] set up, there shall be *a*

[15] See on all this many important details in E. Bickermann, *Der Gott der Makkabäer*, Berlin, 1937, pp. 90–139; 169–183. But one must beware of the extreme conclusions that come forth under the influence of the great number of Jew-hating scholars in Germany; these men have even influenced important Jewish scholars without the latter realizing it.

[16] The profanation of the Temple by Antiochus Epiphanes is called exactly

thousand two hundred and ninety days. Happy is he that waiteth, and cometh to *the thousand three hundred and thirty-five days* (12:11-12).

These numbers amount to more than three and a half years or the 1,150 days that we found above. The numbers could not be made exact, because the author did not know *exactly* when Judas Maccabeus would win such a decisive victory over the Syrians that he could come to Jerusalem and restore the suspended continual burnt-offering to its former condition. Therefore the Book of Daniel was written before the dedication of the Temple by Judas Maccabeus, as has already been said above.

This idea stands forth in Chapter 9 also. Daniel relates that in the first year of Darius the son of Ahasuerus he was meditating "in the books, over the number of the years, whereof the word of the LORD came to Jeremiah the prophet, that He would accomplish for the desolations of Jerusalem seventy years" (9:2).[17] Then he prayed to the LORD that He would turn away His anger from His people and His city. After that came "the man Gabriel" to make him "skilful of understanding" with these words:

Seventy weeks are decreed upon thy people and upon thy holy city, to finish the transgression, and to make an end of sin, and to forgive iniquity, and to bring in everlasting righteousness, and to seal vision and prophet, and to anoint the most holy place. Know therefore and discern, that from the going forth of the word to restore and to build Jerusalem unto one anointed, a prince, shall be seven weeks; and for threescore and two weeks, it shall be built again, with broad place and moat, but in troublous times. And after the threescore and two weeks shall an anointed one be cut off, and be no more; and the people of a prince that shall come shall destroy the city and the sanctuary; but his end shall be with a flood; and unto the end of the war desolations are determined. And he shall make a firm covenant with many for one week; and for half of the week he shall cause the sacrifice and the offering to cease; and upon the wing of detestable things shall be that which causeth appalment; and that until the

the same thing [usual translation "abomination of desolation"] in I Maccabees (1:54). Nestle explains these words thus: *shiqquts* is a term of opprobrium for Baal and *shomem* is Shamayim; thus we have here Baal-Shamayim, which is the name given to Zeus-Jupiter in the Phoenician and Palmyrene inscriptions (see the commentary of M. Lambert on Dan. 8:13; 11:31). See Bickermann, *loc. cit.*

[17] Cf. Jer. 25:11-12; 29:10.

extermination wholly determined be poured out upon that which causeth appalment (9:24-27).

We have arrived at "the matter of the seventy weeks," about which heaps upon heaps of books have been written. Most modern scholars interpret these verses thus: Daniel wishes to vindicate the prophecies of Jeremiah about the seventy years after which Judah will be restored to its previous condition—a prophecy which was not completely fulfilled, since during the Persian and Greek periods Judah was an insignificant and subject state, while in the time of Antiochus misfortunes and ruin had overtaken it; therefore Daniel considers the seventy years of Jeremiah to be seventy sabbatical years, something already intimated at the end of II Chronicles (36:21): "to fulfil the word of the LORD by the mouth of Jeremiah, until the land had been paid her sabbaths; for as long as she lay desolate she kept sabbath, *to fulfil threescore and ten years.*" Seventy weeks (sabbatical years) are, therefore, 490 years. Of this total, "seven weeks," that is, forty-nine years, had passed down to the time of Cyrus ("one anointed, a prince," as we found in Isa. 45:1—"to His anointed, to Cyrus"), when Jerusalem was "restored and built" (586-537). "Threescore and two weeks" are 434 years, and these are the years that passed, in the opinion of the author of the Book of Daniel, from the Edict of Cyrus until "an anointed one" was "cut off," that is, until Onias III was removed from his high-priestly office at the beginning of the reign of Antiochus Epiphanes.[18] These years were "troublous times" for Judah, for she did not then grow great and strong according to the promises of the prophets; indeed, she did not even have independence.

As a matter of fact, from the Edict of Cyrus to the beginning of the reign of Antiochus there passed not 434, but 362 years (537-175). The author of the Book of Daniel erred, therefore, by about seventy years. But this is not to be wondered at, since Josephus made errors like this in his *Antiquities* and *Wars,* and the Alexandrian Jew

---

[18] Wellhausen (*Israel. u. jüd. Geschichte,* 7th ed., 1914, p. 234, Note 1) remarks that in Hebrew the interpretation of "an anointed one shall be cut off" is not that the anointed priest will be slain, but that the high-priestly office will cease to exist.

211

Demetrius [19] (*c.* 200 B.C.E.) erred in the Jewish chronology of the period of the Second Temple by seventy years, *exactly as did the author of the Book of Daniel.*[20]

"For one week" [according to the author of Daniel], that is, for seven years, the first deeds of Antiochus will continue (175–168). He will "destroy the city and the sanctuary" together "with" (according to the reading of the Septuagint) the "prince that shall come" (Jason), and will force many to transgress the holy covenant (or will "make a firm covenant with many" of the Hellenizers). And "for half of the week," that is, for three and a half years ("a time and times and half a time"—"a time, times, and a half"), he will stop sacrifices and offerings and place upon the altar "detestable things that cause appalment" (168–165).[21]

Actually, the service in the Temple was suspended less than three and a half years, since according to I Maccabees the continual burnt-offering was stopped on the 15th of Kislev 145 (Seleucid era) and restored on the 25th of Kislev 148; and in the opinion of Kautzsch,[22] this offering was not stopped until the 25th of Kislev, as would appear from I Maccabees 4:42 and 54. However, as I have already said, the author of the Book of Daniel did not yet know exactly when the dedication of the Temple would take place; but on the basis of the first victories of Judas Maccabeus he expected an early deliverance, to be manifested first of all by the restoration of the divine service in its proper place; and along with this he expected the Jews, "the people of the saints of the Most High," to attain to an everlasting kingdom, while the kingdom of the wicked Antiochus would come to an end and pass away together with the rest of the kingdoms of the Gentiles.

This is the Messianic ideal of the author of the Book of Daniel. It does not contain *material prosperity,* but it does contain a strong

---

[19] Cited by Clement of Alexandria (*Stromata,* 1, 21, 141).

[20] See in detail Schürer, *op. cit.,* III [4], 265–266.

[21] [According to an emended text in 9:26–27.] See the lucid interpretation of Castelli, *Il Messia,* pp. 152–156.

[22] See Note *p* on p. 36 of his translation of I Maccabees in his edition of *Apokryphen und Pseudepigraphen des Alten Testaments,* Vol. I. According to the reckoning of Marti (*op. cit.,* p. 60), the author of the Book of Daniel erred by the short time of forty-five days.

hope for political power and for political and religious authority over all the Gentiles. Nor can it be said that this hope was entirely disappointed. The Hasmoneans were inflamed by a strong faith that the hour had come for the "kingdom of heaven," that is, the kingdom of the God of heaven, to be revealed to the world and for the kingdom of Greece to fall. They established, after severe struggles, a Jewish kingdom, which, to be sure, did not spread over the whole world and did not destroy all the kingdoms of the Gentiles, but did achieve independence, became measurably powerful, and had much to do with the spread of the knowledge of the God of Israel in the pagan world.

However, these Messianic expectations are expectations only for the people Israel as one collective entity. But in the time of Daniel most of the Jews were already far from the old national life, in which the individual was completely swallowed up in the community; therefore, those who went forth to a death of martyrdom and could no longer see with their own eyes the felicity of their nation needed *personal reward and punishment.* So the author of the Book of Daniel supplies this need by the belief in *the resurrection of the dead:* after the downfall of Antiochus there will be a time of trouble for Israel such as never was since they became a nation, and Michael, "the great prince," will fight for them:

And at that time thy people shall be delivered, *every one that shall be found written in the book.*[23] And many of them that sleep in the dust of the earth shall awake, some to everlasting life, and some to reproaches and everlasting abhorrence. And they that are wise shall shine as the brightness of the firmament; and they that turn the many to righteousness [24] as the stars for ever and ever (12:1-3).

The resurrection of the dead, which is mentioned here in such a clear manner for the first time in the Bible, is, therefore, shared by both the good and the bad; but the former rise to everlasting life and

[23] Cf. Mal. 3:16: "And *a book of remembrance* was written before Him, *for them that feared the LORD,* and that thought upon His name" (see above, p. 215). From here came "the book of heaven" in the Ethiopic book of Enoch, and "the heavenly tablets" in the Book of Jubilees, etc.

[24] I.e., those who arouse others also to hold fast to their faith like the righteous. Cf. Isa. 53:11: "by his knowledge shall my righteous servant justify many" (see above, p. 167, Note 35).

the latter to everlasting reproaches. However, it is to be concluded from the word "many" that the clear conception that *all* would rise from the dead had not yet penetrated into the nation.[25] In any case, Judaism was already near the idea of reward and punishment for *each individual* in the nation. The collective national system of rewards and punishments of the ancient prophets was no longer sufficient. Daniel thus served as a progenitor of the Apocrypha and Pseudepigrapha: his Messianic idea eventuates in "the Age to Come" and "the World to Come," in which the dead rise and "the righteous sit enthroned, their crowns on their heads, and enjoy the lustre of the Shekhinah" [Ber. 17a]. The latter idea is already embodied in the words "they that are wise shall shine as the brightness of the firmament." Thus the Messianic idea became bound up with and attached to "eschatology" (not in the sense of "the end of this age" but in the sense of the life after death) something that we find not only in the Pseudepigrapha, but also in Talmud and Midrash from the Mishnah onward.

The age of prophecy had passed and the age of Talmudic Aggadah had come.

[25] Against the opinion of Hühn, *op. cit.*, I, 79, who thinks that the word *rabbim* ("many") is not restrictive, and that the resurrection of the dead in the Book of Daniel is general. See Marti, *op. cit.*, p. 90.

The Name and Personality of
the Messiah

by JOSEPH KLAUSNER

ATTENTION HAS already been called to the fact that the Biblical and post-Biblical Messianic passages differ fundamentally at one point. In the Biblical Messianic idea the point of emphasis is the redemption of Israel and the propagation of the idea of monotheism and divine righteousness. The Messiah himself is sometimes not even mentioned among the promises of redemption; and even if he is mentioned here and there he does not occupy the dominant place that he assumed later. The word *Messiah* ("anointed one") itself, in the sense in which it was used from the second century B.C.E. onward, does not occur in the Old Testament.[1]

It is entirely otherwise with the Messianic expectations of post-Biblical times. Here the Messiah stands in the foreground. He becomes the center of all events, from him proceeds almost everything, and the coming age itself is named after him "the Days of the Messiah" or "the generation of Messiah." [2] Even in the Tannaitic period this emphasis on the personality of the Messiah is already prominent.

But the signs of natural development must not be overlooked. When we survey the very detailed and exaggerated descriptions of the Messiah's every movement and characteristic that come from the post-Tannaitic period; when we take into account the innumerable legends relating to the personality of the Messiah that sprang up like mushrooms in the centuries between the Tannaim and the Cru-

[1] See on this above, pp. 7–8.
[2] See D. Castelli, *Il Messia*, pp. 202–203.

sades—we must admit that, in comparison with these exaggerated flights of fancy, the sayings about the personality of the Messiah transmitted to us in the name of the Tannaim are almost as scanty and as simple as those in the Old Testament. The reason for this is that the Tannaitic sayings are still for the most part close to the original conception. For at the beginning legendary conceptions are always simple and few in number. Only through a more or less lengthy development do they become richer, more poetic, more filled with flights of fancy; but they lose their originality and simplicity. In the Tannaitic period there was still no conception of a "suffering Messiah" or a "pre-existent Messiah." A noble king, a man of the highest moral quality, a political and spiritual leader of the Jewish people in particular and of the human race in general—this, and only this, was the Messiah of the Tannaim.

Before we proceed to a presentation of Tannaitic sayings concerning the name and personality of the Messiah, a remark must be made about one matter: concerning a kingdom of heaven on earth without the ideal king, that is to say, a Messianic kingdom without a Messiah, as sometimes found in the Old Testament and even in the Apocrypha and Pseudepigrapha,[3] the Tannaim know nothing at all. The remark of R. Johanan ben Torta to R. Akiba, "Akiba, grass will be growing up around your jawbones, and still the son of David will not come," is not, as James Drummond thought,[4] proof that R. Johanan ben Torta could imagine the future of Israel without a Messiah. It is simply, as the context shows,[5] a personal criticism of R. Akiba, who had made the mistake of believing in the messiahship of Bar-Cochba. The second saying which Drummond cites as proof of the possibility of the Messianic age without a Messiah, one from Rab Hillel,[6] is Amoraic and belongs to a time when there was a desire to weaken belief in the Messiah's coming as much as possible.[7] Against this it suffices to quote the rule of R. Judah the Patriarch:

[3] This was shown by James Drummond in a special chapter entitled "Conception of the Ideal Kingdom Without a Messiah" (*The Jewish Messiah*, pp. 226–273).
[4] *Ibid.*, pp. 272–273.
[5] Yerushalmi, Taanith 4:8.
[6] See *The Jewish Messiah*, p. 273.
[7] See above, pp. 404–405.

Whoever omits to mention . . . the kingdom of the house of David (that is, "And the throne of Thy servant David do Thou make ready therein speedily") [8] in "Who buildest Jerusalem" (the fourteenth of the Eighteen Benedictions) has not performed his obligation.[9]

The Messiah and his kingdom, a heritage from the house of David, are, therefore, an inseparable part of the Messianic expectations of the Tannaim.

We turn now to the *name* of the Messiah. This name receives rather strange treatment in the Talmudic literature. An unusual Baraitha reads:

Seven things were created before the world was created, and these are they: the Torah, repentance, the Garden of Eden, Gehenna, the Throne of Glory, the Temple, and *the name of the Messiah*. The Torah, for it is written. . . .[10] The name of the Messiah, as it is written (Ps. 72:17), "His name shall endure forever, *before the sun* his name shall exist." [11]

What this name is the Baraitha does not reveal. To conclude from this passage that the Messiah's name preceded the creation of the world (pre-existence) would be senseless. What need would there be for the Messiah's name if the Messiah himself did not yet exist? And that the Messiah himself existed before Creation is nowhere stated in Tannaitic literature. We have no recourse, therefore, but to accept the hypothesis of Maurice Vernes [12] and Meir Friedmann,[13] that "the name of the Messiah" is the *idea* of the Messiah, or, more exactly, *the idea of redemption through the Messiah*. This idea did precede Creation. Before Creation, Israel was predestined to produce from itself a Messiah, to be redeemed by him, and through him to redeem all

[8] Or, according to the Palestinian text of the *Shemoneh Esreh* found in the Genizah (Schechter, *JQR*, X [1898], 654–659): "Have mercy . . . upon the *kingdom* of the house of David, Thy righteous Messiah."

[9] Berakhoth 49a.

[10] Here are given Biblical verses appropriate to each one of the seven things; but the verses may not belong to the Baraitha, since they are introduced by the late (Aramaic) formula "for it is written" instead of the earlier (Hebrew) formula "as it is said."

[11] Pesahim 54a; Nedarim 39b. The same thing is said in the "Parables" of the Ethiopic Enoch, 48:3 (see above, Part II, p. 293). See also the Targum Pseudo-Jonathan on Zech. 4:7.

[12] See M. Vernes, *Histoire des idées messianiques*, pp. 268–269; p. 281, Note 1.

[13] Introduction to Seder Eliyahu, p. 114.

mankind from the evil in the world. That this interpretation of the expression "the name of the Messiah" is not strange to the Talmudic writers is shown by a passage from Midrash Rabbah, a Palestinian work. In it "the name of the Messiah" is numbered among the things which were "contemplated for creation." [14] This existence before the creation of the world is apparently also alluded to in the following Baraitha:

The school of R. Ishmael taught: As a reward for the observance of the three "firsts" (that is, the first days of the three festivals mentioned in Lev. 23:7, 35, 40), they (Israel) merited three other "firsts": to destroy the seed of Esau, the building of the Temple, *and the name of the Messiah.* . . . as it is written (Isa. 41:27), *"First* unto Zion, behold, behold them." [15]

This can only be interpreted in the sense that the idea of the Messiah, like the destruction of the seed of Esau (that is, Edom-Rome), which still remained to be accomplished, and like the future rebuilding of the Temple,[16] had been predestined before Creation (the name of the Messiah is "first"); and by the keeping of the festivals the children of Israel had shown themselves worthy of this "idea" of the Messiah. We have here, in some measure, the Platonic doctrine of ideas.[17]

As to actual names, only a few are known to the Tannaitic period, in contrast to the following period, which knows them in great numbers. The one name that recurs most frequently (but much less in the pre-Hadrianic time) is "Son of David." This occurs frequently not only as a descriptive title but as an actual personal name. A late

14 Gen. R., Chap. 1: "Six things preceded the creation of the world; some of them were actually created, while the creation of the others was already contemplated. The Torah and the Throne of Glory were created. . . . The creation of the Patriarchs . . . , of Israel . . . , of the Temple . . . [and] of the name of Messiah was contemplated." This passage militates against everything which Christian scholars have written on this subject (see, e.g., Schürer, *Geschichte*, II⁴, 616–619).

15 Pesahim 5a.

16 The Temple also, in the Baraitha in Pesahim and Nedarim, and in Genesis Rabbah, is numbered among the things that preceded the creation of the world.

17 The identification of the name with the person of the Messiah, which Bousset-Gressmann (*Das Religion des Judentums,* pp. 262–263 and Note 1, p. 263) wish to make, is not correct, at least so far as the really early Jewish literature is concerned. In that literature the name, *but not the person,* precedes the creation of the world. The idea is perhaps based on the verse "Before the sun his name shall exist" (Ps. 72:17).

Palestinian Baraitha [18] calls him not "Son of David" but simply "David"; [19] but this occurs only once in the Tannaitic period. On the contrary, "Redeemer" was apparently a common designation, since it already occurs in the first benediction of the *Shemoneh Esreh* and in the "Thanksgivings" of Ben-Sira,[20] which are so similar to the *Shemoneh Esreh*. Indeed, this designation occurs in the Old Testament itself.[21]

The other names for the Messiah from the Tannaitic period come from individual Tannaim who, on the basis of their exposition of some Biblical verse, would apply to the Messiah a chance title current only among themselves and their disciples. The following is an example:

R. Jose the Galilean (pre-Hadrianic) says: Also, the Messiah's name is called Peace, for it is written (Isa. 9:5) "Everlasting Father, Prince (called) Peace." [22]

This name did not take root in Jewish literature or become current among common people or scholars; it remained the individual creation of R. Jose the Galilean.

Another name for the Messiah attained even less recognition:

R. Judah [23] expounded as follows: "The burden of the word of the LORD. In the land of Hadrach and in Damascus shall be his resting-place, for the

---

[18] Yerushalmi, Berakhoth 2:4 (f. 5*a*).

[19] This usage is also quoted in the name of the early Amora (semi-Tanna) Rab, Sanhedrin 99*a;* but see above, pp. 46-47.

[20] The "Thanksgivings" occur in the Hebrew text of 51:12. Supplementary Verse 5 reads, "Give thanks unto the *Redeemer* of Israel, for His mercy endureth forever"; here, however, the term is applied to God.

[21] Cf. Isa. 49:7 with 59:20.

[22] *Pereq ha-Shalom* (Chapter on Peace), which is a supplement at the end of Derekh Erets Zuta. See the texts published by M. Higger, *Massekhtoth Zeeroth,* New York, 1929, pp. 101, 104. [The Hebrew words *Sar-Shalom,* if joined together, may mean "Prince of Peace" (as usually translated) or "Prince (called) Peace," as interpreted here by R. Jose. The words may also be separated into two names, "Prince" (and) "Peace" as in San. 94*a*.]

[23] This is the younger disciple of R. Akiba, R. Judah ben Ilai, who taught after the time of Hadrian. But apparently he offered this exposition while still a student, since R. Jose ben Dormaskith was a pre-Hadrianic teacher (Bacher, *Agada der Tannaiten,* I, 293, Heb. trans., Vol. I, Part II, p. 113, Note 15). R. Jose roundly denounces the exposition and calls Judah *Berabbi* ["son (or pupil) of the master"(?), perhaps in sarcasm] (but see article BYRBY in Kohut, *Aruch Completum,* II², 183).

LORD's is the eye of man and all the tribes of Israel" (Zech. 9:1). This (the name Hadrach) is the Messiah, who will be *Had* ("sharp") toward the nations of the world, but *Rach* ("soft") toward Israel.[24]

But this artificial interpretation was immediately rejected by an older pre-Hadrianic Tanna named R. Jose ben Dormaskith,[25] who replied to R. Judah thus:

Son of the master! Why do you twist the Scriptures against us? I call heaven and earth to witness that I am from Damascus and that there is a place there and its name is Hadrach.[26]

This Rabbinic passage is important because it shows us how groundless and hypothetical a Messianic name may sometimes be, even if it comes from the Sages of the pre-Hadrianic period.

Still more so are the names applied by the Amoraim. A whole series of names from a well known Talmudic passage is based purely on paronomasia:

The school of R. Shila said: His name is Shiloh. . . . The school of R. Yannai said: His name is Yinnon. . . . The school of R. Haninah maintained: His name is Haninah. . . . Some say: His name is Menahem ("comforter"), son of Hezekiah. . . . The Rabbis said: His name is "the leper of the school of Rabbi." [27]

Thus each school chooses a name for the Messiah resembling in sound and meaning the name of that school or its head. Only one name found here is introduced by the formula "some say" and is not dependent on paronomasia; therefore this Messianic name is more important, and may come from an earlier period. It is the name "Menahem son of Hezekiah," and it may refer to Menahem, son of Judas the Galilean and grandson of Hezekiah, who played an important

---

[24] Siphre, Deut. 1 (ed. Friedmann, 65*a*).

[25] His mother was apparently a proselyte from Damascus; "Dormaskith" is a special form (similar to the Syriac) of the word meaning "Damascene woman."

[26] Siphre, *loc. cit.* In Pesiqta de-Rab Kahana, section on "Sing, O barren one" [Isa. 54:1] (ed. Buber, 143*a*), R. Nehemiah, the regular opponent of R. Judah, says: "The place is called Hadrach." And of course in the Aramaic inscription of Zakur [Zakar, Zakir], king of Hamath, the city of Ḥazrak (Assyrian Ḥaṭriku)—same as Hadrach in Hebrew—is mentioned. See H. Pognon, *Inscriptions sémitiques de la Syrie et de la Mésopotamie*, Paris, 1907, p. 156.

[27] Sanhedrin 98*b*.

464 of course based

THE MESSIANIC IDEA IN ISRAEL

part at the beginning of the First Revolt (*Wars* 2:17:8–9), and according to Graetz [28] considered himself the Messiah.

But the name can equally well be explained symbolically. The Messiah is *the comforter*, on the basis of Lamentations 1:16: "Because *the comforter* is far from me, even he that should refresh my soul." [29] The symbolic meaning of the name Menahem is obvious since the "redeemer" of the nation is also its "comforter" (on the basis of Isa. 40:1; 51:12). But why is he called "son of Hezekiah"? Here perhaps we may still recognize surviving traces of an earlier and truer understanding of the Messianic prophecies of Isaiah, according to which these prophecies were applied to Hezekiah, king of Judah.[30] We hear the last echoes of this once widely current view in the following exposition by a younger contemporary of R. Judah the Patriarch: [31]

"Of the increase [Heb. le*Marbeh*, with an unusual *m*] of his government and peace there shall be no end" (Isa. 9:6). R. Tanhum said: Bar Kappara expounded in Sepphoris, Why is every other *m* in the middle of a word open, while this one is closed? The Holy One, blessed be He, wished to appoint Hezekiah as the Messiah, and Sennacherib as Gog and Magog; whereupon the Attribute of Justice appeared before the Holy One, blessed be He, and said: 'Sovereign of the Universe! If Thou didst not make David the Messiah, who uttered so many hymns and psalms before Thee, wilt Thou appoint Hezekiah as such, who did not hymn Thee in spite of all these miracles which Thou wroughtest for him?' Therefore it (the *m*) was closed. Straightway the earth opened and said to Him: 'Sovereign of the Universe! Let me utter song before Thee instead of this righteous man (Hezekiah), and make him the Messiah.' So it broke into

---

[28] *Op. cit.*, Hebrew trans. by S. P. Rabbinowitz, II, 80, Note 1. See also J. Klausner, *History of the Second Temple* [Heb.], V, 147–149; idem, *When a Nation Fights for Its Freedom* [Heb.], 8th ed. (1952), pp. 169–170.

[29] Sanhedrin 98*b*; Yerushalmi, Berakhoth 2:4; Lam. R. on 1:16 (ed. Buber, f. 45). Menahem (ben Ammiel) as a name of the Messiah is frequently found in the later literature. Still later Nehemiah (of similar meaning) was used, as in Nehemiah ben Hushiel.

[30] In the time of Justin Martyr, the Jews still held strongly to the idea that some of the Messianic oracles of Isaiah (e.g., Chap. 11) refer to Hezekiah (*Dialogue with Trypho*, Chaps. 43, 67, 68, 71, 77). The opinion of the Amora Rab Hillel (quoted above, p. 404), "There shall be no Messiah for Israel because they have already enjoyed him in the days of Hezekiah," is of course also based on this older view.

[31] Sanhedrin 94*a*.

song before Him, as it is written (Isa. 24:16), "From the uttermost part of the earth have we heard songs: Glory to the righteous one." Then the Prince of the Universe [a special angel] said to Him: 'Sovereign of the Universe! Fulfill the desire [32] of this righteous man. But a heavenly voice cried out, "The secret is mine, the secret is mine" (Isa. 24:16, usual interpretation, "I waste away"; the secret here is that Hezekiah cannot become Messiah). To which the prophet rejoined (Isa. 24:16), "Woe is me, woe is me"; how long (must Israel wait for the Messiah)? The heavenly voice again cried out (Isa. 24:16), "The treacherous deal treacherously, yea the treacherous deal very treacherously." [33]

From this very interesting exposition it is to be seen that the truer interpretation of the Messianic passages in Isaiah was not wholly forgotten in the latter part of the Tannaitic period, even though it was somewhat obscured.[34] We may be fairly certain, therefore, that the saying of Rabban Johanan ben Zakkai, "Make ready a throne for Hezekiah, king of Judah, who is coming," [35] refers to the near approach of the Messiah and not to R. Gamaliel the Patriarch, as was thought by Jacob Levy.[36]

Now I turn from the idea and name of the Messiah to his personality.

In no trustworthy, authentic source of the Tannaitic period is to be found any description of the person and characteristics of the Messiah that goes beyond the bounds of human nature. To be sure, his qualities and his deeds surpass the ordinary standard of human powers. But other righteous and pious persons could also perform signs and wonders, and in the Messianic age the supernatural would become the usual, one might almost say, the natural. The miracles which Elijah had performed in his lifetime and would perform in the Messianic age would be in no wise inferior to those of the King-Messiah.

[32] Heb. *tsivyon*, from the Biblical *tsevi*, with the meaning of the Syriac *tsevyana*.

[33] That is to say, they must wait until woes are piled upon woes, and treacheries upon treacheries. So this passage is interpreted (in San. 94a) by the Amora Raba or R. Isaac. See also Kethubboth 112b (end of the tractate).

[34] See F. Weber, *System d. altsyn. palästin. Theologie*, p. 341.

[35] Berakhoth 28b; Yerushalmi, Sotah 9:16, and Abodah Zarah 3:1; Aboth de-R. Nathan, Recension A, Chap. 25 (ed. Schechter, p. 80). See above, Chap. I, p. 396.

[36] See *Neuhebr. Wörterbuch*, II, 362, where Levy wrongly attributes this saying to R. Eliezer.

Only as a mighty ruler and an exalted and unequaled moral personality would the Messiah be superior to all the rest of the saints and prophets of Israel. He might be "a moral superman," to use an expression of Ahad Ha-Am; but his kingdom is definitely *a kingdom of this world.* Of the *divine* nature of the Messiah, there are perhaps certain indications in the later Midrashim; [37] in the authentic writings of the Tannaitic period there is not a trace. Trypho the Jew says in the book of Justin Martyr: "All of us (Jews) expect the Messiah to come as a man from among men." [38] Thus, even if it were possible to prove that the post-Tannaitic literature does indeed ascribe divine nature to the Messiah (though Castelli and Drummond doubt it), we may assume that this feature was indirectly and unconsciously borrowed from Christianity. Or else we must conclude that the increasingly exaggerated and fantastic veneration of the Messiah did not shrink, from the seventh century c.e. onward, even from making him divine. *But in the earlier literature there is no trace of this.*

The following is an interesting Baraitha concerning the Messiah:

Nine persons entered into Paradise during their lifetime: Enoch son of Jared, Elijah, *the Messiah,* Eliezer the servant of Abraham, Hiram king of Tyre, Ebedmelech the Ethiopian, Jabez son of R. Judah the Patriarch, Bithiah daughter of Pharaoh, and Serah daughter of Asher.[39]

Here we have the supposition that the Messiah already exists in Paradise.[40] Yet it is worthy of notice that even in this Baraitha the Messiah is put on a level with mere human beings, distinguished only for their good deeds. Even certain Gentiles are included: Hiram king of Tyre, Ebedmelech the Ethiopian, and Bithiah daughter of the king of Egypt. This Baraitha is, to be sure, very late, since it mentions the son of R. Judah the Patriarch, the redactor of the Mishnah. There are, of course, variant texts of this Baraitha, in which other personages from the Bible are substituted for the Gentiles and R.

---

[37] Collected by Wünsche, *Die Leiden des Messias,* pp. 42, 76, 77–81. Against this opinion see Castelli, *op. cit.,* pp. 203–209; Drummond, *op. cit.,* chapter on "The Nature of the Messiah," pp. 290–295.

[38] See *Dialogue with Trypho,* Chap. 49, beginning (ἄνθρωπον ἐξ ἀνθρώπων).

[39] Derekh Erets Zuta, end of Chap. 1.

[40] Thus he exists also in Ethiopic Enoch 39:6–7; IV Ezra 12:32; 13:26, 52; 14:9. See Schürer, *op. cit.,* II⁴, 616–619; above, Part II, pp. 293, 358–359.

Judah's son.[41] Yet the very fact that the Messiah could be put on the same level with persons like Eliezer and Serah (who occur in all the texts) proves that the Messiah is "a man from among men."
Another similar Baraitha says:

In the Age to Come the son of David will be in the middle, with Adam, Seth, and Methuselah on his right, and Abraham, Moses, and Jacob on his left.[42]

But this Baraitha is also very late and its text corrupt.[43] Perhaps simply "David" is to be read here instead of "the son of David." [44]
On *the characteristics* of the Messiah we have the following exposition from the time of R. Judah the Patriarch:

R. Tanhum said: Bar Kappara expounded in Sepphoris: Why is it written (Ruth 3:17), "These six [a word missing?] of barley gave he to me"? . . . He (Boaz) symbolically intimated to her (Ruth) that six sons were destined to come forth from her, who should each be blessed with six blessings: David, Messiah, Daniel, Hananiah, Mishael, and Azariah. David, for it is written, . . .[45] The Messiah, for it is written (Isa. 11:2), "And the spirit of the LORD shall rest upon him, the spirit of wisdom and understanding, the spirit of counsel and might, the spirit of knowledge and the fear of the LORD." [46]

The Messiah will inherit, therefore, the six "gifts of the Holy Spirit."
The next verse in Isaiah (11:3) reads:

And his delight [literally "smell"] shall be in the fear of the LORD, and he shall not judge after the sight of his eyes, neither decide after the hearing of his ears.

[41] See the *Haggahoth* (Critical Notes) of Elijah of Vilna, *ad loc.; Tosaphoth*, Yebamoth 16b, on *Pasuq;* M. Friedmann, Introduction to Seder Eliyahu, p. 15.
[42] Kallah Rabbathi, Chap. 7, near end (*Hamishshah Konterisim* [Five Tractates] by N. N. Coronel, Vienna, 1864, 13b.
[43] As is evident from the fact that here Jacob comes not after Abraham, but after Moses.
[44] See Sukkah 52b, where the reading is thus: "David in the middle, with Adam, Seth, and Methuselah on his right, and Abraham, Jacob, and Moses on his left." Cf. Midrash Shoḥer Tob (Tehillim), Ps. 18:29 end (ed. Buber, 79). See also J. Klausner, *Jesus of Nazareth*, 5th Heb. ed., p. 344, Note 2 [Eng. ed., p. 320, Note 12].
[45] Here is quoted I Sam. 16:18 as proof of the blessings which David had received; then follows the discussion of the Amoraim on this verse.
[46] Sanhedrin 93ab.

On this is based another attribute of Messiah, the lack of which caused Bar-Cochba to be recognized as a false Messiah:

Bar Koziba reigned two and a half years, and then said to the Rabbis, "I am the Messiah." They answered, "Of Messiah it is written that he smells and judges (that is, he has an instinct for who is right and who is wrong); let us see whether he (Bar-Cochba) can smell and judge?" When they saw that he could not smell and judge,[47] they killed him.[48]

Thus the Messiah should possess a very deep feeling for what is just and right, and in his judgments he should reach the truth by instinct. But this whole passage seems to me rather late, since it is closely connected with a saying of the Amora Raba.[49] It is written in Aramaic, and *in the existing context* this also points to an Amoraic origin (though sometimes an Aramaic saying is quite early). Obviously the passage came into being many years after Bar-Cochba's failure, and served "after the fact," when the grandiose schemes of "the Son of the Star" had collapsed, as a justification of the frightful defeat which the Jews suffered at Bethar.

In connexion with the saying of R. Jose the Galilean quoted above, concerning Messiah's name, stands this further statement of the same Rabbi:

Great is peace, for in the hour when the King-Messiah is manifested to Israel, he will begin speaking with words of peace, as it is written (Isa. 52:7), "How beautiful upon the mountains are the feet of him that bringeth good tidings, that proclaimeth peace." [50]

This is an important statement. The King-Messiah, who must at times be a mighty warrior, begins his glorious career with words of

[47] This is no doubt a reference to the slaying of the innocent R. Eleazar of Modi'im, whom Bar-Cochba put to death on mere suspicion. On this slaying see Graetz, *Geschichte der Juden*, IV, 175–176 (Heb. trans., II, 247); J. Klausner, "Simon Bar-Cochba" (*When a Nation Fights for Its Freedom* [Heb.], 8th ed., 1952, pp. 243–244).

[48] Sanhedrin 93b.

[49] *Loc. cit.:* "Raba said: He smells and judges, as it is written (Isa. 11:3–4), 'and he shall not judge after the sight of his eyes, . . . but with righteousness shall he judge the poor, and decide with equity for the meek of the land.'"

[50] Derekh Erets Zuta, Chap. 11 (the "Chapter on Peace"); M. Higger, *op. cit.*, p. 101, and note, p. 148; Lev. R., Chap. 9.

225

peace. Below, in Chapter IX, we shall see again the importance of this idea.

It was mentioned in the preceding chapter that the Messiah will be anointed by Elijah, from a marvelous flask of anointing oil, from which have already been anointed the Tabernacle, Aaron and his sons, and many of Israel's high priests and kings. It was also mentioned that Aaron's rod, which budded miraculously in the wilderness, will serve the Messiah as a royal scepter.[51]

This virtually completes the Tannaitic descriptions of the personality of the Messiah. The Tannaim did not add much to the characteristics of the Messiah found in the Scriptures. They only emphasized and heightened his spiritual qualities by the addition of a few pleasing touches. The Amoraim and their still later successors made a greater attempt to glorify the personality of the redeemer, but their highly colored flights of fancy are no longer original and primary. But for the Tannaim, as for the prophets (and the Tannaim were the spiritual heirs of the prophets), the essential thing is not the Messiah, but *the Messianic age*. After all, it is God Himself who will bring redemption in the Messianic age. The Messiah is here in the Tannaitic literature only the instrument of God, albeit the most favored and glorious divine instrument that would ever take bodily form on earth.

[51] See above, in the preceding chapter, pp. 455–456.

III

Jewish and Christian
Doctrine of the Messiah

The Rabbinical Sources

by W. D. DAVIES

When we turn to the rabbinical sources in our attempt to discover what role the Torah was expected to play in the Messianic Age, we must begin by recognizing certain commonplaces. First, it is always dangerous to impose any one mode of thought on Judaism: it could tolerate the widest varieties and even contradictions of beliefs. Moreover, it must be recognized that our rabbinic sources represent the triumph of only one stream within Judaism, the Pharisaic, and even of only one current within that one stream, that of R. Johannan ben Zakkai.[3] Hence the possibility is to be reckoned with that many emphases or tendencies in Judaism in the first century are not represented in our rabbinic sources; and this is a possibility which, in view of the antagonism which arose between the Old Israel and its Torah and the New Israel with its new commandment, is not

[3] H. Danby, *op. cit.* pp. xiv f.

negligible in the present inquiry. Possibly much in the tradition about the nature and role of Torah in the Messianic Age has been either ignored or deliberately suppressed or modified. We have elsewhere emphasized the heterogeneity of first-century Judaism. This has been amply insisted upon in the works of Daube, Goodenough, Lieberman and Morton Smith, and it cannot be overlooked in this quest.

On the other hand, it has to be recognized also that by the first century that movement which received its greatest impulse from Ezra and which was designed to make Jewry a people of the Torah had come to fruition: Pharisaism had become well established even if its first-century signi- ficance has often been over-emphasized.[1] And for many Jews the Torah had become the cornerstone of life. How true this was can be grasped not only from those episodes in Jewish history where loyalty to the Torah was the crucial factor governing religious activity in politics and other spheres, but also from the glorification of Torah in much Jewish thought. As Moore has made so clear, so central was the Torah for Judaism that it could conceive neither of the present nor of the past and future except in terms of Torah. The significance of the Torah in the present is demonstrated by that regulation of all life in its minutest details in accordance with the Torah which ultimately led to the codification of the Mishnah, a codification which was not a mushroom growth, but the fruit of much previous codification which goes back at least to the first century.[2] The significance of the Torah in the past was secured by the development of the belief that the Torah was not only pre-existent—as were certain other pivots of Jewish life—but also, and more vitally, instrumental in the creation of the world.[3] The evidence for this need not be repeated here, because it is only with the Torah in the future that we are concerned, and the place of the Torah in the future was guaranteed by the development of the 'doctrine' which we know as that of the immut- ability of the Torah.

This 'doctrine' we may briefly characterize as follows. The Torah, whether written or oral, had been given to Moses by Yahweh. As the gift of Yahweh and as the ground plan of the Universe it could not but be perfect and unchangeable; it was impossible that it should ever be for- gotten; no prophet could ever arise who would change it, and no new

---

[1] See Morton Smith on 'Palestinian Judaism in the First Century', in *Israel*, ed. M. Davis (New York, 1956), pp. 74 ff.

[2] H. L. Strack, *Introduction to the Talmud and Midrash*, pp. 20 ff.

[3] See G. F. Moore, *op. cit.* I, 263 ff. See also on the above P. Volz, *op. cit.* especially pp. 113 ff. and p. 101.

157

Moses should ever appear to introduce another Law to replace it.[1] This was not only Palestinian belief but also that of Hellenistic Judaism. Philo in a passage where he contrasts the unchanging Torah with the ever-changing laws of other nations writes: 'The provisions of this law alone, stable, unmoved, unshaken, as it were stamped with the seal of nature itself, remain in fixity from the day they were written until now, and for the future we expect them to abide through all time as immortal, so long as the sun and moon and the whole heaven and the world exist.'[2] Moore suggested that the association of the Torah with Wisdom helped in the development of this view.[3] We are also tempted to find, as we shall point out later, that a certain polemic motive entered into the insistence on the 'doctrine'. But whatever be the contributory factors in its rise, and it is far too pronounced and early merely to be a polemic reaction against Christian teaching, we can be certain that the words in Matt. v. 18 a adequately express what came to be the dominant 'doctrine' of rabbinic Judaism.

Thus the developed (rabbinic) Judaism revealed to us in our sources was not a soil in which the belief in any radical changes in the existing Torah was likely to grow nor a soil which would welcome a new Torah. On the one hand, a preliminary consideration—the hospitable comprehensiveness of Judaism—should make us prepared for variety in the treatment of the Torah, while, on the other hand, another preliminary consideration—the dominance even in pre-Christian times of the 'doctrine' of the immutability of the Torah—should make us hesitate before accepting any other view too easily. With these two preliminaries recognized we can now proceed with our task. The following factors are relevant.

(i) *The eschatological role of the rabbinic Elijah.* We begin with the rabbinic treatment of the prophet Elijah. Perhaps because of the vividness of the stories about him in the Old Testament, but, more probably, because of the last words of that volume, Mal. iv. 5: 'Behold, I will send you Elijah the prophet before the great and terrible day of the LORD

---

[1] See G. F. Moore, *loc. cit.*; J. Bonsirven, *Le Judaïsme Palestinien*, I, 301 ff., 452 ff.

[2] G. F. Moore's translation, in *Judaism*, I, 269, of Philo, *Vita Mosis*, II, 3, §§ 14–16.

[3] See also V. Aptowitzer, *Parteipolitik der Hasmonäerzeit*, pp. 116 ff. (Notice that the individual commandments, like the Law as a totality, are said to be eternal; see R. Marcus, *op. cit.* p. 53; cf. S–B, I, 244 ff.)

158

comes', already in pre-Christian Judaism he had become a figure of the End: while not strictly a Messianic figure himself, he was a Messianic 'forerunner'. In the Old Testament, the LXX and the New Testament, three things were connected with him in that capacity—repentance, restoration and resurrection. Although the first of these, repentance, is not a prominent characteristic of the work of *Elias redivivus* in the rabbinic materials, the other two reappear in them also. What concerns us, however, is that the figure of Elijah underwent a process of 'rabbinization'. In the rabbinic sources he appears especially as one who would explain points in the Torah which had baffled the Rabbis. This has been made clear by Ginzberg in his work *Eine unbekannte jüdische Sekte* (New York, 1922), pp. 303 ff.[1] He notes no less than seventeen places where this emerges. These are: TB Berakoth 35*b*; TB Shabbath 108*a*; TB Pesaḥim 13*a*; TB Pesahim 70*a*; Mishnah Shekalim ii. 5; TB Chagigah 25*a*; TB Yebamoth 35*b*, 41*b*, 102*a*; TB Gittin 42*b*; Mishnah Baba Metziah i. 8; iii. 4, 5; TB Menahoth 45*a*; ARN 98, 101 (ed. Schechter); TB Taanith viii. 1; Jer. Berakoth 1*c*; Mishnah Eduyoth viii. 7. This last passage reveals not only that the significance of Elijah was a living issue in first-century Judaism but that possibly it was a living issue in its dialogue with Christianity. It reads as follows:

7 R. Joshua said: I have received as a tradition from Rabban Johanan b. Zakkai, who heard from his teacher, and his teacher from his teacher, as a *Halakah* given to Moses from Sinai, that Elijah will not come to declare unclean or clean, to remove afar or to bring nigh, but to remove afar those [families] that were brought nigh by violence and to bring nigh those [families] that were removed afar by violence. The family of Beth Zerepha was in the land beyond Jordan and Ben Zion removed it afar by force. And yet another [family] was there, and Ben Zion brought it nigh by force. The like of these Elijah will come to declare unclean or clean, to remove afar or to bring nigh. R. Judah says: To bring nigh but not to remove afar. R. Simeon says: To bring agreement where there is matter for dispute. And the Sages say: Neither to remove afar nor to bring nigh, but to make peace in the world, as it is written, *Behold I will send you Elijah the prophet. . .and he shall turn the heart of the fathers to the children and the heart of the children to their fathers.*

Two tasks are assigned to Elijah by the various rabbis mentioned in this passage. He is to pronounce on questions of legitimate Israelitish descent, that is, declare what is clean and unclean, and to create peace. All the

[1] On Elijah, see also R. B. Y. Scott, *The Canadian Journal of Religious Thought*, III (1926), 490–502 on 'The Expectation of Elijah'.

scholars mentioned are entitled 'rabbis', so that the situation which called forth this discussion prevailed after A.D. 70. Since the tradition about Elijah to which appeal is made goes back to an earlier date, Allen[1] is perhaps to be followed in his suggestion that the words, 'God is able of these stones to raise up children unto Abraham' (that is, purity, not blood, is the criterion for inclusion in the Kingdom), may refer to M. Eduyoth viii. 7; Rabban Johannan ben Zakkai's words would agree with such a point of view. But more probably it was the dissension among scholars after A.D. 70, which threatened the unity of Judaism, that called forth this emphasis on the importance of reconciliation. Elijah would come not to engage in legal niceties, but to reconcile the differences among scholars, that is, by implication, to give the true interpretation of the Law. Danby comments on the passage that '[Elijah] will make no change in the Law but only make an end to injustice'. Is the Christian claim to have had its 'Elijah' and his interpretation of the Law, reflected in this insistence on the part of the rabbis that this was not what mattered so much as 'peace'?

Before we leave this section reference must also be made to Ginzberg's emphasis in the volume already cited that, among the rabbis, the Messiah or Messiahs, as such, were not expected to exercise a didactic function. Instead in the Messianic Age this was to be concentrated in the figure of Elijah. On this ground, Ginzberg argued that no new strictly Messianic Torah was anticipated. Although we are fully aware of the danger of presumption in this matter, his position prompts two questions. First, as we have previously implied, may not the 'rabbinization' of Elijah, that is, the concentration of the didactic function in him, have been due to a reaction against Christian claims that their Messiah was the teacher, who had authority? And, secondly, does not the evidence, which we shall adduce below, make Ginzberg's radical rejection of the conception of a New Torah at least dubious? Certainly in such passages as Test. Benj. xi. 2; Test. Levi xviii. 9 the Messiah is the source of new knowledge, and the total evidence is more ambiguous, it seems to us, than Ginzberg allows. Jeremias[2] has even urged that Elijah himself was conceived as the Messiah. This must be regarded as questionable. But as precursor of the Messianic Age, Elijah is a 'Messianic' or 'eschatological' figure, who, in his work of reconciliation, prepares for the Messianic unity. Part of this work had to do with new interpretations of the Law. This justifies our reference to him here: he would be the instrument of changes in the

[1] In the I.C.C. on Matt. xi. 14.
[2] *T.W.Z.N.T.* on Elijah. He is opposed by Giblet, *op. cit.* p. 112.

160

understanding of the Law in Messianic times. This leads us on naturally to the next section.[1]

(ii) Our sources do reveal an awareness that, even though the Torah was immutable, nevertheless modifications of various kinds, at least in certain details, would be necessary.[2] We shall group the material as follows:

(a) *Passages suggesting the cessation of certain enactments concerning Festivals, etc.*[3] There were some who held the view that in the Messianic Age sin would not exist, and it followed that the vast majority of sacrifices, which naturally dealt with the taint of sin, would be irrelevant.[4] A passage in Leviticus Rabbah ix. 7 reads:

R. Phinehas and R. Levi and R. Joḥanan said in the name of R. Menaḥem of Gallia: In the time to come all sacrifices will be annulled, but that of thanks-giving will not be annulled, and all prayers will be annulled, but [that of] thanksgiving will not be annulled. This is [indicated by] what is written: Jer. xxxiii. 11. (Soncino translation.)

The text is:

ר' פנחס ור' לוי ור' יוחנן בשם ר' מנחם דגליא לע"ל כל הקרבנות בטלין
וקרבן תודה אינו בטל כל התפילות בטילות התודה אינה בטילה הה"ד...

Here the phrase referring to the future is לע"ל = לעתיד לבא: its meaning is fluid. Sometimes it refers to the final Age to Come, but at other times it is

---

[1] So too we cannot follow G. Friedrich in his implication that for Judaism the teaching of the Messiah would be insignificant (*T.W.Z.N.T.* II, 723).

[2] It is important to recognize what is meant by the Torah when we refer to its perpetuity. There are passages which claim that only the Torah in the strict sense would persist into the future: the prophets and the hagiographa would cease. See V. Aptowitzer, *op. cit.* p. 261, n. 133, who refers to Jerusalem Meg. 1, 70*d*; also Sh. Spiegel, *H.T.R.* xxiv, 245 ff. The passage in J. Meg. 1, 70, runs:

הנביאים והכתובים עתידין ליבטל וחמשת סיפרי תורה אינן עתידין ליבטל...

(See the translation of the whole section in M. Schwab, *Le Talmud de Jérusalem*, 1882, tome 6, 207.) The words cited only give the view of R. Joḥanan (A.D. 279–320). R. Simeon b. Laḳish (A.D. 279–320) gives an opposite view—not even the festival of Esther, which, because it had not been ordained by Moses, caused great difficulty, would cease; because it was only the ordinances of Moses himself that Lev. xxvii. 34 declared to be eternal. Doubtless for most the Pentateuch, the prophets and the hagiographa were 'eternal'.

[3] Translations of the Babylonian Talmud and Midrash Rabbah, unless otherwise stated, are derived from those of the Soncino Press.

[4] On the place of the cultus generally in the eschatological thinking of Israel see E. Lohmeyer, *Kultus und Evangelium* (Göttingen, 1942), pp. 19 ff.; also pp. 48, 49 ff.

equivalent to the Messianic era.[1] The context, therefore, must decide the particular meaning it may have: and here we are justified in referring it to the Messianic Age; the sense of the passage demands this and the verse from Jer. xxxiii. 11, by which the view is supported, comes from a Messianic prophecy. Notice, however, that the date of the view expressed must be late. Some scholars understand here Menahem of Galilee, reading גלילא. Israelstam[2] reads גליא, and renders as above: the term גליא he takes to refer to a place in Asia Minor. Wünsche[3] and Loewe[4] prefer to read גלילא. Even if we read the latter the date of the passage is A.D. 165–200—the period when Menahem of Galilee flourished.

Another passage refers to the festivals: it comes from Yalqut on Prov. ix. 2 and reads:[5]

All the festivals will cease but not Purim since it is said (Esther ix. 28) '...these days shall be...throughout every generation...and...should not fail from among the Jews...'. R. Eleazar said: The Day of Atonement too will not cease since it is said (Lev. xvi. 34) 'And this shall be unto you an everlasting statute'.

The text runs:

כל המועדים עתידין ליבטל וימי הפורים אינן בטלים לעולם,...א״ר אליעזר
אף יום הכפורים לא יבטל לעולם שנאמר והיתה זאת לכם לחקת עולם:

The date of the passage is uncertain, but it is probably early second century (A.D. 80–120). Here Purim and the Day of Atonement alone among the festivals are to survive into the Messianic Age. The justification for saying that the Day of Atonement would survive is that it is called in Lev. xvi. 34 'an everlasting statute' (חקת עולם). The same phrase is applied elsewhere to other festivals, for example, the Passover (Exod. xii. 17), the Feast of Weeks (Lev. xxiii. 21), Tabernacles (Lev. xxiii. 41). It is arguable therefore that we should not take this passage at its face value, and that it is merely designed to emphasize the importance of Purim and the Day of Atonement. But there is a significant difference between passages dealing with Purim and the Day. of Atonement and those dealing with the other festivals. Thus in Exod. xii. 17 on the Passover the full temporal reference is: 'therefore you shall observe this day, *throughout your generations,* as an ordinance for ever'. Similarly on the Feast of

---

[1] See M. Jastrow, *Dictionary of the Talmud*, p. 1129; J. Bonsirven, *op. cit.* I, 319 f.
[2] Soncino translation: Midrash Rabbah, Leviticus, *ad loc.*
[3] *Bibliotheca Rabbinica*, *ad loc.*   [4] *A Rabbinic Anthology*, *ad rem.*
[5] See Midrash Mishle, ix. 2; J. Klausner, *From Jesus to Paul*, Eng. trans. by W. F. Stinespring, p. 321, n. 13.

162

Weeks in Lev. xxiii. 21 we read: 'it is a statute for ever in all your dwellings *throughout your generations*'. And again in Lev. xxiii. 41 we read on the Feast of Tabernacles, 'it is a statute for ever *throughout your generations...*'. The words in italics are missing in Lev. xvi. 34 on the Day of Atonement, where we only have '*an everlasting statute*', while in Esther ix. 28 on Purim we have the fulsome statement which follows: '*that these days should be remembered and kept throughout every generation, in every family, province, and city, and that these days of Purim should never fall into disuse among the Jews, nor should the commemoration of these days cease among their descendants*'. Thus while at first the claim that Purim and the Day of Atonement alone should be 'eternal festivals' might seem fanciful, it was well grounded by the rabbis in the text of scripture. On the same basis they had to recognize that radical changes in the festivals in the Messianic Age were contemplated. As such this passage is significant for our purpose.[1]

(*b*) *Passages which seem to suggest changes in the laws concerning things clean and unclean, etc.* We begin with a passage from Midrash Tehillim on Ps. cxlvi. 7. This is translated by Braude as follows:[2]

The Lord will loose the bonds (Ps. cxlvi. 7). What does the verse mean by the words *loose the bonds*? Some say that of every animal whose flesh it is forbidden to eat in this world, the Holy One, blessed be He, will declare in the time-to-come that the eating of its flesh is permitted. Thus in the verse *That which hath been is that which shall be, and that which hath been given is that which shall be given* (Eccles. i. 9), the words *that which hath been given* refer to the animals that were given as food before the time of the sons of Noah, for God said: 'Every moving thing that liveth shall be food for you; as the green herb have I given you all' (Gen. ix. 3). That is to say, 'As I give the green herb as food to all, so once I gave both beasts and cattle as food to all'. But why did God declare the flesh of some animals forbidden? In order to see who would accept His commandments and who would not accept them. In the time-to-come, however, God will again permit the eating of that flesh which He has forbidden.

Others say that in the time-to-come, God will not permit this, for it is said *They that...eat swine's flesh, and the detestable thing, and the mouse, shall be*

---

[1] I owe the details in the above to a private communication from Professor Daube.

[2] *Yale Judaica Series*, vol. XIII, *The Midrash on Psalms* (1959), *ad rem*. See also Montefiore and Loewe, *A Rabbinic Anthology*, p. 583. The date of this anonymous passage cannot be fixed. P. R. Weis, of the University of Manchester, in a private note, suggests that in view of the context the passage refers to the 'Final Age' not to the Messianic Age. The phrase לעתיד לבוא שהשכינה ביניהם, which occurs below the above passage, he thinks points to this. But the conditions implied seem to us to be Messianic.

consumed together, saith the Lord (Isa. lxvi. 17). Now if God will cut off and destroy men who eat forbidden flesh, surely he will do the same to the forbidden animals themselves. To what, otherwise, do the words *will loose the bonds* refer? Though nothing is more strongly forbidden than intercourse with a menstruous woman—for when a woman sees blood the Holy One, blessed be He, forbids her to her husband—in the time-to-come, God will permit such intercourse. As Scripture says, *It shall come to pass in that day, saith the Lord of hosts, that...I will cause the prophets and the unclean spirit to pass out of the land* (Zech. xiii. 2), the *unclean* clearly denoting a menstruous woman, and of such it is said '*And thou shalt not approach a woman to uncover her nakedness, as long as she is impure by her uncleanness*' (Lev. xviii. 19).

Still others say that in the time-to-come sexual intercourse will be entirely forbidden. You can see for yourself why it will be. On the day that the Holy One, blessed be He, revealed Himself on Mount Sinai to give the Torah to the children of Israel, He forbade intercourse for three days, as it is said *Be ready against the third day; come not at your wives* (Exod. xix. 15). Now since God, when He revealed Himself for only one day, forbade intercourse for three days, in the time-to-come, when the presence of God dwells continuously in Israel's midst, will not intercourse be entirely forbidden?

What, otherwise, is meant by *bonds* in *will loose the bonds*? The bonds of death and the bonds of the netherworld.

The pertinent Hebrew reads:

ה׳ מתיר אסורים. מהו מתיר אסורים יש אומרים כל הבהמה שנטמאה בעולם הזה מטהר אותה הקב״ה לעתיד לבוא... ומה שנעשה טהורים היו מקודם לבני נח...ולמה אסר אותה, לראות מי שמקבל דבריו, ומי אינו מקבל, ולעתיד לבוא הוא מתיר את כל מה שאסר:

Here distinctions between clean and unclean animals are to be abrogated in the Messianic Age, which is pictured as a return to the primitive or original condition of the world before the disaster of the flood: the idea that the End corresponds to the Beginning is a commonplace of apocalyptic and the principle would seem to be operative here. But there have been objections to the acceptance of this passage and others as rabbinic opinion.[1]

---

[1] Dr Finkelstein writes (19 June 1961): (1) on Gen. Rabbah (see below p. 179), 'Professor Chanoch Albeck, who completed the edition of Theodor, considers chapters xcv–cvi as not part of the original Genesis Rabba. The chapters, in the ordinary editions, do not all correspond to those in the manuscript used by Theodor, and even those included in that manuscript are not considered a part of Genesis Rabba, but of another book. This is on the basis apparently, of internal evidence.' (2) On Midrash Tehillim cxlvi he gives Buber's views. 'Buber's note [in his edition of Tehillim] is, in substance, as follows: "Reitmann has remarked in *Bet Talmud*, III, p. 332 that in Midrash Tehilim, chapter cxlvi there is a very strange passage. This

We notice further that there is an attempt in the passage immediately following to offset the view expressed; and not only so, but it is made clear that in the time to come some of the demands of the Law would be even more severe: thus marital relations would become stricter. Nevertheless this last in itself suggests the possibility of change in the Torah, and as such is again instructive for our purposes.

It is at this point that we can best deal with a passage which is usually cited in favour not merely of the view that the Messianic Age would see changes in the Torah but also that it would bring with it a New Torah. The passage from Leviticus Rabbah xiii. 3 reads as follows:

R. Judan b. R. Simeon said: Behemoth and the Leviathan are to engage in a wild beast contest before the righteous in the Time to Come, and whoever has not been a spectator at the wild beast contests of the heathen nations in this world will be accorded the boon of seeing one in the World to Come. How will they be slaughtered? Behemoth will, with its horns, pull Leviathan down and rend it, and Leviathan will, with its fins, pull Behemoth down and pierce it through. The Sages said: And is this a valid method of slaughter? Have we not learnt the following in a Mishnah: All may slaughter, and one may slaughter at all times (of the day), and with any instrument except with a scythe, or with a saw, or with teeth (in a jaw cut out of a dead animal), beacuse they cause pain as if by choking, or with a nail (of a living body)? R. Abin b. Kahana said: The Holy One, blessed be He, said: Instruction [Torah] shall go forth from Me (Isa. li. 4) [that is, an exceptionsl temporary ruling will go forth from Me]. (Israelstam's Soncino translation.)[1]

is the passage to which he refers. According to him (Reifmann) this passage was added to the Midrash by someone who was quite confused. I (that is, Buber) have discussed this in Bet Talmud, iv, p. 54, at length, trying to show that this is not an addition to the text, but is part of the Midrash which was added at a later time, and is not of the original Midrash Tehilim. The original Midrash was completed only up to the end of Psalm cxviii. This passage also belongs to the later homilist who arranged the passages dealing with these later psalms. However, the question concerning whom the homilist referred to when he said, 'there are those who say', and where he found this passage, I just discovered in the book Yeshuot Meshiho, Rabbi Isaac Abravanel, part 4, chapter 3, who states that an opponent wanted to prove the ultimate nullification of the Torah from a homily which he said occurs in Genesis Rabba of Rabbi Moses Hadarshan in chapter Mikez, which begins with a verse in this very psalm, and according to which all animals which are impure in this world will be purified by God in the future world. Accordingly, the passage which the editor has added in his own supplement to the Midrash Tehilim is taken from the Midrash of Rabbi Moses Hadarshan. The intent of the passage has been very well explained by Rabbi Abravanel, and can be found by the reader in the place quoted."' Rabbi Moses Hadarshan flourished in the eleventh century A.D.

[1] V. Aptowitzer points out a parallel passage. See Jellinek, Beth ha-Midrash iii. 80; iii. 76, which reads, 'In the days of the Messiah Israel will live for 2000 years in

165

The text of the last sentence according to the Wilna and Warsaw editions is:[1]

א״ר אבין בר כהנא אמר הקב״ה תורה ²חדשה מאתי תצא חדוש תורה מאתי
תצא...

Now Edersheim, like Strack–Billerbeck, who, however, qualify their acceptance of this interpretation, took this to refer to a new (Messianic) Torah. Israelstam, however, as we saw, rejects this, and the context favours his interpretation. In his view, the point of the passage is that even though according to the Torah of this world it was not permissible to slay anything with a saw, because this would necessarily involve pain, nevertheless, in the Messianic Age the Leviathan would be permitted to pull down the Behemoth with its fins, which are like saws, in that they have serrated edges. Thus in the contest between Leviathan and Behe-

security, eat from Behemoth, Leviathan, and Ziz. The Ziz and Behemoth will be slaughtered. The Ziz will rend Leviathan and the Behemoth.' Here there is a specific reference to the days of the Messiah when a slaughtering involving pain will be allowed, whereas in the passage quoted in the text a painless slaughtering only will be allowed—this because, V. Aptowitzer argues, it refers not to the Messianic Age but to the Age to Come. But the picture of the wild beast contest probably refers to a Messianic Age on earth, not to the final Age to Come, in both passages, although the possibility is not to be ruled out that the Age to Come itself might be on earth.

[1] In translating Isa. li. 4 J. Israelstam follows the Massoretic text. It is better to understand his translation thus than to suppose that the text of the Midrash gives the text of Isa. li. 4 last, after the comment, and that Israelstam has reversed this by giving the quotation first, then the comment. In the 1890 Warsaw edition and reprints, where there is an error by printer or editor, the reference ישעיה נא is inserted, but in the wrong place. It should come in front of the first תורה not the second תורה. It is also found in some texts between תצא and חדוש, that is, at the end of the verse. Usually, however, the biblical reference is placed in front of the verse, and it is thus that J. Israelstam takes it here. He should, however, have pointed out that he is following the Massoretic text and not that given by the Midrash, which has the adjective חדשה. Professor A. Guttmann thinks that R. Abin bar Kahana may have had an original text, which read חדשה. However this may be, J. Israelstam goes on to translate חדוש תורה מאתי תצא by 'an exceptional temporary ruling will go forth from me' (A. Wünsche renders 'die Erneuerung des Gesetzes wird von mir ausgehen'). But this, as we saw above, is hardly to be accepted. Professor A. Guttmann informs me that J. Israelstam is following David Luria who held that תורה חדשה in the given context means 'temporary ruling' (that is, a ruling for the עתיד לבוא only) הוראת שעה: giving of biblical references, Professor A. Guttmann notes, was not customary in the original texts of the Midrashim. Some editions do not have them, for example the editio princeps, Constantinople, 1512. The second complete edition, Venice, 1545, gives the references in the margin. Yet for our passage, as in the Wilna edition, no reference is given. (The details from Professor Guttmann I gained by correspondence.)

[2] חדשה is read only by the MSS. of London and Paris: see the edition of Wayyikra Rabbah, by M. Margulies (Jerusalem, 1954).

166

moth, which would take place in the presence of the righteous in the Messianic Age, the use of an instrument prohibited in this world by the Torah would be allowed. This would seem to be a possible understanding of the passage: the term חדש is often used of promulgating a new law (not Law) or establishing a new interpretation of a biblical law. But it is desirable that the element of newness in the phrase תורה חדשה should be better preserved than in Israelstam's translation. Israelstam's diminution of the force of the adjective חדשה and his translation of חדוש תורה by 'an exceptional temporary ruling' has been called 'une pirouette d'apologé-tique juive, comme savent en accomplir les apologètes de tous les temps'. Barthélemy insists that since, as we fully recognize, Judaism became increasingly opposed to any suggestion of a New Torah, the reading תורה חדשה in Isa. li. 4 must be early, although he also suggests that it possibly emanated from unorthodox, peripheral circles.[1] So too, Díez Macho has insisted that here we encounter the concept of a New Torah for the Messianic Age.[2] Only by exercising an excess of caution, perhaps, can we favour Israelstam's interpretation over that of Barthélemy and Macho.

(c) *Other passages which seem to imply or actually express the expectation of changes in the Torah.* Bonsirven refers to one passage in Siphre on Deut. xvii. 18, §160, where it is explicitly stated, he thinks, that the Torah will be changed.[3]

The English would roughly be as follows:

He shall write him a copy of this Law (MISHNEH HA-TORAH) for himself (that is), for his own name (person): he should not be content with that of his fathers. MISHNEH (TORAH) (From this) I have no (proof) except for MISHNEH TORAH (that is, Deuteronomy). (As to) the rest of the words of the Torah, Whence (do we know that these too are intended)? Scripture teaches this by

---

[1] In a review in *RB*, LX (1953), 316–18. Barthélemy makes also an important point in the following words: 'Or, dans le Judaïsme du début de l'ère chrétienne, le substantif *ḥiddush* et le verbe *ḥaddesh* ont une signification eschatologique bien établie de "renouvellement apocalyptique", une "transmutation radicale". La première mention formelle d'un tel renouvellement se rencontre dans Jub. 1, 29 où il est dit que "cieux et terre *seront renouvelés*" et que "les luminaires seront renouvelés pour la guérison, la paix et la bénédiction de tous les élus d'Israël". Dans l'hébreu original, il y a très vraisemblablement des formes *hitpaèl* du verbe.' He refers also to Apoc. Baruch xxxii. 6; xvii. 2; 4 Ezra vii. 75.

[2] *Op. cit.*

[3] *Op. cit.* I, 453, n. 9. J. Klausner, *op. cit.* p. 54, interprets 'wohl kann sie theilweise andern (שעתידה להשתנות) aber sie kann nicht abrogirt und durch andere ersetzt werden'.

167

saying (later in this passage) TO KEEP ALL THE WORDS OF THIS LAW, etc.
Why then (does it say) MISHNEH TORAH? Because it was destined to be
changed (le-Hishtannoth) [Hithpaʿēl of *shanah*, to change; also, to repeat, to
copy—the root of *Mishneh*].

The text reads:

וכתב לו את משנה התורה הזאת על ספר לשמו שלא יהא נאות בשל אבותיו:
משנה אין לי אלא משנה תורה שאר ד״ת מנין ת״ל לשמור את כל דברי
התורה הזאת א״כ למה נאמר משנה תורה שעתידה להשתנות . . . .

Bonsirven takes the term להשתנות to refer to a changing of the Torah
itself, and this is a perfectly legitimate possibility. The Hithpaʿēl of שנה
does mean '*to be changed*': moreover, the masculine gender of משנה
makes it impossible to take להשתנות to refer to the copy. Bonsirven's
interpretation is therefore, as stated, fully justified from the language of
this passage taken alone. Unfortunately for our thesis, in the parallel
passage in Tosefta, Sanhedrin iv. 4 ff., the phrase שעתידה להשתנות is
referred, quite specifically, to the change in the *script* which was to be
used in the writing of the Torah. The Hebrew in Tosefta, Sanhedrin iv. 7
reads:

וכתב לו את משנה התורה הזאת וג׳ תורה עתידה להשתנות ולמה נקרא שמה[1]
אשורי על שום שעלה עמהן מאשור ר׳ אומר בכתב אשורי ניתנה תורה
לישראל, וכשחטאו נהפכה להן לְרוֹעֵץ וכשזכו בימי עזרא חזרה להן אשורית:

The English of this would run somewhat as follows:

And he shall for himself write the copy of this law, etc. The Torah is destined
to be changed. And why was it called Assyrian script? because it went up
with them from Assyria. R. (Meir) said: When the Torah was given to Israel
it was given in Assyrian script; and when they sinned it was changed for them
into the form of the Samaritan type, and when they were worthy in the days of
Ezra it went back for them into [or, came back to them in] Assyrian script.

The Tosefta, we may probably safely assume, preserves the oldest
tradition of the meaning of the term להשתנות in this context, and is
therefore to be followed. Hence we must reject Bonsirven's use of the
passage as referring to a change in the Torah itself.

---

[1] The reading שָׁמָה is accepted by Professor A. Guttmann rather than שָׁמָה If
we read שָׁמָה the translation is 'and why was it read there in Assyrian script?' The
Codex Vienna and the *ed. princeps* read שְׁמוֹ, of which שָׁמָה is a corruption; so
Professor Lieberman.

There are two other passages to be discussed here. One, in TB Sanhedrin 51*b*, is sometimes wrongly interpreted to mean that much of the Torah which does not apply to this world will be applicable in the Messianic Age. But the actual meaning is that much of the Torah, meaning sacrifices, temporarily discontinued in this world, owing to adverse conditions, will again be practised in the Messianic Age.[1] It reads:

R. Nahman (A.D. 275–320) said in the name of Rabbah b. Abbuha (A.D. 257–320) in the name of Rab: The *Halachah* is in accordance with the message sent by Rabin in the name of R. Jose b. Hanina. R. Joseph queried: (Do we need) to fix a *halachah* for the days of the Messiah?—Abaye answered: If so, we should not study the laws of sacrifices, as they are also only for the Messianic era. But we say, Study and receive reward; i.e. Learning has its own merit quite apart from any practical utility that may be derived therefrom.

A more important and more often quoted passage occurs in TB Shabbath 151*b* where we find opposing views set in sharp juxtaposition. The passage reads as follows:

R. Simeon b. Eleazar (A.D. 165–200) said: ...*And the years draw nigh, when thou shalt say, I have no pleasure in them*[7]—this refers to the Messianic era, wherein there is neither merit nor guilt. Now, he disagrees with Samuel, who said: The only difference between this world and the Messianic era is in respect of servitude to [foreign] powers, for it is said, *For the poor shall never cease out of the land.*[8] (Note 7 is from Eccles. xii. 1; n. 8 from Deut. xv. 11.)

The context shows that the question as to when the Torah was obligatory and when it was not is the theme of the passage. Samuel apparently regards the Torah as obligatory in the Messianic Age which, he holds, would not differ in this respect from the present age. The meaning of R. Simeon b. Eleazar's (A.D. 165–200) dictum is difficult. Bonsirven[2] would seem to take the words to mean that in the Messianic Age the capacity to sin is obliterated, although he does not state this explicitly, and his meaning is not clear. It seems to us that there are two possibilities as to the interpretation of the phrase לא זכות ולא חובה, which is rendered by Bonsirven, very neatly, 'ni mérite ni démérite', but is better translated as 'no merit and no guilt'. First, the meaning may be that in the Messianic Age the Torah will be so fully obeyed that there will be no guilt, and so spontaneously or easily fulfilled that there will be no merit, a condition of affairs such as Jeremiah, perhaps, may have envisaged and desiderated. This interpretation, it will be agreed, involves a high degree of subtlety.

---

[1] So A. Guttmann in a private note.　　[2] *Le Judaïsme Palestinien*, I, 452.

169

The second meaning is the one that seems to us perhaps most satisfying, namely, that the Torah no longer holds in the Messianic Age, so that questions of reward for observing it and guilt or punishment for refusing to do so do not arise. This would make the condition of those who live in the Messianic Age, in this respect, similar to that of the dead who, according to R. Joḥanan, in the passage immediately preceding, are free from religious duties (see below p. 181, on TB Niddah 61b). The preceding passage in TB Shabbath 151b reads:

It was taught, R. Simeon b. Gamaliel said: For a day-old infant the Sabbath is desecrated; For David, King of Israel, dead, the Sabbath must not be desecrated. 'For a day-old infant the Sabbath is desecrated': the Torah ordered, Desecrate one Sabbath on his account so that he may keep many Sabbaths. 'For David, King of Israel, dead, the Sabbath must not be desecrated': Once man dies he is free from [all] obligations, and thus, R. Joḥanan interpreted: *Among the dead I am free*:[5] once a man is dead he is free from religious duties. (Soncino translation, p. 772; n. 5 refers to Ps. lxxxviii. 6.)

It also implies, as we shall indicate below, that the Messianic Age is like the Age to Come in this matter (see below, pp. 181 ff.).

The evidence presented above sufficiently justifies the claim that despite the 'doctrine' of the immutability of Torah, there were also occasional expressions of expectations that Torah would suffer modification in the Messianic Age. There were some Halakoth which would cease to be applicable in that Age; others, by contrast, would acquire a new relevance. It is important, however, to recognize explicitly that most, if not all, the changes envisaged were deemed to occur within the context of the existing Torah and presuppose the continuance of its validity. Moreover, the changes contemplated imply no necessary diminution in what we may be allowed to term the severity of the yoke of the Torah. On the contrary, that yoke, in some passages, was expected to become even heavier than in this age (see especially Midrash Tehillim cxlvi. 7). In addition we have to point out that much of the traditional Christian interpretation of some of the passages cited does violence to the text and has to be rejected. It may also be helpful to state at this point that in all the passages so far quoted the reference probably is to the Messianic Age as such.

(iii) The third significant factor which we have to notice, is that the Messianic Age, as indeed we might expect, is presented as an era in which certain difficulties or incomprehensibilities which the Torah presented in this Age would be adequately explained and comprehended: now we see in a glass darkly, but then obscurities will be removed. Strack–Billerbeck have dealt with this, and for our purpose the briefest treatment will suffice.[1]

Many of the demands of the Torah seemed inexplicable and irrational: the reasons why certain things had been forbidden or commanded were obscure, and the fact that Jewry could not always give a satisfying apology for much in their practice laid them open to the attacks of Gentile cynicism and criticism. Hence there necessarily developed a considerable activity in the Tannaitic period, and earlier probably, in an attempt to explain why certain things had been commanded which at first seemed even merely stupid. So eager were some to explain the טעמי תורה, 'the grounds or reasons for the Torah's demands', that they were in danger of manipulating their texts, and consequently incurred suspicion. The normative position arrived at was that in this world the demands of Torah were to be obeyed because they were commanded: this was sufficient reason for their observance. This is made clear in the words of R. Joḥanan b. Zakkai (we quote the passage from Numbers Rabbah xix. 8 on xix. 2 because it illustrates the kind of criticism which was made of the demands of the Torah):

An idolater asked R. Joḥanan b. Zakkai: These rites that you perform look like a kind of witchcraft. You bring a heifer, burn it, pound it, and take its ashes. If one of you is defiled by a dead body you sprinkle upon him two or three drops and you say to him: 'Thou art clean.' R. Joḥanan asked him: 'Has the demon of madness ever possessed you?' 'No!' he replied. 'Have you ever seen a man entered by this demon of madness?' 'Yes,' said he. 'And what do you do in such a case?' 'We bring roots,' he replied, 'and make them smoke under him, then we sprinkle water upon the demon and it flees.' Said R. Joḥanan to him: 'Let your ears hear what you utter with your mouth: Precisely so is this spirit a spirit of uncleanness: as it is written, *And also I will cause the prophets and the unclean spirit to pass out of the land* (Zech. xiii. 2). Water of purification is sprinkled upon the unclean and the spirit flees.' When the idolater had gone R. Joḥanan's disciples said to their master: 'Master!' This man you have put off with a mere makeshift but what explanation will you give to us?' Said he to them: 'By your life! It is not the dead that defiles nor the water that purifies! The Holy One, blessed be He, merely says: "I have laid down a statute (חקה),[2] I have issued a decree. You are not allowed to transgress My decree"; as it is written, *This is the statute of the law*' (Num. xix. 2).

[1] *Op. cit.* IV, 2, n. 9: Pesikta, ed. Mandelbaum, p. 71; Mekilta in Siphra, ed. Weiss, p. 86a; also M. Waxman, *J.Q.R.* vol. XLII (October 1951).

[2] This term denotes a command demanding implicit obedience, though the human mind may not comprehend its reason.

171

But although theirs was not to reason why in this world, the rabbis were convinced that the Messianic Age would bring with it an explanation of the inexplicable demands that the Torah made in this world: the טעמי תורה would be revealed. We have previously quoted passages from the Old Testament where the Messianic Age was depicted as a time when God himself would teach his people. This was the firm conviction of the rabbis also. In illustration we shall again quote a passage from Numbers Rabbah xix. 6 on xix. 2, despite its late date, where the reference is not strictly to the Messianic Age, however, but to the final Age to Come:

THAT THEY BRING THEE A RED HEIFER (xix. 2). R. Jose b. Ḥanina (the second half of the third century) expounded: The Holy One, blessed be He, said to Moses: 'To thee I shall disclose the reason for the Heifer, but to anybody else it is a statute.' For R. Huna said: It is written, *When I take the appointed time* [i.e., in the World to Come], *I Myself will judge with equity* (Ps. lxxv. 3) [i.e., reveal the reasons for My Laws], and it is also written, *And it shall come to pass in that day, that there shall not be light, but heavy clouds and thick*—weḳippa'on (Zech. xiv. 6). The written form is 'yeḳippa'on', as much as to say: The things that are concealed from you in this world, you will see in the World to Come, like a blind man who regains his sight, as it is written (Isa. xlii. 16), *And I will bring the blind by a way that they know not. . . .* (Soncino translation, Numbers, vol. II, 756.)[1]

We pass on to the next group of material.[2]

(iv) Despite the changes both in the substance and interpretation of the Torah which they contemplate, those passages which we have so far examined have afforded little if any evidence for the expectation of a New

[1] Sh. Spiegel, *H.T.R.* (October 1931), 261, points out that part of the significance of the predicted coming of Elijah on the threshold of the Messianic Age was that he should settle legal and ritual doubts 'to set straight all dissension, and to compose differences of opinion which could threaten to make of the one law two laws'. He relates this function of Elijah to the doctrine of the perpetual validity of the Law: the difficulties of the existing Law had to be explained because there could be no other Law. Hence the great joy of the rabbis at being able to resolve contradictions between Ezekiel and the Torah: they feared the danger of having to admit the existence of two laws in the canon should these contradictions not be resolved. Compare H. Danby, *op. cit.* p. 12, n. 4, on M. Eduyoth viii. 7.

[2] Professor Muilenburg emphasizes that in the Old Testament, as over against Judaism, the reasons for obedience were given, see *The Way of Israel* (1961), pp. 66 ff. He refers to Exod. xxiii. 8; Deut. v. 12–15; xxv. 3, 15–16; *Hebrew Union College Annual*, XXXII (1961), on 'The Linguistic and Rhetorical Usages of the particle כִּי in the Old Testament', pp. 135 ff. See also B. Gemser, *Congress Volume Copenhagen 1953* (Leiden, 1953), pp. 50–66, on 'The importance of the motive clause in Old Testament law'.

Torah in the Messianic Age. Changes in details and an increase in understanding there would be, but no substitution of the old Torah by a new one was envisaged.[1] In this section we must deal with passages where it has been claimed that it is possible that a New Torah is expressly indicated.

(1) *The Targum on Isa.* xii. 3. The MT reads: וּשְׁאַבְתֶּם־מַיִם בְּשָׂשׂוֹן מִמַּעַיְנֵי הַיְשׁוּעָה, that is, 'And you shall draw water in joy from the wells of salvation'. The whole context of the passage is Messianic: xii. 1–3 reads in its entirety:

> 1 You will say in that day:
> 'I will give thanks to thee, O LORD,
> for though thou wast angry with me,
> thy anger turned away,
> and thou didst comfort me.
> 2 'Behold, God is my salvation;
> I will trust, and will not be afraid;
> for the LORD GOD is my strength and my song,
> and he has become my salvation.'
> 3 With joy you will draw water from the wells of salvation. (RSV.)

The Targum renders xii. 3 as follows:

ותקבלין אולפן חדת בחדוא מבחירי צדיקיא

which is rendered by Stenning:[2] 'And ye shall receive new instruction with joy from the chosen of righteousness.'

The total passage in the Targum reads:

1 And thou shalt say at that time, I will give thanks before thee, O Lord; for because I had sinned before thee, thine anger was upon me; now let thine anger turn from me, and have pity upon me.

2 Behold, in the Memra of the God of my salvation do I trust, and shall not be dismayed; because my strength and my glory is the Terrible One, the Lord: he has spoken by his Merma, and has become my Saviour.

3 And ye shall receive new instruction with joy from the chosen of righteousness.

4 And ye shall say in that time, Give thanks before the Lord; pray in his name; proclaim among the nations his deeds; make mention that his name is mighty.

Israelstam[3] takes אולפן to refer to exposition: he contrasts it sharply with תורה, for which, he claims, usually אוריתא is used: the reference to the

---

[1] The one possible exception would be Leviticus Rabbah xiii. 3, see above, pp. 165 ff.

[2] J. F. Stenning, *The Targum of Isaiah.*

[3] In a private communication.

173

newness of the exposition is prompted by the thought of well-water, that is, fresh or new water (compare M. Aboth ii. 8). But something more than new exposition is expressed here. Daube[1] accepts אולפן in this context as the equivalent of תורה: thus the drawing of water out of the wells of salvation means not only the reception of new teaching or instruction (as in Stenning's translation), but the reception of a New Law. Daube accordingly translates: 'Ye shall receive a new Law from those chosen in righteousness.' He refers this to the Messianic Age. What precisely is understood by 'those chosen in righteousness' is not clear.[2]

(2) *Midrash Qoheleth on* ii. 1 and *on* xi. 8. In the passage, Midrash Qoheleth xi. 8, we read:

תורה שאדם למד בעוה״ז
הבל הוא לפני תורתו של משיח

The Torah which a man learns in this world is vanity compared with the Torah of the Messiah.

This passage carries no date; a somewhat similar passage, slightly more involved, which is given in the name of R. Simon b. Zabdai, is that on ii. 1, which is as follows:

ר׳ חזקיה בש״ר סימון בר זבדי אמר
כל התורה שאת למד בעוה״ז הבל הוא
לפני תורה שבעוה״ב . לפני שבעוה״ז אדם
לומד תורה ושוכח אבל לעתיד לבא מה
כתיב תמן...: נתתי את תורתי בקרבבם:

R. Hezekiah said in the name of Rabbi Simon bar Zabdai: All the Torah which you learn in this world is 'vanity' compared with the Torah in The world to Come. For in This world a man learns and forgets but, as for The time to come, what is written there (Jer. xxxi. 33)? *I will put my Law in their inward parts.*

---

[1] *J.T.S.* XXXIX (1938). To this M. Jastrow lends support, *op. cit.* p. 26. In the Targum on Isa. ii. 3 and xxxii. 6 אולפן and אורייתא are parallel. Dr Daube takes the phrase אולפן חדת of this passage to mean 'that Israel will be given a better Law, a new and final revelation' (*ibid.* p. 55). It is equivalent to תורה חדשה, but this term, he thinks, was probably 'used much more loosely in colloquial speech than it would seem from that particular passage in Targum'. He refers to Tos. Sotah xiv. 9 to prove that 'תורה does not necessarily signify the unique, ideal Law laid down by God. It may mean the Law as understood by one of the various sects; any of them might claim to have the true Torah, in contrast to the Torah of the opponents. It follows that when Jesus added yet another doctrine to those already in existence, he may well have been regarded as founder of a תורה חדשה.' Daube takes διδαχή καινή in Mark i. 27 to mean תלמוד חדש or הוריה חדשה or again הלכה חדשה. The whole article is of first-rate importance.

[2] Water is a familiar figure for the Torah, see S–B, *op. cit.* II, 433.

174

The date of R. Simon b. Zabdai is late (*c.* A.D. 300). But the passage is interesting on more grounds than one. Not only does it help us to understand how the Rabbis understood the Law of the New Covenant of Jeremiah, that is, as referring to the Mosaic Torah, but its context also reveals the background against which we are to place discussions of the problem of the future role of the Torah; because it is noteworthy that in the previous section R. Phinehas (fourth century A.D.) had referred both to the words of the Torah and to the words of מינות (heresy), that is, of sectaries, probably Jewish Christians. Then follows the passage quoted above, the contrast between Torah in this world and that of the world to come: whereas in this world men learn and forget Torah, in the world to come they will learn and not forget; the Torah of God will be in their hearts. The polemic background of the saying is significant, and will occupy us in due course. Now, at first sight, it would appear that the phrase תורה של משיח in xi. 8 implies a contrast between the תורה of this world and that of the world to come, but as Professor A. Guttmann noted to the author, xi. 8 is to be interpreted in the light of ii. 1. The תורה של משיח, he thinks, is to be understood as 'the Torah of the days of the Messiah'. And even if this be not admitted, it is not the Torah that is to be changed in the Age to Come (=the Messianic Age here), but the relation of man to the Torah: that is, the Torah will then be differently and more satisfactorily studied. This is brought out in the Soncino translation: 'in comparison with Torah [which will be learnt] in the World to Come'. Our rendering above is literal.

(3) *Targum on Song of Songs* v. 10:

דודי בכן שריאת כנשתא דישראל למשתעי בשבחא למרי עלמא וכן אמרת
לההוא אלהא רעותי למפלח דעטיף ביממא באצטלא חור כתלגא וזיו יקרא
דיי דאנפוהי זהרין כנורא מסגיאות חוכמתא וסברא דהוא מחדת שמעון חדתין
בכל יומא ועתיד לפרסמנון לעמיה ביומא רבא וטקסיה על רבוא רבון
מלאכין דמשמשין קדמוי:

The English would run somewhat as follows:

My beloved (Cant. v. 10). Then Kenesseth Israel commences to engage in the praise of the Master of the Universe and speaks thus: 'It is my delight to worship God who wraps Himself by day in a robe white as snow and the glorious divine splendour, whose countenance shines like a flame by reason of the greatness of [His] wisdom and thought, who delivers anew every day new traditions (or decisions) which He is to make known to His people on the Great Day, and whose array (or royal authority) extends over a myriad myriads of angels who serve before Him.'

Here Strack–Billerbeck refer, in a paraphrase of the above, to new Halakoth which God will give *by the hand* of the Messiah. But the text does not include a reference to the Messiah. The thought expressed is that new interpretations showing a new ingenuity in exegesis of the Torah will be given in 'the great day' by God himself.

(4) *Yalqut on Isa.* xxvi. 2. Isa. xxvi. 2 in the RSV reads: 'Open the gates, that the righteous nation which keeps faith may enter in.' The Hebrew is: פִּתְחוּ שְׁעָרִים וְיָבֹא גוֹי־צַדִּיק שֹׁמֵר אֱמֻנִים. The comment in Yalqut takes 'which keep faith' to be the equivalent of '*who say Amen*'. That is, they take *Shomer 'emunim* to be *She'omer 'amenim*. On the basis of this the following is developed. We give the translation of Loewe:[1]

For the sake of one single Amen which the wicked respond from Gehinnom, they are rescued therefrom. How so? In time to come, the Holy One, Blessed be He, will take His seat in Eden and expound. All the righteous will sit before Him: all the retinue on high will stand on their feet. The sun and the Zodiac [or, constellations] will be at His right hand and the moon and the stars on His left; *God will sit and expound a new Torah which He will, one day, give by the Messiah's hand* (my italics). When God has finished the recital [Haggadah], Zerubbabel, son of Shealtiel, will rise to his feet and say 'Be His Great Name magnified and sanctified' (that is, the prayer after study, PB p. 86). His voice will reach from one end of the universe to the other and all the inhabitants of the universe will respond 'Amen'. Also the sinners of Israel and the righteous of the Gentiles, who have remained in Gehinnom, will respond 'Amen' out of the midst of Gehinnom. Then the universe will quake, till the sound of their cry is heard by God. He will ask 'What is this sound of great rushing (Ezek. iii. 12, 13) that I hear?' Then the angels of the service make answer, 'Lord of the Universe, these are the sinners of Israel and the righteous of the Gentiles, who remain in Gehinnom. They answer "Amen", and they declare that Thy judgement of them was just.' Immediately God's mercy will be aroused towards them in exceptional measure (*be-yoter*) and He will say: 'What can I do unto them, over and above this judgement, or, what can I do unto them exceptionally, in view of this judgement? For it was but the evil inclination that brought them to this.' At that moment God will take the keys of Gehinnom in His hand and give them to Michael and to Gabriel, in the presence of all the righteous, and say to them, 'Go ye, open the gates of the Gehinnom and bring them up'. Straightway they go with the keys and open the eight thousand gates of Gehinnom. Each single Gehinnom is 300 [parasangs?] long and 300 wide: its thickness is 1000 parasangs and its height 1000 parasangs, so that no single sinner who has fallen therein, can ever get forth. What do Michael and Gabriel do? Immediately they take each sinner by the hand and bring him up, as a man

---

[1] *A Rabbinic Anthology*, p. 558.

raises his fellow from a pit and brings him up by a rope, as it says: 'And he raised me from the horrible pit' (Ps. xl. 3, 2 in EV). Then the angels stand over them, they wash and anoint them; they heal them from the smitings of Gehinnom, clothe them in fair raiment, and bring them into the presence of the Holy One, Blessed be He, and into the presence of all the righteous, when they, the sinners, have been clad as priests and honoured, as it says: 'Let Thy priests be clothed with righteousness and let Thy saints shout for joy' (Ps. cxxxii. 9). 'Thy priests', these are the righteous of the Gentiles, who are God's priests in this world, such as Antoninus and his associates....

The Hebrew of the pertinent words in italics in the above quotation is: והקב״ה דורש להם טעמי תורה חדשה שעתיד הקב״ה ליתן להם על יד מלך המשיח. This seems the most unambiguous reference to a new Messianic Torah. Jewish scholars, such as Israelstam, in correspondence, however, have pointed out that Abarbanel's reading apparently was: טעמי מצוות ע״י מלך המשיה, that is, 'expound the grounds of commands by the hand of king Messiah'. But we can easily see why such an explicit reference to a new Messianic Torah would naturally lead to uneasiness, and possibly give rise to a modified and safer reading. The further attempt to interpret the phrase טעמי תורה חדשה as if it meant טעמי תורה החדשים, that is, 'new grounds of Torah', is suspect for the same reason, although it may be grammatically possible (Gesenius–Kautzsch (1892 ed.), p. 492; see especially 1 Sam. ii. 4; 1 Kings i. 41; Isa. ii. 11; xvi. 8).[1] It is, therefore, to be recognized that we find in this passage an explicit reference to a Messianic Torah new in kind. Notice particularly that this Messianic Torah and the divine exposition of it is in a context of universalism. It is destined not only for Israel, but for 'All the righteous' including those among the Gentiles. And not only so but even the righteous dead among the Gentiles and the unrighteous dead of Israel are brought into the sphere of this new Law. It should, however, be noted that Yalqut as a compilation or thesaurus is not earlier than the thirteenth century, although its component parts are variously dated before this. In fact, the pertinent section above, dealing with the New Torah, comes from the Othiyyoth of R. Akiba, where the reading is טעמי תורה חדשה.[2]

[1] So Israelstam in a private communication.
[2] On these, see Strack, op. cit. pp. 229, 347. See also L. Ginzberg, op. cit. p. 305. He recognized here a New Torah but emphasizes that the source is late, that is, the Alphabet of Akiba. The passage from Midrash Tehillim cxlvi, see above, p. 163, he refers not to the Messianic Age but to the time after the Resurrection (p. 305, n. 5). He writes: 'die alten Quellen kennen weder eine neue Thorah noch die Lehrtätigkeit des Messias' (p. 306). He regards the supposition of Christian influences in this matter as questionable.

(5) *Song of Songs Rabbah* ii. 29 on ii. 13. This is a comment on the words in ii. 13: 'The fig tree putteth forth her green figs.' The whole passage reads, in a literal translation, as follows:

R. Joḥanan said: As for the seven years in which the Son of David comes: the first year will see established what is written (Amos iv) '*And I caused it to rain upon one city*' etc. In the second arrows of hunger shall be sent upon it: in the third a great famine and men and women and children will die, and the pious and the men of 'good works' will be diminished: and the Torah will be forgotten from Israel: in the fourth there will be hunger and no hunger: plenty and no plenty: in the fifth a great plenty: and they shall eat and drink and rejoice and the Torah shall return to its renewal and it will be renewed to Israel. (The Soncino translation gives: 'the Torah will be renewed and restored to Israel': p. 126.)

א״ר יוחנן שבוע שבן דוד בא שנה ראשונה מתקיים מה שנאמ׳ (עמוס ד)
והמטרתי על עיר אחת וגו׳. בשנייה חצי רעב משתלחין בה. בשלישית רעב
גדול ומתים בו אנשים ונשים וטף, וחסדים ואנשי מעשה מתמעטים. והתורה
משתכחת מישראל. ברביעית רעב ולא רעב. שובע ולא שובע. בחמישית שובע
גדול. ואוכלין ושותין ושמחין. התורה חוזרת לחדושה ומתחדשת לישראל.

In his discussion of this Klausner insists that the idea that the Torah would be forgotten from Israel in the days preceding the advent of the Messiah is familiar and early, and that the phrase והתורה חוזרת לחדושה ומתחדשת לישראל is really a late alteration of words which originally meant that in the days of the Messiah the Torah, which had been forgotten, would return to those learning it.[1] This is the force of TB Sanhedrin 97a (Soncino translation, p. 654):

Our Rabbis taught: In the seven-year cycle at the end of which the son of David will come—in the first year, this verse will be fulfilled: *And I will cause it to rain upon one city and cause it not to rain upon another city*; in the second, the arrows of hunger will be sent forth; in the third, a great famine, in the course of which men, women, and children, pious men and saints will die, and the Torah will be forgotten by its students; in the fourth, partial plenty; in the fifth, great plenty, when men will eat, drink and rejoice, and the Torah will return to its disciples; in the sixth, [Heavenly] sounds; in the seventh, wars, and at the conclusion of the septennate the son of David will come.

[1] *Op. cit.* p. 53. J. Klausner points out that in the parallel passage Pesiqta R. 75a (ed. M. Friedmann), the words ומתחדשת לישראל are missing. He rejects Weiss's view that the change from והתורה חוזרת ללומדיה to והתורה חוזרת לחדושה is early. R. Joḥanan died in A.D. 279. In Pesiqta the passage is cited in the name of רבנן: the partial parallel in Sanhedrin 97a is anonymous.

178

Passages beginning with 'Our rabbis taught' [ת״ר] are usually regarded as early. On the other hand, it is easier to understand why the phrase 'The Torah shall return to its renewal...' which *may* be taken to imply a New Torah would be changed to 'The Torah will return to its disciples' than the reverse. But, even if the reading in Song of Songs Rabbah should be the earlier, which is on the whole, however, unlikely, in view of the date of R. Johanan, the phrase חוזרת לחידושה may merely mean, as Klausner insists, 'will return to its original state'. Hence it does not refer to a New Torah which would replace the Old: this latter meaning can only be regarded as a most remote possibility.[1]

(v) There remains one other aspect of Torah in the Messianic Age which should be noted very briefly. There are passages which anticipate that the Gentiles will come to share in the blessings of the Torah in the Messianic Age. This was expressed in the Old Testament passages which we discussed and it is taken up by the rabbis. The chief passage is in Genesis Rabbah xcviii. 9 on Gen. xlix. 11 [But see above p. 164, n. 1]:

HE WASHETH HIS GARMENTS IN WINE, intimates that he [the Messiah] will compose for them words of Torah; AND HIS VESTURE IN THE BLOOD OF GRAPES—that he will restore to them their errors. R. Hanin said: Israel will not require the teaching of the royal Messiah in the future, for it says, *Unto him shall the nations seek* (Isa. xi. 10), but not Israel. If so, for what purpose will the royal Messiah come, and what will he do? He will come to assemble the exiles of Israel and to give them [the Gentiles] thirty precepts, as it says, *And I said unto them: If ye think good, give me my hire; and if not, forbear. So they weighed for my hire thirty pieces of silver* (Zech. xi. 12). Rab said: This alludes to thirty mighty men. R. Johanan said: It alludes to thirty precepts. R. Johanan's disciples said to him: Does not Rab hold that the verse refers only to the nations of the world?—In Rab's view, '*And I said unto them*' means unto Israel, while in R. Johanan's view '*And I said unto them*' means unto the nations of the world.

So Genesis Rabbah xcviii. 8 on Gen. xlix. 10 reads:

UNTIL SHILOH COMETH: this alludes to the royal Messiah. AND UNTO HIM SHALL THE OBEDIENCE (YIKHATH) OF THE PEOPLE BE: he [the Messiah] will come and set on edge (*makheh*) the teeth of the nations of the world.

The first passage seems to imply both that the Messiah will bring his teaching and that he will propound new meanings and interpretations of

---

[1] V. Aptowitzer, *op. cit. ad rem*, compares the phrase with that used to describe the new moon, לבנה בחידושה, Sanhedrin 42a.

Torah, but that he will direct all this to the nations not to Israel, because the latter, presumably, will receive its teaching directly from God, or already had received the requisite teaching.

There were different views as to what demands would be made on the Gentiles: according to some all the minute details of the Torah would be imposed upon them: according to others only three ordinances would be binding upon them: according to still others the Noachian commandments would be placed upon them. We need not here enlarge on the details: it is the fact that is significant: that in the opinion of some rabbis at least the Gentiles would submit to the yoke of the Torah in the Messianic Age.[1]

(vi) So far we have discussed what role the Torah was expected to play in the Messianic Age in a strict sense, and in particular whether Jewish speculation contemplated a New Torah in that Age. We have dealt with the relevant material in the light of the 'doctrine' of the immutability of the Torah which almost dominated Judaism. Next we have to refer to passages which have been held to suggest, not merely that there would be changes in the Torah in the Messianic Age, but that it would be completely abrogated.

The chief passage comes from TB Sanhedrin 97a (end) and Abodah Zarah 9a (middle). The Soncino translation of the former is:

The Tanna debe Eliyyahu taught: The world is to exist six thousand years. In the first two thousand years there was desolation; two thousand years the Torah flourished; and the next two thousand years is the Messianic era [97b] but through our many iniquities all these years have been lost.

The meaning of *The Tanna debe Eliyyahu* in this connexion is defined by Mishcon[2] as 'a Midrash containing chiefly Baraithas compiled by R. Anan, Bab. Amora of the 3rd cent.' We may therefore conclude that the evidence it supplies is fairly early. Baeck[3] on the strength of this, and other passages of lesser importance, has concluded that 'At that time (that is, the first century), the belief was widespread among the Jews that world history consisted of three epochs: first, the period of chaos— tohubohu; then the period of the Torah, beginning with the revelation

[1] See A. Edersheim, *The Life and Times of Jesus the Messiah*, II, 764 ff.; unfortunately there is no attempt made to date the various passages listed.
[2] Soncino translation of TB Abodah Zarah, *ad loc.* The translation of *tohu* may be 'anarchy'; so Morton Smith, *J.B.L.* LXXII (1953), 193.
[3] *The Pharisees*, Eng. trans. (1947), pp. 72 f.

180

on Mount Sinai; and finally, the hoped-for period of the Messiah....In conformity with this, the Gospels say: "Till heaven and earth pass, one jot or one tittle shall in no wise pass from the law, till all be fulfilled" (Matt. v. 18). When all is fulfilled, and the Messiah has come, the period of the law will have come to its close.' The same position is maintained by Silver.[1] Freedman,[2] however, rejects this interpretation of the passage from *The Tanna debe Eliyyahu*, and comments on the reference to the period of the Torah that 'this does not mean that the Torah shall cease thereafter, but is mentioned merely to distinguish it from the next era'. Mishcon makes no reference to the problem posed by the passage.

But we have seen that there is a passage in TB Shabbath 151*b*, which possibly offers some support for Baeck's interpretation, where it is stated that in the Messianic Age there would be neither merit nor guilt (לא זכות ולא חובה). Baeck also refers to TB Niddah 61*b* to confirm his position. It reads: אמר רב יוסף זאת אומרת מצוות בטלות לעתיד לבא, that is, R. Joseph (A.D. 320–75) said: 'This means the commandments shall be abrogated in the time to come.' Baeck refers this passage to the Messianic Age, but the context makes it clear that the reference is to the condition of the dead, who, as we nave seen before, are not subject to the Torah. The point at issue in TB Niddah 61*b* is that of the use of *sha'atnez*, that is, a mixture of wool and linen, which was prohibited to the living but, because death brings exemption from מצות, was, nevertheless, permitted as shrouds for the dead. It seems clear, therefore, that in this passage the phrase לעתיד לבא merely means 'in death', and it is difficult to agree either with Klausner[3] that the context of TB Niddah 61*b* supports the view that the saying does not merely refer to life in the next world but also, by implication, to the Messianic Age, or with Baeck who refers it expressly to the Messianic Age. But that the idea contained in TB Niddah 61*b* may refer to the Age to Come and not merely to the life after death is highly probable, if not certain. It may be permissible for us to refer here to our argument in *Paul and Rabbinic Judaism*[4] that the Age to Come was regarded both as an event, which came into being in time, and also as an eternally existing reality in the heavens, as it were. Hence, in one sense, one entered the Age to Come at death when one became free from the

---

[1] *The History of Messianic Speculation in Israel* (1927), p. 9.
[2] Soncino translation of TB Sanhedrin, II, p. 657, n. 9.
[3] *Jesus of Nazareth*, Eng. trans. p. 275; Klausner regards the passage as earlier than R. Joseph.
[4] Pp. 314 ff.

obligation to obey the מצות. It is to this that TB Niddah 61 *b* explicitly refers. But in another sense the Age to Come was to *come* into history and when this would happen the commandments, that is, the מצות, would also cease then, and by implication TB Niddah 61 *b* can be referred to this Age to Come that is to *come*. We can only refer TB Niddah 61 *b* to the Messianic Age if we can equate or identify this, that is, the Messianic Age, with the Age to Come. That this is a justifiable equation would seem reasonable in many passages: we have seen above that the phrase לעתיד לבא was very fluid and could refer both to the Messianic Age and to the final Age to Come, that is, the post-Messianic period. The distinction between the Age to Come and the Messianic Age is a comparatively late development, and it follows that they were often synonymous terms in early apocalyptic.[1] On the other hand, however, there are passages where the Messianic Age and the Age to Come are sharply distinguished: of the former it was possible to prophesy, but of the latter it was thought that it transcended all human conception. A passage in TB Shabbath 63 *a* (middle) makes this clear:

Samuel said, This world differs from the Messianic Era only in respect to servitude of the exiled; for it is said, *For the poor shall never cease out of the land.* This supports R. Hiyya b. Abba (A.D. 320–59), who said, All the prophets prophesied only for the Messianic Age, but as for The world to come, the eye hath not seen, O Lord, beside thee what he hath prepared for him that waiteth for him....[2]

In view, therefore, of the distinction between the Messianic Age and the Age to Come implied and explicitly stated in such passages as this, it is probably highly precarious to apply TB Niddah 61 *b* too surely to the Messianic Age as such.[3] We can only be sure from this passage that in the Age to Come, that Age that both IS and COMES, the מצות will cease, but we can only regard this as a possibility for the Messianic Age. This point is important for the understanding of the New Testament; and the

---

[1] See R. H. Charles, *Eschatology*, pp. 200 f., and especially J. Klausner, *Die Messianischen Vorstellungen des jüdischen Volkes im Zeitalter der Tannaïten*, pp. 17 ff.

[2] See T. W. Manson, *The Teaching of Jesus*[2], p. 277, n. 2: compare 1 Cor. ii. 9.

[3] L. Ginzberg, *op. cit.* p. 306, n. 1, does not refer it to the Messianic Age but to the time after the Resurrection. S. Lieberman, *Historia Judaica*, v, 2 (October 1943), 91, refers to Tosaphoth Niddah 61 *b* and asserts that 'the abolition of the Law in the future world is a genuine Jewish idea'. He does not define the future world as the Messianic Age, however. On the other hand, J. Z. Lauterbach refers TB Niddah 61 *b* to the Messianic Age, *Rabbinic Essays*, p. 267 n. On the idea that prophecy, which was regarded as the continuation of the voice heard on Sinai, would cease in Messianic times, see S. Schechter, *Some Aspects of Rabbinic Theology*, p. 123. Schechter emphasizes the completeness and finality of the Torah given on Sinai (p. 134).

question forces itself whether the distinction of this age and the Age to Come had come to clear expression in the time of Jesus. This is discussed by Volz, *op. cit.* pp. 63 ff. He concludes that the idea of the Two Ages, in any case, is older than the terms used to express it; we may safely assume that the distinction was a real one in the time of Jesus.[1] Bonsirven[2] thinks that the expressions העולם הזה and העולם הבא appeared at that time.[3]

In the passages treated above we have sought to discover what part the Torah was expected to play in the ideal future whether conceived as a Messianic Age or as the ultimate Age to Come. To recapitulate, we found in the Old Testament, the Apocrypha and Pseudepigrapha and in the rabbinical sources the profound conviction that obedience to the Torah would be a dominating mark of the Messianic Age, and in the prophet Jeremiah a certain tension as to whether this obedience would be spontaneous, in the sense that it would not be directed to, nor governed by, any external code, or whether some form of external Torah would still be

---

[1] See Mark x. 30; Luke xviii. 30; Matt. xii. 32, *et al.* The significance of this will be clear when we recognize that the difficulty of deciding whether Paul, for example, believed that in the Resurrection of Jesus the final Age to Come had arrived or whether that event merely inaugurated the Messianic Age has an important bearing on the Apostle's attitude to the Law. See *P.R.J.*[2] pp. 297 f.; H. J. Schoeps in *Aus Frühchristlicher Zeit: Religionsgeschichtliche Untersuchungen* (Tübingen, 1950) (also *Paulus* (1959), pp. 177 ff.) has dealt with this in 'Paulus als rabbinischer Exeget, 1, Χριστὸς τέλος νόμου', pp. 221 ff. He applies some of the passages which we have examined above to the phrase in Rom. x. 4. 'Die Geltung des Gesetzes als göttlichen Heilsweges ist seit der Auferstehung Jesu von den Toten, die seine Messianität sowohl wie auch den Anbruch der Endzeit beweist, beendigt. Denn das Gesetz ist Herr über den Menschen, solange er lebt' (Rom. vii. 1) (p. 223). In view of our treatment, Schoeps' conclusions would seem to be too bold. The same difficulty must influence our interpretation of Matt. v. 18, on which see my article in *Mélanges bibliques en l'honneur d'A. Robert* (Paris, 1957), pp. 428–46. Leo Baeck in *Judaism and Christianity* (1958), in an essay on *The Faith of Paul*, pp. 139 ff., takes very seriously the need to understand Paul's attitude to the Law in terms of strictly Messianic speculation. The Law was to cease in the Messianic Age. 'The primary question which Paul's faith had to face was: which "period" was it, that of the Torah or that of the Messiah?' (p. 162). As is the case with H J. Schoeps, Baeck seems to be too confident in his claim that the Law was to cease in the Messianic Age. On the other hand, D. Barthélemy, *RB*, LX (1953), 317, argues that, had the concept of the cessation of the Law been a marked element in Pharisaic Judaism in the first century, Paul would have made use of it in Rom. vii. 1–6. Instead he appeals to the principle that the Law was not binding after death. [2] *Op. cit.* 1, 312.

[3] N. Messel, in *Die Einheitlichkeit der jüdischen Eschatologie* (1915), disputed that Jewish eschatology contained the distinction between *This* (*earthly*) *Age* and *the* (*supernatural*) *Age to Come*. The terms refer always, he claimed, to a purely this-worldly and earthly conception. See P. Volz, *op. cit.* p. 66.

183

operative. Generally, however, our sources revealed the expectation that the Torah in its existing form would persist into the Messianic Age, when its obscurities would be made plain, and when there would be certain natural adaptations and changes and, according to some, the inclusion of the Gentiles among those who accepted the yoke of the Torah. The most conscious and general recognition of the need for legal changes in the Messianic Age emerged in the DSS. It turned out to be difficult always to distinguish the Messianic Age from the Age to Come in the final sense, but we found evidence for the belief that this last would transcend all human thought and see the cessation of מצות: but, since the Holy One himself was conceived to be occupied with the study of the Torah in the eternal world, we must not preclude the Torah even from the Age to Come in too radical a fashion.[1]

The evidence for the expectation of a New Torah which the Messiah should bring was not sufficiently definite and unambiguous to make us as certain as were Edersheim and Dalman[2] that this was a well defined and accepted element in the Messianic hope, but neither was it inconsiderable and questionable enough for us to dismiss it, as does Klausner, as merely a late development in a Judaism influenced by Christianity, a point to which we shall return later. Strack–Billerbeck's claim that the Torah of the Messiah would be new merely in the sense that it would expound the Old Torah more fully than was possible in this age probably errs on the side of caution. We can at least affirm that there were elements inchoate in the Messianic hope of Judaism, which could make it possible for some to regard the Messianic Age as marked by a New Torah, new indeed, as Strack–Billerbeck maintain, not in the sense that it contravened the old, but yet not merely in the sense that it affirmed the old on a new level, but in such a way as to justify the adjective חדשה that was applied to it. (Possibly Jeremiah would have thought of a Torah new in kind, but even he, as we suggested, did not exclude the possibility of this new kind of Torah having at the same time an element of *gramma* in it like that of the Old Torah.)

It is perilously easy, however, to systematize what was varied, vague and amorphous. Moreover, the isolation of passages dealing with one theme and their presentation in a concentrated, consecutive manner can too easily create an erroneous impression of their significance: to isolate in this context is to magnify, and to view the passages with which we have dealt in true perspective it is necessary to set them over against the vast

---

[1] G. F. Moore, *Judaism*, I, 273.   [2] *Jesus-Jeshua*, Eng. trans. (1929), p. 85.

184

continent of the rabbinical sources; only then can they be rightly assessed. Nor must it be forgotten that the passages which we have cited are all haggadic, so that they must lack a certain seriousness which more halakic passages would afford.[1] [But see the preface.]

In addition to all this, there is one difficulty, which we mentioned at the beginning of our discussion, which we have not yet met. Those passages which specifically use the term תורה חדשה are late; and Klausner, who apparently accepts this term as referring to a New Torah, claims that the passages concerned are the result of Christian influence, by way of reaction, of course, upon Judaism. At a date earlier than these passages what we usually find is the belief that, before the Messianic Age, Torah would almost fail in Israel but that it would later return. This late date of the passages, it is clear, is a real difficulty, no less than the paucity of their number, but we can submit certain considerations which may serve to offset these two factors.

First, we must emphasize again that the silence of our sources as to an early belief in a New Torah may be due to deliberate surgery. We have previously pointed out that our rabbinic sources represent merely the Pharisaic element in Judaism and that certain polemic tendencies are traceable in them. We do know that the question of the New Torah agitated Judaism. There is a passage in Deuteronomy Rabbah viii. 6 which reads thus:

It is written, 'For this commandment is not in heaven' (Deut. xxx. 11, 12). Moses said to the Israelites, Lest you should say, Another Moses is to arise, and to bring us another Law from heaven, therefore I make it known to you now that it is not in heaven: nothing of it is left in heaven. . . .

The polemical intention is obvious. Paul had used the same kind of midrash on Deut. xxx in Rom. x. 6 ff. in support of the view that God's word had drawn near to men in Christ. Again in Baruch iii. 29 ff. we hear another undertone of controversy where Wisdom is claimed to be inaccessible in the following terms:

Who hath gone up into heaven, and taken her (that is, Wisdom)
And brought her down from the clouds?
Who hath gone over the sea, and found her
And will bring her for choice gold?[2]

---

[1] G. F. Moore, *op. cit.* i, 162. Dr Lieberman insists on this strongly (so orally).
[2] On this see M. Jack Suggs, 'The Word is near you: Note on Rom. x. 6–10', *Report of Society of Biblical Literature and Exegesis* (New York, 1960), p. 8. Paul, he claims, follows a well-established tradition in which the word of Deut. xxx. 12–14 is Wisdom's 'incarnation' in the Torah.

185

JEWISH MESSIANIC EXPECTATION

But in Baruch iv. 1 it is asserted that Wisdom has appeared on earth in the Torah. Justin's *Dialogue with Trypho* makes the same controversy clear: he goes so far as to claim that he has read that there will be a final Law.[1]

Weiss[2] also regarded a complicated passage from TB Shabbath 104*a*, which deals with variant forms of the Hebrew letters and claims that the text of the Torah can suffer no innovations from any prophet, as directed against Paul's attitude towards the Torah. The phrase 'these are the commandments', derived from Lev. xxvii. 34, was taken to teach that 'a prophet may henceforth (that is, after Moses) make no innovations'; and Strack–Billerbeck[3] cite R. Johannan b. Zakkai's famous dictum, which we cited above, as direct polemic comment on Mark vii. 14 ff. (and parallels). In view of all the above, we may safely claim that the early presentation of Christianity as involving a New Law in the *SM* or in the καινὴ ἐντολή of the Fourth Gospel produced counter-claims within Judaism such as we see in Deuteronomy Rabbah viii. 6. But this may also, perhaps, account for the absence in our rabbinic sources of any specific early references to a New Torah, such as may possibly have been once contemplated. By the time that the passages which actually speak of a New Torah are found the separation of Church and Synagogue had become such that speculation among Jews and Christians could be mutually stimulating without being dangerous. It is arguable, at least, that this might account for the greater readiness of later Judaism to speak of a New Torah.[4]

Secondly, a further similar consideration illustrates the kind of situation which may account for the absence of early references to any New Torah. It has been pointed out by Bonsirven that despite the fact that the idea of

---

[1] *Ante-Nicene Christian Library*, II, see pp. 99 f. Justin here claims that he has read 'that there shall be a final law (and an eternal one)'. νυνὶ δὲ ἀνέγνων γάρ, ὦ Τρύφων, ὅτι ἔσοιτο καὶ τελευταῖος νόμος καὶ Διαθήκη κυριωτάτη πασῶν... Αἰώνιός τε ἡμῖν νόμος (Isa. lv. 3; lxi. 8; Jer. xxxii. 40) καὶ τελευταῖος ὁ Χριστὸς ἐδόθη καὶ ἡ διαθήκη πιστή. Text from G. Archambault, *Justin: Dialogue avec Tryphon* (Paris, 1909), I, 51 ff. See especially n. 2.
[2] Cited in Soncino translation of TB Shabbath, p. 499, n. 5.
[3] S–B, *Kommentar*, I, 719.
[4] I have here followed J. Klausner, but I do so with hesitation. I am not quite sure that he is correct in thinking that it would be easier for later Judaism to contemplate a New Torah than it would have been for first-century Judaism. The antipathy to Christianity had become greater, not less. The concept of a New Torah might perhaps have been indigenous and not merely the outcome of Christian influences. Within Christianity the concept of a New Law developed coincidentally with that of the Church as a New Israel. See on this, M. Simon, *Verus Israel* (1948), pp. 100 ff.

186

259

the Covenant dominates Jewish thought, surprisingly enough the idea is relatively little exploited in the rabbinical sources. Bonsirven gives a reason for this: he rightly suggests that the Law had replaced it as the centre of Jewish life and thought;[1] but an additional reason for the fact mentioned surely may be that the covenantal idea was so prominent in Christianity that it became, if not exactly distasteful to Judaism, nevertheless deliberately disused because of its marked Christian associations. It is the same kind of reaction against the New Law preached by early Christians which may have caused the comparative silence of the rabbinic sources on the concept of a New Law.

We are now in a position to turn again to the Matthaean approach to the words of Jesus with which we were concerned in the preceding chapter: how do Jewish expectations illuminate this? It must be recognized at the

---

[1] *Op. cit.* I, 79 f. His words deserve quotation: 'Cette idée de l'alliance domine toute la pensée juive: nous sommes d'autant plus surpris de constater que la littérature rabbinique a relativement peu exploité cette donnée biblique primordiale.' J. Bonsirven asserts that there are very few places where rabbis speculate on the covenantal idea: in the Midrashim comments on the biblical texts dealing with the Covenant are few. He also points out how sectarian movements remained far truer to the Old Testament in this; for example, the Dead Sea Sect governed its life on the covenantal principle. Thus not only Christian concentration on covenantal ideas, but other sectarian tendencies also would tend to reinforce the surprising neglect of the explicit treatment of such texts in the rabbinic sources. To judge from the extant works of Philo the same neglect of the covenantal idea might be found in Hellenistic Judaism, but G. F. Moore pointed out that Philo wrote two lost treatises on the Covenants (see R. Marcus (citing G. F. Moore), *op. cit.* p. 14 n.). (The view expressed by H. J. Schoeps in *Aus frühchristlicher Zeit*, p. 228, that Diaspora Judaism or Septuagint-Judaism, as he describes it, had a false conception of the covenantal relation between Yahweh and Israel, as did also Paul, to speak very mildly, is to be very seriously questioned.) In his *Theologie und Geschichte des Judenchristentums*, p. 90, the same scholar offers parallels to the above mentioned neglect of the covenant concept in the rabbis, parallels which are illuminating. Schoeps is concerned to show the way in which Judaism reacted to the Jewish-Christian emphasis on Christ as the New Moses. He writes: 'Welchen Rang und welche Verbreitung dieses Dogma, vielleicht auf essäische Ursprünge zurückgehend, Christus Jesus–Novus Moses in der jüdischen Christenheit gehabt haben muß, lassen uns auch zwei weitere Umstände erkennen.... Zum anderen der auffällige Verzicht der Tannaiten und frühen Amoräer, Deut. xviii. 15 und 18 auszulegen [see especially p. 90, n. 3, for evidence]. Es begegnet uns hier dieselbe Erscheinung wie bei der Auslegungsgeschichte von Jes. liii; Ps. ii. 7; cx. 1; Jer. xxxi. 31 f.; Hos. ii. 25 usw. *Die jüdische Theologie der ersten Jahrhunderte n. Chr. fand diese Schriftsteller bereits durch die christliche Auslegung präokkupiert und verzichtete daher auf ihre Verwendung innerhalb messianischer Diskussionen oder legte sie betont uneschatologisch aus.*' (Our italics.) Compare also G. Quell, *T.W.Z.N.T.* II, *ad loc.* For the way in which Judaism closed its ranks against Christianity, see S. W. Baron, *A social and religious history of the Jews*[2], II, 2 (Philadelphia, 1952), 130 ff., and the bibliographical details he supplies.

187

outset that the evidence that we have been able to adduce in favour of a *new* Messianic Torah, when set over against the totality of the eschatological expectation of Judaism, is not impressive. In one respect—apart from the comparative paucity of the material—it must appear negative. As we wrote at the beginning of this chapter, could we clearly distinguish the role expected of the Torah in the Messianic Age and in the Age to Come we would be able to set the early Christian attitude to the Law in true perspective. Thus, for example, by determining how the various elements in the New Testament conceived the Resurrection, whether it was regarded as the inauguration of the Messianic Age or of the Age to Come proper, in its ultimate manifestation, we could then discover what attitude to the Law would be natural to them. But this our Jewish sources will not allow us to do, except in the most ambiguous way. Not only was the distinction between the Age to Come and Messianic Age not always clear, so that we had constant difficulty in deciding to which Age a particular passage referred, but it would not be correct to speak of any one generally accepted Jewish expectation as to the role of the Torah in either of these periods. The result of our survey is not in any sense decisive.

On the other hand, the material presented above is sufficiently cogent to illumine for us the Matthaean understanding of the *SM*. Matthew was conscious, as were other early Christians, of living in the Messianic Age: the role of the Law, therefore, inevitably occupied him. We saw that for him the Christian Dispensation, among other things, denies the Old Law on one level, but affirms and fulfils it on another; this is the meaning of the *SM*. Matthew does not explicitly claim to have received a *New* Torah, although the substance of a New Messianic Torah is clearly present to his mind. As the rabbis, and especially as the Dead Sea Sectarians, anticipated, the Messianic Age had brought for Matthew a teaching (תורה, אולפן) with eschatological authority (vii. 28). In his emphasis on the Messianic teaching in the *SM*, Matthew reveals especial affinity, perhaps, with the sectarians, who had very unequivocally contrasted the 'judgements' by which they were to be ruled after the Prophet and the Messiahs of Aaron and Israel had come, with the interim ones to which, until then, they were subject. But, unless the Messiah of Aaron be equated with *Elias redivivus*, which is unlikely, the sectarians had ascribed the giving of these anticipated new judgements to the Prophet, that is, the Messianic function was not strictly connected with the promulgation of new laws. In connecting Jesus, as Messiah, especially with the giving of teaching, Matthew differs from the Sectarians: that is, the teaching in the *SM* is more specifically

188

that of the Messiah in Matthew's view, than would have been the case had the Sectarians found that their Messiahs had come. In his awareness of the significance of the moral teaching of Jesus, as belonging to the Messianic Age, Matthew has Sectarian affinities, but in pinning this down to Jesus as *the Messiah himself* he departs from the Sectarian anticipation. Does he, at this very point, attach himself to the rabbinic anticipation? Ginzberg would have denied this: he insisted strongly that the Messiah of Jewish expectation was not concerned with interpreting the Law. The marks of the Messianic Age in rabbinic tradition would be repentance, liberation from Gentile domination (by the Ephraimitic Messiah), the appearance of Elijah as forerunner of the Davidic Messiah, and finally, the coming of the latter. The 'teaching' of the Age would be in the hands of Elijah.[1] But the passages to which we have appealed justify the view that in some rabbinic circles the Messiah had a didactic function. And it is this emphasis that Matthew found congenial. His is, in this sense, in part a rabbinic Christ, whose words were for him *halakah* and the ground for *halakah* both for Israel and for the Gentile world: both Israel and the latter are addressed in these words of Jesus. At this point again it is impossible to claim Matthew for any single milieu: he reveals both sectarian and rabbinic affinities. One thing is clear: even if the concept of a New Torah in the Messianic Age had not become explicit in Judaism before Christ (which is not at all sure), his figure was a catalyst[2] which gave life to what was inchoate: with him came also a νόμος Χριστοῦ.

[1] *Op. cit. ad rem.*

[2] The situation revealed in Matthew recalls that in the Fourth Gospel. In xvi. 13–16 Jesus is denied to be one of the prophets, nor can xi. 2 be certainly regarded as referring to the expected 'Prophet' rather than to the Messiah himself. The crowds take Jesus to be a prophet in xxi. 46 and, almost certainly, in xxi. 11, but such a generalized concept of a prophet is to be distinguished from that of an eschatological figure 'the Prophet': this emerges from pp. 143 ff. above, and this is rightly emphasized by Bultmann, *Das Evangelium des Johannes* (Göttingen, 1953), p. 61. But the characteristics of 'the Prophet' to come are ascribed by Matthew to Jesus as Messiah. The Matthaean Messiah reminds us also of the Teacher of Righteousness and the Interpreter of the Law of the Scrolls. With the Messianic, Matthew has fused prophetic and rabbinic traits. The same ambiguity emerges in John. In John i. 22 'the Prophet' is distinguished from the Messiah. But in John vi. 14 Jesus is taken by the people to be 'the Prophet' and is, in turn, interpreted as a Messianic figure because they immediately want to make him a king (compare C. H. Dodd, *The Interpretation of the Fourth Gospel*, 1953, p. 345); this is a more natural explanation of John vi. 15 than that an ancient belief in the magic power of the king emerges here (H. Windisch, *Paulus und Christus*, 1934, p. 79). This understanding of the Messiah as 'the Prophet' Bultmann (*op. cit.* p. 61) takes to be a specifically Christian development (Acts iii. 22, vii. 37). Deut. xviii. 15 was not, he claims, Messianically

189

But despite his sense of the didactic significance of Jesus, the Messiah, Matthew, nevertheless, remains sensitive to the niceties of the expectations of Judaism. It was this sensitivity, in part at least, that may have made him hesitate to use the phrase 'new teaching' or 'new Law of the Messiah'. The ambiguity of Jewish expectation has invaded the Evangelist's presentation of the Messianic era. Nevertheless, the phrase 'New Torah' did emerge in Judaism and *may* have already emerged in the first century within Pharisaic Judaism; Paul did not hesitate to speak of 'the Law of Christ' (תורה של משיח) and John of 'the New Commandment', καινὴ ἐντολή, and of ἐντολαὶ τοῦ Χριστοῦ.[1] It is, therefore, probable that it was not only his sensitivity to the niceties of rabbinic and sectarian eschatological anticipations that caused Matthew to change the 'new teaching' of Mark i. 27 to the 'teaching' of vii. 27. There must have been other factors in his world which caused him to temper his language in this way. These we shall explore in the next chapter.

applied in pre-Christian Judaism (*ibid.*), and although he recognizes the Moses-Messiah, New Exodus motif therein (*op. cit.* p. 61, n. 8), he rejects Jeremias's view (*Golgotha*, 1926, p. 83) that 'the Prophet' is a returned Moses (Bultmann, *op. cit.* p. 158, n. 2). As far as the DSS are concerned our examination confirmed Bultmann's separation of 'the Prophet' from the Messiah, but, while the former was not to be a returned Moses, he was a New Moses, that is, a figure like the first Moses. The complexity of Messianic expectation does not allow us to be as unequivocal as Bultmann. We may claim, with some certainty, in the light of Matthew and John that eschatological figures which in Judaism were often distinct, even if they sometimes tended to merge, become identified in primitive Christianity. Is it unreasonable to suggest that this is so because the figure of Jesus historically suggested that he was all these—Messiah, 'the Prophet', Rabbi: it is in this sense that we use the term 'catalyst' of Jesus above. On John vi, see C. K. Barrett, *The Gospel according to St John* (London, 1958), p. 231: 'Several features of this chapter suggest that Jesus was the prophet "like unto Moses"'; and C. H. Dodd, *The Interpretation of the Fourth Gospel*, *ibid.* and p. 339. He takes 'the Prophet' to be a quasi-Messianic designation. Jesus in John vi is New Moses and infinitely more. On the influence of the belief in 'the Prophet', see F. W. Young, *J.B.L.* LXXV (1956), 285 ff.

[1] John xiii. 34; xiv. 15; compare 1 John ii. 7 ff.; 2 John v. In the Epistle to the Hebrews the failure of the old cultus necessarily demands the emergence of a new or, at least, changed Law; see Heb. vii. 12. The New Commandment of John is dealt with in *J.B.L.* LXXIV (1955), 69–79, by Harrisville. He rejects the view that the New Commandment is merely a radicalizing of the old, and Bultmann's claim that it is not new historically, and insists that the 'new commandment' is new in *content* and *historically*—because it belongs to a new aeon that has dawned and is to be practised 'in the light of that love which Jesus is about to show in his death' (p. 79). 'What gives Jesus' words their gravity in John xiii. 34 and their seriousness is that the one who delivers the commandment is about to be sacrificed in order to establish the new eschatological covenant, a covenant by which God orders his relationship to men in a new and final way' (*ibid.*).

190

New Test. Stud. **19**. pp. 246-270

M. DE JONGE

JEWISH EXPECTATIONS ABOUT THE 'MESSIAH' ACCORDING TO THE FOURTH GOSPEL

I. INTRODUCTION

1. This paper will deal with a number of passages in the Fourth Gospel in which Jews express Jewish beliefs concerning the Messiah. Three of these are found in the debates among various groups in Jerusalem which are recorded in chapter vii; they all deal with the *coming* of the Messiah.

vii. 27

ὁ δὲ χριστὸς ὅταν ἔρχηται, οὐδεὶς γινώσκει πόθεν ἐστίν.

vii. 31

ὁ χριστὸς ὅταν ἔλθῃ, μὴ πλείονα σημεῖα ποιήσει ὧν οὗτος ἐποίησεν;

vii. 41 *b*, 42

μὴ γὰρ ἐκ τῆς Γαλιλαίας ὁ χριστὸς ἔρχεται; οὐχ ἡ γραφὴ εἶπεν ὅτι ἐκ τοῦ σπέρματος Δαυίδ, καὶ ἀπὸ Βηθλέεμ τῆς κώμης ὅπου ἦν Δαυίδ, ἔρχεται ὁ χριστός;

To these three must be added the statement in xii. 34, ἡμεῖς ἠκούσαμεν ἐκ τοῦ νόμου ὅτι ὁ χριστὸς μένει εἰς τὸν αἰῶνα, adduced as an objection to Jesus' announcement ὅτι δεῖ ὑψωθῆναι τὸν υἱὸν τοῦ ἀνθρώπου.

Besides these direct statements there is an allusion to Jewish beliefs concerning the Messiah in i. 19-34 where John the Baptist is questioned by representatives of the Jews. On the question 'Who are you?' there seem to be three possible answers: 'the Christ', 'Elijah' and 'the Prophet', obviously in accordance with known variants in Jewish expectation. There is a clear connection (apart from the Elijah-concept) between this section and vii. 40-4 where there are two options: 'the Prophet' or 'the Christ'.

Next i. 35-51 should be mentioned, because in this passage Jesus' first disciples confess their faith in Jesus in terms which are obviously meant to represent various aspects of Jewish expectation. Andrew speaks of ὁ Μεσσίας (translated explicitly as 'the Christ', i. 41); Philip announces 'him about whom Moses in the Law and the Prophets have written' (i. 45, note the emphasis there and here on εὑρήκαμεν!) and Nathanael in his confession speaks of ὁ υἱὸς τοῦ θεοῦ, ὁ βασιλεὺς τοῦ Ἰσραήλ (i. 49).

Similarly iv. 25 points to the Samaritan expectation of (again) the *coming* of the Messiah οἶδα ὅτι Μεσσίας ἔρχεται...ὅταν ἔλθῃ ἐκεῖνος, ἀναγγελεῖ ἡμῖν ἅπαντα.

264

2. In all these cases the Fourth Gospel clearly wishes to confront Jesus' own statements about himself, or pronouncements of others concerning him, with current Jewish (and Samaritan) expectations. Our primary task, therefore, is to investigate how these references to Jewish (or Samaritan) beliefs function in the setting in which they occur, and within the Gospel as a whole.

Secondly, we must ask from what source(s) the evangelist derived his information concerning these expectations about 'the Messiah', and we must try to assess his reliability in reproducing them. Are there parallels in Jewish (or Christian) documents which may corroborate or supplement the statements made by the Jews (and the Samaritans) in the Fourth Gospel, so that we can understand why and how they are introduced in the Gospel? If not, do the statements in the Fourth Gospel supplement what we know from other sources and do they help us to sketch a more coherent picture of Jewish beliefs concerning the Messiah at the time the Fourth Gospel was written? I should like to stress that we cannot deal with the second problem until we have discussed the first. We cannot use the Johannine material without taking into account that the Jews whose opinion is expressed in the Gospel appear on a scene set by a Christian evangelist. They are portrayed as 'representative Jews' and are obviously introduced in the Gospel because it was important to compare John's views on Jesus the Christ with Jewish expectations concerning the Messiah.

If statements made by Jewish opponents or sympathizers in the Fourth Gospel do not agree with expressions or conceptions found in Jewish sources, or show only partial agreements, we may not exclude the possibility that the Gospel, as only source, has preserved truly Jewish notions and beliefs. After all the Jewish material is variegated, and very scanty and haphazard. Yet the Johannine material can only be used to fill in the gaps or to correct the picture after due allowance has been made for its function within the Fourth Gospel.

II. THE FUNCTION OF THE JEWISH STATEMENTS CONCERNING 'THE MESSIAH' IN THE GOSPEL—SOME GENERAL CHARACTERISTICS[1]

Before turning to a more detailed treatment of the individual passages some more general remarks, relating to all passages, may be useful.

1. In an important excursus in his commentary on the Fourth Gospel[2]

---

[1] The points raised in this section are nearly all dealt with at greater length in a number of earlier studies. See 'Nicodemus and Jesus: Some observations on misunderstanding and understanding in the Fourth Gospel', *B.J.R.L.* LIII (1970–71), 337–59 (The Manson Memorial Lecture 1970); 'Onbegrip in Jeruzalem. Jezus en de Joden in Johannes 7', *Rondom het Woord*, XV (1973); 'Jesus as Prophet and King in the Fourth Gospel', *Ephemerides Theologicae Lovanienses*, XLIX (1973), and 'The Use of the Word ΧΡΙΣΤΟΣ in the Johannine Epistles', in *Studies in John* presented to Prof. Dr J. N. Sevenster (*Suppl. N.T.* XXIV) (Leiden, 1970), pp. 66–74.

[2] R. Schnackenburg, *Das Johannesevangelium*, I (Freiburg–Basel–Wien, 1965), pp. 321–8 (further referred to as Commentary 1). See also his 'Die Messiasfrage im Johannesevangelium', in *Neutestamentliche Aufsätze* (Festschrift J. Schmid) (Regensburg, 1963), pp. 240–64.

R. Schnackenburg has emphasized that the entire passage i. 19–51 is purposely centred on the question of the fulfilment of Jewish messianic expectations in Jesus. The Baptist refuses to ascribe any messianic dignity to himself and points to the One who comes after him; the first disciples understand right from the start that various aspects of Jewish messianic expectation converge in this Jesus whom they have met. They need further instruction leading to a deeper insight – and this instruction is given in the later chapters of the Gospel – but clearly this chapter is meant to give a survey of messianic titles and designations and to emphasize that they find their true meaning and fulfilment in Jesus.

In the same way in iv. 1–42 some typical Samaritan reactions are recorded and here again Jesus is portrayed as the one whom the Samaritan woman expects (v. 26) and whom the villagers hail as the Saviour of the world (v. 42).[1] In chapter vii the evangelist deals with various reactions in the crowd and in the leading circles in Jerusalem, and in this framework he brings up one tentative question in favour of Jesus and a number of Jewish objections against his Messiahship – the last of these being reserved to a later occasion, in xii. 34.[2] A similar treatment of the question of Jesus' true identity by means of a report of a debate taking up one theme from various points of view we find in chapter ix, where, however, the title Messiah (Christ) does not occupy a central position. All this, of course, is well known; I mention it here because I want to emphasize the literary character of the treatment of the problem of Jesus' Messiahship. Representative people (disciples, ordinary people: the crowd, Jewish leaders, Samaritans) express representative beliefs and raise representative objections.

2. Though the persons mentioned in the various stories are meant to be representative, they are more like actors in a play, whose utterances help along the course of events and, even more, the development of thought, than identifiable individuals belonging to clearly defined groups, even if we look at the Fourth Gospel by itself, regardless of its links with history. This may be illustrated by a very short survey of the dramatis personae in vii. 10–52.[3]

Here we find in vv. 10–13 two groups among the crowds over against the Jews whom they fear (v. 13). The hostility of 'the Jews'[4] is quite marked here, as it is elsewhere in the Gospel (see e.g. vii. 1, 19 and v. 16, 18; x. 31; xi. 8). Yet in v. 11 (as in v. 35) a broader and not specifically hostile group may be meant. In vv. 14–24 'the Jews' are Jesus' opponents in a discussion which ends with a rabbinical argument, so we might suppose that this term indicates

---

[1] See further the Appendix.
[2] See especially R. Schnackenburg, 'Die Messiasfrage', pp. 249–52, and C. H. Dodd, The Interpretation of the Fourth Gospel (Cambridge, 1953), pp. 89–92 and p. 346, where Dodd says: 'The evangelist has brought together here most of what he has to say in reply to Jewish objections against the messianic claims made for Jesus.'
[3] See also 'Onbegrip in Jeruzalem'.
[4] On οἱ Ἰουδαῖοι see E. Grässer, 'Die antijüdische Polemik im Johannesevangelium', N.T.S. IX (1964–5), 74–90.

the Jewish leaders in Jerusalem.[1] Yet in *v.* 19 ὁ ὄχλος has already appeared again. Moreover, where Jewish leaders are mentioned explicitly in this chapter they are never called 'the Jews'; *v.* 32 speaks of 'the Pharisees' and 'the chief priests and the Pharisees'; in *vv.* 45–52 where we are told of the discussions in the council-chamber the term 'rulers' is also introduced (*v.* 48, cf. *v.* 26). ὁ ὄχλος or οἱ ὄχλοι are never clearly defined or divided groups; the evangelist is clearly not interested in the description of different parties, but contents himself with outlining different reactions (see *vv.* 10–12, 31, 41–3); the picture is further complicated by the introduction of 'some of the people of Jerusalem' in *vv.* 25–30 who stand over against 'the rulers' (*v.* 26). It is not clear whether they belong to the crowd or not, and whether they or a different undefined group (cf. *v.* 25) try to kill Jesus (*v.* 30).

This subject would deserve further treatment, but for the purpose of this paper these illustrations taken from one chapter may suffice. Yet, however vague the description may be, it is useful to note *who* are said to express Jewish messianic beliefs. In vii. 27 the speakers are 'some of the people of Jerusalem'. In vii. 40–4 we meet various groups in the crowd, one of which makes the objection about the Messiah's Davidic descent and his birth in Bethlehem. In xii. 34 it is ὁ ὄχλος that is speaking. In vii. 31 we are told that 'many believed in him'; these believers put the question (to be answered negatively!): 'When the Messiah comes, is it likely that he will perform more signs than this man?' It is after their reaction that the Pharisees decide to take action.

People who are sympathetic towards Jesus occur several times in the Gospel. Sometimes they belong to the common people (ii. 23–5; vi. 2; vii. 40–1; viii. 31; x. 42; xi. 45, 47–8; xii. 11). Sometimes they belong to the leaders (Nicodemus iii. 1–2; vii. 50–2; xix. 38–42; Joseph of Arimathea xix. 38–42; many of the ἄρχοντες xii. 42–3; some of the Pharisees ix. 16). Often this sympathy is called faith (ii. 23–5; vii. 31; viii. 31; x. 42; xi. 45, 48; xii. 11, 42) and Joseph of Arimathea is called a disciple (xix. 38). This faith is often connected with the signs performed by Jesus (ii. 23–5; xi. 45, 47–8; xii. 10–11, 42, cf. vi. 2; x. 42) as it is in vii. 31. We cannot and need not speak about the function of signs in the Fourth Gospel and about the Gospel's effort to define correctly the relationship between faith in Jesus and the signs and works performed by him: it constitutes one of the major themes of Johannine theology.[2] But I should like to emphasize that the people meant here eventually fall under a negative verdict. Their faith needs a fundamental correction; ii. 23–5, the first passage to mention this category of Jewish believers, tells quite plainly: 'Jesus for his part would not trust himself to them. He knew men so well, all of them, that he needed no evidence from others about a man, for he himself could tell what was in a man.'[3]

---

[1] Cf. for example the alternation between οἱ Ἰουδαῖοι (*vv.* 18, 22) and οἱ Φαρισαῖοι (*vv.* 13, 15, 16, 40) in chapter 9.   [2] See below, n. 1, on p. 262.
[3] See 'Nicodemus and Jesus', *passim*, and section IV 4 below.

3. Next, I should like to point out that there is no real discussion about the Jewish statements. In vii. 25–30 Jesus' reaction is significantly introduced by ἔκραξεν ἐν τῷ ἱερῷ διδάσκων (cf. vii. 37).[1] Jesus takes up the πόθεν, explains it in terms of his special mission, which presupposes a unique relationship between Father and Son, but he does not use the word χριστός himself. There is no reaction from Jesus whatever after vii. 31; we are obviously expected to make the necessary adjustments by comparing this statement with the outcome of the discussion between Jesus and Nicodemus in chapter iii, the discourse on the Bread from Heaven in chapter vi and elsewhere. The debate in vii. 40–4 is a typically inner-Jewish discussion in which Jesus himself does not take part; once the problem where he comes from is answered in vii. 25–30 there is no need for further comment on matters like Davidic descent and birth at Bethlehem. In xii. 34 the objection voiced by the crowd concerning Jesus' pronouncement that the Son of Man must be lifted up, and the following question about the identity of this Son of Man, are not answered. Here as in the previous cases the Jewish statements point to a more or less fundamental misunderstanding.[2]

4. In this connection it may be useful to point out that i. 19–51, where various messianic designations, including the word 'Messiah' itself, occur successively, ends with a reference to the Son of Man, his contact with heaven by means of ascending and descending angels. This is not the place to speak about the ascent–descent pattern in the Fourth Gospel; I should like to refer here to W. A. Meeks' fundamental contribution to Johannine studies in his recent article: 'The Man from Heaven in Johannine sectarianism.'[3] It may be useful to emphasize that i. 19–50 stands between i. 18 and i. 51, both dealing with the heavenly status of the One to whom all the designations in the intermediate section point in their own way. The same is true of chapter iii where the term 'a teacher sent by God, performing signs' in v. 2 is corrected and superseded by the expressions (only) Son, Son of God, and Son of Man which designate Jesus' heavenly origin and ultimate authority. We may also mention here chapter ix where the discussion is concerned with Jesus' authority conceived in terms of true prophecy, and where Jesus in a private final conversation with the blind man introduces the term 'Son of Man' in connection with his own mission – as in i. 51 and in iii. 13, 14. Many more examples could be given in order to show that titles like 'prophet', 'teacher sent by God', 'king' or even 'Messiah' do not correspond completely with the real status and authority of Him to whom they point. The terms are not wrong but insufficient; they may be used in a wrong context and are, therefore, in need of further definition.

---

[1] κράζω occurs also in vii. 28, i. 15 and xii. 44. It is used especially of inspired utterances, see R. Bultmann, *Das Evangelium des Johannes* (Göttingen, [12]1952), p. 50 n. 3, who refers to Rom. viii. 15; ix. 27; Gal. iv. 6.

[2] See further 'Jesus as Prophet and King', and 'Onbegrip in Jeruzalem'.

[3] *J.B.L.* xci (1972), 44–72.

In the case of the use of χριστός this further definition is given with the help of the terms Son of Man and Son of God. So i. 51 comes after i. 41; vii. 28, 29 implying Jesus' being Son of the Father come after vii. 27 and correct this basically so that by implication the discussion in vii. 40–4 becomes superficial and superfluous.[1] Also in xii. 34 it is clear that the Jews introduce the term 'Messiah' in a context where Jesus prefers the term 'Son of Man' and connects this Son of Man concept with the notion of 'being lifted up'.

5. The results of II 3 and 4 are fully borne out by a study of the statements about 'the Christ' which have not yet been mentioned. Again there is only time for some short comments.[2]

It is clear that the evangelist realizes that ὁ χριστός is a Jewish designation; we have seen that he uses the transliteration ὁ Μεσσίας and translates it in i. 41. In ix. 22 he tells his readers that a confession of Jesus as ὁ χριστός will necessarily be followed by expulsion from the synagogue. The Fourth Gospel wishes to stress that the use of the title ὁ χριστός for Jesus is the real issue in the debate between synagogue and Christian community. This is also the reason why this term occupies such a prominent place in the arguments used by Jews. Yet the evangelist himself regards the title ὁ χριστός as inadequate and in need of further comment.

The section on John the Baptist in i. 19–34 ends with John's witness to Jesus as the Son of God,[3] not to Jesus as the Christ, though that is the central designation used by the representatives of the Jews (iii. 28 referring to i. 21–3). In his reply to the question of the Jews in x. 24 'If you are the Messiah say so plainly', Jesus refers to the acts performed by him in the name of the Father (x. 25). This passage ends with a very penetrating discourse and debate on the nature of Jesus' sonship and of his unity with the Father (x. 25–30, 31–9). When Martha confesses her faith in xi. 27 she says to Jesus: 'I am convinced (πεπίστευκα) that you are the Messiah, the Son of God, who was to come into the world.' The title ὁ χριστός and the use of the verb ἔρχεσθαι in connection with it are well-known features of Jewish statements in John, as we have seen. But the Christian confession ὁ χριστός is interpreted by the addition ὁ υἱὸς τοῦ θεοῦ. This is also the case in xx. 30, 31, the well-known 'first ending' of the gospel. A number of the signs which Jesus performed in the presence of his disciples were recorded in this book in order that the readers might believe that Jesus is the Christ, the Son of God, and that through this faith they might have life in his name. This shows the inadequacy of the formulation and, therefore, of the faith of the believers among the crowd in vii. 31 who

---

[1] See 'Jesus as Prophet and King', passim.

[2] See R. Schnackenburg, 'Die Messiasfrage', pp. 240–4, 254–6, and M. de Jonge, 'The Use of the word ΧΡΙΣΤΟΣ in the Johannine Epistles', pp. 71–4. In i. 17 and xvii. 3 the expression Ἰησοῦς Χριστός occurs, both times in a context which emphasizes the unity between Father and Son.

[3] The title 'Son of God' is exactly the one we would expect in i. 34, and therefore it is likely to be original. On the other hand it can be argued that the unusual ἐκλεκτός (variant found in ℵ*, some Old Latin and the two Old Syrian versions and in Ambrose) was changed into the more familiar υἱὸς τοῦ θεοῦ.

held that the signs performed by Jesus pointed to his Messiahship. They were right and yet not right, because they did not pay sufficient attention to the fact that this Jesus is the Son of God.

6. This rather rapid and general survey has made clear, I think, that the Jewish statements about the Messiah *either* point to a complete misunderstanding (vii. 27, 41 *b*–42; xii. 34) and are therefore ignored (vii. 41 *b*, 42; xii. 34) or reinterpreted fundamentally (vii. 27); *or* they represent an inadequate formulation of belief in Jesus (vii. 31) which is subsequently implicitly corrected.[1] Christian believers may use and do use 'the Christ' as designation for Jesus (i. 41, cf. vii. 41) – it is the central point in the debate between Jews and Christians – but this title needs to be interpreted. The Gospel interprets it by the title Son of God, pointing to the unity between Jesus and the Father who sent him.

We shall now try to fill in this general picture with the help of the results of a more detailed treatment of the passages concerned and of a comparison of the statements which concern us with data known from other sources.

III. TREATMENT OF INDIVIDUAL PASSAGES

1. *The witness of John the Baptist* (*i*. 19–34)

The first passage to be dealt with is i. 19–34, a section of the Gospel which did not receive much attention in the preceding part of the paper, because it presupposes Jewish beliefs rather than mentioning or correcting them explicitly.[2]

John's explicit and solemn negative confession (*v.* 20: καὶ ὡμολόγησεν καὶ οὐκ ἠρνήσατο, καὶ ὡμολόγησεν!) spoken in front of official representatives of the Jews (*vv.* 19, 22, 24)[3] is an important part of his μαρτυρία. John is portrayed as the ideal witness to Christ (*vv.* 19, 32, 34 and 7–8; iii. 26 and v. 33–6).[4] There is no doubt that he is ἀπεσταλμένος παρὰ θεοῦ (i. 6; iii. 28) and that he witnesses to the truth (v. 33). That is why the section devoted to his preaching is made to end with the perfectly adequate statement: 'He (Jesus) is the Son of God.' Yet John is no more than a witness to the truth, whose testimony is important and essential for those for whom he preached – some of his disciples become disciples of Jesus, and if the Jews whom Jesus

---

[1] Cf. iv. 25. See Appendix.

[2] A useful survey of recent opinion is found in chapter v, 'John the Baptist in the Fourth Gospel', in Walter Wink's *John the Baptist in the Gospel Tradition* (*S.N.T.S. Monograph Ser. 7*) (Cambridge, 1968), pp. 87–106.

[3] It is not clear whether in the present text *v.* 24 refers back to *v.* 19 or introduces a new deputation. On theories of interpretation and redaction regarding *vv.* 22–4 see R. Schnackenburg, Commentary I, pp. 280–1, and R. E. Brown, *The Gospel according to John (I–XII)* (New York, 1966), pp. 67–71.

[4] Walter Wink, *op. cit.* pp. 105–6, calls μαρτυρεῖ in i. 15 and ἀπεσταλμένος εἰμί 'a timeless present'; cf. the use of the perfect in i. 34; v. 33; see also R. Schnackenburg, *Das Johannesevangelium*, II (Freiburg-Basel-Wien, 1971) (= Commentary II), p. 172, on *vv.* 33–5.

addresses in chapter v had accepted John's testimony they would have been saved (*v.* 34) – yet Jesus himself, though announced by John, does not really need him. In v. 34–7 he points to the direct witness of the Father on his behalf; the very works he performs witness to his being sent by the Father.[1] This may be the reason why Jesus' baptism by John is not mentioned in i. 29–33. John came baptizing with water ἵνα φανερωθῇ τῷ 'Ισραήλ (*v.* 31). This passive implies God himself as actor. John himself could only *announce* the one who was to come;[2] he could not *reveal* him, because he did not know who he was. This explicit statement in *v.* 31 is repeated in *v.* 33; God, who sent John to baptize with water, had announced that his successor who would baptize with the Spirit could be recognized by the fact that the Spirit descended upon him and remained on him. Only because God had told him this, could John identify Jesus when he saw this happen (*vv.* 32–3).[3]

In *vv.* 20–2 we hear first of all that John is not the Christ, though John himself chooses the title 'Son of God' to designate Jesus, clearly in accord with the evangelist's deepest intentions. 'The Christ' clearly is the main title in *vv.* 20–2: it is the first to be mentioned in i. 21 (and i. 25), and in iii. 26–30 which refers to the episode related in chapter i it is the *only* title.[4] Why, however, does John also deny that he is Elijah or the Prophet? Jesus is identified with the Prophet by people in the crowd (vi. 14; vii. 40–4) and prophetic notions are very important for the delineation of the Gospel's christology[5] so that the statement of John concerning the Prophet may have been considered necessary. But Jesus is never identified with Elijah! One has pointed to Mark vi. 14–16 par. and viii. 27–9 par. which mention Elijah and 'one of the prophets' besides the 'Christ' as possible 'messianic' options in connection with Jesus.[6] One has even tried to connect the three figures mentioned in i. 20–1 with the three figures expected in 1QS ix. 11.[7] In doing so one overlooks first of all that Elijah is not mentioned anywhere else in this Gospel and that, for example, vii. 40–4 mentions only 'the Prophet' and 'the Christ'; secondly, that the three are mentioned here as Jewish 'messianic possibilities' without any implication that they should appear together at the same time.

The fact that the identification of John the Baptist with Elijah is denied categorically must have something to do with earlier Christian views which

[1] *V.* 37 does not introduce a new μαρτυρία but refers back to *v.* 36 and to the opening statement in *vv.* 31–2; see R. Schnackenburg, Commentary II, p. 174.

[2] Of course John was not a real 'forerunner', because the one whom he announces was already before him, and is, therefore, higher in rank (see i. 15, 27, 30).

[3] See also iii. 27, a general statement clearly referring to the special case of Jesus.

[4] Cf. also Luke iii. 15; Acts xiii. 25.

[5] See 'Jesus as Prophet and King', *passim*, and W. A. Meeks, *The Prophet-King. Moses traditions and the Johannine Christology* (*Suppl. N.T.* XIV) (Leiden, 1967).

[6] So e.g. J. A. T. Robinson, 'Elijah, John and Jesus. An Essay in Detection', *N.T.S.* IV (1957–8), 263–81, esp. p. 270.

[7] See especially G. Richter, 'Bist du Elias? Joh. i. 21', *B.Z.* N.F. VI (1962), 79–92, 238–56, and VII (1963), 63–80. On possible parallels from Qumran see VI, 85–92; on other possible Jewish parallels according to which Elijah might stand on the same level as the Messiah and the Prophet see VII, 70–6. In both cases no evidence is adduced which helps us to understand i. 20–2.

found their expression in Mark and Matthew, and to some extent also in Luke. But why would the Fourth Gospel want to contradict this identification whilst it took over many other things from the tradition concerning John the Baptist, and why did it identify John with 'the voice in the wilderness who helped to prepare the way of the Lord' (in agreement with Mark i. 3), thereby emphasizing John's function as the herald? One can say: John is merely 'a voice', a witness; he no longer conforms to any known figure within the framework of Jewish expectation.[1] But this theory does not explain the explicit denial of John's identification with Elijah.

Now this denial must have christological significance, just like John's denial that he is the Christ and the Prophet. Are we in a position to prove this? I think we are. In i. 26 John tells the people who listen to him that the one who comes after him stands already among them – though they do not know him. The phrase μέσος ὑμῶν στήκει ὃν ὑμεῖς οὐκ οἴδατε is only found in the Fourth Gospel. The Jews who are addressed do not know him, because they do not accept him; i. 10–11 has already made clear that this is a matter of basic misunderstanding and rejection. When i. 31 speaks of a revelation to Israel, it is clear that the true believers among the Jewish people are meant, not just the Jews.[2]

The terminology used here is that of the Fourth Gospel, but there is a link with other traditions concerning an unknown Messiah. Much has been written on the subject: by far the best treatment of it is found in chapter 2, 'Der verborgene Messias im Judentum', in Erik Sjöberg's *Der verborgene Menschensohn in den Evangelien*.[3] Our earliest sources witness to two types of expectation. The one is found in Eth. Enoch, IV Ezra and Syr. Bar., where a pre-existence of the Messiah (or, in the case of Enoch, the Son of Man) in heaven is presupposed. He will appear at the appointed time and it is certain that he will come, for he is already there, though hidden from mortal eyes.[4] Besides that there is the conception that the Messiah is already on earth, incognito and even himself not knowing who he is.[5]

Now it is important to note that in both conceptions mentioned the essential point is the fact that the Messiah *appears*, *is revealed*, that is, is seen by the

---

[1] So e.g. W. Wink, *op. cit.* pp. 89–90, following C. K. Barrett and R. E. Brown.

[2] See i. 49 and xii. 13 where Jesus is called ὁ βασιλεὺς τοῦ Ἰσραήλ, cf. Nathanael as ἀληθῶς Ἰσραηλίτης, and iii. 10 Nicodemus as ὁ διδάσκαλος τοῦ Ἰσραήλ (who because of this position should know better).

[3] Lund, 1955, pp. 41–98; see also Strack–Billerbeck II, 339 f., 488 f.; E. Stauffer, 'Agnostos Christos. Joh. ii 24 und die Eschatologie des vierten Evangeliums' in *The Background of the New Testament and its Eschatology*, ed. W. D. Davies and D. Daube (Cambridge, 1954) (²1964), pp. 281–99, and U. B. Müller, *Messias und Menschensohn in jüdischen Apokalypsen und in der Offenbarung des Johannes* (Gütersloh, 1972), pp. 147–54.

[4] See Eth. En. xlviii. 6 f.; lxii. 7; Syr. Bar. xxix. 3; xxxix. 7; lxxiii. 1; IV Ezra vii. 28; xii. 32; xiii. 26, 32, 52; xiv. 9. U. B. Müller, *op. cit.* p. 152, sees a difference between Eth. Enoch (emphasis on a special heavenly abode and pre-existence before creation of the Son of Man) and IV Ezra (emphasis on 'preservation' of the Messiah, expressing the fact that what is going to happen is determined by God). See also M. de Jonge, *Th.W.N.T.* IX, 507–8.

[5] A third, and later, conception that the Messiah lives on earth, knowing who he is but awaiting God's time need not occupy us here.

people, though not acknowledged by all of them. Speculations about the place where he is hidden, or (in other terms) is preserved by God are clearly of secondary importance.[1] John i. 26 seems to presuppose the second conception, for which Trypho in Justin's *Dialogus cum Tryphone* seems to be the first witness. This is interesting because the same passages in the Dialogue (viii. 3; xlix. 1; cx. 1) provide the earliest evidence for Jewish expectations concerning Elijah as the forerunner, who anoints the Messiah.[2]

The important elements in the picture given in the Dialogue are the following. Even if the Christ has already been born, he is ἄγνωστος; he does not know himself and has no power until Elijah anoints him and φανερὸν πᾶσι ποιήσῃ (viii. 4). Justin refers to this belief in cx. 1, telling Trypho that he is aware of the fact that Jewish teachers are of this opinion. He uses the phrases οὐ γινώσκεται ὅς ἐστιν, ἀλλ' ὅταν ἐμφανὴς καὶ ἔνδοξος γένηται, τότε γνωσθήσεται ὅς ἐστιν.[3] It is important also that in xlix. 1 Trypho connects this with the expectation of a χριστός as ἄνθρωπος ἐξ ἀνθρώπων who is anointed κατ' ἐκλογήν by Elijah and becomes Christ in this way. A conception which is also found in Christianity, as Justin tells us (*Dial.* xlviii)[4] – a view which he respects though he does not share it.

It seems clear that John knows Jewish conceptions like that defended by Trypho and his colleagues, and that he opposes them because (a) the Messiah is not aware of his own mission, (b) is dependent on Elijah for his being revealed to men and (c) is a mere ἄνθρωπος ἐξ ἀνθρώπων. Of course Jesus is not ἐξ ἀνθρώπων; the Fourth Gospel is at great pains to assert that he is ἄνωθεν, ἐκ τοῦ θεοῦ, ἐκ τοῦ οὐρανοῦ (iii. 31; viii. 23, 42; xvi. 28; xviii. 36) and it stresses the fundamental opposition between heaven and earth (see iii. 31–6; viii. 21–9). Therefore Jesus the Christ cannot be dependent on Elijah; the decisive act of φανέρωσις is ascribed to God himself, John is only a witness. The gift of the Spirit is set over against John's baptizing with water; the pouring out of the Spirit could have been called anointing,[5] but then ὁ χριστός is not the most important title in John as we have seen. And of course it is quite inconceivable that Jesus would not have been aware of his own mission. John the Baptist cannot have been Elijah if his being Elijah

[1] So e.g. Sjöberg, *op. cit.* pp. 44–51, 54–6.
[2] See Strack–Billerbeck IV, 2, 779–98, J. Jeremias, art. Ηλ(ε)ίας, *Th.W.N.T.* II, 930–43, and G. Richter, *art. cit.* VII, 70–6.
[3] Cf. *Apol.* xxxv. 1 ὡς δὲ καὶ λήσειν ἔμελλε τοὺς ἄλλους ἀνθρώπους γεννηθεὶς ὁ χριστὸς ἄχρις ἀνδρωθῇ, ὅπερ καὶ γέγονεν, ἀκούσατε... Compare also the relation between David and Samuel in Ps. Philo, *Lib. Ant.* LIX. 4 'et cum veniret propheta non clamaverunt me et quando nominatus est christus obliti sunt me .
[4] See also lxvii. 2.
[5] In Luke iv. 18 and Acts x. 38 Jesus is portrayed as the Anointed by the Spirit – see further M. de Jonge and A. S. van der Woude, '11Q Melchizedek and the New Testament', *N.T.S.* XII (1965–6), 301–26, esp. pp. 309–12 and the literature mentioned there. i. 26–7 and i. 31–3 compare a baptism with the Spirit and one with water; here John clearly uses an earlier Christian tradition in his own way. In i. 25 a connection is made between baptism and the coming of the Messiah, Elijah or the Prophet – Jews are the speakers here, and no clear parallels have yet been found (G. Richter, *art. cit.* VII, 67 'Die Vorstellung einer messianischen Taufe ist bis jetzt nicht bezeugt...'). In any case no connection is made between baptism and anointing, cf. however Luke iii. 16 after iii. 15.

implies the functions ascribed to him by Trypho and his colleagues. *My hypothesis is that in the view of the Fourth Gospel calling John Elijah did imply that.*

I realize, of course, that it is difficult to adduce mid-second-century evidence in order to illustrate the possible background of the Fourth Gospel. Yet if the 'criterion of dissimilarity' may be applied it gives us a strong case. Justin is certainly not dependent on the Fourth Gospel here; he is much more explicit and uses terms the Gospel does not use, and in *Dial.* lxxxviii he gives an entirely different view on the activity of John the Baptist though he does emphasize that John denied that he was the Christ and identified himself with the voice crying aloud.[1] And if we ask whether Justin has christianized Trypho's views the answer must be that this is unlikely,[2] because Trypho's objections here do not really serve Justin's argument either positively or negatively. So, if in Justin's Dialogue we have genuine evidence for the existence of Jewish beliefs in the middle of the second century with regard to Elijah's function in the revealing of the Messiah, it may not be too rash to conclude that the Fourth Gospel presupposes similar notions and criticizes them implicitly but effectively.[3]

Yet we should remember that the Jewish beliefs presupposed or expressed in John i. 19–34 and the passages in Justin's Dialogue are found in Christian writings and function within the context of the debate between Judaism and Christianity. If the Fourth Gospel opposes Jewish notions it may have known them only through the medium of written or oral tradition, the *Sitz im Leben* of which was the Jewish-Christian debate.[4]

[1] See lxxxviii. 7 combining references to John i. 20, 23 and Matt. iii. 11. In *Dial.* xlix the conception of two advents of the Christ is combined with that of two advents of Elijah. The Spirit of God which was in Elijah was also in John (xlix. 3 and xlix. 6, 7, cf. Luke i. 17).

[2] See esp. E. Sjöberg, *op. cit.* p. 82. On the general question of the reliability of Justin's Dialogue as source for Jewish belief see A. von Harnack, *Judentum und Judenchristentum in Justins Dialog mit Trypho* (*T.U.* xxxix, 1) (Leipzig, 1913), pp. 47–98, esp. p. 54 and pp. 61–78.

[3] A polemical attitude towards followers of John the Baptist may also have been of importance for the shaping of this section of the Gospel, but it should not be overrated (so W. Wink, *op. cit.* pp. 98–105). In our case it is important to note that there is no evidence that the Johannine sect ever regarded John as Elijah (so also R. E. Brown, *The Gospel according to St John (I–XII)*, New York, 1966, pp. 47–8).

[4] It may be useful to emphasize a few points in Justin's argumentation in chapter xlviii. At Trypho's remarks that he considers it strange and even foolish to believe προϋπάρχειν θεὸν ὄντα πρὸ αἰώνων τοῦτον τὸν χριστόν (§1), Justin replies that the matter seems to be strange especially to those of Trypho's race, who prefer to believe and to practise what 'your teachers' teach rather than what God asks (τὰ τῶν διδασκάλων ὑμῶν – τὰ τοῦ θεοῦ, implicit reference to Isa. xxix. 13, cf. Matt. xv. 9) (§2). Also with regard to Jewish Christians who maintain that the Christ is a ἄνθρωπος ἐξ ἀνθρώπων he states that the Christ himself commanded not to follow ἀνθρωπείοις διδάγμασι but τοῖς διὰ τῶν μακαρίων προφητῶν κηρυχθεῖσι καὶ δι' αὐτοῦ διδαχθεῖσι (§4). Yet Justin concedes that Divine Sonship, including pre-existence and virgin birth, are not necessary prerequisites for Messiahship. One cannot deny that Jesus is the Christ – ἐὰν φαίνηται ὡς ἄνθρωπος ἐξ ἀνθρώπων γεννηθείς, καὶ ἐκλογῇ γενόμενος εἰς τὸ χριστὸν εἶναι ἀποδεικνύηται.

2. *The statement in vii. 27*

It is possible that the tradition of 'the hidden Messiah' is also hinted at in vii. 27. We have seen that in the two earliest forms of this tradition no stress is laid on the place where the Messiah is hidden. In vii. 27 the central word πόθεν is clearly used in order to lead up to Jesus' reaction. Those who think that they know where Jesus comes from do not really know. Jesus' answer to the πόθεν is: ἐκ τοῦ οὐρανοῦ, i.e. directly sent by the Father.[1] The objection τοῦτον οἴδαμεν πόθεν ἐστίν refers to Jesus' supposed earthly origin; we may compare here vi. 42 'Surely this is Jesus son of Joseph; we know his father and his mother; how can he now say: "I have come down from heaven"?'[2] We cannot prove conclusively that the statement οὐδεὶς γινώσκεται πόθεν ἐστίν refers to the heavenly origin of the Messiah; vi. 42 points in this direction and it is quite possible that the evangelist, with his usual irony, makes the Jerusalemites think of a Messiah of the type found in IV Ezra (and Syr. Bar.). They expect their royal Messiah from heaven[3] and indeed that is where Jesus comes from – only they do not realize this. There is no reason to think that the specific form of the tradition voiced by Trypho is presupposed here.

The essential point in both forms of the tradition of 'the hidden Messiah' was the contrast between 'first hidden'/'finally revealed'.[4] In this connection we may point to vii. 3 where Jesus' unbelieving brothers urge him φανέρωσον σεαυτὸν τῷ κόσμῳ – a fundamental misunderstanding in John's eyes because the revelation takes place in the world but not to the world (xvii. 6!). We should note that the dialectic between 'openness' and 'concealment' is quite marked in chapters vii and viii (vii. 4, 10, 13, 26; viii. 59). Outsiders cannot really know who Jesus is.[5]

3. *The question in vii. 31*

Many authors have already pointed out that according to the available Jewish evidence the Messiah is not expected to perform miracles. There is no need to dwell on this subject at great length, because the situation has been summed up admirably by J. L. Martyn.[6] God's future salvation will include miracles, and there are a few references in Josephus to wonder-workers who led crowds of people into the wilderness and promised the occurrence of signs,

[1] See, again, iii. 31–6; viii. 14, 21–9; ix. 29–30.
[2] In the background of vi. 42 and vii. 27 we may suppose the tradition preserved in Mark vi. 1–6 (par. Matt. xiii. 53–8, cf. Luke iv. 15–30). See also Mark xi. 27–30 (par. Matt. xxi. 23–7, Luke xx. 1–8). In John, however, this is entirely recast in terms of the ascent–descent theme – on which see W. A. Meeks, 'The Man from Heaven in Johannine sectarianism', esp. pp. 59–60 where he assumes the influence of Jewish Wisdom myths on the conception of the apostolic prophet.
[3] The principal texts are summed up in n. 4 on p. 254.
[4] See p. 255 above.
[5] In I Enoch, xlviii. 6, 7 and lxii. 7 speak of a revelation of the hidden Son of Man to the holy and righteous (elect). It is not clear whether this revelation takes place at the end of time or at an earlier period – see U. B. Müller, *op. cit.* pp. 47–51, against E. Sjöberg, *op. cit.* p. 46.
[6] *History and Theology in the Fourth Gospel* (New York and Evanston, 1968), pp. 81–8.

but these people are not called Messiahs. In Tannaitic literature the situation is not essentially different. Klausner's remark: ' *The Messiah* – and this should be carefully noted – *is never mentioned anywhere in the Tannaitic literature as a wonder-worker* per se' is often quoted.[1] Therefore we cannot escape the conclusion that the terminology used in vii. 31 is Christian;[2] we should remember that the statement is said to be made by many people from the crowd *who began to believe in Jesus*! In the N.T. we may point first of all to Matt. xi. 2–6 (par. Luke vii. 18–23) where Jesus' reference to his miracles in his message to John the Baptist is placed under the heading τὰ ἔργα τοῦ χριστοῦ.[3] Next there is Mark xiii. 22 (par. Matt. xxiv. 24) where σημεῖα καὶ τέρατα are ascribed both to pseudo-Messiahs and pseudo-prophets (cf. II Thess. ii. 9).[4] Martyn points out 'that the figures expected by Jews to play roles in the eschatological future … were allowed to coalesce in the most varied ways';[5] and he assumes that 'prophetic elements' have been connected with the figure of the Messiah. In the second part of his book he assumes that the debate between Church and Synagogue centred on the notion of 'the expectation of the Prophet-Messiah' like Moses as opposed to that of 'the presence of the Son of Man'.

Now Martyn is right in emphasizing the merging of various messianic conceptions in Jewish expectation;[6] in 11Q Melch. 18 we have even explicit proof that a prophetic figure could be called 'anointed by the Spirit'.[7] In the Fourth Gospel, however, the prophet and the Messiah are kept separate – also in one of the following episodes in this same chapter, vii. 40–4! The notion of a prophet like Moses is often in the background where Jesus' signs are mentioned (most notably in iii. 2, chapter vi, chapter ix) but the only text which connects σημεῖα with the designation ὁ χριστός is the central statement xx. 30. There, as we have seen, the statement of vii. 31 is supplemented and corrected by the assertion that Jesus is the Christ, *the Son of God*.[8]

---

[1] J. Klausner, *The Messianic Idea in Israel* (transl. W. F. Stinespring) (New York, 1955), p. 506, quoted e.g. by J. L. Martyn, *op. cit.* p. 506, and by F. Hahn, *Christologische Hoheitstitel* (Göttingen, 1963), p. 360 n. 2. [2] So R. Schnackenburg, Commentary II, pp. 205–6.

[3] One should note that the question is σὺ εἶ ὁ ἐρχόμενος; (also in Luke vii. 19).

[4] Miracles are also connected with the Son of David (Mark x. 46–52, par. Matt. xx. 29–34; Matt. ix. 27–31; xii. 22–4; xv. 21–8; xxi. 14–16). This tradition is to be explained differently; there seems to be a connection with Solomon, cf. Sap. Sal. vii. 17–21; Josephus, *Ant.* VIII, 44–9; Testament of Solomon. Contra Chr. Burger, *Jesus als Davidssohn* (Göttingen, 1970). See K. Berger's forthcoming 'Die königlichen Messiastraditionen des N.T.', in *N.T.S.* XIX (1972–3). [5] *Op. cit.* pp. 87–8.

[6] A. S. van der Woude and the present author tried to show that the word Messiah is connected with different figures which play a role in Jewish expectation and also that we cannot speak of 'fixed concepts' – see their contribution 'Messianische Vorstellungen im Spätjudentum' in *Th.W. N.T.* IX, 500–18 (belonging to the article χρίω κτλ.).

[7] See M. de Jonge and A. S. van der Woude, '11Q Melchizedek and the New Testament', pp. 306–7; cf. *C.D.* ii. 12; vi. 1 and 1QM xi. 7.

[8] In vi. 14 the indirect connection between σημεῖα and (a Jewish view on) kingship runs via the προφήτης-title. xii. 18 is (part of) a redactional link between the pericope of the Entrance into Jerusalem and the preceding Lazarus-episode. Thereby also an indirect connection is made between the title ὁ βασιλεύς τοῦ Ἰσραήλ and the σημεῖον. There is no reason to suppose that this was important for the evangelist, nor that he wanted to suggest that this was 'theologically' important for the crowd.

Our conclusion must be: the Fourth Gospel refers here to the views of sympathizing Jews which it corrects further on. Because, however, the terminology used by these Jews is Christian, we may just as well say: the Fourth Gospel refers here to the views of Christians of Jewish descent which it criticizes.[1]

4. The debate in vii. 40–4

This pericope has been mentioned several times already. I have tried to show that the Gospel itself regards the problems raised here as superficial; they are not concerned with the real issue because they are dealt with on an earthly level. Yet the evangelist evidently assumes that objections against Jesus' Messiahship were raised on account of doubts concerning his Davidic descent and his coming from Bethlehem. Now – as many others have pointed out – it is not in the least difficult to find evidence for the Davidic descent of the royal Messiah,[2] but the statement that the Messiah comes from David's village Bethlehem presents us with difficulties. The key passage often quoted here is Targ. Mi. v. 1,[3] which connects the appearance of the Messiah with Bethlehem. This passage is, of course, also quoted by commentators in connection with Matt. ii. 6, where parts of Mi. v. 1 and 3 are adduced in connection with the birthplace of the Messiah by 'the chief priests and the scribes of the people'. Matt. ii. 5, 6 point to an early date of the tradition preserved in the Targum and, on the other hand, this targumic tradition proves that Matthew could be aware of the existence of such a view in Judaism. Yet it is impossible to prove that John in vii. 42, 43 shows knowledge of Jewish views about the Messiah's coming from Bethlehem apart from what he knew of the arguments put forward in the Jewish-Christian debate. It is clear that, by assigning to vii. 40–4 the place in the structure of chapter vii which he did assign to it, he does not only indicate that an inner-Jewish discussion of prophethood and messiahship connected with Jesus does not penetrate into the real secret of Jesus' mission, but also that the matter of Jesus' Davidic descent and the question of his birthplace are not of essential importance. We should not overlook that this implicit criticism is not only concerned with Jewish contributions to the Jewish-Christian debate, either negative, hesitant or positive, but

---

[1] On the question of the right terminology (Jewish sympathizers or Christians of Jewish descent) see below IV 4.

[2] R. Schnackenburg, Commentary II, p. 219 n. 3, follows B. van Iersel, 'Fils de David et Fils de Dieu', in La Venue du Messie (Recherches Bibliques VI) (1962), pp. 113–32, in calling ἐκ σπέρματος Δαυίδ a typically Christian phrase. Van Iersel regards ἐκ σπέρματος Δαυίδ as a Christian 'reduction' of υἱὸς Δαυίδ, in connection with the use of the title 'Son of God' (Rom 1. 3–4). It should be noted, however, that a phrase very similar to ἐκ σπέρματος Δαυίδ occurs in all but the Latin versions of IV Ezra xii. 32 and is likely to be original (see M. de Jonge, Th.W.N.T. IX, 507, following the editions of B. Violet and L. Gry, and U. B. Müller, op. cit. p. 152).

[3] The assertion of the Jews is said to be warranted by Scripture. On this see E. D. Freed, Old Testament Quotations in the Gospel of John (Suppl. N.T. XI) (Leiden, 1965), pp. 39–59. It is interesting to note that the Targum interprets Mi. v. 1 b as referring to the calling of the name of the Messiah from the beginning, cf. I En. xlviii. 3 and further instances in E. Sjöberg, op. cit. p. 58 nn. 2 and 3.

also with those Christians who try to counter the arguments put forward in vii. 44 on the level of their opponents.[1]

This does not mean, of course, that the Fourth Gospel would deny that texts from Scripture can be quoted as proof. It quotes them often and the Johannine Jesus tells quite clearly that 'the Scriptures witness to him' (v. 39). The Gospel also shows acquaintance with typical Jewish argumentation – see for example the midrashic exposition in the discourse on the Bread in chapter vi or the reasoning in accordance with the Jewish principle of *qal-waḥomer* in vii. 19 (to mention only a few examples in the immediate neighbourhood of our passage). And yet, if Scripture is not read and interpreted with the centre of Johannine theology as starting-point one will never discover the truth revealed by God. That is why not only hostile but also sympathetic Jews are considered outsiders, and why Christians who use Jewish arguments from a wrong starting-point are subject to John's criticism. It is clear that John is critical towards argumentation regarding Bethlehem as Jesus' birthplace, his Davidic descent and his divine Sonship as this is found in the birth-stories in Matthew and Luke. By such an approach one will never reach the heart of the matter.

5. *The objection in xii. 34*

The question asked by the crowd in xii. 34 is really an objection. It is not answered and is clearly inserted here in order to show how little the people who listened to Jesus understood what he meant. The sentence πῶς λέγεις σὺ ὅτι δεῖ ὑψωθῆναι τὸν υἱὸν τοῦ ἀνθρώπου; does not bear upon any statement by Jesus in the immediate context, though he has stated in *v.* 23 ἐλήλυθεν ἡ ὥρα ἵνα δοξασθῇ ὁ υἱὸς τοῦ ἀνθρώπου and has spoken of his being lifted up (ὑψωθῶ) from the earth. There is a clear reference to iii. 14 οὕτως ὑψωθῆναι δεῖ τὸν υἱὸν τοῦ ἀνθρώπου and a less clear one to viii. 28. Putting xii. 34 directly behind viii. 28–9[2] does not give any solution; xii. 34 is not intended to function within a coherent picture of a debate between Jesus and people from the crowd – it serves as a further clarification of Johannine christology directed at the reader of the Gospel. In xii. 31–3 Jesus explains the true meaning of his ὑψωθῆναι: it is connected with the victory over ὁ ἄρχων τοῦ κόσμου τούτου, it means that he will draw all people unto him and, paradoxically, it means death on the cross (xviii. 32).[3]

The people in the crowd are not able to follow him. They appeal to Scripture[4] which says that the Messiah is to remain for ever; the nearest scriptural

---

[1] Chr. Burger, *op. cit.* pp. 153–8, is too one-sided when he regards this as a completely inner-Christian controversy in which John's opponents are disqualified as Jews.

[2] So R. Bultmann, *Commentary*, pp. 269–72. Cf. R. Schnackenburg, Commentary II, p. 495: 'Ihm genügt die Anknüpfungsmöglichkeit im Kontext, im übrigen formuliert er nach seinem Kerygma 3, 14...'.

[3] See I. de la Potterie, 'L'Exaltation du Fils de l'homme', *Gregorianum* XLIX (1968), 460–78.

[4] νόμος with the wider meaning of 'Scripture', cf. x. 34; xv. 25 and W. Bauer s.v. νόμος 4*b*, col. 1074.

parallel to be found is Ps. lxxxix. 37, as Van Unnik has shown,[1] but we do not find here a direct quotation. Like vii. 42 this text gives a general statement about expectations connected with the king to be born from the seed of David. The crowd does not explicitly connect the Messiah-title with Jesus, but the evangelist, after vii. 42 and x. 24, clearly implies that it means to say: If one is to think of you as the Messiah and if Scripture tells us clearly that the Messiah remains for ever, how can you say that the Son of Man must be lifted up? The crowd is aware of the fact that Jesus refers to himself when he uses the expression 'Son of Man', and evidently regards ὑψωθῆναι as the opposite of μένειν εἰς τὸν αἰῶνα – whatever it is supposed to understand exactly. The question therefore is not only: How can you say that? but also: Whom do you mean if you cannot mean yourself? τίς ἐστιν οὗτος ὁ υἱὸς τοῦ ἀνθρώπου;[2]

At this point of our investigations a full discussion of the 'Son of Man' problem would be desirable, though I doubt whether it could really shed much light on our text. John wants to make clear that the Jewish Messiah-concept is fixed – it is connected with the expectation of the Davidic King. 'Son of Man' is only used by Jesus himself,[3] and to the Jews who refer to it in xii. 34 this expression does not convey a clear picture. They ask: What do you mean and whom do you mean – didn't you mean yourself? In Jewish literature we find a number of cases where the expressions Messiah and 'Son of Man' occur together, but the combination is brought about in different ways[4] and we cannot speak of any fixed concept. The nearest parallel is – again – provided by Justin's *Dialogus cum Tryphone* where Trypho, in xxxii. 1, speaks of the expectation of 'one who is great and glorious, and takes over the everlasting kingdom from the Ancient of Days as Son of Man'. Trypho implies that this one is the Messiah, for he goes on: 'But this your so-called Christ is without honour and glory, so that He has even fallen into the uttermost curse that is in the Law of God, for he was crucified.'[5] Trypho clearly uses expressions taken from the Son of Man chapter in Daniel as illustrations for the coming of the Messiah. It is by no means certain that the Fourth Gospel presupposes the presence of such ideas in the minds of the interlocutors of the crowd. It is only interested in Jesus' singular use of the expression

---

[1] W. C. van Unnik, 'The quotation from the Old Testament in John 12: 34', *Nov. Test.* III (1959), 174–9.

[2] So also R. Leivestad, in his discussion of this passage on pp. 250–1 of his article 'Exit the Apocalyptic Son of Man', *N.T.S.* XVIII (1971–2), 243–67.

[3] In ix. 35–8 Jesus identifies himself as Son of Man; the blind man has to ask τίς ἐστιν, κύριε, ἵνα πιστεύσω εἰς αὐτόν; before he confesses his faith in the Son of Man, as Jesus requests.

[4] See M. de Jonge, *Th.W.N.T.* IX, 505–6 (on Eth. Enoch) and p. 507 (on IV Ezra). In IV Ezra and Syr. Bar. a distinction is made between the days of the Messiah and the Age to Come. We should note, however, that, nevertheless, in Syr. Bar. xl. 3 the reign of 'my Messiah' is said to last 'for ever', 'until the world of corruption is at an end and until the times aforesaid are fulfilled'.

[5] Translation by A. Lukyn Williams in his *Justin Martyr. The dialogue with Trypho*, Translation, Introduction and Notes (London, 1930). The last sentence presupposes Gal. iii. 13 referring to Deut. xxi. 23. See also R. Schnackenburg, Commentary II, p. 252.

'Son of Man' and in the fundamental difference between his teaching and current expectations connected with the Messiah.

6. Some conclusions

Our further study of the passages concerned has, I think, brought out a few things very clearly.

(a) Not only are these statements entirely subordinate to a clearer exposition of Johannine christology – this was already clear in the use made of them in chapter vii and has now become evident also in our analysis of i. 19–34 – but also the very terminology put into the mouth of Jewish interlocutors often has a Johannine flavour. So the πόθεν in vii. 27 leads up to the typically Johannine statement which follows; in xii. 34 the traditional Messiah-concept comes out clearly but no possible connections between this view on the Messiah and Jewish exegesis of Dan. vii. 13–14, 27. In i. 26 there is at least a typical Johannine ambiguity.

(b) Consequently these statements of 'Johannine Jews' add little or nothing to our knowledge of Jewish expectations concerning the Messiah known from other sources. Where there is disagreement in wording or conception there is always Johannine influence to be considered. Comparison with non-Johannine material proved to be useful, because it brought out more clearly what the Fourth Gospel wanted to emphasize; this is equally true of the passages where direct parallels were found and of those where the Jewish statements in the Fourth Gospel have obviously been adapted to serve its purpose better.

We should note that the tradition concerning the hidden Messiah, attributed by Justin to Trypho and other Jewish teachers, was shown to exist before the middle of the second century, because the Fourth Gospel presupposes and opposes it.

(c) It became clear that the Fourth Gospel criticizes earlier Christian thinking, for example that concerning the σημεῖα – see vii. 31 as compared with xx. 30, 31.[1] In vii. 40–4 and i. 19–34 there is reason to think of a reaction of the Fourth Gospel on issues in earlier or contemporary Christian-Jewish controversies.[2] In both cases it brings out its own theological viewpoint very

---

[1] Whether or not it incorporated and redacted a document dealing with Jesus' σημεῖα, what this source contained and how its christology was criticized explicitly and implicitly need not be decided here. A good survey of recent opinion on this subject is found in J. M. Robinson's 'The Johannine Trajectory' in J. M. Robinson and H. Koester, *Trajectories through Early Christianity* (Philadelphia, 1971), pp. 232–68. See also W. Wilkens, *Zeichen und Werke*, Ein Beitrag zur Theologie des 4. Evangeliums in Erzählungs- und Redestoff (*A.T.A.N.T.* 55) (Zürich, 1969) (and R. Fortna's criticism in *J.B.L.* LXIX (1970), 457–62); B. Lindars, *Behind the Fourth Gospel* (London, 1971), chapter 2, and W. Nicol, *The Semeia in the Fourth Gospel* (*Suppl. N.T.* XXXII) (Leiden, 1972).

[2] R. Schnackenburg, 'Die Messiasfrage', pp. 251–2, would put here also xii. 34. Because we cannot prove that the Jews identify here Messiah and Son of Man a comparison with Justin, *Dial. c. Tryph.* xxxii. 1 remains hazardous. S. himself remarks 'Stärker getrieben aber wird er sicher wieder von seinem positiven christologischen Interesse an die "Erhöhung des Menschensohnes" und den damit gegebenen "Weggang" des Sohnes zum Vater' (p. 252).

clearly, not only in opposition to current Jewish beliefs but, in the case of vii. 42, also with clear implicit criticism of other Christian attempts to answer this Jewish objection.

IV. SOME REMARKS ON THE PURPOSE OF THE FOURTH GOSPEL

1. R. Schnackenburg's treatment of the messianic question in the Gospel of John ends with a discussion of the implications of our views on Johannine christology for our view on the purpose of the Gospel. Against W. C. van Unnik and John A. T. Robinson, who advocate the theory of the Fourth Gospel as a missionary document, he defends the thesis that the Fourth Gospel was written for inner-Church use.[1] Its primary concern is with the christological self-revelation of Jesus and it wants to show all aspects and implications of that revelation. A secondary aim will have been to fortify Christians of Jewish descent in their faith by showing them what they could reply to objections raised by the Jews outside the Church – and the same applies to non-Jewish Christians who are confronted with Jewish opposition. The present investigation leads to the same conclusion (see particularly section II and conclusion (a) in III 6). Schnackenburg also rightly emphasizes that the objections are not just literary 'inventions' used solely to carry the debate a step further – like so many other instances of misunderstanding in the Fourth Gospel. They have that function but they do take into account existing differences of opinion in the Jewish-Christian debate at the time.

2. The Fourth Gospel is not only written for inner-Church use, it also presupposes the community of believers as the place where true insight and real knowledge are granted, preserved and deepened through the activity of the Spirit. This is emphasized very strongly in chapters xiii–xvii which occupy an important place in the present Gospel. Within the community of believers the true 'view' on the facts of Jesus' life, death and glorification is communicated, the true interpretation of his words is given, and consequently also the right interpretation of Scripture (see, apart from the so-called 'Paraclete-passages', also ii. 22; xii. 16, 17; xx. 9). In the chapters i–xii true believers are mentioned besides and over against unbelievers. Faith is the unconditional acceptance of Jesus as the One who is sent by the Father (see for example v. 36–8; vi. 29). Only very seldom do we find explicit reflection on the question why certain people (among these 'the disciples' and 'the twelve') were able to accept Jesus and others rejected him. In the last resort faith is a gift from God, believers are dependent on the divine initiative (i. 12, 13; iii. 3, 5, 8 – here again the Spirit is mentioned! – vi. 37, 44, 65). The 'twelve', who do not leave Jesus unlike so many other disciples (vi. 60–71), have been chosen by Jesus (v. 70).

---

[1] 'Die Messiasfrage', pp. 257–64.

This subject cannot be treated in full within the scope of the present article.[1] The few points just indicated may suffice to show that the Gospel was written (and, very likely, rewritten several times) from the point of view of the community of believers led by the Spirit. The Fourth Gospel, no doubt, intends to present the truth to the entire Church and on behalf of the entire Church. Yet the results reached above in sections II and III compel us to say that the Fourth Gospel de facto presents the theology of a particular group within the Church. Here I agree fully with W. A. Meeks' important article 'The Man from Heaven in Johannine sectarianism',[2] who calls the Fourth Gospel a book for insiders who belong to the Johannine community. 'One of the primary functions of the book, therefore, must have been to provide a reinforcement for the community's social identity ...' he writes.[3] I am not sure that Meeks is right when he supposes that this social identity was largely negative, but I do agree with him that theological and social identity presuppose one another and that Johannine theology is a typical in-group theology. Meeks follows J. L. Martyn who has shown 'that the actual trauma of the Johannine community's separation from the synagogue and its continuing hostile relationships with the synagogue come clearly to expression here'.[4] But I doubt whether this is quite true. Of course, Meeks is right when he thinks that for the Fourth Gospel the true faith in Jesus presupposes membership of the Johannine community and breaking away from the world, particularly the world of Judaism – but the actual situation must have been more complicated.

3. I differ from Schnackenburg and Meeks, in that I would put more emphasis on the fact that Johannine christology is developed not only in contrast with Jewish thinking but also with other christological views. The Johannine community does not only assert its identity by pondering over the true reason for its being separated from the synagogue and by developing christological motifs in explanation of that. It also tries to formulate its own standpoint over against christological discussions in the Church, particularly over against Christian arguments adduced in the debate between Christians and Jews.

Moreover, the fact that the interlocutors remain vague (II 2) and that there is no real discussion on christological issues (II 3) combined with the Gospel's criticism of current Christian argumentation shows, I think, that the Gospel gives theological reflection on the real issues in the debate between Christians and Jews rather than provides arguments in an acute struggle.[5] The

---

[1] See also R. Schnackenburg, 'Die Messiasfrage', pp. 262–3, and F. Mussner, *Die johanneische Sehweise und die Frage nach dem historischen Jesus* (*Questiones Disputatae* 28) (Freiburg–Basel–Wien, 1965).
[2] See p. 250 n. 3.   [3] *Op. cit.* p. 70.
[4] Formulation by Meeks, *op. cit.* p. 69, of the general purport of J. L. Martyn's *History and Theology in the Fourth Gospel*, mentioned already in n. 6 on p. 257.
[5] The same would seem to apply *mutatis mutandis* to the Gospel of Matthew. On the whole the way from a literary document like the Gospel of John to a reconstruction of the actual situation in which it was written is much longer and much more difficult than some authors seem to realize.

very emphasis on the typical Johannine christology which is sometimes set off against Jewish objections but more often is developed quite independently (though presupposing (other) Jewish ways of thought)[1] also points in that direction. In this connection it should be remembered that 'the Jews' in the Fourth Gospel are not only Jews, but also typical representatives of the outside world, of '*the* World'.[2] No doubt the Fourth Gospel was written in a particular situation, but not necessarily *for* that situation; it wants to stress the essential points.[3]

4. A few concluding remarks about texts referring to people who reacted favourably to Jesus' preaching, at least in the beginning (see II 2, end), but who are criticized severely and regarded as outsiders[4] may make my position a bit clearer. They are all Jews, there is no doubt about that; but one might ask whether we should call them Jewish sympathizers or Jewish Christians. In many of the instances listed under II 2 the Gospel uses the expression πιστεύω εἰς (αὐτόν, τὸ ὄνομα αὐτοῦ, τὸν Ἰησοῦν) and this is the expression also used for the real Christian faith.[5] Joseph of Arimathea is called a μαθητὴς [τοῦ] Ἰησοῦ (xix. 38) though in secret, because he was afraid of the Jews. This added phrase rules him out as a true believer as xii. 42-3 shows unmistakably. The same applies to Nicodemus, his companion at the burial of Jesus (xix. 38-42). Though sympathetic towards Jesus and coming to him with a statement of faith, the discussion in iii. 1-21 shows him as a man who cannot understand and does not believe the real secret of Jesus' mission. He belongs to the group mentioned in ii. 23-5 consisting of believers to whom Jesus would not trust himself. Now the Gospel's references to Nicodemus *cum suis*, Joseph and other Jewish leaders[6] all come under the verdict expressed in xii. 42-3. Notwithstanding the use of πιστεύω and μαθητής *we* would call them sympathizing Jews. The same applies to the enthusiastic crowd in vi. 1-15 which hails Jesus as 'the prophet who was coming into the world' but is shown to have only an imperfect understanding of his real being. The discourse on the Bread, and particularly *vv.* 60-71 following it, bring to light that much faith in Jesus was not real faith; many of Jesus' disciples leave him. Are we to think of the people mentioned in *vv.* 60-71 (cf. 73) as Jewish Christians and distinct from the sympathizers in *vv.* 1-15?[7] And what about

[1] This would have to be shown first of all in an analysis of the use of the titles Son, Son of God, Son of Man, and of the ἄνω-κάτω scheme.

[2] See also E. Grässer in the article quoted above (n. 4 on p. 248), esp. pp. 88-90.

[3] Here we should remember that the Fourth Gospel in its present form shows also signs of the beginning of a struggle against docetism (i. 14; vi. 51 b-59; xix. 34-7 and comp. I-II John).

[4] See II2 above, with the reference to my 'Nicodemus and Jesus'.

[5] See i. 12; ii. 11; iii. 16, 18, 36; vi. 29, etc.

[6] See also ix. 16 where some Pharisees react positively without really taking Jesus' side as the sequel shows.

[7] The reaction of the μαθηταί in *v*. 61 is called γογγυσμός, like that of the Jews in *v*. 41, 43. The reaction of the 'disciples' comes, however, after the last part of the discourse (vi. 51 b-58) with its anti-docetic emphasis on the flesh and blood of Jesus. From the Johannine point of view Judaism and docetism, in different ways, deny the same truth, i.e. that Jesus is the Messiah, the Son of God – see e.g. the statement in I John ii. 22, 23 and the present author's comment on it in his *De Brieven van*

the crowds impressed by what happened to Lazarus and hailing Jesus when he entered Jerusalem (xi. 45; xii. 11, 18)? In vii. 31 we are inclined to call the people who speak about the signs of the Messiah Jewish Christians because of their Christian terminology. In viii. 30–1 this would also be right, I think. Here we have people who have come to believe in Jesus and who are admonished to remain in his word (cf. v. 38; xv. 7, 14) in order that they may truly be disciples of Jesus. I am not going into the particular difficulty caused by the fact that there is no indication of a change of scene after vv. 30–2, so that in the present set-up of the Gospel the vehement debate between Jesus and the Jews before v. 30 goes on after v. 32 between Jesus and Jewish Christians.[1]

Whatever the solution of this problem may be, I think that the very confused picture which emerges from our rather rapid survey of these passages shows that our approach is wrong. Only one thing is certain: all these people are outsiders, they do not really understand Jesus, their faith is, therefore, imperfect and insufficient; they do not belong to the group of true believers. Seen from the standpoint of the Johannine group and its theology there is no real difference between sympathizing Jews and Jewish Christians if the latter are still thinking along what the Fourth Gospel considers to be purely Jewish lines.[2] The vagueness of the Fourth Gospel's description of Jewish groups corresponds with its vagueness in describing non-Johannine Christianity of Jewish descent. Everything in the Gospel is centred on its consistent and persistent search for the right terms and conceptions to express the truth about Jesus the Son of God, the Son of Man.

In iv. 25 a representative Samaritan statement concerning the coming of the Messiah is recorded. An encounter between Jesus and the Samaritans is staged in order to confront Jesus' message with typical Samaritan beliefs. The attitude of the Samaritans towards Jesus is, at least at the end, very

---

Johannes (Nijkerk, 1968), pp. 116–24. See also P. Borgen, *Bread from Heaven* (*Suppl. N.T.* x) (Leiden, 1965), pp. 183–92, and N. A. Dahl, 'Der Erstgeborene des Satans und der Vater des Teufels (Polyk. 7: 1 und Joh. 8: 44)' in *Apophoreta. Festschrift E. Haenchen* (*B.Z.N.W.* xxx) (Berlin, 1964), pp. 70–84, esp. pp. 79–81.

[1] On this verse see especially C. H. Dodd, 'A l'arrière-plan d'un dialogue johannique', *R.H.P.R.* xxxvii (1957), 5–17, and a forthcoming publication by B. E. Schein, *The seed of Abraham. John 8: 31–59*; see W. A. Meeks, *J.B.L.* xci (1972), 67 n. 76 (Mr Schein kindly sent me a typescript copy of his paper).

[2] See also E. Allen, 'The Jewish Christian Church in the Fourth Gospel', *J.B.L.* lxxiv (1955), 88–92, and R. M. Grant, 'The Origin of the Fourth Gospel', *J.B.L.* lxix (1950), 305–22. On the Fourth Gospel's anti-Jewish attitude Grant remarks: 'The circumstances under which such an attack would seem advisable would be those in which Jewish Christians insisted that the synoptic gospels (any one of them) were adequate representations of the ministry of Jesus, or in which Jews outside the Church pointed to the Jewishness of Jesus. Naturally Jews outside the Church would influence Christians only slightly unless there were Jewish Christians inside who would be moved by Jewish arguments' (p. 320).

friendly -- as vv. 39-42 show. And Jesus' reply to the statement οἶδα ὅτι Μεσσίας ἔρχεται ... ὅταν ἔλθῃ ἐκεῖνος, ἀναγγελεῖ ἡμῖν ἅπαντα is positive. In fact he declares ἐγώ εἰμι, ὁ λαλῶν σοι. Is it because of the addition 'he will announce all things to us' that Jesus accepts this title for himself – whatever overtones ἐγώ εἰμι may have because of its use further on in this Gospel?

This is not the place to give a full analysis of iv. 1–42, but some remarks can be made which may, perhaps, carry the problem a little further.[1] The woman's reaction: 'I see that you are a prophet' in v. 19 and the statement concerning the Messiah in v. 25 are reactions to previous teaching of Jesus – about the life-giving water as a gift of God (vv. 10–15) and about the woman's personal life (vv. 16–17) and to Jesus' discourse on the worship in spirit and truth (vv. 19–24). Here we do not find Jesus directly or indirectly reacting to statements made by the other partners in the discussion, he conducts the discussion in his own terms and is interrupted by remarks made by the Samaritan woman. It is interesting to note that she is portrayed as being able to say 'you are a (true) prophet', but does not identify Jesus as the Messiah. It is Jesus who has to disclose himself as such (cf. ix. 37; x. 25). And even after this the woman does not go any further than a hesitating 'Could this be the Messiah?' (v. 29). Next, we should note that neither prophet nor Messiah is the final title used in this section. The Samaritans who have come to believe – after the woman's words about Jesus' disclosure of her past and present – and who have deepened their faith and insight in the course of a two-day stay of Jesus in their village, finally profess their faith in the words: 'We have heard him ourselves and we know that he is the Saviour of the World' (v. 42). These Samaritans, one would say, are at least at the same level as the disciples of i. 34–51 who stayed with Jesus (v. 39) and were convinced by his teaching. Yet these disciples appear on the scene, after the woman has run off to her village and before the villagers profess their faith, in order to receive inside information in a special conversation with Jesus. They need it, because they misunderstand completely a word of Jesus concerning the food he has to eat, but they receive it and Jesus' instruction introduces a theme which will be developed further in chapter vi. The essential expression here is 'to do the will of him who sent me' which also recurs several times in the Gospel. In v. 30–6, vi. 38–40 it becomes clear that the unity of will between Jesus and the One who sent him is the unity of will between Son and Father.

Somehow the Samaritans (of whom we hear nothing further on in the Gospel) do not belong to the inner circle of οἱ μαθηταί who receive special instruction and accompany Jesus on his travels, receiving further initiation in the true nature of his message and mission, including that given in the Farewell Discourses (ch. xiii–xvii) announcing the guidance of the Spirit after Jesus'

[1] See also 'Jesus as Prophet and King'.

glorification. In any case 'Messiah' is not the final title and the woman who uses it does not grasp fully the real meaning of this designation as applied to Jesus. Returning to iv. 25 f. we cannot deny that Jesus accepts here the title Messiah as a self-designation. He does so, however, inclusive of the phrase ἀναγγελεῖ ἡμῖν ἅπαντα and, clearly, with his own interpretation of the term Messiah and of this additional phrase – as the context of the chapter shows. Commentators usually do not discuss the meaning of this ὅταν ἔλθῃ ἐκεῖνος, ἀναγγελεῖ ἡμῖν ἅπαντα in the context of the Fourth Gospel, because they are anxious to compare iv. 25 with known Samaritan concepts. W. A. Meeks,[1] however, rightly points to xiii. 19; xviii. 4; xiv. 29; xvi. 4 where Jesus announces what is surely to come. Meeks regards this as a sign of prophetic authenticity to be viewed against the background of Deut. xviii. 18–22.[2] Jesus is more than a prophet, but what is essential for prophecy is also essential for his teaching.

This, of course, leads to the question whether the Samaritans are rightly depicted as expecting a 'prophetic Messiah'. Here we are confronted with a difficult situation. Much has been written lately on the Samaritans and their beliefs. I should like to mention above all J. Macdonald's *The Theology of the Samaritans*,[3] the fifth chapter 'Moses as King and Prophet in Samaritan Sources' in W. A. Meeks' *The Prophet-King*[4] and, most recently, H. G. Kippenberg, *Garizim und Synagoge. Traditionsgeschichtliche Untersuchungen zur samaritanischen Religion der aramäischen Periode*.[5] However, the non-specialist notes with regret that there is no agreement between the specialists with regard to their views on Samaritan eschatological beliefs in the first century A.D. Nearly all our sources are much later and evidently it is not easy to decide which traditions are old and which not. At one point there is no disagreement: the title משיח is not used in Samaritan sources before the sixteenth century.[6] W. A. Meeks is right, therefore, in saying 'that the title Μεσσίας has even been put in the mouth of the Samaritan woman (iv. 25) is a clear sign of the levelling of different terminologies'.[7] But if John is guilty here of 'levelling the different terminologies', like Justin Martyr after him who tells us that both Jews and Samaritans expect τὸν χριστόν,[8] he did so in order to show that Jesus fulfilled Jewish and Samaritan expectations.

---

[1] *The Prophet-King*, p. 46 n. 2.

[2] We may also point here to the activity of the 'Spirit of truth' in xvi. 12–15. He will lead the believers εἰς τὴν ἀλήθειαν πᾶσαν. Like a true prophet he will not speak ἀφ' ἑαυτοῦ but will speak what he hears καὶ τὰ ἐρχόμενα ἀναγγελεῖ ὑμῖν (v. 13, see also vv. 14, 15).

[3] (London, 1964). For our purpose especially Part Four 'Eschatology' (pp. 357–90) is important.

[4] Pp. 216–57.

[5] *Religionsgeschichtliche Versuche und Vorarbeiten* 30 (Berlin–New York, 1971). See especially chapter xi 'Der Taheb' (pp. 276–305) and chapter xii, 'Der Prophet wie Mose' (pp. 306–27).

[6] Kippenberg, *op. cit.* p. 303 n. 218, refers to Abraham haq-Qabbāṣi.

[7] *Op. cit.* p. 318 n. 1. Macdonald, *op. cit.* p. 361, says rather more vaguely on iv. 25: '...though Messiah is hardly the right term in the Samaritan case, for their concept of the one who is to come is not quite like that of Judaism and Christianity'.

[8] *Apol.* liii. 6. Justin adds that they did so ἔχοντες τὸν παρὰ τοῦ θεοῦ λόγον διὰ τῶν προφητῶν παραδοθέντα αὐτοῖς!

It is also clear that the expectation of the Prophet like Moses occupied a very important place in Samaritanism, because the Samaritan Pentateuch adds Deut. v. 28–9; xviii. 18–22; v. 30–1 immediately after Exod. xx. 21, that is after the Decalogue. There are indications that this expectation is early.[1] Do we have to connect this with John iv. 19 or with iv. 25? Kippenberg connects it with *v.* 19[2] but overlooks the fact that in iv. 19 the article is omitted. Jesus is called *a* prophet (and of course a real, *true* prophet is meant) but not *the* prophet who is always called ὁ προφήτης.[3] If there is any connection between the Samaritan expectation of *the* prophet and John's presentation of it we should look to iv. 25 and assume that it was John who introduced the term 'Messiah', while adding the 'prophetic' phrase ἀναγγελεῖ ἡμῖν ἅπαντα.[4]

Traditions regarding the coming of Moses and the Taheb are very variegated and it is not quite clear how they are interrelated and connected with the expectation of the Mosaic prophet;[5] consequently there is also difference of opinion as to the earliest form of these expectations. H. G. Kippenberg states quite clearly: The Taheb is simply the prototype of those who return (to the Lord) and who receive God's compassion. The Taheb is a 'vague' figure and that is the reason why so many different traditions could be connected with it – also prophetic and Mosaic notions. It remains to be asked, however, whether Kippenberg's result – originally strictly divided concepts of prophet like Moses and Taheb, and the return of Moses only as an anti-Dosithean variant of the former one[6] – is not due to his method. His 'Traditionsgeschichte' is mainly a 'Begriffsgeschichte' and he presupposes evidently a development from simplicity to complexity.[7] This presupposition may well be wrong; Samaritan expectation may have been far more complex right from the beginning than Kippenberg thinks. If this is true the background of John iv. 25 may well be more complex too – it may be of importance that we find no less than three times in Memar Marqa that the Taheb 'will reveal the truth'.[8]

[1] See Kippenberg, *op. cit.* chapter xii.

[2] *Op. cit.* p. 313 and pp. 115–17 (on John iv), pp. 324–7 (on 'the prophet', especially in John). Kippenberg's treatment of Johannine texts is, on the whole, disappointing.

[3] So rightly Meeks, *The Prophet-King*, p. 34. This distinction is not important for the use of the prophet-title as starting-point for Johannine christology – see also M. de Jonge, 'Jesus as Prophet and King'.

[4] Besides the Johannine parallels mentioned by W. A. Meeks compare also I Macc. iv. 46 where one stores the stones of the defiled altar somewhere until a prophet will come τοῦ ἀποκριθῆναι περὶ αὐτῶν (cf. xiv. 41). See also *C.D.* vi. 10 f. (the coming of a יורה הצדק with new instructions), and I QS ix. 10 f. (where the prophet and the anointed one(s) of Aaron and Israel have this function); on these and other texts see M. de Jonge, 'The role of Intermediaries in God's final intervention in the future according to the Qumran Scrolls', in O. Michel et al., *Studies on the Jewish Background of the New Testament* (Assen, 1969), pp. 44–63, esp. pp. 54–5.

[5] See W. A. Meeks, *op. cit.* pp. 246–54, and J. Macdonald, *op. cit.* pp. 362–71.

[6] So *op. cit.* chapter xii.   [7] See *op. cit.* pp. 27–9.

[8] *MM* ii, 44, 31 f.; *MM* iv 108, 6 f.; *MM* iv 111, 13 f., see Kippenberg, *op. cit.* pp. 289-93 and his note 159 on p. 293: 'Offensichtlich die wichtigste Tätigkeit des Taheb, da sie zum drittenmal erwähnt wird.'

Finally, it may be remarked that iv. 22–4 dealing with true worship may be a reaction to Samaritan beliefs regarding the restoration of the true worship on Mount Gerizim. Here we have the well-known story in Josephus' *Ant.* xviii, §§85–9 about a Samaritan 'uprising' under Pilate. In the background there is the expectation that in future the Mosaic tabernacle would be restored on Mount Gerizim.[1] In the story told by Josephus there is a connection with Moses-traditions and the leader of the action is a Moses-like figure.

[1] See Kippenberg, *op. cit.* pp. 113–14 and chapter ix, pp. 234–54.

The Jewish and the Christian Messiah *

by JOSEPH KLAUSNER

REMARK ONE:

The subject of this article would require a whole book for its elucidation. Within the limits of a short article I can only indicate the general outlines of the problem and restrict myself to certain important principles. Also, for the sake of brevity, I shall be compelled to cite from the extensive literature on matters pertaining to this subject only what is most relevant.

REMARK TWO:

The conception both of the Jewish Messiah and of the Christian Messiah has changed from period to period. The Jewish Messiah of Isaiah and Jeremiah is not the same as that of Daniel or the Ethiopic Enoch; nor is the conception of the Jewish Messiah in all these like that in the early Talmudic Aggadah, the *Mishneh Torah* of Maimonides, or the Kabbalistic books. It is likewise with respect to the conception of the Christian Messiah: Jesus himself understood his Messiahship very differently from the way in which Paul understood it. The later Church Fathers greatly modified what Paul taught; and the Catholics, Greek Orthodox, and Protestants differ greatly among themselves about how to conceive of the Messiah.

In this brief article I shall deal only with the conception of the Jewish Messiah as it has become crystallized in Biblical-Talmudic Judaism and accepted by most Jews; and with respect to the Christian

* Reprinted from *Sepher Magnes* [Heb.], Jerusalem, 1938.

519

conception of the Messiah I shall deal only with those features now shared by all three branches of the Christian faith. Then I shall attempt to present these two conceptions, the Jewish and the Christian, in contrast with each other, in order to show the difference between them.

I

The Jewish Messiah is a redeemer strong in physical power and in spirit, who in the final days will bring complete redemption, economic and spiritual, to the Jewish people—and along with this, eternal peace, material prosperity, and ethical perfection to the whole human race.

The Jewish Messiah is truly human in origin, of flesh and blood like all mortals. Justin Martyr in his time put this clearly into the mouth of Trypho the Jew, thus: "We Jews all expect that the Messiah will be a man of purely human origin." [1] This human conception of the Messiah remains normative in Judaism to this day. To be sure, a Talmudic Baraitha numbers the name of the Messiah among the seven things which "were created before the world was created"; [2] there is also something of this sort in the "Parables" of the Ethiopic Enoch. [3] But no doubt what is intended is the *idea* of the Messiah or the idea of redemption through the Messiah. [4]

The Messiah is full of the spirit of wisdom and understanding, counsel and might, knowledge and the fear of the LORD. He has a special feeling for justice: he "smells and judges" [that is, he can almost tell a man's guilt or innocence by his sense of smell]. [5] He "shall smite the land (or, the tyrant) with the rod of his mouth, and with the breath of his lips shall he slay the wicked." [6] For "the war against Gog and Magog," who come to destroy Israel, there is a special Mes-

---

1 Ἄνθρωπον ἐξ ἀνθρώπων. See Justin Martyr, *Dialogue with Trypho the Jew*, Chap. 49, beginning.

2 Pesahim 54a; Nedarim 39b.

3 Ethiopic Enoch 48:3.

4 See M. Friedmann, Introduction to Seder Eliyahu Rabbah, Vienna, 1902, p. 114; M. Vernes, *Histoire des idées messianiques*, Paris, 1874, pp. 268–269, 281, note.

5 Sanhedrin 93b; see above, p. 468.

6 Isa. 11:4.

siah—Messiah ben Joseph, who is slain in the war.[7] But Messiah ben David is the king of peace:

When the King-Messiah is revealed to Israel, he will not open his mouth except for peace, as it is written (Isa. 52:7), "How beautiful upon the mountains are the feet of the messenger of good tidings, that announceth peace." [8]

Also, "the Messiah shall be peaceful in his very name, as it is written (Isa. 9:5), 'Everlasting father, prince of peace.' " [9]

What in essence is the task of the King-Messiah?

He redeems Israel from exile and servitude, and he redeems the whole world from oppression, suffering, war, and above all from heathenism and everything which it involves: man's sins both against God and against his fellow man, and particularly the sins of nation against nation. For in the Messianic age all peoples will be converted to Judaism—some of them becoming "true proselytes" and some only "proselytes hanging on" (from self-interest).[10] In the *Alenu* prayer, which is offered by Jews three times daily, we find the hope that speedily

. . . the world will be perfected under the kingdom of the Almighty, and *all the children of flesh* will call upon Thy name, when Thou wilt turn unto Thyself all the wicked of the earth. Let *all the inhabitants of the world* perceive and know that unto Thee *every* knee must bow, *every* tongue must swear . . . and let them *all* accept the yoke of Thy kingdom.[11]

And in the *Shemoneh Esreh* prayer for "Solemn Days" [New Year and Day of Atonement], Jews say: "And let all creatures prostrate themselves before Thee, that they may all form a single band to do Thy will with a perfect heart." In this prayer the Jew prays:

Give then glory, O LORD, unto Thy people, . . . joy to Thy land (Palestine), gladness to Thy city (Jerusalem), a flourishing horn unto

---

[7] Sukkah 52a; see above, pp. 483–501.

[8] Derekh Erets Zuta, Chap. 11 (Section on Peace). See M. Higger, *Minor Tractates* [Heb.], New York, 1929, p. 101, and notes on p. 148; Lev. R., Chap. 9, end.

[9] Derekh Erets Zuta, Section on Peace, Text B (M. Higger, *op. cit.*, p. 104).

[10] *Gerim gerurim.* Cf. Berakhoth 57a and Tosephta, Berakhoth 7(6):2 (and Zuckermandel's notes *ad loc.*) with Abodah Zarah 24a. [See p. 481 above.]

[11] Singer, *Standard Prayer Book*, American ed., p. 94.

David Thy servant, and a clear shining light unto the son of Jesse, Thine anointed.

But at the same time he also prays that "all wickedness shall be wholly consumed like smoke, when Thou makest the dominion of arrogance to pass away from the (whole) earth." [12]

Along with redemption from servitude, from evil, and from heathenism, that is to say, from the evil in man, the Messiah will save man from the evil in nature. No longer will poisonous reptiles and beasts of prey exist; or rather, they will exist, but will do no harm.[13] There will be great material prosperity in the world: the earth will bring forth an abundance of grain and fruit, which man will be able to enjoy without excessive toil.[14] As to the Jewish people, not only will they freely dwell in their own land, but there will also be an "ingathering of exiles," whereby all Jews scattered to the four corners of the earth will be returned to Palestine. All nations will acknowledge the God of Israel and accept His revelation of truth. Thus the King-Messiah, the king of righteousness, will be in a certain sense also the king of all nations, just as the God of Israel will be King over all the earth because He is the One and Only God.

Not every book of prophecy mentions an individual human Messiah. In the books of Nahum, Zephaniah, Habakkuk, Malachi, Joel, and Daniel, God alone is the redeemer. In the books of Amos, Ezekiel, Obadiah, and in the Book of Psalms, there is only a collective Messiah: "deliverers" and "saints" redeem the world by their righteousness and piety. In the books of Haggai and Zechariah, the Messiah is none other than Zerubbabel, a person who is not out of the ordinary except that he is of the house of David. In Deutero-Isaiah and Daniel, the Messiah is not a person at all, but is the whole Jewish people. Likewise, in the Apocryphal books (as distinguished from the Pseudepigrapha), there is no individual Messiah. In the Talmud, Rabbi Hillel (to be distinguished from Hillel the Elder) makes bold to say: "There shall be no Messiah for Israel, because they have already enjoyed him in the days of Hezekiah." [15] To be sure, Rab Joseph rebelled against

[12] *Ibid.*, pp. 350–351.
[13] Siphra, Behuqqothai, Chap. 2, beginning (ed. Weiss, 111a).
[14] See on all this above, pp. 505–512.
[15] Sanhedrin 98b and 99a.

this opinion, saying: "May God forgive R. Hillel for saying this." [16] But the fact remains that it was possible for a Jew faithful to his nation and his religion to conceive of redemption without an individual human redeemer: God Himself would be the redeemer.[17]

This view did not prevail in Judaism. Belief in the coming of the Messiah is the twelfth in the thirteen "Articles of Faith" of Maimonides. But the fact that at one time Judaism could have conceived of redemption without a Messiah is not surprising. For redemption comes from God and through God. The Messiah is only an instrument in the hands of God. He is a human being, flesh and blood, like all mortals. He is but the finest of the human race and the chosen of his nation. And as the chosen of his nation, who is also the choicest of the human race, he must needs be crowned with all the highest virtues to which mortal man can attain.

As the Messiah, he exemplifies both physical and spiritual perfection. Even such an extremely spiritual and ethical person as Philo of Alexandria sees in the Messiah not only the spiritual and ethical side, but also finds in him "all-powerful strength of body" and "might" ($\delta\epsilon\iota\nu\acute{o}\tau\eta s$); for "leading his host to war he will subdue great and populous nations." At the same time Philo finds in the Messiah "holiness and beneficence" ($\sigma\epsilon\mu\nu\acute{o}\tau\eta s$ $\kappa\alpha\grave{\iota}$ $\epsilon\mathring{v}\epsilon\rho\gamma\epsilon\sigma\acute{\iota}\alpha$).[18] Both with respect to holiness, righteousness, truth, and goodness, and with respect to might and authority, the Messiah is the "supreme man" of Judaism, which is very far from Nietzsche's "blond beast." But with all his superior qualities, the Messiah remains a human being. Within the limits of a constantly improving humanity, Judaism has devised the ideal man, or, if we may speak in the language of Kant, "the conception of the [upper] limit of man"—concerning whom we may say with the divinely inspired psalmist, "Thou hast made him but little lower than God." [19] But this "little" leaves the Messiah within the bounds of humanity and does not allow him to pass beyond.

[16] Loc. cit.
[17] See on this, James Drummond, The Jewish Messiah, London, 1877, pp. 226-277.
[18] See Philo, On Rewards and Punishments, Chap. 16, Sects. 95-97 (ed. M., II, 423-424; ed. C.-W., V, 357). See also J. Klausner, Philosophers and Thinkers [Heb.], I, 87-88; above, p. 493.
[19] Ps. 8:6.

The kingdom of the Jewish Messiah is definitely "of this world."
Judaism is not only a religion, but is also the view of life of a single
nation that holds to this religion alone, while the other religions include various nations. It is absolutely necessary, therefore, that
Judaism's ideal for mankind should require first of all the realization
of the yearning of its oppressed, suffering, exiled, and persecuted
nation to return to its own land and recover its former status. But
this ingathering of exiles and this national freedom are closely linked
with the emancipation of all humanity—the destruction of evil and
tyranny in the world, man's conquest of nature (material prosperity
and the elimination of natural forces of destruction), the union of all
peoples into "a single band" to fulfill God's purpose, that is, to do
good and to seek perfection, righteousness, and brotherhood. This is
the "kingdom of heaven" or the "kingdom of the Almighty"; it is the
Messiah's reign or the "Days of the Messiah." But the Messiah is not
the primary figure, although he occupies a central place in this "kingdom of heaven"; "heaven," that is, God, is the primary figure. (The
word "heaven" is used here as a surrogate for God, to avoid blasphemy; hence "kingdom of heaven" and "kingdom of God," or "kingdom of the Almighty," are used interchangeably in the literature of
the end of the period of the Second Temple and later.)

Finally, the "kingdom of heaven" will come only "in the end of the
days." The chief difference [on this point] between Judaism and
Hellenism is that the Greeks and Romans saw the "Golden Age" *in
the past*, at the beginning of history, while the Jews saw it *in the
future*, at the end of history. Humanity is steeped in wickedness and
injustice, and hence is incomplete, or lacking in fulfillment. This fulfillment will come "in the end of the days," when wrongdoing, insolence, and conflict will pass from the earth, when "the wolf shall
dwell with the lamb" and "the earth shall be full of the knowledge
of the LORD as the waters cover the sea." Then those national
achievements for which Israel longs in its exile and bondage will be
realized: the return of the banished, the recovery of the homeland,
the revival of the Hebrew language,[20] and the restoration of the

---

[20] Testaments of the Twelve Patriarchs, Judah 25:3. See on this above, p. 316;
I. Ostersetzer, *The Outside Books* [Heb.], ed. Kahana, I, 1, p. 180; R. H. Charles,

kingdom (the kingdom of the house of David or the kingdom of the Messiah).

This notion of perfection stems from the ardent progressivism that belongs to the very foundation of Judaism. Both present-day Judaism and present-day humanity require completion, that is, they demand and are prepared for development and progress. This completion, the fruition of improvement by means of repentance and good works, will be achieved in the Messianic age. To be sure, the Messiah is reckoned among "three things that come unexpectedly"; [21] but among the "seven things hidden from men" is included also this: "when the kingdom of David will be restored to its former position." [22] Therefore, "unexpectedly" is not to be interpreted to mean that the Messiah will come without preparation, but that it is impossible to know in advance when the preparation will be complete, so that the Messiah *will be able* to come. And therefore, "the advent of Messiah" is not to be contrasted with "the end of the days": "the Messianic time of the end" and "the end of the days" are one and the same. The elimination of imperialistic oppression, the cessation of wars, everlasting peace, the fraternity of nations in "a single band," the removal of evil in man and nature, economic abundance, the flowing of all peoples to "the mountain of the LORD's house"—this whole complex of material and spiritual well-being is the Messianic age or the "kingdom of heaven"; for "heaven" (God) will bring all these things to the world through the Messiah, the exalted instrument of the Divine Will.

This is the Jewish Messiah and these his characteristics and activities.

II

And now by contrast—the Christian Messiah.

Christianity is wholly based on the personality of the Messiah. This statement needs no proof. When the people of Antioch began to

---

Apocrypha and Pseudepigrapha of the Old Testament in English, Oxford, 1913, II, 324, Note 3.

[21] Sanhedrin 97*a*.

[22] Mekhilta, Wayyassa, Chap. 6 (ed. Friedmann, 51*a*; ed. Horowitz-Rabin, p. 171); Pesahim 54*b*, beginning.

make a distinction between the believers in Jesus on the one hand, and Jews expecting the Messiah along with pagan Greeks on the other hand, they could find no more fitting name than "Christians"—a term derived from the Greek translation (*Christos*) of the Hebrew word "Messiah" (*Māshīaḥ*).[23] For at first the only difference between Jews and Christians was that the former believed that the Messiah *was still to come*, and the latter that the Messiah *had already come*.

But because of the fact that the Messiah who had already come was crucified as an ordinary rebel after being scourged and humiliated, and thus was not successful in the political sense, having failed to redeem his people Israel; because of the lowly political status of the Jews at the end of the period of the Second Temple and after the Destruction; and because of the fear that the Romans would persecute believers in a political Messiah—for these reasons there perforce came about a development of ideas, which after centuries of controversy became crystallized in Christianity in the following form:

1. The Messiah did not come to redeem from political oppression and economic wrong, but to redeem from spiritual evil alone.

2. Political oppression is a special problem of the Jews, but spiritual evil is world-wide. Hence Jesus came to redeem the whole world; *not* to redeem the Jewish people and their land *first*, and *then as a consequence* to redeem the whole world, which will forsake idolatry and become like Israel in every respect. And hence the kingdom of the Christian Messiah is "not of this world."

3. Jesus was scourged and humiliated as a common rebel. But he was not a common rebel; he only preached repentance and good works. Therefore, he was a true Messiah and not a false Messiah. Then why did God allow His Chosen One, the Messiah, to undergo frightful suffering and even to be crucified—the most shameful death of all, according to Cicero [24] and Tacitus [25]—and not save him from all these things? The answer can only be that it was the will of God and the will of the Messiah himself that he should be scourged, humiliated, and crucified. But whence came a purpose like this, that

---

[23] Acts 11:26.
[24] See Cicero, *Against Verres*, V 64.
[25] See Tacitus, *Histories*, IV 3 and 11.

would bring about suffering and death without sin? The answer can only be that the suffering was *vicarious* and the death was an *atoning death*. Jesus the Messiah suffered for others, for many, for all humanity. With his blood the Messiah redeemed humanity from sin, *inherited sin*, the sin of Adam, sin which became a part of Adam's nature, bringing death upon him and upon all his descendants. The Messiah went willingly to a disgraceful death in order that humanity might be redeemed from evil, from sin, from suffering, from death, and from the powers of Satan that prevail in the world—that Satan who by his enticement to sin brought death to the world. Support for this belief that the Messiah suffers for the iniquity of others (vicarious suffering) was found in Isaiah 53, which was interpreted not as referring to the persecuted people Israel, but to the suffering Messiah: "Yet he bore the sin of many." [26]

4. But the Messianic suffering which Jesus took upon himself by his own will and by the will of God cannot end in a shameful death. After the Messianic age comes the resurrection of the dead, according to Jewish doctrine. Therefore, of course, the Messiah rose from the dead—the first of men so to rise ("the firstfruits of them that slept," "the firstborn from the dead").[27] And therefore, Jesus is not mortal like other men. The will of God has been revealed in the will of the Messiah, and hence the Messiah is related to God *in a special way*.

5. God says to the Messiah, "Thou art My son, this day have I begotten thee." [28] And Jesus during his lifetime spoke much of "my Father who is in heaven." For Jews this was a common poetic-figurative expression. But the Gentiles, who asserted that certain of their eminent men—Alexander the Great, Plato, Pythagoras—had been fathered by gods who had visited mortal women, saw in this expression an actual genetic relationship of Jesus to God. Saul-Paul of Tarsus, who was a Jew, but one steeped in Greek culture, began to employ the concept "son of God" in a sense close to but not identical with the pagan concept: as Messiah, Jesus is "son of God" in the sense

---

[26] Isa. 53:12.
[27] I Cor. 15:20; Col. 1:18.
[28] Ps. 2:7.

of a "heavenly man" not susceptible to sin nor even to death. By his *temporary* death he atoned for the sin of Adam, and in his resurrection for eternity he ascended into heaven and sits at the right hand of God because he is closer to God than are the angels. This was the first step toward deification. But Paul the Jew did not go so far as to call Jesus "God."

The second step was to identify Jesus with the "Word" by which the world was created according to Judaism,[29] or with the "Logos," which is a sort of angelic being according to Philo of Alexandria.[30] This identification we find in the Gospel of John.[31] But it was natural that the Gentiles whom Paul brought into Christianity should take the third and final step and make Jesus a "God-man"—"one person with two natures"—God and man at one and the same time. Thus Jesus' Messiahship was gradually obscured: Jesus the Messiah gave way to "Jesus the God-man," or "the God Jesus"; and matters finally reached such a pass that the name "Christ" became the essential cognomen of Jesus ("Jesus Christ" and not "Jesus the Messiah"). The Messiahship of Jesus became secondary to his deity.

6. Although Jesus has been elevated to a rank fully equal to that of "God the Father," he still remains "Redeemer," and hence is still Messiah also. He has already come once into the world in the form of a man and has redeemed the world from sin and evil and death and Satan. Yet sin and evil and death and Satan still prevail in the world; therefore we are to expect his second coming, his "Parousia," at which time the Day of Judgment will occur, and Jesus, having taken his seat at the right hand of "his Father," will judge all persons that have ever lived, and will deliver those who believe in him. Then will Satan be conquered, evil will come to an end, sin will cease, and death will pass away; all the powers of darkness will vanish, and the kingdom of heaven will be fully established, though it had already begun with the first appearance of Jesus in the world.

7. Meanwhile, in "this world," men may turn in prayer to Jesus *as* to God his Father *and instead of* God his Father. In this sense he is

---

[29] Aboth 5:1.
[30] See on this in detail J. Klausner, *op. cit.*, I, 78–83.
[31] John 1:1–14.

"mediator" and "Paraclete" between God and man, although actually he himself is God and the true mediator is none other than Mary his mother, the Holy Virgin, "the mother of God" (*Theotokos*) by the Holy Spirit.

This is what happened in Christianity to the Jewish conception of the Messiah. The Christian Messiah ceased to be only a man, and passed beyond the limitations of mortality. Man cannot redeem himself from sin; but the Messiah-God, clothed in the form of a man, is the one who by his own freely shed blood has redeemed mankind. And he will come a second time to redeem humanity, since his first appearance, and even his death on the cross, did not suffice to eradicate evil from the world and to convert all men to belief in him. The first Christians expected this "Parousia" in their own time, and hence would pray, *Marana Tha*—"Our Lord, come!" (and not *Maran Atha* —"Our Lord has come").[32] When their prayer failed to be answered, and the Messiah-God did not again appear, they began to hope for the "thousand-year kingdom" or millennium (chiliasm); and finally they postponed the "Parousia" to an indefinite time.[33]

III

The Christian Messiah is in essence only a further development of the Jewish Messiah. For from Judaism Christianity received the ideas of redemption, the redeemer-Messiah, the Day of Judgment, and the kingdom of heaven. And much of what was common to Judaism and Christianity with respect to Messianic thinking remained even after estrangement and separation between them took place. Nevertheless, the difference between the Jewish and the Christian Messiah is very great.

First of all, Jewish redemption can be conceived without any individual Messiah at all—something which is absolutely impossible in Christianity. Also, "the Redeemer of Israel" for Judaism can mean God alone; in Christianity the Redeemer is Jesus only. Without the

[32] I Cor. 16:22. Cf. Rev. 22:20.
[33] See on this J. Klausner, *History of the Second Temple* [Heb.], V[3] (1952), 125–129; *idem, Jesus of Nazareth*, 5th Heb. ed., Jerusalem, 1945, pp. 432–441 [Eng. ed., pp. 398–407].

Jewish Messiah, Judaism is defective; without the Christian Messiah, Christianity does not exist at all.

Second, there is an irrational side even in the Jewish Messianic conception: where there is no mysticism at all there is no faith. But the irrational and mystical element in the Jewish Messiah is only unnatural, but not anti-natural, not opposed to nature. The unity of God is not affected in any essential way by the Jewish Messiah. In the last analysis, the Jewish Messiah is only, as said above, the instrument of deity—although of course a choice and superb instrument. But in Christianity monotheism is obscured by the Messiah, who is "Son of God," the "Logos," "the Lord," a "God-man," and "one person with two natures." And from this spring the rest of the marked differences between the Jewish and Christian Messiahs: one cannot pray to the Jewish Messiah, he is not a mediator between God and man, he is not a "Paraclete" for man, and so on.

Third, the Jewish Messiah is the redeemer of his people and the redeemer of mankind. But he does not redeem them by his blood; instead, he lends aid to their redemption by his great abilities and deeds. Even Messiah ben Joseph, who is slain, affords no atonement by his blood and his sufferings are not vicarious. Judaism is familiar with "the sin of Adam," but the Jewish Messiah does not with his blood redeem from "original sin," nor from death, nor from Satan. To be sure, Satan will be vanquished in the Messianic age—not by the Messiah, but by God. Man must redeem himself from sin *not by faith alone*, but *by repentance and good works;* then God will redeem him from death and Satan. (Generally speaking, Satan does not occupy in Judaism the central place that he takes in Christianity; Satan in Christianity is almost like the God of Evil of the Persians.) Each man is responsible for himself, and through his good deeds he must find atonement for his sins. He cannot lean upon the Messiah or upon the Messiah's suffering and death.[34]

Fourth and finally, since the Jewish Messiah is only "a righteous man ruling in the fear of God," and since he brings only ethical perfection to the world, the progress of humanity does not depend on him, but *on humanity itself*. Numberless times the Talmud returns to

[34] See A. Büchler, *Studies in Sin and Atonement*, London, 1928, pp. 375-461.

the idea that redemption depends on repentance and good works; well known is the interpretation of the verse "I the LORD will hasten it in its time": [35] "If they are worthy, I will hasten it [the redemption]; if not, it will come in its [own good] time." [36] And the Hebrew people, who were the first to acknowledge faith in One God, the God of goodness, and to whom came prophets of truth and righteousness, can and will be the first to "hasten the redemption" by repentance and good works. In other words, the Jews can and must march at the head of humanity on the road of personal and social progress, on the road to ethical perfection. This will be possible only when they have returned to their own land, have gathered in their exiles, have re-established their own state, and are no longer under the oppression of foreigners; but the "kingdom of heaven" is their goal and their highest aspiration, and without this goal Israel would never be freed from "bondage to foreign powers"—cessation of which will be the obvious external sign that the Days of the Messiah are near. [37]

Therefore, we can say, without being suspected of undue bias toward Judaism, that the Jewish Messianic faith is the seed of progress, which has been planted by Judaism throughout the whole world.

[35] Isa. 60:22.
[36] Sanhedrin 98a; and Yerushalmi, Taanith 1:1 (63d) says, "If you are worthy, I will hasten it; if not, it will come in its [own good] time."
[37] "There is no difference between this age and the Days of the Messiah except bondage to foreign powers" (Ber. 34b and parallels).

"AT THE END OF THE DAYS"

BY

HANS KOSMALA

I

Much has been written on the "eschatology" of the Old Testament prophets in the last 30 or 40 years, but little agreement seems to have been achieved. Statements resulting from these studies range from one extreme to the other, from: "all prophets of the Old Testament, including the pre-exilic prophets, are eschatologists" to "there is no pre-exilic or prophetic eschatology" [1]). On the following pages we shall not discuss the various aspects of the eschatological problems of the Old Testament, but concentrate on the Hebrew expression which seems to be the cause of the confusion: באחרית הימים· It occurs a number of times in various books of the Old Testament, and by no means only in those of the prophets. It appears always in the same form and with the same preposition as a fixed form of speech: Gen. 49, 1; Nu. 24, 14; Dt. 4, 30; 31, 29; Is. 2, 2 (Mi. 4, 1); Jer. 23, 20 (30,24); 48, 47; 49, 39; Ez. 38, 16; Hos. 3, 5; for the occurrences in the book of Daniel see further below. The traditional translations vary slightly. The AV has: "in the latter days", but twice "in the last days"; the RV has throughout "in the latter days"; the RSV: "in the latter days", but twice "in (the) days to come"; the most common modern rendering is: "at the end of the days".

This interpretation of the formula has given rise to two schools of thought:

1) Hugo GRESSMANN, *Der Messias*, 1929, pp. 74-77 and 82-87, says: There are eschatological oracles in the books of the OT, and there is even an older "popular (volkstümliche) eschatology" (*l.c.*, p. 75). Cf. also Paul VOLZ, *Jesaja II*, übersetzt und erklärt, 1932.

2) The literary critics maintain that there is no pre-prophetic or prophetic eschatology. See G. HÖLSCHER, *Die Ursprünge der jüdischen Eschatology*, 1925, and, after him, S. MOWINCKEL, *He That Cometh*, 1956, chapter V, especially pp. 126--133; survey on pp. 126ff.

Both schools take for granted that *b⁽ᵉ⁾aḥ⁽ᵉ⁾rit hayyamim* means "in the last days" or "at the end of the days" tacitly implying the *finis* of this world or at least of this world epoch. They take the expression as an eschatological concept. The first school, therefore, concludes that we find eschatological thought in the books where this and similar expressions (see the list which GRESSMANN gives, *l.c.*, pp. 83f.) are used. The other school, however, feels compelled to postulate that the expression *beᵃḥᵃrit hayyamim* "occurs only in late passages, or late editorial links" (MOWINCKEL, *l.c.*, p. 131, note 2). In other words, "there is no eschatology in the pre-prophetic age" (p. 130), "and the eschatological sayings in the prophetic books belong to the later strata, and come from the age of post-exilic Judaism" (p. 132). HÖLSCHER, therefore, deletes all "eschatological formulas" from the pre-exilic prophets, especially the most suspect of all: "am Ende der Tage" (GRESSMANN, p. 84).

As we see, both views are dependent on the same (traditional) understanding of the formula *beᵃḥᵃrit hayyamim*. But this is not quite what the Hebrew expression conveys. The traditional interpretation of the formula was suggested by the Septuagint which translates it by: ἐπ' ἐσχάτου (ἐσχάτων) τ. ἡμερῶν, ἔσχατον τ.ἡ., ἐν ταῖς ἐσχάταις ἡμέραις —ἔσχατον, of course, meaning simply "the end". However, it should be noted that ἔσχατον does not necessarily denote the "abrupt end", but rather the "furthest", the "utmost", the "extreme", "what comes last". Nevertheless, it is this Greek expression in the commonly accepted sense of "end", which has come to signify in Christian theology "the end of the days", i.e., "the end of the universe as it at present exists". We need not wonder, then, that the quarrel in all discussions on eschatology in the Old Testament turns on the proper definition of the term "eschatology". As it is the creation of Christian theologians, we should realise that it is a *stark belastetes Wort*, tainted by later ideas, which should not be summarily applied to the much earlier and far more primitive Old Testament concept *beᵃḥᵃrit hayyamim* [2]).

II

What is the original meaning of that expression?

The root *'ḥr* points out that something is "behind" or that something (else) "follows". The derivations from this root are applied to both, space and time. *'aḥᵃrit* has never lost the original element of the root. Here are two examples: "(the land or lands) which lie behind (or beyond) the sea" (Ps 139, 9); "... that which will happen: tell us what the earlier things were ... that we may know what followed after them, or let us hear the coming things" (Is. 41, 22). There are a few cases in which '*aḥᵃrit* is used in a loose way in the sense of "end", as for instance in Dt. 11, 12, where the beginning and the end of the ever-recurring agricultural year are described (*re'šit* and '*aḥᵃrit*), where each end is followed by a new beginning; cf. however Job 8, 7, where the two words are used succinctly. The expression '*aḥᵃrit* '*adam* does not necessarily imply the final "end", the death of man, but rather his future time or fate which follows the present situation or circumstances, as in Nu. 23.10; Prov. 19, 20; Job. 8, 7, etc.; cf. here also Sir. 11, 25-28, which deals with the period before and after man's death.

The translation "end" in the expression *bᵃ'aḥᵃrit hayyamim* is in every respect inadequate and can be misleading. *Hayyamim* is never used in the absolute sense for "time" ³). In *hayyom* the article has a demonstrative meaning: *hayyom* is the "present day", "to-day" — the fuller expression being (*'ad*) *hayyom hazzeh*, in contradistinction to *hayyom hahu'*, a (definite) day of the time to come. Likewise *hayyamim* are the (days of the) present time, the present period, and, correspondingly, the fuller, but possibly later expression is *hayyamim ha'elleh*; cf. Zach. 8, 9. 15; Qoh. 7, 10. '*Aḥᵃrit hayyamim*, therefore, signifies "the day, or days, or the time which will follow or come after a certain period, usually the present period" ⁴). It equals the expressions *hayyamim hahem*, or *ba'et hahu'*, or (*hinneh*) *yamim ba'im*, all of which point to a time which is not yet, but will come after the present period has come to an end.

This definition of *bᵃ'aḥᵃrit hayyamim* is borne out by Hos. 3,4f: "**Many days** the Israelites will (shall) dwell without a king ... **Afterwards** they will (shall) return and seek the Lord ... and come in fear to the Lord and his goodness *bᵃ'aḥᵃrit hayyamim*". The word '*aḥar* which introduces the first part of verse 5 makes it quite clear that the parallel expression *bᵃ'aḥᵃrit hayyamim* refers to the "many days" at the beginning of verse 4, describing the period which will have to pass; "afterwards" the events foreseen in verse 5 will take place.

No passage in the Old Testament which has *bᵃ'aḥᵃrit hayyamim* is eschatological in the sense in which we use the word. There is an oracle, Joel 3, 1, which does not contain this expression, but employs the adverb '*aḥᵃrey-ken* instead, in the same sense: "Und es wird sein nach diesem ..." ⁵). Even in so late a passage as Dan. 2, 28f. the expression *bᵃ'aḥᵃrit yomayya'* is still idiomatically used and clearly defined as the time 'aḥᵃrey dᵉnah, the days or time which will come "after this", that is, "after these days". Also in the other places of the Book of Daniel, 'aḥᵃrit must be so understood: 8, 19; 8, 23; 10, 14 bᵉ'aḥᵃrit hayyamim; 12, 8 'aḥᵃrit 'elleh. Both the LXX and Theodotion render it as usual by ἐπ' ἐσχάτου (ἐσχάτων) τῶν ἡμερῶν, with the exception of the last passage, which Theodotion translates τὰ ἔσχατα τούτων, and the LXX ἡ λύσις τοῦ λόγου τούτου, that is, the "interpretation of this word" ⁶).

III

When the Book of Daniel really means the "end", the "conclusion of the final period", or the "final, decisive period" itself, it says so and uses the proper Hebrew word for "end", "finish": qeṣ ⁷). This word is derived from the root qṣṣ, "cut off". All passages containing the word qeṣ are in the Hebrew chapters. Their Greek renderings are interesting. Qeṣ hayyamim we find in 12, 13 (LXX and Theodotion: συντέλεια ἡμερῶν); ʿet qeṣ, the "period of the end", in 8, 17; 11, 35; 11, 40 (LXX: ὥρα καιροῦ, καιρὸς συντελείας, ὥρα συντελείας; Theodotion: πέρας καιροῦ); similarly ʿad qeṣ in 9, 26 or ʿad ʿet qeṣ, in 11, 35 and 12, 9: or just qeṣ in 12, 13 (also more in the sense of ʿet qeṣ). In three places qeṣ is connected with moʿed: 8, 19; 11, 27, 35, with special reference to the "appointed time" of the end. The Greek translations of qeṣ vary to some extent. The LXX renders the word by συντέλεια and καιρός, Theodotion by καιρός mostly together with πέρας (with the exception of 12, 13; see above). Sometimes καιρός stands for moʿed (in connection with qeṣ). A complete list of the Greek translations would show that καιρός became the predominant word for the "end" or the "time of the end", the "appointed time (of the end)". The LXX, it is true, gives some preference to συντέλεια, whilst Theodotion, who lived in the latter part of the sub-apostolic age, evidently found the word καιρός, as applied to eschatological time, already in use and preferred it to συντέλεια. It had already been widely employed as an eschatological term in the New Testament writings. Matthew uses συντέλεια (see further below); there is only one clear example for the eschatological use of the word καιρός, Mat. 8, 29; but cf. also 13, 30; 16, 3; 21, 34. 41 and 26, 18 with eschatological implications (otherwise he uses καιρός as a general word for time).

The Book of Daniel which knows and uses the old Hebraic expression bᵉ'aḥᵃrit hayyamim (even in the Aramaic passage 2, 28) still idiomatically, has a fully developed eschatology in the strict sense. The "end" of the days is a real end. To express this, it uses the word *qeṣ*, which is not used in this sense in the older Biblical texts [8]). The "days of the end" are literally numbered. The end is one of "Heil" and "Unheil", of salvation and doom, and it is the doom by which the days come to an end: the "wrath of God" (8, 19) is bound to come, the doom had been determined (9, 26.27; 11, 36; cf. a. Is. 10, 23; 28, 22).

IV

In spite of the correct use of the term *bᵉʾaḥᵃrit hayyamim* in the Book of Daniel, it was only natural that this expression also came under the spell of eschatology, for it presupposes that the present time or period of days will come to some kind of end, before the things that shall happen will happen.

Although the older translations still distinguish between *ʾaḥᵃrit* and *qeṣ*:

Greek: ἔσχατος—συντέλεια, πέρας, καιρός
Latin: *in novissimis temporibus—finis dierum*
Luther: künftige Zeiten, hernach—Ende der Tage
AV: the latter days—the end of the days
(about the Aramaic translation see last chapter), modern scholars seem to take no notice of this distinction. They translate *bᵉʾaḥᵃrit hayyamim*: "am Ende der Tage" (GRESSMANN, l.c., p. 84), die "Endzeit" (GES.-BUHL, p. 27a), "at the end of the days" (KOEHLER-BAUMGARTNER, p. 33b; MOWINCKEL, p. 131, n. 2). Modern translations should, therefore, be used cautiously, for *ʾaḥᵃrit* and *qeṣ* should be distinguished from each other.

It is on the identification of *ʾaḥᵃrit* with *qeṣ* that the two modern schools base their different conclusions. Because the expression *bᵉʾaḥᵃrit hayyamim* is interpreted as meaning "at the end of the days", the one school says, there is a pre-exilic eschatology, whilst the other school, which says there is none, has to declare that all the passages containing that expression are not original but belong to the age of post-exilic Judaism. As already pointed out, the "eschatological" interpretation of the old-Biblical expression *bᵉʾaḥᵃrit hayyamim* goes back to the Greek translation in its modern understanding, but we should keep in mind that ἔσχατος is originally not quite the same as συντέλεια, τέλος, or πέρας (see the dictionaries).

We do not know when the identification of 'aḥᵉrit (hayyamim) with qeṣ (hayyamim) took place, but we do know that this development was practically completed in New Testament times. Two or three reasons for this trend may be given.

1) There are prophecies of doom in the prophetic writings of the Old Testament. Doom together with salvation forms a necessary and integral part of the (later) eschatological view (cf., for instance, the Biblical quotations in the Damascus document).

2) Some of the OT prophecies had never come true: Is. 2, 2ff., (cf. Jub. 1, 29), Hos. 3, 4f., Joel 3 (cf. Acts 2, 16-25) and 4, and many others. There are a number of references and allusions to Isaiah already in the Book of Daniel.

3) Important events had happened during the exilic and post-exilic period, such as the return to the land of the fathers, the re-erection of the Temple, and we may even include its re-dedication under the Maccabeans. All of them could be understood as fulfilment of former prophecies and evidently they were so understood. However, the dissatisfaction with the priestly kingship of the Hasmoneans, which bore so little resemblance to the prophetic ideals, and the ensuing Roman rule, gave rise to serious doubts. This could not be what the prophets had in mind. The new world-period with a new victorious life of the Jewish people as visualized by the prophets was still to come and to come soon. They conceived it as something utterly different from the present era of spiritual dearth and political subjection.

The authority of the Scriptures was never doubted. God was faithful and the word of his prophets true. The fact that the prophecies had not come true in the past made a new interpretation for the present time of longing and hope necessary. The task was vigorously taken up by the Essenic movement and, after it, together with new aspects, by Early Christianity. The new interpretation became the mainspring of their theologies. "The time of the end", "the end of the time(s)", when all the prophecies of doom and salvation would be fulfilled, was now.

It is true that Jewish apocalyptic thought, especially in its earlier representations, did not always conceive the end as a world catastrophe, cf. for instance the new creation according to Jub. 1, 29; 5, 12; 23, 26 ff.), but the "last" days or times (Test. Levi 14, 1; TIs 6, 1; TZ 8, 2; TD 5, 4; TG 8, 2; TJOs 19, 10) are seen as a real end, a completion, or consummation: τελείωσις χρόνων (TR 6, 8);

συντέλεια τῶν αἰώνων (TL 10, 2; TB 11, 3); καιρὸς συντελείας (TZ 9, 9); *finis saeculi* (4 Ezra 6, 25); *finis temporis, temporum* (2 Bar. 27, 15; 29, 8; 30, 3); *consummatio* (4 Ezra 9, 5); *c. mundi* (2 Bar. 56, 2); *c. saeculi* (83, 7); *c. exitus dierum* (Ass. Mos. 1, 18); (*tempora ?*) *consummentur* (10,13).

V

A few notes on the eschatological expressions in the literature of Qumran and the New Testament may follow here in order to give an idea of the further development of eschatological thought and to show the affinity between its two main trends.

In the Dead Sea Scrolls both expressions (1) *'aḥᵃrit* and (2) *qeṣ* are in use and to some extent still distinguished from each other.

1a) *Bᵊaḥᵃrit hayyamim*. In Sa I, 1 the expression is clearly applied to the "Messianic" time, as the Messiah is already thought to be present in the congregation. It is not quite clear whether this refers to the time of the *qeṣ* or the time after the *qeṣ*. There are two more passages in the Damascus document. D IV, 4 says, that "the elect of Israel . . . shall stand *bᵊaḥᵃrit hayyamim*", that is, evidently, during (IV, 8f.) and after (IV, 10) the "completion of the *qeṣ*". According to D VI, 10f. "the Teacher of Righteousness arises *bᵊaḥᵃrit hayyamim*", that is, after the "*qeṣ* of wickedness".

(1b) *Lᵊaḥᵃrit hayyamim* occurs only in pHab II, 5f. and IX, 6. It should be noted that in these two examples the preposition *bᵊ* has been replaced by the particle *lᵊ*. The difference may not be great, but all translators including the latest (DUPONT-SOMMER and Johann MAIER) render both passages in the same way as those with *bᵊ*: "at the end of the days". It seems that pHab employs the term only in a loose way indicating that the event will take place sometime during the last period. The period thus described begins practically with the day(s) of judgment (cf. also V, 3-6).

(2) *Qeṣ* is definitely, as in the Book of Daniel, "the time of the end", during which the wicked people reign, those who do not believe in the message of the Teacher of Righteousness, "whom God had given . . . to interpret all the words of his servants, the prophets, through whom God had announced all the things that would come over his people . . ." (pHab II, 8-10). The *qeṣ* is, therefore, sometimes described as the *qeṣ riš'ᵃh*, the end-period of wickedness (D VI, 10.14; XII, 23; XV, 7.10; pHab VII, 7.12). The very last part of the end-time is called *qeṣ 'aḥᵃron* (S IV, 16f.; pHab VII, 7.12). The NT equivalent

is καιρὸς ἔσχατος (1 P. 1,5), which is here already the beginning of the new aeon. Qeṣ is sometimes itself the end-period, sometimes the conclusion of this period (S III, 23; or with special reference to the fact that it is fixed by God, qeṣ neḇʳraṣah, S IV, 20.25 and H III, 36 with allusion to Dan. 9, 26f. and 11, 36 and the corresponding passages in Isaiah). S III, 13-15 (qiṣṣim), evidently referring to decisive periods of the past, seems to admit periods of visitation ("Heil" and/or "Unheil").

Summarizing the results of this brief examination of the Scrolls, we may say that the idea of the end is rendered by the word qeṣ with a special emphasis on its wickedness, on judgment, and doom; more generally, however, by 'aḥ°rit hayyamim perhaps with a greater stress on salvation.

VI

Both expressions appear in their Greek form in the New Testament. For b°aḥ°rit hayyamim see the translations of the LXX. Qeṣ is usually rendered by καιρός as in the Greek translations of the Book of Daniel. Both expressions are here even more closely connected with each other: sometimes they are practically identified (cf. 2 Tim. 3, 1).

All passages in John have the singular, "on the last day (ἐν τῇ ἐσχάτῃ ἡμέρᾳ), with reference to the last judgment (12, 48) or the resurrection (6, 39.40.44.54; 11, 24). The plural, "in the last days" (ἐν ταῖς ἐσχάταις ἡμέραις) is used in Acts 2, 17 (quotation of Joel 3, 1ff., which has not b°aḥ°rit hayyamim; see note 5), James 5, 3, and 2 Tim. 3, 1; with ἐπί in 2 P. 3, 3; ἐπ' ἐσχάτου τῶν χρόνων in 1 P. 1,20.

As the present time of the New Testament is "end-time", the word καιρός is very frequent here. Many passages in the New Testament, in which καιρός is usually translated with "time" or, occasionally, "appointed time", actually refer to the present, or almost present, time of the end. It is quite impossible to deal with the concept καιρός without having due regard to the eschatological mood of the context [9]), in which we find it. Admittedly, there are cases where καιρός is used in a more general sense like χρόνος, but there are also other cases where χρόνος is used synonymously with καιρός [10]). About the plural καιροί see examples below.

Here is a list of passages in which the word καιρός can best be studied in its eschatological aspect. The list is not complete.

Mt. 8, 29.
Mk. 1, 15: 10, 30; 13, 33.

Lk. 1, 20; 19, 44; 21, 8.24. 36 (= E 6, 18).
Rom. 3, 26; 12, 11 (*v. l.*); 13, 11.
1. Cor. 4, 5.
Gal. 6, 9.
Eph. 1, 10; 5, 16 (= Col. 4, 5).
1. Thess. 5, 1.
2. Thess. 2, 6.
1. Tim. 2, 6; 4, 1; 6, 15.
2. Tim. 3.1.
Heb. 9, 9 f.
1. P. 1, 11; 4, 17; 5, 6.
Rev. 1, 3; 11, 18; 12, 12. 14; 22, 10.

A number of expressions with *qeṣ*, common in the Scrolls, have their Greek equivalents in the New Testament, although they are not always indentical in meaning.

ad Mk. 1, 15 and Lk. 21, 24 cf. D IV, 10: בשלים קץ (cf. a. LXX Dan. 12, 13 a. Dan. Theodot. 5, 26).

ad Lk. 21, 36 and Eph. 6, 18 cf. D VI, 10; XV, 7.10: בכל קץ

ad Eph. 5, 16, Col. 4, 5; 2 Tim. 3, 1 (Test. Dan. 6, 6) cf. D VI, 10. 14; XII, 23; XV, 7.10; pHab V, 7f.: קץ הרשע(ה)

ad 1 P. 1, 5 (ἐν καιρῷ ἐσχάτῳ) and 1 Tim. 4, 1 (ἐν ὑστέροις καιροῖς) cf. S IV, 16f.; pHab VII, 7.12: (ה)קץ (ה)אחרון.

ad Mat. 16, 3. Lk. 21, 24, Acts 1, 7 and 17, 26 (καιροί) cf. S III, 14f: קצים·
(ad Rom. 13, 11, καιρός + ὥρα, cf. LXX Dan. 8, 17; 11, 35.40).
(ad Lk. 19, 43 cf. D VII, 11).

The word συντέλεια used in the sense of *qeṣ* is peculiar to Matthew: 13, 39.40.49; 24, 3; 28 ,20 (cf. also Heb. 9, 26). It is taken from LXX Dan. 11, 27.35.40; 12, 13; (not in Theodotion).

VII

A few remarks on the Targumim may conclude our observations. All Targumim render *bᵉʾaḥᵃrit hayyamim* by *bᵉsop yomayyaʾ*, although the Aramaic passage in Dan. 2, 28 has *bᵉʾaḥᵃrit yomayyaʾ* (Hebraism?). We see that the Targumists did not follow this precedent, but conceived the Hebrew *ʾaḥᵃrit hayyamim* as "the end of the days". There is no exception. The Aramaic *sop* corresponds to Hebrew *qeṣ*, not to Hebrew *ʾaḥᵃrit*. The common Semitic root means "to take an end", "to be no more", "to cease to exist", "to perish". *Sop*, therefore, denotes the "absolute end". In Hebrew the word *sop* is used as an

Aramaism in a few late passages (s. Ges.-Buhl p. 539 b). In Aramaic it is the common word for "end", the "absolute finish".

The Targumim (together with the literature of Qumran and the New Testament) stand at the end of the development of eschatological thought. For them the 'aḥ"rit is the sop. But in spite of the use of the term sop yomayya', the genuine eschatological mood (from Daniel to the NT) seems to be missing in the Targumim; the eschatological expectation has lost much of its urgency, for we do not get the impression that "the end" is really very near.

---

[1]) See Joh. LINDBLOM, "Gibt es eine Eschatologie bei den alttestamentlichen Propheten?" (STh VI, 2, 1953, pp. 79-114), p. 79, and his bibliographical notes He himself takes a middle course, especially in his latest work Prophecy in Ancient Israel, Oxford 1962. pp. 360-375, where he employs the term "eschatology in the wider sense".

[2]) In LINDBLOM's article (see note 1), p. 80 n. 3, is a reference to an article by A. W. ARGYLE in The Hibbert Journal 51, 1953, pp. 385 ff., who seems to have come to a similar conclusion, namely, that the notion eschaton is inappropriate when one speaks of eschatology in the Old Testament.

[3]) Even the word ʿolam (which comes nearest to this notion of "time", especially in such expressions as meʿolam wrʿad ʿolam, or ʿolamim) very often only means a "long time", a "life-time", or a similar period of some length. For practical purposes we translate the term lʿolam with "for ever", although it refers in each case only to the period in view (cf. Dt. 15, 17; 1 Sam. 1, 22; Is. 42, 14; etc.). The fact that ʿolam denotes a long, but actually limited period made it possible that in post-Biblical Hebrew ʿolam came to mean "world-period" and "world" (αἰών, κόσμος).

The present article does not deal with "time" in the Bible, but rather with the "end" of (the) time(s), that is, with certain limitations of time. It may not be inopportune here to say a few words about the most recent study by James BARR, Biblical Words for Time, 1962, as one of the words for time, καιρός, stands in its centre. One cannot come to a full understanding of "time" in the Bible without taking into account these various limitations which are so often connected with Biblical time or times. I can find only two examples in his book (pp. 38 and 40), where he refers Greek καιρός to Hebrew qeṣ, and that only en passant. The Greek expressions, especially in the NT, must be studied in close connection with their older equivalents in the Bible and now also with those in the Essenic literature. What the author says on p. 118 is so little that it becomes irrelevant. In spite of some pertinent remarks which this book contains, it must be said, that the philosophical approach as the author demonstrates it—he calls it "theological-philosophical"—is insufficient, and it obscures rather than elucidates the meaning of καιρός in many important passages of the NT (see, for instance, his treatment of 1 Cor. 7, 29 on p. 43), where its content cannot be divorced from the ever-present eschatological thought or mood. This is not the place to review his statements in detail. It seems that we shall have to turn back again to some of the results of older Biblical studies which the author so violently criticizes.

[4]) Cf. here Akkadian ina aḥrat umi, which is simply "in future"; the f. pl. aḥriat also means "future"; likewise other derivations from the root aḥr refer to the (sometimes immediate) future; see BEZOLD, Bab.-Ass. Glossar, p. 24b. The

note in KOEHLER-BAUMGARTNER, p. 33b, s.v., that the Akk. expression is an "eschatological term", is incorrect; see now also the brief remarks by Arvid KAPELRUD in his article "Eschatology in the Book of Micah", VT XI, 1961, No. 4., p. 395f.—In Ugaritic texts so far no expression corresponding to the Hebrew and Akkadian has been found; but *baḥr* is here also "afterwards"; *uḥryt (mt)* (only occurence in 2 Aqht VI, 35) is the time after man has spent his present life, i.e., man's future or fate; cp. the Hebrew expression *ʾaḥᵃrit ʾadam* mentioned above.

[5]) It is interesting to note that Luke, when quoting this verse in Acts 2, 17, renders the adverbial expression by ἐν ταῖς ἐσχάταις ἡμέραις. The LXX translation is literal.

[6]) The word λύσις sometimes stands for *pešer*; see KOSMALA, *Hebräer—Essener—Christen*, p. 275, n. 13; p. 350, n.l.

[7]) Th. C. VRIEZEN, "Prophecy and Eschatology" in *VT Supplement* I, 1953, pp. 199-229, says: "For *future* and *end*, for *later* and *last* Hebrew thought has only one word, *ʾaḥᵃrit* . . ." (p. 223 bottom). He does not seem to know the word *qeṣ*, which is the proper word for "end" in the OT, and the Book of Daniel uses it with reference to time.

[8]) A few words should be said here about Amos 8, 2, where *qeṣ* is not a distinct concept of time. For Amos the present time is a time of "sins" (1, 3.6.9.11.13; 2, 1.4.6) especially with regard to Israel, so that God cannot let them go on in that way any longer (cf. 3, 1f.). In other words: "the end (*qeṣ*) is coming to my people Israel" (8, 2; 9, 8), that is, to Israel in its present state, for "days will come" (9, 13), when everything will be repaired (!) (9, 11-15). J. H. GRÖNBAEK ("Zur Frage der Eschatologie in der Verkündigung der Gerichtspropheten", *SEÅ* 24, 1959, pp. 5-21) is right, when he hesitates to call this *Verkündigung* of Amos eschatological (l.c., p. 11).

[9]) Like James BARR; see note 3, second part.

[10]) Even BARR quotes a few such cases, *l.c.*, p. 42.

RECENT STUDY OF THE TERM 'SON OF MAN'

NATHANIEL SCHMIDT

CORNELL UNIVERSITY

THERE are certain problems connected with the term 'son of man' that have not yet been solved in such a manner as to set at rest all reasonable doubt. It is still possible, for instance, to question whether any passage in which Jesus has been supposed to use the phrase בר נשא in its ordinary generic sense is genuine. It is pertinent to inquire whether ὁ υἱὸς τοῦ ἀνθρώπου may not have originated in a mistranslation of בר נשא used in this sense in some Jewish or Jewish-Christian apocalypse. And it is proper to consider whether the term in some form many not have been derived from speculations, of Jewish or pagan origin, concerning the second, the last, or the heavenly Man. But the investigations of the last thirty years have not been in vain. They have affected the methods of research; the questions involved are to-day approached in a new way. They have established some facts, such as these: ὁ υἱὸς τοῦ ἀνθρώπου is a translation of בר נשא, and בר נשא was not a current messianic title. Critical judgment is unmistakably gravitating toward the position that, in the gospels, the Greek term, as understood by the evangelists, is likely to have its earlier home in the eschatological series.

If, nevertheless, there is on many points no consensus of opinion, this is not strange in view of the far-reaching implications and the increasingly rigorous demands of scientific exegesis. The former make caution commendable however attractive a theory may be; the latter enhance the difficulties of the task. Aside from the philological equipment, extensive

326

acquaintance with the relevant literature, and insight into the peculiarities of the various Semitic dialects, there are numerous other requirements which have been justly urged. Textual criticism must be allowed to adhere to its own canons. When primary and secondary strata of tradition are separated, the accretions must be accounted for. A philological observation may furnish a significant clue, but it must be followed through all the literary data, with due regard for the necessary criticism of sources and the main theories propounded in this field. Historical methods must be applied in the sifting of the material and the search for ascertainable facts.

In his valuable contribution to this subject in the Symposium on Eschatology,[1] Bacon mentions at the outset the "distinct relief to students accustomed to think of meekness and lowliness as typical traits in the personal character of Jesus in the authoritative declaration of eminent philologians that the self-designation 'the Son of Man' would be unintelligible in the Palestinian Aramaic of Jesus' time, so that the title with all its connotation of superhuman authority and dignity must be ascribed to the period after the development of the resurrection faith." He then proceeds to give his reasons for not accepting this relief, but preferring a different solution; thus revealing at the same time the scholar's hospitality to new points of view and his sense of duty to test each noteworthy hypothesis in the light of the facts and the apparently assured results of long continued investigations.

Since the discussion of the phrase by so distinguished an Aramaist as Dalman[2] seemed to Bacon to dispose of the conclusions I presented to this Society in 1895[3] and Lietzmann independently reached and published in 1896,[4] and since Bacon's theory is based throughout, with a single exception to be noted below, on what are designated as "Dalman's proofs," it is natural to begin this review with a reference to the character of his arguments. It should be stated that the way was prepared for

[1] *JBL*, XLI, 1922, 143 ff.
[2] *Die Worte Jesu*, 1898.
[3] 'Was בר נשא a Messianic Title?' *JBL*, XV, 1896, 36 ff.
[4] *Der Menschensohn*, 1896, 124 f.

my conclusions and those of Lietzmann by some important hints
of Génébrard, Grotius, Bolten, Uloth, Lagarde, and Wellhausen
and an elaborate study by Eerdmans;[5] and also that they have
been adopted and defended by Wellhausen, Marti, Pfleiderer,
Nöldeke, Merx, Haupt, and other scholars. Dalman's arguments
may here be briefly discussed, as they have already been
examined very carefully by Bevan,[6] Wellhausen,[7] and myself.[8]
Dalman recognizes that בר נשא is the only Aramaic phrase that
can have been translated ὁ υἱὸς τοῦ ἀνθρώπου; that whereever
it is actually found in extant Aramaic literature it has only the
meaning 'der Mensch,' 'man,' 'the man,' 'quidam;' and that it
occurs in this sense with great frequency even in the Galilean
dialect. But he suggests the possibility that it may not have
been used, and not even understood, in Galilee in the first
century A. D. He appeals to the absence of the term in Naba-
taean and Palmyrene inscriptions and the late age of the Palestinian Talmud and the younger Targumim. Its absence in Na-
bataean and Palmyrene inscriptions known to us is not strange
when one considers how seldom 'man' in a generic sense would
be likely to be used and its rare occurrence in the epigraphic
material preserved in any language. Rather is it surprising, in
view of its limited use in Genza and Qolasta, to find it employed
in some of the Mandaic magic formulas published by Montgomery.[9] Fiebig has shown that Simeon b. Jochai and Hoshaya
employed it in the second century A. D. An innovation due to
Edessene influence at so early a date is out of the question. It
is possible that אנשא and גברא were more frequently used than
בר נש; but the collective, and virtually plural, meaning of
אנשא was never quite lost sight of, so that הו בר נשא is found,
but not הו. אנשא. That בר נשא should have been used in
Galilee in the second century, but not even understood a few
generations earlier in the sense it has in Aramaic speech every-

---

[5] Th. Tjidschrift, 1894, 153 ff., 1895, 49 ff. Arnold Meyer called attention
to the hints of Génébrard and Bolten, Jesu Muttersprache, 1896.

[6] Critical Review, IX, 1899, 144 ff.

[7] Skizzen und Vorarbeiten, VI, 1899; Die drei ersten Evangelien,[2] 1911.

[8] 'Son of Man' in Enc. Bibl., 1903; The Prophet of Nazareth, 1905.

[9] Aramaic Incantation Texts from Nippur, 1913, 117, 146.

where, is well nigh inconceivable. The best proof that it was used in this sense in Judaean Aramaic in the second century B. C. is Dan. 7 13. Bacon says: "The linguistic objection seems not to be sustained." It is Dalman's conjecture that has not been sustained. No student familiar with Aramaic has attempted to defend it, and none has indicated his approval.

Even the one scholar who dissents from the generally accepted opinion that ὁ υἱὸς τοῦ ἀνθρώπου is a translation of בר נשא does not express any doubt as to the use and intelligibility of this term in the Galilee of Jesus' time. In an article, remarkable alike for its subtlety of reasoning and its acquaintance with patristic literature, Badham[10] argues in favor of בר אדם. He supposes that Jesus used this term in the sense of son of Adam, second Adam, successor of Adam, and maintains that this suits all the passages in the synoptic gospels. Jesus, he thinks, had constantly in mind the contrast between himself and the first Adam. Healing, physical and spiritual, is quite in harmony with the character of the second Adam. So is forgiveness of sin. The creation of Adam was prior to the creation of the Sabbath, hence the Sabbath was made for Adam, and the second Adam had authority over it. Like the first he is a sower, but of the good seed. He restores the beauty and joy of paradise. Inasmuch as he is man, *he* may be blasphemed, but not the Holy Spirit. Homelessness is the lot of the successor of Adam. The second Adam has come to be a savior. He must suffer and die to expiate the guilt of the first Adam; and he will win the victory, come on the clouds of heaven, and restore paradise. It is in the regeneration, *i. e.,* the new birth of the world, that the second Adam will sit on the throne of his glory. This is in harmony with the predictions of suffering and death, because the final bringing to nought of evil, the destruction of the enemy, is at the same time the rescue of the oppressed. As evidence of the correctness of this interpretation Badham then introduces a wealth of proof-texts from the early fathers of the church, showing that they found in the phrase precisely this allusion to the second Adam in contrast with the first.

10 *Th. Tijdschrift*, 1911, 395 ff.

It is evident, however, that ὁ υἱὸς τοῦ ἀνθρώπου presupposes a term containing the article. The poetic expression אָדָם בֶּן rendered אָדָם בַּר in the Targums which followed the Hebrew, is translated into Greek υἱὸς ἀνθρώπου, but never ὁ υἱὸς τοῦ ἀνθρώπου, though the plural הָאָדָם בְּנֵי is rendered οἱ υἱοὶ τῶν ἀνθρώπων and in Ecclus. even οἱ υἱοὶ τοῦ ἀνθρώπου. On the other hand, the synoptic gospels never use υἱὸς ἀνθρώπου, but always ὁ υἱὸς τοῦ ἀνθρώπου. Other forms like דגברא ברה, דאנשא ברה, and דבר ברה נשא are not found in Jewish writings, but are of Christian origin, being attempts to render the Greek phrase. The only Aramaic term that could have occasioned the unidiomatic ὁ υἱὸς τοῦ ἀνθρώπου is נשא בר. Badham's contention is not strengthened by his interpretation of the gospel passages. Even on the assumption that Jesus regarded himself as the second Adam it must be admitted that the exegesis is often strained and unnatural. But the assumption is extremely difficult. It involves ascribing to him an order of ideas to which he nowhere gives expression in simple and unambiguous language and which seems as much in contrast with his own thought as it is in harmony with later conceptions. Badhams's ingenious endeavor to substitute another Aramaic phrase is no more convincing than Dalman's effort to prove the necessity for another than the ordinary meaning of נשא בר.

Although this term is nowhere found in extant Aramaic literature in any other sense, it has been thought possible that it occurred with a different meaning in the original text of the Parables of Enoch. In 1908,[11] I set forth my reasons for believing that this work was written in Aramaic, and that נשא בר occurred in its earliest form, but only in the ordinary sense. This admirably suits the passages in c. 46: 'I saw one like a man;' 'I asked in regard to that man;' 'he answered: this is the man who has righteousness;' 'this man whom thou hast seen will arouse the kings;' and also 48 2 'in that hour that man was called by the Lord of Spirits.' But it involves the assumption that already the Aramaic text in subsequent

---

[11] 'The Original Language of the Parables of Enoch,' in Old Testament and Semitic Studies in Memory of W. R. Harper, 1908, 329 ff.

sections was tampered with by Christian copyists who introduced the terms ברה דגברא and ברה דבר נשא, and probably,
though perhaps not necessarily, the further assumption that
the Ethiopic text was translated directly from the Aramaic,
for which the utter absence of any sign of acquaintance with
this particular work in patristic literature was cited. Five
years later Charles published an extensive critique of my
position, upholding his former view that the original language
was Hebrew, the term used בן האדם, and the translation in
the supposed Greek version everywhere ὁ υἱὸς τοῦ ἀνθρώπου.
In a study of the Apocalypse of Noah and the Parables of
Enoch contributed to the forthcoming Haupt Memorial Volume,
I have examined in detail the arguments of Charles, showing
that none of the passages quoted presuppose a Hebrew rather
than an Aramaic original, that the only text in patristic
literature (Tertullian, *De cultu feminarum*, 1, 3) cited to prove
acquaintance with the work rather proves the opposite, and
that Christian retouching is obvious in the translation and
probable in the original. It may be added that בן אדם (not בן
האדם) in j. Taanith 65 b has been very satisfactorily explained
by Dalman (*l. c.*, 202 f.), and that Badham also has pointedly
asked "why Justin should not have confuted his Jewish
opponent with the 'son of man' passages if he had known
them," and made some judicious remarks on the subject of
Christian coloring (*l. c.*, 444 f.).

In 4 Ezra 13 1 ff., *quasi similitudinem hominis* and *ille homo*
are also likely to go back to כדמות בר אנש and הו בר נשא.
Wellhausen, who at first was inclined to think of a Hebrew
original (*Skizzen und Vorarbeiten*, VI, 1899, 241), later reached
the conclusion: "Das Original war also jüdisch-aramäisch, wie
das des Enoch." (*Die drei ersten Evangelien*[2], 1911, 124 f.).
This continues to be my conviction even after the arguments
of Box (in Charles, *Apocrypha and Pseudepigrapha of the
O. T.*, 1913). The Syriac version has בר נשא and הו בר נשא,
and the Ethiopic *be'esi*, which may indicate a Greek ὁ ἄνθρωπος. Here, as in En., 'that man' is not a title. It is natural
to suppose an influence of Dan. 7 13. But the man-like being
in En. is not identical with that in Dan., nor is the one in

4 Ezra identical with that in Eth. En. In his excellent outline
of the growth of the messianic idea, Moore rightly observes:
"The 'Son of Man' (in Eth. En.) is not the Messiah pre-
existent in heaven as it is the fashion to say—if that had
been the author's meaning the visions would have read differently."[12] In 4 Ezra 13 1, the one like a man may refer to the
Messiah.

The term ὁ υἱὸς τοῦ ἀνθρώπου is found in all strata of the
gospels, the earlier as well as the later ones. In classifying
the 69 occurrences in the synoptics, obvious duplicates and
passages obelised by critical editors must of course be eliminated. Badham places the distinct sayings in two groups, including in the first group those found in all and also those in
Mt. alone, Mt. and Mk., and Mk. and Lk.; and in the second
those found in Mt. and Lk., but also those in Lk. alone.
Jackson and Lake[13] divide them into four groups: 1. those in
Q, including Mt. 19 28, though the phrase is not found in the
parallel Lk. 22 30, and leaving out Mt. 24 39 = Lk. 17 30;
2. those in Mk., including not only those in all but also those
in Mt. and Mk., and Mk. and Lk.; 3. those in Mt. alone,
leaving out Mt. 26 24 b; and 4. those in Lk. alone. A better
method would seem to be the one I adopted, dividing them
into six groups: 1. those in all (8); 2. in Mt. and Mk. (5);
3. in Mt. and Lk. (8); 4. in Mk. and Lk. (1); 5. in Mt. alone
(9); and 6. in Lk. alone (8). This has been recognized by
Bacon, who follows my tabulation. Jackson and Lake do not
enter into an examination in detail of the later strata, but pay
special attention to Q and Mk.; "for where these agree, if
anywhere, trustworthy information is given." Now in Q there
are four passages referring to the Parousia, and these are
supported by three additional ones in Mk. On the other hand,
there are no passages in Q referring to the Passion. Hence
they infer that the references to the Parousia are earlier than
those to the Passion and more likely to be genuine, as "they

---

[12] In Foakes Jackson and Kirsopp Lake, *The Beginnings of Christianity*,
1922, 346—362.

[13] *The Beginnings of Christianity*, 1922.

are wholly intelligible in the light of contemporary Jewish thought." In them Jesus is understood as speaking objectively concerning the Son of Man, without identifying himself with this personage. There are also two passages in Mk. (2 10, 28) where the phrase is a translation of בר נשא in its generic sense; and one in Q (Mt. 12 31 = Lk. 12 10) where the same is probable, as Mk. 3 28 has 'the sons of men.'

The most important part of the study of these scholars is no doubt the careful reasoning by which they have convinced themselves that the Marcan passages concerning the Passion are late and unauthentic. It is a methodical error to accept both the conclusion that Jesus used, and was understood to mean, בר נשא in its ordinary generic sense and the supposition that it carried a different meaning based on Dalman's conjecture that it was not yet employed and understood in Galilee at the time of Jesus in its generic sense. If the latter were true, the former would be impossible; if the former is true, there is no room for the latter. This applies whether Jesus spoke of himself or concerning some one or some thing else. The idea that he referred, not to himself, but objectively either to his ideal (Brücker, *JPTh* 1886) or to the Coming One (J. Weiss, *Predigt Jesu,* 1892), which has been taken up by Harnack, Heitmüller, Jackson and Lake, Bacon and others, can bring no real relief to those who cling to the thought of a messianic secret cherished by Jesus, if it is admitted that he used the term in its ordinary generic sense, and when it is realized that no evidence has yet been discovered of its employment as a title of the Messiah or of a heavenly being capable of identification with him. It is worth considering also that an unmistakable allusion to the celestial being in Dan. would suggest to his disciples precisely those features of the current messianic ideal, victory and rule over the gentiles, which it is supposed that Jesus wished to remove from their conception of his Messiahship.

Bacon examines in detail the passages in each of the six groups with the result that those in Mt. alone represent changes or expansions made by the evangelist, those in Lk. alone schematic or stylistic improvements, and that in Mk.

and Lk. is not authentic. Of the eight in Q, four, in the eschatological discourse, refer objectively to the Coming One, Jesus intending no identification of himself with this Son of Man; three are suspicious (Mt. 8 20, a proverbial saying, 11 19, unhistorical, 12 40, a misunderstanding); and 12 32 probably shows the generic use of בר נשא. Of those in Mk. seven are regarded as authentic references to the Betrayal and Passion, three objective references to the Coming One, and the rest suspicious, including 2 10, the power to forgive sins, 2 28, authority over the Sabbath, 9 9, transfiguration not to be told until after the resurrection, and 10 45, even the Son of Man came not to be ministered unto. It is not unimportant that so large a number of passages are rejected as due to the evangelists. These were so regarded by many scholars before the last phase of the discussion; and in spite of the reaction against the view based on Aramaic usage it is recognized that the authenticity of about two thirds of the sayings containing the phrase is subject to doubt. While upholding the priority of Q, Bacon attempts, against Jackson and Lake, to render probable the genuineness of the references to the Passion. It is to be noticed also that, though he frankly bases his structure on 'Dalman's proofs,' he nevertheless in one passage resorts to the idea of a בר נשא in the generic sense, which, if Dalman had proved anything, would be impossible. Nor can he quite follow this scholar in his conjecture that the heavenly being that comes on the clouds in Dan. 7 13 "*might* be one who should have passed through suffering and death, and is, in any case, by his very nature no mighty one, no conqueror, no destroyer, but merely a mortal (Menschenkind) whom God has taken under his protection, and for whom he destines great things," though Bacon thinks of him as a "Suppliant before the throne of God." Of all this there is certainly no hint in the text itself. Bacon also makes the concession to Jackson and Lake that "in Mk. no parallel is attempted between Jesus' career and the work and fate of the Isaian 'Servant of Yahwe.'" This weakens the force of his objection to the view of these scholars that it was the actual suffering and death of Jesus that caused the prediction to be put on his lips and transferred the title from the eschatological to the passion series. In Bacon's opinion, Jesus finally identified himself with Daniel's Son of Man and was condemned to death because he declared himself to be the Messiah and predicted that the Sanhedrin would see him sitting on the right hand of power, and coming in the clouds of heaven (Mk. 14 62), which was regarded as blasphemy. In his remarkable book ישו הנו צרי (1922), Klausner also sets forth the view that, in proclaiming himself as the Messiah, Jesus defined his Messiahship by referring to Daniel's Son of Man. Klausner holds that from the beginning of his ministry Jesus thought of himself, not only as a prophet like Ezekiel, but also as a superhuman being, closely related to the deity, like Daniel's Son of Man. The blasphemy consisted in his conception of himself as a Messiah, raised above humanity, and associated with the deity in a manner incompatible with strict monotheism. But what was said in the council chamber is not known; even the Christian witnesses disagree; and none of the disciples was present.

Eduard Meyer[14] does not question that ὁ υἰὸς τοῦ ἀνθρώπου is a translation of בר נשא.[15] He recognizes that the term has its origin, so far as the gospels are concerned, in the eschatological series.[16] He does not ascribe the Synoptic Apocalypse (Mk. 13 and parallels) to Jesus: "es ist ganz klar, daß diese ganze Verkündigung mit dem historischen Jesus nichts zu tun hat, sondern ein Erzeugnis der ersten Generation der Christengemeinde ist, deren Schicksale vorausgesagt werden," perhaps so late as 62 A. D.[17] Whether Jesus spoke of 'the Son of Man' before the High Priest "bleibt mindestens fraglich," since this feature of the confession "trägt die spezifischen Züge der erst nach seinem Tode ausgebildeten christlichen Lehre."[18] Concerning the prediction of the passion he says: "unmöglich ist es, daß Jesus sein Schicksal mit allem Detail vorausgesagt habe, so selbstverständlich es auch nachher

14 *Ursprung und Anfänge des Christentums*, I, 1921; II, 1922.
15 *l. c.*, I, 104.
16 *l. c.*, I, 337.
17 *l. c.*, I, 129 f.
18 *l. c.*, I, 194.

der Christengemeinde erscheinen mußte. Daß ihm dasselbe
Schicksal bevorstehe, wie so vielen Propheten, mochte er
ahnen und aussprechen, die Einzelgestaltung konnte niemand
im voraus wissen."[19] Consequently, he has no confidence in
the genuineness of the bulk of passages in which the term
occurs. There remain then the passages in which it has been
suggested that Jesus originally used בר נשא in the sense it
invariably has in extant Aramaic literature. Here he finds it
'unbegreiflich' that scholars familiar with Aramaic should have
thought it possible that Jesus actually said: "man (בר נשא)
has authority to forgive sins" or "man (בר נשא) is lord of
the Sabbath." Even if it were true that "damit wird eine
philosophische Auffassung hineingetragen, die der Welt des
Judentums wie des Christentums völlig fremd ist und ihren
Begriff der Sünde und der Sündenvergebung geradezu auf-
hebt," such flashes of rare insight, which need not be connected
with any specifically modern philosophical reasoning, are often
characteristic of religious genius. How difficult it would be
to conceive of some ideas and sentiments that seem to us unmistakably expressed in the Book of Job as appearing in any
period of early Jewish history, were the probability of the age
we assign to this work and the accuracy of our modern interpretation to be measured by the generally prevailing views in
Judaism and Christianity! As to the second saying, it is
interesting to observe the different judgment of a man like
Adalbert Merx:[20] "Der Grund für die Tilgung der Worte in
D: 'der Sabbath ist um des Menschen willen gemacht' mit
der daran gehängten Konsequenz, daß der Mensch Herr ist
über den Sabbath, — denn das ist der wahre Sinn, und nicht
etwa der Menschensohn, das bedarf keines Beweises, sondern
ist selbstverständlich, — liegt auf flacher Hand. Mit einem
solchen Prinzip ließ sich ein hierurgischer Kultus weder bei
Juden noch bei Christen aufrecht erhalten. Er war damit
unter die Beurteilung des menschlichen Bewußtseins gestellt,

---

[19] *l. c.*, I, 117.
[20] *Die Evangelien des Markus und Lukas*, 1905, 37; cp. also *Das Evangelium Matthaeus*, 1902, 205.

das der priesterlichen Anforderung gegenüber frei wurde. Solche und ähnliche Prinzipien konnten in der Kirche nicht geduldet werden, sie meistert ihren Meister, indem sie ihn, und nicht etwa den Menschen für den Herrn des Sabbaths erklärt." What is significant in the discussion of this subject by the great Berlin historian is, not his endeavor on the slender basis of a few passages, capable of and fairly demanding a different interpretation, still to maintain the increasingly difficult position of a cryptic Messiahship, involving the occasional, though rare, use by Jesus of the generic term for 'man,' in an esoteric sense, partly to reveal, partly to conceal his somewhat modified Messianic claims, but rather his clear recognition of both the eschatological discourse and the predictions of death and resurrection as products of the Christology of the early church.

Mention should also be made of the ingenious attempt by Bruno Violet[21] to create a new 'son of man' passage. In Mk. 11 14 Jesus says to the figtree: $\mu\eta\kappa\acute{\epsilon}\tau\iota$ $\epsilon\acute{\iota}s$ $\tau\grave{o}\nu$ $a\grave{\iota}\grave{\omega}\nu a$ $\acute{\epsilon}\kappa$ $\sigma o\hat{\upsilon}$ $\mu\eta\delta\epsilon\grave{\iota}s$ $\kappa a\rho\pi\grave{o}\nu$ $\phi\acute{a}\gamma o\iota$. This would imply that he cursed the tree. So it was understood by the scribe who added to the account in Mt. 21 18 ff. the closing words of 19 and 20, not found in Mk. Violet suggests that the Syriac rendering in Peš. need not mean: 'no man *shall* eat,' but may mean: 'no man *will* eat,' and further that in Galilean Aramaic בר נשא may have been used, בר having later dropped out. Taking בר נשא to be Jesus' designation of himself, he then derives this saying: "The Son of Man will never again eat fruits from thee." It is a prediction concerning himself, not a curse of the tree. Jesus is conscious that he is going to his death, and will never again enjoy the fruits of this tree. It is true that the Impf. may mean 'no man will eat.' Merx[22] had already pointed out this possibility, and asked the question whether the story may not be "eine mißverstandene und zur Geschichte umbildete ursprüngliche Parabel." A simpler explanation is

---

[21] In *Forschungen zur Religion und Literatur des Alten und Neuen Testaments*, N. F., XIX, 2.
[22] *Die Evangelien des Markus und Lukas*, 1905, 133.

possible. Jesus is hungry, sees a figtree in the distance, finds
on approaching more closely that it is withered, and remarks:
'no man will ever eat fruits from thee,' reflecting perhaps,
without formulating a parable, on the hopeless condition of his
people. This *obiter dictum,* afterwards remembered, may easily
have been misunderstood and given rise to the idea of a curse
and a selfish, unnecessary and senseless miracle. Whether the
original had אנש אנ, בר אנש, or בר נשא, the meaning would be
the same. But בר נשא is less likely after the negative, and
had it been in the text, it would no doubt have been rendered
ὁ υἱὸς τοῦ ἀνθρώπου and caused no more trouble to a number
of exegetes than in Mk. 2 8 or 2 10.

To most scholars the question whether the references to the
parousia are more genuine than those to the passion seems to
reduce itself to one of the relative age of Q and Mk. If Q is
older, there would be a presumption in favor of the former.
But the problem may not be so simple. Wellhausen argues
for the priority of Mk.; and though Harnack, Heitmüller,
Jülicher (at least so far as Q^1 is concerned), Jackson and
Lake, Bacon and others stress the priority of Q, there is
much disagreement among them. One may, indeed, strongly
maintain the priority of Mk. to our present Mt. and Lk. and
also the posteriority of Mk. to an earlier source or several
such sources without being in sympathy with this or that
theory as regards the degree of Mk.'s originality and the
nature of the earlier source or sources. It is thought by many
scholars that the non-Marcan material found in both Mt. and
Lk. may have been derived from a common source, and it has
become customary to designate it as Q. There can be no
objection to such a *siglum* to indicate this well defined and
available material, if it is deemed desirable. But it should
be borne in mind that the existence of Q as a separate
Greek document is a modern assumption, based on no early
ecclesiastical tradition, and not hinted at either in Mt. or Lk.
It is a supposititious document invented to account for certain
striking similarities between Mt. and Lk. in these sections and
for certain equally striking dissimilarities which appeared to
preclude derivation of one from the other, particularly if the

latter was regarded as coming from an immediate disciple of Jesus. That such a document ever existed can neither be proved nor disproved. Books have been recovered which had apparently left no trace behind them and were unknown even by name; of others only the name has survived; and with many we are acquainted only through obviously very imperfect translations or later versions from these. Nevertheless, such an assumption need not be resorted to, if the facts can equally well be accounted for without it. Is it not conceivable that our present Mt. and Lk. stood in very much the same relation to an earlier form of Mt. as they are assumed to have held to Q? In spite of marked divergencies, the essential identity and, in the main, sequence of sections speak for a common source, the differences being explained as due to the vicissitudes of copying, expansion and contraction, recasting and editorial activity, personal and regional idiosyncrasies of thought, and stylistic preferences. Why should it be considered improbable that the common source was an earlier form of Mt., used with the same freedom both by the later expander and editor of Mt. and by Lk. as is assumed in the case of Q? Harnack[23] has shown that almost invariably the more original form is found in Mt. In the presence of a freely flowing and highly prized oral tradition attaching itself to more than one of the apostles, it is by no means necessary to suppose that one collection, even if ascribed to Matthew, was at all times *maß-gebend.*

When Q is defined as the non-Marcan material common to Mt. and Lk., it should of course be distinguished, not only from Mk., but also from the oldest source, and it should not be pieced out with passages found only in Mt. or only in Lk. Upon this Bacon very justly insists. "The oldest source is not Q," he says. It contained, in his opinion, much beside Q, and Mk. may have used it. That Mk. used this source is indeed highly probable. That he was acquainted with Q is at least incapable of proof, since the Q material is non-Marcan. It is indeed subject to grave doubts. Why should he have so consistently left out all of these

---

[23] *Sprüche und Reden Jesu,* 1907.

statements? The same applies, with equal force, to the assumption that Q was an integral part of the oldest source. What motive can Mk. have had in discarding or passing by in silence everything found in Q? The more one reflects upon this strange procedure, the more plausible it becomes that Mk. did not find the bulk of the Q material in the oldest source. The evidence that he knew and used this earlier source must be looked for chiefly elsewhere. If Mk. is earlier than Q, as Wellhausen thinks, it does not follow that there was not a source earlier than Mk. Mk.'s right to be called the first narrator of the life of Jesus actually known to us need not be questioned, since even if the oldest source had certain headings, introductions, and incidental accounts such as we possess in 'The Words of Amos' and 'The Words of Jeremiah' (⅁), its substance was no doubt a collection of sayings rather than an attempt at a biography. Nor need it be doubted that Mk. furnished the general framework for the later form of Mt. and for Lk. The freedom of Mk.'s gospel from many late elements in the other synoptics is obvious. But the problem of the relative age of Mk. and certain strata in Mt. and Lk. is only confused by the stress laid on manifest accretions, from the infancy stories to the textually doubtful baptismal formula. The right method would seem to be to start with what Mk. has in common with Mt. and Lk. Here such questions as these legitimately arise: Was Mk.'s information derived from a distinct source, so that there was a double tradition, such as Harnack supposes in the case of Mk. and Q? Or does the material in Mt. and Lk. come from Mk.? Or did Mk. use a source also underlying Mt. and Lk.? *A priori* it would be possible to think of two independent strands of tradition, a Petrine and a Matthaean. But it is extremely difficult to conceive of these as running so closely parallel with each other, both in contents and arrangement. A comparison tends to indicate that the more primitive form of a saying is often found in Mt. or Lk. This has been shown by many scholars, notably by Merx,[24] and has again been pointed out

---

[24] *Die vier kanonischen Evangelien*, I, 1902; II, 1905; *passim.*

by those who maintain a pre-Marcan source. The impression has been strengthened by Wellhausen's searching analysis of Mk. and by Bacon's important observations on the advanced position of Mk. on so vital a point as his Christology. It remains most probable that Mk. used an earlier source which to some extent has been preserved in Mt. (and Lk.). This, of course, does not preclude the possibility that many passages now found in all the three gospels were subsequent additions in Mk. which found their way into Mt. and Lk.; or that later additions in Mt. also were incorporated in Mk. and Lk.

The eschatological discourse (Mt. 24, Mk. 13, Lk. 24) may very well be such a later addition, passing from gospel to gospel. Colani (1864) suggested that it is 'a veritable apocalypse,' and Wellhausen (1893) that it came from an originally Jewish apocalypse written just before the fall of Jerusalem. In this apocalypse reference is made (Mk. 13 26 and parallels) objectively to 'the Son of Man.' Wellhausen says: "Nun steht freilich der Vers Mc. 13 26 in einer im Grunde jüdischen Apokalypse, zeigt jedoch den Ausgangspunkt der an Jesus als Menschensohn geknüpften christlichen Parusiehoffnung,"[25] i. e., not the starting point for the hope among the early Christians of the return of Jesus, but for the ascription of this hope to him. It may be added that here also, and not in Q, is likely to be the starting point of the use of ὁ υἱὸς τοῦ ἀνθρώπου as a title and a supposed self-designation. Unfortunately, we do not know how this 'Son of Man' was first introduced in the original apocalypse, whether Jewish or Christian. The first reference may have been similar to that in Dan., Eth. En. and 4 Ezra; or it may, in the original, as Haupt[26] suggests, have had the meaning 'Some One,' the one you know. When this apocalypse was put upon the lips of Jesus, it was evident to all readers that he used it concerning himself; and when the Greek title had once been established as a self-designation, it could then pass to the predictions of his death ascribed to him, and give a new significance to the phrase already used

---

[25] *Die drei ersten Evangelien*[1], 1905, 133.
[26] *The Monist*, 1919, 1 ff.

23*

as a rendering of בר נשא in possibly genuine utterances of
Jesus. Wellhausen's dictum: "Sicher ist, daß, wenn Jesus seine
Jünger nicht zum voraus über seinen Tod und Auferstehung
belehrt hat, so erst recht nicht über seine Parusie"[27] is no
doubt correct historically, but does not show the order in
which this phrase came to be used as a self-designation. A
further indication of the date when this insertion would be
possible may be found in the passage so similar in its tenor
preceding it in Mt. (23 34—38) and split up in Lk. (11 49—51;
13 34—35), with its allusion to the murder of Zechariah b.
Berechiah (Josephus, *Bell. jud.*, IV, 5, 4), if it once formed a
part of the same work. Wellhausen has convincingly shown
that no other Zechariah can be meant, and has set in its right
light the late legend referred to by Moore (*JAOS*, 1906,
317 ff.).[28] That 'The Wisdom of God' is the title of a book
was hinted at by Paulus, van Hengel, Ewald, Bleek, Hilgenfeld, and Gfrörer; that the whole passage belonged to it was
made probable by Strauß (*ZWTh*, 1863, 84 ff.). But the view
that the apocalypse comes from this book, however plausible,
cannot be proved.

Burton[29] distinguishes between four major sources: 1. Mk.;
2. the original Mt. (M); 3. a Galilean source (G); and 4. a
Perean document (P), found in Lk. 9 57—18 14; 19 1—28. In
these sources he gives place to 14 'son of man' passages in
Mk., 6 in M (Mt. 10 23; 13 37, 41; 19 28; 24 30 a; 25 31), 2 in
G (Lk. 6 22; 7 34), and 11 in P (Lk. 9 58; 12 8, 10 a, 40; 11 30;
17 22, 24, 26, 30; 18 8; 19 10). It is interesting to observe that
this eminent New Testament scholar regards 250 verses found
only in Mt. as coming from the *logia* referred to by Papias
so that "the present gospel naturally took the name of that
old document which it alone, of our present gospels at least,
reproduced and of which it might almost be considered only
an enlarged edition."[30] It is also worthy of note that Burton
rejects the hypothesis of Q, and that his G contains only two

[27] *l. c.*[2], 1911, 96.
[28] *l. c.*[2], 1911, 118 ff.
[29] *Principles of Literary Criticism and the Synoptic Problem*, 1904.
[30] *ib.*, 41.

passages referring to the 'son of man,' viz. Lk. 6 22 'for the son of man's sake,' and 7 34 'the son of man is come eating and drinking,' which are both subject to serious doubt. The return to the earliest ecclesiastical tradition seems to be a step in the direction of historic probability, while the abandonment of the theory that the non-Marcan material common to Mt. and Lk. constitutes a distinct document for the assumption of an equally supposititious source G has the disadvantage that its limits must be determined solely by subjective judgment, with the same absence of external testimony. He has been followed in the main by Sharman[31] and Wickes[32]. Sharman, however, either rejects altogether or seriously questions every one of the 'son of man' passages ascribed by Burton to M.[33] Wickes makes a distinction in Burton's P between the material common to Mt. and Lk. and the material not used in Mt. In the part of P regarded by him as Judaean he finds only one 'son of man' passage (19 10). This is loosely attached to what precedes and its character is such that it has long been questioned. None of these scholars seems to have made a special study of the 'son of man' question, or at least taken note of the discussion in their publications. Yet there is an unmistakable tendency on the part of students accepting this new approach to the synoptic problem to eliminate the title entirely from M, G, and the Judaean source in P.

What the earliest source contained can only be a matter of inference and conjecture. Some passages in the so called Q may have had a place in it, though overlooked or intentionally left out by Mk.; some preserved in all three gospels may have formed part of it, others not; some only found in Mt. or Lk. may have been in it. It is by no means improbable that among the sources used by Lk. there was a document not known to either the original Mt. or Mk., and it is possible that it had some such limits as Wickes has conjectured for his second group. In that case Lk. may have dealt with that

[31] *The Teaching of Jesus about the Future according to the Synoptic Gospels*, 1909.
[32] *The Sources of Luke's Perean Section*, 1913.
[33] *l. c.*

source as freely as he apparently did with the earlier form of
Mt. and with Mk. It may also be that he derived this material
from oral tradition on which, like Papias later, he confessedly
leaned to some extent. As to its age and reliability, whether
it came to him in one way or the other, we are obviously
confined to subjective considerations. So far from being able
to say that because a reported saying had a place in the
earliest source it is presumably genuine, we can only conclude
that because of its intrinsic probability it may have belonged
to it, though we cannot be confident even of that. No light is
thrown on its contents by the tradition referred to by Papias.
If, as he avers,[34] Matthew wrote the words of the Lord in the
Hebrew dialect, i. e., in Aramaic, he obviously knew nothing
with certainty concerning this document. Should it ever be
discovered, it would no doubt contain many surprises, and
perhaps raise more questions than it would settle. Even if its
authenticity could be proved, it would still be doubtful whether
it was the first draft or a late copy, and whether the sayings
reported in it were genuine; and behind it would lie oral
tradition with its unavoidable changes.

Even the passages in which Jesus has been supposed to use
the term בר נשא in a generic sense furnish a problem. It
was natural that Bruno Bauer, Volkmar, Jacobsen, Martineau,
Oort, van Manen, Baljou, and Brandt should regard the
Greek term as everywhere a creation of the evangelists. But
Patton[35] has recently taken up the same position, and Bacon
has independently arrived at very nearly the same conclusion
so far as this group is concerned. In regard to Mt. 8 20 and
11 19 I quite agree to-day with Bacon. He has called attention
also to the absence of Mk. 2 27 in D and the minuscules that
go with it. This is important, as D is often relatively free
from interpolations. It should be added that 2 27 a is lacking
in the Sinaitic Syriac; it is also absent in Mt. and Lk. This
weakens the case for 2 28. On the other hand, if 2 27 is an
interpolation, the man who wrote it would seem necessarily to

---

[34] In Eusebius, *Hist. Eccl.*, III, 39.
[35] *American Journal of Religion*, Sept. 1922.

have understood the Greek term as a rendering of בר נשא in its generic sense; and the ὥστε follows more naturally after 2 27, which may have been passed over by D and abbreviated in Sin. Syr. Patton emphasizes the anacoluthon in 2 10 ff. Gen. 3 22—23 has been appealed to as a similar instance; but there we should probably read ונשלחהו for וישלחהו. 'He says to the sick of the palsy' looks like a remark by the evangelist; and in Lk. the people praise God who has given such power to men. In Mt. 12 32 Patton takes umbrage at the distinctively Christian use of the term The Holy Ghost. But the holy spirit is not distinctively Christian, and Bacon's exegesis removes the difficulty. The three passages, Mt. 9 6, 12 8, 32 and parallels, seem to be genuine. They have been interpreted, with rare insight, by Francis A. Henry.[36] The literal unidiomatic translation, reminding of οἱ υἱοὶ τοῦ ἀνθρώπου in Ecclus. may still for some time have conveyed to those who understood Aramaic its original meaning.

Is it possible that the spread of the title from the apocalyptic series to the other groups was facilitated or at least that the common understanding of it in patristic literature can be explained by the Pauline 'second man,' 'last man,' 'man from heaven' or the Gnostic υἱὸς ἀνθρώπου? Moore[37] has shown that there is no evidence of any kind that such terms as 'the last, the second, the coming Adam' were current among Jewish scholars in Palestine as a designation of the Messiah, or ever generally current. The source where Christian scholars have found it, *Neve Shalom,* comes from the end of the 15th century. But the Pauline terms do not give the impression of being innovations by him. It may even be suggested that in 1 Cor. 15 45 a written source is quoted: "And so it is written, the first man Adam was made a living soul; the last man a quickening spirit." Jackson and Lake think that Paul may have disliked the unidiomatic Greek term and translated בר נשא, ὁ ἄνθρωπος. That is improbable. The Gnostic material has been conveniently placed before us by Badham.[38] The

[36] *Jesus and the Christian Religion*[2], 1923, 51 ff.
[37] *JBL*, XVI, 1897, 158.
[38] *l. c.,* 420 ff.

Naasenes, or Ophites, who were a pre-Christian sect, according to Hippolytus "honored as the beginning of all things ἄνθρωπος, 'Man,' and υἱὸς ἀνθρώπου, a 'Son of Man'"; this man is bisexual and is called by them Adam. Irenaeus describes the Ophites as designating the Father of All the first man; and his Idea, ἔννοια, proceeding from him they style Son of Man, the Second Man. Badham questions my inference that both of these terms were used in pre-Christian times, and suggests that the latter was introduced after contact with Christianity. It should be remembered, however, that the necessity for introducing another υἱὸς ἀνθρώπου, son of Yaldabaoth and Achamoth, distinct from the heavenly υἱὸς ἀνθρώπου would not have existed, if there had not been such a prototype in heaven. "Do not lie, Yaldabaoth," says Achamoth; "the Father of All, the first ἄνθρωπος is above thee, and so is ἄνθρωπος, υἱὸς ἀνθρώπου." If there were a Christian contamination, one would expect the article. The two men in the Samothracian mysteries to which the Ophites referred are clearly pre-Christian. When generation is so strongly emphasized, sonship is a natural phrase. The conception of the supreme principle as man may be of mythical or philosophical origin. Reflection on his own nature and meditation on the divine may lead to the idea that what man is in his essence that God is also, and the reverse, hence to consubstantiality, ὁμοουσία, of God and man. This actually took place in India; and it is, therefore, significant that the supreme being, the first principle of the universe, should in the Vedas be called *purusha*, 'man,'[39] and the derived being both *purusha* and

[39] *Rig Veda*, X, 90 (916). Grassmann (*Rig Veda*, II, 1877, 486 f.) regards this hymn as among the latest insertions in the Rig Veda, and relegates it to the *Anhang*. He cites as reasons the apparent references to the Rig-, Sama- and Yajur Vedas and acquaintance with the beginning of the Atharva Veda, the names of the four castes, and the language and character which seem to point to the period of the latest parts of the Atharva Veda. Oldenberg (*Die Religion des Veda*, 1894, 277) recognizes in this hymn describing 'die Entstehung der Menschheit aus dem Leibe des großen tausendfüßigen Urmensch (*purusha*)' 'eine priesterlicherweise schnörkelhaft ausgesponnene, aber möglicherweise uralte Vorstellung.' Obviously *purusha* = man is a

nārāyana, 'son of man.'[40] Here is either an analogy to Gnostic usage, or a borrowing. Chaldaeanism was a syncretistic religion whose elements were not all from ancient Babylonia. Like so many ideas, *e. g.* metempsychosis and atavar, this one may have passed from one end of the world touched by Hellenism to the other. A part of India as well as Phrygia and Babylonia belonged to the Seleucid Empire. But in Babylonian mythology there is also likely to have been a figure spoken of by preference as 'the man.' Gods became men; men became gods. Kristensen[41] thinks the phrase goes back to the Adapa myth. Following Zimmern's suggestion that Adapa = Adam, and that of Jeremias, Zimmern and Winckler that Adapa's designation as *zer ameluti* = בר נשא, he discusses 1) the parallel between Adapa and Adam, 2) the general conception of man in antiquity as one who by virtue of his nature from the beginning has insight into the mysteries of heaven, earth, and the realm below, so that 3) one who in an especial degree possesses this (magician, priest, prophet, king) is in a higher sense than the ordinary a 'man,' a 'son of man,' a typical, ideal *zer ameli* or *sa n si.* This use of the term in a pregnant sense has also been noted by Haupt[42] who calls attention to the fact that *mar ameli* is a gentleman, and בר נשא a man,

designation of the universe, the macrocosm being conceived after the fashion of the microcosm. In X, 90, 5 there seems to be a distinction between purusha, the absolute being, and *purusha* as the first-born. By identification with the Atman in the Upanishads the later conception of the term was developed. Cp. Oldenberg, *Die Lehre der Upanischaden und die Anfänge des Buddhismus,* 1915, *passim.* A special study of this development would be welcome. The distinction between *purusha* and *prakṛti* in the Samkhya and Yoga systems is clearly set forth by Surendranath Dasgupta, *Yoga,* 1925.

[40] Grill (*Untersuchungen über die Entstehung des vierten Evangeliums,* 1902, 348) cites *Māhāna royana Upanishad,* XI, as evidence for the use of *Nārāyana,* 'the one like a man,' 'the son of man' as a designation of *purusha* in the sense of the derived primeval existence. That *Purusha-Nārāyana* is identified with Vishnu does not militate against this. Whether there is a historic connection or not, these Indian speculations correspond with those found in some Gnostic sects.

[41] *Th. Tijdschrift,* 1911, 1 ff.

[42] *The Monist,* 1919, 1 ff.

a noble man, and may be understood as an *exemplar vitae
humanae,* a symbol, *ecce homo!* It is possible, therefore, that
later speculation attached itself to the conception of man in a
pregnant sense, leading even into the realm of mythology; but
a critical examination of the Synoptic material does not justify
the assumption that Jesus himself used the term בר נשא in
any other than the ordinary generic sense.

The impression that meekness and lowliness, modesty and
humility were typical traits in the character of Jesus need not
be given up. There is no necessity for supposing that either
before the episode at Caesarea Philippi or in his last days
Jesus cherished ambitions to lord it over men in one way or
another. Nothing compels the belief that he ever told his
disciples: "Ye shall eat and drink at my table in my kingdom
and sit upon thrones judging the twelve tribes of Israel."[43]
A later scribe, if not Lk., is more likely than the master himself to have picked out prophecies of 'great David's greater
son' in the story of Mephibosheth (2 Sam. 9) and the enthroned
judges of Ps. 122. He may have had his share of erroneous
beliefs and human weaknesses; but there is no evidence that
he surrendered morally, as many others have, to the lure of
kingship, the itch for power over his fellow-men, the passion
for political or spiritual domination. In spite of the growing
idea in the early church that he had not only predicted his
death and resurrection on the third day, but also his return
on the clouds of heaven, clothed with superhuman authority
and dignity, it is permissible to think that he remained faithful unto death, even the death on the cross, to his clearly
expressed convictions, in what may be regarded as genuine
utterances, concerning man's duties, rights, and privileges, his
way of life and service. There is more reverence in honest
doubt than in an easy acceptance of even the salient points in
a late, fluctuating and steadily growing tradition. To remove
the outer wrappings with which loyal love and devout speculation have surrounded him is not to take away from but to
add unto the grandeur and majesty of his personality. These

---

[43] *JBL,* 1922, 182.

garments themselves have had their value, and may in part have been woven with material coming down from primitive times. But the body is more than the raiment. He himself will never be fully known. Each human life has its mystery; it is deepened in the case of a great religious genius. Through ages to come he will, no doubt, remain an object of reverent study. For mankind will not suffer its spiritual heroes to see corruption. In seeking, however, for the permanent place of Jesus in the life of man, students will begin with a quest for the historically probable and learn to free themselves from a mistaken estimate based on questionable data. Without yielding to an unreasonable scepticism that refuses to be guided at all by the only material at our disposal and declines the duty of accounting for its development, without rejecting any part of the tradition simply on the ground that it contravenes an *a priori* judgment of what Jesus could have said and thought concerning himself, without resorting to any but the generally accepted methods of textual, literary and historical criticism, relief from such a conception of the Prophet of Nazareth is still available.

IV

The Two Messiahs

THE MESSIAH OF EPHRAIM AND THE PREMATURE EXODUS OF THE TRIBE OF EPHRAIM

Joseph Heinemann

Department of Hebrew Literature
The Hebrew University, Jerusalem

A considerable number of detailed studies have been devoted to the Messiah of Ephraim (or of Joseph).[1] Among the problems which were raised by scholars are the following: What need was there for the creation of another messianic figure? Why was this second Messiah ascribed to the Joseph tribes in particular? Why and when did the strange motif of the forerunner of the Davidic Messiah, who was doomed to fall in battle, come into being? Does this figure have any connection with the "suffering servant" of Isaiah or, perhaps, with the Christian Messiah, destined to suffer and die?[2]

We must be content with a brief survey of the views of some of the scholars who discussed the topic and who, in turn, quoted and criticised the points made by their predecessors. J. Klausner[3] categorically rejects the claim that the figure of the Messiah who

---

[1] The following abbreviations will be used throughout:
Aptowitzer = V. Aptowitzer, *Parteipolitik der Hasmonäerzeit im rabbinischen und pseudoepigraphischen Schrifttum* (Wien: Kohut-Foundation, 1927).
Dalman = G. H. Dalman, *Der leidende und der sterbende Messias der Synagoge. . .* (Berlin: H. Reuther, 1888).
Ginzberg = L. Ginzberg, "Eine unbekannte jüdische Sekte," *Monatsschrift für Geschichte und Wissenschaft des Judentums* 58 (1914) 159-77, 395-429.
Hurwitz = S. Hurwitz, *Die Gestalt des sterbenden Messias* (Zürich/Stuttgart: Rascher, 1948).
Klausner = J. Klausner, *Die messianischen Vorstellungen des jüdischen Volkes im Zeitalter der Tannaiten* (Berlin: M. Poppelauer, 1904).
Rowley = H. H. Rowley, *The Servant of the Lord and Other Essays on the Old Testament* (London: Lutterworth, 1952) 64ff.
Urbach = E. E. Urbach, *The Sages — Their Concepts and Beliefs* (in Hebrew) (Jerusalem: 1969).

[2] Speculations of this type have already been refuted by Dalman (21f.) and need not concern us any longer; cf. also Rowley, 64f.; Urbach, 619.

[3] Pp. 88-90.

would be killed in battle came into being as a result of the exegesis of Zech 12:10 (and other texts), as Dalman, and others, had proposed;[4] in his opinion, it is not through exegesis that important new ideas or doctrines are created.[5] Nor does he accept the hypothesis of Jacob Levy,[6] that the concept of the Messiah ben Ephraim was created after the failure of the Bar Kokhba revolt in order to make it possible to preserve the messianic faith in spite of this disaster and also in order "to save the honour of R. Akiva," who had publicly proclaimed him the Messiah; by making Bar Kokhba, in the guise of Messiah ben Joseph, the forerunner of the "real" Messiah, his defeat could be accepted without denying his messianic function altogether. Klausner rejects this "rationalistic" view, because "articles of creed" are not created intentionally *ad hoc*, but originate in "deep inner needs" of the people. Moreover, the disappointment after Bar Kokhba's defeat was so immense, as to make it inconceivable that the people (or the sages) should have continued to look upon him as a genuine messianic figure; and, indeed, there is no indication that this was the case. Besides, why should Bar Kokhba be considered a "son of Joseph"?[7]

Klausner himself lays down, first of all, that the earliest datable sources for the concept of the Messiah ben Joseph (B. T. Sukkah 52 a), though tannaitic, need not be earlier than the post-Hadrianic period.[8] He believes the idea of the second, militant Messiah to have come into being, because after the shock caused by the

---

[4] Dalman, 17-18.

[5] I do not accept the general validity of this principle of Klausner, but in this particular case he would seem to be right, if only because the verse in question does not appear to supply the materials necessary for the creation of the legend of the Messiah ben Joseph who will fall in battle.

[6] *Wörterbuch über die Talmudim und Midraschim* (2d ed.; Leipzig: Brockhaus, 1924) *s.v.* מָשִׁיחַ (3. 271); a similar view had already been put forward by Hamburger, cf. Dalman, 21.

[7] We need not discuss the various theories which hold that the figure of the Messiah ben Ephraim had its origin in the Northern Kingdom; for not only is there no evidence whatsoever to support it, but even if there had been such a doctrine prior to the destruction of the Israelite Kingdom, it is impossible to explain its revival in the second century c.e.; cf. Klausner, 90f; Rowley, 69f.; Hurwitz, 171, 180.

[8] Ginsberg (416 n. 2) holds that the R. Dosa mentioned in B. T. *Sukkah* may not be a Tanna at all, but an Amora; but since one of the two sources concerning the Messiah ben Joseph (ibid.) is undoubtedly a *baraita*, this does not alter the position that the motif of the Messiah

destruction of the Temple and the defeat of Bar Kokhba the belief in the "double nature" of the Messiah, incorporating both ideal, spiritual features and military prowess, could no longer be tolerated; hence it was split into the "double Messiah." The second figure, who became the messianic warrior, freed the Messiah ben David of all jarring features. If a second Messiah was postulated, it was obvious, according to Klausner, that he had to be ascribed to Ephraim or Joseph; for only two tribes — Judah and Joseph — had played the part of leaders and rulers in the past. That this additional Messiah would fall in battle was a necessary corollary; for any idea of a possible rivalry between the two Messiahs in the end of the days had to be ruled out.

While a good deal of Klausner's criticism of his predecessors is valid, his own theory is undoubtedly weak and unconvincing. Aptowitzer[9] already made some substantial points against Klausner's argument: if the idea of a militant Messiah had become repugnant, why not abandon it altogether and ascribe the destruction of the nations in the end of the days to God Himself? And why did this additional Messiah have to be of Ephraim, since there were in existence also messianic figures from other tribes?[10] Moreover, the figure of the Messiah of Joseph was undoubtedly the object of hopes and expectations; hence it must have come into being prior to the crushing of all hopes of redemption by military means in consequence of the failure of the Bar Kokhba revolt.

Ginzberg[11] takes the view that the "enigmatic figure" of the Messiah ben Joseph owes its existence, like so many other motifs of Rabbinic eschatology, to the "parallelizing" of the future and the past. The tradition of the premature Exodus of the tribe of Ephraim — which we shall discuss presently — provides the only answer to the question regarding the origin of the Messiah ben Ephraim. Just as in the great salvation of the past a leader of the tribe of Ephraim attempted to bring about the redemption through military action, before the appearance of the truè saviour, Moses, so it is bound to happen in the future, when the military activities of the Messiah ben Ephraim will precede and herald the appear-

---

ben Joseph who is killed is no later than the end of the second century. How much earlier it may be, the sources do not tell us; but see below.

[9] Pp. 105ff.
[10] Especially of Levi; cf. below.
[11] Pp. 414ff.

ance of the Messiah ben David, through whom full redemption will be accomplished. Again Aptowitzer[12] offers some pertinent criticism of this view: The premature Exodus of Ephraim is considered an act of rebellion and of lack of faith, and because of this it ended in total catastrophe; so why project this event into the messianic era? The technique of "analogy," on which Ginzberg bases his argument, is applied only to miracles and the like, not to events which are given a negative evaluation. There is no sign whatsoever in any of the sources of a negative attitude towards the Messiah ben Joseph; on the contrary, he is an object of promise and hope, as e.g. in the statement recurring frequently: "It is an aggadic tradition that Esau will fall by the hands of the sons of Rachel" (Gen. Rabba LXX 5 and parallels; we shall return to this text presently).

While Aptowitzer's own theory is unacceptable, if only because he connects, quite arbitrarily, the creation of the motif of the Messiah ben Joseph with the polemics regarding the usurpation of the monarchy by the Hasmoneans,[13] it is hardly possible to claim that the problem has been solved satisfactorily by any of his predecessors, nor, indeed, by any of the scholars who have dealt with it since.[14] There is a need for a re-examination of the matter, not only because of the insufficiency of all the theories offered so far, but also because the material from Qumran has, to some extent, changed our perspective in the matter of Jewish messianic beliefs around the beginning of the Christian era. While Ginzberg in his essay, published in 1914, which was devoted to the examination of the "Damascus Covenant" — and in which, remarkably enough, he reached the conclusion that this latter was a sectarian document dating from the Hasmonean period — could still argue that there is no sufficient evidence for assuming a belief in two Messiahs, of Judah and of Levi (or Aaron) respectively,[15] to have been prevalent, we know today that the Qumran sect, at least, did expect the coming of the "Messiahs of Aaron and of Israel" (Man. of Discipline IX.11). Hence we have no longer any reason to doubt

---

[12] Pp. 108f.

[13] Cf. A. Marmorstein's detailed review of Aptowitzer's book in *Monatsschrift für Geschichte und Wissenschaft des Judentums* 73 (1929) 244-50, 478-87.

[14] Cf. the summing-up and criticism of recent views: Rowley, 64ff.; Hurwitz, 172ff.

[15] *Sic!* (403f.; 411); and not as stated erroneously by N. Wieder, *JJS* 6 (1955) 14, and by Hurwitz, 196.

evidence to the same effect found in the Testaments of the Patri-archs.[16] Moreover, other messianic figures, such as Melchizedek, are seen to emerge.[17] And while we can not accept Aptowitzer's *idee fixe* of the Hasmonean polemics as the sole and complete explanation of all phenomena, he did adduce considerable evidence that there were yet other messianic figures, as e.g. Elijah (identified at times with Phineas).[18] We need not, therefore, any longer be astonished by the very existence of the Messiah ben Joseph, apart from and besides the Messiah ben David; this is neither an "enig-ma" nor "a curious aberration,"[19] but merely one of many messianic figures which were in existence in the pre-Christian or early Chris-tian era. The question: How did the second messianic figure come into being? need hardly trouble us any longer, but rather the question: How — and when — did it acquire its peculiar feature, viz. that of a Messiah doomed to die in battle?

The only scholar to date to evaluate the figure of the Messiah ben Joseph in the light of the multiplicity of Messiahs in the late Second Temple period, Hurwitz,[20] accepts the argument of Klaus-ner concerning a "splitting" of the messianic figure, but denies that such a split could be due to mere external, historical events; it must of necessity reflect some deep-seated religious-psychological change, related to an "archetypal" background. This "split" he finds expressed not only in the talmudic-midrashic duality of the Davidic and Ephraimite Messiahs, but also in the "Messiahs of Aaron and Israel" of Qumran (and the Testaments of the Tribes). But it remains quite incomprehensible, why the deep-seated psy-chological change, which brought about the split, should in the one case have led to the creation of a priestly Messiah, but in the other to that of a "hero-Messiah." Nor is there any explanation of the fact, that the militant Messiah should come from the tribe of Joseph, and certainly none, why he — but not one of the two

[16] Cf. Aptowitzer, ibid.; Ginzberg, 402ff.; Hurwitz, 194ff.; also N. Wieder, *JJS* 4 (1953) 168, n. 2; 6 (1955) 14f., 24; K. G. Kuhn, "The Two Messiahs of Aaron and Israel," *The Scrolls and the New Testament* (ed. K. Stendahl; New York: Harper & Brothers, 1957) 54ff.; K. Schubert, *Jud* 11 (1955) 216f., 226f.; J. Liver, *HTR* 52 (1959) 149ff.

[17] Cf., e.g., A. S. van der Woude, in *OTS* 14 (1965); R. Meyer in *Volume du congrès international pour l'étude de l'Ancien Testament* (Genève: 1965); J. A. Fitzmyer, "Further Light on Melchizedek from Qumran Cave 11," *JBL* 86 (1967) 25-41.

[18] Aptowitzer, ibid.; cf. also Dalman, 8f.

[19] As G. F. Moore, *Judaism* (Cambridge: Harvard University, 1946) 2. 370, puts it.

[20] Pp. 193ff.

"split" Messiahs of Qumran — must die. Moreover, as we have pointed out already, the evidence suggests not "duality" of Messiahs, but multiplicity; nor does it seem, in view of this evidence, that we can assert with assurance that "originally" there was only one single messianic figure.[21] On the contrary, we gain the impression that in Second Temple times great diversity of messianic doctrines and variety of messianic figures were prevalent.

Furthermore, all scholars who have studied the problem of the Messiah ben Joseph appear to have overlooked a decisive aspect of the evidence in the sources themselves: that only some of the latter speak of the violent death of this Messiah, while others do not mention his tragic end at all and, hence, presumably know nothing of it. If the death in battle of the Messiah ben Joseph was a generally accepted doctrine, it is quite inconceivable that a good many of the sources should ignore it; this is not the sort of "detail" which may accidentally be omitted. We must therefore assume that the motif of the Messiah ben Joseph underwent, at some time, a radical transformation; and there can be no doubt that, if we know this legend in two versions, one of which tells only of the militant, victorious Messiah, while the other adds his death in battle, the one relating his tragic end must be the later one. Those sources which know nothing of the failure and death of this Messiah must reflect an earlier tradition, irrespective of the dates of the literary works in which they appear. And the entire question of the origin of the legend appears in a different perspective, once it is realized that we must account for two separate stages in its development: the creation of the figure of the militant Messiah as such and his subsequent transmutation into the "dying Messiah."

Apart from the two passages in B. T. Sukkah 52a, which speak of the death of the Messiah ben Joseph, his end in battle features prominently also in the "Tosephta"-Targum on Zech 12:10;[22] in addition, it occurs in most of the late medieval "minor" Midrashim, quoted at length in the various studies.[23] But against this must be balanced the following sources: The exposition of the vision of the "four craftsmen" (Zech 2:3f),.which speaks — in different ver-

---

[21] This arbitrary assumption is shared by practically all scholars; cf. especially Klausner, 94f.

[22] Quoter by A. Sperber, *The Bible in Aramaic* (Leiden: Brill, 1962), 3. 495.

[23] E.g., Dalman, 10f.

sions[24] — of either the "Messiah ben Joseph" or of the "Anointed for War," who is undoubtedly identical with the former,[25] but makes no reference to his death.[26] In addition we have several references in the Palestinian Targumim, which, it is generally held today, reflect, at least at times, very early material, viz. Pseudo-Jonathan on Ex 40:11, which speaks of the Messiah ben Eph-raim[27] "through whom the House of Israel will defeat Gog and his associates in the end of the days" and the Targum of Cant. 4.5 and 7.4, which speaks of "two redeemers who will redeem you in the future, the Messiah ben David and the Messiah ben Ephraim." Similar references to the two Messiahs are found in Midrash Psalms 87.6; Tanhuma, ed. Buber I. p. 205, and in a good many of the minor Midrashim. Moreover, there is a whole series of sources to be found in the earliest Midrashim which, though they do not mention the Messiah ben Joseph by name, undoubtedly refer to him, but, again, never to his death: "By whose hand will the kingdom of Edom fall? by the hand of the Anointed for War who will be descended of Joseph. R. Phineas in the name of R. Samuel b. Nahman: It is a tradition that Esau will fall only by the hand of the sons of Rachel, as it is said 'Surely the least (lit. youngest) of the flock shall drag them away' (Jer 49:20); why are they called 'the youngest of the flock'? Because they are the youngest of the tribes (i.e. Jacob's sons)" (Gen. Rabba XCIX; ed. Theodor-Albeck, p. 1274).[28] In Gen. Rabba LXXV.5 (ibid., p. 883) the statement of R. Samuel b. Nahman is preceded by an exposition of Gen 32:5: "'I have sojourned with Laban and stayed until now' — why 'stayed (lit. delayed) until now'? Because Esau's adversary had not yet been born;" while ibid. 6 (ibid. p. 892) the following verse "And I have oxen and asses" (in Hebrew in the — collective — singular) is interpreted: "'Ox' — this is

---

[24] B. T. Sukkah 52b; Pesiqta de Rav Kahana V (ed. Buber, 51a); Pesiqta Rabbati XV (ed. Friedmann, 75a); Cant. Rabba on 2.13; Num. Rabba XIV.1; cf. also Ginzberg, 418f. It is noteworthy that the Munich MS of the Babylonian Talmud has Melchizedek instead of "Kohen Zedeq," cf. R. Rabbinovicz, Variae Lectiones III (Munich: 1870) 170.

[25] Cf. Ginzberg, 421; Dalman, 6f.

[26] The author of this exposition is Shime'on Hasida who, apparently, is a Tanna; cf. Ginzberg, 418 n. 1.

[27] Only this designation is found in all targumic sources.

[28] The latter part of this exposition recurs also in Gen. Rabba LXXIII.7 (ed. Theodor-Albeck, 851, where all parallel passages in which this saying occurs — with only minor variations — are listed in the apparatus).

the Anointed for War, as it is said 'His firstling ox, majesty is his' (Deut 33:17), 'ass' — this is the King Messiah, as it is said 'Lowly, and riding upon an ass'" (Zech 9:9).[29] All the above are comparatively early Midrashic sources; what is more, the third-century R. Samuel b. Nahman already speaks of an "aggadic tradition."[30] But in any case it is obvious, as stated before, that of the two versions the one which does not know of the death of Messiah ben Joseph must be the more ancient one; for it is inconceivable that the death in battle of the Messiah, once maintained, could be quietly ignored subsequently.[31]

Strange as it may seem that all scholars should have failed to read correctly this series of statements and expositions concerning the Messiah ben Joseph,[32] the explanation lies probably in a kind of "optical illusion" which makes one see what is said explicitly in some of the sources also in the ones which know nothing of it. Moreover the illusion was probably fostered by the fact that the Babylonian Talmud is far more familiar to most Jewish scholars than the Palestinian — midrashic or targumic — sources, and the latter are often unconsciously interpreted in the light of the former.

While the existence of the Messiah ben Joseph as such is no harder to accept than that of various other Messiah figures, all known at one and the same time, the crucial problem now is the radical transformation of this legend: when and why was this Messiah sentenced to die? There is every reason to believe that the figure of the victorious warrior Messiah must be pre-Hadrianic, as pointed out by Aptowitzer, whereas it seems extremely likely that its transformation did not occur until after the defeat of Bar Kokhba. Obviously, we must look for a dramatic, even traumatic

---

[29] Cf. also *Tanḥuma* (ed. Buber), 1. 154 and 179.

[30] Cf W. Bacher, *Die exegetische Terminologie der jüdischen Traditionsliteratur* (Leipzig: Hinrichs, 1899), 1. 107f., and 2 (1905) 115.

[31] Nevertheless, teachers of the third century and after faithfully continue to transmit the older version as they received it, even though they must already have been aware of the new conception of the death of Messiah ben Ephraim.

[32] Klausner does not refer to most of this material at all, because he expressly (Introduction, III) limits himself to "Tannaitic material." Others, however, including Dalman and Ginzberg, quote these sources at length. Strangest of all is the case of Aptowitzer, who bases on these very texts his argument against Ginzberg that the Messiah ben Joseph was the object of promises and hopes, without realizing that these sources do not speak of a "dying Messiah" at all.

event to account for this transfiguration of the legend; and no other would supply as likely a cause for the creation of the new version as the defeat and death of Bar Kokhba. Hence J. Levy's theory now appears doubly convincing (especially as his opponents, too, point to the same period of time for the creation of the motif of the dying Messiah).[33] As regards the argument that there is nothing to suggest that Bar Kokhba was still believed to have been a genuine Messianic figure even after his death, it must be stated, first of all, that the midrashic-talmudic sources on this matter are so meagre, as to deprive the *argumentum ex silentio* of any force whatsoever. As regards the use of the name Bar Koziba or Bar Kozba in those sources,[34] this can no longer be held to indicate a derogatory attitude, but is, apparently, merely a variant spelling of his actual name Bar Kosba, now known to us from his letters. And, if we must try to settle the issue by mere speculation, it would seem most unlikely, indeed, that the great leader who for years had led his people in the war against Rome, who had been proclaimed the Messiah by R. Akivah and eventually died a hero's death, should be considered a fraud and a swindler by his former adherents immediately upon his death. Moreover, the Rabbis of the post-Hadrianic generation, who were all, to some degree, disciples of R. Akivah, would hardly have imputed such a gigantic fraud to their master after his martyrdom. On the contrary, this generation must have attempted, by hook or by crook, to achieve the impossible: to uphold Bar Kokhba's messianity in spite of his failure. This paradoxical position could find no more suitable expression than in the highly ambivalent legend of the militant Messiah who is doomed to fall in battle, and yet remains a genuine redeemer, the forerunner of another Messiah who will follow him and complete his mission. The very absurdity of this legend as well as the astounding fact that the Messiah ben Joseph, at first considered victorious, is suddenly transformed into a figure of tragedy, are, in themselves, evidence of an extraordinary situation which gave rise to this self-contradictory conception. Moreover, we shall presently adduce another legend, which similarly attests a highly complex, ambivalent attitude towards the revolt and its failure on the part of

[33] As, e.g., Klausner, cf. above.
[34] E.g., *Lam. Rabba* on 2.2 (ed. Buber, 101f). *P. T. Taᶜan.* IV. 8, 68d; cf. Ginzberg, 415 n. 4; W. Bacher, *Die Agada der Tannaiten* (Strassburg: 1903) 1. 284 n. 3; Str-B 1 (1922) 13.

the generation following it. As the question before us is no longer: Why was the figure of Messiah ben Joseph created?, but: Why was it transformed suddenly into a tragic hero?, we can answer unhesitatingly, that this *volte-face* can reflect no situation other than that in which Bar Kokhba's former supporters found themselves following his defeat.

One problem, however, still needs consideration: what possible connection could there be between Bar Kokhba and the tribe of Joseph or Ephraim? For if the legend about Messiah ben Joseph, after its metamorphosis, was supposed to refer to him, we must be able to account for the association of Bar Kokhba with Ephraim in the consciousness of the ordinary people, for whose sake such legends were created and for whose guidance they were presented in public sermons. This missing link may be provided by the story of the premature Exodus of the sons of Ephraim, a legend which underwent a no less startling and equally revealing transformation at just about the same time.

II.

The story of the Exodus of the Ephraimites, which ended in their being slain in battle by the Philistines, is referred to in the Mekhilta and by Rav in the Babylonian Talmud;[35] but in full dramatic detail it appears in the Palestinian Targumim on Ex 13:17, on Ez 37 and also, more briefly, on Ps 78:9 and 1 Chr 7:20f. The recurrence of the story in so many different targumic passages makes it probable that the legend originally belonged to the targumic tradition, whence it was eventually taken over by the Rabbis. Moreover, the story occurs in a great variety of styles in the different Targum passages as well as in different versions of the Targum to one and the same passage;[36] this again strongly suggests that it was a favourite of the Targumists and used by them frequently. The legend appears to have come into being in the first place through an attempt to make intelligible several obscure Bible passages, especially Ps 78:9 and 1 Chr 7:20f.;[37] by means of

[35] *Mekhilta Beshallaḥ*, beginning (ed. Horovitz-Rabin, 75f.); *B. T. Sanh.* 92b.

[36] Pseudo Jonathan on Ex 13:17 (ed. Ginsburger, 121); *Das Fragmententhargum*, ed. Ginsburger, 31); *Maḥsor Vitry* (ed. Hurwitz, 305); Targum on Ez 37, ibid., 167; Targum on Ez 37 (ed. A. Díez Macho) *Bib* 39 (1958) 201f.

[37] It is no concern of ours here, which ancient and, apparently, long forgotten events these Bible passages may have referred to originally;

"synoptic exegesis" these two passages were made to throw light on, and complement, one another and were built up into a complete and satisfactory narrative. The story obtained in this process was, in turn, found suitable to illuminate yet another difficult verse in Ex 13:17, stating that God did not lead the Israelites by the way of the land of the Philistines "because (sic! in literal translation) that was near . . . lest the people repent when they see war . . .," which could now be explained to mean that the disastrous defeat of the Ephraimites was still "near" (recent) and the people would be deeply shocked and utterly disheartened, when they would be confronted with the bones of their brethren strewn in the fields of Philistia (Mekhilta ibid.). It would seem that the original version of this legend considered the premature Exodus to have been an act of rebellion, stemming from pride and unwillingness to wait for the divine act of redemption: "They kept not the covenant of God, and refused to walk in His law" (Ps 78:10), on which the Mekhilta (ibid.) comments: "They transgressed the appointed time and the oath"; while the Targumim tell that "they prided themselves (to go out) without the salvation of God" and that "they went out (relying) on their own strength and did not wait for the appointed time."[38] However, while these versions unequivocally condemn the act of the Ephraimites, other sources speak of "an error in calculating the end," which caused them to believe that "the end" had come 30 years before the real Exodus.[39] This is based on a contradiction in Scripture between the 400 years of servitude foretold in the "Covenant between the pieces" (Gen 15:13) and the 430 years spoken of in Ex 12:40. This difficulty is solved by assuming that 430 years did, indeed, pass between the Covenant and the Exodus, while the 400 years "that thy seed . . . shall serve them" were to be counted from the birth of Isaac.[40] The Ephraimites, however, counted the 400 years from

---

cf. S. Krauss, *Wiener Zeitschrift f. d. Kunde des Morgenlandes* 38 (1931) 76ff. Krauss's reconstruction of these events on the strength of the versions of this Aggadah, preserved in the latest(!), medieval Midrashim, appears, to say the least, highly questionable.

[38] *Maḥsor Vitry*, 167; "בכוהון" in Hurwitz' edition is an error; the MS has "בכוחהון."

[39] Pseudo-Jonathan on Ex 13:17; *Fragmententhargum*, ibid.; Targum on 1 Chr 7:20f.; Targum on Ps 78:9; Díez Macho, ibid.; cf. also *Cant. Rabba* on 2.7.

[40] Cf. *Mekhilta Bo, Tract. Pasḥa* (ed. Horovitz-Rabin) 50, and the parallels listed there in the apparatus.

the time of the Covenant itself; this error led to their tragic end. In this version, then, they are no longer arrogant rebels, but are guilty only of "calculating the end" — wrongly and disastrously.

In the main, the legend of the premature Exodus would seem to have been inspired by the urge to explain, and harmonize with one another, a series of difficult Bible passages, even though it does, of course, hold up the Epraimite Exodus as a warning either to those who "force the end" or, alternatively, to those who "calculate the end."[41] Various details of the story, peculiar to the targumic tradition, also appear to be the result of a certain technique of interpretation, which draws information from other passages on the strength of verbal analogy. Thus we are told that the Ephraimites numbered 200,000 "mighty men of valour"; and among their armour are mentioned not only the bows of Ps 78:9, but also shields.[42] These details can have been taken only from 2 Chr 17:16-17: ". . . two hundred thousand mighty men of valour . . . armed with bow and shield"; for although this passage refers to military units in the days of Jehoshafat, it has in common with Ps 78:9 the expression "nosheqey qeshet" (which occurs nowhere else).[43]

While the versions of the legend referred to so far may be considered, first and foremost, the result of "creative philology"[44] and of harmonizing exegesis, there is yet another version, so unexpected and, at the same time, so self-contradictory, as to make it certain that it did not originate merely in naive exegesis, but must have been the result of some definite Tendenz. Here the story as above is followed by an additional part: those same Ephraimites who were massacred by the Philistines and whose bones were left scattered in the fields are the dead revived by Ezekiel in the vision

[41] On these categories cf., e.g., B. T. Sanh. 97b and Cant. Rabba on 2.7; see also Urbach, 601ff., 611.

[42] Pseudo-Jonathan and Fragmententhargum, ibid.

[43] Hence those versions of the legend which have numbers other than 200,000 "men of valour" are faulty; cf. Targum on Ez 37 (ed. A. Díez Macho); Pesiqta de Rav Kahana X (ed. Buber, 85a-b); Midrash Or Ha-Afelah (unpublished; quoted by M. Kasher, Torah Shelemah on Ex 13:17). The same applies, of course, to those versions where the error in calculation is not given as 30 years but as 80 years, cf. Pesiqta d. R. K., ibid.

[44] Cf. I. Heinemann, Darkey Ha-Aggadah (Jerusalem: 1950) 6f. and passim.

of the dry bones (Ez 37)![45] The two parts of this composite version express exactly opposite attitudes: while in the first one the Exodus of the sons of Ephraim is considered sinful and, inevitably, resulted in their defeat and death, the second one considers them worthy of a special, "private" re-surrection; hence, in spite of their sin (or error), they must be essentially righteous men, who deserve a miracle such as this, which annulls, in effect, their punishment by restoring them to life. This ingenious re-interpretation of the story — which, incidentally, also offers a solution to another vexatious problem, viz.: who, in fact, were the dead revived by Ezekiel? — must be an indication of a radical change of attitude towards the tendency of the original legend. Far from being the object of derision or condemnation, the Ephraimites now evoke sympathy and are "rehabilitated." But as the first part of the narrative remains unchanged, the addition to it of the re-surrection motif expresses, in fact, if not a contradictory, at least a complex and ambivalent attitude.

In order to evaluate the reason for this radical re-shaping of the story and the change of attitude underlying it, we must attempt to establish some chronological data. The original legend, without the sequel from Ezekiel, is known to the Mekhilta,[46] one of the tannaitic Midrashim; hence it cannot be later than the end of the second century c.e., but may, of course, be earlier. In fact, we must date it at least one generation before the end of the tannaitic period, because the Mekhilta does not actually recount the story, as stated before, but refers to it as well-known; besides, if we are right in assuming that the tale originated in the targumic tradition, some time must be allowed until it would be taken over by the Rabbis for their purposes. The new version, telling of the re-surrection of the Ephraimites, was already known to Rav, the Babylonian Amora, in the first half of the third century. However, he is certainly not its author, for he merely mentions it apropos a discussion on the question, who were the dead revived by Ezekiel. Hence we must postulate in this case, too, that the creation of this new version cannot be later than the last generation

---

[45] Pseudo-Jonathan and *Fragmententhargum*, ibid.; *Maḥsor Vitry*, 167; Díez Macho, ibid.; *B. T. Sanh.* 92b.

[46] In addition, the legend in its original form, without the sequel from Ez 37, has been preserved also in the following sources: Targum on Ps 78:9; Targum on 1 Chr 7:20f.; *Cant. Rabba* on 2.7; *Ex. Rabba* XX.11; *Pirkey R. Eliezer* XLVIII; *Sefer Ha–Yashar*.

of the Tanna'im, around the turn of the second century. In view
of these data it becomes extremely likely that the transformation
of the story through the re-surrection motif must have some connection with the Bar Kokhba revolt. For it is impossible psychologically to ascribe the creation of the original version to the
Tanna'im of the second half of the second century, i.e. to the very
generation who had witnessed the failure of the revolt. We cannot possibly hold this generation responsible for the creation of a
legend, which could have meant, at that particular time and in this
particular situation, only one thing: an out-and-out condemnation
of the rising of Bar Kokhba as an act of arrogance and rebellion
against God, which was punished, rightly, by the total extermination of all concerned. Whatever the attitude of this generation to
Bar Kokhba (and, by implication, to R. Akivah!) may have been,
it cannot have been one of complacent, righteous condemnation.
Hence we are forced to advance the date of the genesis of the
original legend; it must have antedated the Bar Kokhba revolt.
But in the eyes of the generation who had witnessed the disastrous
defeat and had seen "the fallen of Bethar to whom no burial was
given,"[47] the story of the Exodus of Ephraim must have suddenly
acquired a terrible new meaning; it must have seemed to them to
mirror uncannily the events of their own times. However, the
implication that the fate of Ephraim, i.e. of Bar Kokhba and his
followers, was but what they had deserved, because of their over-
bearing pride and presumption, was utterly unacceptable to the
survivors of the revolt. Hence the imperative need to change the
tendency of the legend. Some, apparently, were satisfied with
changing one detail only: the Ephraimites had not been guilty of
rebellion against the will of God, but merely of a tragic error.
Others found a more radical solution: in spite of their transgression and inevitable failure, the Ephraimites had been possessed
by a burning, irresistible desire for redemption, for which they had
sacrificed their lives. Those who had not been satisfied to wait
for salvation, but had taken it into their own hands and attempted
to bring it about before its time, were sinners and deserved their
punishment; yet, at the same time, they were also a shining example
of self-sacrifice and deserving, if not of reward, at least of compensation. And this compensation, most fittingly, takes the form of

[47] P. T. Berakhot I.8, 3d.

the re-surrection before its time of those who died in order to bring about redemption before its time.

Bar Kokhba was not an Ephraimite. But in the legend of the Ephraimite Exodus, his contemporaries, after his defeat, must have found reflected the events of their own time. Thus Bar Kokhba became associated with Ephraim; and it was no longer difficult to take a further step and look upon him as the Messiah of Ephraim. However, both these legends required radical transformation to fit the contemporary situation: the Messiah of Ephraim had to fall in battle; yet the Ephraimites and their leader who had been slain, were held worthy of re-surrection.

THE DOCTRINE OF THE TWO MESSIAHS IN SECTARIAN LITERATURE IN THE TIME OF THE SECOND COMMONWEALTH *

J. LIVER

HEBREW UNIVERSITY, JERUSALEM

I

THE problem of the two Messiahs in Apocryphal literature, especially in the Testaments of the Twelve Patriarchs and in the Damascus Covenant, occupied scholars at the beginning of the present century and has revealed new facets with the discovery of the Dead Sea Scrolls. Especially pertinent to this problem are some of the texts from Qumran Cave 1, and some fragments from Qumran Cave 4, recently published. We shall here endeavor to make clear the distinctive features of these Messiahs, their status and their tasks at the end of days, and to elucidate the historical setting from which the doctrine of the two Messiahs sprang.

Scholars differ as to the time when the scrolls were composed, and they differ even more on the Pseudepigrapha. The greater difficulty in dating the latter is due to their archaizing character and the intentionally obscure way in which the various authors refer to the events of their own age. But there is considerable similarity in ideas, concepts and terminology between some of the Pseudepigrapha — the Ethiopic Enoch, The Book of Jubilees and the Testaments of the Patriarchs — and the Dead Sea Scrolls;[1] fragments from these books were found, together with sectarian writings proper, in the Qumran Caves.[2] We may therefore assume with great probability that, even if these books do not actually belong to the writings of the Qumran Sect, they originated in

* I wish to express my thanks to Dr. D. Flusser, Dr. J. Licht, Mr. S. Safrai and Mr. M. Stern, all of the Hebrew University, who have read the manuscript and given me their advice.

[1] Cf. J. M. Grintz, Sinai 32, 1953, pp. 11 ff., 27 ff. (Hebrew); R. Marcus, The Qumran Scrolls and Early Judaism, Biblical Research, 1, 1952, pp. 12–17.

[2] Cf. Barthélemy — Milik, Qumran Cave 1, Oxford, 1955, pp. 46, 82–91; J. T. Milik, Le Testament de Levi en Araméen, RB, 62, 1955, pp. 398–406; and also RB, 63 (1956), pp. 49–67.

closely related circles [3] and were roughly contemporary with the Sect.

The period in which the Dead Sea Scrolls were composed can be determined from the historical hints contained in the Damascus Covenant [4] and the Sectarian Commentaries, especially the Nahum Commentary: these point quite clearly to the troubled days of Alexander Jannaeus.[5] We may therefore regard the reign of John Hyrcanus I, which preceded his, as the period in which the Sect already took shape and finally separated from the general body of the nation. In this essay I shall show that the historical and social background of the doctrine of the two Messiahs — one a priest and the other a prince or king — must be sought in the Qumran Sect and the Hasmonean period. The fact that we find this doctrine clearly stated in sectarian writings which have reached us in their original form also calls for a thorough examination of the problem of the two Messiahs in the Testaments of the Twelve Patriarchs.

II

From the scrolls so far published, we cannot decide whether the Qumran Sect hoped for a redeeming Messiah or not. However, in matters of salvation as in other respects, the stress in sectarian writings is on the Sect as a whole, which according to them is the only true Israel.[6] The individual — even the head of the community at the end of days — has no standing by himself. The high priest is senior in rank and office in the wars preceding the end of days,[7] as well as subsequently, according to most of the texts before us. On the other hand the prince or "Anointed of

---

[3] Cf. D. Flusser, The Apocryphal Book of Ascensis Isaiae and the Dead Sea Sect, IEJ, 3, 1953, pp. 30 f.

[4] Fragments of the Damascus Covenant were also found among the scrolls in the Qumran Caves. Cf. RB, 63, 1956, p. 61; M. Baillet, ibid., pp. 513–523.

[5] Cf. M. H. Segal, The Habakkuk Commentary and the Damascus Fragments (A Historical Study), JBL, 70, 1951, pp. 131 ff.; J. M. Allegro, Further Light on the History of the Qumran Sect, ibid., 75, 1956, pp. 89 ff.; J. T. Milik, Dix ans de découvertes dans le désert de Juda, Paris, 1957, pp. 51 ff., 103 ff.; F. M. Cross, Ancient Library of Qumran, New York, 1958, pp. 82 ff.

[6] Cf. D. Flusser, The Judean Desert Sect and its Views, Zion, 19, 1954, pp. 89–103 (Hebrew).

[7] Y. Yadin, The War of the Sons of Light with the Sons of Darkness, Jerusalem, 1955, pp. 189 ff. (Hebrew).

Israel" mentioned in these texts is lesser in degree than the high priest, also called most probably "[the priest] [8] head of the congregation of Israel" (1Q 28a, col. II, 12). The precedence of the high priest over the Anointed of Israel at the end of days is evident from the description of the "session of the men of repute called for the council of the community," which is stated in the Rule for the Congregation of Israel at the end of days.[9] According to this description first in the council of the community shall come the priest, head of the congregation of Israel, all the elders of the sons of Aaron, the priests, each according to his rank, shall sit before him; only after them shall come the Anointed One of Israel and all the heads of the families of Israel, each according to his rank (1Q 28a, col. II, 11–17). In the same way, the priest takes precedence over the Anointed of Israel at table (1Q 28a, col. II, 17–21), and this rule is to obtain at all meals where there are ten or more men present (1Q 28a, col. II, 21–22).

The description of the "session of the men of repute" is founded on the "Rule for the session of the many" which expounds the regulations then in force in the Sect. In this passage, it is stated: "The priests shall sit first, and the elders second, and the rest of the people shall sit each according to his position" (1QS VI, 8–9). The regulations of the Sect also forbid members to begin the communal meal before the priest blesses the bread and wine (1QS VI, 4–5; cf. also B. Gittin 59b). These regulations and others indicate the superior position of the priests in the Sect. The description of the "session of the men of repute" in the Rule of the Congregation (1Q 28a) is not a mere repetition of these regulations. It is intended to indicate the superior position of the high priest, and also of the priests in general, at the end of days.

The messianic hope for two leaders, one from Aaron and one

[8] For a different reading cf. F. M. Cross, Qumran Cave 1, JBL, 75, 1956, pp. 124 f.

[9] Cf. Barthélemy — Milik, Qumran Cave 1, Oxford, 1955, pp. 107–118; also, K. G. Kuhn, Die beiden Messias Aarons und Israels, Theologische Literaturzeitung, 79, 1954, pp. 760–761; idem, The Two Messiahs of Aaron and Israel, in The Scrolls and the New Testament, New York, 1957, pp. 54–64, 256–259; K. Schubert, Zwei Messiasse aus dem Regelbuch von Chirbet Qumran, Judaica, 11, 1955, pp. 216–235; E. L. Ehrlich, Ein Beitrag zur Messiaslehre der Qumransekte, ZAW, 68, 1956, pp. 234–243; H. N. Richardson, Some Notes on 1QSa, JBL, 76, 1957, pp. 108–122; A. S. Van der Woude, Die Messianischen Vorstellungen der Gemeinde von Qumran, Assen, 1957, pp. 96–106.

from Israel, who will arise after the end of the epoch of wickedness is expressed in a phrase which recurs in the writings of the Sect, "until the coming of a prophet and the anointed ones of Aaron and Israel" (1QS, IX, 11).[10] In the Damascus Covenant, however, we find the following: "until there shall arise the anointed one of Israel and Aaron" (CD, XII, 22; XIV, 19); "when there shall come the anointed one of Aaron and Israel" (CD, XIX, 11), but the version "anointed one" (משיח) in a medieval copy of the Damascus Covenant is merely a scribal error or an emendation of משיחי, as already pointed out by scholars. This is proved conclusively by the version given in the Manual of Discipline and by the detailed description in the Rule of the Congregation where, together with the priest, head of the congregation of Israel, the Anointed One of Israel is mentioned. The Messiahs of Aaron and Israel are mentioned once more in the Damascus Covenant in the text "until there shall rise an anointed one from Aaron and from Israel" (CD, XX, 1); this is just a shortened phrase meaning an anointed one from Aaron and an anointed one from Israel. A common element in all these passages referring to the anointed ones of Aaron and Israel is the fact that the time of their coming is regarded as the beginning of the end of days. The laws and regulations of the Sect are in force only until that time, and then too the end of the evildoers will come; that is to say, the time when the Messiahs of Aaron and Israel are to arise is equated with the end of days. This fact, moreover, confirms the identification of the anointed of Aaron mentioned in the Manual of Discipline with the priest, head of the congregation of Israel, mentioned together with the anointed of Israel in the Rule of the Congregation.

This identity of the anointed of Aaron and the high priest also emerges from the definition of "anointed" or "Messiah" in the early eschatological writings, the scrolls included. Here the term anointed (משיח) is not limited to the idea of a savior: it still contains the original meaning, "he who is anointed with the oil of unction," i.e., the king or the priest at the end of days. For

---

[10] Cf. N. Wieder, Journal of Jewish Studies, 4, 1943, p. 168, n. 2; and the detailed treatment by H. L. Silberman, The Two "Messiahs" of the Manual of Discipline, VT, 5, 1955, pp. 77–82; Van der Woude, ibid., pp. 27–43, 75–89.

according to rabbinical tradition the oil of unction was hidden away in the reign of Josiah [11] and there was none at the time of the Second Commonwealth. The Halakhah distinguishes between the anointed (high) priest — also called simply "the anointed" [12] (that is, the high priest when the oil of unction is finally restored at the end of days) — and the "priest with manifold garments" who is the high priest in the time of the Second Commonwealth. And although for all practical purposes the "priest with manifold garments" acted as the high priest, there exists in the law a distinction between the two, especially in the regulations dealing with expiatory sacrifice (Mishnah Horayoth). The expiation demanded of the anointed (high priest) is equal to that of the court — i.e., the public — while the prince (i.e., the king) [13] is in this case in the same category as a private person (M. Horayoth, ii:6). But in this matter, which indicates status in juridical decisions, the "priest of manifold garments" is inferior to the anointed high priest. This is expressly stated in the same Mishnaic tractate (iii:4): [14] "And who is the anointed (high priest)? He that is anointed with the oil of unction, but not he that is dedicated by the manifold garments. The (high) priest anointed with the oil of unction differs from the priest of manifold garments only in the bullock offered for (the unwitting transgression of) any of the commandments." In the Babylonian Talmud (Hor., 11b) this distinction in rank is stated in the most extreme terms: "If he is anointed he is the high priest; if he is not anointed he is not the high priest."

In Mishnaic law, only the anointed high priest has full authority, but in view of the absence of the oil of unction there can only be an anointed high priest at the end of days. This Halakhah comes from traditional Judaism, but as it does not in any way run counter to the principles of the Sect, we may reasonably assume that it prevailed among them.

[11] Cf. Tosefta Sotha xiii:1; Tosefta Yoma iii (ii), 7; B. Horayoth 12a; B. Yoma 52b; B. Kerithoth 5b; Yer. Sheqālim vi:1; Yer. Sotha viii:3.

[12] The term anointed (מָשׁיח) for an anointed High Priest is found many times in the Mishnah. Cf. Horayoth ii, passim; Tos. Shebouoth i, 6, etc.

[13] Cf. Mishnah Horayoth iii, 3 — "And who is the Prince (נָשׂיא)? This is the King."

[14] Also, Mishnah Megillah i, 9; Tos. Megillah i, 19; etc.

The identity of the anointed of Aaron with the priestly head of the congregation at the end of days, which is proved by the contents of the sectarian writings, emerges from the precise definition of the term "Anointed of Aaron" (משיח מאהרון) by itself. The term "Anointed of Israel," on the contrary, does not differ from the more general term "anointed." The description of the session of the men of repute in the Rule of the Congregation, according to which the priests sit before the high priest, whereas the heads of the families of Israel sit before the Anointed of Israel, delimits the term in that it excludes the Anointed of Aaron. From this we may conclude that the Anointed of Israel is no less than the future anointed king.

The Anointed of Israel is mentioned in the writings of the Sect only in the expression "the anointed ones of Aaron and Israel" and in the description in the Rule of the Congregation. On the other hand, the Prince of the Congregation is mentioned in the scroll of the War of the Sons of Light (1QM V, 1–2); but he is mentioned only once — and even then not as a leader in war — in contrast to the high priest, who plays a central part in that scroll and is mentioned there many times.[15] In actual fact, only the shield of the Prince of the Congregation is mentioned, on which is written his name with the names of the twelve tribes of Israel and the names of the leaders of the tribes. This does not imply the active participation of the prince in the war, nor does it exclude it.

A benediction for the prince of the congregation is also found in the 1 Qumran Benedictions,[16] which were most probably destined for the end of days. The extant remains of these benedictions include blessings: for them that fear the Lord; the high priest; the priests sons of Zadok, and the Prince of the Congregation. Of the six columns which the benedictions probably comprised there remain only parts of five. The order of the columns is conjectural, but that of the four big fragments which comprise the bottom part of cols. III–V is almost certain,[17] and one of the fragments includes part of col. IV and part of col. V. So the placing

---

[15] Cf. Yadin, op. cit. (supra n. 7), pp. 189 ff.
[16] Cf. Milik, op. cit. (supra n. 9), pp. 118–130.
[17] Cf. ibid., p. 119.

of the benediction for the Prince of the Congregation after the benediction for the high priest and the benediction for the priests sons of Zadok is an established fact. From the contents of the blessing for the Prince of the Congregation we learn (col. V, 20–29) that the Prince of the Congregation is the future ruler who will inherit the kingdom of his people for ever. He will judge the poor justly and admonish the humble of the land. God will lift him to everlasting heights, like a fortified tower; he shall smite nations with the might of his mouth, with his sceptre he shall smite the land. God will raise him to the sceptre of rulers and all the nations will serve him. It is not said here who is to be the Prince of the Congregation, but the contents and even the actual expressions are taken to a great degree from Isaiah, chapter 11, which contains one of the main promises of the future greatness of the house of David; they are taken also from the blessing of Jacob to his son Judah (Genesis xlix, 9–10). The prince is mentioned again in the Damascus Covenant (in an exposition of Numbers xxiv, 17).[18] "The sceptre is the prince of the congregation, and when he arises he shall strike violently all the sons of Seth." (CD VII, 20–21). From the expression "when he arises" (ובעמדו) [19] it is evident that an eschatological prince is meant. In another place in the Damascus Covenant the word prince is used instead of king: "and about the prince it is written, let him not multiply wives [20] unto himself, and David did not read in the sealed book of law, etc." (CD V, 1 ff.). From all this it is clear that the prince is the future secular ruler of the congregation, identical with the Anointed of Israel,[21] and that he is the anointed of David.

---

[18] "There shall step forth a star out of Jacob and a sceptre shall rise out of Israel." This scriptural passage (Num. xxiv, 17) has a central place in the messianic homilies of the Sect. Cf. 4Qp. Gen. xlix; 4Q Testimonia recently published by Allegro, see also below. On messianic exposition of the same passage in rabbinical writings, the Pseudepigrapha; and early Christianity, cf. C. Rabin, The Zadokite Documents, Oxford, 1954, pp. 30 f. Num. xxiv, 17 is also cited in the prayer before battle in 1QM XI, 6–7, but there it does not seem to have any messianic associations. Cf. also Yadin, op. cit. (supra n. 7), p. 323.

[19] Cf. CD XII, 22–24; XIV, 18–19.

[20] Deut. xvii, 17, and there it is distinctly said about the King. Cf. also note 13 above.

[21] Cf. Milik, op. cit. (supra, n. 9), p. 121. On the other hand, I cannot agree with Milik's identification of the hero mentioned in the prayer before battle in

The anointed ones of Aaron and Israel who are destined to arise at the end of days are, as we have shown, identical with the high priest, head of the congregation of Israel, and with the Prince of the Congregation, most probably the future Davidic ruler. The high priest plays a central part in the final war — i.e., the war of the Sons of Light and Darkness — and in the leadership of the people at the end of days. On the other hand, the Prince of the Congregation does not seem to take a very active part in the war and his authority is limited. The high priest takes priority in the session of the council of the community. Moreover, the benediction for the Prince of the Congregation comes after the benedictions for the high priest and priests. All these combined show that according to the texts we have dealt with the people of the Sect attached much greater importance to the Anointed of Aaron than to the Anointed of Israel[22]; and although the Anointed of Israel seems to be of Davidic descent, the fact is not mentioned expressly in these texts.

III

In addition to the above texts we have some further fragments from Qumran 4, published lately by Allegro.[23] In these texts, unlike the ones which only mention the Anointed Ones of Aaron and Israel, we find the expectations for the future ruler, the anointed of righteousness the shoot of David expressly stated. One of the Fragments from a Pesher on Gen. xlix is an exposition of Gen. xlix, 10: ["There shall not] cease a ruler from the tribe of Judah when there be dominion for Israel[24] [and there will not] be cut off an enthroned one (belonging) to (the line of) David,

---

1QM (XI, 6 ff.) with the prince or the Anointed of Israel. Cf. Yadin, op. cit. (supra n. 7), pp. 285, 330-331.

[22] So also in the Testaments of the Twelve Patriarchs; see also below. In rabbinical writings, on the other hand, the King takes precedence over the High Priest (Tosefta Horayoth ii, 9; Bab. Horayoth 13a).

[23] Cf. J. M. Allegro, Further Messianic References in Qumran Literature, JBL, 75, 1956, pp. 174 ff.; Y. Yadin, IEJ, 7, 1957, pp. 66–68; K. Schubert, Die Messiaslehre in den Texten von Chirbet Qumran, Biblische Zeitschrift, 1, 1957, pp. 177–197.

[24] Cf. 1QM I, 5; XVII, 7–8.

(לדויד ‎25‏ כסא יושב) for the staff (מחקק)‎26‏ is the covenant of king-ship and the families of Israel are the feet (הרגלים)‎27‏ until the coming (עד בוא)‎28‏ of the anointed of righteousness the shoot of David.‎29‏ For to him and to his seed has been given the cove-nant of kingship over his people for everlasting generations ‎30‏ which has awaited [the interpreter] ‎31‏ of the law with the men of the community, for it is the assembly of the men of. . . .'' Another fragment from a collection of expectations based on the exposition of Biblical texts ‎32‏ is based on the prophecy of Nathan

‎25‏ The reading of Allegro (ibid.) בוא is erroneous, as already noted by Yadin (ibid.). The words for "and there will not be cut off an enthroned one to David" are a paraphrase of Jer. xxxiii, 17. Cf. also Ps. cxxii, 5.

‎26‏ The מחקק of Gen. xlix, 10; this term was already understood as meaning the Kingdom of the House of David in the Bible (Ps. lx, 9 = cviii, 9). The same Hebrew term is mentioned in Num. xxi, 18. That scriptural passage is interpreted in CD VI, 3–11 to relate to the Book of the Law and the Leaders of the Sect; and there, the Staff מחקק is the Interpreter of the Law (CD VI, 7). The term מחקק is also intended for Moses in rabbinical tradition (cf. Targum to Deut. xxxiii, 21). The Exposition of מחקק in one biblical text about the Interpreter of the Law does not necessarily entail the same exposition in another text. Here מחקק cannot mean anything but the Covenant of Kingship. Cf. also the use of the same term ברית מלכות in relation to the rule of the future king the Shoot of David in the same fragment.

‎27‏ The feet (הרגלים) are those mentioned in Gen. xlix, 10. According to the interpretation of the LXX and the Targum, feet here mean descendants. The families of Israel (אלפי ישראל) may be compared to the chiefs of the families of Israel who according to the Rule of the Congregation are the leaders and will sit before the anointed of Israel (Col. I, 14; Col. II, 14–15 almost certain recon-struction). According to this interpretation the families of Israel, i.e., the mem-bers of the Sect and their leaders are to be considered as legitimately having the authority of Davidic Kingship until the coming of the anointed of righteousness, to whom and to whose descendants the covenant of kingship was given for ever-lasting generations. Yadin, op. cit. (supra n. 23), reads הדגלים, in accordance with the Samaritan Recension of Gen. xlix, 10. The degel is one of the military forma-tions mentioned in the Scroll of the War of the Sons of Light. From the photo-graph of the fragment we are not in a position to decide which of the readings is better. But even so there are many difficulties in Yadin's reading and interpreta-tion.

‎28‏ The words עד בוא represent the words עד כי יבא שילה in Gen. xlix, 10, and their interpretation on the coming of the future anointed king is according to the exegesis of the Targum and the Midrashim. Cf. A. Posnanski, Schilo, Ein Beitrag zur Geschichte der Messiaslehre, Leipzig, 1904. For the expression "עד בוא משיח הצדק" cf. 1QS IX, 14.

‎29‏ This term is founded on Jer. xxiii, 5. Cf. also "את צמח דויד עבדך מהרה תצמיח" in the Eighteen Benedictions (the 'Amidah).

‎30‏ Cf. 2 Samuel vii, 11 ff.; 1Q Benedictions Col. V, 20 ff.; 4QFl, 1 ff. (Cf. infra, n. 32.)

‎31‏ Cf. 4QFl, 2.

‎32‏ Allegro, op. cit., calls this Text 4Q Florilegium, abbreviated to 4QFl.

in 2 Sam. vii, 11–14. This prophecy which is one of the major promises to the house of David in the Bible is already alluded to in the fragment from 4Qp. Gen. xlix.[33] The fragment begins with a somewhat shortened rendering of the biblical text: "And the Lord tells you that he will build a house for you. And I will set up your seed after you and I will establish his royal throne for ever. I shall be to him for a father and he shall be to me for a son." Then comes the exposition which is about the future ruler: "He is the shoot of David who will arise with the interpreter of the law who [in the][34] end of days as it is written:[35] 'And I will raise up the tabernacle of David that is fallen.' That is (היאה)[36] the tabernacle of David that is fallen and after he will arise to save Israel."[37] Another text is a fragment from a Pesher of Isaiah which is an exposition of Is. xi. 1–5, one of the major prophecies on the future greatness of the house of David. Its beginning may be reconstructed[38] "[פשרו על צמח] דויד העומד [פשרו על צמח] דויד העומד באח [רית הימים]" meaning: "Its interpretation concerns the shoot of David who will arise at the end of days," and it goes on to describe his greatness and his glory.

The common elements in these three texts are: (1) the place where they were found, i.e., Qumran Cave 4; (2) the statement of hopes for a Messiah of David; these hopes being based on scriptural passages; (3) the use of the term "shoot of David" in all three passages and "interpreter of the law" in two of them (although in two cases, one of each, an almost certain reconstruc-

---

[33] Cf. n. 31.

[34] The lacuna is at the beginning of the line. There is room for about two words including the two letters "בצ". It is at present impossible to decide whether the words "which . . . in the end of days" apply to the Shoot of David or to the Interpreter of the Law, although I think the latter more probable.

[35] Am. ix, 11. Here and in CD VII, 16: "והקימותי את סוכת דויד" on the other hand M.T. "אקים".

[36] The connecting word "That is" (היאה) rules out the possibility that the repetition is a scribal error. The first time, the tabernacle of David is mentioned in its original biblical meaning; whereas the second mention probably hints at its homiletical exposition. The words, "that is," probably show that it was an exposition well known among the members of the Sect (cf. CD VII, 15 ff.) so that it was enough merely to hint at that exposition. See also below.

[37] The future Davidic king is here probably intended. In 1Q Benedictions too (Col. V, 20 ff.) the delivery of Israel from the yoke of the nations is attributed to the prince of the congregation, i.e., to the future Davidic king.

[38] The restoration is after 4QFl, 3–4: "צמח דויד העומד עם דורש התורה".

tion). We are therefore justified in dealing with all these three texts as one. The hopes for the future king, the shoot of David, the anointed of righteousness stated in these texts, are in varied contrast to the other texts dealt with above, in which there is a disinclination, apparently intentional, to mention the connection of the future king with the House of David.[39] Yet it is quite clear that these new texts too belong to the Sect itself. This we learn not only from their general character, but in particular in view of the specifically sectarian terms "Interpreter of the Law" and "men of the community" which are used there. These texts require a new examination of the conclusions we have stated above with regard to the anointed ones of Aaron and Israel. At the same time, we have to examine in the light of these conclusions, which are based on a scrutiny of all the sectarian writings which are at present available in a more or less complete form, these new texts which Allegro has lately published in fragmentary form. Since, however, the editor chose from the material at his disposal those texts which deal with the Davidic anointed king, we may quite legitimately surmise that in the other texts (as yet unpublished), which deal with the end of days, the future Davidic king is not so prominent. This assumption is strengthened by the fact that the benediction for the prince of the community from the I Qumran benedictions [40] may be compared to these new texts in stressing the exalted position of the future ruler. Only the comparison of the blessing for the prince of the community with the other blessings, and the fact that it is placed after the blessing for the high priest and the blessing for the priests sons of Zadok, indicates his secondary position.

In the fragment from the Pesher to Gen. xlix mentioned above, the hopes for the future Shoot of David are quite clearly expressed. To him and to his seed was given the covenant of kingship over his people for everlasting generations: "the families of Israel are

---

[39] The use of the formula "the anointed ones of Israel and Aaron" implies an intentional avoidance of any direct reference to the Davidic future king. This avoidance is especially noticeable in the texts from the Rule of the Congregation and the Benedictions, dealt with above. In general the Scrolls display a favorable attitude to David, and cf. 1QM XI, 1–3; even in CD V, 1–6, where David's actions are criticized, we find a sentiment favorable to him.

[40] Cf. supra, II.

the feet until the coming of the anointed of David, the shoot of righteousness." And the "families of Israel" (אלפי ישראל) are most probably the people of the community.[41] Here too the dominion of the Shoot of David is presented as a promise which will be fulfilled only in the expected future; in the present this authority is vested in the families of Israel, i.e., in the community as a corporate body. This interpretation is confirmed by the fact that the men of the community and together with them the Interpreter of the Law [דורש התורה] are mentioned further on in the same fragment. The Interpreter of the Law is mentioned in the other fragment 4QFl, and if we examine in detail what is written there ("The Shoot of David who will arise with the interpreter of the law . . . in the end of days"), he is even superior in importance to the Shoot of David. The placing of the Interpreter of the Law together with the Shoot of David is parallel to his placing with the Prince of the Congregation in the Damascus Covenant VII, 19–20. This text in the Damascus Covenant is based on a messianic interpretation of Numbers xxiv, 17: "There shall step forth a star out of Jacob and a sceptre shall arise out of Israel." [42] The star is according to this homiletic interpretation the Interpreter of the Law while the sceptre is the Prince of the Congregation, the Anointed of Israel.[43] In this context there comes in the Damascus Covenant the exposition of Amos ix, 11: "And I will raise up the tabernacle of David that is fallen." The tabernacle of David is expounded there (line 20) as the Books of the Law. In 4QFl too the second citation of Amos ix, 11 most probably hints at a homiletical exposition well known to the members of the Sect [44]; it is quite possible that the exposition is the same as the one given in the Damascus Covenant. This combination of the plain text on the tabernacle of David that God will revive with its homiletic exposition, according to which the tabernacle of the King is, most probably, the Torah, in 4QFl may also hint at the subordination of the anointed king to the laws of the Torah. Also in the Pesher on Isaiah xi, where "the shoot of

---

[41] Cf. n. 27.
[42] Cf. also n. 18.
[43] Cf. supra.
[44] Cf. n. 36.

David who will arise at the end of days," is mentioned, it is also said of him that: "as they teach him (אשׁ[כ]אשׁר יורוהו)[45] so shall he judge." These words come as an exposition of Isaiah xi, 3: "And he shall not judge after the sight of his eyes, neither decide after the hearing of his ears." This is an exposition which implies severe limitations on the power of the future king, and is against the meaning of the text in Isaiah, for instead of the continuation "with righteousness shall he judge the poor" we find in the Pesher "as they teach him," i.e., the priests,[46] the leaders of the Sect.

As we noticed above, there are points of contact between the Interpreter of the Law who shall arise with the Shoot of David at the end of days (in the fragments from Qumran Cave 4), and the Interpreter of the Law in the Damascus Covenant (CD VII, 19–20). This fact lends plausibility to the theory [47] that the Interpreter of the Law, the leader of the Sect after the Teacher of Righteousness, was regarded as the person who is intended to lead Israel at the end of days, clothed in his authority as the anointed of Aaron. It is most probable that the Interpreter of the Law, as well as the Teacher of Righteousness, the first leader of the Sect, was a priest and belonged to the great priestly house of Zadok; [48] and it is not improbable that the sectarians who hoped for salvation in the near future saw in him the destined anointed high priest. But on the other hand, another text in the Damascus Covenant speaks of the Sect as being led in the ways of the Torah by the Interpreter of the Law: "Until there shall arise a teacher of righteousness at the end of days" (CD VI, 11). Therefore we cannot accept the theory that the Interpreter of the Law was regarded as the future priestly leader, as we are then forced to assume that both the Teacher of Righteousness and the Interpreter of the Law were regarded at the very same time as the destined anointed of Aaron.

Indeed, the problem of the relation between the Interpreter of the Law in his eschatological aspects and the Teacher of

[45] Cf. Allegro, op. cit. (supra n. 23), p. 181.
[46] Cf. the Ordinances for the King in Deut. xvii, 18–20, also Deut. xxxiii, 10 in the blessing of Moses on the tribe of Levi.
[47] Cf. D. Flusser in, Studies in the Dead Sea Scrolls, in Memory of E. L. Sukenik, Jerusalem, 1957, p. 86, n. 5; p. 87, n. 8 (Hebrew).
[48] Cf. infra note 100.

Righteousness who will arise at the end of days, requires a fresh treatment in the light of these new texts; [49] it is even doubtful whether the terms "Teacher of Righteousness" and "Interpreter of the Law" are always intended to mean historical personalities, or whether these are just terms with a more general meaning.[50] A possible explanation of the use of the term "Interpreter of the Law" in these new texts from Qumran 4, is to assume that the texts belong to a later period than the time when the historical Interpreter of the Law was active, and that it is signifying a term of honor for the high priest who is intended to lead the nation in the time of salvation, together with the future Davidic king.

The messianic expectations in the texts we have just dealt with come in the form of exposition of biblical texts dealing with the future kingdom of the house of David. Together with the Davidic king we find in them another central personality in the vision of the end of days, namely, the eschatological Interpreter of the Law. The main differences between these texts and the other scrolls concerned with expectations of future salvation are the stress laid on the prominence of the anointed of David, in the new texts, and the intentional avoidance of any explicit mention of the future Davidic king, even when he is implied in the other texts.

As possible explanations of these differences we may suggest the following:

(a) Inside the Sect there was some degree of ideological freedom. Owing to the historical development connected with the growth of the Sect,[51] the authorized leaders of the Sect intended to stress the central position of the priests of the House of Zadok in the future too, and to minimize the importance of the future Davidic king, even though they could not ignore him altogether because of the biblical prophecies of the future Davidic king. But there were others who did

---

[49] Allegro, op. cit. (supra n. 23), p. 176 proposes to identify the Interpreter of the Law with the teacher of righteousness. On previous proposals that the teacher of righteousness is a Messiah redivivus, cf. infra note 72. N. Wieder, The "Law-Interpreter" of the Sect of the Dead Sea: The Second Moses, Journal of Jewish Studies, 4, 1953, pp. 158–175, identified the Interpreter of the Law with the prophet who will herald the coming of the two Messiahs (1QS IX, 11); while Schubert (supra n. 23), is inclined to identify with the future prophet, the Teacher of Righteousness. See also Flusser, ibid. (supra note 47); Cross, ibid. (supra note 5), pp. 171–173.

[50] Cf. 1QS VI, 6: "אִישׁ דּוֹרֵשׁ בַּתּוֹרָה."

[51] Vide infra.

not want to minimize the significance of these prophecies to such an extent, and who expounded these selfsame biblical texts on the future greatness of the House of David. It is also possible that they enlarged on these biblical prophecies for the purpose of the Pesher, without having a conscious theological outlook different from that of the others.

(b) The texts in which the future Davidic king is expressly mentioned date from a different period from those where he is only implied, and in the meantime a certain development inside the Sect gave more weight to the expectations connected with the House of David.[52]

From the regulations in the Manual of Discipline and from the Damascus Covenant we know that the Sect was compactly organized, with a strict internal discipline. It therefore seems to me that we must prefer the second explanation, which links the changed attitude towards the anointed of David with historical development, and not with a difference in views between members of the Sect. This development as well as the growth of the doctrine of the two Messiahs will be dealt with after an examination of the relevant texts from the Book of the Testaments of the Twelve Patriarchs.

IV

A major difficulty when dealing with the Book of the Testaments of the Twelve Patriarchs is determining what is its original text,

---

[52] We need not take into account the possibility that the texts which expressly mention the future ruler of the House of David are earlier than the others and that the expectation of a ruler from the House of David progressively lessened because: (a) The major texts (in the present state of publication) are those which do not mention expressly a future Davidic ruler; and it does not seem probable that future publication will alter the situation much. (b) The Sect was established under the leadership of the priests, sons of Zadok (vide infra), and they, hoping for the end of days in the near future, were surely not interested in stressing the importance of the future Davidic king. (c) After the decline of the Hasmonean dynasty and the beginning of Roman oppression, we find evidence of messianic yearnings connected with the House of David in sources which definitely do not belong to the Dead Sea Sect or its adherents (for the first time in the Psalms of Solomon, especially Psalms xvii and xviii), whereas in the earlier apocalyptic literature the Davidic Messiah is not mentioned at all. Cf. also infra n. 106. I am dealing with the historical development of Davidic Expectations in detail, in my book, The House of David from the Fall of the Kingdom of Judah to the Fall of the Second Commonwealth and After, Jerusalem, 1959 (Hebrew).

and what are late additions; a matter which is still in dispute.[53] The Book of the Testaments of the Twelve Patriarchs, originally written in Hebrew,[54] is known to us only in its Greek form, and in ancient translations from the Greek. In all these versions Christian interpolations have crept in, but the extent of these interpolations is the subject of disagreement. It is also debated to what extent the book was added to still earlier by Jewish hands, and the divergence of opinion is particularly marked in regard to texts dealing with future destined saviors of Israel. But the close connection between the Book of the Testaments and the Dead Sea Sect literature, which emerges also from these parts of the Testament whose originality is not disputed, helps us to determine its date; and the preceding discussion of the future Messiahs in the scrolls is also of assistance in understanding the system of the two saviors, as expounded in the Book of the Testaments of the Twelve Patriarchs.

Before the scrolls were discovered, and before it became clear that there were sectarian circles in Israel who hoped for two Messiahs, one of Aaron and one of Israel, and were at the same time in opposition to the ruling priests of Judea, it was difficult to reconcile the doctrine of the two Messiahs of the Testaments of the Twelve Patriarchs with what was then known of Jewish religion in the time of the Second Commonwealth. On the other hand, the attempts to explain the two Messiahs in the Book of the Testaments brought forth various theories on the development of the messianic idea in the period of the Second Commonwealth. The system of Charles, who related the book to circles close to the Hasmoneans, and was inclined to see in the king and priest mentioned there John Hyrcanus, was the one most widely accepted by scholars. Charles supposed that in the original writing there was only one Messiah from the tribe of Levi who was both king and priest, and that only after the rift between Hyrcanus and the Pharisees had become open, and the opposition to Hasmonean

---

[53] Cf. R. H. Charles, The Testaments of the Twelve Patriarchs, London, 1908; M. De Jonge, The Testaments of the Twelve Patriarchs, Leiden, 1953, and there pp. 10–12 a review of the different views.

[54] R. H. Charles, The Greek Versions of the Testaments of the Twelve Patriarchs, London, 1908, pp. XXIII–XXXIII. The notation of the different recensions and Mss. is according to this edition.

rule hardened, was the book newly edited and paragraphs concerning the future savior from Judah added. Charles even claimed [55] that in the thirty years between the rule of Simeon and the end of the reign of John Hyrcanus, the Jewish people jettisoned the idea of a Messiah from David and adopted the idea of a Messiah from Levi. A different explanation was given by K. Kohler and L. Ginzberg.[56] According to them, the Messiah from Levi belongs to a later secondary stratum of the book, while the original book is mainly concerned with the Messiah from Judah, in accordance with accepted Jewish beliefs. Besides these, there were other scholars who maintained the doctrine of two Messiahs but only as applied to part of the texts concerned, and tried to explain it in different ways; [57] and still others who thought that according to the system of the book the Messiah would emerge from the union of the two tribes Levi and Judah.[58] The fact that the system of the two Messiahs was in force in the Dead Sea Sect enables us to reject entirely the supposition of two different strata in the book, in one of which the Messiah is from Levi and in the other from

[55] Charles, Testaments, pp. XCVII ff.; idem, the Apocrypha and Pseudepigrapha, 2, Oxford, 1913, p. 294. V. Aptovitzer (Parteipolitik der Hasmonäerzeit, Wien, 1927) goes even further in his conclusions than Charles. According to Aptovitzer the Testaments are a polemical treatise against the adversaries of the Hasmonean rulers (ibid., pp. 82 ff.). The starting point of the debate, according to Aptovitzer, was the exposition of Ps. cx, 4, "The Lord hath sworn and will not repent thou art a priest for ever after the order of Melchizedek"; the Hasmonean party claimed that according to this verse a priest would be the Messiah, while their opponents thought the same verse meant that the Messiah (who would be from the tribe of Judah) would also be a priest. According to Aptovitzer the book of Testaments of the Twelve Patriarchs, which speaks of a king from the tribe of Levi, was composed inside the Hasmonean party, whose adherents claimed that the king would arise out of the tribe of Levi and the tribe of Judah together, and that the Hasmonean rulers were not only the descendants of Aaron but also the descendants of Judah. On the other hand their opponents, whose opinions are stated, according to Aptovitzer, in some of the Midrashim, admitted that the Messiah would be descended from the two tribes, but claimed that it was David who traced his descent both from Judah and from Levi. Aptovitzer's whole edifice lacks any factual basis, and he twists the sources he uses in order to "prove" his points. Cf. J. Klausner, Qiryath-Sefer, 5, 1929, pp. 348–350; M. H. Segal, Tarbiz 21, 1950, pp. 135–136 (Hebrew).

[56] K. Kohler, Jewish Encyclopedia, xii, pp. 113 f.; L. Ginzberg, Eine unbekannte jüdische Sekte, Monatsch. z. Gesch. u. Wissensch. d. Judenth., 58, 1914, pp. 403–411.

[57] Cf. G. R. Beasley-Murray, The Two Messiahs in the Testaments of the Twelve Patriarchs, Journal Theol. Studies, 48, 1947, pp. 1–12. (This paper was not available to me.)

[58] Cf. M. H. Segal, Tarbiz 21, 1950, p. 134 (Hebrew); A. J. B. Higgins, Priest and Messiah, VT, 3, 1953, pp. 323 f.

Judah. The lack of contradiction between the different parts of the book in the matter of the two Messiahs and its agreement with the scrolls [59] will become clear from careful examination of the pertinent texts.

When we come to examine the doctrine of the Testaments of the Twelve Patriarchs on future salvation and on priesthood and kingship, we have to remember that it is a Pseudepigraph which purports to give the words of the sons of Jacob, the fathers of the tribes of Israel. The future events in the lives of their descendants — that is the history of the nation down to the author's own days — must find expression in the book. We have to distinguish in the Book of the Testaments between the appreciation of the past in the vision of the patriarchs and the vision of the end of days which is the future age to the author himself. We must also remember that most of the Book of the Testaments is one work, and the division into twelve testaments is intentional. The details given in the different testaments should therefore be regarded as a unity. We will give here, in the order in which they appear in the Book of Testaments, those texts which deal with kingship and prophecy, saviors from Levi and Judah, and the salvation of Israel.

Reuben vi, 7–12: For to Levi God gave the dominion and to Judah with him and to me also and to Dan and Joseph that we should be for rulers.[60] Therefore I command you to hearken to Levi because he shall know the Law of the Lord and shall give ordinances for judgment and shall sacrifice for all Israel until the end of days of the anointed High Priest [61] of whom the Lord spake. I adjure you

---

[59] J. H. Grintz, Sinai, 32, 1953, pp. 30 f. (Hebrew), already pointed to the fact. Cf. also, Kuhn, ibid. (supra n. 7); and lately Van der Woude, ibid. (supra n. 7), pp. 190–216. Van der Woude's book arrived in Jerusalem after the paper had already been forwarded to the editors, and it agrees in some details with those reached independently in this paper.

[60] Charles considers as a "foolish interpolation" the inclusion of Judah, Reuben, Dan and Joseph in this verse and thinks that the verse deals only with the supremacy of Levi (Greek Versions, p. 13; Testaments, pp. 13 f.), while De Jonge (Testaments, p. 88) thinks that only Reuben, Dan and Joseph are interpolated. But it is most probable that the four tribes were here mentioned as an allusion to the four standards: the standard of the camp of Judah, the standard of the camp of Reuben, the standard of the camp of Ephraim-Joseph, and the standard of the camp of Dan, according to which the children of Israel pitched camp round the tent of meeting in the desert (Num. ch. ii). Cf. Segal, op. cit. (supra n. 58), p. 132.

[61] ἀρχιερέως χριστοῦ so in most Greek Mss. and the Slavonic Version. One Greek Ms. (h): ἀρχιερεὺς χριστοῦ — "The high priest of the anointed"; which is mean-

by the God of heaven to do truth each one unto his neighbour and to entertain love each for his brother. And you draw near to Levi in humbleness of heart, that you may receive a blessing from his mouth. For he shall bless Israel, and Judah (τὸν Ἰσραηλ καὶ τὸν Ἰουδαν) because him (ὅτι ἐν αὐτῷ) hath the Lord chosen to be king over all the nation. And bow down before his seed, for on your behalf he will die in wars visible and invisible [62] and will be king for ever.

This passage in the Testament of Reuben begins with the dominion that God gave to Levi and Judah. It applies in a general way to the Government that was in the hands of the tribe of Levi before the foundation of the Israelite Kingdom and during the Second Commonwealth, and to the Kingship of the Davidic dynasty before the Babylonian Exile. Then comes the exhortation to hearken to Levi because he has been given the offices of judgment and sacrifice, and the eschatological anointed priest is also referred to. After that is mentioned the Kingship of Judah whom God has chosen to be king over all the nation and it is expressly stated that from his seed shall come forth the King Messiah.

According to Charles [63] the words: "because him hath God chosen to be king" apply to Levi, while the words "and Judah" are connected only with the preceding part of the sentence where it is said that Levi shall bless Israel and Judah. According to him both the priesthood and royalty of Levi are here mentioned and are intended to mean the dominion of the Hasmoneans. But even in the text as it stands the words: "because him hath God

---

ingless, and which Charles corrects to ἀρχιερεὺς χριστός — "The anointed high priest." According to the emendation of Charles the meaning of the text is that the anointed high priest, i.e., the Hasmonean ruler, shall sacrifice until the end of days. Not only is Charles' reading based on the one Ms. in which these words are corrupt, but as we have already seen (supra II), the expression "anointed priest" necessarily means the high priest at the end of days.

[62] The expression, "for on your behalf he will die in wars visible and invisible," is difficult. Charles (Testaments, p. 16), retranslating it into Hebrew, proposes יעמוד — "will stand forth" instead of ימות — "will die," and at the beginning of the verse זרעו — "his arm," "his might," instead of זרעו — "his seed," and interprets his emended text on the wars of the Hasmonean high priests. Not only are the emendations and interpretation offered by Charles improbable in themselves, but the verse as a whole is intended for Judah and not for Levi. The one who fights these wars is the future king from the tribe of Judah.

[63] Cf. Charles, Testaments, p. 16.

chosen to be king," definitely apply to Judah and not to Levi.[64] Furthermore we may assume that the text originally was: "And you draw near to Levi . . . for he shall bless Israel and to Judah [65] because him hath God chosen to be king." In any case, we have here the promise of priesthood to Levi as against the promise of royalty to Judah.

In the Testament of Reuben the position is this: Hegemony among the tribes of Israel to Levi and to Judah; Levi has a more prominent standing than Judah; Messianic hopes connected with an anointed priest from Levi and a king from Judah.

> Simeon vii, 1–2: And now my children obey Levi and Judah, and be not lifted up against these two tribes for from them shall arise unto you the salvation of God. For there shall arise from Levi as if it were High Priest and from Judah as if it were King God and man and he shall save all the nations and the race of Israel.

The expressions: "God and man" and "all the nations" are obvious Christian interpolations,[66] and the whole phrase from "God and man" appears to have been rewritten from a Christian point of view. Originally it was probably something like — and through them shall all Israel be saved.

The Testament of Simeon gives the following: Hegemony to Levi and Judah; priesthood to Levi and royalty to Judah; salvation of Israel in Levi and in Judah.

The Testament of Levi stands out from the others. At the beginning comes a vision (Levi ii,5 — v,6), in which Levi sees sights similar to those described in the Ethiopic Book of Enoch. Levi beholds the seven firmaments of heaven, the angels of the Lord and the glorious presence of the Most High. Towards the end of the vision he is destined to priesthood (v,2). Then comes a second vision (ch.viii) in which Levi sees seven men in white raiment, who clothe him in the robe of priesthood and the other paraphernalia of the High Priest, and authorize him to serve the Lord as a priest. And then they say to him (viii,11–16):

---

[64] And if we retain the present text, the words, "because him hath God chosen" signify the reason why Judah was given a special blessing.

[65] We may assume that the Greek translator understood the Hebrew "וליהודה" as accusative and translated "καὶ τὸν Ἰουδαν." Cf. Grintz, op. cit. (supra n. 1), p. 31.

[66] Cf. Charles, Greek Versions, pp. 25–26.

Levi, thy seed shall be divided into three offices, for a sign of the glory of the Lord that is to come. And the first portion shall be great, greater than it shall be none. The second shall be in the priesthood. And the third shall be called by a new name, because a king shall arise from Judah (ἐκ τοῦ Ιουδα) and shall establish a new priesthood after the fashion of the nations to all the nations (read, "because a king like all the nations shall arise from Judah and shall establish a new priesthood")[67] and his presence is beloved as a prophet of the Most High, the seed of Abraham our father.

The first two who are to arise from the seed of Levi are agreed by most scholars to be Moses and Aaron. Charles[68] wanted to see Hyrcanus in the third one and instead of a "King shall arise from Judah" (ἐκ τοῦ Ιουδα) i.e., Judah the tribe, which is given in all the extant manuscripts of the Testaments he wished to read "a king shall arise in Judah" (ἐν τῷ) i.e., Judah the land; accordingly, he interprets the text on a king from Levi who shall arise in the land of Judah. But this is quite arbitrary,[69] and, even if we accept it, the identification with Hyrcanus is rather far-fetched. According to the actual text, the third one from the seed of Levi is a priest who will be established in his office with the help of the king from Judah, and this description most probably applies to the priest Zadok,[70] who according to the tradition in Chronicles was already placed at the head of the intricate priestly organization in the time of David; and until the time of the Hasmoneans the high priestly family were regarded as his descendants. What is more, the expression "and his presence is beloved as a prophet of the Most High; the seed of Abraham our

---

[67] The words, "after the fashion of the nations to all the nations" represent a dittography in the Hebrew text. The correct reading is no doubt "like all the nations" (ככל הגוים) and it applies, as Dr. D. Flusser has pointed out to me, to the king who shall arise from Judah. Cf. Deut. xvii, 14, "I will set a king over me like all the nations that are around me"; I Sam. viii, 5: "Now make us a king to judge us like all the nations." The phrase, "A king like all the nations shall arise from Judah" tallies with the Scriptures. On the other hand, priesthood after the fashion of the nations, which means equating the priesthood with the priesthood of idol-worshippers, does not harmonize in any way with the views of the author of the Testaments.

[68] Charles, Testaments, p. 45; followed by many others.

[69] Cf. Ginsberg, op. cit. (supra n. 56), pp. 407 f.

[70] Cf. T. W. Manson, Journal Theol. Studies, 48, 1947, pp. 60–61 (this was unavailable to me); Grintz, op. cit. (supra n. 1), p. 32.

father" is more applicable to David than to any other king of Israel.

Together with the glorification of the descendants of Levi we find in the Testament of Levi the most violent denunciations of the priesthood. The misdeeds of priests in future generations are described with remarkable vividness (Levi ch. x; chaps. xiv–xv, especially xiv, 5–7).[71] After this there comes an apocalyptic vision describing the decline of the priesthood from generation to generation (chaps. xvi–xvii) — from the first who is anointed to priesthood and shall speak to the Lord, and his priesthood shall be perfect (xvii, 2), down to the last priests who are lovers of money, adulterers, idolaters, and lascivious abusers of children and beasts. God will take his vengeance upon the evil priests, and will then raise up a new priest [72] (ch. xviii), by whom all the words of the Lord shall be revealed. He shall execute righteous judgment on earth, and his star shall arise in heaven as of a king. He shall shine forth as the sun, the heavens shall be opened and from the heavens shall come upon him sanctification. In the time of his priesthood the expected end of days shall come, evil shall cease

[71] The description of the degeneration and decline of the high priesthood in these chapters, and in the Testament of Levi ch. xvii, is parallel to the description in the Psalms of Solomon ch. viii. These descriptions are founded on the deeds of the hellenizing priests in the days of Antiochus IV, but are very much exaggerated. Their origin is in the polemical literature of the first Hassidim. This literature was most probably read by the sectarians and used in their accusations against their opponents the priests of Jerusalem; we need not regard these descriptions as intended to mean specific Hasmonean rulers.

[72] Charles, Testaments, pp. 62 f., regards the evil priests as the hellenizing priests in the time of Antiochus IV, while the new priest who shall arise after them is, according to him, the Hasmonean house and especially John Hyrcanus. But in the Testament of Levi, ch. xviii an eschatological priest is described and even if we did not know about the points of contact between the Dead Sea Sect and the Testaments of the Twelve Patriarchs it would be impossible to agree with Charles' identification. Dupont-Sommer (Nouveaux aperçus sur les manuscrits de la Mer Morte, Paris, 1953, pp. 64–84) identifies the seven anointed priests in the Test. of Levi xvii as the Hasmoneans. The first he identifies as Judas Maccabaeus and the seventh as Aristobulus II. The new priest, according to Dupont-Sommer, is the teacher of righteousness who (according to him) was killed during the time of Aristobulus II and was expected to rise again as the anointed one (ibid. p. 79). However, the identification of the anointed priest in Testament of Levi xvii which Dupont-Sommer offers is unfounded, and, what is more, based in some places on a misinterpretation of the text. Cf. also B. Otzen, Studia Theologica 7, 1954, 146 f.; Cross, ibid. (supra note 5), pp. 118 f. The theory that the new priest is the teacher of righteousness redivivus (a theory first propounded by S. Schechter, Documents of Jewish Sectaries I, Cambridge, 1910, pp. XII ff.) is also doubtful.

and the righteous shall rejoice. This new priest is described in the vivid colors of a Messiah, but it is nowhere said that he will be a king or even that there will not be a king at that time; on the contrary, it is his priesthood that is emphasized.

In this apocalyptic vision in the Testament of Levi we have emphasis on the superiority of the priesthood; and hope for a new priest who shall arise at the end of days. It thus has many points of similarity with the doctrine of the Dead Sea Scrolls where we also find a preference of the priests, especially the sons of Zadok, coupled with serious accusations against the priests of Jerusalem, and expectation of a future anointed priest. The total effect is, of course, different, but the points of similarity we have enumerated lead us to assume that if these testaments were not composed in the Sect itself, they originated in circles whose social and ideological background was very close to that of the Dead Sea Sect.

In the Testament of Levi there is no kingship of Levi to be found, the kingship is for Judah and the priesthood for Levi; at the end of days a messianic new priest will arise.

> Judah xxi, 1–2: And now, my children, I command you, love Levi, that you may abide and exalt not yourselves against him lest you be utterly destroyed. For to me the Lord gave the kingdom and to him the priesthood, and he set the kingdom beneath the priesthood.

A similar verse to Judah xxi, 12 is found in a fragment from the so-called Aramaic Testaments from Qumran Cave 1: ולך ולב[ניך מלכות כהנותא רבא מן מלכות]א [73] — "to you and to your sons kingship. The priesthood is superior to the kingship." The stress upon the superiority of Levi over Judah and of course over all the other tribes recurs in Judah ch. xxv.

---

[73] Barthélemy-Milik, op. cit. (supra n. 2), p. 88. Milik reads the first letter כ but ג seems better. P. Grelot, Notes sur le Testament araméen de Levi, RB 63, 1956, p. 396, n. 2 offers the reconstruction:
"ולך ולב[ניך מלכות כהנותא רבא מן מלכות [חרבא"
explaining it as pointing to two kingships, the kingship of priesthood and the kingship of the sword. But while the proposed reconstruction of the beginning of the line is very plausible, his reconstruction at the end of the line and the way in which he explains the whole, are most improbable. The reconstruction and explanation offered in the text above, which are in complete concord with the Testament of Judah xxi, 2, are to be preferred.

In chs. xxi–xxiii we have a short survey of the history of Israel from the point of view of the acts and behavior of the kings, followed by a promise that God will renew the Kingdom of Judah after its destruction and will not destroy the kingdom from the seed of Judah for ever (xxii, 2–3). Charles [74] argues that a whole section of the Testament of Judah xxi, 6–xxiii, 5 is not in its proper place, but is a later addition which should be interpreted as a severe polemic against the Hasmonean kings Aristobulus II and Hyrcanus II. But Charles does not bring any concrete reasons for his argument; the passage seems rather to be an organic part of the Testament of Judah dealing with the future of his descendants. Just as in the Testament of Levi (chs. xvi–xviii), after the survey of the history of the tribe comes a vision which is messianic in content (xxiv, 1–6):

> And after these things shall a star arise to you from Jacob in peace and a man shall arise from my seed like a sun of righteousness walking with the sons of men in meekness and righteousness and no sin shall be found in him.[75] And the heavens shall be opened unto him to pour out the spirit, (even) the blessing of the Holy Father.[76] And he shall pour out the spirit of grace upon you. And you shall be unto him sons in truth, and you shall walk in his commandments first and last. This branch of God most high, and this fountain giving life unto all.[77] Then shall the sceptre of my kingdom shine forth, and from your root shall arise a stem and from it shall grow a rod of righteousness to the nations, to judge and to save all that call upon the Lord.

Charles [78] finds in this chapter two separate messianic prophecies, both of them out of place. The first (xxiv, 1–4) concerns the Messiah from Levi, the second is a later addition. De Jonge [79]

---

[74] Charles, Testaments, p. 91.

[75] The Armenian Version is much shorter, "And after these things shall arise a star of peace and he shall walk with men in meekness and righteousness and the heavens, etc."

[76] πατρὸς ἁγίου — the expression in its present form is Christian.

[77] So in some Greek Mss. (c, h, i); in the others we have, "This fountain unto life for all flesh." According to Charles (Testaments, p. 97) the whole verse is an interpolation. In the Armenian Version we have, "Then a branch shall go forth from me."

[78] Charles, Testaments, pp. 95 f.

[79] De Jonge, Testaments, pp. 89 f.

claims that this chapter and the whole book of the Testaments are Christian, and that this prophecy concerns Jesus. But it is hardly credible that in the Testament of Judah there should be no messianic expectations for the House of David; moreover, the fact that before this vision (xxi, 1–2) as well as after it (xxv, 1–2), the superiority of Levi over Judah is stressed, rules out any assumption of the Christian character of these chapters as a whole.

Expectations for the future in the Testament of Judah (xxiv) are restrained in comparison with those in Levi (xviii) and are mainly concerned with the sceptre of Judah as a king. Also in Judah xxiv, 1, instead of "a man shall arise from my seed," it may be that we should read "from his seed," [80] i.e., from the seed of the star of Jacob mentioned in the first part of the verse, which is not necessarily Judah. From this assumption we may conclude that verses 1–4, 5–6 in the Testament of Judah xxiv are not concerned with the same person, and in view of the great similarity in content and expressions between Judah xxiv, 1–4 and Levi xviii, 3–4, it is not improbable that the first part of Judah xxiv was originally intended for the savior from Levi under whose leadership salvation will be brought and justice will prevail. And then the sceptre of the kingdom of the ruler from Judah shall shine forth. This theory is supported by the fact that in these chapters in the Testament of Judah, the superiority of Levi over Judah is stressed; and it may be that the exposition of Num. xxiv, 17 ("There shall step forth a star out of Jacob") in the Testament of Judah xxiv, 1 ("and after all these shall a star arise to you from Jacob") suggests the star of the new priest in the Testament of Levi (xviii, 2–3: "And then shall the Lord raise up a new priest . . . and his star shall arise in Heaven"). In the second part of the chapter, in verse 5, we have the expression "sceptre of my kingdom" which hints at the second part of the same verse in Num. xxiv, 17 ("and a sceptre shall arise out of Israel"). An exposition of Num. xxiv, 17 on two different persons is also found in the Covenant of Damascus VII, 18–21,[81] where the

---

[80] In the Hebrew text "מזרעו" instead of "מזרעי," i.e., ו instead of י. In some of the Dead Sea Scrolls (so the Isaiah Scroll A) the ו is sometimes written with a short stem and is almost indistinguishable from the י.

[81] Cf. supra, III.

sceptre is expounded as meaning the future prince of the congregation. We may assume here too that the verse is expounded to mean the new priest from Levi and the future king from Judah.[82] The Testament of Judah gives special emphasis to the superiority of Levi over Judah; we also have here a prophecy of a future king from the tribe of Judah, and perhaps of two anointed ones from Levi and Judah.

Issachar v, 7: And Levi and Judah were extolled by the Lord even among the sons of Jacob; for the Lord gave them an inheritance, and to Levi he gave the priesthood and to Judah the kingdom.

[82] After this paper was completed a study by K. Schubert, Testamentum Judah 24 im Lichte der Texte von Chirbet Qumran, appeared in the Wiener Zeitschrift fur die Kunde des Morgenlandes, 53, 1957, pp. 227–236. Schubert also points out the close similarity between Test. Judah xxiv and the messianic expectations of the Dead Sea Sect. He even attempts to reconstruct the Hebrew original of this chapter, drawing upon the theological terminology of the Sect. His conclusions are founded on the Hebrew text that he reconstructed. This experiment is most enlightening; but on the other hand if we recast the Testaments into a proposed Hebrew original we cannot, in the present state of research, use that reconstructed text to prove a point.

Schubert is inclined to regard Test. Judah xxiv as referring to the anointed of David, and only in verse 1 does he find an intimation of the two anointed ones. Schubert's theory is based on: (1) a reconstruction of verse 1 as follows, "ואחר כך ידרוך כוכב מיעקב בשמים ויקם גבר משבטי כשמש הצדק" (כשמים being an emendation of בשלום which the Greek indicates). Here Schubert seems to find a clear inference to Num. xxiv, 17, "There shall come a star out of Jacob and a sceptre (שבט) shall rise out of Israel," and as this biblical text is connected, in the writings of the Sect, with the expectations of the anointed ones of Aaron and Israel (vide supra), the beginning of Test. Judah xxiv points to the same figures. (2) Schubert's theory is also based on several terms or expressions which are traditionally connected with the Davidic Messiah; some of these in verses 5–6, verses which are undoubtedly intended for the Davidic future king; but one of these terms "צמח" appears according to Schubert in verse 4, which in the Greek versions belongs to the first part of Test. Judah xxiv, i.e., that part of the chapter which I regard as applying to the anointed one of Aaron.

It is especially on these two points that Schubert's reconstruction is, at least, unfounded: (1) In verse 1 he retranslates the Greek into Hebrew, "ויקום גבר משבטי" (and a man shall arise from my tribe [= שבט]); but the Greek σπέρμα usually means seed, and never a tribe or sceptre. If we reject this unfounded emendation there is nothing more to support Schubert's view that in this verse the sceptre of Num. xxiv, 17 is mentioned or even implied. (2) In verse 4 Schubert translates, "צמח לאל עליון" (sic.) "הואה" (He is the "shoot" of the God most high). The Greek word βλαστός which Schubert translates as "צמח" (the inverted commas are in Schubert's German translation) is used in the LXX for some Hebrew words connected with growth and sprouting, but never for "צמח." The word for "צמח" in the LXX is usually Ἀνατολή. Cf. also Van der Woude, ibid. (supra notes 9, 59) pp. 206 f.

Here we have hegemony among the tribes to Levi and Judah; priesthood to Levi and kingship to Judah.

> Dan v, 4: I know that in the last days you shall depart from the Lord, and you shall provoke Levi to anger and fight against Judah but you shall not prevail against them. For an angel of the Lord shall guide them both; for by them shall Israel stand.
>
> Dan v, 9–10: And so when you return to the Lord you shall obtain mercy and he shall bring you into His sanctuary, and He shall give you peace and there shall arise unto you from the tribe of Judah and of Levi (ἐκ τῆς φυλῆς Ἰουδα καὶ τοῦ Λευι) the salvation of the Lord. And He shall make war against Beliar, etc.

Charles [83] regards the word Judah in verse 10 as an interpolation and reads: "there shall arise unto you from the tribe of Levi the salvation of the Lord." According to him this is to be proved from the fact that in the text before us we have "from the tribe of" and not "from the tribes of." But it is much more probable that the word "tribe" is to be regarded as the interpolation, and the original text was "from Judah and Levi" or "from Levi and Judah." The rest of this verse "And He shall make war, etc." as well as the previous verse (Dan v, 9) is concerned with God and not with Levi or Judah.[84]

According to the Testament of Dan, the salvation of the Lord shall be from the two tribes Levi and Judah. This testament does not concern itself with the historical priesthood or kingship; this has already been dealt with at length in the previous testaments.

> Naphtali viii, 2–3: Do you also charge your children that they be united to Levi and to Judah. For through Judah shall come the salvation of Israel and in him shall Jacob be blessed. For through his tribe, etc.

---

[83] Charles, Greek Versions, p. 138.

[84] The verse which comes after these cited above, Dan v, 11, "And the captivity shall He take from Beliar; the souls of the saints, and turn the disobedient hearts unto the Lord and give to them that call upon Him the eternal peace," evidently concerns God, and not the human savior, even though in the text that is before us it is written that He shall turn the disobedient hearts, "unto the Lord" and not "unto Him."

Here apparently the salvation of Israel is only in Judah, although Levi is also mentioned. Charles [85] emends the verse as follows: "For through them (Levi and Judah) shall come the salvation, etc." Segal [86] offers the reading: "For through Judah shall come the salvation of Israel and in Levi shall Jacob be blessed." But the whole passage shows definite signs of Christian elaboration, and in verse 3 we even find a characteristic Christian expression such as: "Shall God, dwelling among men, appear on earth." We cannot, therefore, place here too much importance on the exact wording, but the general meaning is the supremacy of the two tribes Levi and Judah. In Naphtali v, 3–4 there comes a vision in which Naphtali sees Levi grasping the sun while Judah seizes the moon, i.e., the supremacy of Levi over Judah is most clearly stated.

> Gad viii, 1: Do you also tell these things to your children, that they honour Judah and Levi for from them shall the Lord raise up [87] salvation to Israel.[88]

In the Testament of Gad we have salvation of Israel in Judah and in Levi. Like the Testament of Dan, it does not concern itself with the historical priesthood and kingship.

Joseph xix, 11–12:

Greek Mss. and Slavonic Recension	Armenian Version [89]
Do you therefore my children observe the commandments of the Lord, and honour Levi and Ju-	And do you my children honour Levi and Judah for from them shall arise the salvation of Israel.

---

[85] Charles, Greek Versions, pp. 155 f.

[86] Segal, op. cit. (supra note 56), p. 133. If we follow Segal's suggestion, we have only to read "וּבלוי" instead of "ובו," i.e., the error was already in the Hebrew text of the Greek translator.

[87] ἀνατελεῖ — this word may mean "arise" as well as "raise up."

[88] σωτηρίαν — so in the Greek Mss. c, g, h, i, and in the Armenian Version. We have to prefer this reading to the reading of Ms. b — σωτῆρα, only according to the reading of this one Ms. can we interpret the verse to mean that the Lord shall raise up the savior of Israel from the two tribes. The reading in Mss. a, d, e, f — σωτήρ has a Christian character, for according to this reading the verse means that there shall arise (cf. the preceding note) from the two tribes the Lord savior of Israel.

[89] According to the translation of Charles, Greek Versions, pp. 211 f.; Testaments, pp. 195 f.

dah. For from them shall arise unto you the lamb of God who shall take away the sin of the world saving all the nations and Israel. For his kingdom is an everlasting kingdom which shall not pass away, but my kingdom among you shall come to an end as a watcher's hammock which disappears after the summer.

For my kingdom which is among you shall come to an end as a watcher's hammock which will not appear after the summer.

In the Greek Version we have expressions such as: "The lamb of God who shall take away the sin of the world saving all the nations" which is most clearly a Christian interpolation. The expression: "For his kingdom is an everlasting kingdom which shall not pass away" also seems to be of Christian origin. Whereas the shorter Armenian Version seems to be nearer to the original.[90] The main difference between the Armenian and the Greek in the parallel parts is in verse 11. Whereas in the Greek we have: "For from there shall arise unto you the one who shall save," i.e., a savior from the two tribes, we have in the Armenian the non-committal: "For from them shall arise the salvation of Israel." Here too we are to prefer the text that underlies the Armenian version; for in other Testaments (Simeon vii, 1; Dan v, 10; Gad viii, 1; etc.) we do find in the Greek as well as in the Armenian the same formula: "Salvation of Israel" or "Salvation of the Lord," as applied to Levi and Judah. The kingdom that shall come to an end, in these verses from the Testament of Joseph, is the Northern Kingdom of the Ten Tribes. Of Levi and Judah it is here simply said: "Do you therefore my children honour

[90] Cf. Charles, Testaments, p. 191. Christian interpolations are also found in the Testament of Benjamin xi, 2. In one of the Mss. (c). we find: "And there shall arise in the end of days one beloved of the Lord from the tribe of Judah and Levi, a doer of His good pleasure in his mouth." In other Greek Mss. and the Slavonic recension we have here a passage most clearly pointing to Paul. On the other hand in the Armenian version Benjamin says about his own tribe: "And I shall no longer be called a captain of robbers and a wolf on account of your ravages, but one beloved of the Lord and a doer of the good pleasure of His mouth" (cf. Gen. xlix, 27; Deut. xxxiii, 12). Cf. also Charles, The Greek Versions, pp. 230 f.; Segal, op. cit. (n. 56 supra), p. 133, n. 17.

Levi and Judah for from them shall arise the salvation of Israel." From the texts we have examined, and they are all the texts in the Book of the Testaments of the Twelve Patriarchs which concern this subject, we have obtained a consistent picture.[91] Kingship from Judah and priesthood from Levi in the historical past as well as in the messianic future; hopes for the salvation of Israel in Levi as well as in Judah; superiority of the priesthood over kingship, i.e., of Levi over Judah. We do not have in the Book of the Testaments a savior or ruler who will emerge from both tribes, nor do we have a concentration of the offices of king and priest in the hands of a ruler from the tribe of Levi.

A similar attitude to priesthood and kingship is found in the Book of Jubilees. According to Jub. xxxi, 9 ff., Isaac blesses in a spirit of prophecy before his death Levi and Judah; he lays his right hand on Levi and his left on Judah as a sign of the superiority of Levi over Judah.[92] He also blesses Levi first. In this blessing (xxxi, 13–18) the holiness, greatness and glory of the sons of Levi are described, and their great honor as servants of the Lord and teachers of his Law, who bless the people in the name of the Lord. They shall be judges and princes and chiefs to all the seed of Jacob. The blessing over Judah (xxxi, 18–21) is much shorter, and the stress is on the rule of Judah as king, his strength in war and power, and the fear of the nations before him. The blessings

[91] Table summing up the attitude to Levi and Judah in the different Testaments:

	Reuben	Simeon	Levi	Judah	Issa-char	Dan	Naph-tali	Gad	Joseph
Superiority of Levi over Judah	vi:7,11			xxi:1–2 xxv:1–2			v:3–4		
Priesthood to Levi; Kingship to Judah	vi:8,10	vii:2	viii:11–16		v:7				
Salvation of Israel in Levi and Judah		vii:1				v:4,7	viii:2–3	viii:1	xix:11
The new priest at the end of days	vi:8	vii:2?	xviii:1ff.	xxiv:1–4?					
The messianic King at the end of days	vi:12	vii:2?		xxii:2–3 xxiv:5–6					

[92] According to Jub. xxxii, 8–9, Levi officiated as a priest in Bethel before his father Jacob and also received from his father tithes. Cf. also Jub. xxx, 18–19; 32:1.

in the main apply to the historical Levi and Judah, but the picture given by the author of the Book of Jubilees (who belonged to the same sectarian circles [93] as the author of the Book of the Testaments of the Twelve Patriarchs) is in accord with the description of the future messianic time in the Book of the Testaments, which is also most probably that of the author of the Book of Jubilees.

V

The doctrine of the two anointed ones, one from Aaron and the other from Israel (i.e., David), and the special position of the anointed of Aaron as against the anointed of Israel is rooted in the particular social and religious background of the sects at the time of Hasmonean rule. It is only in sectarian writings that we find this doctrine clearly expressed and expounded.

Indeed the anointed ones of Aaron and Israel are not saviors in the true sense of the word, but leaders of the people in the time of salvation, and we also find a cosmic redeemer appointed from the beginning of time, who is hinted at in sectarian writings [94] and explicitly mentioned in related works.[95] But there is no real contradiction between this superhuman figure and the anointed ones of Aaron and Israel. And furthermore in later eschatological systems we find a savior with both human and cosmic characteristics that cannot logically be combined. The most celebrated example is Jesus, who is regarded in the Gospels as both human and divine. In a lesser degree we find this feature in Judaism too.[96] Moreover, the different aspects of the character of the savior and the various eschatological systems left their mark even after they had passed

[93] Cf. supra, I.

[94] The wondrous councillor whose supernatural birth is described in The Thanksgiving Scroll (1QH III, 10 f.); cf. also, J. Licht, The Thanksgiving Scroll. Jerusalem, 1957, pp. 51, 76 ff. (Hebrew).

[95] The Son of Man in the Ethiopic Book of Enoch, chs. xxxvii–lxxi (The Similitudes of Enoch). Cf. H. H. Rowley, The Relevance of Apocalyptic², New York, 1946, pp. 58 ff.

[96] Cf. P. Volz, Die Eschatologie der jüdischen Gemeinde im Neutestamentlichen Zeitalter, Tübingen, 1934, pp. 173 ff.; J. Klausner, The Messianic Idea in Israel (Trans. from the 3rd Hebrew Ed.), New York, 1955, passim.

away, and we find in rabbinic literature [97] as well as in Christianity [98] traces of a priestly Messiah.

The central position of the anointed of Aaron in the eschatological system of the Dead Sea Sect is the result of a long historical development on the one hand and of the circumstances of the formation of the Sect on the other. The rise of the priesthood to a position of authority and rule in Judea had already begun after the return from Babylonian exile, and at the end of the Persian period, or shortly afterwards, the high priest was already ruler of Judea and its official representative to the foreign governing power; even the changes which came over Judea with the rise of the Hasmonean house maintained the rule in the hands of the high priesthood. In the prophecies of Zechariah in the vision of the two anointed ones (iv, 1–5, 11–14) and the prophecy on the shoot (vi, 12–13) the high priest already appears as equal to the future king, or at least not much inferior. In the song of praise at the end of the Book of Ecclesiasticus we also find, alongside the benediction "to Him that makes a horn to sprout for the house of David" (li, 12), the benediction "to Him that chooses the sons of Zadok to be priests" (ibid.). Even after the upheaval that took place in Judea, when the Hasmonean house arose and the sons of Zadok [99] came down from their exalted position, the

[97] Cf. Cant. Rabba 2: 29; Bab. Sukkah 52b, etc. Cf. Ginzberg, op. cit. (supra n. 56), pp. 411–428; Grintz, op. cit. (supra n. 1), p. 32. Some hints of a priestly Messiah are probably also found in Karaite literature; cf. N. Wieder, The Doctrine of the Two Messiahs among the Karaites, Journal of Jewish Studies, 6, 1955, pp. 14–25.

[98] Cf. Hebrews, passim. Cf. also Y. Yadin, The Dead Sea Scrolls and the Epistle to the Hebrews, Aspects of the Dead Sea Scrolls, Jerusalem, 1957, pp. 36–55. On efforts to find the conception that the Messiah is also a priest, in other books of the New Testament, cf. F. Friedrich, Beobachtungen zur messianischen Hohepriestererwartung in den Synoptikenn, Zeitschrift für Theologie und Kirche, 53, 1956, pp. 265–311, esp. pp. 275 ff.

[99] The Hasmoneans, who were provincial priests and belonged to the division of Jehoiarib (1 Macc. ii, 1) most probably did not belong to the house of Zadok. The fact that the blessing, "to Him that chooseth the sons of Zadok to be priests," which comes in the song of praise at the end of the Hebrew Ecclesiasticus (li, 12) is not repeated in the later prayers, and that the whole song of praise does not come in the Greek translation of Ecclesiasticus, may show that from the time of the Hasmoneans and onward the sons of Zadok did not generally officiate as high priests. The special emphasis in the writings of the Dead Sea Sect that the men of the Sect separated themselves from the remainder of the nation under the leadership of the sons of Zadok ("When they shall gather [in the assembly to] walk according to the Law of the priests sons of Zadok and the men of their covenant

leadership of the people and the rule of the country was yet retained in the hands of the high priests.

The beginning of the Dead Sea Sect was after the sons of Zadok came down, but not a long time afterwards; the leaders of the Sect were descended from the sons of Zadok [100] who strove to restore their former glory. The Sect grew most probably from the extreme pietists, the Hasidim, at the time of the persecutions of Antiochus IV.[101] These fled to the desert, hid in caves and gave their lives to uphold the Torah (1 Macc. ii, 29–42). Among them were also priests from the aristocratic house of Zadok. Evidence of the presence of priests of high lineage among them is preserved in rabbinical tradition on Jose ben Joezer, who was most pious in priesthood — חסיד שבכהונה (Mishnah Hagigah ii, 7), and was also the uncle of Yaqum-Alcimus,[102] the high priest at the time of persecution of Antiochus. We learn of the conservatism of those circles and their adherence to the leadership of the house of Zadok from the fact that the Hasidim were ready to accept the peace offers of that same Alcimus who was made high priest by Antiochus

---

who forsook [the way] of the people, they are the men of His counsel who kept His covenant in the midst of wickedness"; Rule of the Congregation Col. I, 1 f.; cf. for the proposed readings 1QS V, 1–3; etc.) also probably shows that the Hasmoneans did not belong to the family of Zadok. And one of the reasons for their severe antagonism to the Hasmonean high priest (The Wicked Priest 1Q p. Hab. passim, cf. M. H. Segal, The Habakkuk Commentary and the Damascus Fragments, JBL, 70, 1951, pp. 137 ff.) was most probably that in their opinion the Hasmoneans were not properly qualified to act as high priests.

[100] On the status of the priests in the Sect, cf. 1QS II, 19–21; IX, 7; Rule of the Congregation Col. II, 13–14; CD XIV, 3; and especially on the status of the sons of Zadok, 1QS V, 2–3; Rule of the Congregation, passim; etc. On the leadership of the Sect from its foundation by the son of Zadok, cf..supra note 99. It is most probable that the founder of the Sect, the Teacher of Righteousness, as well as the Interpreter of the Law (the leader of the Sect after him) belonged to the high priestly family of Zadok. That the Teacher of Righteousness was a priest we learn from the fragments of a Pesher to Psalm xxxvii published by Allegro (PEQ, 1954, pp. 69–75) where it is said, "its interpretation concerns the priest the teacher of righteousness" פשרו על הכהן מורה ה]צדק[," p. 71, Col. II, 15). Cf. also 1Q p. Hab., II, 7–8; and further fragments from p. Ps. xxxvii (J. M. Allegro, JBL, 75, 1956, pp. 94–95). The Interpreter of the Law was also most probably a priest, as we learn from the fact that the interpretation of the law was one of the offices of the priests (cf. 1QS V, 9–10; VI, 6; CD XIII, 1–3; XIV, 6–8); this is affirmed by his position, in the various texts dealt with above, as the leader who is to stand at the end of days together with the Davidic king.

[101] On the history of the Sect cf. the works mentioned in note 5 supra.

[102] Cf. Gen. Rabba 65: 18 — Jakum of Zeraroth (i.e., Alcimus) was the nephew of Rabbi Jose ben Joezer of Zeredah, etc.

after Menelaus (2 Macc. xiv, 3, 7), mainly because he was from the legitimate high priestly family (cf. 1 Macc. vii, 12–14). It seems most probable that a considerable number of the Hasidim and especially the priests sons of Zadok among them were op-posed at a later date to the taking over of the high priesthood by the Hasmonean house from the sons of Zadok. And when the rule of the Hasmonean house was made permanent and the high priests from the Hasmonean house embarked upon wars of con-quest, entered into political alliance with Gentiles and adapted themselves to the ways of life of the Hellenistic rulers, this opposition intensified. At the same time, during the reign of Hyrcanus I or even earlier, the priestly Teacher of Righteousness arose, who was most probably from the Zadokite family of high priests, and organized the Sect [103] as a united and compact body. This Sect separated itself, as we have already remarked, from the mass of the nation and considered itself to be the only true Israel.

The striving for redemption of the Dead Sea Sect, the fact that for hundreds of years it had been customary to see in the high priest the only ruler and leader of the people, and the central posi-tion of the sons of Zadok in the Sect brought about the formation of a doctrine which placed at the head of the congregation of Israel in future times a high priest — the anointed of Aaron. But the unlimited authority of the Bible, which the Sect shared with the rest of the people of Israel, required the appearance of a Davidic Messiah in any eschatological system where redemption is brought by earthly persons. And so, when they formed this image of an eschatological priest, they could not disregard the prophecies on the house of David in the Bible; and they placed at the side of the anointed of Aaron the anointed of Israel, that is, the king who would arise from the house of David.

According to the Dead Sea Sect, the anointed of Aaron would probably arise from the family of Zadok, from which house the leaders of the Sect came. On the other hand, families whose de-scent from the house of David was confirmed no longer existed in Palestine at that time either inside or outside the Sect.[104] But

---

[103] Vide CD I, 7–10, and cf. supra note 100.

[104] Cf. J. Liver, The Problem of the Genealogy of the Davidic Family after the Biblical Period, Tarbiz, 26, 1957, pp. 229–254 (Hebrew; English summary ibid. pp. I–III).

the hope for an anointed of David was not connected with the physical presence of a family tracing its descent from the house of David at that time. This hope was connected with the belief that the house of David did exist inside the nation, even if it was not known who its representatives were, and the Davidic Messiah would appear at the appointed time, even though before his appearance his identity might be unknown. The announcement of the coming of the future time and the establishment of the identity of the anointed of Aaron from the house of Zadok and the anointed of Israel from Israel — the Sect, are among the functions of the prophet who would arise at the end of days.[105]

The doctrine of the two Messiahs in the Book of the Testaments of the Twelve Patriarchs is identical, as we have shown, with that found in the writings of the Dead Sea Sect; and those parts in the Book of the Testaments which are concerned with the Messiahs of Judah and Levi belong either to the Sect itself or to circles close to it. We have no evidence at all for the existence of a doctrine of two Messiahs outside the Dead Sea Sect and its related circles. From the decline of the Hasmonean kingdom onward we find the belief in a messianic ruler from the house of David in Israel in full force, while in the apocalyptic visions in the Book of Daniel which belong to the time before the Hasmonean rule, there is no terrestrial Messiah at all.[106] It may not seem improbable on the face of it that the doctrine of two Messiahs — the one from Aaron being the more important — should arise among the adherents of the Hasmonean priestly rulers, but these were well established in their rule and it is rather far-fetched to assume that they encouraged eschatological hopes whose realization would

---

[105] Vide 1QS IX, 10–11, "until the coming of a prophet and the anointed ones of Aaron and Israel," and cf. 1 Macc. iv, 46. See also Silberman, op. cit. (supra n. 10), where this question is dealt with in detail.

[106] The expression anointed one (מָשִׁיחַ) nevertheless occurs in the Book of Daniel. In Dan. ix, 25 "one anointed the prince" is mentioned and in verse 26 it is said, "And after the three score and two weeks shall an anointed one be cut off." No eschatological ruler is meant here but only a king or high priest, according to the usual meaning of this term in the Bible. The period of the first of these anointed ones is after the Babylonian exile and he is usually identified with Cyrus (cf. Isa. xlv, 1), Zerubbabel or the High Priest Joshua. The other anointed one is usually identified with the High Priest Onias IV who was removed from office by Antiochus IV. Cf. J. A. Montgomery, The Book of Daniel, Edinburgh, 1927, pp. 378 ff.; A. Bentzen, Daniel, Tübingen, 1952, pp. 74 f.

limit their authority. Insofar as we have evidence, during the whole period of Hasmonean rule the belief in a future messianic king from the house of David was present as a vague hope for the very distant future.[107] This belief was general, and only among sectarians was there added the figure of a priestly Messiah, and the doctrine of two Messiahs peculiar to them took shape. We may assume that in its later history the Sect underwent a certain development which gave more prominence to the future expectations connected with the house of David. That this really was so we learn from the new texts from Qumran Cave 4 where more stress is placed on the Davidic future king than in most of the other texts. This development most probably happened after the persecutions which the Sect underwent, and after the disappointment at the delay in the coming of expected salvation.[108] It is also possible that the general trend at the time of the decline of Hasmonean rule — which brought about the rise of the hope for

---

[107] For the belief in a future king from the House of David among the Hasmoneans and their adherents, we may turn to the words that the author of the First Book of Maccabees puts into the mouth of Mattathias in his last speech to his sons, "David for being merciful inherited the throne of kingship for ever" (1 Macc. ii, 56), which furthermore implies a belief in the eternity of the House of David. In the same trend he tells of the confirmation of Simon in his office, "and the Jews and the priests are well pleased that Simon shall be their prince and high priest for ever until a true prophet shall arise" (1 Macc. xiv, 41). Appointing a permanent order "until a true prophet shall arise" may be regarded as proof that the Hasmoneans distinguished clearly between the duration of their rule and the future salvation; for the coming of the true prophet is the first stage towards that end. Compare the use of that same formula in the Dead Sea Scrolls (cf. supra n. 105). On the other hand, the fact that the Hasmonean rulers proclaimed themselves kings and the early Halakhah regards them as the legitimate kings for their time (cf. G. Alon, Sinai 12, 1943, p. 25 ff.; Hebrew) may teach us that the Hasmoneans and their adherents, as well as the people and the Pharisee rabbis, regarded the hope for the renewal of the Davidic kingdom as an expectation for a distant future age. And cf. the Baraitha in Bab. Talmud Sotah 48b, "Come and hear: When the First Temple was destroyed, the cities with pasture land were abolished, the Urim and Thummim ceased, there was no more king from the House of David. And if anyone incites you to quote 'And the governor said unto them that they shall not eat of the most holy things till there stand up a priest with Urim and Thummim' [reply to him] as when one man says to another 'until the dead revive and the Messiah son of David comes' (i.e., it is only a phrase for the very remote future)"; also cf. Yer. Kid. 4:1. On the other hand the pious author of the Psalms of Solomon, who wrote at the time of the last Hasmonean princes, after the Roman conquest of Jerusalem, and hoped for redemption and salvation in the near future, accuses the Hasmonean kings of having usurped the throne reserved for the descendants of David (Ps. xvii). Cf. also supra n. 52.

[108] Cf. Flusser, op. cit. (supra n. 6), pp. 97 ff.

a Davidic Messiah — influenced the members of the Sect indirectly. This trend found expression in sectarian writings in the emphasis laid on the prominence and royal status of the Prince of the Congregation at the end of days, who is explicitly called "the Shoot of Righteousness, the Anointed of David"; but all this without leaving to any marked degree the framework of faith and doctrine which traditionally prevailed in the Sect, and most probably without giving up the central position of the anointed of Aaron in its eschatological system.

V

Messianic Phenomena—
Speculation and Calculation

משה בֵּר

משהו על רב יהודה אחוה דרב סלא חסידא

לזכרו של דודי המנוח,

ר׳ דב יששכר בער, ז״ל, היועץ המשפטי של משרד הדתוה.

רב יהודה אחוה דרב סלא חסידא נמנה בין אלה אמוראי בבל שאין
בידינו לעמוד על טיבם ועל תורתם. לפיכך כל ידיעה, ולו הקטנה ביותר, שאפשר
להעלותה מן המקורות ושיש בכוחה להאיר אישיותו של אחד מחכמי התלמוד,
טמונה בה ברכה.

להלן ייעשה הנסיון לדון על אישיותו של רב יהודה אחוה דרב סלא
חסידא מתוך הסיפורים על גילויי אליהו שנתגלו לו לחכם זה. ובינתיים נסכם
בקצרה את הפרטים הביוגראפיים המעטים הידועים לנו על אמורא בבלי זה.

הוא חי במחציתה הראשונה של המאה הרביעית בעיר נהרדעא,
כמסופר בשבת קיב, א. שם נמסר דיון בעניין הלכי בין רב יהודה לבין אביי;
ואילו על מקום מגוריו אפשר לעמוד מתוך דברי "אביי ואיתימא רב נחמן בר
יצחק" שנשתמרו ביומא יט, ב. על מעמדו הכללי של רב יהודה אפשר להסיק
מתוך הסוגיא בשבת, שם. במהלכה של הסוגיא הנזכרת, בה מוסב הדיון על נעילת
הסנדל בשבת ובדינים הקשורים בה, מביאים לדוגמא את רב יהודה אחוה דרב סלא
חסידא, שהוא ובנו נעלו חליפות אותו זוג סנדלים עצמו. מכאן, שלא היה אמיד אם
לא פחות מזה [1]. אלו הן כל הידיעות הביוגראפיות שנשתמרו על רב יהודה [2]. מהן
מצטיירת דמותו של תלמיד חכם לא אמיד, ובעל משפחה, שחי בישוב יהודי קדום
ומרכזי של יהודי בבל שירד מגדולתו.

אולם אין בפרטים מועטים אלה, כאמור, כדי להעמיד אותנו על עולמו הדתי-
הרוחני של ת״ח זה. ולשם כך עלינו לעיין בתוכנם של גילויי אליהו, שזכה רב
יהודה ונתגלה לו. ועל שלושה גילויים נמסר לנו בתלמוד הבבלי.

גילויים אלה נתייחד להם מקום מיוחד, שכן מצד תכנם הם שונים, שינוי
מהותי, מאותם גילויי אליהו שנתגלו להם לאמוראים האחרים בבבל [3]. אולם בטרם
שנעמוד על ייחודם נציע את המקורות עצמם:

"אמר ליה אליהו לרב יהודה אחוה דרב סלא חסידא: אין העולם פחות

---

1 על פרט זה כבר עמד הײַמאן, בתולדות תנאים ואמוראים, חלק ב, עמ׳ 552.

2 מ. איש־שלום, במבוא למהדורתו לסדר אליהו רבה... מהדורה שניה, עמ׳ 34
סבור, שהמאורע עליו מסופר בברכות ה, ב : "רב הונא תקיפו ליה מאה דני דחמרא..."
מדובר ברב יהודה שלנו. אולם זו טעות, שכן מבחינה כרונולוגית אי אפשר להעלות על הדעת
שבמחציתה השניה של המאה השלישית הוכיח, תוכחה נמרצת למדי, רב יהודה זה את רב
הונא הגדול ממנו בשנים מרובות. ובאמת יש שם "ואמרי לה" והמסופר הוא ברב אדא בר
אהבה, חבירו של רב הונא. וראה גם בדקדוקי סופרים למקום.

3 את גילויי־אליהו המרובים בספרות חז״ל אסף איש־שלום במבואותיו לסדר אליהו רבה.

משמונים וחמשה יובלות וביובל האחרון בן דוד בא. א״ל: בתחילתו או בסופו?
א״ל: איני יודע; כלה או אינו כלה? א״ל: איני יודע. רב אשי אמר: הכי אמר ליה:
עד הכא לא תיסתכי ליה, מכאן ואילך איסתכי ליה״ [4].

דו־שיח זה מגלה באופן חד־משמעי, שרב יהודה חי תוך ציפיה משיחית
אינטנסיבית ביותר. נתברר לו, לרב יהודה, שבן דוד לא יבוא בימיו, אלא לכל
המוקדם במחציתה השניה של המאה החמישית. וקרוב לומר, שהיה בו, בגילוי זה,
בשורה שדכאה את רוחו של רב יהודה.

ציפיתו־כמיהתו של רב יהודה למשיח עולה גם מן הגילוי הבא: „דאמר
ליה אליהו לרב יהודה אחוה דרב סלא חסידא: אמריתו, אמאי לא אתי משיח?
והא האידנא יומא דכיפורי הוא ואבעול כמה בתולתא בנהרדעא! א״ל: הקב״ה מאי
אמר? אמר ליה: ,לפתח חטאת רובץ׳ (בראשית ד). ושטן מאי אמר? א״ל: שטן
ביומא דכיפורי לית ליה רשות לאסטוני״ [5].

אמנם, יש הבדל ניכר בין שני הגילויים הנזכרים, שכן תכנו של הגילוי
הראשון הוא אינפורמטיבי והוא מגלה את זמנה של הגאולה. והוא תשובה לתמיהתו
של רב יהודה בבעיית ה„מתי״. בעוד שהגילוי השני בא להשיב על התלבטותו
של רב יהודה בבעיית ה„למה״. למה לא בא בן דוד ביום הכיפורים, שבו בני
ישראל נקיי עוון. אולם, הצד השווה בין שני הגילויים הוא העדות, והיא עדות
מכוונת, שרב יהודה היה בעל חוויה דתית ערה, שהענין המשיחי תפס בה מקום
נרחב למדי.

בעצם, אף במשנתם של אמוראי בבל אחרים תפס הענין המשיחי מקום רחב.
אלא אם נשווה את הגותם המשיחית של אלה [6] לזו של רב יהודה, נמצא הבדל חשוב.
רוב מאמריהם של אמוראי בבל, שדן בענייני הגאולה, עוסק בעיקרו בתנאים
הדרושים כדי להחיש את בואו של הגואל, או במה שעתיד להיות ולהתרחש בדור
בו יבוא בן דוד, וכיוצא בו. הם דנים בעניינים אלה מתוך דיסטאנס מסויים ומתוך
דיון שהוא לרוב נטול כל תקיפות סוביקטיבית. בעוד שרב יהודה דן בענייני הגאולה,
במידה שהגילויים המועטים מאפשרים לשפוט על כך, מתוך תקיפות סוביקטיבית.
הענין דוחק לו ואליהו מתגלה לו ומוסר לו מה שמוסר.

וכאן מתעוררת השאלה: מה גרם לשוני הנזכר. האם יש כאן רק הבדלים
פסיכולוגיים, שוני שבמזג, או שפעלו כאן גורמים היסטוריים־ריאליים שהשפיעו
וקבעו את העמדות השונות שבתפיסה המשיחית ואת דחיפותה?

לכאורה, נועד כאן לענין הפסיכולוגי מקום חשוב. שכן שני המקורות
הנזכרים הם גילויי אליהו. כלומר, תופעה פסיכולוגית־סוביקטיבית מובהקת. והם
עצמם עדים נאמנים למידת רגישותו הנפשית של רב יהודה בענין זה. אולם דומה,
שהסיבה הפסיכולוגית כשלעצמה אין ביכולתה לבאר אל נכון את כמיהתו המשיחית
של אמורא זה. קרוב לומר, שרגישותו הנפשית של רב יהודה ניזונה במישרין
ממאורעות היסטוריים־ריאליים.

ונסקור להלן רק בקצרה אחדות מן הפורענויות שפקדו את יהודי בבל

---

4 סנהדרין צז, רע״ב. ובכ״י מינכן: סכ״י.

5 יומא יט, ב ובכ״י מינכן בשינויים קלים. מקור זה נתפרש בצורה בלתי מניחה את
הדעת. ראה, למשל, י. מ. גוטמן, מפתח התלמוד, כרך ג, עמ׳ 40.

6 עי׳, למשל, סנהדרין פרק י.

ושניתן לשער שהן הן שגרמו להתעוררות דתית־משיחית בחוגם של ת״ח. החל
משנות העשרים של המאה השלישית, פקדו את יהודי בבל מספר מאורעות טראגיים.
יהדות זו, שחיה את חייה במשך מאות שנים, תוך שלווה יחסית נזדעזעה עם עלותה
של השושלת הסאסנידית לשלטון. שורה של פגיעות דתיות באו להם לפתע וערערו
את בטחונם [7], וכשוך חמתם וקנאותם הדתית של הכובשים החדשים עלה עליהם, על
יהודי בבל, צבא השודדים של התדמורים בהנהגתו של פפא בר נצר. וביחוד ייזכר
כאן כיבושה של נהרדעא והריסתה בסופה של שנת 259 או בתחילתה של שנת 260 [8],
שגרמה סבל מרובה לתושביו של מרכז עתיק זה [9]. ואין ספק, שמאורע טראגי זה
גרם זעזוע ליהודי בבל כולה, מלבד סבלם של פליטי העיר [10] וביותר של השבויים
המרובים, שנשבו ע״י גדודיו של פפא בר נצר. אולם, המאורעות שעשויים היו
לגרום להתעוררות משיחית ולעיצוב תפיסתה היו ההתנגשויות הקשות והממושכות
בין רומי ופרס. שתי המעצמות העולמיות של אותה תקופה, גרמו לשורה ארוכה
של פגעים חמורים ליהודי בבל, שנתפרשו על ידם כמלחמת גוג ומגוג ועוררו
בקרבם תקוות משיחיות [11], אולם במחציתה הראשונה של המאה הרביעית נתרבה
סבלם של יהודי בבל והתקוות המשיחיות נתבדו. המוני ערבים התפרצו לישוביהם
לשם שוד וביזה ואונס. עד כמה שידוע לי היה נולדקה [12] הראשון, שהעמיד על
מאורעות אלה. גרם להם מזלם ליהודי פומבדיתא, נהרדעא (שנשתקמה במקצת),
הגרוניא, מתא מחסיא, סורא, כפרי נרש, ואחרים, ששכנו על גבול המדבר ולפיכך
היו הם הראשונים שסבלו קשות מידיהם של הערבים־המתנפלים.

אולם גם בתחום המצב הדתי נתרחש ובא מפנה גדול במחציתה הראשונה
של המאה הרביעית. עלייתו של קונסטנטין לשלטון גרמה לכך ששיפור השני החל
ברדיפה שיטתית ואכזרית אחרי הנוצרים. שיפור השני ראה בהם, בנוצרים, אויבים
בכוח, שלבם במערב ומושבם במזרח. לא ברור לגמרי מה היה גורלם של יהודי
בבל בזמן הרדיפות [13] בין כה וכה יש להביא בחשבון את המתיחות הפרסית־
נוצרית, שלשבה ממדים נרחבים וקבלה אופי מרטירולוגי. קל לשער שבאווירה
כזאת גברה והלכה התסיסה המשיחית בקרב חוגים שונים של יהודי בבל וביחוד
בחוגם של ת״ח.

ייתכן ונפשו הרגישה של רב יהודה ניזונה ממאורעות הטראגיים הנזכרים,
שעיצבו את תפיסתו המשיחית וגרמו לו לדחוק את הקץ. ואם יש בה, בהנחתנו, מן
האמת הרי אז גם קל לשער מה מידת האכזבה שנגרמה לו לרב יהודה כאשר נתבדו
תקוותיו המשיחיות. את מקומן של אותן הציפיות תפסו האכזבה והדכאון.

ומתוך הסתייגות וזהירות מרובה יש לשאול : האם אין בגילוי אליהו השלישי

7 ראה להלן הערה 11.

8 עיין Mommsen, Römische Geschichte, V 3, Berlin, 1886, s. 430, ff.
וג. אלון, תולדות היהודים . . . ב, עמ' 171 והערה 43.

9 עי' קדמוניות היהודים ליוסף בן מתתיהו, ספר יט, פרק ט.

10 על גורל בנותיו של שמואל, עי' ירושלמי כתובות פ״ב, ה״י (כו, סע״ג).

11 ראה בספרו של פונק, Die Juden in Babylonien, I. Berlin, 1902, s. 75.

12 בתרגומו הגרמני של טאבארי, ליידען, 1879, עמ' 68—52. יש להוסיף את המקורות
הבאים : כתובות ג, ב ; חולין מו, א. ועוד.

13 ראה נולדקה, שם.

שנתגלה לו לרב יהודה משום עדות על מצבו הפסיכי הקשה. על גילוי זה נמסר
לנו בברכות כט, ב: "א"ל אליהו לרב יהודה אחוה דרב סלא חסידא: לא תרתח
ולא תחטי ולא תרוי ולא תחטי. וכשאתה יוצא לדרך המלך בקונך וצא".

דבריו אלה של אליהו הם ספק עצה ספק תוכחה. סופם של הדברים האמורים
הם סתומים למדי. האמוראים פרשום שכוונתם לתפילת הדרך. אולם קשה במקצת
להלום פירוש זה. שכן היכן נמצא בספרות חז"ל הביטוי "המלך בקונך" כסינונים
לתפילה? יתר על כן, וכי אליהו נתגלה לו לרב יהודה כדי ללמדו חובת תפילת
הדרך, שאותה כבר התפללו התנאים? מטבעם של גילויי אליהו, כשתוכנם בעניני
הלכה, שהם באים לחדש הלכה ובעיקרם לפרש הלכה שלא נתפרשה כראוי ע"י ת"ח
שנתלבטו בה. ביטוי זה עושה רושם שיש לפרשו, על דרך ההשאלה, אולם אין
בידנו לפרשו כראוי. ברם, גם דבריו הראשונים של אליהו הם תמוהים במקצת.
אמנם ייתכן, שגם אמורא נכשל באורח חייו ומרבה לכעוס ולשתות ודבריו של אליהו
מכוונים להוכיח את רב יהודה שיחדול מחטאים אלה. אלא שאפשר, כאמור למעלה,
לראות בריתחתו ובשתיה המוגזמת מעין עדות לדכאונו ולמצבו הנפשי של רב
יהודה בכלל. אולם אין כמובן להכריע הכרע של ממש, אם אמנם יש לראות במקור
זה קשר אל שני הגילויים הנזכרים אם לאו.

מה שעולה לנו משני הגילויים הראשונים הוא שרב יהודה אחוה דרב
סלא חסידא נמנה על אותם אמוראי בבל, והם אינם מרובים ביותר,
שציפו באופן אינטנסיבי לביאת הגואל ולא ראו בבבל את מולדתם אלא גולה
שיש להיגאל ממנה.

Power

JACOB NEUSNER

i. JEWISH POWERLESSNESS

From the perspective of the Sasanian government at Ctesiphon, the Jews, like other minority communities, did not exercise much power. They fielded no armies, exerted no influence in affairs of state, controlled no appointments in the government bureaucracy, shaped no foreign policies or domestic programs. For example, Jews may, at least for a time, have served as canal inspectors. However, they did not decide whether and where to build canals, nor did they supply the capital needed for construction.

Their prosperity and their very lives depended upon the imperial regime. In times of war they were mere pawns. In A.D. 363 when the Roman emperor Julian invaded Babylonia, his historian, Ammianus Marcellinus, reported that a Jewish town was razed and the inhabitants fled. They were able to return only after Shapur II's brilliant strategy forced the Roman invaders to retreat. But the Jews themselves had done nothing to contribute to shaping or effecting that strategy. The government was able to move populations here and there in its empire. From Armenia, Jews and Christians were deported to Persia; neither group had much say in their removal. However, generally the exalted Sasanian king of kings and his ministers looked benignly on the Jewish group, did what they thought good for them, served as patrons for their welfare, and, on the whole, made a success of it.

44

The Jews, for their part, looked to "the *King* of the king of kings, the Holy One, blessed be he." As discussed in Chapter One, they sought in their own way to exercise another kind of power, that which derived from heaven. On earth they regarded the trivial affairs of their villages and towns as having supernatural importance. If their activities seemed petty to the great ministers of state, to the people of the villages they did not. This was quite natural. While one may have wanted to share in the decisions on whether Iran should go to war against Rome or whether the state should intensify its investment in the water supply and agriculture of a vast region, he could exercise a say-so concerning only humble matters: food served on the table, conduct in the local marketplace, prayers said in the synagogue, planting crops, raising children, and making marriages. Somewhat paradoxically, these seemingly petty matters were understood by the rabbis and by ordinary Jews as well to be of greater weight in the final determination of world history than the amassing of vast armies and the siege of great cities.

At the head of the Jewish community from the first century onward stood the *exilarch*, the ruler of the Jewish community in exile. He was supported by the Iranian government in power, first the Parthians, later, after an interval, the Sasanians. His authority over the Jews depended upon that support. Normally, Jews could not appeal over his head to the government, and his decisions therefore had the effect of law for Jewry. He certainly wielded the force necessary to carry out his will. He collected the governmental taxes levied upon Jewry as a whole and transmitted them to the court at Ctesiphon. He represented Jewry at court, when needed, and effected government policies among the Jews. At the head of the state stood the all-powerful king of kings, radiating power through various bureaus and departments of government down to the farms and streets of the empire; at the head of the Jewish state-within-the-state stood the exilarch.

The exilarch's government consisted of local bureaus, or courts, which adjudicated disputes, supervised commerce and trade, enforced the law, collected taxes, and did all the other things at the village level for which the exilarch was responsible to the court at Ctesiphon. As will be seen, the staffing of some of these local courts by rabbis was at first an effort to secure better-trained and more effective, disciplined administration. The neat pyramid described above was a fantasy. For several reasons no government could ac-

45

tually work as efficiently as the scheme suggests. First, communication was poor. What was done in a village could not be readily supervised, nor could errors be rapidly rectified. The will of the exilarch might be expressed, but an intervening, second-level bureaucracy which would oversee the work of the local courts was rarely available. Local prejudice, custom, and vested interests thwarted the ready realization of the exilarch's—or the emperor's —wishes. Second, regardless of the authority at the disposal of the exilarch, he would have required a considerable police force to oversee and carry out his policies. The Jews did not live in a single, compact territory, but were spread through the canal system of the region. One man could not be everywhere. Even under the best circumstances, government in antiquity was considerably less efficient than it is today.

The power available within the Jewish community may be characterized as derivative, episodic, and inconsequential. It derived from the wishes of men and from forces external to Jewry. Dependent upon local practices, it was effected only when instruments for its realization were present, and these were available not routinely, but only on occasion. And what Jews did, did not make a great deal of difference in the larger world in which Jews found themselves. Therefore, when one speaks of power and of the structure by which power was organized, mediated, and brought to bear, he must use incongruously grand concepts to explain trivialities. That structure, as observed, was loose, fragile, and one-dimensional. It consisted of a power-center—the subordinated exilarch and his little administration—with local authorities standing in a loose relationship to the center, in control of the administrative courts of the villages and towns.

ii. THE EXILARCH

The exilarchate began to function effectively in the second half of the first century. Whether it actually was older than that—possibly dating back to the time of Jehoiachin at the beginning of the sixth century B.C., as was commonly believed—cannot be said. However, the only concrete information presently available about the politics of first-century A.D. Babylonian Jewry contains no reference to an exilarch, even while discussing important matters in which an exilarch, if there were one, should have been involved.

46

During the troubled time in the first half of the first century, when one Parthian pretender after another seized the throne, Babylonia, like the rest of the Parthian empire, enjoyed no secure government at all. As noted in Chapter One, two Jewish brothers, Anilai and Asinai, during the confusion seized power in central Babylonia, ruling not only the Jewish communities but the whole area. They set up their own government, which lasted for nearly two decades.

The chaos began to abate with the rise of the Parthian emperor, Vologases I, in the middle of the first century A.D. While the indecisive struggle between Parthia and Rome, ending in about A.D. 65, may have weakened his government, a number of his constructive efforts curbed the power of the Parthian nobles and established a secure frontier with both Rome and Armenia (although Roman preoccupation with Palestine from A.D. 66 to 73 must also be considered as a factor). Vologases I achieved something which had been unknown in Parthia for more than half a century: he held power through several decades, managing to avoid both foreign disasters and internal strife. His foundation of Vologasia, near Seleucia-Ctesiphon, doubtless greatly assisted the expansion of the silk trade with China on the east and with Palmyra and the Mediterranean coast, and this increasingly profitable trade probably provided new financial resources for the throne.

If the story of the Jewish "barony" of Anilai and Asinai in and around Nehardea from *ca.* A.D. 20 to 36 is historical, then the Parthian central government must have had to give considerable attention to the government of this numerous ethnic minority. The very position of the great areas of Jewish settlement required it, for the Jews formed a large segment of the settled population around the winter capital of Ctesiphon, the Greek city of Seleucia, and the new emporium at Vologasia. The Jewish population surrounding the heart of the empire had to be suitably governed. From the Babylonian Jews' establishment of their own state in *ca.* A.D. 20-36, it must have been clear to the reforming administration of Vologases that Jews in Babylonia were not adequately controlled.

What choices were open to the Parthian authorities? First, they could, of course, ignore the problem, allowing events to take their natural course in the Jewish territories and settlements. This was manifestly unsatisfactory, for Vologases sought to establish effective government and could not overlook the inevitable chaos that would have resulted from ignoring the behavior of the Jews in Babylonia,

47

where his capital was located. Second, they could attempt to include the government of the Jewish ethnic groups within the territorial sovereignties of other places. The Jews around Seleucia could have been placed under the Greek authorities of that city (as doubtless those in the city itself were). But this course of action would have been unsatisfactory, since the Greek cities at this time were not the regime's most loyal adherents. Furthermore the Jews and the Greeks hated each other; the Greeks had fought Anilai and Asinai. And the Jewish settlements were too extensive for incorporation into surrounding political units; at the same time they were not sufficiently compact or concentrated to form a separate unit.

An ideal solution was to establish among the Jews in Babylonia an ethnic authority of their own, much like that which probably existed after the destruction of the first Temple in Babylonian and in Achemenid times. If such an authority could develop and win the loyalty of the Jewish population to the regime, then the Parthian government would have accomplished several useful purposes. First, it would assure an effective government in the Jewish villages and towns and over Jewish minorities in the Greek and Iranian settlements. Second, it would secure the peace of strategically vital territories near the capital. Third, in time the Parthians might make use of the authority so constituted to advance their own foreign policy through an exploitation of the Jewish authority's connections with Jews in Roman Palestine. There is every evidence that some Jews in Palestine and throughout the upper Mesopotamian valley did act in a manner favorable to Parthian interests at a number of crucial points in the second century. Thus it was in the interest of the Parthian government, both during its period of reorganization under Vologases I and afterwards, either to found or to encourage and support the foundation of a Jewish ethnarch, or exilarch, in Babylonia.

A further factor played a part in Parthian consideration of the Jews' administration. The destruction of the Temple in Jerusalem in A.D. 70 posed a serious problem to the Parthian government. In former times, Babylonian Jewry, like that in other parts of the diaspora, had been loyal to the Temple. Pilgrims went up to Jerusalem, and Temple collections of a half-*sheqel* were gathered regularly in Nehardea in the south and in Nisibis in the north and forwarded in armed caravans to the Temple. The Temple authorities, for their part, sent letters to Babylonia to advise the Jews on

48

the sacred calendar and other religious issues. After the destruction, the authority of the Temple was assumed by the remnants of the Pharisaic party at Yavneh, where, with Roman approval, the powers formerly exercised by the Temple administration became vested in Yoḥanan b. Zakkai. The Parthians enjoyed the services of an excellent intelligence bureau, and they must have known that the Palestinian Jewish authority would no longer be exercised by quasi-independent officials, but would be very closely supervised by the Romans.

If the Parthians had been willing to allow a limited, and on the whole politically neutral, authority to be exerted from the Jerusalem Temple over their subjects, they would never have permitted such authority to be exerted by what they assumed was a Roman functionary. On the contrary, just as the Romans sought to mobilize Jewish support and to use Jewish officials for their own purposes, so too the Parthians exploited the fact that within their hereditary enemy's territories flourished a large religious-ethnic group with strong ties across the Euphrates and a deep sense of grievance against Rome. They continuously tried to foment unrest among minority groups within the Roman Empire. The Romans, for their part, were keenly aware of the danger of leaving substantial ethnic groups to straddle their borders; for this reason they had invaded Britain and attempted to retain Armenia in the preceding century and a half. They were, moreover, deeply concerned about Jewish public opinion in Parthia, and as a public relations effort had hired Josephus to convey their view of war guilt to the Jews across the Euphrates.

The evidence that the exilarchate was actually created at this time is slight; however, it ought not to be ignored. The silence of Josephus on this point is made very striking indeed by his testimony about how Jews actually were governed by Anilai and Asinai at this time. If there was an exilarch between A.D. 20 and 40, there is no evidence that he was of any import. He certainly did not exert any authority or affect events in any observable way. Evidence that an exilarchic line was founded after A.D. 70 appears in the list of exilarchs given in the *Seder 'Olam Zuta* (Small History of the World). Among those people listed from the time of the first destruction of Jerusalem to A.D. 70, the *Seder 'Olam Zuta* preserves no names or traditions worth taking seriously, and one may conclude that its eighth-century author had no reliable information on the

49

subject. However, the listings after 70 include names that *are* attested in other sources. Following is the list of exilarchs from *ca.* 70 to *ca.* 275:

And at this time Shemaiah died. And there arose after him Shekheniah his son, who is the tenth generation of Jehoiachin the King at the time of the destruction of the Second Temple. . . .

Shekheniah died and Hezekiah his son arose. Hezekiah died and was buried in the land of Israel in the valley of Arbella in the east of the city. 'Aqov his son arose. 'Aqov died and Naḥum his son arose after him.

There were sages with him, their names being R. Huna and R. Ḥinena, R. Matennah and R. Ḥananel. Naḥum died. After him arose Yoḥanan his brother, son of 'Aqov.

His sage was R. Ḥananel. Yoḥanan died. After him arose Shefet his son. Shefet died. 'Anan his son arose. When 'Anan died Nathan remained in his mother's womb.

He is Nathan of Ṣusita, *Rosh Golah* [exilarch]. Nathan died. After him arose R. Huna his son. Rav [d. *ca.* 250] and Samuel were his sages.

Since Rav and Samuel date from the end of the Parthian period, we may conclude that the above list covers the period from *ca.* A.D. 70 to 226. Some of the names on it, particularly Naḥum and Huna, are attested in earlier sources; and the tradition recorded in *Seder 'Olam Zuta* may well imply the beginning of sound information on an exilarch sometime in the latter half of the first century.

The exilarchate in Parthian Babylonia, like the patriarchate in Roman Palestine, was the most convenient means to manage a potentially useful ethnic group's affairs at home and to exploit its connections abroad. It was a way of annulling whatever influence Jewish functionaries of Rome might exert over Babylonian Jewry by providing an alternate, home-born authority, supported and closely supervised by the Parthian government. Both the exilarch and patriarch were backed by imperial troops. Judah, the Palestinian patriarch [*ca.* A.D. 170-210], had a detachment of Goths at his command. The exilarch possessed an armed retinue. Both eventually achieved great spiritual as well as political influence over their respective Jewish communities. Each was created in part because of the destruction of Jerusalem. The patriarchate was a means of governing internal Jewish affairs in which the Romans had no special interest, while at the same time keeping peace in Palestine. The exilarchate had the same function in Babylonia. At the same time

50

both were intended to prevent aliens from influencing Jews under their control; they themselves were to exert malevolent influence across the frontier where possible.

In the second century, the exilarchate developed into a powerful instrument of government, with its agents enjoying the perquisites of the Iranian nobility. It inflicted the death penalty and governed the Jews by its own lights, enforcing its judgment with military force when it chose. If the several Jewish revolts against Rome, which at times were highly propitious from the Parthian viewpoint, were in fact instigated by its agents, and if the support given in the crisis of Trajan's invasion was the result of exilarchic influence, then the Parthians must have judged the exilarch to be a great success indeed. By the end of the second century, the exilarch Huna was regarded with a mixture of respect and apprehension in Palestine, where his claim to Davidic ancestry in the male line (superior to Judah's allegedly in the female line) was recognized. Among the Jews and Parthians alike, the exilarchate played a major political and administrative role.

iii. The Rabbi

The rabbis were originally a Palestinian group. Babylonian Jews' first contact with them may have antedated the Bar Kokhba War (ca. A.D. 132-135) by a century, but the rabbinical movement first established its characteristic institution, the academy, during that war. Refugee sages, fleeing the terrible struggle and its aftermath, settled in Babylonia.

The main point of interest for this study is the exilarch's relationship to the rabbis. In ca. A.D. 140 Nathan, son of the Babylonian exilarch, was sent to school under rabbinical auspices, and he later continued his studies in Palestinian schools. Several other Babylonians in the Palestinian schools, including Hiyya, his sons, and his nephew Rav, were probably related to the exilarch. The evidence thus points to the existence of a few rabbis from Babylonia, and a few others in Babylonia, in the second century. Generally those rabbis who lived in Babylonia were colleagues or disciples of R. 'Aqiba and R. Ishmael, the leading masters in Yavneh before the Bar Kokhba War. Those who came from Babylonia were exilarchic relatives. When law-teachers came to Babylonia during and after the war, the exilarch must have provided the means for conducting

51

law schools, just as he had sent his son and was to send his relatives later to study in the Palestinian schools.

The settlement of rabbis in Babylonia was encouraged by the exilarch in his effort to secure well-trained officials. What accounts for the pro-rabbinical sentiment of the exilarch? The exilarch must have had to contend with other Jewish authorities, particularly powerful local figures like Arda, Pyl-y Barish, Anilai, and Asinai. These potentially dangerous competitors for the rule of Jewry were seen to be "assimilated" to Parthian culture. Babylonian Jewish officials were "Parthian" in many ways. They were upper-class Jews who possessed wealth and influence, much like the exilarch himself. One good way of circumventing their influence over the ordinary Jews (who would have had much less contact with Parthian politics, court life, and, therefore, general culture) would have been for the exilarch to present himself as the protagonist of the ancient tradition of Moses, against the local Iranized Jewish elite competing with him for power. The exilarch would then have been able to claim that his rule was legitimate, not merely effective. When the people listened to him, they were obeying the Torah of Moses, and he therefore stood for the ancient revelation of Moses at Sinai. The local Jewish strong-men, however, ruled by force of arms, not by the right rules laid down by Moses. So the ordinary Jews would have been given good reason to favor the central authority of the exilarch over the local rulers.

But how to establish such a public image? How better than to associate oneself with the Palestinian rabbis whose prestige had been rising ever since the destruction of the Temple, and who could send disciplined, learned, and charismatic rabbis to serve the exilarch, to help build his administration, and to bolster his claim of descent from David? Allegedly knowledgeable in the Mosaic law, the rabbis were believed to be holy men and were accredited with wonderful powers. Because of their standing in the community, they could lend prestige to the peculiar political claim of the exilarch. Against such holy men, what could local strong-men or powerful upper-class leaders offer? The exilarchate was a relatively new institution. Because of the terrible invasions and unsettled domestic conditions of the second century, the Parthian government, which had created the exilarchate, was unable to provide necessary support. As a result the exilarch had his hands full simply establishing his preeminence over other, older kinds of local Jewish authori-

52

ties. The Palestinian rabbis, as well as those Babylonians trained by them, provided a ready and inviting aid in setting up an effective and "legitimate" administration.

Thus the rabbis served to enhance the legitimacy of the exilarchate by providing stronger theological foundations for the exilarch's political power and by attesting to the validity of his claim to be descended from David. Their learning, holiness, and magical powers won the assent of ordinary people to their legal and exegetical doctrines. They were useful to the exilarch, for they could give him what he lacked: a means of influencing the masses, and a source of administrative talent and disciplined, reliable local leadership. In return the rabbis were prepared to collaborate with any political leader who would give them power over Jewry to achieve their religious program. Together the rabbis and exilarch might outweigh the competing, centrifugal forces constituted by older, local grandees of various sorts and in various places.

By the turn of the third century, the rabbinical movement in Babylonia included a few local authorities, such as Samuel, and a larger number of trained and authorized Palestinian rabbis. The movement hardly dominated Babylonian Jewish life, and it posed no threat whatever to the exilarch, who made use of rabbis for his own purposes and was probably glad to have more of them. The exilarch provided the chief source of financial support for the rabbinical schools and of employment for their graduates. He was equally eager to accept the credentials of Palestine-trained rabbis, and to authorize Palestinian rabbinical newcomers to serve in his system of courts as lawyers, judges, and communal administrators.

The exilarch, moreover, was particularly anxious to employ men who could apply in Babylonia the newly promulgated Mishnah which had just been issued in Palestine by the patriarch Judah ca. A.D. 200. Whatever old traditions and ad hoc decisions existed in Babylonia, the new Mishnah had irresistible appeal. Based upon a viable and supple exegetical method, it was organized according to logical categories, and, most important, was advertised as the very will of God revealed, along with the written Torah, by God to Moses at Mount Sinai and transmitted from that time to the present by faithful prophets, sages, and rabbis. Still a relatively new institution, the exilarchate was glad to associate itself and its administration with so grand a prestige as accrued to the Mishnah in the minds of those rabbis who accepted the rabbinical claim of its origin in the

53

revelation of Sinai. Among these were the exilarch's own son Nathan; his relatives, Ḥiyya and Rav; and others close to him. He, too, therefore, was probably a believer. The exilarch claimed to be of the seed of David. How better to win the loyalty and conformity of ordinary people than to couple that claim with the equally impressive one: "In the Jewish courts we at last apply not merely the scattered, though hoary, traditions of our forefathers of the exile, but the whole revelation of Sinai itself."

In the decades after the redaction and promulgation of the Mishnah by the patriarch in Palestine, the exilarch gladly accepted its authority, and therefore hired men who would apply it—under exilarchic auspices to be sure. The rabbinical movement, small and possessing little influence and authority in Babylonia in the beginning, received the enthusiastic backing of the exilarch, who had earlier sent his representatives to the Palestinian schools. Whatever other schools there were must have either ceased to exist or begun to teach the Mishnah and its accompanying traditions, exegetical methods, and rules. In response the rabbis ruled that it was only with the authorization of the exilarch that one might judge cases in Jewish Babylonia. "Authorization" in rabbinic discourse meant actual bureaucratic appointment by the exilarch, and so an alliance was forged between the rabbis, needing political support, and the exilarch, requiring prestigious and qualified functionaries.

iv. MESSIAH VS. TORAH

How did the two groups—the exilarch and his circle on one side, and the rabbinical estate on the other—understand, themselves, and explain to others the power they exercised over the Jewish community at large? Two quite different claims of normative authority or legitimacy were put forward in Babylonian Judaism. Both were based upon myth, stories about or statements of ultimate reality in highly symbolic form. Although interrelated, the myths were different. One, the Torah-myth, served the purposes of the rabbis; the other, the Messiah-myth, was advanced by the exilarch.

The rabbis' political myth is examined in the following story (b. Git. 62a) about Geniva, a rabbinical master of the second half of the third century who was finally put to death by the exilarch of the day, Mar 'Uqba:

54

R. Huna and R. Hisda were sitting, when Geniva happened by. One said to the other, "Let us arise before him, for he is master of Torah." The other said, "Shall we arise before a man of division?" Meanwhile he came, and said to them, "Peace be unto you, Kings, peace be unto you, Kings." They said to him, "How do you know that rabbis are called kings?" He said to them, "As it is said, *By me, kings rule*" (Prov. 8:15, referring to wisdom).

"And how do you know that a double greeting is given to kings?"

"As Rav Judah said in the name of Rav, 'How do you know that a double greeting is given to the king?' As it is said, *Then the spirit came upon Amasai who was chief of the thirty* (I Chron 12:18, continuing 'Peace, peace be upon you') ."

They said to him, "Would you care for a bite with us?" He replied . . .

The story of his trial and execution is as follows (b. Giṭ. 7a) :

Mar 'Uqba sent to R. Eleazar [ben Pedat], "Men are opposing me, and it is in my power to hand them over to the government. What is to be done?"

He drew a line and wrote to him, *"I said, I will take heed to my ways, that I sin not with my tongue, I will keep a curb upon my mouth while the wicked is before me* [Ps. 39:2], that is, even though the wicked is against me, I shall guard my mouth with a muzzle."

Again he said to him, "They are greatly troubling me, and I cannot overcome them."

He replied, *"Resign thyself unto the Lord and wait patiently for him* (Ps. 37:7) that is, wait for the Lord and he will bring them down prostrate before you. Arise early and stay late in the academy, and they will perish of themselves."

The matter had scarcely left the mouth of R. Eleazar when they placed Geniva in a collar to lead him to execution.

The difficulty Geniva gave the exilarch Mar 'Uqba was based on the relationship between the rabbi and the exilarch. Geniva and his party had said or done something the exilarch found extremely irritating, and the latter, having no capital jurisdiction over the Jews, handed him over to the Iranian government for punishment. The Iranian regime would, of course, properly support its functionary's authority.

Since the bulk of Geniva's reported sayings were quite standard rabbinical traditions, only the passage on the "double greeting" provides a hint of how he might have offended Mar 'Uqba. It may

55

be supposed that he had publicly declared something the rabbis previously kept to themselves: their belief that the exilarch, who judged cases according to Persian law, derived his authority not from knowledge of the rabbinical traditions but from the support of a heathen government; that he collaborated in the affairs of that government; and that such a person was not really qualified to administer Jewry's affairs. Instead the rabbis felt that since they themselves were kings, they should rule.

This threat to the exilarchic position could have elicited only one response—to put the troublemaker out of the way. Until that could be arranged, the exilarch would have encouraged other rabbis to keep their distance from Geniva, despite his obvious mastery of traditions. Indeed, R. Huna and R. Ḥisda, who was Mar 'Uqba's teacher, were well aware of the dangers of associating with the "man of division." Their respect for his learning was tempered by their hesitation to have anything at all to do with him. Geniva for his part responded by quoting traditions deriving from their own master, Rav—traditions which they quite obviously did not know. By stressing their "kingship" he meant to point out the egregious quality of the relationship: they should not serve one lesser than themselves. They were rabbis, therefore kings, and Scripture had said so.

The exilarch's political myth is revealed in a saying by one of his own rabbinical adherents, Naḥman b. Jacob, who lived at the same time as Geniva. He stated (b. Sanh. 98b):

"If [the messiah] is among the living, he is such a one as I, as it is said, *And their nobles shall be of themselves, and their governors shall proceed from the midst of them* (Jer. 30:21)."

As part of the exilarchate, Naḥman saw himself in an extraordinary light. Jeremiah refers to the time of the Messiah when the fortunes of Jacob will be restored. The restoration would be signified by the Jews' once again governing themselves.

Naḥman inferred that the rule of the exilarchate certified, and might in time mark the fulfillment of, that particular Messianic promise. Such a saying reflected the political theology of the exilarch. Being both scion of David and recognized governor of the Jews, the exilarch represented the fulfillment of prophetic hopes for the restoration of a Jewish monarch of the Davidic line. Hence his rule

56

was legitimate and should be obeyed. Naḥman's citation of Jeremiah provides one of the few glimpses into the way the exilarch explained his rule to the Jews. It shows that not merely Persian approval and support, but a wholly "proper" basis in Jewish genealogy and history provided the theoretical foundation of his power. By contrast, the rabbis maintained that not Davidic overlordship, but full obedience to the Torah would signify the advent of Messianic rule.

The Davidic origins of the exilarch were first referred to in the time of Judah, the patriarch of Palestinian Jewry at the end of the second century A.D., in a colloquy between Judah and Ḥiyya (b. Hor. 11b):

Rabbi [Judah the Prince] inquired of R. Ḥiyya [a Babylonian related to the exilarch], "Is one like myself to bring a he-goat [as a sin-offering of a ruler, according to Lev. 4:23]?"

"You have your rival in Babylonia," he replied.

"The kings of Israel and the kings of the house of David," he objected, "bring sacrifices independently of one another."

"There," Ḥiyya replied, "they were not subordinate to one another. Here [in Palestine] we are subordinate to them [in Babylonia]."

R. Safra taught thus: Rabbi [Judah] inquired to R. Ḥiyya, "Is one like me to bring a he-goat?"

"There is the scepter, here is only the law-giver, as it was taught, *The scepter shall not depart from Judah*, refers to the Exilarch in Babylonia who rules Israel with the scepter, *nor the ruler's staff between his feet* [Gen. 49:10] refers to the grandchildren of Hillel who teach the Torah to Israel in public."

The reference to Gen. 49:10, *"The scepter shall not depart from Judah,"* is striking, for it shows that the Davidic claim was tied to the exercise of political authority. So far as the Palestinians were concerned, the exilarch's claim was taken as fact.

As earlier noted, the rabbis believed that, along with the written Torah, God had revealed to Moses at Mount Sinai an oral, unwritten Torah, which had been preserved and handed on from prophets to sages and finally to rabbis. Israel's life was to be shaped by divine revelation; the rabbis alone knew the full configuration of the will of God, and their claim to rule rested upon the belief in the oral Torah. They thus clashed with the exilarch, who, using equally theological terms, maintained that he was qualified to rule because he was descended from the seed of David. Moreover, rab-

57

binic political theology ran counter to the widespread conviction of Jews that *anyone* holding political power over them had better be able to claim Davidic ancestry.

The rabbis authenticated their claim to power not only by their teaching of Torah, but also by their knowledge of the secrets of creation—including the names of God by which miracles may be produced, and the mysteries of astrology, medicine, and practical magic—and by their day-to-day conduct as a class of religious virtuosi and illuminati. For their schools they eagerly recruited students who would join with them in the task of studying the "whole Torah," and go forth afterward to exemplify and enforce its teaching among the ordinary people. They were seeking totally to reform the life of Israel so that it would conform to the Torah as they taught it. They believed that if Israel would live according to the will of "their Father in heaven," then no nation or race could rule over them, but the Anointed of God would do so. History as a succession of pagan empires would come to an end; Israel would live in peace in its own land; an endless age of prosperity because of Israel's reconciliation with God would follow. So the issues were not inconsiderable.

"How do you know that rabbis are called kings?" The reply is, "Scripture says, 'By me kings rule.'" Such was not the view of the exilarch, who wanted it to be believed that he ruled because he was heir of David. It is worth quoting the entire biblical passage (Prov. 8:15) to which Geniva made reference:

> By me kings rule
>   and rulers decree what is just
> By me princes rule
>   and nobles govern the earth.

This passage was part of a key proof text for the rabbinical schools, for in it, "Torah" (which they believed they alone properly expounded) is described as the beginning of the works of creation; as the foundation for right politics; and as the sole source of righteousness, justice, and knowledge. Torah came before creation, and so provided the design for the world. The chapter (Prov. 8:34-36) closes:

> Happy is the man who listens to me,
>   watching daily at my gates,

58

waiting beside my doors.
For he who finds me finds life
and obtains favor from the Lord;
But he who misses me injures himself;
all who hate me love death.

It was far more than a matter of power politics. When the rabbis read a reference to the gates and doors of Torah, they knew what it meant—the gates of their academies.

The crux of the matter was: How was redemption to be gained? The rabbis believed it was through a legal reformation of Israel. The exilarch and his relatives thought differently, for Nahman supposed that their Davidic connection ought to prove sufficient in time to produce a Messiah, possibly even in their own day if God willed it. Redemption would proceed either from the academies or from the Davidides; the two were mutually exclusive. Beyond the concrete issues of the day, the question of redemption smoldered in the shadows, lending eschatological significance to a politics which was, from today's perspective, concerned with trivialities. "Torah" was central in the redemptive process. A legal reformation would effect "Torah" and so bring about the Messiah's coming. "All who hate me love death." The exilarchs were seen by their enemies as hating Torah. Had the exilarch subordinated himself to the academies and accepted their direction, the potential conflict between the opposing legacies might never have been realized.

But the exilarch had a powerful claim too. He was of David's seed, and from him or from one of his relatives would come the Messiah. That claim was probably far older and better established in the mind of Babylonian Jewry than that of the rabbis, and for better reasons. The exilarch had no reason to subordinate himself to the academy, and he had very good reason not to.

From the rabbis' perspective, the exilarch was a merely political figure, while they themselves were endowed with the sanctity deriving from Torah, revelation. In modern terms, they would have called themselves "the church" and the exilarch "the state." And— "By me, kings rule." But the exilarch's viewpoint could not have conformed to theirs. As far as he was concerned, his rule was as the surrogate of the Messiah; indeed his presence was the best assurance that the Messiah would one day come—and would come from his own household. Israel was not rejected by God as long as she

59

governed herself, and the exilarch's rule was therefore proof of the continued validity of the covenant, of the enduring Messianic hope; the scepter had *not* departed from Judah. *Not* a secular authority, the exilarch claimed to descend from David, to be the link between the rule of David in the ideal past and the rule of David in the ideal future. The Torah-myth thus came into conflict with the Messiah-myth.

It cannot be said, however, that the exilarch, a "merely political figure," was alone in making use of a religious myth for political purposes. The rabbis too sought to control political institutions—the courts and administrative agencies of Babylonian Jewry. They wanted to make use of those political institutions for religious purposes, that is, to coerce ordinary Jews to conform to the Torah as they taught it.

Both the rabbis and the exilarch claimed to be "the church" and therefore to be the state also. No distinction was recognized between politics and religion. If one ruled, it was because God wanted him to do so. If another obeyed, he obeyed heaven and revelation, not merely the arbitrary fiat of a temporarily powerful individual. Society should be governed by God's law; on this, everyone agreed. The issue was, Who knew that law? And who should be the one to interpret and apply it? Political argument was phrased in theological language, and only by accepting the claim of one party and rejecting that of the other can one be described as "the church," and the other as "the state." Political theory obviously was subsumed under the eschatological and Messianic issue: how is Israel to be saved?

The exilarch certainly expected that someday the Lord would send the Messiah, raising him up out of the house of the exilarch, related as it was to the Davidic family. That commonplace theory probably represented the older political view of both Babylonian and Palestinian Jewry. It was believed that redemption would come in God's own time, through David's descendant, and anyone presuming to exercise political authority over Jews had best begin with a claim to derive from the Davidic household. It is known that Davidic ancestry was alleged by practically every important Jewish figure in the political life of the late antiquity; included were the Hasmoneans, Jesus, the patriarchal family in Palestine, the exilarch —and even Herod!

In Iranian culture, it was conventional to claim to be an heir of the Achemenids, Cyrus and Darius, for example. The Parthians

60

did so, not at the outset of their rule, but only in the first century when they found that military superiority no longer could sustain their throne. On the other hand, the Sasanians stated from the very outset that they were heirs of the Achemenids. Maintaining that the Parthians were illegitimate, the Sasanians asserted that they were the restorers of the ancient, rightful dynasty of Iran. The claim to be descended from a remote, glorious emperor was a widespread political convention in this time; what was strikingly unconventional was the rabbis' Torah-myth and its political expression.

It apparently was not sufficient for anyone to claim rulership because he had power, because he was wise, or because custom dictated it. Jewish politics revolved around the Messianic issue. Others could obey because it was expedient or merely necessary, but Jews would listen only to the Messiah's surrogate, obey only the word of God. In the humblest details of daily conduct they sought significance of grand, metahistorical dimensions. Ruling no government like other governments, Jews entered a fantasy in which what they did control, despite its worldly triviality, was believed to possess far greater significance than even the deeds of great and impressive empires held by others: "Others are ruled by the court of Ctesiphon, by the king of kings. We obey the King of kings of kings, the Holy One." The debate centered, therefore, on what obedience to God entailed—whether God's will was contained in the Torah of the rabbis or whether it was expressed through the rule of the exilarch, the scion of David. Theology imposed itself on politics probably because theology was all the Jews had left to render their politics worthwhile.

v. Conflict of Myths

The practical conflict between the power of the exilarch and that of the rabbis may best be described in terms of an issue debated in the early fourth century: Should rabbis pay taxes?

The exilarch imposed and collected taxes, dividing them among Jews of various towns and groups, and transmitting them to the state on specified occasions. It would hardly enhance his authority if he could not impose his will upon everyone, including rabbis. Choosing to make the payment of the poll tax the decisive issue, the rabbis asserted that they were not like other Jews, but formed a special class which was subjected neither to the authority of the

61

exilarch nor to the control of the state. For his part, the exilarch saw no reason to change the status quo of nearly three centuries' standing.

Why did rabbis choose just this time to claim exemption from taxation? A partial reason was that they were convinced they had no other correct course; furthermore, the time seemed promising. During the period from Shapur I's death in A.D. 273, to the end of the minority of Shapur II in about 325, the central government was distracted by disastrous foreign wars, the suppression of the Manichaeans, dynastic struggles every few years, and finally the centrifugal effects of the weak regency. When Shapur II came to power, his attention was drawn to international and military issues. The Sasanian government in his time never paid the Jews much attention while the revenues were forthcoming and nothing subversive happened. Both conditions were met. Subversion by the rabbis was not directed at the Sasanian government. So long as the full quota of head taxes was paid, it hardly mattered in the state who actually paid them or who did not. The Jewish question was an inconsequential local matter, and greater affairs of state must have occupied not only Shapur, who certainly was not even consulted on such a minor question, but also the ministers of Ctesiphon.

Had it been otherwise, the ministers of Shapur would have been perfectly well prepared to investigate anti-government activity and to punish those they thought guilty. The same satraps and Mobads who in the fourth century tortured Christian monks and nuns, priests, bishops, and laity of Babylonia and Adiabene for not paying taxes were quite capable of persecuting rabbis, if not the Jews as a group, had they thought it useful to the security of the state. They did nothing of the sort; presumably they saw no reason to.

Moreover, once the great persecution against the Christians had begun, in ca. 340, the exilarch could hardly have called to his aid those whose capacities for bloody mischief now stood fully revealed. Had he asked for state aid in suppressing the rabbinate as a class, he would have embittered the ordinary Jews against himself; and the record of rabbinical martyrdoms, accompanied by the conventional miracles done by both heavenly messengers and earthly saints, would have rendered him totally distasteful to common folk. So the exilarch at first was unwilling, and later quite unable to enlist the powers of the state. The state, unknowing and uninterested, paid attention to quite different matters. Still, in such a circumstance

62

rebellion against the exilarch was a chancy thing. The rabbis took that chance.

The exilarch was prepared to grant unusual favors to the rabbis as an estate. They had special privileges at court; they were given advantages in marketing their produce. The exilarch was quoted as instructing Rava to see whether a certain man who was claiming rabbinical status was really a scholar. If so, Rava was to reserve a market privilege for him, so that he might sell his produce before others. Since the rabbis staffed exilarchic courts, it certainly was advantageous to protect them.

The rabbis' claim to be exempt from the poll tax was quite another matter, however. The exilarch could not exempt rabbis from the poll tax. One of the principal guarantees of continued peace for the Jewish community was the efficient collection of taxes, and the exilarch himself would have had to make up any deficit. All he could do was shift the burden of taxes to others, so that the rabbis' share would devolve upon ordinary Jews. He was not ready to do so, and it is extremely unlikely that ordinary people would have wanted him to. The tax rates already were so high that poor people struggled to find the money to pay them. References abound to people's selling their property, or themselves into slavery, to raise the necessary money. The state could not afford to compromise. War was necessary to protect its territory, including first and foremost Babylonia itself. Armies were expensive, and contributions were required of everyone, particularly of those who lived in so rich and fertile a region. Moreover, those living closest to the capital were least able to evade the taxes. So the exilarch could hardly accede to the rabbis' demand. The Iranians would not allow the lightening of taxes; the ordinary Jews could not bear an additional burden if it were shifted to them.

The rabbis' claim of tax-exemption was phrased in scriptural terms. They were certain that from most ancient times rabbis were not supposed to pay taxes and that it would be a transgression of scriptural precedent if they now did so. A positive claim was made by R. Naḥman b. Isaac (b. B.B. 8a) :

R. Naḥman b. R. Ḥisda [an exilarchic representative] applied the head-tax to the sages.

R. Naḥman b. Isaac said to him, "You have transgressed against the teachings of the Torah, the Prophets, and the Writings. Against the Torah,

63

as it is written, *Although he loves the people, all his saints are in your hand* (Deut. 33:3).

"You have transgressed against the Prophets, as it is written, *Even when they study* [lit.: *Give] among the nations, now I shall gather them, and a few of them shall be free from the burden of kings and princes* (Hosea 8:10).

"You have transgressed against the Writings, as it is written, *It shall not be lawful to impose upon them* [*priests and Levites*] *minda, belo, and halakh* (Ezra 7:24), and Rav Judah explained, '*Minda* means the portion of the king, *belo* is the poll-tax, and *halakh* is the *annona* [corvée].' "

The several Scriptures are not of equal weight. The passage in Deuteronomy suggests that "his saints" (believed by the rabbis to be themselves) are in God's hand. Therefore, they do not require the protection of walls or armies and should not have to pay for them. Likewise, R. Judah b. Ezekiel had said that everyone must contribute to the building of doors for the town walls and gates except rabbis, who do not require the protection of walls and gates.

The meaning of the passage in Hosea is quite clear: when the Jews study the Torah among the gentiles (i.e., in Babylonia), a few should not have to pay taxes; and these few, quite obviously, are the rabbis. The citation from Ezra explicitly states that priests do not have to pay the "portion of the king" or the poll tax. What was not made explicit, because everyone in the schools knew it, was that the rabbis believed they had inherited the rights and privileges of the priesthood, since study of Torah was now equivalent to the priestly offerings in Temple times. Therefore, according to Artaxerxes' order reported by Ezra, rabbis do not have to pay the head tax. This was plainly stated in Scripture, and the rabbis felt it was beyond question. Even the Iranian government should not impose the poll tax on them, they supposed. Rava threatened that the rabbis would apostasize (b. Ned. 62b):

Rava said, "It is permitted for a rabbinical disciple to say, 'I will not pay the toll-tax,' as it is written, *It shall not be lawful to impose minda, belo, or halakh*" (Ezra 7:24).
Rava moreover stated, "A rabbinical disciple is permitted to say, 'I am a servant of fire and do not pay the poll tax.' "
What is the reason? It is only said in order to drive away a lion.

Rava's remarkable saying that a rabbinical disciple could lie to evade the poll tax or even deny that he was a Jew, tells nothing about

64

what would have happened had he done so. The tax-collectors in the Jewish community were Jews, not Iranians. What Rava has in mind was a Jew telling the Jewish collector that he was an apostate. There might have been an implied threat: "If you do not leave me alone, I shall become a servant of fire." It is doubtful that Rava imagined a rabbinical disciple would make such an assertion before a Mobad, who knew full well how to assess such a claim. His thought was that it was so wrong to collect the poll tax from rabbis, that the disciples could perjure themselves or even pretend to commit overt apostasy. It was a very strong assertion.

The only sources currently available do not reveal what the exilarch said or did in response to the rabbinical tax rebellion. If Torah, Prophecy, and Writings are brought to testify, and public apostasy theoretically was permitted to a rabbinical disciple, one can hardly suppose that rabbis were not under pressure. The greater likelihood is that they paid their tax but resisted as powerfully as they could through their most effective weapons—ascription of their tax exemption to Moses, Hosea, and Artaxerxes, and public announcements of permission to evade the taxes by any means. The exilarch exerted great pressure, because he both had to and wanted to. The vehemence of the rabbis' traditions on the subject must be interpreted as evidence of his success.

It is not known whether R. Naḥman b. Isaac ever managed to intimidate R. Naḥman b. R. Hisda, or, for that matter, whether any young rabbinical disciples actually lied to the tax-collectors. It is known, however, that Shapur II's police from A.D. 339 to 379 executed Christian tax-resisters. Since there is no evidence of "martyrdom" of rabbis because of nonpayment of taxes, it is very likely that there was none. The rabbis protested, but they must have paid. To the exilarch, that would have been all that really mattered.

But the rabbis would have been embittered not only because they had lost money, which would have especially bothered the poorer ones, but also because they were forced to transgress their religious convictions about their own rights and privileges. Their view of the sanctity of the rabbinate is clear: they were the "saints" in God's hand. It was a sin for them to pay the poll tax, and it was a still greater sin for the exilarch to force them to do so.

The exilarch had to respond publicly to the criticism and disloyalty of hostile elements in the rabbinate. His response probably would have taken the form of propaganda which would have been

65

not less venomous than that of the rabbis. To begin with, he would have stressed his descent from the house of David, for that was the foundation of his politics. He would, moreover, have alluded to the cost to other Jews of the rabbinical tax exemption and maintained that the rabbis refused to pay their fair share of the rising imposts. The rabbis wanted to establish a second Jewish government, which the Persians would never allow. "In these troubled times, when Christians are giving evidence of what happens to minority-communities that fall afoul of the state," the exilarch would have pointed out, "it will not pay to solicit Persian hostility!"

Furthermore, according to the exilarch, the condition of the Jews themselves would have provided the best testimony to the soundness of exilarchic rule: "Consider the fact that while others are persecuted, Jews are secure. Chaos reigns everywhere, but at home there is order, or as much order as responsible government can bring when faced with such dissident, provocative elements." The exilarch could therefore have concluded his message by asking, "How many wish to enslave themselves to pay heavier taxes so that rabbis may now enjoy the full benefit of their private, fantastic, and self-serving scriptural exegesis? Not all rabbis, to be sure, but only a minority of them are guilty of such intended subversion. Most of them remain loyal to the house of David and its living representative." The living representative was, of course, the exilarch himself.

Three centuries earlier, Yoḥanan b. Zakkai, excluded from the bastions of power in Jerusalem and displeased with the Temple priesthood's administration of its holy office, had found a suitable polemic in the words of Qohelet 4:18, *Guard your foot when you go to the house of God and be ready to hearken.* He said that it was better to listen to the words of the wise than to offer the sacrifices of fools, meaning the ancient priesthood. Now his words found an echo in the saying attributed to Rava (b. Ber. 23a):

And be ready to listen. Rava said, "Be ready to listen to the words of the sages, for if they sin, they bring an offering and carry out penance." *It is better than when fools give.* "Do you be like fools who sin and bring an offering, but do not do penance."

vi. RECONCILIATION

During the next fifty years, from *ca.* 330 to *ca.* 380, the exilarch was able to reassert complete control over the rabbinical schools. At

66

the same time, however, he made certain that his functionaries and heirs received an excellent rabbinical education. So in effect he capitulated by becoming a rabbi himself, that is, by getting a sound knowledge of the Torah as taught by rabbis. But he insisted that the schools where Jews became rabbis remain under his very close supervision. No true victor can therefore be designated in the struggle for power in the Jewish community. The rabbis rabbinized the exilarchate; the exilarch exercised substantial control over the rabbinate.

These two groups suffered in a disaster which occurred during the reign of the Sasanian emperor Peroz, when both leading rabbis and the exilarch, believing the Messiah would come in 468—four hundred years after the destruction of Jerusalem—foolishly acted upon the consequences of that belief. Jewish government was wiped out. It was an ironic denouement. The rabbis followed the exilarch's Messianism and endorsed it. If, therefore, the exilarch was "rabbinized," the rabbis were "Messianized." The two theories were united; the two parties suffered together.

A detailed examination of this disaster will set into perspective the consideration of power within Babylonian Judaism. The essential weakness of the Jewish community and all its institutions, including both the exilarchate and the rabbinate, become apparent in this study. Until *ca.* A.D. 450, Judaism had been a licit religion. After that time, for close to half a century, Judaism was treated as an illicit religion, and some Jews were punished for practicing it. To find a similarly severe crisis one has to look backward to the brief but vicious Hadrianic repression following the Bar Kokhba War. First a review of the Peroz catastrophe as it appears in several sources and traditions:

R. Nahman b. R. Huna died in the year 455 A.D. Then a persecution took place, for Yazdagird [the Iranian king of kings] decreed to annul the Sabbath.

(*Letter of R. Sherira Gaon,* ed. B. M. Lewin
[Haifa, 1921], pp. 94, 1. 12-13; 95, 1. 1-2)

In the year 455 R. Nahman b. R. Huna died. And Argazur [sic!] the King of the Persians decreed against our fathers that they profane Sabbaths. In the year 468 Rabbah b. R. Ashi died. In the year 471 R. Hama son of Rava died. Huna b. Mar Zutra the exilarch was killed, and the Jews were given over to the government. In the year 467 the schools were

67

destroyed. And they decreed against the Jews to be subject to Persian law. And Rabbah Tosfa'ah died.

(Seder Tannaim ve Amoraim, ed. M. Grosberg [London, 1908], Chapter II, p. 65)

A later tradition provides the following account of the insertion of the *Shema'* in the *Qedushah,* the sanctification-prayer:

Because in the time of R. Naḥman, Yuzgard [sic!] the king of Persia decreed that the *Shema'* should not be read. Forthwith what did the sages of that generation do? They decreed to include it in the midst of every *Qedushah.* . . . And why did they decree to say it by swallowing [= inclusion elsewhere]? So that the *Shema'* should not be forgotten by the children. And they sought mercy from heaven. Thereupon a serpent came at noonday and swallowed Yuzgard the king in his bed, and the decree was annulled.

The *Letter of R. Sherira* further states that an important rabbi died in 459 at the time of the persecution decreed by Yazdagird.

Rabbana Amemar bar Mar Yenuqa, Huna Mar bar R. Ashi the exilarch, and Mesharshia b. Peqod were imprisoned. On the 18th day of Ṭevet, Huna bar Mar Zuṭra the *Nasi* [= exilarch] and Mesharshia were killed, and in Adar of the same year Rabbana Amemar bar Mar Yenuqa was killed.

And in the year 470 all the synagogues in Babylonia were closed, and the children of the Jews were seized by the Magi.

(Letter of R. Sherira Gaon, pp. 96, 1. 14-16; 95, 1. 1-9)

The same event appears in the *Book of Tradition (Sefer HaQabbalah)* of Abraham ibn Daud:

Before this [the Moslem conquest], however, the Almighty, blessed be He, had turned their heart to hate His people, so that the Persian king seized three Jewish notables: Amemar bar Mar Yanqa bar Mar Zuṭra, the colleague of R. Ashi, R. Mesharshia, and the exilarch, whose name was Huna Mar, and put them to death. He also seized Jewish youths and compelled them to leave the fold.

(The Book of Tradition [Philadelphia: Jewish Publication Society of America, 1968], ed. and trans. Gerson D. Cohen, IV, 1. 158-64, pp. 41-42)

68

According to the Iranian historian Hamza Işfahani, in the eleventh year of Peroz' reign (468), Jews of Işfahan flayed two Magi (Zoroastrian priests) alive. As a result, half the Jewish population of Işfahan was slaughtered, and the children were handed over to the service of the fire-temple at Harvan.

What is the import of these medieval accounts? It is known that Yazdagird II and Peroz persecuted Christianity. Just as they directed their efforts against priests, nuns, and monks, so in the Jewish case they are said to have imprisoned and then put to death both rabbis, particularly those who were heads of schools, and the exilarch. Since the Christian case was primarily a religious persecution, without the usual attribution of political motives, it is striking that the Jewish accounts report decrees against keeping the Sabbath, the conduct of schools, and similar, fundamental Jewish religious practices, not to mention the abolition of Jewish self-government. So the persecutions of the two religious communities exhibit similar qualities.

Moreover, the independent account from Işfahan provides a measure of verification for the Jewish stories. For example, the detail about seizure of Jewish children for Mazdean purposes appears in both Jewish and Iranian traditions. But of still greater significance in the Işfahan version is the reason for the persecution. Jewish and Christian traditions claim that it was directed against their religious practices, and therefore presumably was motivated by religious "fanaticism"; the Iranian story is that Jews had mistreated Magi and as a result were punished. Iranians viewed the "persecution" as a *local* action against the malfeasance of a *local* community.

There are stories available from Christian sources of Christian saints burning down fire-temples during the reign of Yazdagird I, *ca.* A.D. 410. It is by no means incredible that Jews did something of the same sort in Işfahan. The Christians acted because they thought Yazdagird I would follow the path of Constantine and become a Christian.

The Jews had a tradition that the Messiah could come in the year 468, that is, four hundred years after the destruction of the Temple:

Said R. Ḥanina, "From the year 400 after the destruction [of the Temple, dated by the rabbis in 68] if someone says to you, 'Buy a field worth a thousand *denarii* for one *denar*,' do not buy it."

In a *beraita* we learn, "From the year 4231 of the Creation of the World

69

onward [= A.D. 471], if someone says to you, 'Buy a field worth a thousand *denarii* for a *denar,*' do not buy it."

(b. A. Z. 9b)

R. Hanina lived in the third century in Palestine, but it is known that his tradition was preserved in the Babylonian schools a century and a half later. Some Jews, including leading rabbis, expected the Messiah to come in 468 or shortly thereafter, and the preliminary destruction of pagan temples and murder of their priests followed as a consequence of such a belief. No information is currently available on what happened, if anything, in Iṣfahan in 468. But it is plausible that some Jews would have done what later Iranian tradition claimed they did. If so, the local pogrom would have been a natural result.

It is puzzling that the state engaged in such a far-reaching repression of Judaism as a religion. If Magi went so far as to seize Jews and interrogate them about religious matters, investigate and legislate concerning the content of Jewish worship, close synagogues, snatch away Jewish children, and the like, and if the state supported these actions, surely some motive or provocation far more profound than political or economic necessity must have been at hand. And if Jews provoked these severe repressions, as the Isfahani tradition says they did, they surely must have had a considerable reason.

In the background of every Jewish act of political or religious violence lies the Messianic expectation. Therefore the conviction that the Messiah would come in 468 or in 471 must be taken very seriously. In the days of Shapur II, in 362-363, a movement similar to that in Iṣfahani took shape in Mahoza, and the king was compelled to send troops to massacre the Messianists. Later more movements appeared, coalescing around local figures in Babylonia and Mesopotamia, as well as in Byzantine territories. In the second and third decades of the fifth century, Messianic movements were rampant both in Jewish Palestine and in the Greek diaspora. Obviously Messianism constituted a powerful force in Babylonian Judaism, and Jewish Messianists invariably took active measures in support of their convictions. A bloody war was fought in Hadrianic times when they had believed Bar Kokhba to be the Messiah (a belief that had been confirmed by some rabbis). The natural result of this religion was repression not only of the war but also of those Judaic religious practices which the Romans believed had caused it.

70

Similarly, when the Iranians conquered Jerusalem in A.D. 614, Palestinian Jews again believed the Messiah was about to come. As a consequence of the capture of Jerusalem, they murdered many local Christians, particularly the religious.

The fact that the Sabbath was prohibited, certain central prayers were outlawed, and important rabbis—including the exilarch himself—were put to death in the years between *ca.* 455 and *ca.* 475, seems to be illuminated by the Messianic expectations attached to this period. Whatever the religious convictions of Yazdagird and Peroz, Jews may well have followed the dictates of their *own* piety, with disastrous results. The earlier persecutions combined with the older tradition about what would happen in 468 served to arouse this expectation. It was a self-fulfilling prophecy. The involvement and death of the exilarch is particularly striking, because the rabbis had taught (and presumably the exilarch did as well) that the Messiah would come forth from the Davidic household of the exilarch. If the exilarch was implicated in a rebellion, his government would naturally have been outlawed.

The disaster of 468 is a fitting end to this account of the institutions and theories of power in Babylonian Judaism. It underlines how little actual power was in the hands of Jews; they could not even control their own destiny. So far as the myths that explained and shaped history served to reconcile the Jews to their situation of weakness, they proved adaptive and functional. But when those myths led to the expectation that Jews might take into their own hands the worldly side of the Messianic task, they became dysfunctional and destructive. The competition between exilarch and rabbi, therefore, was in accord with the political realities of Jewish life. It focused partisan energies upon internal issues and thus kept the community out of trouble. But the reconciliation between the two released those energies, bringing catastrophe.

71

The Five Methods

by A. H. SILVER

Messianic calculators may be said to have employed five methods in their technique.

A. The Book of Daniel

The most common and the earliest was to decipher the specific dates given in the Book of Daniel. As early as the first century, men were already engaged in this work. The Book of Daniel gives at least six Messianic dates:[1] (1) time, times and half a time, (2) 2300, (3) 70 weeks (also 7 weeks, 62 weeks and 1 week), (4) season, seasons and half a season, (5) 1290 days, (6) 1335 days. These were challenging and tantalizing figures. What were the terminals of these cryptic dates? Surely they cannot be mutually exclusive. They must all be graded historical moments in the great drama of Israel's Redemption leading up to the ultimate Messianic day. Do the days mean years? Do the weeks mean seven years? How long is "time"? Is "times" the same as "seasons"? Is "time, times and half a time" equal to two and a half, or three and a half times? Were there perhaps more than one Redemption year given, dependent upon the merit of the people? What are the four kingdoms and the four beasts? And who is "the little horn"? And who is the king of the South and the king of the North, and all the other persons and powers alluded to in the revelations? Above all, what is the starting point from which all these periods of time are to be reckoned? These and numerous other questions presented themselves to those who embarked upon the fascinating enterprise of unraveling the great mystery.

[1] See *supra*, p. 124.

243

244 MESSIANIC SPECULATION IN ISRAEL

B. Other Biblical Texts

A second method was to determine from Scriptural passages (other than those of Daniel), phrases or words, especially those alluding to the future and redolent of promise, the length of the Messianic age, and to fix upon a certain important moment in the history of the people as the starting point from which to reckon this age. Many such *termini a quo* were fixed upon by the calculators through the ages.

C. Other Exiles

The third method was to turn to the earlier exiles, the Egyptian and the Babylonian, and from their duration and attendant circumstances learn the secret of the third exile. Clearly there was some divine logic in fixing the term of the Egyptian exile to 400 (also 210 and 430) years, and that of the Babylonian to 70 (also 52) years. A similar logic undoubtedly controls the duration of this last exile. What is it?

D. Gematria

One of the most fruitful methods employed by Jewish adventists in their calculations was Gematria (the interpretation of a word according to the numerical value of its letters), and its related pseudo-sciences, Notarikon (taking each letter of a word as the initial of some other word = acrostics), Ẓiruf or Ḥiluf (the interpretation of a word by transposing its letters = anagram), and Temurah (substituting one letter for another). Gematria was a never-failing medium and its scope was limited only by the ingenuity of the speculator.

It was a time-honored device, and the medieval student had ample authority for employing it. R. Eliezer ben Jose, the Galilean (second half of 2 c.), had included Gematria among the thirty-two hermeneutic rules by which the Torah may be interpreted. R. Yoḥanan ben Zakkai studied Gematria.[2] This device was actually used

[2] *B. B.*, p. 134a.

in connection with redemption from exile—in this case the Egyptian exile. R. Abba bar Kahana interpreted the word[3] רדו as indicating the number of years (210, in Gematria) which the children of Israel would remain in Egypt.[4] R. Levi pointed out that the word בזאת[5] indicated the length of the duration of the first Temple, 410 years.[6] It is of interest that both of these Gematriot were frequently used by later calculators.

R. Yoḥanan, quoting R. Jose ben Zimra, proved that Notarikon is found in the Torah.[7] There are close to a hundred and fifty cases of Gematria in Talmudic literature.

The science of Ẓiruf was employed in discovering the will of God through the Urim and Tumim. R. Yoḥanan declared that the answer to the High Priests' query was given by the letters thrusting themselves upward. Resh Lakish said by the automatic combinations of the letters.[8]

That number mysticism was also employed by the early Christians in connection with the Messiah is evident by the sharp and lengthy criticism which Irenaeus (2 c.) directs against it.[9]

Under the influence of Kabbala this science was highly developed and elaborated in post-Talmudic times. The Sefer Yeẓirah, the Otiot de R. Akiba and many other treatises on alphabetic theosophy gave great impetus to Gematria. The Sefer Yeẓirah declared, "By means of 32 mysterious paths of wisdom did the Lord of hosts . . . ordain and create his universe" (i. e. the 22 letters, plus 10 sefirot, or vowels).[10] "The 22 fundamental letters God appointed, established, combined, weighed and changed them, and through them He formed all things existent and

---

[3] Gen. 42.2.
[4] Ber. R. 91.2.
[5] Lev. 16.3: בזאת יבא אהרן.
[6] Lev. R. 21.8.
[7] Sab. 105a: מנין ללשון נוטריקון מן התורה; see also the six Notarikons given in that passage.
[8] כיצד נעשית: רבי יוחנן אומר בולטות. ריש לקיש אומר מצטרפות (Yoma 73b).
[9] "Against Heresies," Bk. II, Chaps. XXIV–XXV in The Ante-Nicene Fathers, I.
[10] Op. cit., 1.1.

destined to exist.[11] The planetary system, the Zodiac, the days of the week, the organs of the human body and all the moral qualities were fashioned by the aid of the basic alphabet. Similarly, the *Otiot de R. Akiba* declared, "R. Akiba said: 'the 22 letters by which the Torah was given to Israel are engraved with a flaming pen upon the fearful and awful crown of God; and when God wished to create the universe, all the letters descended and stood before God, and each one said, 'Through me create thou the universe.'"[12]

Letter mysticism made tremendous strides during the Middle Ages. Hardly a Biblical commentary outside the classic Spanish school but what employed alphabetic metaphysics on a smaller or larger scale. In the thirteenth century Abulafia maintained that letters, vowels and numerals are the highest subjects of speculation, and their mystic interpretation the profoundest tradition of the prophets.[13] In the sixteenth century Cordovero declared that the letters have their source in God and from Him they emanate as very light spirits and descend in successive stages until their pilgrimage is ended.[14] The vowels have even a higher mystic value.[15] Likewise are the accents of supreme mystic import. They belong to the very source of the first sefirah. Cordovero characterizes the letters as persons (נפשות), the vowels as powers (כחות), and the accents as souls (נשמות).[16] In the *Tikkune ha-Zohar*, one of the Zoharitic compositions, it is stated that the accents are the souls (נשמתין), the vowels are the spirits (רוחין) and the letters are the persons (נפשות).[17] This is an interesting application of the doctrine of the three souls, sensuous, emotional and intellectual, of the Platonic system. The *Sefer ha-Bahir*, a pre-Zoharitic Kabbalistic text book, declared that the vowels are like the soul which lives in the body of a man.[18]

The true interpretation of the Torah, declared Cordovero, can be had only through the medium of letter mysticism in all its endless ramfications: "We can arrive at a knowledge of the secrets of our Holy Torah, by means of anagrams, Gematriot, substitutions, initial, middle and final letters, the beginning or ends of verses, skipping of letters and the contraction of letters. These matters are very exalted and occult, and their secret is beyond our full comprehension, for by means of these methods they may change endlessly and to infinity."[19]

David ben Solomon ibn Abi Zimra (1479–1589), teacher of Isaac Luria and author of a work on the mystic significance of the alphabet, accurately sums up the nigh universally accepted belief of the Middle Ages regarding the sanctity of the letters of the Hebrew alphabet. He quotes approvingly and substantiates Maimonides' opinion that "The script which we now employ is the Assyrian script,[20] and that it is the script in which God wrote the Torah."[21] "This is the script," writes the Radbaz, "in which the Torah and the Tables were given; and all the secrets of their forms, their flourishes and their crownlets, majuscular letters and minuscular, crooked and looped, bent and straight, and all their intimations and mysteries were revealed to Moses, just like all the rest of the oral law, and this script has a sanctity all of its own." והוא הכתב שיש בו קדושה מצד עצמו [22] So also Abraham Portaleone, the physician (d. 1612), writes in his שלטי הגבורים[23]: והנה זה משלמות התורה ומהרמזים הצפונים באותיותיה כי על כן באו בתורה אותיות הפוכות ותלויות וכן עקומות ומלופפות וכן גדולות וקטנות וכן מנומרות ומנוקרות כי יתגלו מתוכן חמשים שערי בינה שנגלו לו למשה. As late as the year 1863 Aaron Kornfeld wrote a book, ציונים לדברי הקבלה in which he catalogues over

---

[18] ספר הבהיר, ed. Wilna, 1883, p. 23). (see ודמין באתוותא לנשמתא דחיי בגופא דאינשא

[19] ספר פרדס רמונים, ed. Koretz, 1780–1, Gate 30, p. 176b.

[20] כתב אשורי as against כתב עברי.

[21] *Yadayim* 4.5.

[22] מגן דוד, ed. Amsterdam, 1713, end of Intro.

[23] Ed. Mantua, 1613, p. 174a.

300 Rabbinic laws and interpretations derived *per Gematriam* from Biblical verses. He maintains that God in writing the Torah had intended that these verses should lend themselves to such use if for no other reason than as an aid to man's memory.[24]

ולסבה הזאת אין רחוק לומר כי ה' יתבר' בכתבו התורה כוון גם לזה למען יועיל
לחרותם בזכרון לבלתי ישכח כל כך מהרה.

The Radbaz calls his book מגן דוד, because 'מ'ג'ן' suggests the three ways by which he intends to interpret every letter: מסורת (traditional sound and form of the letter), גימטריא (numerical value), and נוטריקון (initials).[25] "God is the whiteness of the parchment which underlies, penetrates and supports the letters of the alphabet."[26]

The Neo-Platonic influence which is strong in Kabbala, and which had incorporated the Pythagorean science of numbers and letters, gave to Jewish mysticism a strong impetus in this direction, although the origin of it need not be sought, as we have seen, outside of Jewish thought. It was well developed among the Rabbis of the early centuries of the common era, but whereas among the Rabbis this study was regarded as פרפראות לחכמה, mere after-courses to wisdom,[27] among the Kabbalists in the decadent period it had suplanted חכמה herself.

As regards this method of computing the end the Jewish adventists had a great advantage over the Christian. The latter, in their speculations, were limited to those passages in the Old and the New Testaments which contained clear Messianic references, where specific dates and figures are given, such as those of Daniel and Revelations. Few of them had access to the original Hebrew of the Old Testament. The Old Testament was known to them largely in the Latin translation, and the New in its Greek original, or in its Latin translation. They could not, by means of the highly elastic art of Gematria, force a secret from any passage they chose. The science of Anagram

[24] Ed. Prague, 1865, Intro.
[25] *Op. cit.*, p. 1a.
[26] *Ibid.*, p. 1b
[27] *Abot* 3.23.

and Gematria was, of course, known to them, but they were limited to the use of a language which was not "the language of God." The Jewish adventist was in possession of the divine speech itself. To him Hebrew was the language of God actually, not figuratively. To him the phrase, "by the word of God were the heavens created," was more than a figure of speech. The "word" was made up of letters and vowels. These letters and vowels were Hebrew letters and vowels—the twenty-two letters of the alphabet and the ten vowels. Not alone were words channels of revelation, but every letter of the Bible and every vowel held a profound mystery. Not alone did each word possess a literal meaning (פשט), an allegoric meaning (רמז), an homiletic meaning (דרוש) and an anagogic meaning (סוד), but the very letters of the word and their permutations, combinations and numerical value contained recondite truth—had, as it were, marvelous halftones and overtones. Not alone were the Biblical laws and teachings divine, but the very words which expressed them had a divinity of their own and a meaning of their own. Cordovero gives the most complete exposition of the spiritual autonomy of the Hebrew alphabet. It is altogether unlike the alphabet of any other language. All other alphabets are the formal and inert channels of thought. The Hebrew alphabet is thought itself. When a doctor writes a medical treatise his object is to suggest some cure. He does not intend to make *the book itself* a cure. When his thought is once grasped there is no more need for the book. Not so the Torah. It has an inviolable sanctity beyond the ideas which it conveys. So that even an ignorant man reading it without understanding is greatly benefited. The surface narratives and chronicles of the Torah, says Cordovero, elaborating upon a theme of the *Zohar*,[28] are only the outer garment (לבוש עליון), the legal and Aggadic interpretations of it are the body (גופא), the Kabbalistic interpretation of it is the soul (נשמה), but the mystic interpretation of its letters, their permuta-

[28] Par. בהעלותך, p. 152a.

tions and combinations, is the real spiritual essence of it
(רוחניות), the knowledge of which would enable a man to
create worlds.[29]

Every letter was a visible revelation of invisible truth.
The Rabbis had already employed words and part of words
in their hermeneutics and dialectics to expound the law
and to develop it, as well as in their Aggadic peregrinations.
The mystic employed the same strategy in his excursions.
The letter never restrained him. On the contrary, he
moved bravely on to his destination on a vehicle which
always responded to his will.

This may perhaps account for the fact that the Jewish
mystic seldom, if ever, found himself in direct opposition
to the "written word." We find no Jewish mystic who
attacked the Bible, but many of the Christian mystics
fretted under the constraint of the "letter which killeth."
The Jewish mystic could find his complete freedom in the
Bible, for by means of his highly refined methodology the
very letters dissolved into a world of spirituality. Spiritual
autonomy, which is the very life-blood of mysticism, drove
the Christian mystic away from the Book. It drove the
Jewish mystic *into* the Book. Rufus Jones, in outlining
Sebastian Franck's (16 c.) attitude to the Scriptures,
accurately sums up the essential viewpoint of many of
the Christian mystics: "Franck insists that from its
inherent nature, a written Scripture cannot be the final
authority in religion: (a) it is outward, external, while
the seat of religion is in the soul of man; (b) it is transitory
and shifting, for language is always in the process of
change, and written words have different meanings to
different ages and in different countries . . .; (c) the
Scripture is full of mystery, contradiction and paradox,
which only 'the key of David'—the inner experience of
the heart, can unlock . . .; and (d) Scripture at best
brings only knowledge."[30]

The Jewish mystic, however, said הפך בה והפך בה דכלא בה
"Turn it about and about, for *everything* is in it". To

[29] פרדס רמונים, p. 167a, b, c.
[30] *Spiritual Reformers in the 16th and 17th Centuries*, p. 60.

the Christian mystic the Book was at best a temporary guide, a pedagogic help, a shadow of reality. To the Jewish mystic it was the *whole of reality*. It was the Living Word.

Jewish mysticism in general based its authority not upon vision or revelation, but upon an inspired and occult interpretation of the words of the Bible. When the Jewish adventist, therefore, sought the key to the solution of his problems, he felt free to go to any passage in the Bible, to the words or letters of any sacred text, which to him seemed freighted with mystery and prophetic of marvelous matter.

The rôle which Gematria played in Messianic calculations cannot be overestimated. Especially was it of importance in the seventeenth century and in the Shabbetian movement. It is astounding to see how often the weapons which were employed by the opposing sides in the Shabbetian controversy were those of Gematria.

Rabbi Joshua Neneto, of Alexandria, writing to the community of Leghorn, points to the numerous passages in the Bible which, *per Gematriam*, clearly establish the Messiahship of Shabbetai Zebi. He states that these passages are almost endless, and that they are sufficient and valid proof.[31] This view was shared by all the adherents of Shabbetai Zebi. They pointed with conviction to the fact that the name of Shabbetai Zebi, שבתי צבי was equal to the name of God, שדי taken in its integrated form: ש'ד'י ד'ל'ת' י'ו'ד'=814.[32] It is also equal to ו'ש'נ'ת' נ'א'ו'ל'י' ב'א'ה' =814 ("And my year of redemption is come").[33] Zebi (צבי) is also the Notarikon of צ'דיק ב'אמונתו י'חיה ("the righteous shall live by his faith").[34]

[31] ומצאנו בתורה 'נביאים וכתובים פסוקים נרמזים על שמו לאין חקר ולאין מספר (see קיצור צנ'צ, p. 25).

[32] *Ibid.*

[33] Is. 63.4. Emden's תורת הקנאות, ed. Lemberg, 1870, Chap. XVI, and Cahana's תילדות השבתאים והחסידים, p. 96.

[34] Hab. 2.4. There is another Notarikon for שבתי צבי in Ezek. 20.15: הביא אותם אל הארץ אשר נתתי' זבת' חלב' ודבש' צ'ב'י (see A. Freimann, עניני שבתי צבי, p. 98; also the elaborate Notarikon built upon the two verses in Gen. 41.1, 2. יהי מקץ שנתים, reprinted in Cahana's תולדות הש' והה
, App. IV, pp. 142–3.)

The opponents countered by pointing out that שבתי צבי is equal to י׳י׳ד׳ ע׳ צ׳י׳ד׳ א׳י׳ש ש׳ד׳ה׳ ("And he (Esau) was a cunning hunter, a man of the field").[35]   Also that שבתי is equal to ב׳ל׳ע׳ם ר׳ש׳ע׳ = Balaam, the wicked.   Also that שבתי צבי is equal to עמלק הרשע = Amalek the wicked, and ר׳ו׳ח ש׳ק׳ר׳ = the lying spirit.[36]

The year of Shabbetai Zebi's revelation was also established by Gematria. It was based on the Zoharitic Messianic year 1648, which in turn was based on the verse בשנת היובל הזאת תשובו = 5408 = 1648 ("In this year of the Jubilee shall ye return").[37]   This was the year when Shabbetai Zebi first began to reveal his true character to his disciples in Smyrna. It was in the eighth year of the Jubilee cycle. Within the remaining 42 years of that cycle, i. e. up to 1690, the restoration must take place. The year 1666, when Shabbetai again made public avowal of his Messiahship, was indicated in ישראל נ׳ש׳ע׳ בה׳ = 1666 ("O, Israel, thou art saved by the Lord").[38]   Nathan of Gaza proclaimed that the restoration will take place before the year 5430 = 1670.[39]   When this year did not bring about the promised Redemption, the disciples found Gematria for other years: 1675, 1680, 1686, 1692, 1706, 1710.[40]

The extensive use of secret Gematria codes in the charms and amulets of the eighteenth century, coupling the name of Shabbetai Zebi with that of God, was responsible for the prolonged and bitter Emden-Eybeschütz controversy.

This method, of course, was not unopposed. There were many who sensed the menace of such a free and

[35] Gen. 25.27.

[36] צנ׳צ, קיצור, pp. 63, 65–66.

[37] Lev. 25.13.

[38] Is. 45.17, צ׳צ, קיצור, p. 13a.

[39] A Gematria was discovered for that year, too. כמנדל דוד צוארך בנוי לתלפיות אלף המגן תלוי עליו כל שלטי הגבורים ("Thy neck is like the Tower of David, builded with turrets, whereon there hang a thousand shields, all the armor of the mighty men," Songs of Songs, 4.4). The Tower of David is Shabbetai Zebi—The Messiah ben David—who will rebuild the Temple in the year (פיות) ה׳ת׳ל׳ ל׳ =5430=1670, according to the testimony (לתהל) פ׳י׳ר׳ת׳ of Nathan the Prophet, in the fifth millennium אלף ה׳מן (קיצור צנ׳צ) p. 8).

[40] See צ׳צ קיצור, pp. 73, 77, 83; also ספר טריבת קדש in עניני שבתי צבי, pp. 12, 37.

undisciplined reading of sacred text. Maimonides, for example, was strongly opposed to the whole system of alphabetic theosophy. In his *Guide* he writes: "You must beware of sharing the error of those who write amulets. Whatever you hear from them or read in their works, especially in reference to the names which they form by combinations, is utterly senseless; they call these combinations "shemot" (names—combinations of the letters of the Tetragrammaton), and believe that their pronunciation demands sanctification and purification, and that by using them they are enabled to work miracles. Rational persons ought not to listen to such men, nor in any way believe their assertions."[41] There were many others who shared Maimonides' view. We have also seen the vigorous onslaught upon this pseudo-science by Modena. In spite of them this pseudo-science progressed unchecked in Jewry.

E. Astrology

Astrology was another means of Messianic calculation. It, too, was well grounded in Jewish tradition. We might with safety assume that already in their nomadic period the tribes of Israel, like almost all Semitic peoples, had developed some crude astrological system. The nomadic Hebrew undoubtedly shared in the pan-vitalistic supposition of primitive man. And this would inevitably result in ascribing life and conscious existence to the heavenly bodies. Under Canaanitish and Assyrian influence astral worship as well as astrology developed in Israel, for wherever there is worship of heavenly bodies there is also astral divination, i. e. astrology. The historical books of the Bible abound in references to this form of idolatry. In the period of the prophets the worship of the "host of heaven" was prevalent in Israel, and the prophets from Amos down exerted themselves to the utmost to suppress it. Amos and Isaiah denounced it.[42] Zephaniah and

[41] *Guide For the Perplexed*, Friedlander, London, 1910, Bk. I, Chap. LVi' p. 91.
[42] Amos 5.26; Is. 17.8.

Jeremiah inveighed against it.[43] Deuteronomy is strenuous in its opposition.[44] It is doubtful whether the Deuteronomic reformation succeeded in putting even a temporary check upon this idolatry. Deutero-Isaiah indirectly wages war upon it by insisting that Yahweh is the sole creator and Lord of all the hosts of heaven.[45] Job speaks of the sinfulness of it.[46] The worship in some form or another survived throughout post-exilic times and traces of it are found in very late Talmudic sources.

The official religion, under prophetic impetus, began quite early to oppose astrological divination. Occasionally, however, even in the Bible the predictive powers of the heavenly bodies are acknowledged. Thus in Gen. 1.14 it is declared: "And they (the sun, moon and stars) shall be for *signs* and for seasons." But as a rule the official religion frowned upon it, and at times vigorously opposed it. It compromised with the principle of monotheism, and it endangered the doctrine of free will and moral responsibility. Herein Judaism moved in advance of all the other religions of antiquity, which never outgrew it. Judaism, in keeping with its practice of ascribing to all forms of Israelitish idolatry a foreign nativity, branded astrology "a custom of the heathen." Thus Jeremiah urges upon the people, "be not afraid of the signs of the heavens," and calls it "the way of the heathen."[47] Judaism did not deny astral influences as such. It simply denied their efficacy in the case of Israel. Israel, being God's own people, was beyond the control of stars or planets. This was also the position taken in subsequent times. Abraham, the Rabbis held, employed astrology until he was favored with a revelation from Yahweh. With it came the command, "Forsake astrology."[48]

When the Christian Church in the early centuries was

---

[43] Zeph. 1.5; Jer. 7.18; 8.2; 19.15; 32.29.
[44] Deut. 1.19; 17.13.
[45] Is. 40.26; 45.12.
[46] Job. 31.26–7.
[47] Jer. 10.2.
[48] צא מאיצטגנינות שלך (*Ber. R.* 44.14; *Sab.* 156a). See Philo *Migration of Abraham* XXXII; *Dreams* X; also Halevi, *Kuzari* 4.27.

THE FIVE METHODS 255

confronted with the need of opposing astrology, it adopted a similar strategy. In the face of what seemed to be over-whelming evidence for astrology, it contented itself with declaring that astrology was the particular domain of the devil and other evil spirits, and that with the coming of Christ all astrological divination was prohibited. Thus Tertullian wrote: "One proposition I lay down: that those angels, the deserters from God, the lovers of women, were likewise the discoverers of this curious art (astrology), on that account also condemned by God. . . . But, how-ever, that science has been allowed until the Gospel, in order that after Christ's birth no one should thenceforward interpret anyone's nativity by the heaven."[49]

The Sibylline Book III counts it among the virtues of "the race of most righteous men," the Jews, that they do not study the predictions of Chaldaean astrology, nor do they astronomize, for all these things are in their nature prone to deceive."[50] According to Enoch the evil spirit Baraquijal taught men astrology, and Kokabel the con-stellation.[51] But while the official religion proscribed it, the popular religion retained it.

The practice of forecasting the future by means of heavenly bodies was therefore not new in Israel. It gained widespread recognition among the people in the early centuries of the common era through Graeco-Roman influence. The thought of the Mediterranean world was thoroughly saturated with this pseudo-science, and its finest minds, such as Pliny, Seneca, Ptolemy, Galen, Plutarch, Lucian and many others believed in it and expounded it. Above all, it was universally accepted and practiced by the masses of the people of the Mediterranean world, and it was approved by the official religions of the day.

In spite of occasional expressions of opposition to astrology found in the Talmud and the Midrash, such as

[49] *On Idolatry*, chap. 9.
[50] The Sibylline Books III, l. 227–8.
[51] Book of Enoch 8.3.

"There are no planets for Israel,"[52] and "One must not consult Chaldeans," (astrologers)[53], the preponderately favorable allusions prove conclusively that it was widely held and practiced in Israel. Some Rabbis, like Samuel (3 c.), may have practiced it in their leisure time, when they were not engaged in the study of the Torah, and may have scrupulously refrained from combining the two studies.[54]   But it is clear from statements such as the following that this science had a strong hold over the minds even of some of the leaders of the people. R. Simon said, "There isn't a blade of grass which has not a planet in the heavens which strikes it and commands it to grow."[55]   Raba (4 c.) declared, "Life, offspring and sustenance do not depend upon merit but upon the planets."[56] Elsewhere in the Talmud we find quite an elaborate account of natal astrology.[57] as well as the categoric assertion of R. Ḥanina that "the planet makes a man wise and the planet makes a man rich, and there is a planet governing the fortunes of Israel." That certain constellations are good and certain others are evil[58] and that each nation is under the sovereignty of a particular star was widely held.[59]   Both Philo and Josephus believed in some form of astrology. It is noteworthy, however, that we find in Talmudic literature no *Messianic calculation* based on astrology.

But it was in the Middle Ages under Arabic influence that the belief in astrology among the Jews became well-nigh universal. The Arabs appropriated the whole astrological gallery of the Graeco-Roman world and added thereto. Jews and Christians alike were their eager disciples. A perusal of the list of translations of astrological works made by the Jews of the Middle Ages, will

[52] אין מזל לישראל (*Sab.* 156a).
[53] אין שואלים בכלדיים (*Pes.* 113b).
[54] *Deut. R.* 8.6.
[55] *Gen. R.* 10.7.
[56] *Mo'ed Ḳat.* 28a.
[57] *Sab.* 156a.
[58] *Ta'an* 29b.
[59] See E. Bischoff, *Babylonisch-Astrales im Weltbilde des Thalmud und Midrasch*, Leipsig, 1907, pp. 115 ff.

indicate the high regard in which this science was held by them.[60] The Jews proved to be important channels through which this science invaded Christian Europe in the twelfth and thirteenth centuries. They came into vital contact with Arabic culture at a somewhat earlier time than the European Christians. Accordingly astrology was wide-spread among them at an earlier time.

Ibn Ezra, who at times practiced astrology as a profession, called the heavens the "Book of Life in which men's destinies are inscribed the day they are born."[61] He declared that "all the affairs below depend upon the powers above, and from the heavens are all deeds determined."[62] Also "good or evil, honor or disgrace, which befall a man are all the work of the conjunction of the stars."[63] The *Zohar* declared "everything depends upon the planets, even the Scrolls in the Temple."[64]

Abraham Bar Ḥiyya vigorously defended astrology in the twelfth century. In answer to an attack which was made upon him because he advised a bridegroom to postpone the hour of his wedding to a time when the constellation would be more propitious, he wrote a lengthy defense of astrology in a letter to R. Judah ben Barzillai.[65] He declared that he had studied this science all his life.[66] He finds it not at all incompatible with Judaism. The Rabbis engaged in it;[67] even Abraham studied it.[68] The powers of the heavenly bodies are of course granted to them by God.[69] Through righteousness and prayer their evil decrees may be averted. This is an especial favor

[60] See Steinschneider, *Die Heb. Übersetzungen des Mittelalters*, p. 525 ff.
[61] Com. on Ps. 69.29. See Krochmal, מורה נבוכי הזמן, Warsaw, 1894, pp. 306, 311 ff.
[62] Com. on Gen. 11.5.
[63] Comm. on Ps. 67. See also Ibn Ezra's ספר למשאלה בקדרות, ed. Manasseh Grossberg, London, 1902, p. 3, note 6.
[64] Par. נשא, p. 134a.
[65] Published by A. Z. Schwarz, in *Festschrift Adolf Schwarz*, Vienna, 1917, pp. 23–26.
[66] *Op. cit.*, p. 36.
[67] *Ibid.*, p. 26.
[68] *Ibid.*, p. 27.
[69] *Ibid.*, pp. 25, 30.

granted by God to Israel in which the Gentiles do not share.[70] He is convinced that Jews ought to study astrology and believe in it.[71]

In the thirteenth century Judah ben Solomon Ha-Kohen ibn Matkah of Toledo rose to a similar defense of astrology.[72]

Even those who opposed it did not entirely deny that the heavenly bodies were active intelligences. Thus Halevi gives astrology an ancillary position to prophecy, but he does not deny its validity. One cannot arrive at a knowledge of God or at religious truth by means of astrology any more than one can by means of philosophy. Even Maimonides, who alone among his contemporaries vigorously attacked genethlialogy and judicial astrology,[73] calling it "stupidity" and "falsehood," shared the universal belief that the heavenly bodies were living, active intelligences who controlled, through their influences, the mundane world.[74] Under the influence of Arabic thought the orthodox opposition to astrology in Israel well-nigh broke down, as was also the case in the Christian world.[75]

It is not surprising, therefore, that Jewish adventists resorted to this method in their calculations. It was employed by them before the days of Ibn Ezra.[76] It was extensively used in the fourteenth and fifteenth centuries.[77] It was generally held that the seven planets in their progress through the signs of the zodiac and in the variety

[70] *Ibid.*, p. 27.

[71] ומכל אשר קדמנו תבאר שחכמת הכוכבים ראויה ללמוד אותה ולהחזיק בה (*ibid.*, p. 18).

[72] See Alexander Marx, "The Correspondence Between the Rabbis of Southern France and Maimonides about Astrology," *Hebrew Union College Annual*, III, Cincinnati, 1926, p. 314.

[73] See his *Responsum* to the letter of inquiry sent to him by the Rabbis of Southern France concerning Astrology, published anew and corrected from new MSS. by Professor Alexander Marx (*op. cit.*, pp. 349 ff.). In connection with Maimonides' thoroughgoing opposition to astrology, Professor Marx states that to his knowledge only one other Hebrew writer—Isaac Pulgar (14 c.), author of '*Ezer ha-Dat*—fully endorsed Maimonides' position (*ibid.*, p. 324).

[74] See his *Guide Bk.* II, 2.5, and 10.

[75] See T. O. Wedel, *The Medieval Attitude Toward Astrology*, Yale Univ. Press, 1920, pp. 69 ff.

[76] See his *Com. Dan.* 11.29; see also *Me'or 'Enayim*, chap. 43.

[77] "Zunz, Eine merkwürdige Medaille," in his *Ges. Schr.*, III, pp. 94 ff.

of their conjunctions influenced the affairs of men and nations. Each stage in the progress and each conjunction had a particular significance. They predicted mighty events and great changes in the world. Of particular significance for Israel was the conjunction of the two highest planets, Jupiter and Saturn. This conjunction was regarded as significant also by Christians. Six years before the birth of Jesus, it was pointed out, such a conjunction took place in the tenth revolution of Saturn, which always predicts the advent of a great historic personage.[78]

The prevalence of this belief in the twelfth century is attested by Petahia of Ratisbon. In Nineveh the traveler Patahia consulted an astrologer *to learn the Messianic year:* "At Nineveh there was an astrologer whose name was Rabbi Solomon. There is among all the sages in Nineveh and in the land of Ashur none as expert in the planets as he. Rabbi Petahia asked him when the Messiah will come. And he told him, 'I have seen this often distinctly in the planets.' But Rabbi Judah the Pious (who probably transcribed Petahia's account of his travels) would not write it down, lest he should be suspected of believing the words of Rabbi Solomon."[79]

[78] See Thorndike, *Magic and Experimental Science*, II, p. 672; also p. 896.
[79] *Travels of R. Petachia*, trans. Benisch, London, 1861, p. 13.

חבלי משיח
מאיר וכסמן

אורך הגלות, כאמור, לא מעט את השאיפה לגאולה כי אם העמיק
אותה ומזמן לזמן כאשר כבד עול הגלות התעוררה ביתר עוז ביחוד לרגלי
כל מקרה בלתי רגיל בעולם. מקרה כזה בין בחיים הכלליים בין בחיי
היהודים ובין בטבע עורר את התקוה כי הגאולה הולכת ומתקרבת.
מסורה עתיקה, שראשיתה אנו מוצאים בספרים האפוקליפטיים כמו
עזרא ד', חזון ברוך ועוד ושיסודה הוא כי הגאולה היא לא רק מהגלות
אבל גם גאולת העולם מהרע, הדגישה כי בטרם ביאת המשיח יתגלה
הרע בעולם, בין הרע המוסרי ובין הרע הגשמי בכל תקפו. ורק בבואו
אל שיאו אז יתגלה המשיח. מסורה זו עברה בחלקה הגדול גם אל הספרות
התלמודית. סימני התקרבות הגאולה קבלו שם מיוחד „חבלי המשיח",
כלומר, הצרות מעידות שהקץ מתקרב. יסוד השם הוא בדברי הנביאים
שדמו את הגאולה ללדת של האשה הבאה אחרי צירים וחבלים[69]. תאור
הדברים האלה נמצאו לכל הפחות כשש פעמים בספרות התלמודית־מדרשית[70].

הפסקה הראשית הי בסנהדרין צ"ז, „ת"ר שבוע (כלומר, שבע השנים)
שבן דוד בא שנה ראשונה מתקים והמטרתי על עיר אחת ועל עיר אחת
לא אמטיר (עמוס, ד', ז), כלומר בצורת חלקית; שנה השניה חצי רעב
משתלחין; שנה שלישית רעב גדול ומתים אנשים, נשים וטף, חסידים
ואנשי מעשה ותורה משתכחת מלומדיה; ברביעית שובע ואינו שובע;
בחמישית שובע גדול ואוכלין ושותין ותורה חוזרת ללומדיה; בששית
קולות ובשביעית מלחמות; במוצאי שביעית בן דוד בא". המובן קולות
אינו ברור. רש"י מביא שני פירושים, אחד כי „קולות" כונתן שמועות
נפוצות שמשיח בא, והשני תקיעות שופר מלמעלה המודיעות על ביאת
המשיח. ואמנם מוצאים אנו במדרשים על תקיעת שופר לפני

---

[69] ישעיה, כ"ו, י"ז „כמו הרה תקריב ללדת תחיל תזעק בחבליה כן היינו
מפניך ה' "; שם ס"ו ח' „היוחל ארץ ביום אחד, אם יולד גוי פעם אחת כי חלה גם
ילדה ציון את בניה".

[70] סנהדרין צ"ז, א'; סוטה מ"ה; דרך ארץ זוטא שהש"ר פ' ב', י"ג־י"ד; פסיקתא
דרב כהנא, הוצ. בובר ע' מ"ו פסיקתא רבתי הוצ. פרידמן ע' ע"ה.

[71] עיין להלן.

התגלות המשיח על ידי אליהו או המשיח בעצמו [71], אבל תקיעות אלו באות
תיכף לביאת המשיח ולא כשנה קודם. קרוב איפא שבפסקא זו שומעים
אנו הד מספר החצוני עזרא ד' ששמה נזכר בסיפור על חבלי משיח קולות
שופר שישמעו אנשים ויחרדו לקולם [72].

פסקא זו מובאה בסנהדרין כברייתא סתמית. בדרך ארץ זוטא בשם
ר' שמעון בן יוחאי, בפסיקתא דר' כהנא ובפסיקתא רבתי בשם „רבנן
אמרי" אולם בשיר השירים רבה בשם ר' יוחנן. מזה אפשר להוכיח כי
בעוד שהמסורה עצמה היתה רוחה לא היה ברור מי האומרה. אפשר איפא
לקבל כי הרעיון של חבלי משיח הוא מתקופת התנאים כנוסחת רוב הפסק
אות והשם ר' יוחנן במדרש שיר השירים בא מפני שלפני הפסקה בסנהדרין
בא מאמר ר' יוחנן על צרות כלליות שתקרינה בדור שהמשיח בא.

חבלי משיח לפי פסקא זו הם טבעיות ואנושיות דברים
הנקרים הרבה פעמים במשך ההיסטוריה, ולא לחנם פקפק רב יוסף
בסמכותה של מסורה זו ואמר „הא כמה שביעית דהוה כן ולא אתא"
והוצרכו לענותו כי סדר המקרים עיקר, כלומר, שמוכרחין לבוא כסדרם [73].
אולם באותו הדף ישנם מאמרים אחרים, חוץ מזה של ר' יוחנן המדבר סתם
על צרות וגזרות על ישראל [74], המדגישים צד אחר מחבלי משיח. ר' יהודה
תלמידו של ר' עקיבא מדבר על ירידה מוסרית בדור שלפני ביאת המשיח
כגון מעוט למוד התורה, רבוי העזות והשקר וחוסר הבושה עד כי אפשר
יהיה להגיד כי „פני הדור כפני הכלב". ר' נהוראי מוסיף פרטי הירידה
ואומר „כי נערים ילבינו פני זקנים, בת קמה באמה וכלה בחמותה", על פי
דברי הפסוק מיכה ז' ו', ור' נחמיה מוסיף ואומר „דור שבן דוד בא
תרבה העזות, היוקר יעות הגפן יתן פריו והיין ביוקר [75] וכל המלכות
תהפך למינות ואין תוכחה". פה ישנם מקרים טבעיים אחדים אבל ההדגשה
היא על הצד המוסרי וביחוד על חוסר האמונה בעולם — דברי ר' יהודה
ר' נהורא ור' נחמיה הנזכרים פה כמאמרי יחידים נחתמו בגושפנקא
כללית של דעות החכמים בזה שנרשמו במשנה סוטה ט' ט' באופן סתמי

<hr>

[72] עיין עזרא ד' פ' ו', כ"ג.

[73] אביי אמר לו „בששת קולות בשביעית מלחמות מי הוה, ועוד מי הוו כסדרן".
מדברי אביי אפשר להוכיח כי המובן של המלה „קולות" בברייתא אינו כהשערתי
בפנים תקיעות שופר מחרדות, אבל סתם שמועות רעות.

[74] שם.

[75] מובן המלים „היוקר יעות" הוא לפי רש"י הכבוד יעות דרכו, כלומר, שלא
יכבדו את הראוים לזה, אולם במשנה סוטה הגרסא היא היוקר יאמיר, כלומר יוקר
ממש, יעלה עד למעלה, כמו אמיר. המלים הגפן תתן פריה והיין ביוקר מובנים אף
על פי שהגפן יתן פריו אבל הפרי לא יהיה טוב ולכן היין יקר, או כי יתרבו השכורים,
ולכן יהיה היין יקר.

בהקדמה כללית „בעקבתא דמשיחא חוצפה יסגי" ואחרי כן באים הפרטים
שהובאו בשם התנאים האמורים.

בכל אלה התאורים של חבלי משיח בספרות התלמודית־מדרשית
מרגישים אנו נטיה ריאלית. החבלים הם בעיקר טבעיים ורעות מוסריות.
לעומת זה בספרים הגנוזים עזרא ד' וחזון ברוך סימני גאולה מעורבבים
במקרים על טבעיים כמו נפילת אש מן השמים וכי ים המלח ישליך מתוכו
מספר גדול של דגים; מים מתוקים יהפכו למלוחים והמעינות יתיבשו
במשך שלוש שעות וכדומה. וזה מראה על הכוון הכללי של הספרות
שאנו דנים בה הנוטה לפכחות והתקרבות למציאות. קביעות ענין של חבלי
משיח במשנה נתנה לדעה זו סמכות מסוימה והיא נעשתה לחוליה בשלשלת
הרעיון הכללי של רעיון המשיחיות במשך הדורות.

חדוש העולם
מ א י ר ו כ ס מ ן

כפי שראינו למעלה בפרקים על הספרות החצונית תופסת הדעה
על חדוש העולם, כפן מהתמונה הכללית של עולם הבא, מקום מסוים
בספרות זו. יסודה הוא כפי שציננו דברי הנביא ,,כי הנני בורא שמים
חדשים וארץ חדשה" (ישעיה, ס"ה, י"ז) שבזמן המאוחר הבינו אותן
כפשוטן. אין להתפלא איפא שנזכרת היא גם בספרות התלמודית-מדרשית
מספר פעמים, אולם ככל הדעות על העתיד שדננו עליהן אין מהותה
ואפיה קביעות ומוצקות. ידועה היתה דעה זו גם בדורות התנאים. קוראים
אנו במכילתא ,,ר'אלעזר המודעי אומר, אם תזכולשמור את השבת עתיד
הקב"ה ליתן לכם שש מדות טובות, ארץ ישראל ועולם הבא ועולם חדש
ומלכות בית דוד וכהונה ולויה" [287]. והנה אף כי הדברים אינם ברורים,
כי רוב המדות שהוא חושב שיכים לימות המשיח והוא אינו מזכירים.
עלינו איפא לקבל כי המונח עולם הבא במאמר זה מזדהה עם ימות המשיח
כבמספר מאמרים שהבאנו למעלה. עולם חדש, הנבדל פה מעולם הבא
הוא העולם הבא האמתי אלא שהתנא מכנהו בשם זה לפי הדעה הרוחה
כי מלבד כל תכונותיו של עולם זה יצטין גם בחדושו.

ענין חדוש עולם נדון גם במקומות אחדים בסנהדרין, המאמר
הראשון הוא בשם תנא דבי אליהו והוא ,,צדיקים שעתיד הקב"ה להתחיותן
אינם חוזרין לעפרם שנאמר והיה הנשאר בציון והנותר בירושלים קדוש
יאמר לו כל הכתוב לחיים בירושלים (ישעיה ד', ג'). מה קדוש לעולם קים
אף הם לעולם קימין. ואם תאמר אותן שנים שעתיד הקב"ה לחדש את
עולמו שנאמר ,ונשגב ה' לבדו ביום ההוא' (שם ב' י"א), צדיקים מה
הם עושין הקב"ה עושה להם כנפים ושטין על פני המים שנאמר ,על
כן לא נירא בהמיר ארץ במוט הרים בלב ימים' " (תהלים, מ"ו, ג') [288].
והנה מאמר זה מלבד הקושי שיש בו בענין תחית המתים שכנראה מדבריו
תקדם לעולם הבא וחדוש העולם ושכבר דננו בו למעלה. אינו מגביל
לא את זמן החדוש ולא את הזמן המבדיל בין העולם הזה ובין העולם החדש,
אלא מדבר על החדוש ועל חורבן קודם לו כעל דבר ידוע ומקובל כנראה

---

[287] מכילתא דר' ישמעאל הוצ' לויטרבך כ' ב' ע' 120. מאמר זה נזכר עוד
פעם בספר זה שם ע' 175. אולם במקום ר' אלעזר המודעי בא ר' אליעזר, וגם המאמר
בא בקשר עם דרשה אחרת. אבל מהותו לא נשתנה.
[288] סנהדרין צ"ב, א'.

מהשאלה מה יעשו הצדיקים בזמן הקודם לחדוש כלומר בזמן החורבן [289].
אולם שני מקומות אחרים דנים בחדוש ביתר בהירות ופרטות ככה ,,אמר
רב קטינא שית אלפי שני הוי עלמא ואחד חרוב שנאמר ונשגב ה' לבדו
ביום ההוא. אביי אמר תרי חרוב שנאמר ,יחינו מיומים, ביום השלישי
יקימנו ונחיה (הושע ב'). תניא כותיה דרב קטינא כשם שהשביעית משמטת
שנה אחת לז' שנים כך העולם משמט אלף שנים לשבעת אלפים שנה שנאמר
ונשגב ה' לבדו ביום ההוא'' ואומר מזמור שיר ליום השבת ליום שכולו
שבת [290]. המובן בדברים אלה הוא כי אחר ששת אלפים שנה הכוללים גם
ימות המשיח יחרב העולם אלף שנה, כלומר, על סמך הפסוק שה' בעצמו
ימצא יום אחד בעולם, ויום ה' הוא אלף שנים. אביי על סמך דרשה
אחרת אומר כי העולם יהיה חרב אלפים שנה, כלומר, שני ימים של
הקב"ה. הברייתא אומרת בפירוש כי רק אלף שנה יהא חרב — החורבן
מובע במונח שמיטה — והחדוש יבוא אחרי כן. ובאותו הדף במקום אחר
נאמר ,,כי אין הקב"ה מחדש עולמו אלא לאחר ז' אלפים שנה'' [290]. הדעה
המקובלת היא כנראה זו של הברייתא כי ההפסק יתקים אלף שנה ודעת
אביי היא רק דעת יחיד. אולם אפשר ללמוד מאותה הדרשה שלו כי העולם
החדש יתחיל בתחית המתים כי הוא מדגיש את המלים ,,יקימנו ונחיה''
וכבר העירונו למעלה על האפשרות של שתי תחיות מצומצמה בימות
המשיח וכללית בראשית עולם הבא.

מענין הוא המונח ,,יום שכולו שבת'' הנמצא בפסקא זו וגם במשנה
סוף תמיד, והשאלה אם מובנו של מונח זה בשני מקומות אלה הוא אחד
או משתנה לפי הענין צריכה דיון וברור. פירושו של רש"י למונח בסנהדרין
הוא ,,שכולו שבת, שהעולם משמט'', כלומר, חרב. והרע"ב בפירושו לפסקא
בסוף תמיד ,,מזמור שיר לעתיד לבוא ליום שכולו שבת ומנוחה לחיי
העולמים'' אומר ,,האי תנא סבר לה כמאן דאמר שתא אלפי שני הוי
עלמא וחד חרוב, ועל שם שבאלף השביעי לא יהיה כי אם הקב"ה שנאמר
ונשגב ה' לבדו ביום ההוא. לכך אומרים בשבת מזמור שיר ליום השבת,
לאלף השביעי שיומו של הקב"ה הוא אלף שנה [291]. פירושו זה של הרע"ב
מיוסד על פירוש רש"י לחלק הראשון של פסקא זו ,,מזמור שיר ליום
שבת ליום שכולו שבת'' הנמצא לא בתמיד כי אם בראש השנה ל"א [292].

---

[289] אמנם אפשר שהפסקא המתחילה ,,ואם תאמר'' וכו' אינו מגוף הקובץ
הקדום הנקרא תנא דבי אליהו אבל מסתמא דגמרא, אבל השאלה מוכיחה שהדעה על
חדוש העולם היתה רווחה בימי האמוראים.
[290] סנהדרין צ"ז, א'-ב'.
[291] הרמב"ם שפירושו לפרקים אחדים בתמיד נדפס בהוצאת ש"ס ווילנא עובר
על הפסקא בשתיקה.
[292] הוא אומר שם: ,,ליום שכולו שבת שעתיד שבת העולם להיות חרב, ואין אדם
וכל המלאכות שובתות, על אותו יום אומרים שיר של שבת''.

אולם למרות סמכות גדולי הפרשנים קשה לקבל מובן זה של המונח במשנה בסוף תמיד כי אין הענין מתאים לזה. המונח "לעתיד לבוא" המקדים את המונח "יום שכולו שבת" אם אינו מכון לימות המשיח, הרי משמעותו הוא על פי הרוב לעולם הבא. וחוץ מזה מה הוא מובן של המלים "ומנוחה לחיי העולמים"? המובן היותר פשוט הוא כי החיים בעתיד לבוא יהיו חיי עולם, כלומר נצחיים אמנם הרע"ב גורס לא חיי העולמים אבל חי העולמים ומבאר את זה, כנראה, על האלוהים שהוא חי לעולם[293], אבל המובן עדין אינו ברור כי למה הוסיפו "ומנוחה" האם ה' כביכול צריך מנוחה? האם יגע מעבודתו?

אבל חוץ מזה יש לפקפק גם על פירושו של רש"י עצמו שלאור הענין בראש השנה נראה כדחוק. הרצאת הדברים שם הוא ככה "תניא אמר ר' יהודה בשם רבי עקיבא. בראשון (כלומר שיר של יום ביום ראשון לשבוע) מה היו אומרים לה' הארץ ומלואה על שם שקנה (כלומר ברא שמים וארץ) והקנה ושליט בעולמו. בשני מה היו אומרים "גדול ה' ומהולל מאד" על שם שחלק מעשיו (הבדיל את הרקיע בין מים למים) ומלך עליהן. בשלישי היו אומרים "אלהים נצב בעדת אל" על שם שגלה ארץ בחכמתו והכין תבל לעדתו (ביום ג' נראתה היבשה). ברביעי מה היו אומרים "אל נקמות ה'" על שם שברא חמה ולבנה ועתיד לפרע מעובדיהן. בחמישי מה היו אומרים הרנינו לאלהים עוזנו על שם שברא עופות ודגים לשבח לשמו. בששי מה היו אומרים, "ה' מלך גאות לבש" על שם שגמר מלאכתו ומלך עליהן. בשביעי מה היו אומרים מזמור שיר ליום השבת ליום שכולו שבת". אלה הם דברי רבי עקיבא. על זה אומר רבי נחמיה "מה ראו חכמים לחלק בין הפרקים", כלומר, מדוע כל שירי ימי שבוע הם על מקרי ימי הבריאה ושיר של יום השבת הוא על העתיד? לכן הוא מסכים לטעמי שיר שאר ימי השבוע אבל בנוגע לשיר של יום השבת הוא הוא "על שם ששבת", כלומר לזכר השביתה בשבוע של הבריאה. והנה אין הכרח כלל לפרש את המונח "ליום שכולו שבת" בדברי רבי עקיבא כמו שמפרש רש"י יום שעתיד העולם להיות חרב ואין אדם

---

[293] והנה בכל הנוסחאות הנדפסות של המשנה הגרסא היא לחיי העולמים ולא חי העולמים. וכן היא הגרסא בפירושו של הראש למשנה זו. אמנם התוספות יום טוב בהערתו על דברי הרע"ב משתדל להראות כי אין הבדל בין חיי העולמים ובין חי העולמים כי לפי דעתו מובן שניהם, הוא ה' שהוא חיי העולם והוא קורא חי בצירי. והנה ידועה היא המחלוקת על מובן הבטוי חי העולמים הנמצא בתפלת ברוך שאמר ובישתבחה. הרמב"ם במורה נבוכים א' ע"ב, והכוזרי ד' ס' ג' מבארים את זה במובן ה' שהוא חיי העולם, אבל ר' נסים גאון בפירושו לברכות ע' ל"ב ואבודרהם בפירושו לתפלת ברוך שאמר ואחרים מבארים חי העולמים, חי לעולם, והנה חי הוא נסמך מחי (בפתח) ומובנו חי לעולם, אבל חיי עולמים משמעותם יותר קרוב חיים נצחיים.

וכל המלאכות שובתות. הרבה יותר פשוט הוא המובן כי ביום ההוא תהיה
מנוחה לעולם מן כל מלחמות והמחלוקות בין בני אדם ומלכות שמים
תתפשט ולא יהיו עובדים לאלילים. וטענתו של ר' נחמיה היא כאמור שגם
שיר זה הוא על העבר. אבל אחד מבעלי סתמא דגמרא הבין את המחלוקת
בין ר' עקיבא ור' נחמיה באופן אחר ואמר "וקא מפליגי בדרב קטינא
דאמר רב קטינא שתא אלפי שני הוי עלמא וחד חרוב שנאמר 'ונשגב ה'
לבדו ביום ההוא". אביי אמר תרי חרוב שנאמר יחינו מיומים" מובן דברים
אלה הוא כי ר' נחמיה חושב כאביי כי העולם יחרב אלפים שנה, כלומר,
שני ימים וממילא אי אפשר לשיר שיר על יום אחד מפני שהם שנים
(רש"י). וזה הכריח את רש"י לפרש את המונח "יום שכולו שבת" בדברי
ר' עקיבא על החורבן. אולם קרוב מאד שלא ר' עקיבא ולא ר' נחמיה כונו
כלל לענין תורבן העולם והמשך זמנו. והמחלוקת ביניהם היא אם השיר
מכוון על העתיד או על העבר. והמובן של "יום שכולו שבת" הוא העולם
הבא. וככה בארה המשנה הסתמית בסוף תמיד הכוללת את דברי ר'
עקיבא את מובנו של מונח זה וליתר ברור הוסיפה את המלים "לעתיד
לבוא" "ומנוחה לחיי העולמים" שהכונה היא זמן שבו יהיו חיים נצחיים
ושלוה עולמית.

ראיה יותר מוכחת כי החכמים בדורות התנאים הבינו את המונח
"יום שכולו שבת" במובן עולם הבא מוצאים אנו בפסקא באבות דר'
נתן ששם מובא אותו המאמר על המזמורים סתם, לא בשם רבי עקיבא
ומוסיף באור "יום שכולו שבת שאין בו לא אכילה ולא שתיה ולא משא
ומתן אלא צדיקים יושבין ונזונין מזיו השכינה שנאמר 'ויחזו את האלהים
ויאכלו וישתו' כמלאכי השרת" [294]. הרי ברור שככה הבינו את המונח
במשנה "יום שכולו שבת" הוא עולם הבא אלא שבעל המאמר באבות
דר' נתן דעתו הוא כי עולם יהיה רוחני כדעת רב והבריתא. אמנם בבריתא,
אם זו היא באמת בריתא, בסנהדרין צ"ז, תניא כותיה דר' קטינא וכו",
המובן של "יום שכולו שבת" הוא על ההפסק בין שני העולמות כי זה
מובא בקשר עם אלף שנה הפסק שהיא דעת ר' קטינא. אבל אין זה
מוכיח על המובן של המשנה בסוף תמיד. בעל הבריתא או מי שהוא
פירש ככה את דברי ר' עקיבא כמו שעשה האומר בראש השנה ל"א,
"וקמפליגי בדברי רב קטינא".

ההפסק של אלף שנים בין חורבנו של העולם הזה ובין העולם

---

[294] אבות דרבי נתן פ' א', ח'. אגב אורחא חפץ אני להעיר כי הגרסא "ונזונין"
היא יותר נכונה מהגרסא "נהנין". הגמצאת בשני מקומות אחרים: בדברי רב (ברכות
י"ז) ובבריתא בכלה רבתי פרק ב', הפסוק המובא בתור ראיה "ויחזו את האלוהים
ויאכלו וישתו" (שמות, כ"ד, י"א) מעיד על זה. פירוש הפסוק הוא ככה לפי דברי
בעל המאמר, אם רואים את האלוהים הרי זה להם כאכילה ושתיה.

החדש נזכר רק בתלמוד. הספר האפוקליפטיתי עזרא, ד' שגם הוא יודע מהפסק זה קובע את זמנו לז' ימים של חורבן [295]. הפרקי דר' אליעזר בשם חכמים אומר כי רק שני ימים יהיה העולם חרב ,,וכל יושבי הארץ יטעמו טעם מיתה שאין נפש אדם ובהמה על הארץ שנאמר ,,ויושביה כמו כן ימותון" (ישעיה, נ"א, י'), וביום השלישי מתחדש אותם ומחיה אותם ומקים אותם לפניו שנאמר וביום השלישי יקימנו ונחיה" (הושע, ו', ב') [296]. והנה גם פה מובא הפסוק מהושע אבל הימים מובנים כפשוטם ולא כימי הקב"ה שהם אלפים שנה כבאור אביי. נראה שכל ענין חדוש זה לא היה קבוע ומוחלט ושונות בו הדעות, אבל הזמן של אלף שנה כנראה היה יותר רוח.

גם ענין החדוש עצמו, מהותו ואפיו לא ברור, ועל השאלה אם כונת החדוש היא בריאה ממש של שמים וארץ חדשים, או רק יצירה חדשה של החומר של העולם קשה לתת תשובה ברורה. ישנן כנראה שתי דעות בזה. מהמאמר בסנהדרין צ"ב, ששמה נתנת תשובה על השאלה מה יעשו הצדיקים שקמו לתחיה בעת החורבן, כי הקב"ה יעשה להם כנפים והם ישוטו על פני המים, אפשר להחליט כי אין פה בריאה חדשה כי אם יצירה חדשה של החומר הקים, כי הרי ישנן מים וקרקע מתחתם, וכן הבטוי בסנהדרין צ"ז תנא דבי אליהו שתא אלפי שני הוי עלמא וחד חרוב, מראה על חורבן ויצירה חדשה של החומר הקים. ועוד יותר ברורה היא דעה זו ממאמר באותו הפרק בפרקי דר' אליעזר ,,ר' אליעזר אומר כל צבא השמים עתידין לעבור ולהתחדש מהכתוב עליהם, וכל צבאם יבול כנבול עלה מגפן (ישעיה, ל"ד, ד'), מה הגפן והתאנה נובל עלה מהם והם עומדים עץ יבש ותוזרות ופורחות ונוצצות וצומחות ומוציאים עליהם חדשים כך כל צבא השמים יבולו וחוזרין ופורחין ונוצצין וצומחים ומתחדשים במקומן" [297]. הרי רואים אנו רק כליון הצורה ולא החומר. וגם קודם לזה בדברי חכמים הנזכרים ,,יגגולו כספר השמים", כאדם שהוא קורא בספר וגולל אותו כך עתיד הקב"ה לגלגול את השמים; ,,והארץ כבגד תבלה' (ישעיה נ"א ו') כאדם שהוא פושט את טליתו והוא מכיל (כלומר מודד) אותה וחוזר ומקפל אותה, כך מקפל את הארץ וחוזר ומתדש אותה למקומה כטלית" [298]. הרי רואים אנו שהכול קים רק יהיה חרב.

לעומת זה אנחנו מוצאים דעה אחרת. לכל הפחות בשני מקומות,

---

[295] עזרא ד', ה' פסוק ל'.

[296] פרקי דר' אליעזר, פ' נ"א.

[297] שם.

[298] על מאמר זה יסד הקליר את דבריו בפיוט למלכיות ליום א' של ראש השנה ,,לראי (כלומר השמים שהם ראי מראה יקפיל וחדשים יכפיל.

במדרש בראשית רבה „ר' הונא בשם ר' אליעזר בנו של ר' יוסי הגלילי
אומר אפילו אותן הן כי הנני בורא שמים חדשים" (ישעיה, ס"ה,
י"ז) כבר ברואין הן משמת ימי בראשית. הדה הוא דכתיב כי כאשר השמים
החדשים והארץ התדשה, חדשה אין כתיב כאן אלא החדשה" 299, כלומר,
בהא הידיעה זו שנבראה קודם ועומדת מזומנת. הרי רואים אנו כי עולם
זה ממש נברא, ובאותיות דר' עקיבא 300 נאמר „ומנין שאף שמים וארץ
שעתידין להתחדש אין נבראין אלא בה"א שנאמר השמים החדשים והארץ
החדשה". נאמר פה איפא מפורש על בריאה שלשמה של העולם שתתקים
בעתיד באותו האופן של הבריאה הראשונה. אולם ממאמר מדרשי אחר
אפשר להוכיח שחכמים אחדים הבינו את המושג של חדוש העולם, באופן
של שנוים באפיו „עשרה דברים עתיד הקב"ה לחדש לעתיד לבוא" והוא
הולך ומונה: (א) כי הוא בעצמו יאיר לעולם (ב) יוציא מים חיים מירושלים
וירפא כל המתלות (ג) האילנות יתנו פירותיהן בכל חודש. (ד) כל הערים
החרבות תבנינה ואפילו סדום ועמורה (ה) ירושלים תבנה באבני ספיר
(ו)שלום בין החיות (ז) שלום בין החיות עופות ורמשים עם ישראל (ח)
אין בכי בעולם (ט) חדלון המות (י) חדלון היגון ושלטון השמחה התמידית 301,
כל החדושים הנחמדים מיוסדים על דרשות בפסוקי הנביאים. אולם אין
פה חדוש העולם עצמו באיזה אופן. אלא חדושים באופי העולם וביחוד
בחיי האדם והסביבה קרוב לקבל שחכמים אחדים איפא הבינו את מובן
החדוש באופן המתואר, וזה הוא לפי דעתם התדוש הנזכר בישעיה ס"ה,
י"ז. ואם כן ישנן לפנינו דעות שונות ואי אפשר לקבוע מסמרות בדבר,
אף כי הרעיון בכללו הוא מקובל. ואי אפשר לטעות שהמלים „לעתיד לבוא"
מכונים לימות המשיח, אף כי אתדים מחדושים נזכרים במקומות אחרים
שהבאנו למעלה כי יחולו בימות המשיח. אבל הסימן המובהק של עולם
הבא חדלון המות מעיד כי הזמן הוא עולם הבא.

---

299 בראשית, רבה, א' י"ג מובא גם בתנחומא בובר בראשית, ט' ובילקוט
בראשית רמז ג' ובישעיה רמז שע"ב.
300 ראשית אות ה', מדרש זה סדורו מאוחר. אבל החומר שלו קדום.
301 שמות רבה, פ' ט"ו.

תקופות ימות המשיח ומלחמת גוג ומגוג
מ א י ר   ו כ ס מ ן

בנוגע לתכונת תקופת ימות המשיח אפשר לסמן בתאורים השונים
והמרובים בתלמוד מדרשים שני זרמים. הראשון מציר ימים אלה כימי
גאולה אנושית פשוטה שהיסוד הלאומי מתבלט בה, מטרת גאולה זו
היא להסיר את עול הגלות ולהחזיר את מלכות ישראל כמקדם מבלי שמקרה
זה בחיי עמנו יהא מלווה בהופעות על-טבעיות. זרם זה מוצא בטויו העקרי
במאמר יחידי בתלמוד שנאמנם הוא נשנה מספר פעמים, מאמרו של שמואל
„אין בין העולם הזה לימות המשיח אלא שעבוד מלכיות בלבד" [80]. מאמר
זה הוא סתום ואינו מפרש כלל איך תתהוה הגאולה על ידי המשיח אם על
ידי מלחמה אנושית שהמשיח יתגבר על אויבי ישראל בדרך טבעי, או
בדרך פלאי כפי מסורת הדורות שיסודה בדברי הנביאים והלכה והתעבתה
במשך מאות בשנים דרך כל הספרות החצונית. אולם ישנם גם רמזים
אחרים לדעה זו הרואה את ימות המשיח מנקודה אנושית-טבעית. כאלה
הם מאמרו של ר׳ שמעון בן חלפתא כי „גאולתן של ישראל תתגלה קמעה
קמעה" [81] וגם מאמרו של רב נחמן שהעיר בדיון על שמו של המשיח
ועל זהותו „אם מן חייא הוא כגון אבא" [82], כלומר, אם המשיח יקום בדורנו
אז יוכל להיות איש כמוני שהוא מבית דוד ויש לו כוח שלטון; כי כידוע
רב נחמן היה חתנא דבי ריש גלותא וקרוב מאד שגם הוא היה מבית
דוד. סמוך לזה יש גם מאמרו של רב, „אי מן חייא כגון רבנו הקדוש
אי מן מתיא כגון דניאל איש חמודות" [83], כלומר, אם הוא מבין החיים
אז יהיה איש הדומה בתכונותיו לרבי ואם מן המתים יהא דומה לדניאל.
בדברי רב אלה כבר מבצבצת נימה על-טבעית כי מסתפק הוא באישיותו
ואפשר כי יקום לתחיה גם מבין אלה שכבר מתו [84], אולם האפשרות

---

80 ברכות, ל״ג, שבת, ס״ג; סנהדרין צ״ט.

81 ירושלמי ברכות, הל׳ א׳.

82 סנהדרין צ״ט.

83 רש״י עובר בשתיקה על דברי רב נחמן, אבל המהרש״א מעיר כי רב נחמן
המביא ראיה לדעתו מדברי הכתוב (ירמיה, ל׳, כ״א) „והיה אדירו ממנו ומושלו
מקרבו יצא" מבאר אותם ככה כי המשיח שהוא האדיר המרומז יצא מאותם בני דוד
שעדין יש להם ממשלה גם בגלות כמו משפחת ריש גלותא, ונראים דבריו.

84 שם, רש״י מביא שני פירושים בדברי רב האחד כנזכר למעלה שהמשיח
יוכל להיות או מבין החיים או מבין המתים והשני ככה : רב אומר „אם יש דוגמתו

218

שהמשיח יהיה מבין החיים ואישיות דומה לזו של רבי מראה שהאופן
הטבעי של הגאולה לא רחוקה היתה ממחשבותיהם של החכמים, ביחוד
חכמי בבל כי בעלי מאמרים אלה הם בבליים. מאמרים אלה מרמזים,
כאמור על נטיה מסוימה בתאור ימות המשיח. כי התקופה המשיחית ואישיות
המשיח והופעתו קשורים זה בזה.

אולם נראה הדבר כי נטיה זו לא הכתה שרשים בחיי היהודים
וממילא לא בספרות שעיקר מטרתה בדיוני נושא זה היה לעודד את העם
לסבול את עול הגלות על ידי תאורים מזהירים של הגאולה העתידה.
ומובן הוא שבמדה שצבעי תאור עתיד זה היו יותר מפליאים באותה
המדה היו יותר מתאימים לרוח העם כי היו משעשעים את דמיונו
ומניחים אותו בעמלו וסבלונו. נוסף לזה כבר נשתרשה מסורת משיחית
שהיא על־טבעית פלאית אם במדרגות שונות. לכן אין להתפלא כי התאורים
של הזרם השני המפליאים הן בפתאומיותן והן במהותם תופסים מקום
גדול בתאורי ימות המשיח בספרות התלמודית־מדרשית.

הפן הראשון בדרמה גדולה זו של ימות המשיח היא תקופת ההכנה
למאורע זה. כבר הזכרנו את הרעיון על חבלי משיח הסימנים המעידים על
קרבת הגאולה. אבל המה רק מבשרים את הגאולה ומעידים על בואה.
אולם גם לגאולה עצמה ישנם, כנראה לפי הרבה מקורות, שני מדורות,
הפרוזדור והטרקלין. ולכל מדור, כמו שנראה להלן יש משיח משלו.
תאורי התקופה הראשונה של הגאולה מעטים בספרות התלמודית־מדרשית
וכמעט שאין פנים כלל על התחלתה ופרטיה, אבל מרמזים אליה בקשר

בחיים הוא רבנו הקדוש ואם דוגמא הוא למתים היינו כגון דניאל איש חמודות"
לפי פירוש זה שמסתמא קבל רש"י מרבותיו הבינו את דברי רב באופן זה : המשיח
יהיה מבין החיים אך השאלה היא על תכונתו אם ישנה אישיות כזו המתאימה לתכונתו
בדורו של רב או לאו. חושבני שפירוש זה הוא נכון מפני שמיד אחרי מאמר זה
של רב מובא מאמר אחר על ידי רב יהודה בשם רב: "עתיד הקב"ה להעמיד להם
דוד אחר שנאמר "ועבדו את ה' אלוהיהם ואת דוד מלכם אשר אקים להם")ירמיה,
(ל', ט') הקים לא נאמר אלא אקים", מתוך קושיא שרב פפא שאל לאביי מכתוב
אחר ודוד עבדי נשיא להם לעולם" (יחזקאל, ל"ז, כ"ה) — התשובה היא כי דוד
יהא אנטי־קסר, כלומר, משנה אבל המשיח יהיה המלך אפשר להוכיח כי דברי רב
היו מכונים כנגד הדעה שהמשיח יהיה מבין המתים שיקומו לתחיה. אמנם נמצא גם
מאמר אחר דומה לזה של רב "רבנן אמרי אהי מלכא משיחא אימן חייא דוד שמיה
אי מן דמכיא (המתים) דוד שמיה" (ירושלמי ברכות פ' ב', הל' ד'). אבל ממאמר
זה אין להביא ראיה על תאור אישיותו של המשיח כי ההדגשה היא על השם. לעומת
זה דרשות רב מדגישות את ההתנגדות לדעה כי המשיח יהא שיקום לתחיה
וכי יהיה איש בעתיד שה' יקים להם, והמלים במאמרם שעתיד הקב"ה להעמיד להם דוד
אחר" מובנן הוא לא כי שמו יהיה דוד, אבל מלך אחר — והוא המשיח. ומהתנגדות
זו אפשר להחליט על השקפתו של רב כי אישיותו של המשיח תהא אנושית טבעית
ולא על טבעית.

עם מספר תאורים של ימות המשיח ושני המשיחים כעל עובדה ודבר
ידוע. יסוד הדעה על תקופה זו שתשמש כעין הכנה לימות המשיח עצמם
הוא כנראה במסורת עתיקה שהתבססה על נבואת יחזקאל. נביא גולה זה
המדבר כל כך הרבה על תקופת העתיד מקדיש אחת מנבואותיו (ל״ח-ל״ט)
לתאור מלחמה עתידה בין קבוצת עמים שבראשם עומד גוג מארץ מגוג
נשיא ראש משך ותובל, עם ישראל. הנבואה היא לאחרית הימים (ל״ח,
ט״ז) כלומר לזמן בלתי מוגבל והיא קשורה עם פסקה בפרק הקודם (ל״ז,
כ״ד-כ״ח) המדברת על השיבה מן הגלות. מובן נבואה זו היא כי היא אחרי
שישובו בני ישראל מן הגולה וישבו כבר על ארצם זמן רב אז יעלה גוג
וקבוצת העמים שלו על ישראל. נראה גם כן כי היתה מסורה נבואית
קדומה על מלחמה זו כי הנביא אומר לגוג ״האתה הוא אשר דברתי בימים
קדמונים ביד עבדי ישראל הנביאים בימים ההם שנים להביא
אותך עליהם״ (ל״ח, י״ז) [85]. קבוצת העמים היא גדולה אולם העיקר בהם
הם עמי הצפון משך ותובל ואליהם ילוו גם עמים אחרים הגרים גם בדרום
כמו כוש (ל״ח, ד׳), אם מובן השם הזה הוא אטיפיה, כמו בהרבה מקומות
אחרים [86].

כונת נבואה זו היא להגיד כי באחרית הימים יתגלה ה׳ לעיני
כל הגוים אפילו הרחוקים ביותר, כי מלחמה זו תגמר במפלת העמים האלה
שהתקוממו לא רק כנגד ישראל אבל גם כנגד ה׳ בעצמו. מפלה זו תלוה
על ידי אותות ונפלאות כמו רעש האדמה והתמוטטות ההרים (ל״ח, י״ט,
כ׳). אולם אף כי נבואה זו היא לאחרית הימים אין לה קשר כפי שהיא
מסורה במקרא עם ימות המשיח כפי שהם משקפים במסורת והסכרות
התלמודית־מדרשית, כי כאמור קבוץ גלויות והקמת מלכות ישראל קודמים
לה בזמן. בפרק ל״ז מדבר הנביא על קבוץ הגלויות ועל זה שמלך ששמו

---

[85] הנוסח המסורתי הוא ״האתה״ בהא השאלה והכונה היא כי הנבואה העתיקה
לא הזכירה את גוג ומגוג ושאר העמים. השבעים אמנם קראו אתה בלא הא, כלומר,
כי נבאו על גוג עוד בזמן קדום אבל אין ספק שנוסחת המסורה היא הנכונה.

[86] קשה להחליט אם המלה ״ראש״ אחרי ״נשיא״ מובנה שם אומה כמושתרגמו
השבעים או הכונה היא הנשיא הראשי של משך ותובל. רוב המפרשים וגם התרגום
מפרשים ככה. חוקרי המקרא השתדלו לזהות אומות אלה ולהגביל את מקומם. משך
ותובל נזכרים אצל יחזקאל פעמים, כ״ז, י״ג ביחד עם יון וגם בבראשית י׳ ב׳. עמים
אלה באים בקבוצה אחת עם יון שהם יושבי איונינה באסיה הקטנה. הרבה חוקרים
איפא חושבים כי משך ותובל ישבו בדרומית מזרחית לים השחור ואולי הם הסקיטים,
ששבטיהם התפשטו בסוף המאה השביעית על ארצות פרס ובבל וגם עד ארץ ישראל
הגיעו. גוג הוא מנהיג קבוצת עמים אלה מגוג היא ארצו כמו שכתוב ״גוג מארץ
מגוג״ אולם מגוג הוא גם שם העם היושב בארץ זו, ולכן אין להביא ראיה כמו
שעושה החכם קליונער בספרו הנ״ל ע׳ 323 מהשמוש הרגיל בתלמוד במונח ״מלחמת
גוג ומגוג״ כי גוג הוא שם קבוצי. הכונה היא מלחמת גוג המנהיג ועמו מגוג.

דוד, שמובנו הוא מלך מבית דוד ימשול על ישראל בארצם (ל״ז-כ״ב).
נראה שיחזקאל, כנזכר למעלה, תאר את שיבת הגולים לארצם ויסוד
מלכות ישראל באופן טבעי ואנושי אף כי אינו מזכיר פרטי מאורע זה
אלא מדבר עליו באופן כללי.

אך למרות חוסר הקשר במקרא בין מלחמת גוג ומגוג ובין תקופת
המשיחיות ראו חכמי התלמוד והאגדה קשר הדוק בין שני אלה אלא
שאין דעה קבועה בנוגע לזמן מלחמה זו. מקורות אחדים מקדימים אותה
אפילו לקבוץ גלויות ואחרים קובעים אותה בתקופת המשיחיות הראשונה
או הפרוזדור. ואחרים מאחרים אותה עוד יותר. מלחמת גוג ומגוג וסופה
המעציב, כלומר מפלת העמים נזכרו במשנה. בין מספר מאמרים המיוחסים
לר׳ עקיבא (עדיות פ׳ ב׳ שנה י׳) המדברים על קביעת זמן של י״ב חודש
להמשך דברים שונים נזכר גם המאמר כי משפט גוג ומגוג לעתיד
לבוא ימשך י״ב חודש. מובן מאמר זה לפי פירוש הראב״ד ותוספות
שאנץ שנמשכו אחריו היא כי לא ינגפו בבת אחת אבל מפלתן תמשך
כל הזמן הזה. הזמן שבו תתקים מלחמת גוג ומגוג מסומן פה במלים
״לעתיד לבוא״ שמובנם הכללי בספרות זו הוא ימות המשיח, אמרתי הכללי,
מפני שממספר פעמים המונח הזה מזדהה עם עולם הבא (עיין להלן).
בכל אופן חכמי התלמוד מקשרים מלחמה זו עם ימות המשיח או בראשיתה
כעין הכנה או באמצעיתה של תקופה זו ולפעמים אפילו בסופה. אולם
תמיד מבדילים ביניהם. ככה דרשו ״אהבתי כי ישמע קולי — לימות
המשיח; אסרו חג בעבותים — לימות גוג ומגוג; אלי אתה ואודך —
לעתיד לבוא״.[87] במאמר זה המונח ״לעתיד לבוא״ מזדהה כנראה עם
עולם הבא וגוג ומגוג בא באמצע בין ימות המשיח ועולם הבא, אולי
בסוף ימות המשיח. במקום אחר נאמר ״לעתיד לבוא באים גוים ומתגיירין״
שואלין הלא למדנו שאין מקבלין גרים לימות המשיח? והתשובה באה
״נעשו גרים גרורים ומניחים תפילין בראשיהם, תפילין בזרועותיהם,
ציצית בבגדיהם ומזוזות על פתחיהן. כיון שרואין את מלחמת גוג ומגוג
אומרים להם למה באתם, עונים על ה׳ ועל משיחו מיד כל אחד מנתק
מצותו והולך״[88] במאמר זה ״לעתיד לבוא״ וימות המשיח הם אחד ומלחמת
גוג ומגוג באה אחר התחלת ימות המשיח. וגם מאמר אחר שהובא כבר
למעלה מוכיח כי זמן גוג ומגוג היא בהתחלת ימות המשיח, כי מצאו
כתוב במגלה שלאחר ארבעת אלפים ורצ״א, או יותר טוב רל״א שנה העולם
יתום מהם מלחמות תנינים, מהן מלחמות גוג ומגוג ושאר ימות המשיח
ואין הקב״ה מתדש עולמו אלא לאחר שבעת אלפים שנה. פה מפורש כי לכל

---

[87] ירושלמי ברכות פ׳ ב׳ הל׳ ד׳.

[88] עבודה זרה, ג׳ ב׳.

הפחות חלק גדול של ימות המשיח בא אחרי מלחמת גוג ומגוג כמשמעות
הדברים „וישאר ימות המשיח" [89] אולם ישנה גם גרסא שרש"י מביא
הקוראת „והשאר ימות המשיח" ולפיה מלחמה זו תקדם לגמרי לימות
המשיח. וגרסה זו מוצאה סיוע ממספר מאמרים אחדים המבדילים בין
שני אלה. בדרשה על הפסוק „הופיע מהר פארן" (דברים ל"ג, ג') נאמר
„ארבע הופעות של ה' כלומר, התגלות כוחו והן: ראשונה במצרים,
שניה בשעת מתן תורה; שלישית לימות גוג ומגוג; רביעית לימות
המשיח" [90]. מלחמת גוג ומגוג קודמת איפא לימות המשיח. וכן אומר ר'
אליעזר „אם תזכו לשמור את השבת תנצלו משלוש פורענות מחבלו של
משיח, מיומו של גוג, ומיום הדין הגדול" [91] „ופה בא יומו של גוג מיד
אחר הבלו של משיח וזה מראה כי מלחמה זו תהא בראשית ימות המשיח
אחרי סימני הגאולה. „יום הדין הגדול" קשור כפי שנראה או עם ימות
המשיח עצמן או עם סופן קודם תחית המתים.

וכן במקום אחר דורש ר' יונה בשם ר' אבא בר' ירמיה וגם ר' אבא
בר כהנא את הפסוק „חכמות בנתה ביתה חצבה עמודיה שבעה" (משלי,
ח' א') ככה: חכמות בנתה ביתה זה בנין בית המקדש חצבה עמודיה שבעה
אלו ז' שנים של גוג והוא מבאר בעצמו כי המה הז' שנים שהכתוב אומר
עליהם (יחזקאל, ל"ט י"א) כי בני ישראל ישתמשו בכלי הזין של האויבים
להסקת התנורים ולצרכי שריפה והוא מוסיף כי אלה השנים תהינה
שנים טובות לצדיקים כמו משתה ימי הנשואים [91] הכוונה היא כי דברי

<hr>

[89] כי פירוש המלים „יתום העולם" הוא כי יבוא שנוי בסדר העולם, כבר
העירונו למעלה. סוף המאמר על זמן חדוש העולם מעיד על זה ועיין הערה — המובן
של הדברים „מלחמות תנינים" הוא לא כפירוש רש"י דגים, כי אם כמו שכבר העיר
המהרש"א כי המלה תנינים משמשת סמל לעמים חזקים שכן יחזקאל מכנה את פרעה
בשם זה (כ"ט, ג') וגם ישעיה קורא לעמים ידועים בשם זה (כ"ז, א'). לפי דעת מאמר
זה תהינה בראשונה מלחמות בין העמים עצמם, ואחר כך מלחמת קבוצת עמים
עם בני ישראל שישבו אז כבר בארצם. כדאי להעיר כי לפי מאמר זה ימשכו ימות
המשיח זמן רב, כי מלחמות העמים לא תוכלנה להמשיך יותר ממספר שנים, וזמן
מלחמת גוג ומגוג נזכר במשנה עדיות המובאה למעלה הוא י"ב חודש ואם אפילו
נקבל כי אומר מאמר זה מסכים עם הדעה המובעה במאמרים הקודמים של רב קטינא
ועוד כי העולם יחרב במשך אלף שנה (האלף השביעי) עדין נשאר, — אחר נכוי של
רצ"א או רל"א שנה מן האלף החמשי ועשרות שנים אחדות למלחמות — יותר מט"ו
מאה שנה לימות המשיח.

[90] ספרי, דברים ס' שמ"ג.

[91] מכילתא הוצ. לויטרבך, כ' ב' עמודים 120 וגם 123.

[92] ויקרא רבה, פ' י"א, ב', חלק מאותו המאמר נמצא גם בירושלמי שבועות
פ' ה' הל ג. והאומר הוא גם כן ר' יונא „המת בשבע שנות גוג אין לו חלק לעתיד
לבוא וסימנא דאכיל פרוטגמיא אכיל משתותא" מובן מאמר זה הוא מערפל ותלוי
במובן המלה פרוטגמיא. הערוך בערכו אינה מפרשה אבל בערך „משתותא" הוא

הכתוב שישתמשו בכלי הנשק לצורך שרפה המה רק סמל לטובה מרובה.
והמובן הכללי של המאמר הוא כי בנין בית המקדש יבוא אחרי שבע
שנים טובות אלה שהם תהיינה כעין הכנה לו כמו שהבית נסמך על עמודים,
כפרוש המהרז"ו ולא כמו שטעה בפירוש המאמר החכם ובר בספרו על
התיאולוגיה היהודית. והנה בנין המקדש הוא אחד המאורעות החשובים
של ימות המשיח, הרי רואים אנו כי מלחמת גוג ומגוג באה בראשית ימות
המשיח. ומאמרו של ר׳ יונה מתחיל במלים „פתר קריא בגוג לעתיד לבוא"
שפה הוא המובן ימות המשיח.

אולם התרגום ירושלמי לבמדבר י"א כ"ו אומר כי אלדד ומידד היו
מתנבאים כי באחרית הימים יעלה גוג וחיליו על ירושלים אולם יפלו
בידי מלך המשיח ובני ישראל ישתמשו בעצי כלי הזין שלהם שבע שנים
ולא יצטרכו לקצוץ אלנות מן היערות, רואים אנו איפא כי מדברי התרגום
אפשר להוכיח כי מלחמת גוג ומפלתו באה לכל היותר באמצע תקופת
המשיח והמשיח הוא יהיה המנצח של גוג ומגוג[93].

אמנם ישנם גם מאמרים אחרים המאחרים את מלחמת גוג ומגוג.
המאמר הראשון שהבאנו מירושלמי ברכות הדורש את פסוקי הלל ומקדים
ימות המשיח לגוג ומגוג. ודומה לזה נמצאת דרשה על הפסוק כוס ישועות
אשא האומרת „כוס ישועה אין כתיב כאן אלא כוס ישועות אחד לימות

מבאר את זה כעין פרקמטיא ואומר דאכל סחורות בעולם הזה כגון פרקמטיא
אכל משתה שלו שהיה מזומן לו לעתיד לבוא, כלומר, לא נשתיר לו מה לאכול לעתיד
לבוא" פרוש זה אינו מתאים לענין, כי המאמר מדבר לא על העולם הזה הרגיל אבל
על ז׳ שנות גוג ומגוג שהן לכל הדעות התחלת העתיד לבוא או ימות המשיח,
ואולי היתה לפניו נוסחא אחרת. ובכלל מדוע יפסיד הצדיק את חלקו אם ראה בטובה
גם בעולם הזה ? לכן נכון הוא פירושם של בנימין מוספיא וקהוט כי המלה
פרוגמטיא היא מלשון יונית ומובנה נשואים ראשונים, כלומר, ירוסין וזה מתאים
לענין בין במדרש ובין בירושלמי, במדרש המובן הוא כי אם שנוכח בזמן הארוסין,
זה הוא ז׳ שנים הטובות הבאות אחרי מפלת גוג שהן הכנה לימות המשיח העקריים
יהא במשתה, כלומר, יהנה גם בשנים אלה גם אחרי כן. ובירושלמי המובן — אם
לא נגרוס מי שמת „קודם" שבע שני גוג אין לו חלק — אז עלינו לקבל כי הכונה
במלים „בשבע שני גוג" היא כי הוא מת בתחלתן, „ואין לו חלק" משמעותן שהוא
מפסיד את הטובה בשנים אלה. ואם גם יקום לתחיה בעולם הבא, החיים אז אפשר
כפי שנראה יהיו רוחניים. ולא תהיה טובה גשמית. בכל אופן מאמר הירושלמי
מראה שגוג ומגוג באים קודם ימי המשיח העקריים.

[93] אמנם בנוסחא אחרת בתרגום המיוחס ליונתן לפסוק זה נאמר כי ה׳ בעצמו
יפיל את חילות גוג וישרוף אותם באש מתחת כסא הכבוד, ומיד אחרי מפלתם תהא
תחית המתים. דעה זו קרובה למובן הפשוט של ענין זה שאינה
מזכירה את המשיח אבל אומרת שמפלת גוג וחיליו תבוא על ידי התגלות כוח ה׳
בעצמו, אלא שהתרגום מוסיף את אמצעי הכליון היינו אש מתחת כסא הכבוד. אולם
מזה שהוא מסמיך את תחית המתים למפלת גוג אפשר להוכיח כי הוא מאחר אותה

המשיח ואחד לימות גוג[94]. אבל מאמרים אלה מעטים הם בערך לעומת
המאמרים המקדימים את מלחמת גוג ומגוג לימות המשיח או קובעים
אותה בתחלתה או לכל היותר באמצעיתה, והרוב מכריע, כי דעה זו הכתה
שרשים בלב העם כי גוג ומגוג יבוא אמנם אחרי קבוץ גלויות כי לולי
זאת לא יהיה לו עם מי ילחם! אבל מאורע זה יקדם לימות המשיח העקריים.
ואין יסוד לדברי חוקרים נוצרים אחדים המאחרים את מלחמת גוג ומגוג
עד לסוף ימי המשיח כהקדמה לעולם הבא[95].

לסוף ימי המשיח כמבוא לעולם הבא. אולם אם ישנה דעה שהקדימה תחית המתים
לימות המשיח על זה נדון להלן.
[94] בראשית רבה פ׳ פ״ח, ה׳.
[95] החכם וובר בספרו   Juedische Theologie   משתדל להוכיח על פי מספר
מאמרים שמלחמת גוג ומגוג תהא המערכה האחרונה בתקופת המשיח כעין פרוזדור
לעולם הבא (עמודים 389‎-387). אבל הוא לא השגיח במספר גדול של מאמרים המדגישים
בפירוש את קדימת מלחמה זו לראשית או באמצע התקופה המשיחית, וגם טעה
במובן של מאמרים אחדים שהביא. ככה הוא אומר למשל, על סמך המדרש ויקרא
רבה, י״א, ב׳ כי ימי גוג ימשכו שבע שנים וכבר הראינו למעלה על טעותו ועל
המובן האמתי של פסקה זו כי, כאמור. הרוב מכריע, ורוב המאמרים מקדימים יום
גוג ומגוג לימות המשיח. כי היתה גם דעה המאחרת מלחמה זו, המשקפה במספר
מועט של מאמרים שהבאנו אין להסתפק, אבל דעת ההקדם היתה רווחה.

THE ASSUMPTION OF MOSES AND THE REVOLT OF BAR KOKBA

Studies in the Apocalyptic Literature

By SOLOMON ZEITLIN, Dropsie College

THE little volume which we possess today under the name of the *Assumption of Moses* is actually a composite work consisting of two books, *The Testament of Moses* and a treatise known to the Church Fathers as *The Assumption of Moses*. In his *De Principiis*, Origen mentioned an apocryphal book entitled *The Assumption of Moses*,[1] and, in the *Acts of the Second Nicene Council*, 787 C. E.,[2] a reference is found to a book of the same name.[2a] In a list of apocryphal works, however, mention is made of the *Testament of Moses*.[3]

Now, it chanced that nearly ninety years ago a renowned Italian scholar, Ceriani, discovered in the Ambrosian Library of Milan a palimpsest manuscript of the sixth century which bore no title, but which Ceriani identified

---

[1] *Et primo quidem in Genesi serpens Evam seduxisse describitur: de quo in Adscensione Mosis, cujus libelli meminit in epistola sua apostolus Judas, Michael archangelus cum diabolo disputans de corpore Mosis, ait a diabolo inspiratum serpentem causam exstitisse praevaricationis Adae et Evae.* Lib. III, 2, pp. 303–4. Origenis, *Opera Omnia*, ed. C. H. E. Lommatzsch, t. XXX, Berlini, 1847.

[2] *Acta Synodi Nicaenae* II.

[2a] See below note 4.

[3] See A. Hilgenfeld, *Messias Judaeorum, Libris Eorum Paulo Ante Et Paulo Post Christum Natum Conscriptis Illustratus*. Lipsiae, 1869; pp. 461–2; G. Volkmar, *Mose Prophetie, Und Himmelfahrt*. Leipzig, 1867; pp. 7–9.

1

with the passage quoted in the *Acts of the Second Nicene Council*.[4] Since that passage was quoted in the name of the *Assumption of Moses*, Ceriani named the work he discovered *The Assumption of Moses*. Schürer[5] and Charles,[6] however, have pointed out that this *Assumption of Moses* is actually *The Testament of Moses*, while only a small portion of it is *The Assumption of Moses*.

The manuscript which was discovered by Ceriani is defective and badly preserved. Its Latin rendering is imperfect and, at times, ungrammatical.[7] It has no division of chapters and verses, and often many of the letters are undecipherable. The palimpsest itself comes from the sixth century. Undoubtedly, this Latin version was rendered from the Greek, and hence, it may be assumed that it was made not later than the end of the fifth century or the beginning of the sixth. The original language of this book was without doubt Hebrew,[8] but both the Hebrew and the Greek text have been lost.

---

[4] The passage in the Acts of the *Second Nicene Council* reads as follows: Μέλλων ὁ προφήτης Μωυσῆς ἐξιέναι τοῦ βίου ὡς γέγραπται ἐν βίβλῳ Ἀναλήψεως Μωυσέως προσκαλεσάμενος Ἰησοῦν υἱὸν Ναυὴ καὶ διαλεγόμενος πρὸς αὐτὸν ἔφη. Καὶ προεθεάσατό με ὁ θεὸς πρὸ καταβολῆς κόσμου εἶναί με τῆς διαθήκης αὐτοῦ μεσίτην. Ceriani identified this with the follwing words found in the manuscript: *Itaque excogitavit et invenit me, qui ab initio orbis terrarum praeparatus sum, ut sim arbiter testamenti illius.* Thus, he came to the conclusion that the manuscript is the *Assumption of Moses* mentioned by the Church Fathers.

[5] *Geschichte*, vol. III.

[6] *Apocrypha and Pseudepigrapha*, vol. II.

[7] Eg. *tunc* for *nunc*, *lib* for *tribus*, *scenae testimonium* for *scenom testimonii*, *cum Moyses* for *tum Moyses*, *occidit* for *occidet*, *docentes* for *dicentes*, *et leges* for *leges et*, *in domum* for *in dominum*. The Greek, as well, of which the Latin is a translation, must have contained some serious mistakes. Comp. note 132.

[8] See Charles, *op. cit.* Comp. *idem. The Assumption of Moses, Translated From The Latin Sixth Century Ms., The Unemended Text Of Which Is Published Herewith, Together With The Text In Its Restored And Critically Emended Form*, London, 1897, pp. XXXVIII–L.

Ceriani published *The Assumption of Moses* in the *Monumenta sacra et profana* in 1861. Five years later Hilgenfeld edited the text;[9] then Volkmar followed and provided a German translation and a commentary.[10] In 1868, Schmidt and Merx again edited this Latin version,[11] and three years later Fritzsche included it in his *Libri Apocryphi Vet Testamenti Graece*, publishing the text of Ceriani on one page and the emended text on the opposite.

The Assumption of Moses which we now have, begins with the statement that in the year two thousand five hundred from the creation of the world[12] Moses summoned Joshua to tell him that he (Moses) was about to pass away, and he gave Joshua instructions how to administer the people. We are also informed that Moses told Joshua to preserve the books which he delivered to him, to set them in order, and to "anoint them with oil of cedar and put them away in earthen vessels in the place which He made from the beginning of the creation of the world." The author then deals briefly with the period from the death of Moses down to his own time. He shows familiarity with the history of the Jewish people — their exile by the Babylonians, their restoration to the land of their fathers, and their tribulations under Antiochus Epiphanes. Next, he tells about the Hasmoneans who usurped the high priesthood and the kingdom. He is aware that Herod ruled for thirty-four years and calls him an "insolent king."[13] Towards the end, the author relates the rest of the history of the Jews, revealing his conviction that the salvation of

[9] *Op. cit.*

[10] *Op. cit.*, pp. 137–152.

[11] "Die Assumptio Moses, mit Einleitung und erklärenden Anmerkungen herausgegeben" (*Archiv für wissenschaftliche Erforschung des Alten Testaments*, I. ii 1868).

[12] *Qui est bis millesimus et quingentesimus annus a creatura orbis terrae.*

[13] *Rex petulans.*

Israel would come through the establishment of a theocratic state.

The general opinion is that this book was compiled shortly after the death of Herod, that is, in the first two decades of the first century C. E.[14] As to the authorship of the book, scholars are divided, some maintaining that the author was a Pharisaic Quietist,[15] others that he was a Zealot.[16] Before determining the authorship and the date of the book, however, we must clarify a few important obscurities.

TAXO

In chapter 9, we read: "Then (in that day there) will (be) arise a man of the tribe of Levi, whose name will be Taxo, who, having seven sons, will speak to them."[17]

A considerable literature has been written about the identity of Taxo. Scholars believe that in the identification of Taxo lies the real significance of the book. Hilgenfeld,[18] for example, assumed that the name Taxo means Messiah. He arrived at this conclusion through *gematria*, the letters $T\xi\gamma$ equal 363, and those of המשיח likewise equal 363. Volkmar assumed that the word $T\acute{a}\xi\omega$ was corrupted from $T\alpha\xi\iota o$, and believed again through *gematria* that it meant Rabbi Akiba, for $T\alpha\xi\iota o$ equals 431 and רבון עקבא equals 431.[19] Colani holds the opinion that Taxo meant Rabbi Jehuda ben Baba, who was put to death at the time of the Hadrianic persecutions; Colani also arrived at his opinion

---

[14] See below p. 10.

[15] Charles, *op. cit.*

[16] W. J. Deane, *Pseudepigrapha: An Account Of Certain Apocryphal Sacred Writings Of The Jews And Early Christians*, Edinburgh, 1891, pp. 105–6.

[17] *Tunc illo (die erit) [dicente] homo de tribu Levi, cujus nomen erit Taxo, qui habens VII filios dicet ad eos rogans.*

[18] *Op. cit.*, pp. 466–7.

[19] *Op. cit.*, p. 60. However, the name of Akiba has a *yod* in it, עקיבא.

through *gematria*.[20] Hausrath thinks that by the substitutive method of *at bash* שלה was transformed into תכמו, the Greek translator erroneously taking the מ as ס.[21] *Shiloh* stands here for Messiah. Wieseler thinks that Taxo refers back to חשי, "the badger-like one."[22] This designation he suggests is derived from the fact that the pious dwelt in caves in the earth.[23] Rosenthal points out that שילה is numerically equal to משה and says it has reference to a second Moses who was to rise again.[24] Lattey agrees with Hausrath that Taxo is Shiloh, and that Taxo thus stands for the Messiah.[25] Burkitt[26] and Charles identify Taxo with Eleazar of *II Maccabees*.[27] Holscher agrees with Burkitt that Taxo refers to Eleazar, but says he is another Eleazar of the time of Bar Kokba.[28] Torrey[29] states that Taxo is Mattathis, "the father of the Maccabees and all the Hasmonean dynasty." He writes, "In the numerical value of the letters used, 'Taxo' corresponds exactly to 'the Hasmonean,' in Aramaic, but not in Hebrew.'[30]

These theories cannot be seriously entertained. Some of them are ingenious, but they do not answer the question who is Taxo, who had seven sons and who exhorted them, as we are informed, to observe the law and to die rather than transgress the commands of God. He could not be

[20] *Revue de Theologie*, 1868, pp. 90–4.
[21] *Neutestamentl Zeitgesch*. IV, p. 77.
[22] *Jahr. f. d. Th*. 1868, p. 629. Comp. also Deane, *op. cit*., p. 119.
[23] Deane is of the opinion that Taxo "is probably the Low-Latin word meaning 'a badger,' equivalent to the Hebrew החש *tachash*."
[24] *Vier Apokryphische Bücher*, Leipzig, 1885, p. 31.
[25] *Catholic Biblical Quarterly*, 1942. Comp. H. H. Rowley, *The Relevance Of Apocalyptic*, pp. 128–30.
[26] *Jewish And Christian Apocalypses*, The Schweich Lectures 1913, London, 1914, pp. 37–39.
[27] Charles, *op. cit*., p. 30.
[28] *Zeitschrift für die neutestamentliche Wissenschaft*, 1916, 117–8.
[29] *The Apocryphal Literature*, New Haven, 1945, pp. 114–16.
[30] P. 116.

Mattathis, as Dr. Torrey believes, because Mattathis encouraged his sons to resist and fight the Greeks,[31], while Taxo was opposed to combatting the enemy.[32] Dr. Torrey is of the opinion that the seven sons represent "the seven Hasmonean rulers, from Judas to Antigonus."[33] But, as a matter of fact, there were ten rulers from Judas to Antigonus.[34] These are not the only objections that can be raised against Dr. Torrey's theories, as well as those of other scholars. Is it not anomalous that the author of *The Assumption of Moses* should make use of *gematria* for the names Messiah, Hasmonean, Mattathis, Shiloh. Certainly, he would not use the method of *gematria* to arrive at the word Messiah, for none of the apocryphal writers ever adopted this method of *gematria*. Furthermore, the use of *gematria*, I believe, was not known to the Jews during the Second Commonwealth. None of the scholars has suggested any reason why the author should substitute the name of Taxo for that of Messiah or Hasmonean.

I venture to say that the word Taxo is the Greek word Τόξον latinized by the author. *Toxon* means a bow, in the Hebrew *keshet*.

The word *keshet* occupied a conspicuous place in the early Jewish theology. Rabbi Joshua ben Levi said that when a Jew sees the *keshet* in the sky he must fall to the

[31] See I Mac. 2.64–66 ... ἰσχύσατε καὶ ἀνδρίζεσθε ἐν τῷ νόμῳ ... οὗτος ὑμῖν ἔσται ἄρχων στρατιᾶς καὶ πολεμήσει πόλεμον λαῶν.

[32] Ch. 9. In making use of chapter divisions, I follow the edition of Fritzsche. The manuscript itself, as I have said, has no chapter divisions.

[33] *Op. cit.*, p. 116. Comp. also *idem. Jour. Bib. Lit.*, 1943. Comp. also W. Bousset, *Die Religion des Judentums im Späthellenistischen Zeitalter*, 1926, p. 232; J. Lagrange, *Le Judaism, Avant Jesus Christ*, 1931, pp. 237–242.

[34] Judas, Jonathan, Simon, John Hyrkanus I, Aristobulus I, Alexander Jannaeus, Alexandra, John Hyrkanus II, Aristobulus II, Antigonus.

ground.[35] According to the Talmud, the *keshet* was created on the sixth day (Friday) at twilight.[36] From the Book of Genesis, we learn that when God made a covenant with Noah that "neither shall there any more be a flood to destroy the earth" the *keshet* (bow) was to be the token of the covenant between God and Noah.[37] In the Book of Ezekiel, it is related that when Ezekiel saw the chariot, he declared: "As the appearance of the *bow* that is in the cloud in the day of rain, so was the appearance of the brightness around about, this was the appearance of the likeness of the glory of God."[38] The author of the Book of Revelation wrote that he saw "a white horse: and he that sat on him had a *bow*; and a crown was given unto him: and he went forth conquering and to conquer."[39] The Zohar connects the *keshet* with the coming of the Messiah. It affirms that when the *keshet* appears in very bright colors and the world is lit up by it, then the coming of the Messiah will be near.[40] Thus, we see that the *keshet* occupied an important position in the early Jewish theology.

[35] א'ר אלכסנדרי אמר ר' יהושע בן לוי הרואה את הקשת בענן צריך שיפול על פניו. שנאמר כמראה הקשת אשר יהיה בענן . . . הוא מראה דמות כבוד ד' וראאה ואפל על פני. Ber. 59a.

[36] עשרה דברים נבראו בערב שבת בין השמשות ואלו הן . . . והקשת. Abot 5.

[37] את קשתי נתתי בענן והיתה לאות ברית ביני ובין הארץ . . . והיתה הקשת בענן וראיתיה לזכר ברית עולם בין אלהים ובין כל נפש חיה. Gen. 9.12–16.

[38] Ezek. 1.28.

[39] καὶ ἰδοὺ· ἵππος λευκός καὶ ὁ καθήμενος ἐπ᾽ αὐτόν ἔχων τόξον καὶ ἐδόθη αὐτῷ στέφανος καὶ ἐξῆλθεν νικῶν καὶ ἵνα νικήσῃ. Rev. 6.2. See also Sirah, 43.11, ἴδε τόξον καὶ εὐλόγησον τὸν ποιήσαντα αὐτο; 50. 7, ὡς ἥλιος ἐκλάμπων ἐπὶ ναόν ὑψίστου καί ὡς τόξον φωτίζον ἐν νεφέλαις δόξης.

[40] וכד יפקון ישראל מן גלותא זמינא האי קשת לאתקשטא בגווני ככלה דא דמתקשטא לבעלה אמר ליה ההוא יודאי כך אמר לי אבא כד הוה מסתלק מעלמא לא תצפי לרגלי דמשיחא עד דיתחזי האי קשת בעלמא מתקשטא בגוונין נהירין ויתנהיר לעלמא וכדין צפי לי למשיח (פ' נח); כמראה הקשת זה הי עלמין וזה את קשתי נתתי בענן דא מלכות נתתי מן יומא דאתחברי עלמא . . . (בראשית); את קשתי נתתי בענן הנין דהההוא קשת אשלחת לבושי ויהיב למשה ובהההוא לבושא סליק משה לטורא ומינה חמא מה דחמא מכלא עד ההוא אתר (פ' משפטים); קום אנת ר' יוסי הגלילי ואימא דהא מלין שפירין קאמרת בחבורא קדמאה דקשת לא אתייא אלא לאגנא על עלמא למלכא דבכל זמנא דבריה

The author of the *Assumption of Moses* when he wrote אז (τοξον) יקום (יהיה) איש (אדם) משבט לוי ושמו יהיה קשת "*Tunc illo (die erit) [dicente] homo de tribu Levi, cujus nomen erit Taxo,*" "then will arise a man of the tribe of Levi whose name will be Taxo" may have had in mind the prophecy of Zech. 6.12. כה אמר ד' צבאות לאמר הנה איש צמח שמו ומתחתיו יצמח ובנה את היכל ד'.[40a] The Church Fathers maintained that this passage referred to Jesus. The Septuagint translates the word צמח by Ἀνατολή branch or offshoot. Justin Martyr maintained that this passage of Zechariah referred to Jesus.[41] He also rendered the word צמח by Ἀνατολή, but in the sense of East. The Vulgate renders this passage: *Haec ait Dominus exercitum, dicens: ECCE VIR ORIENS NOMEN EIUS: et subter eum orietur, et aedificabit templum Domino. Et ipse extruet templum Domino.* The word צמח is generally translated in the Vulgate by *germen*.[42] In this passage, however, the Vulgate renders it *ORIENS, East*. Thus, the Vulgate definitely follows Justin Martyr in that it gives the translation of Zechariah as "a man whose name is East," meaning, of course, Jesus. The rabbis, likewise, interpret the word צמח as referring to the Messiah.[43]

The words of Zech. 6.12 present a certain ambiguity. Does this prophecy refer to Joshua, the priest of the tribe

---

חב ומלכא חזי למטרוניתא סליק רוגזא דבריה . . . אלא ודאי ההוא קשת דאתגלייא בגולתא לא איהו אלא מטטרון דאתקרי שד"י ואיהו עבדו זקן ביתו דשליט בכל דילה (רעיא מהימנא, פ' פנחס). According to the Zohar, *keshet* is Mattatron, who is the chief of the angels and is even called שד"י, the Almighty.

[40a] He only substituted the word קשת for צמח.

[41] Καὶ Πάλιν Ἀνατολή ὄνομα αὐτοῦ Ζαχαρίας φησί. *Dialogue with Trypho*, 121.

[42] E. g. Jer. 23.5; 33.15; Ezek. 16.7.

[43] Mid. R. Lam. 1, מה שמו של מלך המשיח . . . ר' יהושע בן לוי אמר צמח שמו שנאמר הנה איש צמח שמו ומתחתיו יצמח ר' יודן בש"ר איבו אמר מנחם שמו שנא' כי רחק ממני מנחם. א"ר חניא ולא פליגא חושבנא דדין כחושבנא דדין הוא מנחם הוא צמח הא נברא משיחא שמיה עתיד דיתגלי ויתרבי. See also Targum Jonathan *ad loc.* ויבני ית היכלא. Comp. also Rashi *ad loc.* ויש פותרים אותו במלך המשיח אבל כל העניין הזה מדבר בבית שני.

of Levi, or to Zerubbabel of the tribe of Judah? The rabbinic tradition holds that it refers to Zerubbabel.[44] From the text itself, however, we may infer that it refers to Joshua of the tribe of Levi.

A study of the *Assumption of Moses* reveals the fact that the author did not believe in a Messiah but held that God would reveal Himself in this world. The man named Taxo, *keshet*, would herald the coming of God in His full majesty.[45]

Assuming that the word Taxo actually is a latinized Greek word $\tau o \xi o \nu$ the fact that in this Latin text we have a Greek word does not present any difficulty. This is not the only place where the author did not translate the Greek but rather transliterated it. Examples of this are: *chedrio*[46] (cedar) $\kappa \epsilon \delta \rho \acute{o} \omega$; *heremus*[47] (wilderness) $\dot{\epsilon} \rho \widetilde{\eta} \mu o s$; and *acrobistia*[48] (uncircumcised) $\dot{\alpha} \kappa \rho o \beta \upsilon \sigma \tau \acute{\iota} a$. As to the word Taxo instead of *toxon*, as we should expect if this word is a transliteration of the Greek, we must bear in mind that the Latin translation in general is faulty. There are many other errors both in textual structure as well as in grammar.[48a]

DATE OF COMPOSITION

The same wide divergence of opinion that exists with regard to the word Taxo also exists as to the date of composition and the authorship of *The Assumption of Moses*. Ewald,[49] Wieseler[50] and Dillmann[51] are of the opinion that

---

[44] See Rashi *ibid*. ‎צמח שמו הוא זרובבל.
[45] Comp. ch. 10.
[46] Ch. 1, 17.
[47] Ch. 3, 11.
[48] Ch. 8, 3.
[48a] See note 7.
[49] *Gesch. des Volkes Israel*, vol. 6.
[50] *Op. cit.*
[51] See the literature given in Herzong's *Real-Encyc.* 3rd ed., XVI, pp. 242–44.

this book was compiled during the first decades C. E. Torrey also accepts this date.[52] Hilgenfeld holds that the book was composed about the year 44–45 C. E.[53] Charles is firm in his belief that it was composed between 7 and 30 C. E.[54] On the other hand, Schmidt and Merx insist that the composition of the book took place sometime between 54 and 64 C. E.[55] Volkmar argues for a still later date, sometime between 137–138 C. E.[56] General opinion among scholars is, however, that *The Assumption of Moses* was compiled *before* the destruction of the Second Temple. This date is out of question and need not even be considered.

The author gives the date of Moses' death as two thousand five hundred years after the creation of the world and thus helps us inadvertantly to establish the date when he lived and wrote it. Now, during the Second Commonwealth, this manner of designating an era by *Anno Mundi*, was not used by the Jews. In the Bible, different eras are given, for example, the era of the Exodus,[57] the era of the destruction of the Temple of Solomon,[58] the era of the different kings.[59] In the Second Commonwealth we also find different eras by which the Jews reckoned their chronology: the era of the Seleucides,[60] the era of the establishment of the Jewish state in the time of Simon the Hasmonean,[61] the

---

[52] *Op. cit.* p. 116.

[53] *Op. cit.* p. LXXIV.

[54] *Op. cit.*

[55] *Op. cit.*

[56] *Op. cit.* pp. 57–72.

[57] E. g. I Kings 6.1 ויהי בשמונים שנה וארבע מאות שנה לצאת בני ישראל ממצרים.

[58] Ezek. 1.1; 8.1; 20.1; 24.1. See also Yer. R. H. 1.

[59] The dates of the Persian kings are given in the books of the Bible of the post-exilic period, בשנת שתים לדריוש, בשנת שלש לכרש.

[60] This chronology was used in the books of the Maccabees and by Josephus in his book *Antiquities*.

[61] השנה הראשונה לגאולת ישראל.

era of the different kings,[62] but nowhere is the era of the creation used.[63] Only after the destruction of the Second Temple did this manner of designating the era come into vogue.[62a]

Thus, we may say with certainty that this book, *The Assumption of Moses*, could have been composed only *after* the destruction of the Second Temple.

Those who are of the opinion that the book was composed in the first two decades of the first century C. E. maintain that the author referred to Herod when he said "He will beget children who, succeeding him, will rule for shorter periods." The statement about the rule of his children for shorter periods is true only regarding Archelaus, who ruled for nine years. It may possibly apply to Herod's grandson, who ruled for four years. But it does not apply to his other children, Philip and Herod Antipas, who reigned longer than their father Herod who ruled for thirty-four years.[64] The scholars therefore concluded that the book could have been written only after the removal of Archelaus in 6 C. E. and before Philip and Herod Antipas died. This would fix the date of the composition of this book before 30 C. E. However, this is not sufficient proof to assign the book to this early date. The author of our book, in his statement

---

[62] So Josephus, in his book *The Jewish Wars*, gives the dates of the Roman emperors.

[62a] See also IV Ezra 14.48.

[63] Josephus, in his book *Antiquities* 1, 3, 3, gives the date of the flood as 2262 after the birth of Adam, the first man. χρόνος δὲ οὗτος ἀπὸ Ἀδάμου τοῦ πρώτου γεγονότος ... In book 8, 3, 1, Josephus ‚says: "From the birth of Adam the first man to the time when Solomon built the Temple there elapsed altogether 3102 years. ἀπὸ δὲ τοῦ πρώτου γεννηθέντος Ἀδάμου ἕως οὗ τὸν ναὸν ᾠκοδόμησε Σολομών .... Josephus never used the term ἀπὸ τῆς κτίσεως τοῦ κόσμου (לבריאת העולם) "after the creation of the world," since there was no such era known to the Jews at the time of the Second Commonwealth.

[64] From the year 38 to 4 B. C. E.

"Children who, succeeding him, will reign for shorter periods," may refer to those who were kings of Judaea, but Philip and Herod Antipas never ruled over Judaea.

AUTHORSHIP

On the authorship of the book, wide differences of opinion also exist. Scholars are divided in regard to the sect to which the author belonged. Some hold that he was a Pharisee,[65] while others believe him a Sadducee.[66] Still others are of the opinion that he was an Essene.[66a] On the other hand, some consider him a Zealot,[67] while others maintain that he belonged to the Pharisaic Quietist group.[68] All these scholars who differ as to the authorship of this book base their theories on Chapter VII, which contains, in their opinion, the crux of the argument in the determination of the authorship as well as the date of the book.

As stated above, the condition of the text of this book is unsatisfactory. The Latin translation is full of errors of transcription and, in some places, the text itself is very hard to decipher. Chapter VII is more than defective; it is mutilated. The text of this chapter as it was found reads as follows:[69]

ex quo facto finien	. . . . . . ae . . . . pos . .
tur tempors momen	. . . . initiis tribus ad
to . . . . etur cursus	exitus viiii propter
a . . . . horae iiii ue	initium tres sep
niant coguntur secun	timae secunda tria

[65] Dillmann, *op. cit.* Comp. also Schürer, *op. cit.*
[66] See Volkmar, *op. cit.* pp. 105–6.
[66a] Schmidt-Merx, *op. cit.*
[67] See Deane, *op. cit.*
[68] Charles, *op. cit.*
[69] The text here is from the original manuscript published by Fritzsche.

in tertia duae h . .ra . .   tores quaeru . . .
tae et regnarunt   fallaces celantes se
de his homines pes   ne possent cognos
tilentiosi et impii   ci impii in scelere
docentes se esse   pleni et iniquitate
iustos et hi susci   ab oriente usque ad
tabunt iram animo   occidentem dicen
rum suorum qui   tes habebimus dis
erunt homines do   cubitiones et luxu
losi sibi placentes   riam edentes et
ficti in omnibus suis   bibentes
et omni hora diei   Et putauimus nos
amantes convivia   tamquam principes
deuoratores gulae   erimus et manus
s . . . n . . . ca . . . .   eorum et mentes
. . . . . nus diis . . . .   inmunda tractantes
. . . . omnis . . . .   et os eorum loque
. . . .   tur ingentia et su
. . . . u . . . . o . . . .   per dicent noli . . . .
rae . . . . . elen   tange ni inquines
tes . . . . . rum bo   me loco in quo . . . s . . .
norum comesto   . . . is d . . . .
res dicentes se haec   su . . . . . us . . . . .
facere propter mi   in . . . .
sericordiam qu . . .   re . . . . raui . . . .
se et extermina

This text was emended and edited by Schmidt and Merx[70] and later re-edited critically by Fritzsche.[71] The English translation by Charles based mainly on these two editions is as follows: "And when this is done the times will be ended, in a moment the (second) course will be (ended),

[70] *Op. cit.*
[71] *Op. cit.*

the four hours will come. They will be forced . . . .
And, in the time of these, pestilent[72] and impious men will
rule, saying that they are just. And these will conceal the
wrath of their minds, being treacherous men, self-pleasers,
dissemblers in all their own affairs and lovers of banquets at
every hour of the day, gluttons, gourmands . . . .
Devourers of the goods of the poor saying that they do so
on the ground of their justice, but (in reality) to destroy
them, complainers, deceitful, concealing themselves lest
they should be recognised, impious, filled with lawlessness
and iniquity from sunrise to sunset: Saying: "We shall
have feastings and luxury, eating and drinking, yea we
shall drink our fill, we shall be as princes." And though
their hands and their minds touch unclean things, yet their
mouth will speak great things, and they will say furthermore: "Do not touch me lest thou shouldst pollute me in
the place where I stand" . . . .

Who were the "pestilent and impious men" to whom
the author refers? And whom did he have in mind when he
said "lovers of banquets at every hour of the day, gluttons,
gourmands . . . . "? Hilgenfeld thinks that they were
the Herodian princes.[73] Ewald,[74] Dillmann[75] and Schürer[76]
believe them to be Pharisees of the first decades after
Herod's death. This passage refers to the Pharisees and
to the Sadducees, according to Wieseler.[77] Rosenthal's
view is that some verses allude to the Sadducees and others
to the Pharisees.[78] Geiger concludes that the passage
refers only to the Sadducees.[79] Other scholars say that the

---

[72] *Pestilentiosi et impii.*
[73] *Op. cit.*
[74] *Op. cit.*
[75] *Op. cit.*
[76] *Op. cit.*
[77] *Op. cit.*
[78] *Op. cit.* pp. 19–22.
[79] See *Jüdische Zeitschrift*, 1868.

author had the Roman procurators in mind,[80] while Volkmar, on the other hand, says that he was thinking of the Sadducees of the time of Nerva and Trajan.[81]

These opinions are untenable. The Pharisees were not inclined towards gluttony nor were they addicted to wine. They were never charged with these vices, even by their bitterest opponents. Furthermore, the book could not have been written by a Sadducee. Neither can we accept the theory that this passage is applicable to the Sadducees of the time of Nerva and Trajan, because, after the destruction of the Temple, the Sadducees as a sect ceased to exist. The assumption that one or two verses of this chapter refer to the Pharisees while another verse or two point to the Sadducees is not valid. Neither can we accept the theory that this chapter refers to the Herodian princes or to the Roman procurators. I previously showed that the author's use of the manner of designating an era of the Creation proves unquestionably that this book could not have been written *before* the destruction of the Temple. After the destruction there were no Herodian princes. For the same reason, also, we must reject the opinion that this book was written by a Zealot, because the Zealots, as a party, came into existence in the year 66 C. E., under the leadership of Eleazar, the son of Simon. (Incidentally, we must correct the erroneous assumption of the scholars that the Zealots came into existence at the time of Herod under the leadership of Judas of Galilee . . . Josephus, in his book *The Jewish Wars*, used the term Zealots forty-eight times. In all but one passage, he refers to the party which was led by Eleazar, the son of Simon.)[82] Since we have refuted the theories of

---

[80] Beldensperger, *Das Selbstbewusstsein Jesu*, 1888, p. 31.

[81] *Op. cit.*

[82] The assertion that the Zealots as a party arose at the time of Quirinius is historically wrong. Josephus applies the term Zealots only to a particular party led by Eleazar, the son of Simon — a party equally

the scholars in reference to Chapter VII, the question now arises as to whom the author indeed had in mind.

To answer this question we must give a short survey of the different parties that existed in Judaea before the destruction of the Temple and of those that survived this catastrophe. It is well known that during the Second Commonwealth three different parties existed among the Jews, the Sadducees, the Pharisees and the Essenes. The Sadducees, besides denying predestination, the Divine influence on man's acts and the authority of the Oral Law, were interested in the Jewish state as a national state, and from time to time they were imperialists. They also denied that God made a covenant with David, thus rejecting the leadership of the Davidic family over the Jews. The ideas of the Pharisees ran diametrically opposite to those of the Sadducees. They believed in Divine Providence, in reward and punishment in the future world and stressed the importance of the Oral Law. They were humble. They held that God made a covenant with David and that the kingdom should belong to his children.[82a] The Pharisees exerted great influence over the masses. The Essenes were successors to the early *Hasidim*. They were highly individualistic in their attitude toward Jewish life. They were strict in their observance of the laws of the Bible, and since they could not observe these laws in the cities where the Pharisees had modified the *Halakot*, they formed communities of their own outside of the cities, where they found it possible to practise their own customs and live their own way of life.

opposed to the provisional government, to John of Gischala, and to Simon, son of Giora. The Fourth Philosophy originated at the time of Quirinius under the leadership of Judas of Galilee, while the party of Zealots came into existence in the year 66 and was organized by Eleazar ben Simon. See S. Zeitlin, *JQR*, 1943, pp. 351–2.

[82a] See S. Zeitlin, *Who Crucified Jesus?* Ch. VI.

Besides these three branches of Judaism, there were two others, the Fourth Philosophy and the Apocalyptists. Both of these parties were actually offshoots of the Pharisees.[83] Both believed that God was the only ruler and that there should be no lordship of man over man. Both had a strong attachment to liberty. They preferred to die rather than to accept man as a ruler. Their methods of achieving the freedom of the people, however, were different. The Fourth Philosophy believed in the use of force. They held that terror must oppose terror. Their successors were the *Sicarii*, who were so called because of their use of the *sica*, or dagger.[84] The Apocalyptists were opposed to the use of force or terror. They believed in the revelation of God. They looked forward to the time when God would either reveal Himself and save His people, the Jews, from their foreign yoke, or when He would send a Messiah, a supernatural person, who would save the Jews.

With the fall of the state of Judaea and the destruction of the Temple, the Sadducees disappeared as a group. There was no reason for their existence; there was no longer a Jewish state. The Essenes likewise disappeared as a group; it was no longer possible for them to live under the Romans. The Pharisees, who really were never a group in the strict sense of the word (even the name Pharisees was coined by the Sadducees),[84a] continued to exist after the catastrophe. They were the founders of what has come to be known as Normative Judaism. They adjusted themselves to the new conditions. The *Sicarii* and the Apocalyptists, disregarding the calamities which befell the Jews, clung tenaciously to their views. They continued to preach that God had not forsaken the Jews, that the

---

[83] Comp. *The Jewish Wars*, 2, 8, 2; *Ant.* 18, 1, 6.
[84] *The Jewish Wars*, 2, 17, 6.
[84a] S. Zeitlin, הצדוקים והפרושים.

destruction of the state and the burning of the Temple
had only been a test of their piety. God had made them
suffer but He would never forsake them. He would reveal
Himself or would send a Messiah to save the Jews and
punish all their oppressors.

THE SICARII AND THE REVOLT OF BAR KOKBA

The *Sicarii* became more of a secular than a religious
group. They were the forerunners or perhaps the very
leaders of the Bar Kokba revolt. On the other hand, the
Apocalyptists were a purely religious group. Many of
them, after the destruction of the Temple, particularly
those who believed in a Messiah, joined the Christians.
They were the Judeo-Christians. Other members of the
Apocalyptists, under the weight of the great catastrophe
of the burning of the Temple and the destruction of the
Holy City of Jerusalem, became more religious-nationalis-
tic. They believed that God could not have forsaken His
chosen people and that He would punish the pagans.
They looked forward to a day not remote when God would
reveal Himself to His people. This group (the Apocalyptists), whom Josephus called wicked, deceivers and impostors, who, under the pretense of divine inspiration,
fostered revolutions,[85] were not the cause of the Bar Kokba
revolt. This revolt was of a national-secular character.

---

[85] *The Jewish Wars* II, 13, 3–4. "Besides these there arose another
body of villains, with purer hands but more impious intentions, who
no less than the assassins ruined the peace of the city. Deceivers and
impostors, under the pretense of divine inspiration fostering revolutionary changes, they persuaded the multitude to act like madmen, and
led them out into the desert under the belief that God would there give
them tokens of deliverance." ... πλάνοι γὰρ ἄνθρωποι καί ἀπατεῶνες
προσχήματι θειασμοῦ νεωτερισμοὺς καὶ μεταβολὰς πραγματευόμενοι
δαιμονᾶν τὸ πλῆθος ἔπειθον καὶ πρῆγον εἰς τὴν ἐρημίαν ὡς ἐκεῖ τοῦ
θεου δείξοντος αὐτοῖς σημεῖα ἐλευθερίας.

It was fomented by the ideas of the *Sicarii*. The Palestinian Talmud relates that Bar Kokba himself before battle used to address God as follows: "We do not need Your assistance, but do not help our foe."[86] Also, there is a similar story in the Midrash about two brothers, apparently among the leaders of the revolt, who once went out to fight the Romans. An elderly man met them at the gates of the village and wished them Divine assistance. To this they answered that they did not need His assistance, but hoped that He would not help their foe.[87] This clearly indicates that the Bar Kokba revolt was not a religious but a national-secular revolt to restore the Jewish national state.

It is probable that the Apocalyptists, who believed in the establishment of the Kingdom of God, suffered during this revolt because they did not believe in a Messiah and were not even interested in establishing a Jewish state. Justin Martyr related that during the revolt, Bar Kokba persecuted the Christians, and forced them to deny Jesus.[88] If this was so, it is quite understandable why the Judeo-Christians were persecuted. At that time, they were still a part of the Jewish people. They believed that Jesus was the promised Messiah. They were opposed to a Jewish state. It was to their interest that the revolt of Bar Kokba should fail. They even informed the Roman authorities about the activities of the Jews preparing for the revolt.

---

[86] וכדדהוה נפק לקרבא הוה אמר ריבונה דעלמא לא תסעוד ולא תכסוף (Yer. Tan. 4).

[87] Midrash Lam. 2, שני אחין היו בכפר הרובא ולא הוה שבקין רומאי עבר תמן דלא הוה קטלי יתיה אמרי כל סמא דמילא ניתי כלילא דאדריאנוס וניתיב בראשו של שמעון דהא רומאי אתון מן דנפקין פגע בהון חד סבא א'ל ברייא בסעדיכון מן אליון אמרו ליה לא נסעוד ולא נכסוף. See also Yer. Tan. 4.

[88] Καὶ γὰρ ἐν τῷ νῦν γεγενημένῳ ἰουδαϊκῷ πολέμῳ Βαρχωχέβας ὁ τῆς Ἰουδαίων ἀποστάσεως ἀρχηγέτης Χριστιανοὺς μόνους εἰς τιμωρίας δεινὰς εἰ μὴ ἀρνοῖντο Ἰησοῦν τὸν Χριστὸν καὶ βλασφημοῖεν ἐκέλευεν ἀπάγεσθαι. *The First Apology*, 31.

For them Jesus was a High Priest and a descendant of the House of David. The leaders of the revolt, on the other hand, regarded them as enemies of the Jewish people, as obstructionists of the revolt and informers to the Romans.

There was a strong division in regard to the revolt even among the leaders of the Jewish people. Many of the rabbis looked upon this revolt as a suicidal act of the Jewish people. Rabban Johanan ben Zaccai had been greatly opposed to the revolt in the time of Nero and Vespasian and had only been saved from death at the hands of the leaders of the revolt by his disciples, who carried him out of the city of Jerusalem in a coffin.[89] In the revolt of Bar Kokba, Rabbi Eleazar of Modin was among those opposed to it. It is said that Bar Kokba heard that Rabbi Eleazar was willing to deliver the city to the Romans, and therefore killed him.[90]

According to the Talmud, the leaders of the revolt during the time of Nero-Vespasian were called בריוני, rebels.[91] Josephus called them λῃσταί, lestai, robbers, bandits.[92] According to the Gospel of Mark Jesus was crucified between two lestai (robbers).[93] The men who were crucified with Jesus were undoubtedly members of the Sicarii who were called lestai (robbers). Probably, the

---

[89] . . . ולימרי דנח נפשיך . . . נכנס בו ר' אליעזר מצד אחד ור' See Git. 56a

. . . בין ווי לוה נמלט רבן יוחנן .See also Midrash Lam. 1, יהושע מצד אחד

בן זכאי . . . אמר אפקוני בדמות דמית טען ר"א ברישה ור' יהושע ברגליה ובן בטיח מהלך קומי

[90] Ibid, 2, . . . אזלין ואמרין לבר כוזיבא חביבך ר' אלעזר בעי לאשלמא מדינתא

עם אדריאנוס . . . נתמלא רוגזה לבו כוזיבא יהב לי חד בעיטא ברגליה וקטליה .See also Yer. Tan. 4.

[91] Git. 56a, הנהו בריינו אמרו להו רבנן ניפוק ונעבוד שלמא בהדייהו לא שבקינהו .

[92] The Jewish Wars 2. 13, 3 . . . . ἕτερον εἶδος λῃστῶν ἐν Ἱεροσο-λύμοις ἐπεφύετο οἱ καλούμενοι σικάριοι.

[93] Καὶ σὺν αὐτῳ σταυροῦσιν δύο λῃστάς. Mark 15.27. See also Mat. 27.38. The rendering in the King James version is "thieves," but is incorrect. The word "thief" in the Gospels is rendered in Greek by the word κλέπτης.

leaders in the revolt of Bar Kokba were also designated
by their opponents *lestai*, bandits. A story is told in the
Midrash that the son of Rabbi Haninah ben Tradyon
joined the לסטים, *lestai* and later disclosed their secrets.
For this they killed him.[94] Most likely, the son of Rabbi
Haninah ben Tradyon did not join ordinary robbers but
the revolutionary group who organized the revolt against
the Romans and who were called *lestai* (robbers) by their
opponents.

It is true that one of the greatest spiritual leaders of
that time, Rabbi Akiba, believed that Bar Kokba was the
King Messiah.[95] However, most of his colleagues did not
agree with him. One of Akiba's colleagues said to him,
"grass will grow through thy jaws and the son of David
will not yet have appeared,"[95a] which means that when
you will be dead and buried the Messiah will not yet have
come. The phenomenon of Rabbi Akiba, one of the greatest
teachers of the Jewish religion, joining a secular-national
movement is not without parallel in history. There are
many cases of men who join movements which are in
opposition to the ideology of their social class. Even some
of Akiba's devoted disciples did not share his point of view
and were not in favor of the revolt against the Romans.
Rabbi Judah even tried to justify the enemy. Rabbi Jose

[94] Mid. Lam. 3, מעשה בבנו של חניה בן הרדיון שנתחבר ללסטים וגלה את רזון
מעשה בבנו של ר' חניה בן. Comp. also Sem. 12, והרנהו וטלאו פיו עפר וצרורות
והרנהו שיצא לתרבות רעה ותפסוהו לסטים בן תרדיון. That the son of R. Haninah
ben Teradyon was a learned person and was consulted by rabbis on
matters of law is evident from the following Tosefta, תנור מאימתי מקבל
טומאה . . . מאימתי טהרתו, אמר ר' חלפתא איש כפר חנניא שאלתי את שמעון בן חנניא
ששאל את בנו של ר' חנניא בן תרדיון ואמר משיסיענו ממקומו ובתו אומרת משיפשטו את
חלקו כשנאמרו דברי לפני ר' יהודה בן בבא אמר יפה אמרה בתו מבנו (כלים, ב'ק,ד')
This Tosefta confirms my hypothesis that he did not join ordinary
robbers but rather *lestai*, "terrorists," followers of Bar Kokba.
[95] Ibid. 2, ר' עקיבא כד חמי ליה להדין (בר כוכבא) בר כוזיבא אמר היינו מלכא
משיחא.
[95a] Ibid. א'ל ר' יוחנן בן תורתא יעלו עשבים בלחייך ועדיין בן דוד לא בא.

refused to express an opinion in reference to the Romans
Only Rabbi Simon was very militant against them.[96]

Rabbi Joshua, who in his youth witnessed the catastrophe[97] which befell Judaea at the time of Vespasian and
lived to see the preparation for the revolt against Hadrian,
opposed it. A Midrash relates that when the Jews assembled to take counsel about starting the revolt, Rabbi
Joshua told them the well-known fable about the lion and
the crane. A lion was choking because a bone was sticking
in his throat. He offered a reward to anyone who whould
remove the bone. A crane responded to the offer, and,
probing the lion's throat with her long bill, removed the
bone. When the crane demanded her reward, the lion
said to her: "You are very well rewarded by coming out
of the lion's throat alive."[98] Rabbi Joshua, in relating this
fable, indicated that the Jews were fortunate in that they
were left alive while among the lions (Romans). It is
probable that Rabbi Joshua had in mind the betrayal of
the Jews by the Roman government. When Hadrian
became emperor after the death of Trajan in the year
117 C. E., while the rightful successor to the throne,
Quietus, was still alive and the revolt of the Jews in Northern Africa was still fresh in the emperor's mind,[99] he prom-

---

[96] Shab. 33b, ‏ר' יוסי ... זו אומה של מעשיהן נאים כמה ואמר יהודה ר' פתח‎
‏נשרים ... עצמ' לצרך אלא תקנו לא שתקנו מה כל ואמר יחאי בן שמעון ר' נענה שתק‎
‏יהודה אמרו למלכות, ונשמעו דבריהם וסיפר גרים בן יהודה הלך מכס, מהם ליטול‎
‏יהרג שגינה שמעון לצפורי יגלה ששתק יוסי יתעלה שעילה‎.

[97] We know from the Talmud that Rabbi Joshua attended to duties
in the Temple. See Ar. 11b, ‏בהנפת לסייע שהלך חנניא בן יהושע בר' מעשה‎
‏דלתות‎.

[98] Gen. Rab. 64, ‏כתביא דאחון כיון רמון, דבית בקעתא בהדה מצמתין קהליא והוון‎
‏ודרש ועאל ... חנניה בן יהושע ר' יעול אמרין ... מלכותא על לממרד בעיין בכיין שרון‎
‏הדין אתא אגריה, ליה יהיב אנא יהיב ליה מפיק דאתי כל בגרונו עצם ועמד טרף טרף ארי‎
‏מלגלג ההא זיל א'ל אגרי, לי הב א'ל ואפקי' מוקריה יהיב ארוך דמוקריה מיצראה קוהא‎
‏בשלום זו לאומה שנכנסנו דיינו כך בשלום, ונפקת בשלום דאריה לפומא דעלית ואומר‎
‏בשלום ויצאנו‎.

[99] See S. Zeitlin, The Apocrypha, *JQR*, 1947.

ised the Jews of Judaea that he would permit them to
rebuild their Temple.[100] In 122, when Hadrian was already

[100] בימי ר' יהושע בן חנניה גזרה מלכות הרשעה שיבנה ביהמ'ק, Gen. Rab. 64,
הושיבו פפוס ולוליאנוס מעכו עד אנטוכיא והיו מספקין לעולי גולה כסף וזהב
כל צרכם אולין אילין כותאי ואמרין ידוע להוא למלכא דהדין קרותא מרדתא תתבנא . . .
ואמר להון מה נעבוד וגזירות, אמרין ליה שלח ואמר להון או ישנון יתה מאתריה אין
הון בהון חזרין . . . ומן גרמיהון אנון . . . יוספון. Lulianus and Pappas were undoubtedly among the leaders of the revolt of Bar Kokba. With many others,
they both were killed in Lydda and were called הרוגי לוד. The rabbis
were divided in their opinion about the "slain of Lydda," particularly
about Lulianus and Pappas. Some rabbis believed that they were
ordinary הרוגי מלכות, "slain by the government," while others believed
them "slain for the sake of the Jews and the cause of Judaism." In
the Talmud Tan. 18b, the following account is given about Lulianus and
Pappas. אמר כשבקש טורייגוס להרוג את לולינוס ופפוס אחיו בלודקיא אמר להם
אם מעמו של חנניה מישאל ועזריה אתם ובא אלהיכם ויציל אתכם מידי כדרך שהציל
את חנניה מישאל ועזריה מיד נבוכדנצר, אמרו לו חנניה מישאל ועזריה צדקים גמורין
היו וראוין היו ליעשות להם נס ונבוכדנצר מלך הגון היה וראוי ליעשות נס על ידו (ואותו
רשע הדיוט) ואתה מלך רשע ואינו ראוי ליעשות נס על ידך, ואנו נתחייבנו כליה למקום
ואם אין אתה הורגנו הרבה הורגים יש למקום הרבה דובים . . . אלא לא מסרנו הקדוש
ברוך הוא בידך אלא שעתיד ליפרע דמינו מידך. "Said he to them: 'If ye be of
the people of Hananiah, Mishael, and Azariah, your God will come and
save you from my hands as he saved Hananiah, Mishael, and Azariah
from the hands of Nebuchadnezzar.' They replied: 'Hananiah, Mishael,
and Azariah were righteous and pious men and Nebuchadnezzar a
noble monarch who was worthy that a miracle should be wrought
through him, whilst thou art a wicked king and not fit that a miracle
be performed through thee. We deserve death, and if thou wilt not slay
us, God hath many other agencies through which to kill us, many
bears . . . but if thou killest us the Lord will demand our blood of thy
hand.' The story concludes that he killed them nevertheless. From
this story, it is apparent that Lulianus and Pappas were not considered
righteous men like Hananiah, Mishael, Azariah. This story is also
given in the tractate Sem. 8. However, there is a gloss אבל כשנמות תדע
שאנו מבני בניהם של חנניה מישאל ועזריה. "They said to the king: 'If we shall
be killed, then you should know that we are of the children of Hananiah,
Mishael and Azariah." Apparently, the author of this gloss considered
Lulianus and Pappas righteous men. (Comp. also the Scholia to
Megillat Taanit.)

In the Sifra on Lev. 26.19 ושברתי את גאון עזכם "and I shall break the
power of your pride," the Rabbis said: אילו הגיאים שהם גאונם של ישראל
כגון פפוס בן יהודה ולוליינוס אלכסנדרי וחבריו "that is, the haughty who are
the pride of Israel like Pappas ben Judah and Lulianus the Alexandrian
and their fellows." From this *Sifra*, it is apparent that the rabbis looked
upon these two men with an element of contempt. Comp. also Ber. 61b,

secure upon his throne, since Quietus had been executed,[101] he so modified the permission to rebuild that it was tantamount to revoking it. When the Jews found that they had been betrayed by the Romans, they prepared to revolt. Rabbi Joshua, in relating the fable, implied that they should not fight the Romans. However, his advice was not heeded. Rabbi Joshua, who was one of the few sages who experienced the war against Vespasian, also witnessed the beginning of the revolt of Bar Kokba. Rabban Gamaliel, as well as Rabbi Eleazar[102] and most of the disciples of Rabban Johanan ben Zaccai, had died before that revolt had begun. There was no real leadership now. No other Nasi, president, had been chosen in Rabban Gamaliel's place. Some believed that his son, Simon, was not appointed in his father's place because of his youth. In my

אשריך ר' עקיבא שנתפסת על דברי תורה אוי לו לפפוס (בן יהודה) שנתפס על דברים
בטלים;

In the *Midrash Koheleth* Rab. 9.8, the following story is related:
ר' אחא הוה מתחמיד למחמי אפוי דר' אלכסנדרי אתחמי לי בחלמיה, הראהו תרין מילין,
הרוני לוד אין לפנים ממחיצתם (ברוך שהעביר חרפתן של לוליאנוס ופפוס), ואשרי מי
שבא לכאן ותלמודו בידו "Rabbi Alexandri appeared to Rabbi Aha in his dream and showed him two things (I disagree with my friend Dr. Lieberman who insisted that the original reading had "three things"): no compartment beyond that of the slain of Lydda (blessed be He who removed the revilement of Lulianus and Pappas) and happy is he who came here equipped with learning." Rabbi Aha saw in his dream that the "slain of Lydda" were in the future world considered righteous people and thus he proclaimed his thanks to God that the revilement against Lulianus and Pappas was removed. The word חרפה is not to be translated "shame" but "revilement, abuse." Comp. שומעים את חרפתם. Some scribe who erroneously thought that ברוך שהעביר חרפתן של לוליאנוס ופפוס is a part of R. Aha's dream changed תרין "two" to תלת "three."
This Midrash is based on the Talmud Pes. 50 אומרים שהיו ושמעתי ...
(1) אשרי מי שבא לכאן ותלמודו בידו, (2) ושמעתי שהיו אומרים הרוני מלכות
אין אדם יכול לעמוד במחיצתן ומאן נינהו אלימא רבי עקיבא וחבריו משום הרוני
לוד הרוני אלא לא והו מלכות. For other interpretations of the "slain of Lydda," see S. Lieberman, I. Sonne, *JQR* 1945, pp. 163-69; 1946, pp. 243-46; 1947, pp. 317-23.
[101] Quietus was killed either late in the summer or early in the autumn of 118 C. E.
[102] See B. M. 59b; Sanh. 68a.

opinion, he was not appointed because there was great opposition to religious leadership.[103] Whatever the reason for not choosing him in his father's place, the fact is that the Jews had no Nasi, and no central religious authority existed. There was, indeed, a spiritual vacuum. Rabbi Joshua[104] expressed himself about this period as follows: "Insolence will increase and honor dwindle, the nobility will pervert (justice), the wine will be abundant but wine will be dear."[105] He meant to say that although there would be a good harvest of grapes, the price of wine would rise because of a great demand for it since many people would be addicted to drunkenness.[106] Another younger contemporary, by the name of Phineas ben Jair (the Hasid), said: "Men of arm and men of speech grew powerful."[107] By this he meant to imply that demagogues and men of violence (unscrupulous) would rule the Jews.[107a]

According to the Talmud, two rabbis of great prominence whose parents suffered under the Roman government, were appointed by the Roman government to stamp out robbers and thieves. One was Rabbi Eleazar, the son of Rabbi Simon who, to save his life, had to hide in a cave for many years. The second was Rabbi Ishmael, the son of Rabbi Jose who, in fear of death, fled the country.

---

[103] We may assume from the Talmud R. H. that Rabbi Simon had already attained intellectual maturity before the revolt of Bar Kokba. אמר ר' שמעון בן גמליאל לא היו נוהגין כן ביבנא. Comp. also Yer. *ibid.* 4.

[104] The name of Rabbi Eliezer appears in our printed editions of the Talmud. However, in the Munich manuscript, as well as in עין יעקב, the name of Rabbi Joshua is given. Comp. also משנה ed. H. Lowe.

[105] Sota 9, 16. בעקבות משיחא חוצפא יסגא ויוקר יאמיר הגפן תתן פרייה והיין ביוקר.

[106] See also Targum to Eccl. 7.4, ולב שטיא בחדות בית ליצנוחהון אכלין ושתין ומתפנקין ולא יתבין על לבהון סינוף אחיהון.

[107] *Ibid.* רבי פנחס בן יאיר אומר משחרב בית המקדש ... ונברו בעלי זרוע ובעלי לשון.

[107a] Comp. M. Sota 3, הוא היה אומר (ר' יהושע) חסיד שוטה ורשע ערום ואשה פרושה ומכות פרושים הרי אלו מבלי עולם.

The Talmud conceals the story about these two appointees under a veil of legend. When Rabbi Eleazar was reproached for undertaking this work for the government, he replied that he was only "removing the thorns from the vineyard."[108] When Rabbi Ishmael, according to the Talmud, was reproached by Elijah, he said that he had to accept the appointment because it was the decree of the government.[109]

Why did two rabbis of such prominence become informers to help the Roman government eradicate robbers and thieves? Perhaps these so-called "robbers" were the remnants of the rebels who had been active in the revolt of Bar Kokba. It is also possible that some wicked men who had selfish motives took advantage of the revolutionary movement and made use of it for their own designs and attempted to give to their murderous acts the sanction of the party with which they asserted they were affiliated. This was during the time of the revolt against the Romans in the years 65–70.[110] As a matter of fact, whenever revo-

---

[108] B. M. 83b, אתיוה לרבי אלעזר ברבי שמעון וקא תפיס גנבי ואזיל שלח לו . . .
ר' יהושע בן קרחא חומץ בן יין עד מתי אתה מוסר עמו של אלהינו להריגה שלח ליה
קוצים אני מכלה מן הכרם שלח ליה יבא בעל הכרם ויכלה את קוציו.
[109] Ibid. 84a, ואף ר' ישמעאל ברבי יוסי מטא כי האי מעשה לידיה פגע ביה אליהו
אמר עד מתי אתה מוסר עמו של אלהינו להריגה אמר ליה מאי אעבוד הרמנא דמלכא
הוא אמר ליה אבוך ערק לאסיא את ערק ללודקיא.
[110] Comp. S. Zeitlin, *Studies in the Beginnings of Christianity*, 1923.
"As a matter of course, whenever revolution is agitated·in any nation, some wicked people who have selfish motives will take advantage of the movement and make use of it for their own designs and attempt to give to their act the sanction of the party with which they claim to be affiliated. Thus, it was during the early period of the revolutionary agitation in Judaea, when some bands of robbers, adopting the methods of the Sicarii, killed well-to-do persons, taking their lands and cattle under the pretext that these persons were pro-Romans. Some of the Procurators even extended protection to these robbers and not only had an understanding with them but were often guided by political motives. Their purpose was to bring about a reaction among the Jews against the revolutionists. Their plan was to confuse the rank and file of the people who could not readily distinguish between plain robbers and real revolutionaries whose motives were pure."

lution is agitated in any country, criminals often take advantage of it for their own benefit by adopting the methods of the revolutionists. We thus can understand why these two prominent rabbis, the sons of two great patriots, took upon themselves the task of helping the Romans wipe out this type of criminal who committed crimes while pretending to be acting for the love of the Jews. In any event, we can see from this story the chaotic state of the Jews after the revolt of Bar Kokba.

THE ASSUMPTION OF MOSES AND THE REVOLT OF BAR KOKBA

From the facts given in our short survey of the life of the Jews after the destruction of the Second Temple and bearing in mind that *The Assumption of Moses* was written since that destruction, we may assume that Chapter VII refers to the period prior to the revolt of Bar Kokba. The "pestilent"[111] and "impious men," who, the author says, "will rule," refers to the leaders of the Bar Kokba period. He also calls them "deceitful" and "devourers of the goods of the poor."[112] He was strongly opposed to the revolt. He did not believe in a Messiah. He held that God would rule the world. He even gave the exact time for the revelation of God in this world, which would be 250 "times"

---

[111] *Homines pestilentiosi.* The Greek undoubtedly read λοιμοί while the original Hebrew had פרצים. The passage in Dan. 11.14 בני פריצי עמך is rendered by the Septuagint thus υἱοὶ τῶν λοιμῶν τοῦ λαοῦ. We learn from I Maccabees (15.16–21) that during the time of Simon the Hasmonean the Romans granted the Jewish state the right to extradite and to punish according to the Jewish law any "pestilent" fellows λοιμοί, (Vulgate) *pestilentes.* The word λοιμὸν has a political connotation. The Book of Acts (24) relates that the high priest accused Paul before the Roman governor Felix, calling him λοιμὸν a troublemaker and a mover of sedition among all the Jews throughout the world. See also Taeubler, *JQR*, 1946, pp. 23–6.

[112] *(Paupe)rum bonorum comestores.*

after the death of Moses.[113] Since "time" meant a period
of seven years, a sabbatical year,[114] 250 times "seven years"
equals 1750 years. Since, according to the author, Moses'
death occurred in the year 2500 after the Creation, [and
1750 years had passed since his death, therefore] the advent
of God would be in the year 4250 A. M., that is, 490 C. E.

In Chapter VIII, the author speaks of "a vengeance"
and "wrath" that will visit the Jews as had never afflicted
them before. He says that God will stir up against them
a king of the kings who will crucify those practicing circumcision. They will be compelled to wear idols in public.
They will also be forced to blaspheme their God.[115] The
scholars who are of the opinion that this book was written
in the first two decades of the first century C. E. regard
what is said in this and the following chapters as a forecast
of what will happen to the Jews before the advent of God's
kingdom. However, Schürer and Charles[116] do not think
that these chapters present a forecast but are rather accounts of the tribulations which had already befallen the
Jews. They believe that these referred to the persecutions
of Antiochus IV. Charles was perplexed by the fact that
Chapter VIII appears after the chapter giving an account
of the Hasmoneans and Herod. He, therefore, assumed
that this chapter was transposed and believed that it
belonged after Chapter V.[116a] This theory is unacceptable.
There may be dislocations in this difficult book, but, as we
pointed out before, it could not have been written before
the destruction of the Second Temple. Furthermore, in

[113] *Erunt enim a morte — receptione — m(ea) usque ad adventum illius
tempora CCL quae fient.*

[114] See Charles, *op. cit.* Volkmar, *op. cit.*

[115] *Et cogentur palam baiulare idola eorum inquinata, quomodo sunt
pariter continentibus ea.*

[116] *Op. cit.*

[116a] *Op. cit.*

Chapter IX the author speaks of a man whose name is Taxo, and this chapter is certainly connected with Chapter VIII. Taxo, as we have shown, could not have been Eleazar of the Maccabean period, as Charles assumes. Chapter VIII undoubtedly refers to the Hadrianic persecutions and is not a forecast of future events but is a narration of past events. It is well known that Hadrian suppressed the revolt of Bar Kokba with inhuman cruelty. He not only changed the name of Jerusalem to Aelia Capitolina[117] but strove to destroy the Jewish religion. The edict against circumcision was enforced.[118] The decree against the study of the Torah was likewise enforced.[119] Whoever was found observing the Jewish religion was first tortured and then put to death. Chapter VIII is really an account of the persecutions and tribulations of the Jews after the revolt of Bar Kokba.[120]

We have suggested that Taxo is a latinized Greek word, which means *keshet*, bow. Some have held that the reference to Taxo's seven sons indicates that he was a real person and not an ideal figure.[121] It is probable that the author had Rabbi Joshua in mind when he spoke of Taxo. We must bear in mind that this book is a testament of Moses to Joshua. The verse of Zech. 6.12, which says "behold the man whose name is Zemaḥ (Branch)," referred to Joshua, the high priest. Therefore, we may assume that the word *keshet*, bow, was suggested by the words of Zech. 6.12, and that the author had in mind Rabbi Joshua, who was

---

[117] See Dio, *Roman History*, 69; Eusebius, *The Church History*, 4.

[118] Yer. Yeb. 8.

[119] Tan. 18a, (כוכבא) הרבה משוכין היו בימי בן כוזבא.

[120] The question may arise, why there was no mention of the destruction of the city and of the burning of the Temple, if the *Assumption of Moses* was compiled after the time of Bar Kokba. We must bear in mind that the text is defective and incomplete. Many passages are missing.

[121] H. H. Rowley, *The Relevance of Apocalyptic.*

opposed to the revolt. Note that Rabbi Joshua was of the tribe of Levi.[122] We must also remember that this verse of Zechariah, which is said to refer to Jesus, is not mentioned by the authors of the New Testament nor by the Apostolic Fathers, although they assumed that numerous passages from the Bible indicated that Jesus was the true Messiah. The first person to associate this verse with Jesus was Justin Martyr who lived in the time of Bar Kokba and hence was a contemporary of our author.[123] We must bear in mind the struggle among the Jewish Apocalyptists in regard to a Messiah. Our author was emphatically opposed to the idea of a Messiah; he believed in the kingdom of God ushered in by God Himself without the instrumentality of a Messiah.

As to the seven sons of Taxo, it is well known that the rabbis called their disciples "sons." We do not know how many disciples Rabbi Joshua had. The author may have had in mind a particular group of seven rabbis as disciples, "sons of Rabbi Joshua." A Midrash tells us that after the revolt was crushed seven rabbis assembled in the city of Usha: Rabbi Judah, Rabbi Meir, Rabbi Jose, Rabbi Nehmiah, Rabbi Simon ben Yochia, Rabbi Eleazar ben Jose, and Rabbi Eleazar ben Jacob.[124]

There is also a possibility that the seven sons were not real persons but were suggested by the prophecy of Zechariah: "For behold the stone that I have laid before Joshua;

---

[122] Comp. Ma'as. Sh. 5, 4; Yer. *ibid.*

[123] Justin Martyr used this verse in a dialogue with Trypho, the Jew. Whether he actually had a debate with a Jew named Trypho is questionable. But it is certain that Justin Martyr wanted to prove to the Jews that Jesus was the true Messiah by quoting a passage from Zechariah.

[124] Mid. R. Song of Songs, 2, בשלפי השמד נתכנסו רבותינו לאושא ואלו הן ר' יהודה ור' נחמיה ור' מאיר ור' יוסי ור' שמעון בן יוחai ור' אליעזר בנו של ר' יוסי הגלילי ור' אליעזר בן יעקב. In the Bab. Talmud Ber. 63b, the text has Jabneh instead of Usha. However, the text of the Midrash is correct, since these rabbis were of the post-Bar Kokba period.

upon one stone shall be seven eyes . . . and I will remove
the iniquity of the land in one day."[125] The prophecy of
Zechariah also speaks of a candlestick of gold with seven
lamps.[126] It is well known that the number seven was very
popular among the Jews, and there was a great deal of
messianic speculation about it.[127]

THE KINGDOM OF GOD

The author tells us that Taxo said to his seven sons:
"Let us fast three (days) and on the fourth day let us go
into a cave which is in the field;" and that he added: "and
let us rather die than to transgress the commands of the
Lord of lords, the God of our fathers. For if we do this
and die, our blood will be avenged before the Lord." In
the passage following, he describes the kingdom of God.
He says that when the Heavenly One will arise from His
royal throne, His wrath will burn on account of His sons
and the earth will tremble, the high mountains will be
made low, and the hills will be shaken and fall. He will
appear in order to punish the Gentiles and He will destroy
all their idols. Israel will then be happy.[128]

The text is very obscure. There is nothing, however, in
it to indicate that the death of Taxo and his seven sons
will effect the establishment of the kingdom of God. Furthermore, Taxo said to his seven sons: "Let us fast for the
space of three (days)."[129] On the fourth day, they were to

[125] 3.9, כי הנה האבן אשר נתתי לפני יהושע על אבן אחת שבעה עינים.
[126] 4.2, מנורת זהב . . . ושבעה נרתיה עליה.
[127] Comp. also the Book of Revelation where the number seven is of
great significance.
[128] *Quia exurget Summus, Deus aeternus solus, Et palam veniet ut
vindicet gentes, Et perdet omnia idola eorum. Tunc felix eris tu Istrahel.*
[129] *Jejunemus triduo, et quarto die intremus in speluncam quae est in
agro est, et moriamur potius, quam praetereamus mandata Domini Domi-
morum, Dei parentum nostrorum. Hoc enim si faciemus et moriemur,
sanguis noster vindicabitur coram Domino.*

enter a cave and perish there rather than to transgress the laws of God. "If we do this and die," Taxo said, "our blood will be avenged." It is true that the number three frequently occurs in the Bible. But why did Taxo tell his sons to fast three days and then to enter a cave to perish there, after which God would avenge their blood?

First, we must take into consideration the original Hebrew of the text and the manner in which the book was written. The original Hebrew had צמו or even תענו, which may have the connotation not of *fasting* but of *suffering* and of *affliction*. Neither does the word *triduo* refer to three days. The author of this book frequently avails himself of the use of cryptograms. It was noted before that when the author said "250 times" he actually meant 250 cycles of seven years.[130] Scholars have already noted that when the author said in Chapter I, "They shall be ruled by chiefs and kings for eighteen years," he actually referred to the fifteen judges[131] and three kings, Saul, David, and Solomon. And when he said "during nineteen years, the ten tribes will be apostates," he actually referred to the nineteen kings of Israel.[132] When the author said in

---

[130] See Hilgenfeld, *op. cit.* p. 462; Charles, *op. cit.*

[131] Othniel the son of Kenaz, Ehud the son of Gera, Shomgar the son of Anoth, Deborah, Gibeon, Abimelech, Tola the son of Puah, Jair the Gileadite, Jephthah, Ibzan, Elon the Zebulunith, Abdon the son of Hillel, Samson, Eli (the priest), Samuel.

[132] Jeroboam, Nadab, Boasha, Elah, Zimri, Omri, Ahab, Ahaziah, Jehoram, Jehu, Jehoahoz, Jehoash, Jeroboam, Zechariah, Shallum, Menahem, Pekahiah, Pekah, Hoshea.

Further, when the author says "seven will entrench the walls" *Et VII circumvallabunt muros* Charles took this to mean that seven kings will bolster the strength and advance the prosperity of Judah. The seven kings, according to Charles, were Rehoboam, Abigah, Asa, Jehoshaphat, Jehoram, Ahaziah, and Athaliah. The Midrash interprets the verse of Jer. 15.9 אומללה יולדת השבעה "she that had borne seven languisheth" as referring to seven wicked kings of Judah, Jehoram, Joash, Ahaz, Manasseh, Amon, Jehoiakim and Zedekiah. אלו שבעה מלכי יהודה רשעים יהורם יהואש אחז מנשה אמון יהויקים צדקיה (מדרש תנחומא, ילקוט

Chapter II, "And they will offer sacrifices throughout twenty years," he really meant twenty rulers of Judah, from Rehoboam to Zedekiah, including Athaliah.

Thus, we clearly see that the author of *The Assumption of Moses* resorted to the use of cryptograms. Instead of rulers, kings, he used the word "years." I venture to say that, when he said "three (days)," he actually had in mind 300 years. We must also bear in mind that the original reading was שלשה ימים. The word ימים sometimes had the connotation of "a year."[132a] We may even assume that the author used *gematria*, since the *Assumption of Moses* was compiled seventy years after the destruction of the Temple. The word ימים *equals* 100. Hence, שלשה ימים actually meant 300 years.

Taxo's statement to his seven sons that they should fast for three (days) meant that they should suffer for 300 years and that in the fourth hundred year they should go into the cave since the kingdom of God would come. By the words "let us go into the cave," the author had in mind the prophecy of Isaiah that, before the advent

שמעוני). Is this Midrash in contradiction to the *Assumption of Moses*? I believe not. On the contrary, they corroborate each other. The original Hebrew text had חמה *fury, anger,* but the Greek translator took the word חמה to mean *walls.* It is well known that homograph words which have the same spelling but differ in meaning are often mistranslated. Hence, the passage in the Midrash is most likely based on the *Assumption of Moses.*

It is worthwhile to note another mistranslation of the Hebrew. Joshua calls Moses "the lord of the word" *dominum verbi.* Charles remarks "I cannot suggest the origin of this phrase." There is no question in my mind that the Hebrew text had דבר leader. The translator took this to mean דבר word. Comp. Sanh. 8a א'ל משה ליהושע אתה והזקנים שבדור . . . אמר לו הקב'ה טול מקל והך על קדקדם דבר אחד לדור ואין שני דברין לדור. Moses was called אדון הדברין the master of the leaders, or דבר רבה like ספרא רבה (Sota 13b).

[132a] Comp. Gen. 24.55, השב הנערה אתנו ימים, the Targum of Jonathan renders the word ימים as "a year" תיסב ריבא עמנו יומי שתא חדא. Comp. also Lev. 25.29.

of God, the people would go into the caves: "And they shall go into the holes of the rocks and into the caves of the earth for the fear of the Lord and for the glory of His majesty, when He ariseth to shake terribly the earth."[133] The author of the Book of Revelation also says that before the coming of God the people would hide in caves: "And the kings of the earth and the great men and the rich men and the chief captains and the mighty men and every bond man and every free man hide themselves in the caves and in the rocks of the mountains."[134]

THE YEAR OF THE ADVENT OF GOD AND THE YEAR OF THE COMPILATION OF THE BOOK

The author of *The Assumption of Moses* awaited the establishment of the kingdom of God in the fourth century after the compilation of the book. Hence, we can actually fix the date of the writing of this book. We previously pointed out that the advent of God would be in the year 4250 A. M., i. e. 490 C. E.[135] According to the Talmud, the son of David will arrive in the eighty-fifth Jubilee.[136] A Jubilee consists of fifty years. Eighty-five times fifty are 4250 years = 490 C. E. Thus, the Messianic Age given in the Talmud corresponds exactly to the date in *The Assumption of Moses*. Another passage in the Talmud says that the Messiah will come in the year 4291 A. M.[137] I had occasion to point out that the actual reading was 4231,

[133] 2.17–9, ונשגב ד' לבדו ביום ההוא, והאלילים כליל יחלף, ובאו במערות צרים ובמחלת עפר מפני פחד ד' ומהדר גאונו בקומו לערץ הארץ.

[134] 6, 15, Καὶ οἱ βασιλεῖς τῆς γῆς καὶ οἱ μεγιστᾶνες καὶ οἱ χιλίαρχοι καὶ οἱ πλούσιοι καὶ οἱ ἰσχυροὶ καὶ πᾶς δοῦλος καὶ ἐλεύθερος ἔκρυψαν ἑαυτοὺς εἰς τὰ σπήλαια καὶ εἰς τὰς πέτρας τῶν ὀρέων.

[135] See above p. 28.

[136] Sanh. 97b, אמר ליה אליהו לרב יהודה אחוה דרב סלא חסידא אין העולם פחות משמונים וחמשה יובלות וביובל האחרון בא אמר ליה בתחלתו או בסופו . . . אמר ליה עד הכא לא תיסתכי ליה מכאן ואילך איסתכי ליה.

[137] *Ibid.* ד' אלפים ומאתים ותשעים ואחד שנה לבריאתו של עולם.

that is, in the year 471 C. E.[138] Why is 4231 designated as
the year of the Messianic age? It is because eighty-four
Jubilees are 4200 years; and thirty-one years constitute
a majority of the years and decades of the eighty-fifth
Jubilee.[139] I believe therefore we may say with certainty
that the book, *The Assumption of Moses*, was composed in
the year 140 C. E. Three hundred years of tribulations,
which the author says the Jews will suffer, would give
us 440 C. E. i. e. 4200 A. M., or eighty-four Jubilees.
When Taxo told his sons to go into caves on the "fourth"
(hundred) because of the beginning of the age of the
advent of God, he really meant the eighty-fifth Jubilee,
which the Talmud also assigned as the Jubilee of the
Messianic Age. The advent of God was expected in the
thirty-first year of this Jubilee, i. e. 4231 A. M., or 471 C. E.
Thus, 140 C. E., when *The Assumption of Moses* was composed, plus 331 gives us 471, i. e. 4231 A. M., which is the
beginning of the Messianic Age.

In a Baraita quoted in the Talmud of Abodah Zarah,
it is stated: "If in the year 4231 A. M. (471 C. E.) a man
offers you a field worth a thousand denarii for one denarius
do not buy it."[140] The reason for this was that the Jews

---

[138] *JQR*, 1946, 166. After I emended the text, I noticed that Rabbi
Elijah of Wilno had also emended the text to read שלשים ואחד instead of
תשעים ואחד. See הנהות הגר'א, נ'ב שלשים ונ'ב נמחק ותשעים.

[139] See also Tosefot Ab. Zarah 9b כשיעבור רוב יובל האחרון. In the book
of Revelation, it is said that the second millenium "is six hundred
threescore and six," because six hundred is a majority of a thousand
and three score is a majority of a century and six is a majority of ten.
Incidentally, the year 1666 was considered to be the year of the Second
Coming and this belief led to the spreading of the movement of Sabatai
Zevi, who proclaimed that in the year 1666 he would reveal himself in
the Holy Land as the Messiah.

[140] *Ibid.,* אמר ר' חנינא אחר ארבע מאות לחורבן הבית אם יאמר לך אדם קח שדה שוה
אלף דינרים בדינר אחד אל תקח, במתניתא תנא (אחר) ארבעת אלפים ומאתים ושלשים
ואחת שנה לבריאת עולם אם יאמר לך אדם קח לך שדה שוה אלף דינרים בדינר אחד
אל תקח.

either expected the advent of the Messiah or the advent of the Kingdom of God. I have often wondered what was the source of the Talmud for this Messianic Age, 4231 A. M. (471 C. E.). Now we may say with assurance that the source was the book, *The Asssumption of Moses*. As a matter of fact, the rabbis of the Talmud knew about this book. This is evident from a story related in the Tractate Sanhedrin that Rab Hanan sent a message to Rab Joseph, in which he said: "I met a man and he had a scroll written in Assyrian script and in the sacred tongue and he said that he enlisted in the Roman army and among the treasures of Rome he found a scroll, in which it was written that after 4231 A. M. (471 C. E.) the Messianic Age will arrive."[141] This scroll, which was found among the treasures of the Roman Empire, was undoubted'y *The Assumption of Moses*.[141a] We may conclude that not only did the Talmud make use of *The Assumption of Moses*, but that this book was composed in the year 140 C. E., since the date of the Messianic Age given in the Talmud corresponds exactly to the date specified in *The Assumption of Moses*.

Taxo said to his sons: "Let us die rather than transgress the commands of the Lord of lords, the God of our

---

[141] שלח ליה רב חנן בר תחליפא לרב יוסף מצאתי אדם אחד ובידו מגילה 97b, אחת כתובה אשורית ולשון קדש אמרתי לו זו מנין לך אמר לי לחיילות של רומי נשכרתי ובין גנזי רומי מצאתיה וכתוב בה לאחר ד' אלפים ומאתים (ותשעים) ושלשים ואחד שנה לבריאתו של עולם יותם מהן מלחמת חנינים מהן מלחמת גוג ומגוג והשאר ימות המשיח.

[141a] Isaac Abravanel assumed that this Megilah was written by Joseph ben Gorion. (ברומי) והמגלה ההיא דעתי שיוסף בן גריון כתבה והניחה שמה כשאר ספריו וכבר יורה על זה מה שכתב בסוף מאמר הה' מהספר שכתב אל היהודים ובספר שכתבתי אל הרומאים ספרתי כל הפלאות אשר מדינת רומי... נם כתבתי. אליהם את כל העתידות אחרי מותי עד חרב ותשומם כאשר קבלתי מפי' חכמי ישראל קרובים לנביאים וגם מפי חכמי הגוים הנאמנים בחכמתם' (מעיני הישועה, על לניאל). It is indeed strange that a man of such great knowledge was unaware that Josippon was not written by Josephus but was composed sometime at the end of the *fourth century* C. E. This is particularly surprising since Josephus had already been translated into Latin and was read by the scholarly world in the early sixteenth century.

fathers." Scholars improperly interpret this passage to mean that he told them to die in the cave and that God would avenge their blood.[142] But this passage is not connected with the previous passages when Taxo said to his sons: "Let us fast (suffer) for three (centuries) and on the fourth let us go into a cave." When Taxo said to his sons that they should die rather than transgress the commands of the Lord he emphasized that the Jews should not engage in open war against their oppressors but if they were compelled to transgress the precepts of God they should rather die than transgress. He concluded with the following words: "If we do this and die, our blood will be avenged when God will reveal Himself in His full majesty."

The idea that the Jews should not defy their oppressors, the Gentiles, by open warfare is also expressed in a story in the Midrash. The Midrash on Genesis relates that two disciples of Rabbi Joshua changed their clothes during the time of the persecutions (so that they should not be recognized as Jews and be killed). They encountered a Roman captain who said to them: "If you are the sons of the Torah, then you have to give your life for it, and if you are not, then why are you being slaughtered for it?" They answered him: "We are the sons of the Torah and we are ready to be slaughtered for the sake of the Torah but it is not the custom for human beings to commit suicide."[143]

---

[142] See Charles, op. cit.

[143] M. R. 82, שני תלמידים מטל ר' יהושע שינו עטיפתן בשעת השמד פגע בהם סרדיוט אחד אמר להם אם אתם בניה של תורה חנו נפשכם עליה, ואם אין אתם בניה למה אתם נהרנים עליה אמרו לו בניה אנו ועליה אנו נהרנים אלא שאין דרכו של אדם לאבד את עצמו לדעת. See also Ab. Zarah 18a, ת'ר כשחלה ר' יוסי בן קיסמא הלך ר' חנינא בן תרדיון לבקרו אמר לו חנינא אחי אי אתה יודע שאומה זו מן השמים המליכוה שהחריבה את ביתו ושרפה את היכלו והרנה את חסידיו ואיבדה את טוביו ועדיין היא קיימת ואני שמעתי עליך שאתה יושב ועוסק בתורה ומקהיל קהלות ברבים וספר תורה מונחת לך בחיקך אמר לו מן השמים ירחמו אמר לו אני אומר לך דברים של טעם ואתה אומר לי מן השמים ירחמו, "When Rabbi Jose ben Kisma was ill, Rabbi Hanina ben Teradion went to visit him. He said to him: 'Brother Hanina, knowest thou not that Heaven (God) has ordained this na-

The Fourth Ezra, the Apocalypse (Second) Baruch and The Assumption of Moses

The Assumption of Moses is the last of the three books of Apocrypha literature which we possess written in the second century C. E. The other two are the Fourth Ezra and the Apocalypse of Baruch. These three books present different philosophic views on Judaism and on the Messianic Age. The authors differ in their attitude toward the Jewish people. According to the Fourth Ezra, a Man—Vir— whom the Most High kept in reserve for centuries, would appear and destroy all the nations that had oppressed His chosen people.[144] *Vir* (the Messiah) would herald the kingdom of God. All the nations would join the Israelites.[145]

---

tion (Rome) to reign? For though she laid waste His House, burned His Temple, slew His pious and brought His best to destruction, still she is well established. Yet I have heard about thee that thou sittest and occupiest thyself with the Torah and gatherest assemblies and keepest a book of the Law in thy bosom.' He replied: 'Heaven (God) will show mercy.' " To this, Rabbi Jose replied: "I am talking sense to thee and thou sayest Heaven will show mercy."

This story clearly indicates that many of the sages opposed open defiance of the Roman government. Many of the rabbis looked with disapproval upon the revolt of Bar Kokba. The rabbis of the later generations considered this revolt as forcing the coming of the Messiah ahead of time, and hence taught that the Jews committed a transgression. See Mid. Rab. Song of Songs, ארבעה שבועות השביען כנגד ד' דורות שדחקו את הקץ. See also Targum on Song of Songs, השבעתי ...וכשלו. ...ואחד בימי כוזבא יאמר מלכא משיחא משביע אנא עליכון עמי בית ישראל מה דין אתון מתגרין בעמי ארעא למפק מן נלותא ומה דין אתון מרדין בחילותיה דגוג ומגוג אתעכיבו פון זעיר עד די שיצון עמסיא די עלו לאנחא קרבא לירושלים ובתר כן ידכר מרי עלמא רחמי דקמוהי למפרקכון צדקיא ויהא רעוא מן קדמוהי למפרקכון. This Midrash conveyed the following idea: The King Messiah pleaded with the Jews not to revolt against the Roman authorities and not to fight their armies, but to wait until God would redeem them.

[144] *Et tunc revelabitur filius meus, quem vidisti ut virum ascendentem . . . ipse autem filius meus arguet quae advenerunt gentes impietates eorum, has quae tempestati adpropiaverunt, et improperabit coram eis mala cogitamenta eorum et cruciamenta quibus incipient cruciari, quae assimilatae sunt flammae, et perdet eos sine labore per legem quae igni assimilata est. 13.29–38.*

[145] See S. Zeitlin, *JQR*, 1947.

There is no mention in the Fourth Ezra of the rebuilding of Jerusalem, Zion and the Temple. The author pictures the Messianic Age as the time of the establishment of the Kingdom of God. On the other hand, the author of Baruch viewed the Messianic Age as the time when the Messiah would establish a Jewish state in Judaea.[146] The author of Baruch states that the kingdom which destroyed Zion would itself be overthrown and subjugated by another which, in turn, would be overthrown, when a third kingdom would arise which also would be destroyed, and then a fourth kingdom would take its place, which would be more terrible than all that had preceded it. And when the time for the fourth kingdom to be destroyed would come, the Messiah would then be revealed.[147] The people of Israel would again find happiness, Jerusalem would be rebuilt, sacrifices would be resumed, the priests would return to their duties.[148] The nations which had not persecuted the children of Israel would be spared by the Messiah, but all those who ruled over the people of Israel would be destroyed by the sword.[149]

[146] *Et illo tempore post modicum iterum aedificabitur Sion, et constituentur iterum oblationes eius, et sacerdotes revertentur ad ministerium suum, et iterum venient gentes ut glorificent eam; veruntamen non plene sicut in initio: sed erit post haec, erit ruina gentium multarum. hae sunt aquae lucidae, quas vidisti.* 44; 68.5–6.

[147] *Ecce dies veniunt, et corrumpetur regnum istud quod olim corrupit Sion, et subiicietur illi quod venturum est post ipsum. iterum autem et illud post tempus corrumpetur, et surget aliud tertium, et dominabitur etiam illud tempore suo et corrumpetur. et post ista surget regnum quartum, cuius potestas erit dura et mala magis quam illa quae fuerunt ante ipsum . . . et erit, cum appropinquaverit tempus finis eius ut cadat, tunc revelabitur principatus Messiae mei,* 39, 3–7.

These four kingdoms are undoubtedly Babylon, Persia, Greece and Rome, the last of which the author calls the most terrible.

[148] See note 146.

[149] *Omnis populus qui non noscit Israel, neque conculcavit semen Iacob, ipse est qui vivet; et hoc, quia subiicientur ex omnibus gentibus populo tuo. omnes illi autem qui dominati sunt vobis, aut noverunt vos, isti omnes in gladium tradentur."* 72, 4–6.

The author of *The Assumption of Moses* believed that God would reveal Himself to His people and that His kingdom would be established the world over. Like the author of the Fourth Ezra, he did not approve of the restoration of Zion as a national state and of the rebuilding of the Temple. However, his ideas differ from those of the author of the Fourth Ezra. According to the latter, *Vir* (Messiah) will conquer the enemies of Israel with the sword.[150] According to the author of *The Assumption of Moses*, God will reveal Himself by His own majesty.[151]

The Fourth Ezra was composed in the first decade of the second century before the revolt of the Jews against the pagans in Cyrene and in Egypt.[152] The Book of Baruch was written in Palestine shortly before the revolt of Bar Kokba.[153] The author of *The Assumption of Moses*, who witnessed the suffering of the Jews and the catastrophe which brought about these two revolts, strongly opposed open warfare by the Jews against the Romans. He blamed the "pestilent" (troublemakers) Jews who were responsible for the calamities that befell the Jews as a consequence of the revolt of Bar Kokba. He disapproved of nationalist Jews who believed that Bar Kokba was a Messiah. He was also set against the Judeo-Christians who believed that Jesus was the Messiah.

These three Apocalyptic books are very important for a proper understanding of Jewish history and a true evaluation of Jewish life from the time of the revolt against Trajan to that against Hadrian by Bar Kokba. There are few sources for the history of this revolt. The Roman

[150] See note 144.

[151] *Quia exurget Summus, Deus aeternus solus, Et palam veniet ut vindicet gentes, Et perdet omnia idola eorum.* 10, 7.

[152] See S. Zeitlin, *JQR* 1947, p. 246.

[153] *Idem., ibid.*

historian Dio[154] and the Church historian Eusebius[155] gave only fragmentary data about them. References to these revolts in the Talmud and the Midrash are not only fragmentary but are covered with a veil of mystery and legend. Thus, these three books form a great contribution to the comprehension of Judaism and Jewish life in that period. The Fourth Ezra and the Apocalypse of Baruch respectively helped to foment these two revolts. On the other hand, the author of *The Assumption of Moses* regarded the teachings of the authors of these two books as responsible for the acts of the "pestilent" men and the great sufferings of the Jews after the suppression of the Bar Kokba revolt.

The Assumption of Moses was written in Hebrew. The author could not hope to have any influence on the Jews unless the book was written in the sacred tongue. It could not come from Moses in any other tongue than Hebrew. It is true that some Aramaic words are found in this book, but Aramaic words also appear in the Bible, even in the Pentateuch, but the entire language of *The Assumption of Moses* is in the sacred tongue.

Of course, this book is not a testament of Moses to his disciple Joshua. We cannot assume, however, that the author (and for that matter, all the authors of Apocryphal literature) was a deceiver, and really intended to tell the Jews that he had a book written by Moses. On the contrary, we know that all these authors were pious, sincere and humble Jews. There is a possibility that the authors of these books believed that by signing the names of Moses, Enoch, Ezra, Baruch, etc. the books would have a great influence upon the Jews.

There is another possibility that the author of *The Assumption of Moses* believed that if Moses lived in those

[154] *Op. cit.*
[155] *Op. cit.*

troublesome times his message to the Jews would have been the same as his own. Thus, the author concealed his identity in his devotion to his ideas and ideals. Since the author was an Apocalyptist, he may even have had a vision in which he saw Moses who gave him his testament to put into writing.

The Assumption of Moses had a great influence on Jewish thought. As we have seen before, even the date of the Messianic Age, 4231 A. M.–471 C. E. was actually based on this book. This book, however, had no influence on the Church. The ideas in it are diametrically opposed to the ideas of the Church. The author did not believe in a Messiah. One of the purposes of his writing was to oppose the view that Jesus was the Messiah. He does not mention either resurrection, or reward and punishment in a Future World.

Origen says that verse 9 of the Epistle of Jude, "yet Michael the archangel, when contending with the devil, he disputed about the body of Moses, durst not bring against him a railing accusation, but said, the Lord rebuke thee,"[156] is based on *The Assumption of Moses*. This is not historically correct. The archangel Michael is not mentioned in *The Assumption of Moses*. The story of the struggle between the archangel Michael and Satan over the burial of Moses is based on an old Midrash.[157] The fact that Origen mentioned *The Assumption of Moses* in connection with the Epistle of Jude rescued this book from total oblivion. Bishop Evodius, in his Epistle to Augus-

---

[156] See note 1.

[157] Comp. Sifre Deut., אמר לו הקב׳ה למלאך המות לך והבא לי נשמתו של משה הלך ועמד לפניו אמר לו משה במקום שאני יושב אין לך רשות לעמוד ואתה אומר לי חן לי נשמתך גער בו ויצא בנזיפה. Comp. also Mid. R. Deut. 11, כך היה סמאל הרשע מצפה נשמתו של משה ואומר יהיה מיכאל בוכה ואני ממלא פי שחוק . . . באותה שעה אמר הקב׳ה לגבריאל נבריאל צא והבא נשמתו של משה . . . אמר למיכאל צא והבא נשמתו של משה.

tine, also says: "In the Apocrypha and in the Mysteries of Moses, a writing which is wholly devoid of authority, it is indeed said that at the time when he (Moses) ascended to the mount to die . . . there was one body which was committed to the earth, and another which was joined to the angel who accompanied him."[158] This story is likewise based on a Midrash.[159]

The Assumption of Moses is the last literary composition we have of Apocryphal literature. The earliest book is Jubilees, composed in the fifth century B. C. E.[160] Thus, the period of Apocryphal writing extended over half a millenium. This literature represents the *dissenting ideas* in Judaism during the Second Commonwealth. The leaders of Normative Judaism considered these writings pernicious and dangerous. Therefore, the rabbis who called these books "outside books"[161] prohibited the Jews from reading them. They pronounced that "anyone who reads outside books will not have a portion in the future world."[162]

[158] *Quamquam et in apocryphis et in secretis ipsius Moysi, quae scriptura caret auctoritate, tunc, cum ascenderet in montem, ut moreretur, ui corporis efficitur, ut aliud esset, quod terrae mandaretur, aliud, quod angelo comitanti sociaretur. sed non satis urguet me apocryphorum proferre sententiam illis superioribus rebus definitis. Epistularum 158.*

[159] Comp. Mid. R. Deut. 11, באותה שעה עמד משה וקידש את עצמו כשרפים וירד הקב"ה משמי שמים העליונים ליטול נשמתו של משה ונ' מלאכי השרת עמו מיכאל וגבריאל וזגנאל... א"ל הקב"ה נשמה צאי אל האחרי ואני מעלה אותך לשמי שמים העליונים ואני מושיבך תחת כסא כבודי אצל כרובים ושרפים. The story about the burial of Moses as given by Clement of Alexandria *The Stromata*, 6, 15, is also based on a Midrash. Comp. also Sota 13b–14a, מלמד שהיה משה מוטל בכנפי שכינה... היכן משה קבור עמדו למעלה נדמה להם למטה, למטה נדמו להם למעלה נחלקו לשתי כיתות אותן שעמדו למעלה נדמה להן למטה, למטה נדמו להן למעלה. See also Targum of Jerusalem, Deut. 34.6. Some scholars are of the opinion that the phrase "mediator" ἐν χειρὶ μεσίτου, in the Epistle of the Galatians, shows evidence that the author of this epistle was acquainted with the *Assumption of Moses* where Moses is called "mediator" *ut sim arbiter testamenti illius* (1, 14). However, Philo had already called Moses a mediator μεσίτης. *The Life of Moses* III, 19.

[160] See S. Zeitlin, *The Book of Jubilees*, 1939.

[161] ספרים חצונים.   [162] כל הקורא בהן אין לו חלק לעולם הבא.

After the catstrophe of Bar Kokba, Normative Judaism became well established. When the rabbis assembled in the town Usha they laid the foundation for the codification of the *Halaka*. The Apocalyptists who, before the revolt of Bar Kokba, still speculated about mysticism, were no longer a power to be reckoned with. Christianity ceased to be a Jewish heretical sect. It became a different religion. It was no longer dominated by Judeo-Christians.

While Normative Judaism then prevailed and there was no longer a struggle between Normative Judaism and the mysticism of the Apocalyptists, nevertheless, the rabbis did not succeed in entirely eradicating the Apocalyptic ideas. During the Middle Ages, we again note the fruits of the Apocalyptists in a new mystic literature upon which the rabbis were again compelled to launch an attack.

In times of crisis, the ideas of the Apocalyptists usually take hold of great masses of the Jewish people. As in the days of the Second Commonwealth, the Apocalyptists, whom Josephus called "deceivers," brought about much suffering of the Jews.[163] Thus, in the Middle Ages, the Cabbalists, the successors of the Apocalyptists, brought great misfortune upon the Jewish people. I refer to Sabbatai Zevi and his followers.

The history of the Second Jewish Commonwealth was written mostly by the students of the New Testament, since they were interested in the origin of Christianity. These writers gave preference to one set of sources: Josephus, the New Testament and the Hellenistic literature. The tannaitic literature, particularly the Halaka, was entirely ignored. It is well known that the legal structure of a nation is the foundation of its existence and that the laws are based on the social, economic and religious life of

[163] See note 85.

the people. The Apocryphal literature was improperly used by the historians because of the numerous errors in the Greek translations and to the improper dating of these books. The Jews had almost entirely ignored this literature. To understand Judaism and the Jewish people, however, we must not only make a study of the literature of Normative Judaism but also of the literature of the *dissenters*. This literature presents a phase of thought among the Jewish people and it had an important influence upon the development of Judaism throughout the ages.[164] Nevertheless, in order to make use of the Apocryphal literature, we must first establish a proper text. There is indeed a crying need for editing anew this great literature which has been so greatly instrumental in shaping western civilization.

---

[164] It is surprising that Dr. G. Scholem, in his book *The Major Trends of Mysticism*, did not take cognizance of the influence of the apocalyptic literature on the Cabbala.

The Essenes and Messianic Expectations

by S. ZEITLIN

The Essenes believed in fate, that all things were pre-ordained by God. They held that anyone who was appointed ruler should be respected, and that no ruler attained his office except by the will of God.[65] This applied not only to their own rulers but also to the rulers of the Judaeans. A king like Herod, they believed, should be respected because it was God's will that he attained this high office.[66]

They believed in immortality of the soul, that it is imperishable and never dies. As Josephus says, they believed the soul emanates from the finest ether, that it is a prisoner of the body but is freed from it after death.[67] They believed the righteous would be rewarded after death, while the souls of the wicked would undergo everlasting punishment. The Essenes, according to Philo, used to assemble in the synagogue on the Sabbath,[68] to read the

---

[65] *Jewish War*, 2.140.

[66] Comp. *Ant.* 15.37–4. Menahem the Essene said to Herod: "You will reign for God has deemed you worthy."

[67] *Jewish War*, 2.154–5. "The body is corruptible and its constituent matter impermanent, but that the soul is immortal and imperishable. Emanating from the finest ether αἰθέρος, these souls become entangled, as it were, in the prison-house of the body, to which they are dragged down by a sort of natural spell: but when once they are released from the bonds of the flesh, then, as though liberated from a long servitude, they rejoice and are borne aloft."

[68] οἵ καλοῦνται συναγωγαί.

102

Torah. One would read aloud and another would expound difficult passages. Josephus does not use the word synagogue. He says they used to come together in a particular place.[69] The practice of assembling on the Sabbath to read the Torah was not singularly an Essenaic custom. Josephus tells us in his book *Contra Apionem* that the Jews used to assemble on the Sabbath to listen to the reading of the Torah.[70] The term synagogue in Philo may have the connotation of assembly for any purpose as well as for the reading of the Torah, but not for the saying of prayers. They had another term for the house of prayers, *proseuche*.[71]

Hippolytus says that all the Jewish sects expected a Messiah. Undoubtedly this was true in the end of the second century CE.[72] Most of the Jews expected a Redeemer to free them from the Romans, and to reestablish their state and rebuild the Holy Temple. During the Second Commonwealth, however, the Jews did not expect a Messiah in the sense that we understand the term today. They believed that God would help them to vanquish their enemies as he had done in the time of David and Judah Maccabee. Only one group, the Apocalyptists, a Pharisaic sect, believed that a Redeemer would eventually free the Jews from their oppressors, and that he would be the Messiah endowed with supernatural powers.

The word משיח Messiah has the meaning of anointed one. The priests and kings during the period of the First Temple all were anointed with oil.[72a] This anointment was considered divine and they were called the Lord's anointed משיח ה'. Even a pagan king who was anointed was surnamed Mes-

[69] *Op. cit.*
[70] 2.175.
[71] Comp. S. Zeitlin, "The Origin of the Synagogue," *AAJR*, 1931.
[72] Comp. note 42.
[72a] Comp. also *The Testament of Levi*, 8.4, "anointed me with holy oil"; Ps. 23.5; 45.18; 133.2.

siah, like King Cyrus.[73] In the time of the Second Commonwealth neither the priests nor the kings of Judaea were
anointed.[73a] They were no longer called the Lord's anointed.
The term Messiah came to have a new meaning, — those
who were anointed by the holy spirit. Jesus who was called
Messiah, Christ, by his followers was never anointed with
oil. The gospels do not record that Jesus was ever anointed
with oil by John the Baptist or any one else.[74]

There were two offshoots from the Pharisees. One was
the sect organized by Judah, the Galilean which sponsored
the Fourth Philosophy, whose aim was to fight the Romans
and force the leaders of the Jews to make war against them.[75]
Its methods were terroristic. It was a minority group, and
as it could not expect victory in open battle it resorted to
other tactics. All the members of this sect kept a sica
(dagger) hidden under their garments and assassinated
anyone whom they suspected of being pro-Roman. They
spread terror among the leaders of the Jews. Because of
their practice of carrying a *sica* concealed in their garments
Josephus called them *Sicarii*.[76]

The other offshoot of the Pharisees was called the "Apocalyptists" because they believed in the revelation of God.
Their views agreed with followers of the Fourth Philosophy
in their hatred of the Romans, and they regarded their own
leaders wicked and traitorous because they sold themselves
out to the Romans. They were opposed, however, to
terroristic methods. Being against fighting the Romans
with arms, they looked for divine intervention for the

---

[73] Isa. 45.1. ‏כה אמר ה' למשיחו לכורש‎.

[73a] Comp. also Yoma, 52, ‏משנגז . . . שמן המשחה‎.

[74] It is never stated in the apocalyptic literature where the name
Messiah frequently occurs, and his functions described, that he will
be anointed with oil.

[75] Comp. Josephus, *Jewish War*, 2.118.

[76] *Ibid.* 254–57; 7.252–55.

freedom of Israel. They preached that the day would come when the Messiah would be sent by God to free them and punish their oppressors and all evildoers. They believed that the Messiah existed before creation, and that he would eventually reveal himself and be glorified by all the people of the earth. He would sit on the throne of his father David.[77] The *Apocalyptists* were the forerunners of Christianity.

Only in apocalyptic literature like the Book of Enoch, Psalms of Solomon, The Testament of the Twelve Patriarchs, etc., is the idea of the Messiah well developed, while in the apocryphal literature such as the four books of the Maccabees, Judith, The Wisdom of Solomon, the Letter of Aristeas, Tobit, etc., regardless of where the books were written, in Judaea or the Diaspora, there *is no mention* of Messianic expectations.

The Jews of the Second Commonwealth did not look toward a Messiah. Most if not all histories of the Second Jewish Commonwealth *are vitiated* with the idea of Messianic expectations. Jewish as well as Christian theologians have interpreted certain biblical and apocryphal passages as referring to a Messiah, the Christian theologians to their Messiah and the Jewish to theirs. I have no quarrel with them. On the contrary, I admire their theological efforts. All honor to the theologians. A people must have a sacred theology. My objections are to the historians who are deluded by the idea that Messianic expectations occupied the Jews during the Second Commonwealth, and who write books on Messianic expectations.[78] They not only deceive

[77] Comp. Psalms of Solomon; Enoch; The Testaments of the Twelve Patriarchs.

[78] I refer to writers who speculate on the Messianic expectation and its origin during the Second Commonwealth. The Jews then except the Apocalyptists, did not expect a Messiah. I do not refer to authors who deal with Messianic expectations after the destruction of the

their readers, *but they distort the entire Jewish history of that period*. Messianic expectations came in only after the destruction of the Second Temple. During the Second Commonwealth, the *Apocalyptists* expected a Messiah, but the Jews in general did not have any notion about the coming of a Messiah. It originated with the *Apocalyptists* who, because they were opposed to terroristic methods, propagated the doctrine that God would send them a prophet, a man of supernatural power to vanquish their enemy.

In neither the works of Philo nor of Josephus is there any mention of a Messiah or any inkling of Messianic expectations. It has been generally assumed that Josephus did not mention the Messiah because he feared his benefactors, the Flavian family. This assumption has no validity. If he had been aware that the Jews expected a Messiah, he would have said so, but he probably would have used in this connection such appellatives as "charlatan" and "imposter," so that the Romans should not suspect him of any seditious views. In describing the *Apocalyptists* he says, "They were deceivers and imposters, under the pretense of divine inspiration fostering revolutionary changes. They persuaded the multitude to act like madmen and led them out into the desert under the belief that there God would give them tokens of deliverance."[79] If Josephus had known of the Messianic expectations among the Jews he would have given an account of the movement in such a way as to make sure that the Roman authorities would not suspect him of belief in such expectations.

Temple. The Jews at that time speculated on the coming of the Messiah. The book of Dr. A. H. Silver, *A History of Messianic Speculations in Israel*, is an important and valuable work.

[79] *Jewish War*, 2.258–9. Comp. also *ibid*. "Besides these (the Sicarii) there arose another body of villains, with purer hands but more impious intentions, who no less than the assassins ruined the peace of the city." ·

Hippolytus says that the Jews believed in a Messiah but
denied that Christ was the Messiah, and that they held he
would be a scion of David, "not from a virgin and the Holy
Spirit, but from a woman and a man." ... "They [the
Jews] allege," he writes, "that this Messiah will be king
over them, a warlike and powerful individual, who after
having gathered the entire nation of the Jews and having
done battle with all the Nations, will restore for them
Jerusalem the royal city. And into this city he will collect
the entire nation, and restore the ancient customs, that it
may fulfil the royal and priestly functions, and dwell in
confidence for a period of time, and that a war would next
be waged against them after being thus congregated, and
in this war Messiah would fall by the edge of the sword.
Shortly after this there will be the conflagration and
termination of the universe."[80]

Hippolytus' account of the Jewish belief in the Messiah,
which undoubtedly reflects in some way the ideas of the
Jews of his time, is illuminating. It sheds light on rabbinic
utterances in regard to the Messiah. According to a talmudic statement the Jews believed in two Messiahs, one
of the tribe of Joseph, or rather who was an Ephraimite,
and the other a scion of David. The Messiah ben Ephraim
would be killed in battle[81] and then the ben David Messiah
would arrive. Thus the Talmud corroborates Hippolytus

---

[80] γένεσιν μὲν γὰρ αὐτοῦ ἐσομενην λέγουσιν ἐκ γένους Δαβίδ
ἀλλ᾽ οὐκ ἐκ παρθένου καὶ ἁγίου πνεύματος, ἀλλ᾽ ἐκ γυναικὸς καὶ
ἀνδρός ... φάσκοντες τοῦτον ἐσόμενον βασιλέα ἐπ᾽ αὐτούς, ἄνδρα
πολεμιστὴν καὶ δυνατόν, ὃς ἐπισυνάξας τὸ πᾶν ἔθνος Ἰουδαίων
πάντα τὰ ἔθνη πολεμήσας, ἀναστήσει αὐτοῖς τὴν Ἱερουσαλὴμ
πόλιν βασιλίδα, εἰς ἣν ἐπισυνάξει ἅπαν τὸ ἔθνος καὶ πάλιν ἐπί
τὰ ἀρχαῖα ἔθη ἀποκαταστήσει βασιλεῦον καὶ ἱερατεῦον καὶ κατοικοῦν
ἐν πεποιθήσει ἐν χρόνοις ἱκανοῖς. ἔπειτα ἐπαναστῆναι κατ᾽ αὐτῶν
πόλεμον ἐπισυναχθέντων. ἐν ἐκείνῳ τῷ πολέμῳ πεσεῖν τὸν Χριστὸν
ἐν μαχαίρῃ, ἔπειτα μετ᾽ οὐ πολὺ τὴν συντέλειαν καὶ ἐκπύρωσιν
τοῦ παντὸς ἐπιστῆναι.

[81] Tal. Suk. 52. שרה משיח בן יוסף ששהרג. Comp. also IV Ezra, 7.28.

that a Messiah would be killed in battle. Most scholars hold that the conception of a Messiah ben Ephraim is based on the 12th chapter of Zechariah.[82] A conception using this type of reasoning is not sound and historians should not accept it. It belongs in the realm of theology rather than in that of history. An idea which becomes deeply rooted in a people may be the outgrowth of religious, political, or social conditions. Leaders in order to propagate the idea then quote scripture to support it.

After the destruction of the Second Temple, the adherents of the Fourth Philosophy whom Josephus called the *Sicarii*, continued to agitate for a new revolt against Rome. They caused disturbances in Egypt,[83] in Cyrenaica[84] and in Judaea proper. This agitation gained many recruits. When Trajan died in 117 during the war with the Parthians, the Jew of Judaea began to prepare for war against the Romans. This preparation which began in 122 culminated in an open struggle in 132. The man who headed this revolt was named Simon, and many proclaimed him King Messiah. One of his great followers was Rabbi Akiba. Simon was named bar Kokba, i. e., King Messiah,[85] and he apparently maintained that he was of the family of David.[86] The revolt ended with the greatest catastrophe for the Jews.

After this debacle the Jews were in a state of deep gloom and depression. Their national and spiritual life suffered a great setback. The explanation which was advanced that Simon was not the Messiah but was a deceiver, *Bar Koseba*,

[82] Comp. *ibid.* ‎וכפדה הארץ . . . חד אמר על משיה בן יוכף שנהרג‎.
[83] *Jewish War*, 2.410–19.
[84] *Ibid.* 7.437–44.
[85] Comp. Yer. Tan. 4. ‎ר׳ עקיבה כד הוה חמי בר כוזבה [בר כוכבה] אמר‎ ‎דרך כוכב . . . כד‎ Comp. also Targum Numb. 24.17 ‎דין הוא מלכא משיחא‎. ‎יקום מלכא מיעקב ויתרבא משיחא‎ Comp., also *The Testament of Judah*, 24.1, "shall arise the star," ‎כוכב‎, i.e. Messiah.
[86] Yer. *ibid.* ‎עקיבה יעלו עשבים בלחייך ועדיין בן דוד לא בא‎.

gave them no solace. They looked to their leaders for a
better explanation than that they had been deceived. A
theory was set up that this collapse was only temporary,
that although Simon was the Messiah, he was not of the
Davidic family, but of the Ephraim family, and that as a
matter of fact the killing of the Ephraimite Messiah had
already been foretold by the Prophet Zechariah. Subsequently the other Messiah who would be of the Davidic
family would appear and wreak vengeance upon the gentiles. This had been foretold by Zechariah.[87] Some were
of the opinion that there would be no Messiah, but that
God would reveal himself and destroy all the enemies of the
Jews, and that He would gather all the Jews from the four
corners of the earth into the Holy Land. These enemies
were designated under a collective name, *Gog* and *Magog*.
These names were derived from Ezekiel.[88]

The reason the Jews expected a Messiah of the Davidic
family is well known; however, the source of the expectation
that another Messiah would come and that he would be an
Ephraimite still needs clarification.

There had been rivalry between the Judaean and the
Ephraimite tribes. The first king over the ten tribes was
Jeroboam, an Ephraimite, who revolted against Solomon.
We learn from the Pentateuch that when Moses sent men
on the mission to investigate the land of Canaan, they came
with discouraging reports, except Caleb of the tribe of
Judah, and Joshua the son of Nun, of the tribe of Ephraim.[89]
Since the two latter brought in good reports about the land of
Canaan, God rewarded both tribes. David was of the tribe
of Judah, while Joshua, the first ruler after Moses, came

---

[87] On the Messiah ben Ephraim, see C. Torrey, *JBL*, 1947; H. H.
Rowley, *The Servant of the Lord*, pp. 64–75.

[88] 38–39. Comp. Eduy. 2.10.

[89] Num. 13–14.

from the tribe of Ephraim. These two tribes would later be associated in that the first Messiah would be an Ephraimite,[90] and the second would be of the Davidic family.

There is a legend in rabbinic literature that the Ephraimites left Egypt before the day God set for the exodus, and consequently they were slain.[91] This is analogous to a second redemption. In the first redemption the Ephraimites were killed, because they forced the time of the redemption in leaving Egypt ahead of the time set. Later the Messiah of Ephraim was also killed because the Jews forced the time of redemption before the predestined time.

On the other hand, some Jews even after the time of Bar Kokba did not believe in any Messiah. They expected God himself to save and redeem them from their enemies. The author of the book The Assumption of Moses, which was composed in the year 140 CE,[92] calls those who led the Bar Kokba revolt pestilent men and deceivers. Normative Judaism or Pharisaic Judaism still continued to oppose any idea of a Messiah. Rabbi (Judah the prince) who was the leader in normative Judaism composed the Mishne[92a] which was to be second in authority to the Bible. He does not

[90] Comp. Targum of Jonathan, Ex. 40.11, דעל ידוי . . . דהושע כביל יהושע. עהידא ארעא דישראל לאיהפלאא ומשיחא בר אפרים דנפיק כינה.
[91] See Tal. Sanh. 92, בני אפרים שמנו לקץ וטעו; Targum of Jonathan Ps. 78.9, כד הוו יתבין במצרים אהרברבו בני אפרים כנו קצא וטעו ונפקו הלתין. שנים קדם קצא . . . ואתקטלו ביום קדרי קרבא. Comp. Midrash R. Song of Songs, 2, צדהקו את הקץ ונכשלו . . . ואחד ביםי כובא ואחד ביםי שוהלה בן אפרים.
[92] Comp. S. Zeitlin, "The Assumption of Moses and the Revolt of Bar Kokba," JQR, 1947.
[92a] The word משנה has the connotation "study" and "second." The halakot which Rabbi Judah collected and codified was called כ'שנה i.e., second to the Pentateuch. The transliteration of the word כ'שנה Mishna hitherto used is incorrect. In the edict issued by the Roman government forbidding the study of the כ'שנה the term δευτερωσις (second) was employed. (Comp. Justinian Novellae, 146.1-2) Thus it is evident that in Palestine the word כשנה was pronounced Mishne. In this essay I therefore transliterate the word כ'שנה Mishne. I hope to present a full study of the Mishne and Tosefta in the near future.

mention Messiah — an omission which would be impossible
if normative Judaism believed in one. It is true that the
words "the days of Messiah" occur in the first chapter of
Berakot[93] and in the last chapter of *Sota*;[94] however, these
passages are later additions after the death of Rabbi. As
the name of Rabbi is mentioned in the passage of Sota,[95]
we may assume that these words were introduced after his
death. In the passage of Mishne *Berakot* of the Babylonian
Talmud, the text reads כל להביא לימות המשיח, whereas in the
Mishne of the Palestinian Talmud the text has as follows: כל
ימי חייך עולם הבא להביא את ימות המשיח. In my opinion the words
ימות המשיח "the days of Messiah" point to a later interpretation; however, it is *a fact that Messiah is not mentioned
in the entire Mishne*. It is stated there that all the Israelites
would have a share in the future world. Those who did not
believe that the Torah was revealed by God would not have
such a share. Resurrection, the Future World, and Revelation are stressed in the Mishne.[95a] Since Messiah is not
mentioned, we have conclusive proof that even after the
destruction of the Temple, normative Judaism for a
century and a half did not entertain the idea of a Messiah.

Pharisaic or normative Judaism dominated Jewish life
after the Bar Kokba catastrophe. The books of the
Apocalyptists were banned and the people were forbidden
to read them under the risk of losing their portion in the
future world.[96] Nevertheless the ideas of the Apocalyptists,
particularly in reference to the idea of a Messiah, were not
eradicated. In times of persecution and under suffering and

---

[93] והכמים אומרים ימי חייך העולם הזה כל להביא ימות המשיח.

[94] בעקבות משיחא הוצפא יכנא.

[95] משכה רבי בכל ענוה ויראת דטא.

[95a] (Comp. also Yer. Pea 1) האומר אין תהיית המתים ואין תורה מן השמים.

[96] ואלו שאין להם הלק לעולם הבא...ר' עקיבא אומר אף הקורא בספרים
החצונים. See Joshua Bloch, *On the Apocalyptic in Judaism*, Philadelphia,
1952.

distress, the Jews did turn to the idea of a Messiah, believing he would save them and take revenge on their enemies. The Jewish sages, the Tannaim and Amoraim, were occupied with the idea of the advent of a Messiah. Some of them foretold the day of his coming, and also described the turmoil and anguish which would precede it.[97] Christianity undoubtedly gave an impetus in shaping the conception of the supernatural Messiah among the Jews.

The idea of a Messiah undoubtedly afforded great spiritual comfort to the Jews, especially during their persecutions, but it also brought many catastrophies to them. Many false Messiahs appeared, and the Jews suffered spiritually as well as politically. After the great massacre of the Jews in 1648, a false Messiah named Sabbatai Zevi appeared, and he held great sway over the Jewish people regardless of class distinction. The ignorant as well as the learned accepted him as the true Messiah. The Jews had to have an outlet for their great misfortunes in which almost a third of the people, was destroyed.

We may say with some assurance that the recent establishment of the State of Israel has saved the Jewish people from the rise of a false Messiah, as an aftermath of one of the greatest catastrophies which has befallen the Jews, when about six million, more than a third of their number, the flower of the people, were exterminated. Such a catastrophe could not but have raised great mental disquietude, particularly among the orthodox Jews. The questions would have been raised, where was Providence, where was the God of Israel, the protector of His people? The answer might have been the rise of false Messiahs as an outlet. But the establishment of the State of Israel gave a partial answer to various perplexities. The State of Israel is,

97 Comp. Tal. Sanh. 97–9. Many rabbis vehemently opposed those who set dates for the coming of the Messiah.

according to the belief of some orthodox Jews אתחלתא
דגאולה "the beginning of the redemption."

Although the Jews have not succumbed to false Messiahs,
they did not escape the intellectual decline characteristic
of pseudo-Messianism. We refer to the literature of sym-
bolism and mysticism which has become prevalent among
the Jews, — a literature which is a synchronized Judaism
and Christianity, but is neither Judaism nor Christianity.
The literature is the production of so-called neo-orthodox.
Neither the orthodox nor the liberals indulge in such a
literature.[98] Unfortunately it is published by creditable
publishers and national organizations, although it surely
is a passing fad; nevertheless it does great harm to the youth
who are not well versed in Judaism. In Israel, however,
the people do not indulge in this pseudo-theological
literature.

[98] We may safely assume that Maimonides even in his time, the
thirteenth century, would have branded such literature as belonging to
the type of obscurantism.

Bibliography

Abbott, Edwin A. *The Son of Man,* Cambridge, 1910.

Allegro, J. M. "Further Messianic References in Qumran Literature" *JBL* 75 (1956), pp. 174–87.

Aptowitzer, V. "Die Zukunftshoffnung Israels in der Assyrischen Zeit." *Theologische Abhandlungen Holtzman's Festgabe.* Leipzig, 1902.

Bamberger, B. J. "Revelation of Torah after Sinai." *HUCA* 16 (1941), pp. 97–113.

Beasley-Murray, G. R. "The Two Messiahs in the Testament of the Twelve Patriarchs. *JTS* 48 (1947), pp. 1–12.

Ber, M. "Mashehu al R. Judah Aḥave d'R. Sella Ḥasida." *Sinai* 48 (1961), pp. 299–302.

Borenstein, "Ta'arikei Israel." *Hatekufah* 9, pp. 222 ff.

Böklen, E. *Die Verwandschaft der jüdischen-christlichen mit der Pärsischen Eschatologie.* Göttingen, 1902.

Bousset-Gressman, Wm. *Die Religion des Judentums im Neutestamentlichen Zeitalter.* Berlin, 1903.

Briggs, C. A. *Messianic Prophecy.* New York, 1886.

Cohen, B. "Letter and Spirit in Jewish and Roman Law." *M. Kaplan Jubilee Volume,* pp. 109–36. New York, 1953.

Cohen, Gerson. *Messianic Postures of Ashkenazim and Sephardim.* Leo Baeck Memorial Lecture IX. New York, 1967.

Dalman, G. H. *Der leidende und sterbende Messias der Synagoge.* Berlin, 1888.

Davies, W. D. *Christian Origins and Judaism.* London, 1962.

———. *Paul and Rabbinic Judaism.* London, 1953.

———. *The Setting of the Sermon on the Mount.* Cambridge, 1964.

———. *Torah in the Messianic Age.* Philadelphia, 1952.

De Jonge, Marnius. "Jewish Expectations about the 'Messiah'According to the Fourth Gospel." *NTS* 14 (1972), pp. 246–70.

Dix, G. H. "The Messiah ben Joseph." *JTS* (1926), pp. 130–43.

Drummond, J. *The Jewish Messiah.* London, 1877.

Dürr L., "Ursprünge und Ausbau der Israelitisch-jüdischen Heilandserwartung." *Theologische Literaturzeitung* 18 (1926).

Ehrlich, E. L. *"Ein Beitrag zur Messiaslehre der Qumransekte."* *ZAW* 68 (1956), pp. 234–43.

Eshkoli, A. Z. *HaTenuot HaMeshiḥiyut beYisrael.* Jerusalem, 1956.

515

Finkelstein, L. "Some Aspects of Early Rabbinic Nationalism." *Brandeis Avuḳah Annual of 1932*, pp. 78–96.

Friedman, M. *Introduction to Seder Eliyahu,* pp. 2–44. Vienna, 1902.

Friedrich, F. "Beobachtungen zur messianischen Hohepriester erwartung in den Synoptikenn." *Zeitschrift für Theologie und Kirche* 53 (1956), pp. 265–311.

Goodspeed, E. J. *Israel's Messianic Hope*. New York, 1960.

Greenstone, J. *The Messiah Idea in Jewish History*. Philadelphia, 1906.

Gressman, Hugo. *Der Messias*. Göttingen, 1929.

————. *Der Ursprung der Israelitisch-jüdischen Eschatologie*. 1905.

————. "The Sources of Israel's Messianic Hope." *AJT* 17 (1913), pp. 173–94.

Haran, M. "The Conceptions of the 'Taheb' in the Samaritan Religion." *Tarbiz* 23 (1942), pp. 96–111.

Heinemann, I. "Messianismus und Mysterienreligion." *MGWJ* 69 (1925), pp. 343–55.

Heinemann, J. "The Messiah of Ephraim and the Premature Exodus of the Tribe of Ephraim." *HTR* 68 (1975), pp. 1–15.

Higgins, A. J. B. "Jewish Messianic Belief in Justin Martyr's *Dialogue with Trypho*." *NT* 9 (1967), pp. 298–305.

————. "Priest and Messiah." *VT* 3 (1953), pp. 321–36.

————. "The Priestly Messiah." *NTS* 13 (1967), pp. 211–39.

Holdheim, S. *Das Ceremonialgesetz im Messiasreich*. Schwerin, 1845.

Hölscher, G. *Die Ursprünge der jüdischen Eschatologie*. Giessen, 1925.

Holtzmann, Das Messias bewusstsein Jesu u. seine neuste Bestreitung, Giessen, 1902.

Hruby, Kurt Von. "Die Messiaserwartung in der Talmudischen Zeit, mit besonderer Berücksichtigung des Leiden den Messias." *Judaica* 20 (1964), pp. 6–22, 73–90, 193–212; 21 (1965), pp. 100–122.

Hühn, E. *Die Messianische Weissagungen*. Freiburg, 1899.

Hurwitz, S. *Die Gestalt des sterbenden Messias*. Zurich, 1948.

Isser, S. "Dositheus, Jesus, and a Moses Arethology." *Christianity, Judaism and other Greco-Roman Cults IV,* ed. J. Neusner, pp. 167–89. Leiden, 1975.

Kaufmann, J. *Midrashe Geulah*. Jerusalem, 1954.

Kasher, M. *Hateḳufah Hagedolah*. Jerusalem, 1969.

Klausner, J. *Die messianischen Vorstellung des jüdischen Volkes im Zeitalter der Tannaiten*. Berlin, 1904.

————. *The Messianic Idea in Israel*. New York, 1955.

Kosmala, H. "At the End of the Days." *Annual of the Swedish Theological Institute* 11 (1963), pp. 27–37.

Kuhn, K. G. "The Two Messiahs of Aaron and Israel." *The Scroll and the New Testament,* ed. K. Stendhal. New York, 1957.

Liver, Jacob. "The Doctrine of the Two Messiahs in Sectarian Literature in the Time of the Second Commonwealth." *HTR* 52 (1952), pp. 149–85.

———. *Toldot Bet David.* Jerusalem, 1959.

Löwy, M. "Die Paulinische Lehre vom Gesetz." *MGWJ,* (1903), pp. 322–39, 417–33, 534–44; (1904), 267–76, 321–27.

Marmorstein, A. "Meḥashvei Ḳitzim." *HaIvri,* 10, pp. 12–13.

———. "Rayon HaGeulah beAggadat haTannaim." *Sefer Zikkaron likhbod A. Marmorstein,* pp. 16–76. London, 1950.

———. "Zur Aptowitzer's Parteipolitik d. Hasmonäerzeit." *MGWJ* 73 (1929), pp. 244–50, 478–87.

Meyer, E. *Ursprung und Anfänge des Christentums* I (1921); II (1922).

Moore, G. F. *Judaism,* vol. II, pp. 323–76. Cambridge, 1966.

Mowinckel, S. *He That Cometh.* Oxford, 1956.

Oesterley, W. O. E. *The Evolution of the Messianic Idea.* New York, 1909.

Parker, Pierson. "The Meaning of 'Son of Man.'" *JBL* 60 (1941), pp. 151–57.

Posnanski, A. *Schilo, Ein Beitrag zur Geschichte der Messiaslehre.* Leipzig, 1909.

Rowley, H. H. *The Servant of the Lord and Other Essays on the Old Testament.* London, 1952.

Sarachek, J. *The Doctrine of the Messiah in Medieval Jewish Literature.* New York, 1932.

Scheftelowitz, J. *Die altpersische Religion und das Judentum.* 1920.

Schmidt, N. "The Origin of Jewish Eschatology." *JBL* 41 (1922), pp. 102–14.

———. "Recent Study of the Term 'Son of Man.'" *JBL* 45 (1926), pp. 326–49.

———. "Was בר אנש a Messianic Title?" *JBL* 15 (1896), pp. 36–53.

Scholem, Gershom. *The Messianic Idea in Judaism.* New York, 1971.

———. "Zur Verständnis der messianische Idee im Judentum." *Eranos-Jahrbuch* 28 (1959), pp. 193–239.

Schubert, K. "Zwei Messiasse aus dem Regelbuch von Chirbet Qumran." *Judaica* 2 (1955), pp. 216–35.

Silberman, H. L. "The Two 'Messiahs' of the Manual of Discipline." *VT* 5 (1955), p. 77–82.

Silver, A. H. *A History of Messianic Speculation in Israel.* Boston, 1959.

Smith, H. P. "The Origin of the Messianic Hope in Israel." *AJT* 14 (1910), pp. 337–60.

Spiegel, Sh. "Ezekiel and Pseudo-Ezekiel?" *HTR* 24 (1931), pp. 245–321.

Stanton, V. H. *The Jewish and the Christian Messiah.* Edinburgh, 1886.

Stone, M. "The Concept of the Messiah in IV Ezra." *Studies in the History of Religion* 14 (Leiden, 1968), pp. 295–312.

Torrey, C. C. "The Messiah Son of Ephraim." *JBL* 66 (1947), pp. 253–77.

Urbach, E. E. "On Redemption." *The Sages,* 1, pp. 649–92; 2, pp. 990–1009. Jerusalem, 1975.

Van der Wonde, A. S. *Die Messianischen Vorstellungen der Gemeinde von Qumran.* Assen, 1957.

Volz, P. *Die Eschatologie der jüdischen Gemeinde im Neutestamentlichen Zeitalters.* Tübingen, 1934.

Waxman, Meyer. *Galut veGeulah beSifrut Yisrael.* New York, 1952.

Wieder, N. "The Doctrine of the Two Messiahs among the Karaites." *JJS* 6 (1955), p. 14–25.

———. "The 'Law-Interpreter' of the Sect of the Dead Sea Scrolls: The Second Moses." *JJS* 4 (1953), pp. 158–75.

Wilder, A. N. "The Nature of Jewish Eschatology." *JBL* 50 (1931), pp. 201–6.

Wünsche, A. *Die Leiden des Messias.* Leipzig, 1890.

Yeivin, Sh. *Milḥemet Bar Kokhba.* Jerusalem, 1947.

Zeitlin, S. "The Assumption of Moses and the Revolt of Bar Kokba." *JQR* 38 (1947), pp. 1–45.

———. "The Essenes and Messianic Expectations." *JQR* 45 (1954), pp. 83–119.

———. "The Origin of the Idea of the Messiah." *In Time of Harvest.* pp. 447–59. New York, 1963.

Zobel, M. *Gottes Gesalbter, der Messias und die Messianische Zeit im Talmud und Midrasch.* Berlin, 1938.